Building Accounting Systems
Using Access 2003

James T. Perry, Ph.D.
The University of San Diego School of Business

Gary P. Schneider, Ph.D., CPA
The University of San Diego School of Business

THOMSON
SOUTH-WESTERN

Australia · Canada · Mexico · Singapore · Spain · United Kingdom · United States

Building Accounting Systems Using Access 2003
By James T. Perry and Gary P. Schneider

Vice President/Editorial Director
Jack Calhoun

Vice President/Editor-in-Chief
George Werthman

Publisher
Rob Dewey

Acquisitions Editor
Julie Moulton

Developmental Editor
Carol Bennett

Marketing Manager
Chip Kislack

Sr. Production Editor
Tim Bailey

Technology Project Editor
Sally Nieman

Sr. Media Editor
Robin Browning

Editorial Assistant
Allison Rolfes

Design Project Manager
Michael H. Stratton

Manufacturing Coordinator
Doug Wilke

Production
Litten Editing and Production, Inc.

Composition
GGS Information Services, Inc.

Printer
Phoenix Book Technology

Preface

To the Student

Traditional methods of recording economic events and accumulating accounting information have given way to database technology in today's accounting information systems. As we write this sixth edition of *Building Accounting Systems*, we find that organizations increasingly depend on databases that include accounting and other operating data for mission-critical information. Accounting information systems—or the accounting views of enterprise-wide databases—contain much of the information managers use to make decisions and control operations. These databases also store the information that accountants use to prepare the formal accounting reports, such as year-end financial statements, that organizations issue to external users. As a professional accountant, you will play a central role in ensuring that the accounting systems you use, audit, and help design will deliver timely, accurate, and complete information. This book will help you learn how to perform that role effectively.

This text describes how database management systems provide design tools that information systems professionals and accountants can use to build accounting systems. The text begins by explaining how database systems are a part of your everyday life. The text then helps you develop a basic understanding of the theory and practice of relational database management systems. The book then builds on that foundation and shows you how to build the elements of accounting systems using Microsoft Access, one of the most widely available database management software packages for personal computers.

The book begins by explaining how to use the Windows operating environment. It then reviews the history and theory of relational database systems and describes practical uses of Microsoft Access. The book explains accounting transaction cycles and shows you how to use the database theory and tools you learned in the earlier chapters to build accounting system elements for each of the four main transaction cycles: revenue, purchase, payroll, and production.

Chapter 1 provides a firm grounding in the fundamentals of the Windows XP operating system. This chapter may be a review for some of you; for others, this will be your first hands-on introduction to the Windows operating system. Chapter 2 introduces Microsoft Access database management software. You will learn the basics of using tables to store information, displaying database contents, finding answers to questions with database queries, using forms to enter data, and printing database reports. Chapter 3 presents a concise yet thorough introduction to database theory. You will learn how to use normalization rules to structure your data in ways that avoid redundancy and data loss. This chapter also introduces user views and entity-relationship modeling. Additionally, you will learn the differences between database accounting systems and double-entry bookkeeping systems and the advantages of the database approach. You will learn how to classify business activities by level of complexity. You will also learn to identify the business activities that occur in the four main transaction cycles we use in this book. Finally, you will learn how to perform basic database operations that enable you to locate subsets of table rows or columns and to collect information from several related database tables. In Chapter 4 you create several tables and queries—tasks for which we provide step-by-step guidance. You will be happy to know that you can perform all of these database functions *without writing a single line of program code*. When you have finished Chapter 4, you will have the database skills you need to create both tables and queries—the fundamental database building blocks that deliver data to the remaining basic accounting system components. Chapter 5 provides an in-depth discussion of designing and creating Access forms and reports. You will learn how to create forms based on one table and multiple tables. Similarly, you will learn how to design and create reports using the Access Report Wizard and how to manually create reports based on queries.

Chapters 6 through 9 apply database concepts and techniques to the specific challenges of building accounting information systems. In Chapter 6, you will begin your walk through the accounting transaction cycles with the revenue cycle. For example, you will learn how to use tables and forms to record sales and cash collections. Chapter 7 shows database applications in the purchase cycle, which include creating purchase orders, recording the receipt of goods ordered, and paying vendors. In Chapter 8, you will build the database elements that businesses use to handle the many details of payroll accounting. You will learn how to combine records of time worked with employee information to calculate gross pay, deductions, and net pay. Chapter 9 describes the production cycle and shows you how to build accounting database elements that track materials, labor, and overhead costs into production using job order cost accumulation examples. The chapter also explains how you can extend these examples to build process, hybrid, and activity-based cost accounting databases. Chapter 10 shows you how to add "icing" to the database "cake" with enhancements to the database elements you created in the preceding chapters. These enhancements include custom buttons for simplifying database operations and Visual Basic for Applications procedures that enforce business rules and validate user input.

We hope you will become an active participant as you read the text and work through the step-by-step examples. You will best retain what you have read by working through the book on a computer. To reinforce your learning, we have included four types of review questions at the end of each chapter:

- Multiple-choice questions, which refresh your memory about key points in a chapter.
- Discussion questions, which are more general and provide a basis for interesting small group discussions of the topics.
- Practice Exercises, which are short problems that require you to use Access to create a solution.
- Problems, which are more comprehensive problems that require you to use Access to create your own accounting databases or extend the examples in the text.

By studying the text carefully, working through the examples, and using the end-of-chapter materials to reinforce your knowledge, you will learn how to use database management software to design and build accounting systems that deliver timely, accurate information to managers and financial statement users.

To the Instructor

Many accounting professors feel that the accounting information systems course is the greatest teaching challenge in the curriculum. One of our goals in writing this book was to help make your job of teaching accounting systems easier. Accounting practice has evolved from manual journals and ledgers to database accounting systems—even in very small firms. At the same time, many introductory accounting courses have shifted to financial statement user and managerial decision-maker orientations from the more traditional preparer orientations. Despite this decreased emphasis on the mechanics of accounting in the introductory courses, accounting majors still need to understand how accounting systems record, classify, and aggregate economic events. This book serves as a powerful tool that can help you give your students a solid introduction to database principles *and* valuable hands-on experience in constructing accounting systems. By using Microsoft Access—object-based software that features an intuitive graphic user interface—this book vastly reduces the amount of class time you must spend on nonaccounting systems matters. The text's step-by-step instructions can reduce your time and drudgery in the computer lab. The time you do spend with students in class or in the computer lab will not be wasted on mundane "click here and then click there" instructing, because we have filled this book with detailed instructions and examples to save you that kind of work.

We are convinced that there are at least as many different ways of teaching the accounting systems course as there are professors teaching it. Therefore, this book was designed to be flexible. In a junior- or senior-level course, the book can effectively supplement any accounting information systems text currently on the market. Most of these texts are organized around transaction cycles that are identical or similar to the transaction cycles we use in this book. Adopters of this book's earlier editions have used it successfully with many different accounting information systems texts. Some instructors have used this book as the main course text, supplementing it with readings from the current literature on internal control and systems design. Instructors have incorporated the book into their courses in various ways. Some cover all or part of the book in class. Others assign the book as a series of computer lab assignments or as outside reading.

Many accounting systems courses include some type of systems design project. A number of instructors have used earlier editions of this book as an effective springboard for such projects. Students can extend the book's examples or use them as analogs for the real-world systems they design and build in their projects. Students will feel better prepared to take on the challenge of a systems design project after they have experienced successes with creating the example accounting systems in this book.

Although we designed this book to meet the needs of the undergraduate accounting major systems class, it is flexible enough to be used in other settings. Many community colleges now offer a computer accounting course. This book would serve well as either the main text or a supplement in such a course. Instructors of graduate accounting systems courses may wish to assign this book as a project for those students who lack undergraduate systems course work or for students whose undergraduate systems exposure is dated. Instructors of information systems auditing courses at the graduate level have also found the book to be a useful supplement in those courses.

The book includes a number of features that will make your teaching easier:

- A concise introduction to database theory that includes thorough discussions of normalization and entity-relationship modeling.
- An exposition of the database approach to accounting systems that includes a comparison to double-entry bookkeeping procedures.
- Step-by-step instructions in all chapters that guide the student through each example.
- Numerous figures that show the computer screen at key points in each task and that show finished forms and printed reports.
- A Companion CD that contains tables, files, queries, forms, reports, and other information to help students complete the exercises and follow along with the examples in the text.

We have taken special care to include database tables, forms, queries, and reports so that students can use any chapter independently of other chapters. You will find that many of the tables include comprehensive examples of significant size. By including these very large tables, we hope to give students an experience that resembles working with real-world databases.

An Instructor's Manual available to adopters includes detailed lecture suggestions for each chapter and solutions to all end-of-chapter questions and exercises. The Instructor's Resource CD (ISBN: 0-324-30203-7) contains the Instructor's Manual, in both Microsoft Word and Adobe PDF formats, to help you create customized lecture notes, transparencies, and presentation software slide shows for classroom use. The Instructor's Resource CD also includes solutions to all computer exercises in the form of Microsoft Access tables, forms, queries, and reports.

Organization of the Book

The text contains ten chapters. The first five chapters introduce the Windows XP operating system, Microsoft Access, and basic database modeling. The next four chapters show students how to use the database theory and tools from the earlier chapters to build functional accounting system database elements. Chapter 10 describes advanced features of Microsoft Access, including automating database procedures and validity-checking features with custom-built Visual Basic for Applications (VBA) code.

Chapter 1 is an overview of Windows XP and emphasizes fundamental operations such as launching programs, examining object properties, and manipulating windows. This chapter will help students who are computer novices attain sufficient Windows proficiency to use any Windows database management product. You can skip Chapter 1 if you feel your students already have sufficient knowledge about using Windows XP. Chapter 2 familiarizes students with the Microsoft Access database management system. The chapter illustrates all major database elements, including tables, queries, forms, and reports. Chapter 3 presents a brief history of databases; describes the requirements for databases to be in first, second, and third normal forms; and describes how database accounting differs from double-entry bookkeeping and why firms are using database accounting systems. Chapter 3 also identifies firms as service, merchandising, or manufacturing; discusses the transaction cycle elements that exist in each type of firm; and gives students sufficient grounding in database theory to create well-designed, anomaly-free databases. Chapter 4 provides students with hands-on experience in building database tables and queries. Chapter 5 contains a thorough discussion about designing and building Access forms for data entry, data viewing, and Access reports to supply management with hard copy output. Building on a foundation of tables and queries, the forms and reports discussion provides the capstone Microsoft Access experience needed to completely understand the role of a database management system in producing accounting objects.

The next four chapters of the book show students how to apply the tools and techniques from the first five chapters to the specific tasks of building accounting system elements. We use four transaction cycles to organize these four chapters: revenue, purchase, payroll, and production. Each of these four chapters begins with a description of an example company and an entity-relationship diagram of its data model. The data model feature is new in this edition. We included it in response to requests from many users of previous editions.

We define the revenue cycle to include cash receipts and the purchase cycle to include cash disbursements. Chapter 6 shows students how to track customer information, sales, and cash receipts in the revenue cycle. In Chapter 7, students get to see the purchase cycle as a mirror image of the revenue cycle. They learn how to track vendor information and record purchase orders, receipt of goods ordered, and cash disbursements. Chapter 8 presents students with a straightforward payroll system example that they can easily extend to accommodate greater levels of complexity. Chapter 9, which covers the production cycle, shows students how to track materials, labor, and overhead costs in a job order cost accumulation system. Chapter 9 also explains how students can extend these job order examples to build process, hybrid, and activity-based cost accounting database systems.

Chapter 10 concludes the book with instructions for enhancing database systems with command buttons to validate data input, enforce business rules, and automate common database procedures. These enhancements require the student to write macros and VBA code; however, we provide step-by-step instructions that make this a pleasant exercise. Even the most computer-phobic accounting student should find writing these short code snippets tolerable.

Paths Through the Book

The chapters need not be assigned in sequence. You can follow several paths through the book. If your students are familiar with the Windows operating environment you will be using, you can skip Chapter 1 or assign it as review reading. Chapters 2, 3, 4, and 5 should be assigned in order, since Chapters 4 and 5 integrate the Chapter 2 introduction to Microsoft Access with the Chapter 3 treatment of database principles and their application to accounting systems.

Many instructors will want to cover all four of the transaction cycle chapters, assigning Chapters 6, 7, 8, and 9 in sequence. Some instructors prefer to focus on one or two transaction cycles each semester. Chapter 6, the revenue cycle, and Chapter 7, the purchase cycle, are ideal candidates for such a focus. You can go directly to Chapter 8 from Chapter 5 if you wish. Chapters 8 and 9 are independent of each other, but students will find these chapters easier if they have first worked through Chapter 7. Although Chapter 9 includes a brief introduction to cost accounting concepts, most students will find the material in this chapter to be somewhat difficult if they have not already had a cost accounting course.

We made Chapter 10 the last chapter because some instructors may wish to omit it. The chapter includes advanced database software techniques that students can use to enhance the accounting systems that they build. If your students are comfortable with Windows productivity software such as word processors or spreadsheets—particularly if they have written macros or VBA code—then you should be able to assign Chapter 10 any time after Chapter 5. None of the book's other chapters require students to have mastered the material in Chapter 10, so you may wish to cover this material at the end of the course if time permits.

Access Installation Note

This book assumes that you have installed Microsoft Office Access 2003 on your computer. The installation that Microsoft provides as part of its default "Typical" installation option does not install all of the program elements that you will need to complete the exercises in this book. You must include the set of program features titled "Additional Wizards" when you install Access 2003. The installation dialog box in which you make this selection appears in Figure P.1.

If your original installation did not include the "Additional Wizards" option, then you can reinstall Access 2003 by inserting your Office Access 2003 or Microsoft Office

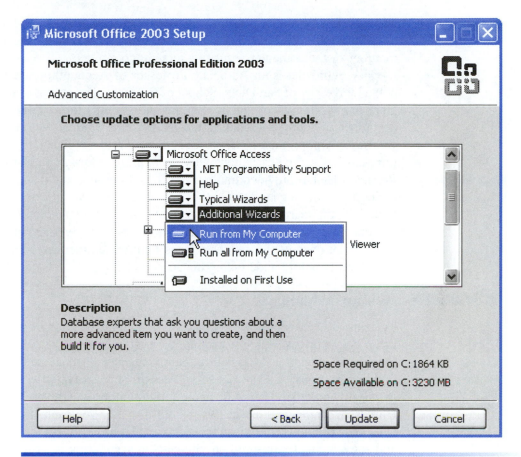

Figure P.1   Installing the Microsoft Office Access 2003 Additional Wizards option.

System 2003 installation CD and selecting *install*. The options that were selected during the last installation on that computer will appear in the dialog box. Change the Additional Wizards option as shown in Figure P.1 and continue with the installation. The reinstallation will not delete any Access files that you have created. It will only update the Access program files to include the additional program features you have selected.

About the Authors

Jim Perry is a Professor of Management Information Systems at the University of San Diego School of Business. He is the author or co-author of 80 textbooks and trade books and over a dozen articles on computer security, database management systems, multimedia delivery systems, and chief programmer teams. Jim is a charter member of the Association for Information Systems. He holds a Ph.D. in computer science from the Pennsylvania State University and a Bachelor of Science in mathematics from Purdue University. Jim has worked as a computer security consultant to various private and governmental organizations, including the Jet Propulsion Laboratory. He was a consultant on the Strategic Defense Initiative ("Star Wars") project and served as a member of the computer security oversight committee.

Gary Schneider is an Associate Professor of Accounting and Information Systems at the University of San Diego School of Business. The author or co-author of 40 books, Gary has written widely on accounting and systems topics. His work has appeared in a number of journals including the *IS Audit & Control Journal*, *Interfaces*, and the *Journal of Information Systems*. Gary is active in the American Accounting Association and has served as editor of its *Accounting Information Systems and Technology Reporter*. He has provided training and consulting services to a number of major clients, including AlliedSignal, the Gartner Group, and Qualcomm. In 1999, he was named a Fellow of the Gartner Institute. Gary holds a Ph.D. in accounting from the University of Tennessee, an MBA in accounting from Xavier University, and a BA in economics from the University of Cincinnati. He is a CPA and practiced public accounting in Ohio for 14 years before undertaking his academic career.

Acknowledgments

Creating a successful book is always a collaborative effort between authors and publisher. We work as a team to provide the best book possible. We want to thank the following reviewers for the insightful comments and suggestions they gave us on this and previous editions: A. Faye Borthick, Georgia State University; Severin Grabski, Michigan State University; Mary R. Scott, Grambling State University; and Jerry D. Siebel, University of South Florida. We would also like to thank the many professors who have used previous editions in their classes and have provided us with valuable insights and suggestions for this edition. Students in accounting information systems classes at the University of San Diego and at Georgia State University have used various versions of the manuscripts for this and previous editions of the book. We appreciate the many helpful suggestions these students provided.

The authors especially want to acknowledge the work of the professionals at South-Western College Publishing. We extend special thanks to George Werthman, Julie Moulton, Carol Bennett, and the other members of the Accounting Team at South-Western. We appreciate the care and attention to detail with which everyone at South-Western handled the development and production of this edition.

Finally, we want to express deep appreciation to our spouses, Nancy Perry and Cathy Cosby, for their remarkable patience as we worked both ends of the clock to complete this edition of the book on a very tight schedule.

If you would like to contact us about the book, we would enjoy hearing from you. We welcome comments and suggestions that we might incorporate into future editions of the book. You can e-mail book-related messages to us at **debit@sandiego.edu**. For the latest information about *Building Accounting Systems* and related resources, please visit our Web site at **http://perry.swlearning.com**.

Dedication

This text is dedicated to Nancy C. Perry and Cathryn A. Cosby.

Trademark List

The following trademarks and registered trademarks appear in this book:

1. Microsoft, Windows, Access, Word, Excel, Exchange, Internet Explorer, FoxPro, Paint, Office, and The Microsoft Network are registered trademarks of Microsoft Corporation. Any reference to Microsoft Windows, Access, Word, Excel, Exchange, Internet Explorer, FoxPro, Paint, Office, or The Microsoft Network refers to this note.
2. Adobe is a registered trademark of Adobe Systems Incorporated. Any references to Adobe refer to this note.

Contents

3   DATABASES AND ACCOUNTING SYSTEMS 105

CHAPTER 1
Working with Windows

OBJECTIVES

This chapter presents an overview of the Microsoft Windows environment available on millions of microcomputers around the world. For those unfamiliar with Windows, you will learn the skills essential for working with it. All references in this chapter apply to Windows XP unless specifically noted. Those of you familiar with Windows will probably discover some new techniques while reading this chapter. Several key Windows features are presented. In particular, you will learn how to:

- Understand what objects are found on the desktop.
- Open, close, maximize, and minimize windows.
- Launch an application using the Start button.
- Use a dialog box.
- Exit an application.
- Use Windows Explorer to manage files and programs and to launch a program.
- Create folders with Windows Explorer.
- Get help on the current application.
- Launch multiple applications and switch between them.
- Pass data between Windows programs.
- Create and use desktop shortcuts.
- Modify the Start menu.
- Relocate the Taskbar.

AN OVERVIEW OF WINDOWS

Microsoft Windows provides a convenient work surface from which you can run applications, manage files, and run your business. By simply clicking the Start button and selecting a program, you can launch Microsoft Office Word, Microsoft Office Access, or any of the thousands of Windows programs available. Windows allows you to run more than one program at a time. For instance, you could be writing a memo to your sales manager using your favorite word processing program, Word. When you are ready to summarize last month's sales figures, you can quickly switch to Excel, your tried

1

and true spreadsheet program, to review the sales figures found in last quarter's spreadsheet. Switching between applications is as easy as clicking a button.

Transferring data between Windows programs is easy. Suppose you want to mail letters to customers in a particular state—Washington, for example—informing them about a special product promotion available for a limited time only. You need to create Word documents for each customer in Washington containing details about the promotion. This would be a daunting task if you had to actually type each letter individually. However, you know that Word can use Windows tools to retrieve information from an Access database containing your customers' names and addresses. Microsoft Office Word and Microsoft Office Access work together seamlessly to deliver database information to Word documents on demand. With Windows, Word, and Access, it is simple to create a form letter for each customer as well as mailing labels. Figure 1.1 shows an example of a Word document (bottom), a sheet of Avery 5160 mailing labels, and an Access database (right) that dynamically supplies customer addresses to both forms.

Another way that applications can share information is called *Object Linking and Embedding,* or *OLE*. OLE actually embeds a copy of the data into another document. For instance, you could place a copy of the customer database, or a subset of it, into a Word document. In this example, the Word document is the container, and the Access

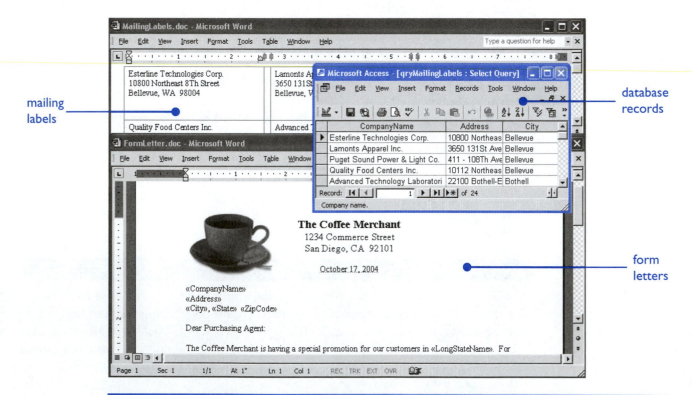

Figure 1.1 Linking database information to Word documents.

database, supplying the database information to the document, is known as the *server*. (You will see this container/server relationship illustrated throughout this text.)

Because of its ease of use and the advantages mentioned, Windows is a well-established standard among PC users. In the sections that follow, you will learn the most important features of Windows—those skills and techniques essential to thriving in today's business world.

Starting Windows

Windows automatically executes after your computer is turned on and has successfully completed some hardware tests. Depending on how you have set up Windows, you may be asked to type a user name and password. Alternatively, the operating system may ask you to log in by pressing Ctrl+Alt+Delete and then signing in. Follow the prompts, and fill in the appropriate information when necessary.

The Desktop

Windows uses the desktop metaphor whereby the computer screen simulates, through icons, one's desktop containing various objects. Everything on the desktop is an object, meaning it is a thing having properties or characteristics. Examples of objects on the desktop include My Computer, My Network Places, and so on. You can even add shortcuts to programs, printers, and documents. Figure 1.2 shows an example of a Windows desktop. Keep in mind that your desktop may look different because it may contain a varying number of objects that are arranged in unique ways. However, our figure is representative of the major elements found on the desktop.

Your desktop may contain the My Computer icon. My Computer is the entrance to all the disk drives and files on your computer. Through My Computer you can examine the floppy disk drive, hard drives, CD drives, and the system configuration.

The Recycle Bin icon holds files and folders that have been deleted. Anything in the Recycle Bin can either be recovered or removed permanently. Once objects have been removed, they cannot be restored.

Your desktop may show an Internet Explorer icon. It provides a convenient way to access the World Wide Web (Web) using Microsoft's full-featured Internet Explorer. Navigating the Web couldn't be simpler, because it uses a page metaphor to display information.

Your desktop may also contain My Briefcase. This icon enables you to keep various copies of your files synchronized and up to date whether you are working on the road, at home, or in the office. When you are finished working on a file on your laptop computer, for instance, you can use My Briefcase to update the file on your main computer when you get back to the office. Files are automatically and nearly effortlessly maintained so that you need not worry about which file is the latest version and which file should be deleted.

The Taskbar is the area that normally rests on the bottom of your screen. (You can move the Taskbar to the top or sides of the screen if you wish, and you can even hide it until it is needed.) The Windows Taskbar contains the Start button (see Figure 1.2),

Figure 1.2 Windows desktop example.

which you can use to quickly find a file or start a program; buttons representing programs that are currently running; and the task tray. Two programs are currently running, and the buttons on the Taskbar indicate their names: Microsoft Word and Microsoft Access. The *task tray* contains small icons representing programs that are always in memory. For example, the task tray shown in Figure 1.2 shows several icons representing a network connection, an antivirus program, and other important programs. The arrow on the left side of the task tray indicates some task-tray icons are hidden. The task tray also displays the current time, an option you can set on or off.

Using the Mouse

Before we examine Windows any further, it is important to understand how to use the essential pointing device, the mouse. Although you can use Windows without a mouse, it is considerably more difficult. Five terms, describing different ways to use the mouse, occur throughout this text: point, click, right-click, double-click, and drag.

When we ask you to "point to Programs" or "point to Find in the Start menu," we simply mean you should move the mouse pointer so that its tip is directly over the desired object on the screen. Pointing with your mouse opens displays, menus, or submenus.

When you are instructed to "click the mouse" or "click," press and release the left mouse button. If you are asked to click a particular button, move the mouse pointer to it and then press and quickly release the left mouse button once. Select an item on-screen by moving the mouse pointer to the item and clicking once with the left mouse button. Once you select an item, you can perform various activities. For example, after you have selected an icon, you can move it from one place on your desktop to another.

Right-clicking the mouse is similar to clicking except that you use the right mouse button. For example, if you want to learn about a desktop icon's properties, you first right-click the icon to display a shortcut menu and then click (left-click) the mouse to display the icon's properties.

Frequently, we will ask you to double-click some object on the Windows work surface. When you double-click an icon representing a program, that program is activated. To double-click, quickly click the left mouse button twice. If you don't click rapidly enough, you will simply select the object twice instead of activating it.

Another way to use the mouse is to drag an object. In a word processing program, for example, you might want to move a sentence from one place to another. You can do this by dragging it. To drag any object, select the object (click it), press and hold down the left mouse button, and move the mouse. It takes a little practice, but you will master it quickly. Dragging is useful in several circumstances. For instance, you can enlarge a window by dragging its border or corner. You can also reduce or enlarge a Windows help frame by dragging a border toward or away from the opposite border.

BECOMING MORE FAMILIAR WITH WINDOWS

Anatomy of a Window

Most windows contain the same elements. Figure 1.3 shows a typical window that opens when you double-click My Computer. A window has a frame or border that defines its outer edges. The My Computer window shown can be sized—that is, the window can be stretched or shrunk by dragging any edge. In the lower right corner is the size grip, which is a special handle to make obvious to the user how to resize a window. Along the window's top is a Title bar containing the name of the application, current topic, or current document. The current application, My Computer, is displayed in this case. When a window is active, its Title bar is a darker color than the Title bars of other windows.

On the extreme left of the Title bar is a control icon, which can be opened to manipulate the window with the keyboard. You can close a window by double-clicking its control icon, though you will find it far easier to use the mouse for most actions. Three window buttons appear on the right end of each window's Title bar. These are called the Minimize, Maximize/Restore, and Close buttons. You would click the Minimize button (the button that looks like a dash) to remove the window from view (the program remains running). If the window does not fill the screen, then the middle button, called Maximize, causes the window to fill the screen when you click

Control icon

Title bar

Restore button

Minimize button

Close button

menu bar

toolbar

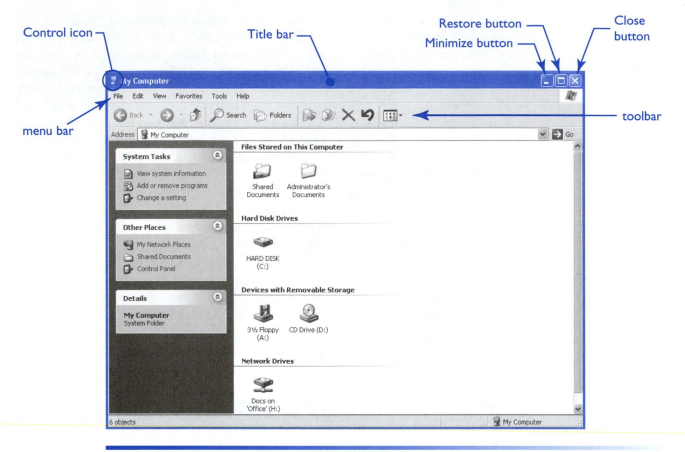

Figure 1.3   Components of a window.

it. If the window is already maximized, then the middle button looks like two over-lapping windows and is called the Restore button. When you click Restore, the window is reduced to less than full screen. You use the Close button in the upper right corner of a window to close the window with one click. If the window represents a program, rather than a group, then clicking the Close button terminates execution of the application.

Below the Title bar is the menu bar. Clicking any of the menu items displays a drop-down menu, which contains commands that you can select. If you click the My Computer's Edit menu, for instance, you will see the drop-down menu shown in Figure 1.4. A list of commands is associated with each menu of any Windows program. When you select a menu, its pull-down menu is displayed. You can select a menu either by clicking it with the mouse or by pressing the Alt key and the letter underlined in the menu name. For example, notice that the letter E in the Edit menu (see Figure 1.4) is underlined. Pressing Alt and then E simultaneously displays the Edit menu. Throughout the text, we use a standard notation to indicate keys that you press simultaneously. For example, Alt+E denotes pressing and holding the Alt key and pressing and releasing

unavailable
commands
are dimmed

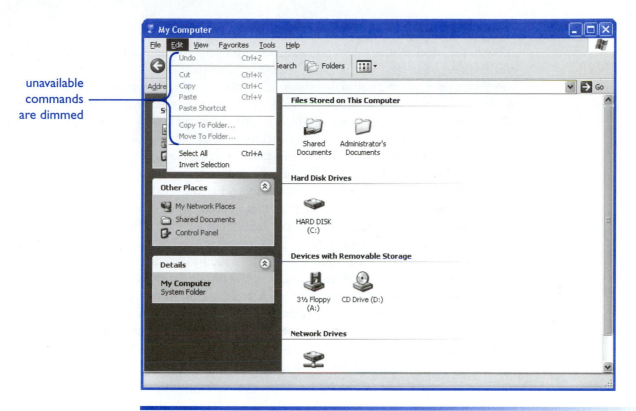

Figure 1.4 A typical Windows pull-down menu.

the letter E to invoke the Edit menu. The key that follows *Alt* varies depending on which menu you wish to select.

When you want to select a command in a pull-down menu, simply point to it with the mouse. The selection bar highlights the designated command. To execute a highlighted command, simply click the mouse. Alternatively, you can use the arrow keys to move up and down the pull-down list of commands and press Enter at any point to execute the highlighted command. Some commands are inapplicable in certain situations. Whenever you are not allowed to select a command, it is dimmed (light gray). The Undo, Cut, Copy, Paste, Paste Shortcut, Copy To Folder, and Move to Folder commands are dimmed in Figure 1.4. Only the Select All and Invert Selection commands are bold and therefore available.

Along the window's bottom edge is the status bar. The status bar displays useful information about the window, such as the number of objects it holds or a description of a command you have selected when the window contains a running application.

When there is more information than can be displayed in the window, scroll bars automatically appear on the right and bottom window edges. By sliding the scroll boxes or using the scroll arrows, you can pan the window up, down, left, or right to see otherwise hidden parts of the object within the window.

Manipulating Windows

As with the other sections that follow, this section actively involves you in learning several Windows features. You will manipulate program and document windows in several ways, including moving and sizing them. To help you learn and reinforce these Windows skills, we ask you to reinforce your reading by practicing each task described herein. There are two types of activities in which you can participate: Try It tasks and Exercises.

Try It tasks are smaller, more easily accomplished computer activities that take only a few moments to complete. For example, a Try It task might be to minimize, maximize, and restore a window, or it might be a description of how to switch between Microsoft Office Access and Windows Explorer using Taskbar buttons. The phrase *Try It* introduces a paragraph describing these types of activities. If a task comprises several steps, the individual steps are not numbered.

Exercises are more comprehensive activities that are central to some ongoing and important process or project that is being described in a chapter. Exercises typically consist of two or more numbered steps. Completing an exercise helps you to achieve some important goal. An example of an exercise is the series of steps that illustrate how to launch several Windows applications, open document windows in each application, and copy information between open windows. Such an exercise reinforces how to implement information sharing between, for example, Access and Word—an essential task in business. Your first Try It task follows.

TRY IT

Double-click the My Computer icon (see Figure 1.2). What happens if you click a desktop icon only once? You simply select the icon. To activate it, double-click. The My Computer window will open, displaying icons representing hardware on your computer and your network similar to Figure 1.3. Maximize the My Computer window. Right-click the icon representing drive C. The shortcut menu appears. Locate *Properties* in the menu (near the bottom of the list) and click it. A tabbed dialog box, showing the properties of the selected object, appears. Click the General tab, if necessary, to go to the page containing a pie graph. It illustrates how much space is either occupied or available on drive C. After you have had a chance to examine the display, click the question mark button called *What's This?* Notice that the mouse pointer changes to an arrow with a question mark attached to its right side. After clicking What's This?, you can move to any object and click it to obtain context-sensitive help. Move the mouse pointer down to the pie graph and click it. A brief explanation of the clicked object appears (see Figure 1.5). Click the light yellow help box to make it disappear. Click the Close button on the Properties dialog box to close it. Finally, click the Close button on My Computer to close it. The desktop reappears. Moving windows about the desktop, changing their size, and closing them is intuitive in Windows. We'll direct you through some fundamental window manipulation activities next.

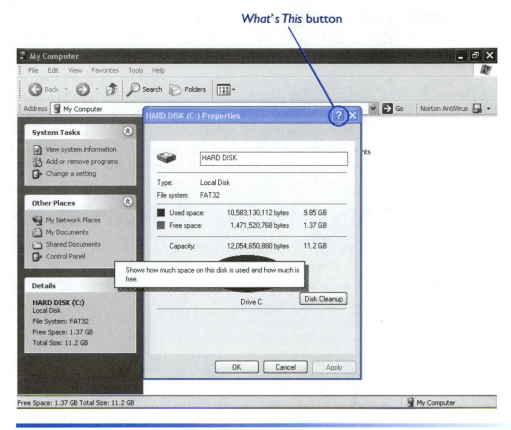

Figure 1.5 Obtaining help with the What's This? button.

TRY IT

Open the My Computer window again (double-click its desktop icon). Maximize the window, if necessary, so that it fills the screen. Restore the window so it occupies only part of the work surface by clicking the Restore button. Make the window virtually disappear by pressing the Minimize button. Where did the My Computer window go? When you minimize a program, Windows places a button on the Taskbar representing the minimized program. Though the window disappears, its Taskbar button remains. By clicking a program's Taskbar button, you can switch from one program to another. Restore the My Computer window by clicking the Taskbar button labeled My Computer. Click and drag the My Computer window's size grip (the dotted triangle in the lower right corner of the dialog box) away from its opposite corner to increase the window's size. Similarly, drag the size grip towards its opposite corner to reduce the window's size. You can create an infinite number of window sizes this way. Move the My Computer dialog box to the top left of your screen by dragging its title bar. Then, move it so it is approximately in the center of your screen. Finally, close the My Computer window.

Getting Help

Help is available in all Windows programs in a variety of ways. Context-sensitive help provides assistance for almost every object on the screen. Microsoft products have help screens that are actually Web pages. That is, help for Microsoft products including Windows and Microsoft Access are formatted as Web pages complete with hyperlinks that take you to related information when you click them. You have already used What's This? to obtain information about an object on the screen. ToolTips are another form of context-sensitive help. ToolTips are small pop-up banners that briefly appear when you hover the mouse over an object, such as a toolbar button.

TRY IT

Move the mouse pointer over the Start button, which is located at the left end of the Taskbar. After a second or two, a ToolTip appears indicating you should "Click here to begin." Likewise, you can see the date if you move the mouse pointer to the time display located in the task tray.

Windows programs supply explicit help through a Help menu. Extensive help is available on the computer. The Windows Help system provides search features, as well as contents and indexing capabilities. Windows help, available from the Start button (you will learn more about the Start button in the next section), is an excellent choice.

EXERCISE 1.1: GETTING SPECIFIC HELP

1. Click the Start button (the Start button is explained fully in the next section). The Start menu is displayed.
2. Click Help and Support in the right panel of the Start menu.
3. The Help and Support Center dialog box opens. Click the window's Maximize button, if necessary, to maximize the window.
4. Type **formatting** into the Search text box (you will search for help on formatting disks) and then click the Start searching icon to the right of the Search text box. The help system displays several results in the Search Results panel.
5. Click the hyperlink *Format a basic volume* in the Search Results. The right panel in the Help and Support Center dialog box describes how to format a disk (see Figure 1.6).
6. Click the Help and Support Center Close button after reading the help information.

THE START MENU

The Start button, located on the left end of the Taskbar, provides the major access point for programs, documents, and other objects. The Start menu, a cascading menu, appears when you click the Start button. Submenus cascade—logically flow from—the main menu items (see Figure 1.7).

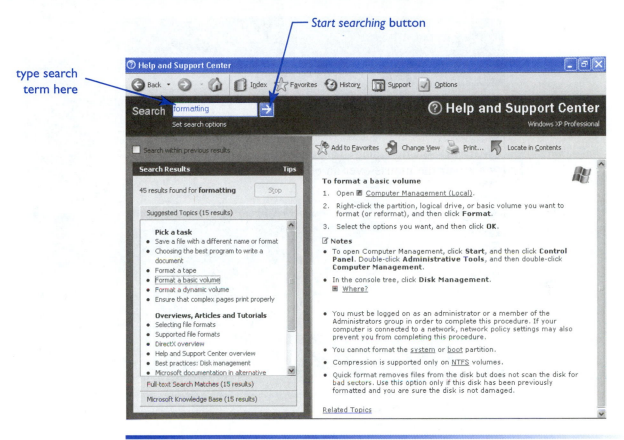

Figure 1.6 Locating help on formatting disks.

Opening the Start Menu

The Start menu items vary from one computer to another because Windows adds program icons for programs you invoke frequently. The right panel of the Start menu generally contains entries such as My Computer, My Network Places, Control Panel, Connect To, Printers and Faxes, Help and Support, and Search. The left panel contains icons representing programs you use frequently, but you can add your own icons to the Start menu to provide convenient access. Some of the menu items have right arrows. These arrows indicate that the menu item leads to a submenu, which opens when you merely point to the menu item by moving the mouse over the item and pausing briefly.

The Programs Menu Item

When you point to the *All Programs* menu item, located in the lower left corner of the Start menu, it opens to reveal program items and program group items. Only executable items are found in the Programs menu, not data or other nonexecutable objects. Programs include Windows Explorer and other application programs you have installed on your computer. When you point to a group item, Windows reveals more entries. For

the Start menu

Figure 1.7   The Start menu.

example, Accessories is a group item that contains the usual collection of standard Windows groups and programs (see Figure 1.8). You simply point to Accessories and then select a program or group item from the cascaded menu. You can close each of the cascading menus in turn by selecting a menu item from a previous menu. Similarly, you can close all menus except the Start menu by moving the mouse pointer to one of the Start menu items that doesn't cascade, such as Run or Help and Support.

Windows provides keyboard alternatives to the mouse. For instance, you can press Ctrl+Esc to open the Start menu. Once open, the Start menu lists items that you can select by using the arrow keys. The up and down arrow keys move up and down an open menu, and the right and left arrow keys move to a cascading menu or the previous menu, respectively. Press the Alt key to close all open menus.

TRY IT

Click the Start menu and then move the mouse pointer to All Programs. Pause and the cascade menu opens. Next, move to the right and point to Accessories. Move the mouse pointer down the menu items to WordPad (probably the last entry in the list of programs). Finally, close all menus.

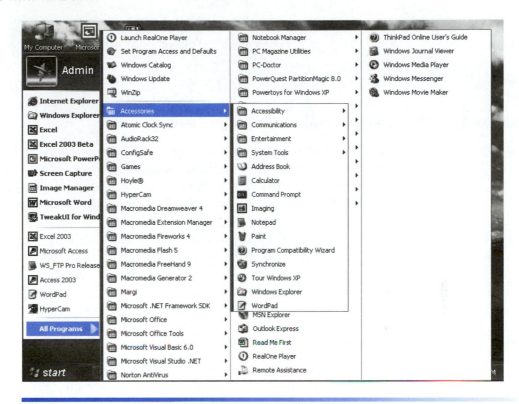

Figure 1.8   Displaying submenus of the Start menu.

The Documents Menu Item

The My Recent Documents menu item displays a list of the 15 objects you have most recently used. If you worked on an Access database named accounts *payable.mdb* and then opened Microsoft Word to write a letter you later saved as *NewAccounts.doc*, then those two document names would appear in the My Recent Documents menu item list. The My Recent Documents menu facilitates returning quickly and easily to the items with which you have recently worked. For example, you return to your computer after a day's absence, start Windows, click the Start menu button, point to My Recent Documents, and then select the document with which you want to work. (In this context, the word document refers to a variety of objects, including a word processing document, a spreadsheet, a database, or a graphic image.) This reinforces the notion that you focus on the object that you want to work with, rather than worrying about which program or tool is required to load and manipulate the document.

TRY IT

See what documents people using your computer have recently used. Click Start and point to My Recent Documents. The cascade menu will reveal the document names, or it will be empty if the list has been erased. (You will learn how to clear the My Recent Documents list later.)

The Control Panel Menu Item

The Control Panel allows you to customize the appearance and functionality of your computer, remove or add programs, and set up user accounts and network connections. The Control Panel contains icons representing a large number of system settings you can change and actions you can take. For example, you can add or remove programs from the Control Panel group, change your monitor's display characteristics, or alter the date and time. The Printers and Faxes menu item allows you to add, delete, or modify printers available to your system. Right-clicking the Taskbar displays a pop-up menu from which you can click Properties and alter the characteristics of the Taskbar and associated task tray. For example, you could choose to hide the Taskbar or hide the clock, which is customarily displayed in the task tray on the right end of the Taskbar.

The Search Menu Item

Having a document-centric system like Windows aids your productivity; however, it is not useful if you cannot locate the document you want. That's when the Search menu item goes to work. You can use Search to locate files or folders on any disk drive, including floppy drives. In addition, you can find files or folders on any computer on any network to which your computer is attached. If you have opted to use the online service Microsoft Network, you can locate files on it as well. If you cannot find a file on your hard disk, you can invoke the Search menu item to search through every file on your hard drive.

TRY IT

See if you can use Search to locate the Windows file called *msaccess*. Click the Start button, click Search in the Start menu. When the Search Results dialog box opens, type **msaccess** in the *Search for files or folders named* text box and ensure that the Look in text box contains *My Computer*. If it does not, then click the list box drop-down list arrow, scroll to the top of the list, and click My Computer. Click the Search Options hyperlink below the Look in list box. Click the Advanced Options check box to place a check mark in it, and then click the Search system folders check box to place a check mark in it. Click the Search Now button to start the search process. Windows begins searching for any files or folders that begin with *msaccess*. Shortly thereafter, files are displayed in the search results window. After you have reviewed the names, click the dialog box's Close button.

The Help and Support Menu Item

The Help and Support menu item, which you used earlier, provides systemwide help at the click of a button. Select Help and Support whenever you want to find more information on a Windows topic. Product-specific help is best obtained through the Help and Support menu of the product itself, because software product manufacturers supply rich help content along with their programs. If you want help on Microsoft Access, it is best to seek help from the Help menu within Access. Help on creating Windows shortcuts—a topic that is common across applications—can be found by using the Start menu Help and Support menu item.

The Run Menu Item

The Run menu item allows one to run a program by simply typing the program's name and pressing Enter. You can use the Run command to launch infrequently used programs that might not be represented on the Start menu or its submenus. When you want to launch a program from the Run menu item, click Start, click Run, and enter the program's name, including the full path, in the Open text box. If you do not know the program's exact location on the disk, you can click the Browse button and search through folders until you locate it. Or you can use Search to locate the program. If you use the latter method, then you can double-click the program within the search results list to execute it. If you find yourself using the Run command frequently for a particular program, consider placing the program in the Start menu or placing it on the desktop as a shortcut to the program. You will learn how to do that later in this chapter.

The Turn Off Computer Item

It is incorrect to simply turn off your computer when you are finished using Windows. In fact, Windows requires you to follow a simple procedure to shut down your computer. Doing so protects files and other data from being corrupted or saved improperly. In short, never turn off your computer while Windows is running. A Turn Off menu item is available as a simple Windows exit procedure. To shut down Windows, click the Start menu and click Turn Off Computer. A dialog box containing your options is displayed (see Figure 1.9). Click the Turn Off button if you want to turn off your computer for an extended period (more than a few hours). If you want to restart your computer, then click "Restart" in the list of choices. If you want your computer to hibernate for an indefinite period, then click the Stand By button. Finally, if you want to simply resume processing, click the Cancel button to return to Windows.

Use caution. If you are using a computer in a laboratory with several computers, you probably should not stop Windows. Always check with your instructor or an available lab assistant before selecting the Turn Off option. If you merely want to restore the computer desktop to its original state before leaving the lab, then select the option "Restart."

Figure 1.9 The Shut Down Windows dialog box.

WORKING WITH PROGRAMS AND DATA

WordPad, a close relative of the full-featured Microsoft Word, is a word processor that comes with Windows. You will use WordPad to help illustrate several mouse and keyboard techniques that you can use in all Windows programs. Perhaps the best way for you to become better acquainted with the Windows environment is to go through a complete cycle including launching a program, opening a document, altering some of the document's text, and printing the final result. The following paragraphs describe these procedures.

Launching Applications Directly

The following exercise guides you through the process of executing (sometimes called launching) the WordPad program. Subsequent exercises continue the cycle to its conclusion—a finished letter ready for mailing.

EXERCISE 1.2: LAUNCHING AN APPLICATION

1. Click the Start button.
2. Point to All Programs in the Start menu.
3. Point to Accessories in the menu that cascades from All Programs.
4. Locate the WordPad menu item and click it once. If necessary, maximize the WordPad window. WordPad opens and displays an empty document.

Next, you will open a document and make a change to it. Doing this gives you practice using a typical Windows application menu. To read a document from a disk or CD in the WordPad window, you open a document. Open is a command found in the File menu of almost any Windows application.

First, let's discuss a few disk-naming conventions we will use throughout the text. Because the exact names of your internal hard disk, floppy disk(s), DVD, and CD drives vary depending on the configuration of your computer, we adopt the following disk names to keep things simple and consistent. We refer to your floppy drive as drive A, though it could be drive A or B. We assume you have at least one hard drive (though you may have more than one), which we refer to as drive C. Finally, drive D refers to the CD drive. Naturally, you may have any type of removable drive including a CD-R, a DVD drive, and so on. So, simply remember this: Drive A is the floppy disk drive, drive C is the hard disk drive, and drive D is the CD drive.

To prepare for the next exercise, place the Companion CD, which came with your text, into your CD drive. If your CD drive is E, for example, simply substitute E whenever we refer to drive D. Note: If an AutoPlay dialog box automatically opens shortly after you insert your CD, Windows is trying to help. It thinks you want to install new software from the CD. Simply click the dialog box Close button to remove the dialog box and proceed to the next exercise.

EXERCISE 1.3: OPENING A DOCUMENT

1. With WordPad still open, click the File menu to display its menu. Note that you can also press Alt+F to open the File menu.
2. Click Open, and then press Enter. The Open dialog box appears. Dialog boxes require you to supply additional information and, occasionally, to make decisions by clicking various check boxes, option buttons, and other objects within the dialog box. A list of file names (if any) found on one of the available disk drives is displayed in the File Name list box. Notice, however, that only files with .rtf extensions are displayed. Those files are stored in a form compatible with both WordPad and Word.
3. Click the arrow on the Look in drop-down list box, and select the CD drive (drive D or E). A list of ten folders called *Ch01 through Supplement* appears.
4. Double-click the Ch01 folder to open it, click the Files of Type list arrow, and then click the Word for Windows (*.doc) choice in the drop-down list (see Figure 1.10).
5. Open the file *FallWashPromotion.doc* by double-clicking its file name.

The document you see in WordPad is a letter to selected customers of The Coffee Merchant. It will be mailed to customers in the Washington state area promoting a special sale for a limited time. The letter displayed in WordPad illustrates a few typical Windows operations and WordPad procedures.

WordPad's Edit menu commands are similar to those found in other Windows products such as Excel or Word. With the *FallWashPromotion.doc* document still visible, let's locate and replace the two placeholder-phrases *company-city* and *company-state* with an actual customer's city and state. There is no need to replace the other placeholder tags that you see in the inside address right now. We just want you to briefly experience a typical replace operation.

EXERCISE 1.4: SEARCH AND REPLACE

1. Click the Edit menu (click Edit or press Alt+E).
2. Click the Replace command (notice the shortcut key combination Ctrl+H invokes replace without first selecting the Edit menu).

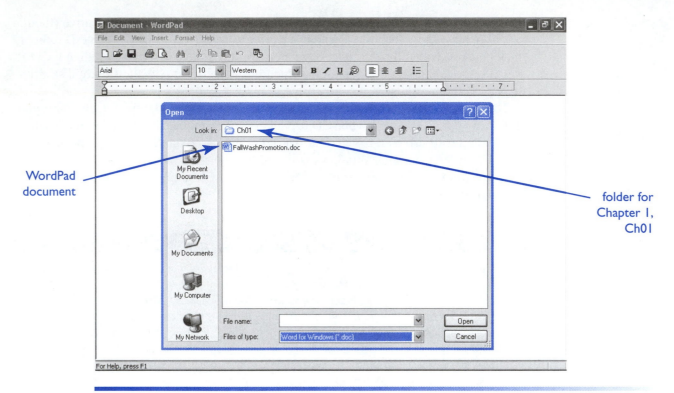

WordPad document

folder for Chapter 1, Ch01

Figure 1.10 Open dialog box.

The insertion point, a blinking vertical bar, is in the leftmost position in the Find what text box. The insertion point indicates where typed characters will appear.

3. In the *Find what* text box of the Find dialog box, type **company-city** and press Tab to move to the *Replace with* text box.
4. In the *Replace with* text box, type **Seattle** (see Figure 1.11), which is the replacement string consisting of those characters that replace any or all occurrences of the search string *company-city*.
5. Click the Replace All button to replace all occurrences of *company-city* with *Seattle*.
6. Click OK when the search ends.
7. Repeat steps 3 through 6, typing **company-state** in step 3 and **Washington** in step 4.
8. Click the Close button in the Replace dialog box title bar to close the dialog box.

EXERCISE 1.5: PRINTING PAGES AND EXITING

1. Click File on the menu bar, and then click Print. The Print dialog box opens.
2. Click the Pages option button found in the Page Range panel. The bullet to the left of Pages is darkened, indicating that it is the current choice among the Print Range options.
3. Type **1** to print only page 1. The completed dialog box is shown in Figure 1.12.
4. Click the Print button to print the file.
5. Click File, click Exit, and then click No when asked if you want to save changes. The document closes, and Windows closes the WordPad application.

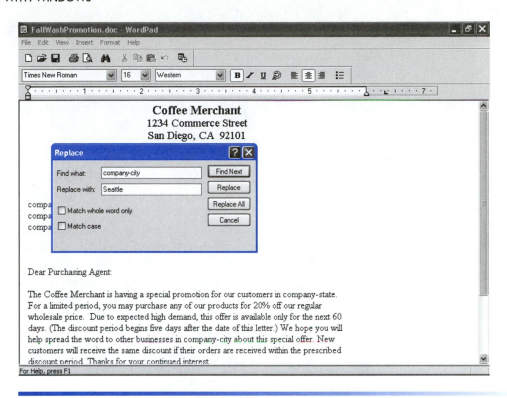

Figure 1.11 Replace dialog box.

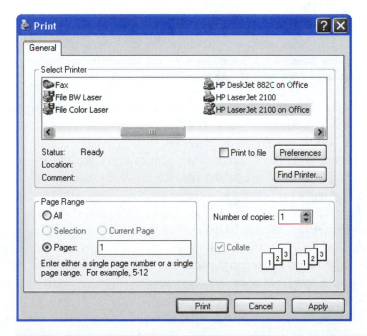

Figure 1.12 Print dialog box.

Launching an Application from a File

In this section, we introduce you briefly to this faster method to launch a program. Instead of directing you to a program and then a file to be manipulated by a program, we'll simply tell you the name of a data file on the Companion CD and ask you to find the data and launch the program that created it. Two questions come to mind. First, how does one find the file—especially considering the size of the CD and the number of files it contains? Second, what program must be launched in order to view or modify the data file? The answer to the first question is that you let the system search the entire Companion CD for you. As for the second question, the system automatically associates a program with a data file as long as the file has a recognized *secondary name* (or *extension*, as it is sometimes called).

Try this approach by finding a file and load its associated program. The next two exercises show you how to do that. In the first exercise, you will use a program called Search. Search locates files and directories by name on any disk drive. Suppose you know that a particular file is stored on the Companion CD, but you cannot remember where. All you remember is part of the file name—the first part of the file name is *Olympic* and has something to do with the Olympic games.

EXERCISE 1.6: FINDING A FILE

1. Click the Start button and then click Search. The Search Results dialog box opens.
2. Click in the *For Files or Folders Named* text box, type **Olympic** in the *Search for files or folders named* text box. This is the partial file name that the Search program will attempt to locate.
3. Ensure that your Companion CD is in the CD drive. Then, click the list arrow on the Look in list box. Then, click your CD drive. We call this navigating to your file.
4. Click the Search Now button to begin the search. (Keep the Search Results window open because you are going to use it again shortly.)

Within a short time, the Search program locates and displays all file or folder names that match the file name you specified. Figure 1.13 shows that it found only one file on the CD, *OlympicHostCountries.wri*.

Now that you have found the file, you can modify it. Suppose you don't know what program was used to create the file. That's okay, because the file name extension (or secondary name) is usually associated with a particular program. Files ending with .xls, for example, are Microsoft Office Excel files. Similarly, files ending with .mdb are Microsoft Office Access database files. You don't have to know these facts in order to invoke the program that created the file. The system remembers associations like those—file name extensions and their related programs. The next exercise shows you how simple it is to execute the program associated with the file that the Find program just located.

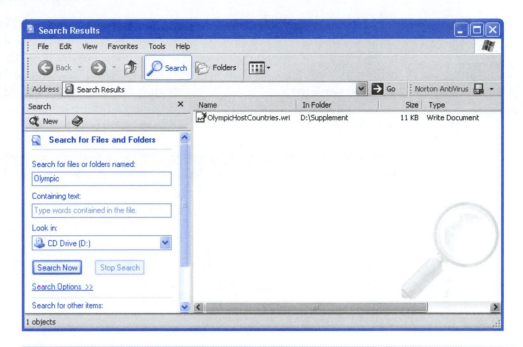

Figure 1.13 Locating a file using Search.

EXERCISE 1.7: LAUNCHING A PROGRAM FROM A DATA FILE

1. Make sure the Search Results window is still available and displays the file *OlympicHostCountries.wri.*
2. Double-click the file name *OlympicHostCountries.wri* displayed in the list of located files.
3. Windows launches WordPad, a Windows-supplied word processing program, and the Olympic document appears in a WordPad document window. The document lists information about the modern Olympics, including the host countries and number of participants.
4. Click WordPad's Maximize button so the document and WordPad fill the screen.
5. Move the insertion point to the top of the document and press Enter twice to open up two new lines. Click the topmost line, press Tab four times to move to the right in the new, first line, and type your name. (The font may be too large for your liking. In that case, select your name, click Format, click Font, and select a smaller point size.)
6. Click File on the menu bar, and then click Print to print the document.
7. Right-click the Search Results button on the Taskbar and click Close to close the Search program. Leave WordPad running, because you will use it in the next section.

Switching Between Applications

Windows is a *multitasking* operating system, which means it is capable of running more than one program at a time. You probably will find that it is most convenient to have several programs running and at the ready simultaneously. Perhaps you are working with accounts receivable files stored in Access and you are also writing letters to customers using Word or WordPad. To appreciate how handy the multitasking capabilities are, you have to experience it. Windows multitasking is smooth and intuitive. To illustrate how easy it is, you will start another program and practice switching between programs. Then you will learn how simple it is for two applications to share information.

EXERCISE 1.8: LAUNCH ANOTHER PROGRAM

1. Make sure that WordPad is still running.
2. Click the Start button on the Taskbar, and point to All Programs.
3. Point to the Accessories group, and locate and click Paint in the Accessories cascade menu. Paint appears (see Figure 1.14).

Now two programs are loaded and available simultaneously—WordPad and Paint. Examine the Taskbar (usually located at the bottom of your screen, though you can drag it to any of the four edges of your screen). Two Taskbar buttons represent the loaded programs.

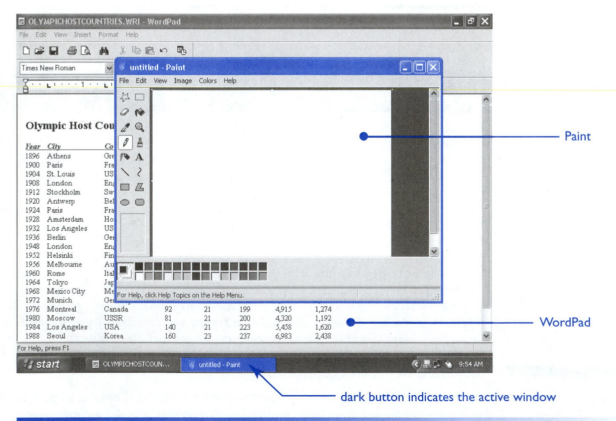

Figure 1.14   Paint and WordPad programs running simultaneously.

Program Taskbar buttons provide a convenient way to switch back and forth between programs, especially when programs are minimized. There are three ways to move from one running program to another. Each method operates slightly differently, and you may eventually select a favorite way to switch between applications. The first method uses the Taskbar to switch between tasks.

EXERCISE 1.9: USING THE TASKBAR TO SWITCH BETWEEN PROGRAMS

1. With WordPad and Paint still open, switch to WordPad by clicking the WordPad button (displaying the partial name of the document) on the Taskbar. The WordPad window becomes active.
2. Switch back to Paint by clicking its Taskbar button.

Another equally effective way to move to another program that is running is to use the keystroke shortcut Alt+Tab. Using the Alt+Tab key sequence is convenient for touch typists because it allows one to switch quickly between programs without using the mouse.

EXERCISE 1.10: USING ALT+TAB TO SWITCH BETWEEN PROGRAMS

1. Press and hold down the Alt key and tap and release the Tab key. With the Tab key released, continue holding down the Alt key for a moment. Windows displays in the middle of the screen a marquee of running programs. A border surrounds the program icon that will be displayed if you release the Alt key (see Figure 1.15).
2. Practice toggling between the two program icons by tapping the Tab key as you continue to hold down the Alt key.
3. Release the Tab key when the border is on the WordPad icon, and then release the Alt key to move to that program.

Occasionally, you may want to minimize all open windows on the desktop so that you can move to one of your desktop shortcuts. To do so, right-click the Taskbar (place the mouse in any unoccupied area of the Taskbar—avoiding any Taskbar buttons and the Task tray on the right end of the Taskbar) and click Show the Desktop from the shortcut menu. Using this method can save you time when the desktop is filled with several windows and you want a clear shot at the desktop.

The next section briefly describes how to share information between Windows applications. The particular method, called object linking and embedding, or OLE for short, simplifies producing mailing labels in Word from a subset of your customers' addresses in an Access database, for example.

Sharing Data Among Applications

Data from one program can be shared with another. In this simple but typical example, you will create a graphic in Paint and transfer the graphic to a WordPad document. The combined data—a graphic inside a document—is known as a *compound document*.

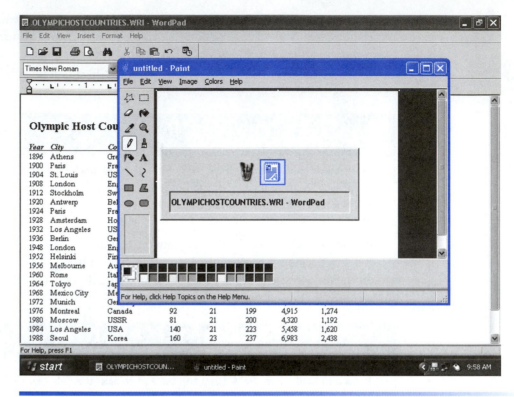

Figure 1.15   Using Alt+Tab to move between running programs.

TRY IT

First, make sure that WordPad and Paint are still running and that WordPad is the active program. Open (execute File, Open) the file called *RecycleLetter.wri*, which is also found in the Ch01 folder on your Companion CD. (Remember to set the file type in WordPad to *Windows Write (*.wri)* in the Files of type list box.) If Windows displays a dialog box asking if you want to save changes to the Olympic document, click No. Insert a blank line at the top of the document where the graphic will be placed. Switch to Paint. On the Paint menu bar, click File, click Open, and navigate to the Ch01 folder on your Companion CD, click *WeRecycle.bmp*, and click the Open button to open the graphic in Paint. Click the Select tool (the dashed rectangle), and click and drag the dashed line so that it just encompasses the graphic, including the text at the top. Then, click Edit and click Copy to place the graphic on the Clipboard. Switch back to WordPad, click Edit, click Paste, and move the graphic by dragging it so that it does not intersect any text. Click anywhere outside the pasted graphic to deselect it. Print the document. Figure 1.16 shows the completed compound document. When you are finished, close both the WordPad and Paint applications without saving the changes to any document or graphic.

embedded
graphic

Figure 1.16 Graphic embedded in a WordPad document.

What is important to remember from the preceding example is that you pass information between Windows applications by copying from one application—placing the object on the Clipboard—and then pasting the object into the recipient (container) document. This works for all Windows-compliant programs, including Access, Excel, and Word.

USING WINDOWS EXPLORER

Windows provides an advanced browser and file manager called Windows Explorer. Windows Explorer allows you to perform file management duties, open and close documents, and run programs. In fact, you may find that Windows Explorer is the interface you use most often, because it is frequently more convenient to find a file and work with it using Windows Explorer. Windows Explorer is found in the Programs group of the Start menu. It may be located elsewhere on your institution's computers, but it is easy to find.

TRY IT

Launch Windows Explorer so that you can see its interface. Click the Start button, and then point to All Programs. Click the Accessories group, and click Windows Explorer. (You can also launch Explorer by right-clicking the Start button and selecting Explore from the short-cut menu. This is probably the most convenient method.) If there are no folders in the left panel, then click Folders button.

The Folders pane presents a tree structure of your entire computer system including desktop objects. You can expand or collapse each branch of the tree as you desire. The right panel is the Contents pane. It displays the folders, files, and other objects found in the folder that is selected and open in the Folders pane.

Normally, Explorer displays a view of your computer system beginning with your desktop—the "root" of the hierarchical or tree structure of files and devices. Emphasizing the outline structure of your disk file structure, each folder displayed can contain files and other folders. Figure 1.17 shows a typical Explorer window with folders and files. Of course, your display will be different.

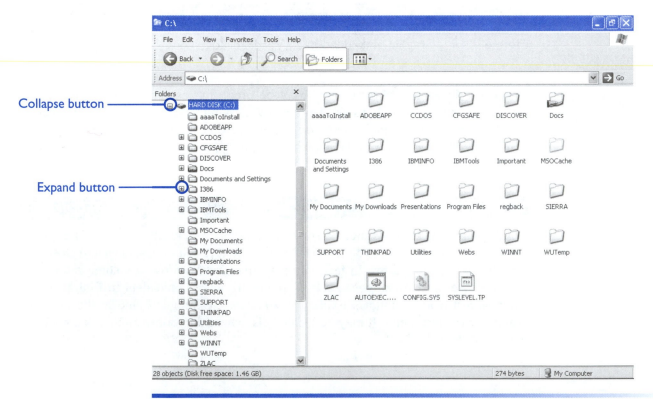

Figure 1.17 Typical Explorer window showing folders and files.

The lines in the Folders pane emphasize the relationships between folders and the folders and files that they contain. Notice the plus and minus signs at the intersection of horizontal and vertical lines in the Folders pane. A small box with a plus sign—called the Expand button—indicates that the object contains other objects that you can reveal by clicking the Expand button. Likewise, boxes with minus signs are called Collapse buttons. Clicking a Collapse button implodes the structure, revealing less detail.

Opening Drives, Files, and Folders

The Contents pane can show only one level of detail at a time. Therefore, you must click the Expand button on the particular drive or folder until you reach the particular file or folder for which you are looking. Suppose, for example, that you want to see what is on the Companion CD. Using Explorer, you can "walk" down through each of the folders and files, noting what files are stored in which folders. Practice expanding and collapsing folders in Explorer.

TRY IT

If Explorer is not running, start it (click the Start button, point to All Programs, click Accessories, and click Windows Explorer). Open the Folders pane, if necessary, by clicking Folders. In the Folders pane, click the Expand button next to My Computer, and click the icon representing the C drive in the Folders pane. Click the View button on the Standard Buttons toolbar, and click Icons. Your display should roughly resemble Figure 1.17, though the exact folder and file names on your disk will differ from the figure. Click the folder named Program Files in the Folders pane on the C drive. You may have to use the Folders pane scroll bar to move down the hierarchy of folders until the Program Files folder appears. Note, the Folders pane never displays file names. File names are displayed only in the Contents pane. Leave Windows Explorer open for an exercise that follows.

The preceding exercise illustrates the fundamental way you explore the disks and their contents. If you want to look at the contents of your Companion CD, simply click the drive icon corresponding to your CD or DVD drive and look at the Contents pane.

Formatting a Floppy Disk

One of the useful activities you can perform while running Explorer is formatting a disk. In particular, you can format your floppy disk, because it is highly unlikely you will want to format your hard disk(s) and you should not try to format your Companion CD. You may want to save your database files, temporary files, and other documents you develop while reading this book. The logical place to save information, especially while working in a university computing laboratory, is on a floppy disk or other removable devices such as a Zip disk. Disks such as Iomega Zip disks store several hundred times the information a floppy disk does. Zip disks, floppy disks, and rewritable CD disks are all highly portable. Formatting most rewritable devices follows the same general steps as formatting a floppy disk; so, it's a good idea to learn how to format a floppy disk. Warning: If you have a formatted disk containing valuable data, then do not use that disk for this exercise. Once formatted, a disk's files lost during the formatting process cannot be recovered.

EXERCISE 1.11: FORMATTING A FLOPPY DISK WITH EXPLORER

1. Launch Windows Explorer, if necessary, and place a floppy disk in drive A.
2. In the Folders pane of the Windows Explorer window, right-click the drive A icon (not the Expand button). (If drive A is not visible in the Folders pane, then slide the Folders pane scroll button to the top of the scroll bar. The icon for drive A will come into view.)
3. Click Format in the pop-up menu.
4. Click the Start button, and click OK if a warning message appears indicating you will erase the disk's contents.
5. Once the formatting process is complete, click OK to close the dialog box indicating formatting is complete, and then click the Close button to close the Format dialog box. (Leave Windows Explorer running, however.)

Creating Folders

Folders, like their physical counterparts in filing cabinet systems, are a convenient way to store and organize your files and other folders. Folders provide a way to partition and separate one group of project files from another. For instance, you may find it convenient to keep each chapter's homework, databases, and other work in its own folder whose name clearly indicates which chapter's material is stored therein (for example, a folder named Chapter 1). The next exercise guides you through this process using Windows Explorer. To prepare for this exercise, place a floppy disk in drive A. You may want to use the disk you formatted in the previous exercise.

EXERCISE 1.12: CREATING FOLDERS WITH WINDOWS EXPLORER

1. Ensure that Windows Explorer is running, and switch to it by clicking its button on the Taskbar.
2. Place a formatted floppy in drive A, and click the drive A icon in the Windows Explorer Folders pane.
3. Click File on the menu bar, point to New, and click Folder from the cascade menu. Windows creates a folder called New Folder and displays it in the Contents pane.
4. With the folder called "New Folder" still highlighted, type Chapter 2, and press Enter. Windows renames the folder **Chapter 2**
5. Click the Views icon on the Windows Explorer toolbar and then click Icons to display icons in the Contents pane.

6. Click the drive A Expand button in the Folders pane to display the new folder in the Folders and Contents panes. Figure 1.18 shows the new folder in place.
7. Click the Close button on Windows Explorer's title bar to terminate the program.

Now you know how to make new folders in which you can store files or other folders. Perhaps the most important subtlety in creating a folder is to ensure that you have selected the appropriate folder or disk before creating a new folder. Windows creates new folders below the folder or disk currently selected in the Folders pane. Therefore, if you want to create a folder labeled *Chapter 3* alongside the Chapter 2 folder, then first select the drive A icon. Otherwise, if Chapter 2 is highlighted in the Folders pane, Windows will create a new folder as a subfolder of Chapter 2.

Copying, Moving, Naming, and Deleting Files

The problem with opening and using Access databases that are stored on your Companion CD is that Access opens databases in a mode called read/write, whereby Access can both read and write database records. Unless you are using a writable CD drive or DVD drive, you cannot write data to a CD. When you open a database on your CD, Access displays a warning dialog box indicating the database is read-only. Here's a

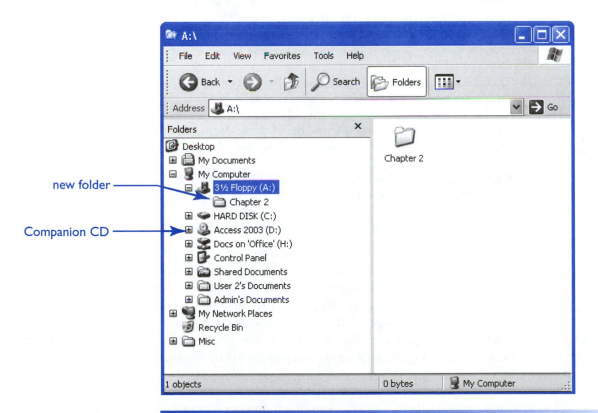

Figure 1.18 Creating a folder.

solution to this dilemma—one which you will use repeatedly while reading this text and using the associated databases.

Your Companion CD contains several databases, tables, and other objects that you will use as you read this textbook and work on the problems. In order for you to both read and write to Access databases, you have to copy files from the Companion CD to your computer's hard drive (preferable) or to your floppy disk (slower operating). Then, you must alter the Read-only file property so that the database can be both read and modified. After you do that, you will be able to operate normally on the copy of the database. That's why we want you to pay close attention to Exercises 1.13 and 1.14. In the following exercise, you will copy the file *Ch02.mdb* from the CD to the folder you just created, Chapter 2, on your floppy disk. In preparation for the exercise, launch Windows Explorer, if necessary, insert the floppy disk you formatted in the preceding exercise into drive A, and insert your Companion CD into the CD drive.

EXERCISE 1.13: COPYING A FILE FROM OUR COMPANION CD TO A DISK

1. Launch Windows Explorer, click the drive A icon, click its Expand button, and click the Windows Explorer Maximize button so that the Chapter 2 folder is displayed in the Folders pane and Windows Explorer fills the screen.
2. Scroll down the Folders pane display, locating the icon for your CD. Click the icon corresponding to your CD drive. Windows displays the folders in both the Folders pane and the Contents pane.
3. Click the Ch02 folder in the Folders pane. The contents of the folder, an Access database file, appear in Windows Explorer's Contents pane.
4. Click and drag the file *Ch02.mdb* in the Contents pane to the drive A icon in the Folders pane. (If drive A is not visible near the top of the Folders pane, continue dragging by moving the mouse to the top of the Folders pane. The pane will scroll down and reveal the floppy disk, drive A.)
5. Continue dragging the file until the dimmed file name, which represents the mouse, is directly over the Chapter 2 folder in the Folders pane. The folder will be highlighted when the mouse is properly positioned.
6. Release the left mouse button, dropping the file into the folder.

When you drag and drop a file from one disk to a different disk, Windows *copies* the file. However, if you drag and drop a file from one folder on a disk to another folder on the same disk, Windows *moves* the file. You can have more control over the action by right-clicking the selected file to drag it (we call this action right-drag for short). When you drop the file into its destination folder, a pop-up menu is displayed from which you can choose either to copy or move the file by clicking which action you'd like. Figure 1.19 shows the pop-up menu displayed when you right-drag a file.

Moving a file from one place to another is a cut and paste operation. The easiest way to move a file is by right-clicking it and then dragging it from one location to another. When you release the right mouse, a pop-up menu appears. From the menu, you

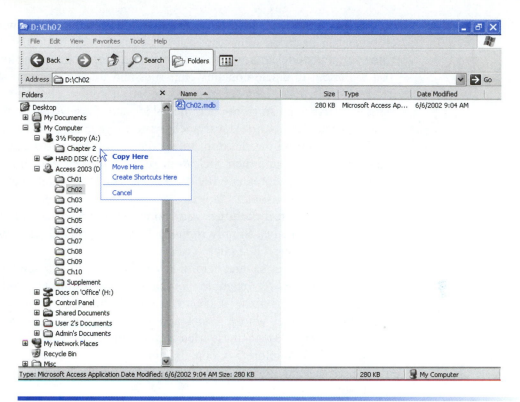

Figure 1.19   Pop-up menu displayed after right-dragging a file.

can select Move. Using the keyboard is perhaps the fastest way to copy or move a file from one place to another:

- Locate and click the file to be copied.
- Press Ctrl+C (to copy) or Ctrl+X (to move).
- Locate the target folder in Windows Explorer's Folders pane, and select the folder (the target).
- Finally, press Ctrl+V to paste the file into the target folder.

You can copy or move entire files or a collection of files from one folder to another using copy or cut and paste keystrokes identical to those you use when copying objects between programs and the Clipboard.

Eventually, files and folders are no longer useful to you and you can delete them. The folder and file you created on drive A—the folder called Chapter 2 and the file *Ch02.mdb*—are merely useful for demonstration purposes, and you no longer need them. When you delete files or folders from your hard disk, Windows places them in a special folder called the *Recycle Bin* where they remain until you empty the bin. If you delete files from a floppy disk, they are not placed in the Recycle Bin. In the latter case, you cannot recover deleted files.

You delete folders in the same way as files. However, the consequences of deleting a folder can be more significant than deleting one or more files. When you delete a folder, you also delete any files and folders it may contain. Make sure that the folder you are about to delete contains only files and folders that you are sure you want to delete. To delete a folder, select it in Windows Explorer and drag it to the Recycle Bin. Alternatively, you can right-click the folder and click Delete in the pop-up menu.

Restoring files you previously deleted from your hard disk is simple. Double-click the Recycle Bin on the desktop, select file(s) you want to restore (ctrl-click or shift-click—see below), and then click *Restore the selected items* in the Recycle Bin Tasks panel. Windows restores any files or folders you select and places them back in their original locations.

Whenever you feel the urge, you can empty the Recycle Bin, permanently removing all files it contains. Simply right-click the Recycle Bin and select the option titled Empty Recycle Bin. Then click Yes.

Windows provides several helpful keystroke shortcuts for selecting files. While using Windows Explorer, for example, you can press and hold Ctrl and click file names to select noncontiguous files. Hold Shift and click the first and last of a group of contiguous files (those files whose names appear in sequence next to one another) to select the whole group. Besides these tried and true methods, you can drag the mouse pointer across Windows Explorer's Contents window, creating a rectangular dashed line. Any file names the line touches will be selected when you release the mouse pointer. Try it yourself.

You can rename a folder or file by right-clicking it and then click Rename from the pop-up menu. Finally, type the object's new name and press Enter. You can cancel the pop-up menu and choose to take no action by clicking anywhere outside the menu. Another, perhaps simpler, way to rename a file or folder is to select it and then press F2. Or you can slowly click twice (do not double-click) a file or folder name. A vertical, blinking cursor appears at the end of the object's name. You can retype the name or use the arrow keys to move the cursor left or right to make small changes in the name. Practice clicking slowly twice to master the procedure. If you are too quick, you'll end up launching the application that is associated with the file whose name you double-clicked. Stick with one of the other renaming techniques if you have difficulty using the two-click method.

Setting File and Folder Properties

Files and folders have hidden attributes or properties that both limit actions you can take on the objects and display information about the objects. Which properties you can alter depends on the type of object. Files and folders have a common set of properties that you can access from Windows Explorer either by right-clicking the object or by selecting Properties from Explorer's File menu. Four properties that all file types and folders have in common are called Archive, Read-only, Hidden, and System. Of these, only one is important to us—the Read-only property.

Access database files, which you will use throughout this book, will not open properly if their Read-only attributes are set. When you copy a database file from a CD to a floppy disk or hard disk, some versions of the Windows operating system leave the Read-only attribute set. (We use the term *set* to mean "has the value of yes" or "is enabled.") The next exercise shows you how to clear (remove) a file's Read-only property, regardless of the operating system you are using, thereby ensuring you can alter its contents and then save it back to its original file.

EXERCISE 1.14: CLEARING A FILE'S READ-ONLY PROPERTY

1. Navigate to drive A in the Folders pane and select the folder Chapter 2, which contains the file *Ch02.mdb* you copied in Exercise 1.13.
2. In Windows Explorer's Contents pane, right-click the file *Ch02.mdb* and click Properties from the pop-up list. The Properties dialog box opens.
3. Click the Read-only check box to clear it (see Figure 1.20). (If the box has a check mark, clicking it will erase the check mark—clear it.) Notice that the Apply button, dimmed prior to your action, is now available.
4. Finally, click OK to affirm the change and return to Windows Explorer.

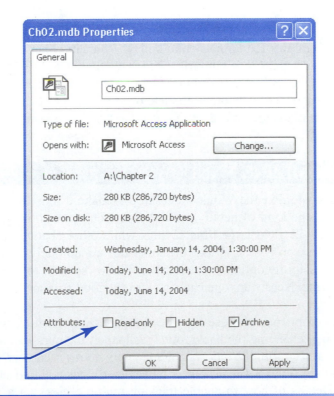

Read-only property

Figure 1.20 Clearing a file's Read-only property.

Launching a Program from Explorer

As you become more comfortable with Windows, you may use Windows Explorer as your default work surface for beginning your Access database work. Because most files are associated with an application, it is usually easiest to launch Explorer, locate the database file you want to work with, and then launch Access by double-clicking the file. This is a simple, efficient approach to starting a program and opening a file to work on. You have practiced this once already, in Exercise 1.7, Launching a Program from a Data File. In that exercise, you located a file with Search and then double-clicked the file name to launch WordPad. When you locate with Windows Explorer the database file you want to open, simply double-click its name to launch Microsoft Access.

Generally, the pattern you should follow in working with database files supplied with this text is to first copy the particular chapter's database file to drive C, your computer's hard drive, so that Access can read, write, and modify database information rapidly. This way, you will be able to make needed database modifications as you read the text and see the effects of your changes. Of course, you can open the Companion CD databases directly on the CD, but Access allows you to read the data only. You cannot post any changes to the database stored on the CD.

Exiting Windows Explorer

Exiting Windows Explorer is child's play. You can either choose Close from the File menu or click the Close button located in the upper right corner of the Explorer window. If you haven't closed Explorer yet, do so now using either method. The Windows desktop reappears (or another application if any are still running). Make sure all running applications are closed so that you have a clear view of the desktop.

CUSTOMIZING WINDOWS

You can customize the Windows desktop to make it more efficient for you to use and to provide the kind of detail you like. Some customization features, such as desktop shortcuts, will yield large time savings while other changes you make simply establish the desktop—your virtual office space—as uniquely yours. Windows also provides accessibility options, which make Windows easier to use for those with physical impairments. Nearly anyone can find several good reasons to customize the Windows desktop.

Different people who use a single computer may wish to customize the desktop to their liking, changing the background wallpaper, the number and types of icons on the desktop, and so forth. Windows automatically tracks each user's preferences and saves them in their own profile. The user name determines which desktop environment is selected. Details of how to enable tracking multiple users on a single machine are beyond the scope of this chapter.

Creating and Using Shortcuts

A shortcut is an icon representing a program or other object that provides a quick way to access a particular object. The Start menu items, for example, are shortcuts to programs. Shortcuts inherit the same icon as the object to which they point, thus making it sometimes difficult to distinguish between them. However, shortcut icons also contain a small arrow, which distinguishes the shortcut icon from the icon actually representing a program or other object.

The most common reason to create a desktop shortcut is to provide quick access to frequently used applications. There is practically no limit to the number of shortcuts you can create and place on the desktop, but we advise restraint. If you create too many shortcuts, the desktop can become cluttered and unreadable and you are almost back to where you started—unable to find a particular application or other object quickly. On the other hand, you may want to create shortcuts for lots of objects and then later cull the collection to the 20 percent of the shortcuts you use 80 percent of the time (the often observed "20/80" rule). In any case, it is simple enough to delete unwanted shortcuts later. Let's see how to create desktop shortcuts by creating one of your own. Bear in mind that your university computer laboratory may be set up to prevent this type of desktop customization. It can't hurt to try, though.

EXERCISE 1.15: CREATING A DESKTOP SHORTCUT

1. Close any open applications so that the desktop is clearly visible.
2. Click the Taskbar Start button, point to All Programs, and point to the Accessories group.
3. Right-click WordPad.
4. Point to *Send To* (see Figure 1.21), and click *Desktop (create shortcut)* in the cascade menu. Windows places a shortcut on the desktop.
5. Click the Start button to close its menu.

The shortcut appears on the desktop. The shortcut icon matches WordPad's icon in every respect except that an arrow appears in the lower left corner. This identifies the icon as a shortcut (see Figure 1.22).

Use folders on the desktop to group shortcuts if your desktop becomes too cluttered. This way, you can find a shortcut by opening the folder containing related shortcuts. Creating a desktop folder is a basic, five-step procedure: Right-click any blank area on the desktop, point to New, click Folder, type the folder's name, and press Enter. With a folder on the desktop, you can drag shortcuts from the desktop and drop them into the folder. Because the desktop is both the source and destination of the operation, the shortcut is moved to a folder by default when you drag and drop it. To remove an object from a desktop folder and place it back on the desktop, double-click the folder to open it and then drag the object from the open folder onto the desktop. Delete a folder by selecting it and then pressing the Delete key. Click Yes to confirm the delete operation.

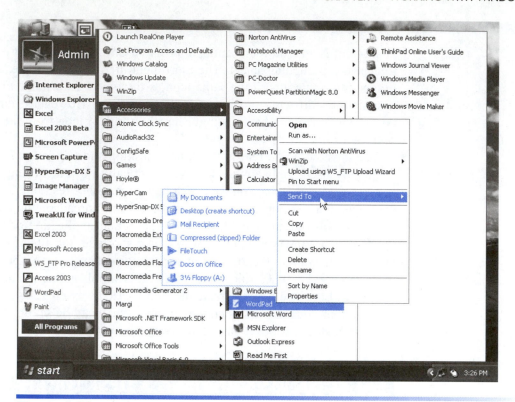

Figure 1.21   Creating a shortcut.

Placing Shortcuts on the Start Menu

You can customize the Start menu like other Windows objects. A time saver is to place shortcuts to frequently used programs on the Start menu. Because the real estate available on the Start menu is limited, restrict what you place there to the select programs you use the most. Remember, too, if you are working in a university computing laboratory, you probably will not be able to customize the Start button. The following exercise explains how to place a shortcut on the Start menu.

TRY IT

Right-click the WordPad shortcut you just placed on the desktop, drag it to the Start button, and release the right mouse. (If you click and drag the WordPad shortcut from the desktop and drop it on the Start menu, the shortcut is *moved*, not copied, to the Start menu.) Click the Start button and locate the WordPad shortcut in the Start menu (see Figure 1.23).

Figure 1.22   WordPad shortcut.

Removing Start Menu Items

You can remove shortcuts from the Start menu easily. If you followed the suggestion above and added a shortcut to the Start menu, then try the following exercise to remove the item. Otherwise, simply read the steps that follow.

EXERCISE 1.16: REMOVING A SHORTCUT FROM THE START MENU

1. Click the Start menu.
2. Right-click the WordPad entry in the Start menu. A pop-up menu appears (see Figure 1.24).
3. Click *Remove from This List* in the pop-up menu.

Clearing the Start Menu Documents Window

The My Recent Documents menu displays the names of the last 15 documents that you accessed. For instance, the document *FallWashPromotion.doc* appears in the My Recent Documents window if you opened that document recently. Similarly, if you open a database, the name of that database is placed in the My Recent Documents menu. When the number of document names exceeds 15, the oldest name is removed

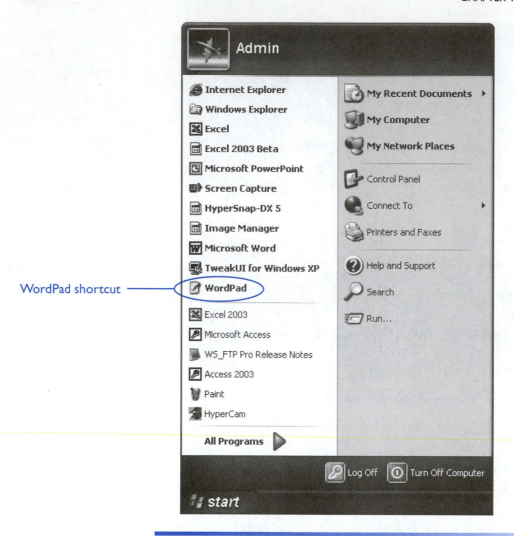

WordPad shortcut

Figure 1.23 WordPad shortcut on the Start menu.

from the bottom of the list and the newest name is placed at the top. The Document window provides a quick way to return to a document you were working with recently—whether it is a Word document, Access database, or Notepad memo.

There's a slightly faster way to display the Taskbar Properties sheet. Simply right-click any *gray* area of the Taskbar (a gray area is any Taskbar area that is not occupied by a program button or the Status area). Then choose Properties from the pop-up menu. Remember this time-saver when you deal with the Start menu or the Taskbar.

Take a moment to look at the My Recent Documents menu on your computer to see what names appear there: Click the Start button, and then point to My Recent Documents. Sometimes people are sensitive about document names appearing in the My Recent Documents window. For instance, suppose you had just worked on a letter named *IncomeTaxesDue.doc* containing sensitive tax and income information. You

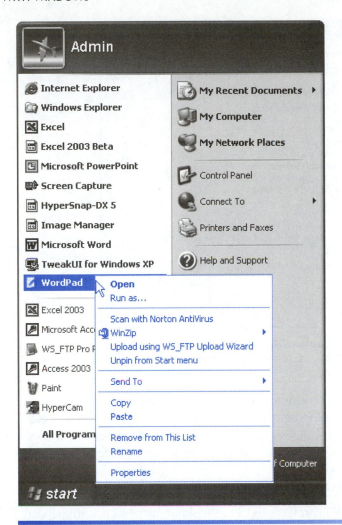

Figure 1.24 Removing a shortcut from the Start menu.

certainly do not want an unauthorized person reading the document. Clearing the file names from that list is a matter of remembering a few keystrokes. The next exercise illustrates the required steps.

EXERCISE 1.17: CLEARING THE DOCUMENTS MENU

1. Right-click the Start button.
2. Click Properties from the pop-up menu, and then click the Customize button.
3. Click the Advanced tab (see Figure 1.25).
4. Click the Clear List button. The document names are cleared from My Recent Documents, and the Clear button is dimmed.
5. Click the OK button to close the dialog box, and click OK to close the Taskbar and Start Menu Properties dialog box.

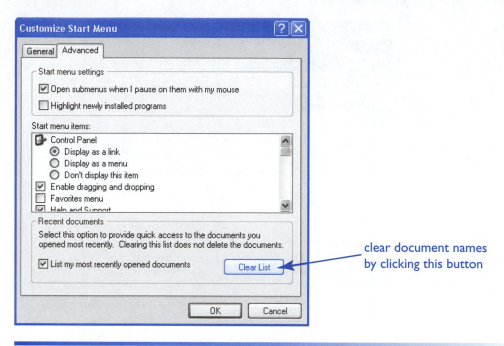

Figure 1.25   Clearing document names from the My Recent Documents list.

Now if you examine the Start menu My Recent Documents list, you will see a single item indicating that the list is empty. Emptying the My Recent Documents list does not prevent someone from accessing your documents, but it does prevent someone else from knowing what documents you accessed recently.

Customizing the Taskbar

Some people prefer to have the Taskbar out of sight until needed. Others like the Taskbar placed in a different location on the desktop. You can customize the Taskbar to suit your needs. We show you how to alter both the location and behavior of the Taskbar. However, we want to remind you to be considerate of others who may use the computer after you are done. Anyone using a public-access computer such as a college laboratory computer expects to find shortcuts and Start menu items in familiar places. Change the Taskbar all you want, but be sure to return the computer to its original state prior to leaving the laboratory. If you hide the Taskbar, the next student who uses the computer may not know how to make the Taskbar reappear. Be sure to clear the Auto-hide Taskbar property before leaving the computer.

To change the height of the Taskbar, move the pointer to the upper edge of the Taskbar. When the pointer changes to a double-headed arrow, drag the upper border towards the center of the screen to widen the Taskbar. Similarly, drag the top edge of the Taskbar towards the edge of the screen to make the Taskbar narrower. Try altering the Taskbar's size. Widen it to almost half the height of the screen, and then restore it to its standard height.

Changing the location of the Taskbar from its default position at the bottom of the screen is a straightforward procedure. Simply drag the Taskbar to one of the four edges of the screen to place it in that position.

TRY IT

Click any empty area of the Taskbar, and drag it to the top of the screen. Notice that the Taskbar docks itself up against the top of the display, and desktop icons automatically shift down slightly to accommodate the Taskbar. Drag the Taskbar to the right or left side of the desktop. Again, desktop shortcuts move out of the way accordingly.

Sometimes the Taskbar is unnecessary or is using up valuable screen space. You can hide the Taskbar until you need it again by setting its Auto-hide property. To change the Taskbar's display behavior, right-click an empty area of the Taskbar and then click Properties. Check the Auto-hide check box to place a checkmark in it (see Figure 1.26), and click OK. The dialog box closes, and the Taskbar moves off the screen until you move the cursor near the Taskbar's former location.

Experiment yourself. Set the Auto-hide property, and then move the cursor near the edge of the screen where the Taskbar usually appears. The Taskbar reappears. When

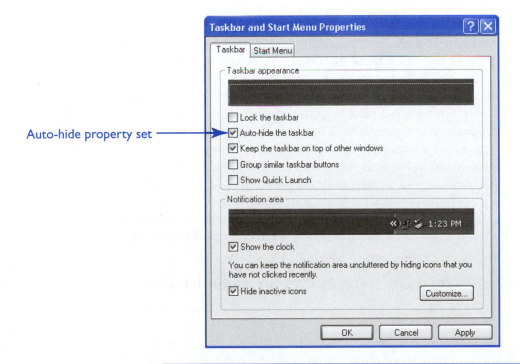

Figure 1.26 Setting the Taskbar's Auto-hide property.

you move the pointer away from the edge of the screen, the Taskbar slips out of sight. Clearing the Auto-hide property reverses this behavior. Bring the Taskbar into sight, right-click in a blank area, select Properties, and clear Auto-hide in the Taskbar appearance panel of the Taskbar and Start Menu Properties dialog box. Finally, click OK to establish the Taskbar characteristics.

Another property, Show clock, determines whether the time is displayed on the Taskbar. Clearing it removes the clock. Setting it displays the clock.

You probably noticed the Apply button on the Taskbar and Start Menu Properties dialog box. It serves a different function from the OK button. Clicking Apply establishes the properties you have selected but leaves the dialog box open. You can make additional Taskbar changes if you wish. Clicking OK establishes the properties you have selected and closes the dialog box, precluding further property changes until the dialog box is reopened.

RESTARTING WINDOWS

Sometimes an error occurs that causes the keyboard to freeze, in which case you may need to restart Windows. Windows indicates that an error has occurred and instructs you to restart, or you may need to log off your network and reconnect as a different user. The first case requires you to simply restart Windows but not necessarily reinitialize the entire machine. The latter case, logging on as a different user, is useful for several reasons. Whenever you restart Windows, you may be asked to specify your user name and password. If your computer is on a network, you may also have to provide a user name and password to log on to the Local Area Network (LAN). The network and Windows user names and passwords can be the same to simplify the task of connecting to both the network and Windows. To focus our discussion on Windows itself, let's assume for a moment that your computer is not connected to a LAN. Why then are a user name and password required or even useful on a standalone Windows computer? One major reason is that Windows can accommodate and keep track of multiple users' desktop preferences with user names. This way, several people, each with a self-assigned user name, can log on to a particular computer. Then, Windows restores the user's desktop icons, Start menu settings, and other work environment information for each identified user. Preserved desktop settings and environment are saved in user profiles. User profiles provide customized desktop configurations that allow people using the computer to work most efficiently. Forcing everyone who uses a particular computer to use a fixed set of shortcuts hinders creativity and efficiency.

 Go to http://perry.swlearning.com for an in-depth tutorial.

SUMMARY

This chapter describes the Windows environment. You have launched Windows, logged on to Windows, examined what is on the desktop, and used the mouse. You have learned how to use a typical Windows dialog box and what menu items are found in the Start menu. You understand how to launch programs directly from the All Programs item on the Start menu. You learned how to share data between running programs by embedding a Paint graphic inside a WordPad document. You learned how easily you can switch from one program to another by using the program buttons located on the Taskbar.

After working with the Windows interface, you examined Windows Explorer. You opened disk drives, folders, and files; formatted a floppy disk for first-time use; created a folder on your floppy disk; and copied files from the Companion CD to your floppy disk. Using Explorer, you discovered how to delete and rename files, how to set selected file properties, and how to launch applications from associated data files.

You discovered that shortcuts are a very convenient and flexible Windows feature. You used existing shortcuts and learned how to create your own desktop shortcuts. You found that you could place shortcuts on the Start menu to provide quick, global access to your most often used programs. You learned that the Document menu's list of recently accessed files provided automatic and fast access to items you recently worked on. You learned how to clear the My Recent Document list to eliminate the file names from prying eyes. Moving the Taskbar to other edges of the screen, you realized yet another way to customize the Windows desktop.

QUESTIONS AND PROBLEMS FOR REVIEW

Multiple-Choice Questions

1. Where would you find the Control icon, which is used to manipulate the window with the keyboard?
   a. Control panel
   b. Menu bar
   c. Tool bar
   d. Title bar

2. The terms *point, click, drag, double-click,* and *right-click* describe different ways to use
   a. the keyboard.
   b. the mouse.
   c. the Taskbar.
   d. none of the above.

3. The Documents menu displays a list of the most recent objects you have used. It is unique in that these objects
   a. can only be from the same program or the same tool.
   b. are limited to objects used a minimum number of times.
   c. are all from your current session.
   d. can be from any program or tool.

4. Creating and using file folders are helpful in that
   a. they are a convenient way to store files and other folders.
   b. they help you to be organized by separating one group of project files from another.
   c. they make searching for a specific file easier and more efficient.
   d. all of the above.

5. If you mistakenly delete a file or folder, from where can you retrieve it?
   a. The Documents menu
   b. The desktop
   c. You can't retrieve it
   d. The Recycle bin

6. You can rename a folder or file by
   a. right-clicking it and then selecting Rename from the pop-up menu.
   b. selecting it and pressing F4.
   c. quickly clicking it twice and retyping the name.
   d. using Save As from the File menu.

7. Shortcut icons represent what?
   a. A quick way to access a particular object
   b. Applications only
   c. Files or folders only
   d. The most efficient way to shut down an application

8. You can launch a program from
   a. a shortcut icon or a file.
   b. Explorer.
   c. programs via the Start menu.
   d. all of the above.

9. Customized desktop configurations are saved in what?
   a. The Desktop
   b. The Start menu
   c. User profiles
   d. The Control Panel

10. The advanced browser and file manager that allows you to open, close, and run documents is called
    a. Windows Explorer.
    b. Accessories.
    c. My Computer.
    d. Desktop.

Discussion Questions

1. Describe in a few sentences how you would use Windows Explorer. Start by explaining the structure of the Windows Explorer panels. What types of operations can you do on files?

2. Briefly describe at least five applications contained in the Accessories folder. (Click Start, point to All Programs, and click Accessories.)

3. Explain two ways to create a shortcut to a program or document.

4. Describe the ways to get help on Windows in general. How would you obtain help using cut and paste in WordPad?

5. Discuss what, in general terms, is found in the folder called My Recent Documents. What steps can you take to empty that folder?

Practice Exercises

1. Create a folder on your desktop called Practice Problems. Create another folder inside Practice Problems called Chapter 1 Problems. Launch WordPad. In two sentences describe what skills you hope to develop using this text. Include your name and date in the document. Save the file as *Practice Problem 1* in the Chapter 1 Problems folder. Close all windows. Using Windows Explorer, find your WordPad file and print it.

2. You might find it handy to have a calculator at your fingertips. Search for the Windows application file called *Calc*. Create a shortcut on your desktop of this application. Move this shortcut to the Start menu. Delete the duplicate shortcut from the desktop.

3. Insert your Companion CD into your drive. Open in WordPad the file called *PracticeExercise3.rtf* in the Ch01 folder. Clear the Read-only Attribute, if needed. Replace "student name" with your name. Save the file as *PE3.rtf* on your computer in a location of your choice. Reopen the file and print.

4. Close any Windows application you currently have running. Launch Microsoft WordPad. Type your name on the first line, and minimize the window. Go to the Start menu, and restart your computer. What happened? Hopefully, Windows reminded you to save your work and close WordPad. Cancel any messages, close WordPad without saving the file, and now restart your computer.

5. Get prepared and organized for this class (as well as others) by creating homework folders for the first three chapters. If you are using a computer that is not your own, create these folders on a disk. Logically name the folders and organize them (i.e., place folders inside other folders where it makes sense) so that you can easily save future work and find it quickly.

Problems

1. Using WordPad, write a short, two-paragraph summary of the main points covered in one of your recent classes. For instance, write about your latest accounting information systems class lecture. Be sure to include your name on the document so you can easily identify it. After you have created a document, save it on your floppy disk. Then print the document.

2. If you have a new, unused floppy disk, use Windows Explorer to format your disk. In addition, label the new disk with your last name. Next, using either the new disk or one that already has information on it, use Windows Explorer to create two folders called *Notes* and *Homework* on your disk.

3. Create a new company logo using Microsoft Paint. The logo should contain at least your company's name. Try the Airbrush, Brush, Line, and Pencil tools. Change colors. Be creative. This might be your future company's logo, after all! Choose 256 Color Bitmap in the *Save as type* list box. Save the graphic on your disk in any folder as the file *MyLogo.bmp*. Launch the WordPad program. Start the document by embedding your logo into the new document, and then write some text on the lines below your logo. Save the document as *MyLogo.wri* on your floppy disk, and print the document. Be sure your name is either in the logo or near the top of the typed material so that you can easily distinguish your output. Finally, close both Paint and WordPad.

4. Launch the following programs, one after the other: WordPad, Paint, Notepad, and Windows Explorer. Minimize all applications so they are buttons on the Taskbar. Right-click a program's Taskbar button, and select Close from the pop-up menu to stop and unload the program. Repeat the program-exiting process for all remaining programs. How many ways can you think of to exit the programs you launched?

5. Learn about Windows by consulting Help. Click Start, and then click *Help and Support*. Type **Copying files** in the Search text box, and click the Start searching icon. Click any of the resulting topics in the Search Results panel, and click the Print icon to print the help topic you are exploring. Close the Help and Support Center window when you are done.

CHAPTER 2
Introduction to Microsoft Access

OBJECTIVES

This chapter introduces you to using the Microsoft Office Access database. You will use existing databases to browse data, use Microsoft Access menus, and create several types of information forms. The purpose of this chapter is to provide you a level footing in using Access. If you have used Microsoft Office Access extensively, then you can skip this chapter. Important topics covered in this chapter include:

- Starting and exiting Access.
- Understanding the Access work surface icons.
- Using the Access objects, including tables, queries, forms, and reports.
- Opening and displaying database tables.
- Retrieving information with queries.
- Modifying tables' contents with action queries.
- Creating and using forms to display and query tables and databases.
- Designing and using database reports.

We feature a small, fictitious stock brokerage firm to illustrate how organizations use databases to manipulate and store crucial business information. The brokerage firm must maintain a record of each client's portfolio of stocks, bonds, etc. Among the important information stored is client information (such as name and address) and portfolio information (such as the stock purchased, purchase date, and number of shares bought). As we work with the database package in this chapter, we will reveal various information items kept by the stock brokerage firm. More importantly, this chapter demonstrates that a relational database system can be built to track and maintain critical business information and economic events.

INTRODUCTION

Modern computer-based systems, including most accounting systems, have a database system. An accounts receivable program, for example, frequently stores its information in a special system known as a database. The information is subsequently extracted, summarized, and displayed by a program especially adept at storing, organizing, and quickly retrieving facts stored in a database. Such systems are known as database management systems.

What Is Microsoft Office Access?

You will study and use one such database management system written for microcomputers, called Microsoft Office Access. Once you learn the fundamentals of Microsoft Office Access, you will be able to create your own accounting systems with this powerful database system. (We usually use the shorthand term "Access" in this textbook rather than the longer term "Microsoft Office Access.")

What Is a Relational Database?

Access is a relational database management system. A relational database system is founded on the rules, created and published by Dr. E. F. Codd, that collectively define a relational database management system. Of the several database management system types, the relational database management systems are the most widely used today. We will uncover some of Codd's rules for relational database systems in Chapters 3 and 4 and elsewhere in the text.

The fundamental storage entity for a relational database system is easy to visualize—it is a two-dimensional object having rows and columns called a table. A table holds data, and each row corresponds to one instance of data. Each of a table's columns corresponds to a different characteristic, called an *attribute*. For example, consider a table holding employee information. A particular row of the table represents an individual employee. There are as many rows in an employee table as there are employees in the company, division, or department. The employee table's columns hold data such as employees' first names, last names, hire dates, social security numbers, genders, birth dates, and so on. Each column holds only one "fact." For instance, a given column always contains employees' hire dates and nothing else; another column holds only employees' last names.

A database often is comprised of more than one table. For instance, the employee table might be only one of several tables that collectively describe a company's employees, their skills, and their complete productivity histories. Almost always, more than one table is used to store information. A collection of tables that are related and collectively describe an entity is known as a database. You can imagine that an accounts receivable database contains many tables that are related to one another: a customer table, a salesperson table, an inventory table (you sell goods from inventory), and so on. Although most databases contain several tables, the terms *database* and *table* frequently are used interchangeably. *Flat file* is the term given for a database consisting of one table—a very rare occurrence in business.

Most databases used in business and government are large, often consisting of hundreds of tables. We will not subject you to such a large system in our examples or exercises. However, our databases do contain more than one table, and some of those tables have several hundred rows. Manipulating several, larger tables will give you an idea of what real corporate databases entail. The reason for using multiple tables to represent related information will become clear as you continue to read.

To better understand the concept of tables and their relationships, begin by launching Access and looking at a few tables we have prepared.

Starting Microsoft Access

Your first exercise in this chapter is to launch Access. First, launch Windows if necessary. Access is usually stored with other Microsoft Office products. Locate Access, whose file name is *Msaccess.exe*, with Windows Explorer. If you have difficulty, then use Find in the Start menu and search for the file name. Once you find it, you can launch Access directly from the Find dialog box.

EXERCISE 2.1: STARTING ACCESS

1. Click Start, point to All Programs, and locate and click the Microsoft Access program in the All Programs list.
2. Access opens and displays the Task Pane (see Figure 2.1). If the Task Pane is not open, then click View on the menu bar, point to Toolbars, and click Task Pane to open it.

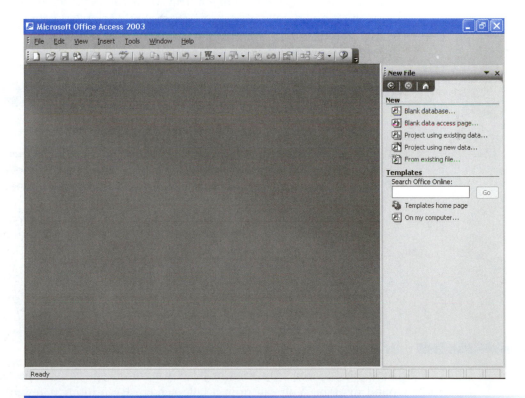

Figure 2.1 Access Open dialog box in the Startup window.

The Access Startup window that appears to the left of the Task Pane is the principal workspace. All Access windows are opened in the Access Startup window, and they are wholly contained in it. Each type of Access window you will encounter appears in its own window. Tables are always displayed in a Table window. You view forms, described in the section *Using Forms* (page 91) in this chapter, in a Form window, reports in a Report window, and so on. Each window has its own distinct commands and functions that apply only to that type of window. You will see these windows and the commands contained in them when we discuss each type of window. Take a moment to examine the Access window (see Figure 2.1 if you are not using the computer right now).

Along the top of the window are the Title bar and the Minimize, Restore, and Close buttons. Just below the Title bar is the Startup window menu bar, containing the File, Edit, View, Insert, Tools, Window, and Help menus. Below the menu bar is the Database toolbar, displaying buttons appropriate for the current window. (Many icons are dim because they cannot be clicked without a database being open.) When you move the mouse over the toolbar buttons, their names appear after a short delay. They are called toolbar ScreenTips.

Obtaining Help

It is important to know how to get help when you get stuck or would just like to know more about a particular aspect of Access. Let's see what help is available on creating forms. Make sure the Access Startup window is visible and active, and then do the following exercise.

EXERCISE 2.2: DISPLAYING HELP

1. Click Help on the menu bar and then click Microsoft Access Help. The Microsoft Access Help panel appears in the task pane.
2. Type **form** in the Search text box at the top of the Microsoft Access Help panel, and then click the Start searching button (the green arrow icon to the right of the Search text box).
3. Click *Create a form* from the list of choices in the Search results panel. Help about creating forms appears in a separate Microsoft Access Help dialog box.
4. Click the Maximize button in the Microsoft Access Help dialog box, and then click the Show All link in the upper right corner to expand the help topics (see Figure 2.2).
5. After you have examined the help screen for a moment, click the Close button on the Microsoft Access Help title bar.
6. Click View on the menu bar, and then click Task Pane to close the task pane. (Shortcut: Click the Close button on the Search results pane of the task pane to close the task pane quickly.)

Printing Help

Occasionally, you may wish to jot down some especially important information you found in Help. You can print a help screen. By printing a few of the important help screens, you can have a handy reference within easy reach—even if you aren't near a

print button

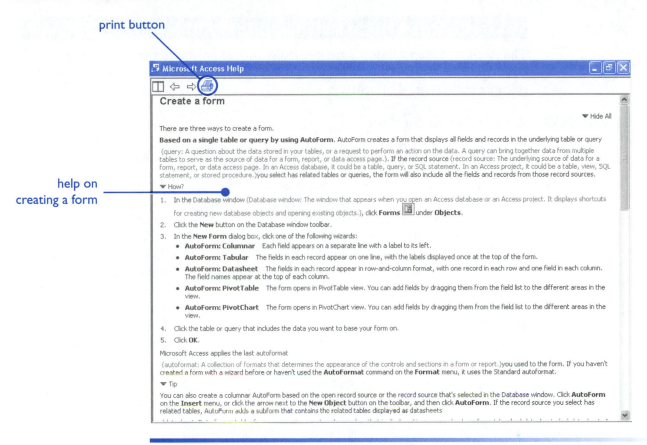

help on
creating a form

Figure 2.2   Obtaining help.

computer. Once you have located the help screen you want to print, click the Help page Print button (see Figure 2.2), then select a printer, determine whether you want to print the entire help page(s) or a smaller number of pages, and click the Print button. Windows prints the help screen information. That is all there is to it. (Print the Create a form help screen you located in the preceding exercise to ensure that you understand the printing process.)

Exiting Access

After completing all of your database work, you should always exit Access. If you are using a database stored on a floppy disk, it is especially important to remember to exit Access before removing the floppy disk. Otherwise, you risk losing data. Exiting Access signals the program to do its housekeeping chores such as posting any changes you have made to your database on your disk, closing other information sources, and returning to Windows. Exit Access by selecting Exit from the File menu found on the Access menu bar. Access quickly closes any open databases and returns to Windows.

EXAMINING THE ACCESS ENVIRONMENT

The Access Startup window's toolbar icons change as you move to other parts of Access. Toolbar buttons that are applicable in a particular window appear in color. Inapplicable buttons are dimmed.

Access Work Surface

The Startup window's menus function like those of other Windows products. Through the File menu, for instance, you can open files (database files in this case) and exit Access. The File menu contains commands to create a new database and open any hidden windows. Two very important File menu commands are New and Open. Executing New allows you to create a database, whereas executing Open makes available an existing Access database. Figure 2.3 shows the screen display after selecting the Open command. Alternatively, you can click the Blank Database link in the New panel of the Task Pane to accomplish the same result. You may find the latter method easier and more accessible.

After you either create a new database or locate and open one of the available databases, Microsoft Access displays the Database window within the Microsoft Access window. The Database window is the central control point from which you conduct all

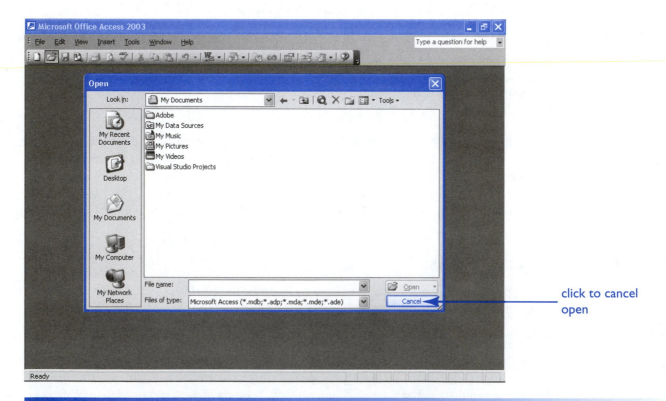

Figure 2.3 Preparing to open a database.

database activities. Figure 2.4 shows the Database window for one of the databases, *Ch02.mdb*, found on your Companion CD.

The File menu changes once a Database window is open. Additional File menu commands become available including Get External Data, Close, Save As, Back Up Database, Export, Print Preview, Print, Send To, and Database Properties. These commands allow you to import data from other sources, close the current database, save the database under a new name or export it to another data type, alter database properties, and perform standard Windows print activities. You will use some of the File menu commands as you read this text and work through its examples.

Other menus on the menu bar include Edit, View, Insert, Tools, and Window. The Edit menu contains familiar commands such as Cut, Copy, and Paste as well as Create Shortcut, Delete, Rename, Groups, and Add to Group. The Create Shortcut, Delete, and Rename commands allow you to create a desktop shortcut to any database object, delete an object, or rename an object, respectively.

The View menu lets you display different types of objects in the Database window. You can select Tables, Queries, Forms, Reports, Pages, Macros, or Modules from the Database Objects menu item, for instance. Or you can select those objects by clicking their names in the Objects bar on the left side of the Database window. Another group of commands—Large Icons, Small Icons, List, Details, and Arrange Icons—provides

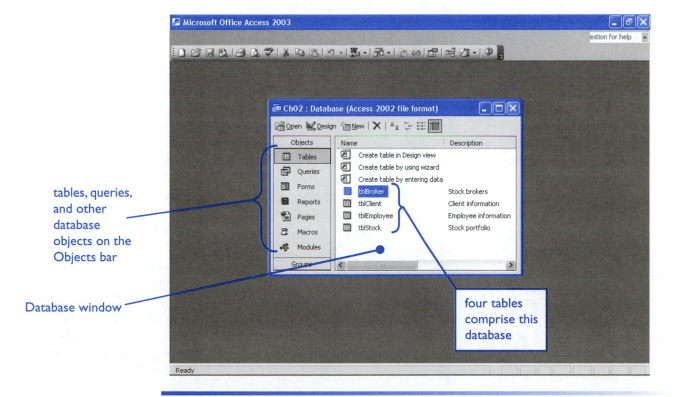

Figure 2.4 The Database window.

alternative views of the objects in the Database window. The Properties command displays summary information about a table or other database object. The Code command opens the Code window. You use the Toolbars command to display or hide one or more of the several special toolbars.

The Insert menu contains commands to insert tables, forms, queries, and other database objects into the current database. AutoForm and AutoReport create a new form and a new report based on the currently selected table or query. We will use these commands in this text.

The Tools menu contains Spelling, Office Links, Speech, Online Collaboration, which facilitate integration with office products and collaboration with colleagues; Relationships, which lets you establish relationships between tables; Analyze, which provides tools for evaluation and analysis of the efficiency of database objects; Database Utilities to convert your database to earlier formats, compact it, and back up the database; Security to keep your database secure; and Options, which allows you to set database-wide default values and conditions. There are other commands in the Tools menu, but they are beyond the scope of this text.

The Window menu contains six commands. (If you see fewer than six commands, then click the double arrow at the end of the drop-down list to reveal all of them.) They are Tile Horizontally, Tile Vertically, Cascade, Arrange Icons, Hide, and Unhide. Tile Horizontally and Tile Vertically arrange all Access windows so that they do not overlap one another. The orientation depends on which of the two you choose. Cascade presents windows so that only the title bar of each open but inactive Access window is displayed. The active window is placed on top. When Access windows are reduced to icons, the Arrange Icons command lines up the icons along the bottom edge of the Access window in the same order as it found them. Finally, the Hide command hides the active window from view, whereas the Unhide command reveals a hidden window.

Figure 2.5 shows an example of several database tables. Two tables and the Database window are cascaded, and one table is reduced to an icon. It is in the lower left corner of the Access window. (Later in this chapter you will look more closely at each of these three tables.)

Help is the rightmost menu on the Database window. Clicking Help and then clicking the Microsoft Access Help command opens the Microsoft Access Help panel in the task pane. We have presented an overview of the Help menu already, so you are already familiar with it.

Look at Figure 2.5 again. Notice the several toolbar buttons. Those buttons represent shortcuts to commands accessed from the menu bar. The buttons that are unavailable in a particular situation are dimmed. Buttons that are not dimmed may be clicked to rapidly accomplish various tasks. The buttons provide a shortcut to menu commands; they do not replace the menu commands. You will use both the buttons and menus to create and modify various database objects as you read through this text.

menu bar

toolbar

three cascaded windows

minimized window containing the *tblBroker* table

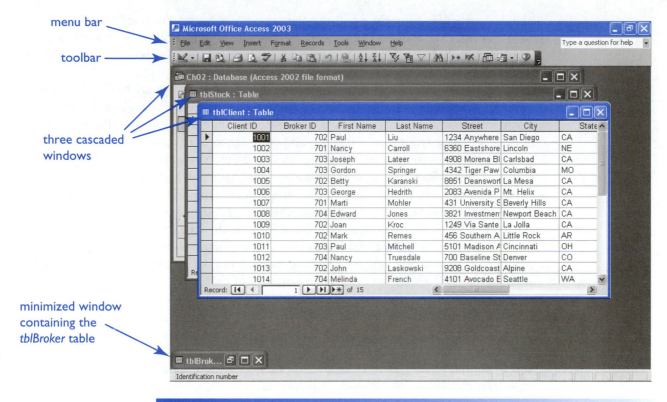

Figure 2.5 Icons and cascaded windows.

Access Objects

Access provides many ways to store, display, and report your data. The structures and methods you employ to store and display your data are called objects. Access objects include tables, queries, forms, reports, pages, macros, and modules. This text explains how to use these objects, placing emphasis on the first four of them—tables, queries, forms, and reports. This section presents an overview of four of these seven important object classes, and it shows how you can use each to building accounting information systems. Sections that follow use tables, queries, forms, and reports we have already created. Exploring the objects illustrates how information is organized and retrieved with a database system located at the heart of an accounting information system. At various points in the chapter, we ask you to create some small tables, short queries, simple forms, and small reports for a very limited system.

First, let's see what these objects are that are the building blocks of a database management system that you will be using to build your accounting information systems.

TABLES. *Tables* are the fundamental storage structures for data, a company's information resource. Like spreadsheet models you may have seen and used, tables are two-dimensional objects with columns and rows. Each row contains all available information about a particular item. (We will use the term *record* interchangeably with *row*.) All rows contain exactly the same number of columns, though not every column of every row necessarily has a value. Sometimes an entry is empty—database folks say the entry is *null*.

Consider a table holding employee information. A small company having 50 employees could store employee data—name, date of birth, hire date, etc.—in a 50-row table. Each employee column would be a particular information field. (The terms *field* and *column* are used synonymously in this and other texts.) Each column contains one type (or category) of information. For instance, one column contains each employee's hire date, another column holds each employee's last name, and yet another column holds each employee's birth date. Figure 2.6 shows an example of a small Access table that stores employee data. The main difference between this employee table and an industrial-strength table is size—most employee tables contain hundreds, if not thousands, of rows. Moreover, employee data tables usually have many columns—not just five. This example is purposefully small so you can understand the principles of database tables without the added complexity of large volumes of data.

Observe that each column holds only one type of data—an important rule to keep in mind when you create your own tables. Each row contains information about an employee, and only one employee's data is stored in a given row. As you can see, several types of data can be stored in a table: text, memo, number, date/time, currency, and hyperlink. Access tables can also hold other types of data including AutoNumber (a unique number), Yes/No, and OLE objects.

At the top of each column is the column's name, called an *attribute*, which uniquely identifies a column. Each row corresponds to one employee. A row is indivisible. That is, the data in a row remains with the row, even if the rows are sorted or displayed in a different order. Though the rows are unsorted, they can be organized into a more meaningful arrangement whenever necessary. This is one of the advantages of a relational database system: the order of rows in a table is unimportant. In other words, you do not have to be worried about inputting data into a table in an orderly way. No row is more important than another.

Similarly, the columns are placed in an arbitrary order left to right. Is there some arcane rule that states columns must be arranged in a particular order? No. We have designed the *tblEmployee* table so that the employee identification number is first, but no other implicit meaning or significance exists in the columns' arrangement. (Though it is not necessary to put all rows' unique identifier column first, it is customary and convenient.) You can rearrange columns so that the EmpSalary field is second, the EmpName field is last, and so on. This is another advantage of relational databases: the order of table columns is unimportant. The field EmpID contains mutually unique values. No two employees share the same identification number. This type of field is called a table's *primary key*. You will learn more about primary keys later.

QUERIES. There are several types of queries, but the most common query is called a *selection query*, or simply, *query*. A selection query is a question you can ask about your database. (Because selection queries are the most commonly used type, they are

each column holds a different characteristic
about the row it decribes

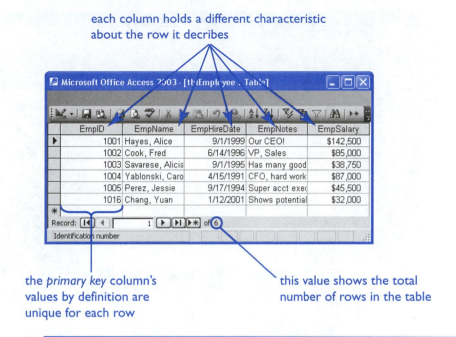

the *primary key* column's
values by definition are
unique for each row

this value shows the total
number of rows in the table

Figure 2.6   Example table containing employee data.

simply called *queries*.) For instance, a query stated in English is "How many employees earn more than $50,000?" or "What customers' invoices are over 60 days past due?" Queries are especially helpful for combining information from several related tables into a single, cohesive result. Queries also provide a way to reduce the data volume by returning and displaying only the subset of table rows in which you are interested. You can use queries to summarize data, displaying only the aggregate results. For instance, you can ask Access to total all outstanding invoices. Other types of queries insert new data into a table, delete unwanted data from a table, or change values in a table. With Access queries, you can select which tables are the subjects of your questions, designate the columns you would like to see, and specify which table rows are to be returned.

The structure of a query is called its *design*. The query result, called the *dynaset*, is displayed in a Query window. Figure 2.7 shows an example of a query's design and its dynaset, each in its own window. Notice the query design window. Only the columns appearing in the query design are displayed in the dynaset. Check marks (three of them in this example) in the query grid's Show row prescribe which columns appear in the dynaset, and the expression >50000, called a selection criterion, filters the rows. Selection criteria restrict the rows that are returned to those that meet the conditions specified by the criteria—in this case, rows whose Salary field is greater than $50,000.

FORMS. Frequently, it is better to work with table data one row at a time. Tables are not an intuitive interface for many people, especially those who are not accustomed to working with databases. Access forms solve this problem. Forms display data from

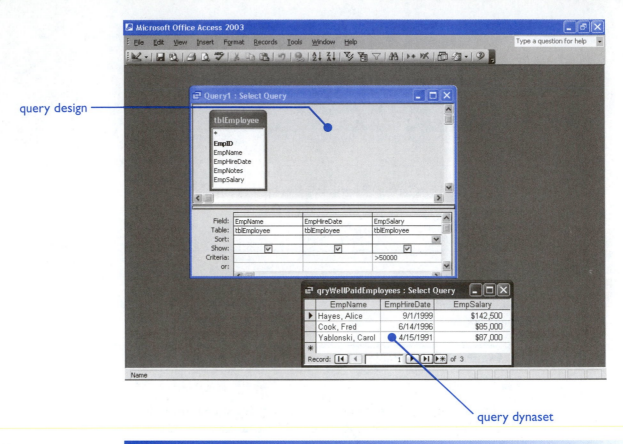

query design

query dynaset

Figure 2.7 Example query and dynaset.

a table or a query in a format that is easier to understand. You can see one row or many rows of a table. Figure 2.8 shows an example of a form displaying the Employee table data in an attractive and intuitive layout.

A form may be an easier way to view and change data stored in your databases. One of several records appears in the form. You can move to the next record, the previous record, or the first or last record by clicking the navigation buttons located in the lower left corner of the window. You can move directly to a specific record by pressing F5, typing a record number, and pressing Enter. The single, right-pointing arrow button moves one record at a time, displaying the next record in the form. The right-pointing arrow button with a vertical line to its right moves directly to the last record. The opposite actions take place for the left-pointing navigation buttons.

REPORTS. Imagine showing several people in a meeting a financial statement displayed on your notebook computer's screen. That would be awkward and unprofessional. Hard copy output, a report, is a better solution. That way, the report can be distributed easily to an assembled group. Access provides a comprehensive report-producing facility.

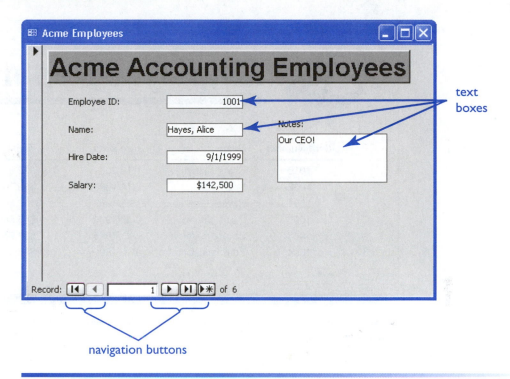

Figure 2.8   Example form displaying an Employee table row.

Access reports are often the main output produced by a database system. While it is important to store accounts receivable information in a database and to query that database for answers, a far more important activity is to produce a printed output. For instance, you might want a list of all customers whose payments are over 60 days past due. If there are more than a few dozen of those customers, then a printed report is the most useful output. You can scan the list, marking accounts that deserve special attention. You can also make copies of a hard copy output for distribution to appropriate departments and managers.

You can use Access's report design features and tools to customize a report to look any way you would like. A report can display data from one table or from several tables that have been linked together. Figure 2.9 shows an example of a simple report employing a drop shadow around the title, a graphic (a company logo), bold column headings, and sorted employee names from the Employee table. The simple report is easy to create, and the results are professional looking. Unlike using Access, it might take several hours to create an equivalent report using a programming language such as Java or C++ and require a few hundred lines of code.

The sections that follow describe the process of using and creating tables, queries, forms, and reports. We encourage you to participate in the exercises, because the remainder of the chapter is interactive. You will learn the most if you duplicate the steps we present and actually use and create the objects that we do. To help you in this

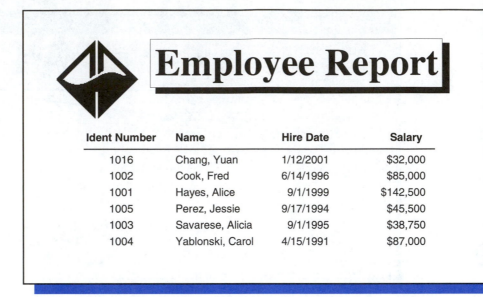

Figure 2.9 Example report.

process, we have supplied many of the required tables, queries, forms, and reports so that you can try them out. In addition, you will create a few of your own.

WORKING WITH DATABASES AND TABLES

The foundation of any database system rests on its tables. Tables hold the data that is transformed into information. In this section you will learn how to use tables that we have provided, create your own tables, modify the order in which table columns are displayed, and link tables together.

Important Note: Before you work on the tables found on your Companion CD, you should first copy the database from the Companion CD to the hard disk, drive C, of the computer on which you are working (Exercise 1.13, page 30). Remember to clear the copied file's Read-only attribute (Exercise 1.14, page 33). Do these two activities before beginning your work session. (Not all operating systems require you to clear the attribute, but be aware that it may be set.) That way, you will be able to make changes to your tables, queries, and other objects stored in the databases we supply with the textbook. You should avoid using databases directly from your Companion CD because Access limits your activities to "read-only." That means you cannot make any changes either to the structure of tables or other objects, and you cannot alter the data stored in the tables. When you have completed your work on a database, simply copy the database from your hard disk to a floppy disk. That way, you can transport your database work from one machine to another if necessary. (All database files in this textbook are designed to individually fit on one floppy disk.)

The only database you need to copy from the Companion CD for this chapter is found in the folder called *Ch02*. The database is called *Ch02.mdb*. Copy this file to your hard disk now, before you start working with the database. We will assume from this point on that you have copied each chapter's database(s) from the CD to drive C prior to working through a chapter. (Recall from Chapter 1 that you can use Windows Explorer to copy files from one place to another.) At the end of each work session—after you copy your database file to a floppy disk—you may want to erase the database from the hard disk. Simply locate the file on the hard disk with Explorer, select it, and press the Delete key to remove the database. You always have the original database file on your Companion CD, whose contents cannot be erased.

Before you work on your database with Access, be sure to tell Access where to find your database objects. This simple procedure is called *opening a database*. We describe this process next.

Opening a Database

Whether you are using a stand-alone computer (one not connected to a network of computers) or a computer in a laboratory on a local network, you must first open a database. A *database* is a collection of objects that are related, including tables, queries, forms, reports, macros, and modules. Access stores all the objects of a particular database within one file. Access fetches and stores information in whichever database is open, but only one database may be open at one time.

All exercises in this text refer to the Companion CD that comes with this text. (You used the CD-ROM in an exercise in Chapter 1.) We have segregated files of all types needed for each chapter into separate databases so that you can isolate all changes and activities by chapter. Here is how the disk directories are set up. All files needed for Chapter 2 are found in the directory Ch02 (C-h-zero-two), all files needed for Chapter 3 are found in the directory Ch03, and so on. Whenever you are working with a chapter, you can locate databases and files in the associated chapter directory on your Companion CD. The next exercise shows you how to open a database that has been copied to drive C from your Companion CD so the data are available to Microsoft Access.

EXERCISE 2.3: OPENING A DATABASE

1. Launch Access by double-clicking the Access icon (locate it in the Start menu list of programs). The Getting Started panel of the task pane opens.
2. Click *More* in the task pane section called *Open*.
3. Click the Look in list box, and navigate to the disk drive and folder containing *Ch02.mdb* (see Figure 2.10).
4. In the large list box displaying folder names and file names, click *Ch02.mdb*, and click the Open button. (Alternatively, you can double-click the database file name to open it.) Microsoft Access displays the Ch02 Database window and closes the task pane (see Figure 2.11).

The Database window displays the names of all tables in the database. There are other objects held in the database including queries, forms, and reports. The names of forms in this database can be seen if you click Forms on the Objects bar. Likewise, you can

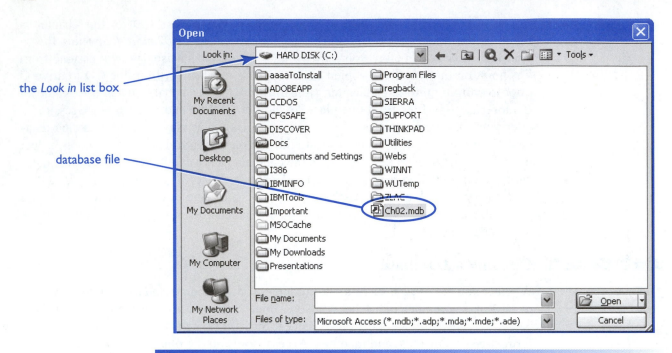

the *Look in* list box

database file

Figure 2.10   Open Database dialog box.

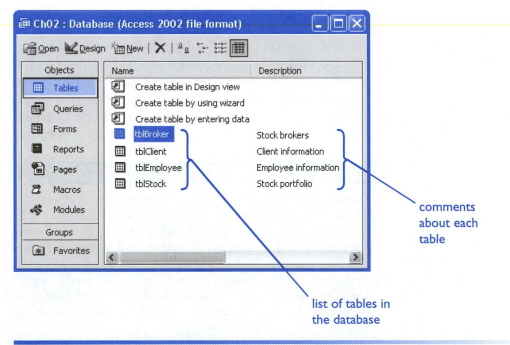

comments
about each
table

list of tables in
the database

Figure 2.11   Database window.

see all queries by clicking Queries. If the table objects show icons or show more information, then your view setting has been changed. If your table list match doesn't match the list in Figure 2.11, click View and then click Details (or click the Details button on the Database window toolbar). Now the two should look alike.

Looking at Your Data through Different Windows

Access provides several ways to view your data. You can inspect your data in a Table window, which displays data in columns and rows called a Datasheet view—just like a spreadsheet's data. Or you can use a Form window to display one or more rows in a nontabular format. Forms provide an attractive way to view and change data, because they can be designed to resemble paper forms with which you are already familiar. (You can also view a form in Datasheet view.) Alternatively, you can view your data in a report format with the Report window. The Report window provides a preview of a printed report so that you can review it as you would a hard copy report prior to printing it.

Because each view appears in a separate window, you can display several different views simultaneously. Figure 2.12 shows both a Table window and a Form window of the Employee table. Because the Form window is active (notice the Form window Title bar is darker), the menu bar and toolbar are the ones used in a Form window.

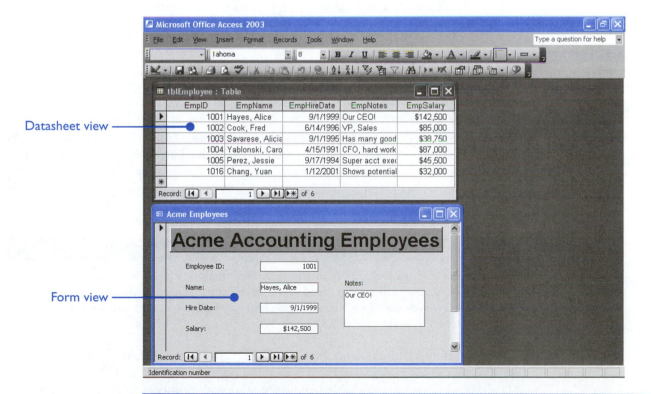

Figure 2.12 Two views of the same data.

One of the Companion CD databases contains information about a fictitious stock brokerage firm. This small database consists of four tables, three of which are related to one another: Broker (*tblBroker*), Client (*tblClient*), and Stock (*tblStock*). We follow the object naming convention that all tables begin with the prefix *tbl* followed immediately by the rest of the object name. Queries begin with *qry* and the rest of the object name, forms begin with *frm* and the rest of the object name, and reports begin with *rpt* and the remainder of the name. (For simplicity, we refer to the tables in this textbook without their prefixes.) The Broker table contains information about four of the brokerage firm's employees, all stockbrokers. Client contains the names, addresses, and other data about selected brokerage clients. The Stock table lists the stocks currently held by each customer whose name is in the Client list. All of these tables are smaller than corresponding tables in a real brokerage house. We want you to comprehend the process of extracting meaningful information from the data, not marvel at the size of the database. It is easier to understand database concepts using several small tables. Client, for instance, contains 15 rows, one for each customer. Broker contains 4 rows, which contain a few facts about the brokers. Finally, Stock contains 173 rows. Whenever a customer purchases an individual stock, that transaction is recorded and saved in the Stock table.

You may be interested in more details about what these three tables contain. Details about each of the brokerage firm tables are revealed as we describe fundamental Access operations and procedures in this chapter. We begin by examining the use of Access tables, the elemental building block of all database applications.

Opening a Table

The Table window is one way to view your data. When you open a table, the menu bar and toolbar change to menus and icons that are appropriate for table operations. You can better understand this process if you open an existing table and experience firsthand how some of the toolbar buttons and menus operate. In preparation for the exercise that follows, execute Access and the Ch02 database you have copied to drive C. If you forget how to open a database, review the previous exercise to refresh your memory. Now you are ready to follow the steps in the next exercise to open one of the tables on your disk.

EXERCISE 2.4: OPENING A TABLE

1. Click Tables in the Objects bar to display the list of tables in the Ch02 database.
2. Double-click the table *tblClient* found in the list of tables. (Alternatively, you can select *tblClient* and click the Open button in the Database window.) Access opens the Client table in Datasheet view (see Figure 2.13).

Take a moment to examine the Client table. Notice the Datasheet navigation buttons located in the Navigation bar found at the bottom edge of the Table window. The Database window may be visible behind the table and slightly to its left. (Your arrangement of windows will probably be slightly different.) Below the Access Title bar is the

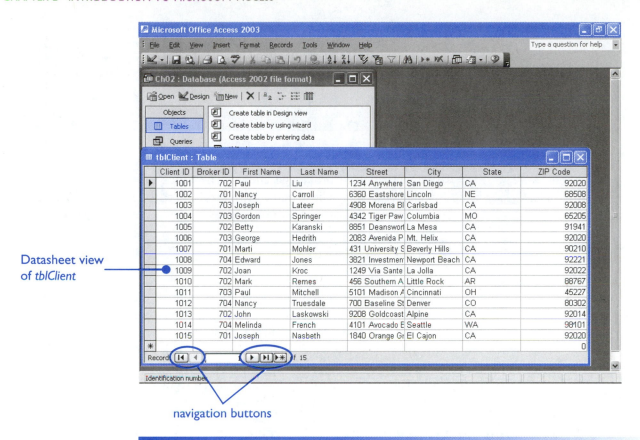

Figure 2.13 The Client table (*tblClient*).

Table window menu bar. The menu bar's contents vary depending on what type of window is active (Table, Form, and so on). Below the menu bar is the toolbar. The contents of the toolbar vary with the active window. The Table Datasheet toolbar, shown in Figure 2.14, is displayed when a Table window is active and you are viewing a Datasheet (a table). The Form Design toolbar is displayed when the Form Design window is active.

Some Datasheet toolbar buttons are familiar, because they are similar to those found in other Windows products. Familiar toolbar buttons include Print, Print Preview, Cut, Copy, and Paste, which are on the left side of the toolbar. The Print button is a familiar icon that you can click to print a table. Hover the mouse pointer over the Print button. When you hover the mouse pointer over any toolbar button, you will see text, called a *ScreenTip*, appearing just below the button. The ScreenTip displays the toolbar button's name.

Binoculars on the toolbar are used to search the table. Other toolbar buttons allow you to modify the table's design (Design view), sort the table into ascending or descending order, apply filter criteria to select particular records, and create forms and reports from the table. You will use some of these latter buttons later in this chapter.

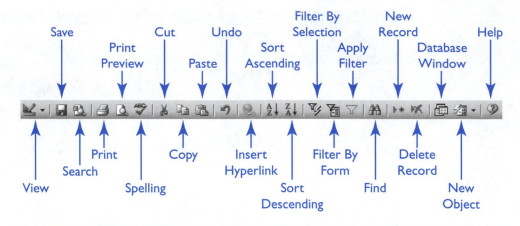

Figure 2.14 Table Datasheet toolbar.

When a horizontal scroll bar appears along the bottom of the Table window, it indicates that some table columns are out of view. The scroll bar works like any other Windows scroll bar: drag the scroll box to the right and the window pans to the right; click the scroll arrows and the window shifts for each click in the indicated direction. Vertical scroll bars appear whenever any rows of the table cannot be seen, as is frequently the case. The vertical scroll bar, located on the right side of the Table window, operates similarly to the horizontal scroll bar.

Moving Around a Table

When you open a large table, only the first few rows display on the screen. There are several ways to move through a table so that its rows are displayed in the Table window. You can select one of the movement choices from the Go To selection of the Edit menu: First, Last, Next, Previous, or New Record. You can also use the keyboard: the up arrow, down arrow, PgUp, and PgDn keys move up one row, down one row, up one screen, and down one screen, respectively. Perhaps the easiest way to scroll through a table's rows is to use the navigation buttons (see Figure 2.13). Left to right, they move to the top of the table, up one row, to a specific numbered record, down one row, to the last record in the table, or add a new row to the table. The last button opens a new record, which is placed immediately following the last record in the table. The New Record button is a convenient way to add a new record to a table. Try the navigation buttons. With the Client table still displayed in a Table window, first go to the top of the database. Then, click the Last Record navigation button to go to the last record. (We use the term *record* interchangeably with the term *row*.)

Notice that the dark row pointer rests in one row of the record selector column. The record selector column is to the left of the table's leftmost column (see Figure 2.13). As you move around the table with the navigation buttons, the record selector moves to another row. Pressing the right and left arrow keys moves the cursor to a different column in the same row.

Searching for a Value in a Column

Searching for a particular record in a table based on the value of one of its columns is straightforward. Though nearly all the data is visible in this small Client table example, most corporate tables contain thousands and hundreds of thousands of rows. Finding a particular client's record in such a large table would be extremely difficult without a database system. Imagine that the Client table contains many rows and you want to find a client whose name begins with the letters "Lasko" but you do not remember the exact spelling. Your task, in the next exercise, is to locate the client's record. If necessary, open the table *tblClient*.

EXERCISE 2.5: SEARCHING FOR A ROW CONTAINING A PARTICULAR VALUE

1. With the *tblClient* datasheet displayed, click the topmost name in the Last Name column. That moves the cursor to the column you will ask Access to search.
2. Click the Find button (it looks like a pair of binoculars) and type **Lask*** in the Find What text box. Be sure to include the asterisk, a wildcard, following the last letter of the partial name.
3. Select Down from the Search drop-down list.
4. Click the Find Next button to start the search process. Access searches the Last Name column for a match and moves the record selector to the row containing the name Laskowski; the matching name is highlighted.
5. Close the Find and Replace dialog box. This provides an unrestricted view of your table and the record that Access located.
6. Move the record pointer to the first record in the *tblClient* table by using the appropriate navigation button. (Leave the Client table open for the next set of steps.)

Try a few other search operations. For instance, locate the record whose City column contains "Seattle." What happens if there is no match? A dialog box is displayed indicating the search was unsuccessful.

Changing a Table's Display Characteristics

You can change the visual properties of any table you are viewing. For instance, you can move columns left or right in a table, alter individual column display widths, and remove the grid lines that separate the rows and columns. You can change a column's display properties by right-clicking the table column name above the first row of data. Even though you may change a table's display characteristics, you are not changing the table's structure or contents. For instance, if you move the FirstName column to the left of its current position, the underlying table structure is unaffected. Only the display characteristics of the *tblClient* table are affected. (Access gives you the opportunity to save a table's display characteristics permanently when you close the table.)

Let's change two display properties for the Client table temporarily. The next exercise moves the ClientName column to the first column, just to the right of the record selector column. You will also make one other visual change: You will optimize the widths of all columns so no data are obscured. Before starting the exercise, make sure

Access is loaded, the database Ch02 is open, and the Client (*tblClient*) datasheet appears in Datasheet view. Maximize the Table window so you can see more of the table.

EXERCISE 2.6: CHANGING A TABLE'S DISPLAY PROPERTIES

1. Move the pointer to the First Name *field selector* (column heading). When the mouse pointer is over the column heading, it changes to a down-pointing arrow. (When the pointer is within the data column, it changes to an I-beam shape.)
2. Click and drag the mouse to the right until both the First Name and the Last Name columns darken, and then release the mouse button.
3. Click inside either darkened column's field selector (*not* the data below the field selector), drag to the leftmost position in the table, and release the mouse button. (The columns remain darkened after you release the mouse.)
4. With the columns still selected, right-click the mouse anywhere in the First Name column. A pop-up menu appears.
5. Click Column Width from the list of pop-up menu choices.
6. Click the Best Fit button. The columns resize to the smallest width that will display both the column label and the widest entry in each column.
7. Click any entry in the Client ID column to deselect the highlighted columns, and then move the mouse to the Client ID column field selector. When the mouse changes to a down-pointing arrow, click and drag it to the right, selecting the column field selectors for Client ID through ZIP Code. Release the mouse.
8. With all columns except First Name and Last Name darkened (selected), position the pointer on the right border of any darkened field selector and double-click the mouse to produce the best-fit width for all the selected columns.
9. Click any data entry in the table to deselect the columns. Figure 2.15 shows the reformatted *tblClient* datasheet.

We are finished with this exercise and do not want to permanently change the Client datasheet display characteristics; so, close the table by clicking the Close button on the *tblClient* title bar. A dialog box opens indicating the layout for *tblClient* has changed and asks whether you want to save the new layout. Click No to discard the table display changes you have made.

Sorting Table Rows

Often you can locate a record or group of records more quickly if the table is sorted. For instance, it is somewhat difficult to scan the Client table, as small as it is, and determine quickly whether a client named Toadvine is among the last names in your client list. You can imagine how difficult searching for clients by name would be for a much longer client list containing thousands of records, especially when the records are not sorted by name. The Client table is already sorted on one of its fields, Client ID.

There are two ways to sort any table. One way is to perform a quick sort to organize the table on a single column. Another way is to create and apply a filter, which allows you to accomplish more complex, multicolumn sort operations. No matter which method you choose, the table returns to its original order once it is closed.

two name columns moved to the leftmost position

	First Name	Last Name	Client ID	Broker ID	Street	City	State	ZIP Code
▶	Paul	Liu	1001	702	1234 Anywhere Street	San Diego	CA	92020
	Nancy	Carroll	1002	701	6360 Eastshore Drive	Lincoln	NE	68508
	Joseph	Lateer	1003	703	4908 Morena Blvd	Carlsbad	CA	92008
	Gordon	Springer	1004	703	4342 Tiger Paw Lane	Columbia	MO	65205
	Betty	Karanski	1005	702	8851 Deansworthy Street	La Mesa	CA	91941
	George	Hedrith	1006	703	2083 Avenida Picante	Mt. Helix	CA	92020
	Marti	Mohler	1007	701	431 University Street	Beverly Hills	CA	90210
	Edward	Jones	1008	704	3821 Investments Heights Dr.	Newport Beach	CA	92221
	Joan	Kroc	1009	702	1249 Via Sante Fe	La Jolla	CA	92022
	Mark	Remes	1010	702	456 Southern Accent Way	Little Rock	AR	88767
	Paul	Mitchell	1011	703	5101 Madison Avenue	Cincinnati	OH	45227
	Nancy	Truesdale	1012	704	700 Baseline Street	Denver	CO	80302
	John	Laskowski	1013	702	9208 Goldcoast Drive	Alpine	CA	92014
	Melinda	French	1014	704	4101 Avocado Blvd	Seattle	WA	98101
	Joseph	Nasbeth	1015	701	1840 Orange Grove	El Cajon	CA	92020
✱								0

tblClient : Table

Record: 1 of 15

Figure 2.15 Changing a table's display properties.

Some tables are automatically organized because they have key field(s). Client, for instance, is organized on the Client ID field because that field was designated a primary key field when the table was constructed. (Primary key fields ensure that each row of a particular table is unique and uniquely identifiable.) You will sort the Client table into ascending name order in the next exercise. In preparation for the exercise, ensure that Access is still running and that the Ch02 database is open. Click Tables in the Objects bar of the Database window to display the list of tables in Ch02. Then, open the Client table (*tblClient*).

EXERCISE 2.7: SORTING A TABLE

1. With the Client table displayed in Datasheet view, click any data value in the Last Name column.
2. Click Records on the menu bar, point to Sort, and click Sort Ascending. The datasheet is sorted into ascending order by clients' last names. Do not close the table yet.

Another way to sort a table is to create an Advanced Filter/Sort. When you do, you can select multiple table sort columns (for instance, ascending order by State and then ascending order by City within any State). You can select column names from a list, place each sort column into a sort grid, and select either an Ascending or Descending sort order for each column. Once you create an Advanced Filter/Sort, you apply it by clicking the Apply Filter button found on the toolbar (it is the unembellished funnel).

You redisplay the datasheet in its original order by selecting Remove Filter/Sort from the Records menu. Experiment a bit with these. They can do no harm, because the table's actual record order is unaffected. Only a datasheet's displayed row order is changed.

After you are done experimenting with sorting, close the Client table by clicking the Table window Close button. When the dialog box appears asking if you want to save the changes to the design of the table, click No. The Database window becomes active. Be careful not to click the Access application Close button, because the entire application will close and you will have to restart Access.

Printing a Table

To print a database table, select the table (it need not be open in a window to print its contents) or display the table in Datasheet view and then click Print from the File menu. You can also click the toolbar Print button. However, be aware that you cannot control the number of pages or other print parameters if you use the toolbar Print button. Clicking the button starts printing the table immediately. We suggest you always select Print from the File menu to maintain greater control over the content and volume that you want printed.

When you select Print from the File menu, a Print dialog box appears (see Figure 2.16). You can choose to print all pages or a range of pages. Select a page range by entering From and To page numbers. Normally, you need only one copy of the report. However, if multiple copies are needed, simply alter the value in the Number of Copies spin control box. When you are ready to print the table, click the OK button. Otherwise, click the Cancel button to nullify the print process and return to the Table window.

A printed table is created using a default format. The table's contents are printed in columns with horizontal and vertical table grid lines. Today's date appears in the upper right corner of the report, and the table's name appears centered above the table. At the bottom center of the page is a page number. Additional pages are printed whenever a table's columns are wider than can be printed on a single page.

The table report is functional but far from beautiful. Access provides tools for producing boardroom-quality reports replete with fonts, specialty features such as underlining and boldface, etc. Later in this chapter we describe how to create and use Access reports. Table printouts are quick and easy to produce and allow you to quickly check values in various columns.

Printing a Table's Structure

Printing information about the structure and definition of any table is a bit more complicated. Click Tools, point to Analyze, and then click Documenter Check the box corresponding to the name of the object(s), *tblClient*, for instance (see Figure 2.17). Click OK. Then, select Print from the File menu to print detailed information such as properties, relationships, permissions, data names, data types, and sizes. A printed copy of a table's definition provides good system documentation.

selected printer

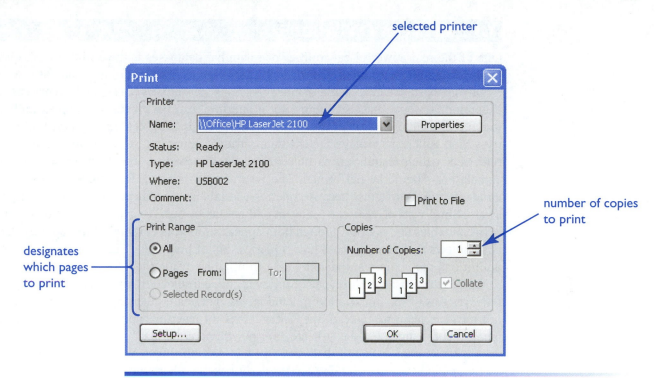

designates
which pages
to print

number of copies
to print

Figure 2.16   Print dialog box.

click other tabs to select additional objects

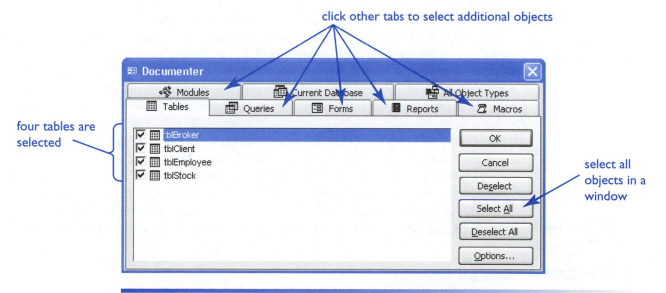

four tables are
selected

select all
objects in a
window

Figure 2.17   Using Documenter to print table structure information.

QUERYING A DATABASE

One of the real powerful capabilities of relational databases is the ability to ask questions that return interesting and meaningful answers derived from a database. Relational database systems make asking questions particularly easy, and Access is no exception. A *query*, the usual name for a question, can be simple or complex and can involve one table, dozens of tables, or even hundreds of tables. In a query, you specify which tables are involved in the data retrieval operation, which columns are to be retrieved, which records are to be returned, how to sort the returned rows, and what calculations should be performed. The result is also a table. Relational database systems are closed systems, because queries use tables as input and return tables as answers. Simply stated, you put tables in and get tables out. A very important distinction between tables and queries, though both appear similar, is that tables are the only database objects that actually hold data. Queries do not hold data. They are merely stored definitions that extract and display data from tables when they are run.

One of the most popular types of query is called a selection query. A *selection query* retrieves rows from one or more related tables. There are other types of queries that do not retrieve answers. Instead, they alter tables by inserting new records, deleting existing records, updating data, or creating new table columns.

All of the examples and discussion in this section illustrate selection queries. The section called *Creating Action Queries* describes the other types of queries—those that alter table data.

What are examples of the kinds of information you could retrieve with a query, and why not simply print a table? Consider a larger version of the Client table. Suppose it contained information on over 14,000 clients and your supervisor wants to know how many clients are located in California. Or perhaps another manager wants to know how many clients are served by broker number 701. You probably would not print a 14,000-row client table and then manually look for the answers. That could take hours and be fraught with error and frustration. To compound the problem of sifting through data, the File Print command does not allow you to regulate which rows or which columns print.

Queries give you flexibility in deciding which rows and columns of a table should be printed and provide an easy way to sift through large volumes of data. That is, queries provide a simple way to pose ad hoc questions that return subsets of table rows, columns, or both. Access uses a query method called *Query by Example*, or *QBE*. QBE is a method of stating a query whereby you give Access an example of the result you want, and Access uses that model to return a result in a table-like structure called a *dynaset*.

Using a Query

Suppose you are a stockbroker and you want a list of all your California clients. Furthermore, you want the list sorted by city. Because you are planning to mail literature to those customers, you want to see the clients' name and address fields (including zip code). However, you do not need to see the clients' identification numbers nor their assigned brokers' numbers. To extract the needed information, you create a query by opening a Query window and showing Access an example of what you want. Figure 2.18 shows both the query's design and the resulting dynaset.

Let's try running the preceding query just to see how the question formation process works. The query shown in the Query window of Figure 2.18 has been saved in the Ch02 database under the name *qryCaliforniaClients*. By using the "qry" prefix on all query names[1], we can easily distinguish queries from other database objects.

In the next section you will build a new query from scratch. The next exercise illustrates using an existing query. First, launch Access, if necessary, and ensure that database Ch02 is open. Then, complete the following exercise to open and run a query.

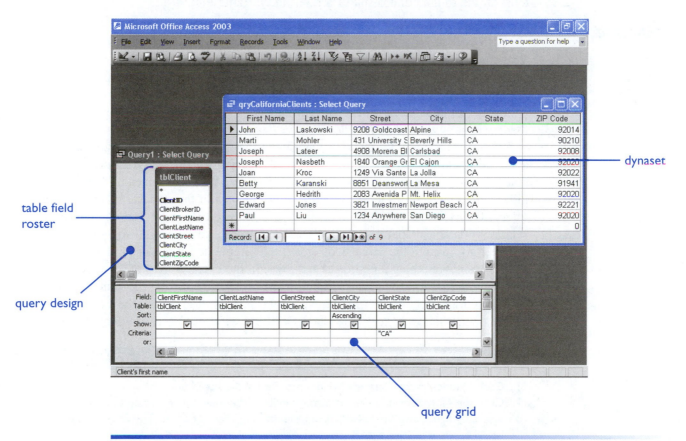

Figure 2.18 A query design and resulting dynaset.

[1]*A note about naming objects:* We follow the convention that query names have the prefix *qry* followed by the query name. No object name contains embedded blanks. Blanks in object names can be troublesome, and you should avoid them. For instance, the name *qryNewCustomers* is preferable to the name *qry New Customers*, with blanks between the words. Squash the separate words together, and distinguish them by using initial capital letters for each word except the prefix (tbl, qry, frm, and rpt).

EXERCISE 2.8: RUNNING A QUERY

1. Click Queries in the Database window's Objects bar to display a list of the queries stored in the Chapter 2 database, *Ch02.mdb*.
2. Double-click the query *qryCaliforniaClients*. (Double-clicking a database object's name is a fast way to open it in nondesign view. Alternatively, you can click the query name and then click the Open button.) A dynaset will appear displaying the query's result.
3. After you have examined the results, click the Query window Close button.

The preceding dynaset displays clients living in California, sorted by city. Candidate rows are drawn from a table called *tblClient*. If you are curious about how the query is structured, you can click the toolbar Design View button. It is the leftmost icon on the toolbar and displays a ruler and a triangle.

Creating a One-Table Query

You can create new queries using the Query by Example (QBE) method. For instance, suppose you want to see a list of all customer invoices that are over 60 days past due. Printing or displaying the Invoice table would not be the answer, since all invoices would be printed. What you want is to sift through all the invoices and display only those whose invoice date is older than 59 days.

You create a query by clicking Queries in the Objects bar of the Database window and then clicking the New button. When the query grid appears, you construct a query that tells Access to search through the Invoice table for all invoices more than 59 days old. Rows that satisfy the age condition will appear in the dynaset when you run the query. Queries that restrict which rows are returned (by using some criteria) use a relational database operation called *selection*. (You specify which rows to *select*.)

Let's go through the process of creating a simple selection query that searches the *tblStock* table, returning a portion of the rows. In the exercise that follows, we will create a query that lists all stock transaction information for the client whose number is 1015. One table holds all the information we want: *tblStock*. Prepare for the exercise by closing all open windows except the Ch02 Database window. Then, complete the exercise.

EXERCISE 2.9: CREATING A ONE-TABLE QUERY

1. Click Queries in the Database window to display the list of queries.
2. Click the New button in the Database window. The New Query dialog box opens.
3. Select Design View, if necessary, from the list, and then click OK. The Show Table dialog box appears (see Figure 2.19).
4. Click the Stock table (*tblStock*), and then click the Add button. Microsoft Access adds the Stock table to the query.
5. Click the Show Table dialog box Close button to indicate that no more tables are to be part of the query definition. The Show Table dialog box closes.
6. Drag the asterisk (*) field from the *tblStock* field list to the first cell in the Field row of the Query by Example (QBE) grid. (The asterisk stands for all fields in the table.) Dragging the asterisk saves time. You avoid dragging individual fields to the QBE grid, but you lose control over the left-to-right placement of fields.

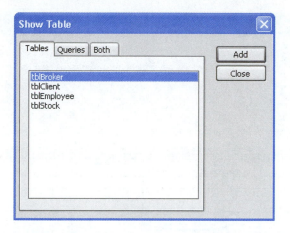

Figure 2.19   Show Table dialog box.

7. Drag the ClientID field from the *tblStock* field list to the second cell in the Field row of the QBE grid. (A shortcut is to double-click the field name in the list of fields to place it in the next available Field row cell of the QBE grid.)
8. Click the Show row check box under the ClientID column to clear (erase) it. There's no need for ClientID to be displayed twice, but we want to select only rows containing a particular value for ClientID. Therefore, we include, but do not display, a separate column to hold selection criteria.

    Next, we limit the search for records to those that satisfy our criteria: rows whose ClientID is 1015. That is, we want only client 1015's rows displayed in the dynaset, not all rows. We limit rows by entering the example value 1015 in the Criteria row of the ClientID column in the QBE grid.
9. Click the cell in the Criteria row under the ClientID column, and type 1015 (see Figure 2.20).
10. Click the Datasheet View button on the toolbar (it is the grid-looking icon leftmost in the toolbar). The dynaset displays the results of this query (see Figure 2.21). Adjust the height and width of the dynaset dialog box by dragging its bottom and left borders, if necessary, to reveal its 14 rows and 6 columns.

Saving a Query

You can execute queries periodically to produce current lists of clients, spare parts, invoices over 60 days past due, etc. Always save queries so that you do not have to recreate them. By saving a query, you can later rerun it to obtain accurate, timely information about changing data. Note that you cannot save the dynaset, because it is not an object. It merely displays data from the underlying table that pass the criteria test. (You can create a special query, called a *Make-Table query*, which can save the dynaset as a table. We explore this and other special query types later in the chapter.)

You save a new query by selecting either Save or Save As from the File menu and then entering a name in the Query Name text box. Click OK, and the query is saved. Let's check it out by saving the current query.

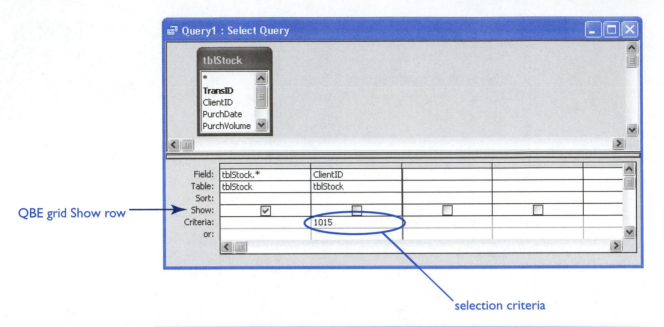

QBE grid Show row

selection criteria

Figure 2.20   One-table query, Design view.

	TransID	ClientID	Date	Volume	Price	Name
▶	20210	1015	12/17/2002	100	$124.25	America Online
	20471	1015	3/11/2003	75	$27.87	Walt Disney Co
	20476	1015	3/18/2003	125	$24.25	Quantum Corp.
	20575	1015	4/1/2003	150	$71.44	Fannie Mae
	20725	1015	5/10/2003	150	$16.38	Computer Task
	20748	1015	5/21/2003	150	$43.69	Unisys
	20787	1015	6/8/2003	250	$3.59	ZI Corp
	20792	1015	6/8/2003	125	$26.83	Compaq Compu
	20941	1015	8/4/2003	250	$72.81	Ameritech
	21093	1015	9/9/2003	150	$94.00	Microsoft
	21134	1015	9/20/2003	250	$17.25	Sequent Compu
	21234	1015	10/15/2003	150	$146.32	Texas Instrumer
	21626	1015	8/5/2004	125	$24.13	Comdisco
	21770	1015	11/1/2004	250	$14.56	Ducommun

Record: ⏮ ◀   1 ▶ ⏭ ▶✱ of 14

only rows with *1015* in the ClientID
column appear in the dynaset

Figure 2.21   One-table query dynaset.

TRY IT

Select the Save command from the File menu. The Save As dialog box appears. Type the name **qryClient1015** in the Query Name text box. Click OK. The query is saved in the Ch02 database in the Queries window with the name qryClient1015. We have saved the query in your database under the name *qryClient1015Stock* on your Companion CD in case you choose not to save your query.

For any existing query you may have altered, the procedure to save it is almost the same. Simply select Save from the File menu, and the query will be saved under the existing name in your database. Keep in mind that if there are several query windows open simultaneously, only the active query—the one whose window is active—is saved.

Sorting the Results

Normally, Access displays a dynaset in order by the primary key of the underlying table. (For instance, the *tblClient* table's key column is ClientID.) If the table referenced by a query has no primary key, then the dynaset's rows display in no particular order. However, you can specify your own sort requirements so that dynaset rows will be in a more meaningful order. You select a sort order by selecting either Ascending or Descending beneath the appropriate column(s) in the QBE grid Sort row.

TRY IT

Display in Design view the query *qryCaliforniaClients*, and click in the Sort row beneath the first column. Select either Ascending or Descending from the drop-down list. Continue selecting, if desired, other columns to the right in the QBE grid. You can select Ascending or Descending for any number of columns, but the leftmost column having the Sort row cell filled is the primary sort column. The significance of other sort columns are determined by their relative position in the QBE sort grid, left to right. You may wish to drag one or more columns to the left to enhance their influence on the final sort order. Better yet, you can add columns to the right specifying sort orders for each column. Clear the Show check box of any duplicate columns so they are used to sort, but are not displayed, in the dynaset.

Using More Complex Selection Criteria

Suppose the manager of the stock brokerage firm wants to know the number of stock transactions and the volume of each purchase that occurred in her office during the month of January. She is considering sending most of her brokers on vacation for

January if activity is sufficiently low during that month. Let's see how we could answer that question with a query.

To answer the preceding request, the manager can formulate a query that returns all Stock table rows for which the value in the Date column is greater than 12/31 of the previous year and less than 2/1 of the current year. The criteria clearly involves two conditions—two different dates. Furthermore, both conditions must be true for a row to be returned in the Answer table. For situations like this, the criteria must use an AND operator. In fact, you can use the AND operator in the criteria whenever you select rows based on a range of values for a single column of a table. Let's create a new query to select all rows representing January stock purchases.

For this query we need not list all columns of the Stock table, because the manager is interested only in gross numbers of transactions, their volume, and the price of each trade. It is sufficient to list only the client identification number (ClientID), the purchase date (Date), number of shares purchased (Volume), and the purchase price (Price) columns. We are using the projection operation. A projection operation is one in which a subset of a table's columns is displayed. In this example, we include a subset of the Stock table's columns in the dynaset returned by the query. Projection is one of the important operations available with relational database systems such as Access. In preparation for the next exercise, close all windows except the Database window.

EXERCISE 2.10: WRITING A QUERY USING AN "AND" OPERATOR

1. Close any open windows except the Database window.
2. Click Queries in the Objects bar of the Database window, and then click the New button.
3. Select Design View in the New Query dialog box, and click OK.
4. Double-click the *tblStock* table from the list shown in the Show Table dialog box, and click the Close button.
5. Click ClientID in the *tblStock* table field roster, hold down the Ctrl key, and click, in turn, the following fields: PurchDate, PurchVolume, and PurchPrice. Release the Ctrl key.
6. Click inside any of the selected fields in the table field roster, drag the list to the first cell in the Field row, and release the mouse. When you release the mouse, Access places the four fields in separate Field row cells in the QBE grid.
7. Click the Criteria cell below the PurchDate column and type **>#12/31/2002# And <#2/1/2003#**, the selection criteria. Be sure to include the > and < symbols and to surround the date constants with the # symbols.
8. Click the Datasheet View button to see the results of your query (see Figure 2.22).
9. When you are finished, click the Query window Close button to close it.
10. Click No when you are asked if you want to save the newly created query. The query is already saved as *qryJanuaryStockPurchases* on your Companion CD in the Ch02 database.

Look carefully at the expression in the QBE grid in Figure 2.22 in the Criteria row of the Date column. That expression filters rows, selecting only those rows whose Date value falls within the specified range.

Three new symbols and a logical operator are introduced in the criteria. The *And* operator separates two expressions. This indicates that the conditions to its left and

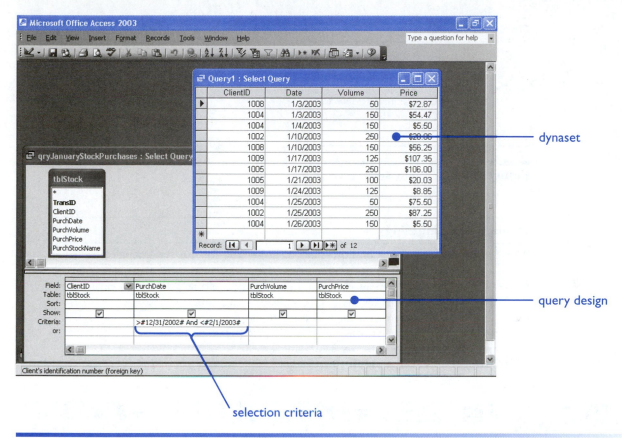

Figure 2.22 Selection and projection operations with an *and* operator used in the criteria.

right must be met simultaneously. In other words, rows are displayed only if the Date value is after December 31, 2002, and before February 1, 2003. Pound signs (#) enclose each date value. Embedding dates in # symbols ensures that Access recognizes the enclosed values as dates rather than arithmetic expressions. An alternative way to write an expression having the same effect is the criterion **Between #1/1/2003# And #1/31/2003#**. Most people prefer to use this form when dealing with lower and upper date (or value) ranges.

You probably are already familiar with the greater than (>) and less than (<) symbols. These are just two of the comparison operators that bracket the date range. A complete list of comparison operators is given in Figure 2.23. Among the logical operators is "And." The list of logical operators is given in Figure 2.24.

When you want to use criteria on two or more fields simultaneously, you place those conditions under the respective column names in the query image. For instance, suppose you want to list all stock purchases made by a particular client in a particular month of a given year, which involves a combination of queries similar to those you created in previous exercises.

Operator	Meaning
<	Less than
>	Greater than
=	Equal to
<=	Less than or equal to
>=	Greater than or equal to
<>	Not equal to

Figure 2.23   Comparison operators.

Operator	Meaning
And	Conditions on both sides must be true for the statement to be true. Otherwise, the statement is false.
Or	The statement is true if a condition on either side is true or if both conditions are true. Otherwise, the statement is false.
Not	A unary operator, it negates the logic it precedes.

Figure 2.24   Logical operators.

TRY IT

Modify the preceding query, *qryJanuaryStockPurchases*, to answer your new question. Click the Criteria row in the ClientID column, and type **1008**. Displaying the Datasheet view shows rows whose ClientID value equals 1008 and whose Date column value is any day in January 2003. The value 1008 is an exact match criterion, whereas the Date criterion is a value range criterion. What you have learned is that AND queries involving different fields of a table are created by entering all of the criteria in the same Criteria row of the QBE grid.

Creating Selection Criteria Using the "OR" Operator

You are likely to encounter queries similar to the following: "List the purchases in which clients have purchased either item A or item B." Another example is this one: "List all client records whose stock purchase price is less than $3.50 or whose stock name is Microsoft, regardless of purchase price." Both of the preceding questions involve two conditions, either of which is reason enough to list the record. That is, the criteria are called OR conditions. Unlike AND conditions, in which all conditions must be true to select and return a row to the dynaset, only one of the conditions need be true for a row to be returned.

How do you form a query involving OR conditions? Let's examine the latter example in the previous paragraph and see exactly what is needed to form a query. Two independent criteria are involved. There are two basic ways to formulate OR criteria, depending on whether the criteria concern one field or different fields. If two different fields are involved (stock price and stock name, in our example), then you create a query containing two Criteria rows—one row for each condition. If a criterion involves only one field, then you can place alternate acceptable values in one field, separating them with the word *Or*.

The next exercise uses the first method, since two different fields are involved. Close any open Access windows, but leave the Ch02 Database window open.

EXERCISE 2.11: FORMING AN "OR" QUERY

1. Click Queries in the Objects bar to ensure you are about to create a query, not a table, form, or some other object.
2. Click the New button, select Design View in the New Query dialog box, and click OK.
3. Double-click the *tblStock* table in the Show Table dialog box, and then click the Close button to close the Show Table dialog box.
4. Drag the asterisk (*) from the *tblStock* field list to the first cell in the Field row of the QBE grid.
5. Drag the PurchPrice and PurchStockName fields from the field list to the second and third cells in the Field row.
6. Clear the check boxes under the PurchPrice and PurchStockName columns so Access does not display values in those columns.
7. Click the Criteria cell under the PurchPrice column in the QBE grid, press Shift+F2 to enlarge the Criteria cell (this action is called "invoking the Zoom window"), and type the criterion **<3.5**
8. Click the OK button to close the Zoom window.
9. Click the second Criteria row under the PurchStockName column. Type the expression **"microsoft"** (type the quotation marks). Although Access automatically surrounds any text criterion with double quotation marks when you click another cell in the QBE grid, it's a good idea to get used to typing them. Access ignores capitalization when searching for matches.
10. Click the Datasheet View button to see the query results.

The dynaset, whose rows are in TransID order (because TransID is the table's primary key), is shown. Figure 2.25 shows both the query and the returned dynaset. (Normally, you can see either the query or the dynaset, since they are opposite sides of the same "coin." We have created a second query so you can see both at once.)

Notice that to form an OR query, you have as many Criteria rows in the query grid as there are independent selection criteria. Each row contains characters, a value, or an expression below a single column. When OR conditions involve only one field, there is an alternative way to write the criteria. For instance, suppose you want to display Stock table rows for anyone who has purchased either Microsoft or Biogen stock. Because both criteria involve the same field, StockName, you can write both criteria in one query image row, separating the criteria with the reserved word *OR* (either upper-case or lowercase):

"Microsoft" Or Like "Biogen*"

Normally, when dealing with character fields in a table, capitalization is significant. However, Access ignores capitalization and locates matching rows based on spelling alone. Character matching rules vary from one database product to another, however. Be sure to experiment with it first. *BIOGEN* in a query may not match *Biogen* in the database if you are not using Microsoft Access.

The asterisk following the word *Biogen* is one of the *wildcard* characters. Asterisk can stand for none or for any number of letters. This allows a match on a string such as *Biogen, Inc.*, *BIOGEN LTD.*, and so on. The asterisk can be used on either or both ends of any query string. Whenever you use a wildcard with a character string, Access automatically inserts the word *Like* ahead of it. Of course, the order of the strings separated by OR does not matter.

What would happen if you formed a query with only one row and placed the expression <3.5 beneath PurchPrice and (in the same criteria row) placed MICROSOFT beneath PurchStockName? No rows would be returned in the dynaset because no table rows satisfy both criteria simultaneously. The latter query is an example of specifying AND criteria. Simply stated, each Criteria row states conditions that must all be satisfied before any rows are selected by that particular criteria for inclusion in the dynaset. Of course, if there are other Criteria rows, they too may select rows to be retrieved. You should try the AND criteria as described above with Price and StockName values. Verify that no rows are returned for the data we have supplied.

Including Expressions in a Query

For most applications, it is informative to calculate values that are not stored in the database. Accounting applications are no exception. For instance, brokers keep a watchful eye on their larger accounts. One measure of a client's account size is the total purchase price of each stock a client owns. However, the Stock database does not record that value. There are two approaches to solving this problem; one is correct and the other is wholly incorrect.

An incorrect solution would be to create a new *tblStock* table column that holds the total purchase price of a stock. While this might be an acceptable solution when using a spreadsheet product, doing this with a database can lead to inconsistencies in the database and trouble later on. Why? Suppose that the total purchase price is calculated as the product of the PurchPrice and PurchVolume columns (that is, purchase price is the product of price per share and the number of shares purchased). Now, suppose someone discovers a mistake made in transcribing the volume purchased for a particular transaction. Instead of recording 200 shares, someone recorded the transaction volume as 100 shares. Someone enters the correct value 200.

Even though the PurchVolume value is now correct in the database record for a particular errant transaction, the total purchase price is not. Unlike a spreadsheet, a

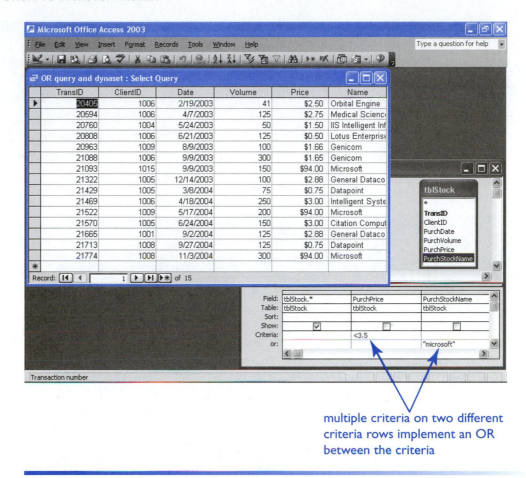

multiple criteria on two different criteria rows implement an OR between the criteria

Figure 2.25 OR query and dynaset.

field value in a database row does not change automatically when other values on which it depends change. Here's an important rule covering this situation: *Never store in a table any value (field) that is functionally dependent on two or more fields in the record.* That's a simplification of a rule that will be described in Chapter 3, but it merely states you shouldn't store in a database a value you can calculate or derive from the database.

So, what is the correct way to arrive at the total purchase price for each stock for every customer? The correct way is to include an *expression* in the query QBE grid to calculate the desired value dynamically—each time the query is executed. Instead of having you go through the process of creating such a query, we have provided an example for you to simply execute. You will find a query containing a calculation stored in your Ch02 database on the Companion CD, called *qryStockValue*.

TRY IT

Click Queries in the Objects bar of the Database window. Then, double-click the query *qryStockValue*. The query displays rows from the *tblStock* table as well as each transaction's total value. Examine the query in Figure 2.26 as well as the dynaset showing the retrieved and calculated results.

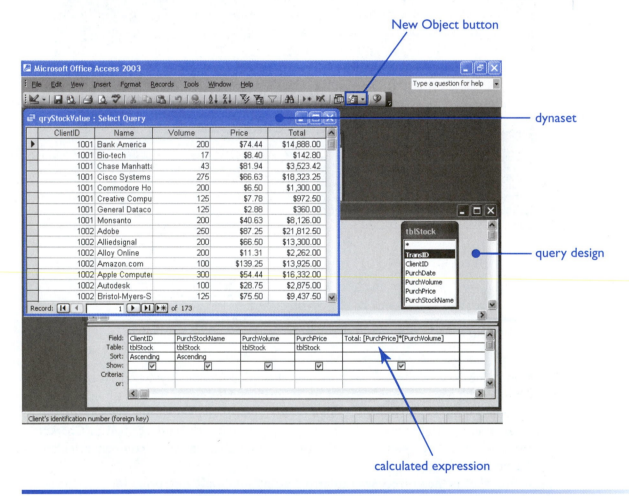

Figure 2.26 A query calculating a value with an expression.

Click the Design View button, and examine the query. Pay particular attention to the expression in the Field row. (You may have to click the horizontal scroll bar to bring the field into view.) The expression *Total: [PurchPrice]*[PurchVolume]* is in the Field row. The expression computes total stock purchase price for each row in turn and creates a new column in the dynaset. The word *Total* followed by a colon and a space is the column's name (also called an *alias*). The expression variables *[PurchPrice]* and *[PurchVolume]* reference table field names and get their values from the columns Price and Volume, respectively.

Printing Dynasets

To print a query's resulting dynaset, first display the dynaset (click the Datasheet View button if necessary). Before printing, always check the dynaset to make sure it contains the results you expected. Occasionally, you may pose a query that is too broad and encompasses too many database records. Or perhaps you inadvertently omitted a needed column. Always preview the query's result first. Print it only when you are satisfied.

Print the dynaset by clicking File and then clicking Print. The now familiar Print dialog box (see Figure 2.16) appears. Make any changes necessary, perhaps limiting the range of pages to print, and then click OK to print the dynaset.

Printing Query Definitions

Printing a query's definition is just like printing a table's definition, which you learned earlier. Here's an overview of how to print the documentation for the *qryStockValue* query. Open the Query window by clicking Queries in the Objects bar of the Database window. Select the Tools menu. Then, point to Analyze, and click Documenter. The Documenter dialog box opens. Click the Queries tab, if necessary. All of the query names appear along with their check boxes. Click the *qryStockValue* check box and any other queries whose definition you want to print (Figure 2.27). Finally, click OK to preview the definition report. If you are satisfied with the report preview, select Print from the File menu to print the query definition report.

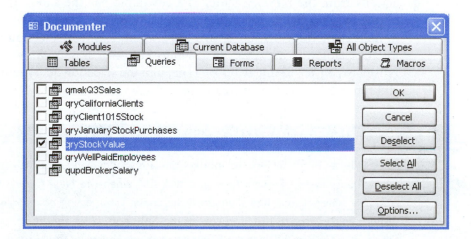

Figure 2.27   Preparing to print a query's definition.

CREATING ACTION QUERIES

Besides selection queries, you can create another type of Access query called an *action query*. Action queries provide a powerful means to make changes to a database's tables. Action queries can create a new table, remove records from an existing table, update one or more fields of an existing table, and add new records to an existing table. Action queries resemble selection queries such as those discussed in the previous section. The major difference is that they *alter* the database in some way, not merely display results from the database. Action queries include make-table, update, delete, append, and crosstab.

With a *make-table* query, you can retrieve a subset of rows from one or more tables and save the dynaset as a table. Perhaps you want to concentrate on the smaller table or you want to export the smaller table to Excel to analyze it further. Update queries allow you to change existing database information. You can create or run an update query to increase all programmers' hourly pay rates by 8 percent, for instance. A delete query selects and removes records from one or more tables. You could run a delete query to purge records of clients who have not contacted your office in over two years. With an append query, you can add new records to an existing table. Finally, a crosstab query summarizes and combines data from more than one source to present a compact, spreadsheet-like result. You might use a crosstab query to sum stock sales by broker for the first quarter of 2004—a statistic that is not apparent by observing tables alone. We present a concise description of how to create and run four of these action query types next.

Make-Table Query

You can create a new table from existing tables by using a make-table query. Suppose you want to create a new table containing only third quarter 2003 stock sales transactions from the *tblStock* table. The new table has the same structure, but contains only July, August, and September transactions. You could create a make-table query to deliver the information in two steps. First, create a selection query based on the *tblStock* table that retrieves all columns but only those rows whose transaction date falls between 7/1/03 and 9/30/03. Then, turn the selection query into a make-table query and run it to create the desired table.

TRY IT

Click Queries in the Objects bar of the Database window, and click the New button to create a new query. Select Design View, and click OK when the New Query dialog box appears. Add the table *tblStock*, and then close the Show Table dialog box. Drag all fields from the *tblStock* field roster to the Field row of the QBE grid. Drag another copy of the PurchDate field to the QBE grid. Clear the Show box corresponding to the second copy of PurchDate. In the Criteria row beneath the second copy of PurchDate, enter the selection criteria

Between #7/1/2003# And #9/30/2003#, and select Datasheet from the View menu to preview the new table. Select Design from the View menu to return to the Design view window. In the Design view window, select Make-Table Query from the Query menu. Enter a new table name, **tblThirdQuarterSales**, and click OK. Click File on the menu bar, click Save, and type **qmakThirdQuarterSales** to name the query. (The prefix *qmak* indicates the query is a make-table query.) Now you can run the query to create a new table: In Design view, select Run from the Query menu. A warning dialog box indicates "You are about to run a make-table query that will modify data in your table." Click Yes to approve creating the new table.

After you run the make-table query, a new table appears among those listed when you click Tables in the Objects bar. Of course, you can delete the table (you may want to save the query, however) by selecting the table, choosing Delete from the Edit menu, and clicking Yes when asked to confirm the deletion. You can also right-click the table and select Delete from the pop-up menu.

Update Query

Update queries allow you to make changes to many records in a table. You can update one field, or you can simultaneously update several. Update queries alter individual table fields, replacing them with new values. For instance, suppose you want to make a mid-year adjustment to female brokers' salaries. You determine that they should receive a 5 percent raise across the board. (Their male counterparts will have to wait an additional six months to qualify for a raise.) An update query is what is needed to make mass changes to the table containing brokers' salaries. Of course, our table is small, but this is an example of the kind of database change that would be laborious if it were done manually, one record at a time. The following activity leads you through making an update query. You can choose to create and then run your own query, or you can run the one saved in your Ch02 database called *qupdBrokerSalary*.

TRY IT

Create a new selection query, based on the table *tblBroker*, of the records to be updated, placing in the QBE grid only the fields to be updated or used for criteria. In this case, place only the fields BrokerSalary and BrokerGender in the QBE grid. (Salary will be updated, but Gender is used to select which rows' salary values are updated.) In the Criteria row, type **"F"** below the BrokerGender column. Before proceeding, view the affected records to ensure your selection criteria are in good shape. Select the Datasheet View button to view the selected records (two records). Switch back to Design view and continue. Click Query on the menu bar, and then click Update Query. Notice that the QBE grid changes with the addition of a new "Update To" row. In the Update To row beneath the BrokerSalary column, type the expression **[BrokerSalary]*1.05** (be sure to enclose BrokerSalary in square brackets). Figure 2.28 shows the design of the completed update query prior to execution. You can run the query to update the BrokerSalary fields of the *tblBroker* table by clicking Query and then clicking Run. Alternatively, you can click the Run button on the Query Design toolbar.

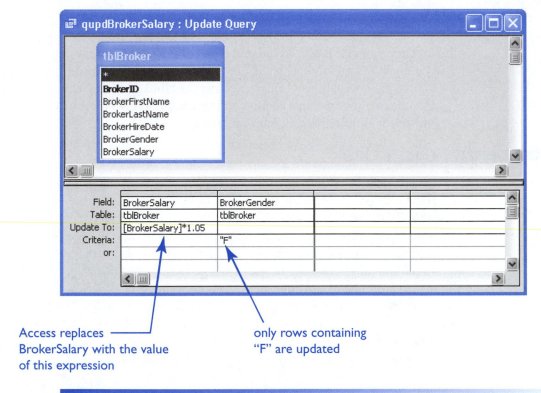

Access replaces BrokerSalary with the value of this expression

only rows containing "F" are updated

Figure 2.28   An update query example.

Beware: Access cannot reverse an update operation. In other words, you cannot click the Undo command following this operation. You can undo some update operations by formulating a new update query to restore updated values, but many update operations are irreversible. For instance, suppose you choose to update the location field of an employee's work address to "New York" for all employees whose city is currently Indianapolis. This will effectively move all Indianapolis employees to New York. However, you cannot easily reverse the change if other employees already are listed as living in New York. It is not a matter of changing the City field of New York back to Indianapolis, because some are New Yorkers who were never located in Indianapolis in the first place! Always select Datasheet View before running an update query to check the scope of your changes.

Delete Query

A delete query is used to delete records from tables. It is not used to delete entire tables. To delete an entire table, not just the records it contains, you click Tables in the Database window, select the table, and press the Delete key. The entire table, plus data, is removed from the database. Deleting records is a much more subtle activity. Suppose, for instance, that you want to remove from the *tblStock* table all transactions that occurred on or before December 31, 2003. In other words, you want to "clear the books" for a new year, 2004. A delete query with the proper selection criteria will do the trick. First, create a selection query, and then examine its Datasheet view to ensure that proper records will be deleted when the query is transformed to a delete query. To create a delete query from a selection query, ensure the query is displayed in Design view and then select Delete Query from the Query menu.

Once you have properly defined a delete query, simply run it to delete the targeted records. Figure 2.29 shows an example of a delete query that removes from the table *tblStock* all stock transactions that occurred before 2004. The delete query, called *qdelOldTransactions*, is stored in your database, Ch02. Notice that the only fields that are needed in the QBE grid are those being used for criteria. In this example, only the PurchDate field is required, because that is the sole selection criterion—the purchase transaction date. Of course, Access will delete the entire record.

Append Query

You use an append query to add records from a table or query to the end of another table. For instance, you would use an append query to create a comprehensive employee table containing all employees in all divisions. The table *tblEmployee*, for instance, represents only one division of a larger company. By creating an append query, you can add other divisions' employee records to the *tblEmployee* table.

To create an append query, simply create a selection query including fields from the source tables that are in the target (destination) table and any fields that are used as criteria. In the Criteria row of the query, establish the conditions that are used to select records from the other table to append to the current table (for instance, only Division 1 and Division 2 employees). View the potential new records by clicking the Datasheet View button. Then, switch back to Design view and select Append Query from the Query menu to turn the selection query into an append query. When prompted for the target table name by the Append dialog box, enter the target table's name or select it from the Table Name drop-down list. Click OK to complete the query definition. Figure 2.30 shows an example in which a fictitious division's employee records are to be appended to the *tblEmployee* table.

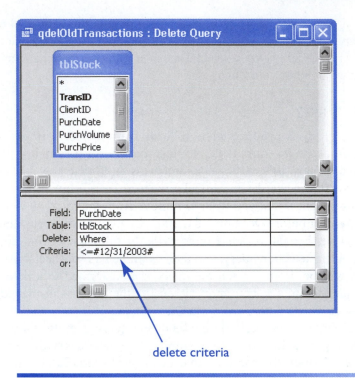

delete criteria

Figure 2.29 A delete query example.

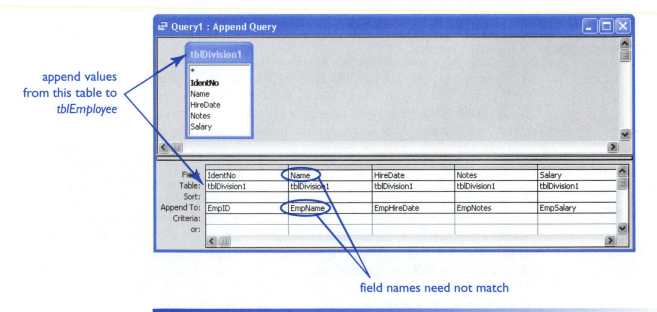

append values from this table to *tblEmployee*

field names need not match

Figure 2.30 An append query example.

USING FORMS

A form provides a convenient, less cluttered work surface through which you can enter or alter information in your tables. A form can display information from one or more tables. Additionally, a form can display information from a query (that is, the query's dynaset).

One of the advantages of using a form to enter or change data is that the form can resemble a paper form with which you or your clients are already familiar. When the form on the screen mimics a paper form, those using the form will intuitively know what information goes where, and they usually feel more comfortable with a familiar interface. Entering data directly into a table can be more confusing and error-prone, especially for anyone not familiar with databases in general or Access in particular. Another advantage of a form is that you can enforce a medley of validation checks on values that are entered in a table through a form.

Viewing a Table Through a Form

To help you better understand a form, we have created one that displays information from the Client table (*tblClient*), which is shown in Figures 2.13 and 2.15. The form is found on your Companion CD and is called *frmClient*. (All forms on the Companion CD have the prefix *frm*.) Work through the next exercise to open a Form view of the *tblClient* table.

EXERCISE 2.12: OPENING AND USING A FORM

1. Close all open windows except the Database window. (This isn't necessary, but it reduces screen clutter.)
2. Click Forms in the Objects bar of the Database window to display all forms in the Ch02 database.
3. Double-click the form *frmClient*. The Client form appears (see Figure 2.31).
4. Close the form after you have examined it.

All fields from the Client table (Figure 2.13) appear in a nice arrangement in the form in Figure 2.31. Familiar navigation buttons appear along the bottom edge of the Form window. Those buttons perform the usual actions: move to the top of the table, move up one row, and so forth. Look at the 15 records one at a time by clicking the Next Record navigation button. After you have moved to the last record, click the First Record navigation button. The first record appears in the form. Notice that the form displays records in order by ClientID. The form is built from the *tblClient* table whose primary key, ClientID, maintains the table (and thus the form) rows in order by the ClientID field. If you want rows displayed in the form in name order, you could create a query that returns rows sorted on ClientLastName (specify Ascending sort in the QBE grid under ClientLastName). Then you can build a form based on the query. We illustrate a query-based form in the next section.

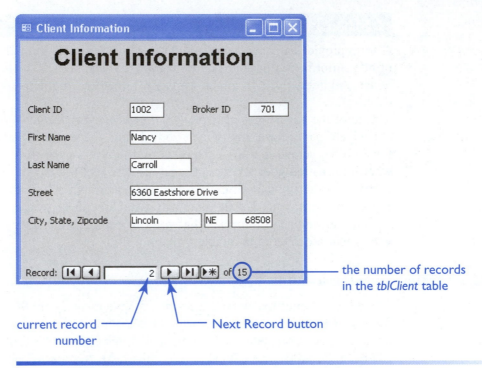

Figure 2.31   A client form.

Several interesting design elements have been employed in the Client form so that it is at once intuitive and attractive. Along the top is a simple title, in Arial typeface, identifying the form. In the upper left part of the form is the client's identification number. It is entered first. Below it are the client's name and address.

Viewing a Query Through a Form

You can create forms from queries as well as tables. It makes no difference whether the form displays a table's contents or a query's contents. Figure 2.32 shows a form that displays a subset of the fields from the *qryStockValue* query, which is shown in Figure 2.26. Unlike the previous form, this one has no Minimize or Restore buttons available in the form's Title bar. Notice that the Form window status line displays the current record and the total number of records. In this case, the total number of records depends on how many rows are selected by the query upon which the form is built. It is likely that you will create and use many forms based on queries. The form shown in Figure 2.32 is stored on your Companion CD in the Ch02 database as *frmStockValue*. Try it out yourself.

Creating a Form Quickly

When you want to enter data into a table one record at a time, the best user interface may be a form. We illustrate how easy it is to create a functional and attractive form

**no Minimize or
Maximize button is available**

Client Stock Purchases

Client ID	1001
Stock Name	Cisco Systems
Stock Volume	275
Purchase Price	$66.63
Total	$18,323.25

Record: 4 of 173 ———— **record count**

Figure 2.32 Form based on the query, *qryStockValue*.

by simply choosing a table and clicking a button. Let's create a simple form for the *tblBroker* table through which we can observe or alter information. First, switch to the Database window (the fastest way is to click the Database Window button on the toolbar). Then, create an AutoForm by completing the steps in the following activity.

TRY IT

Click Tables in the Objects bar of the Database window to display a list of the Ch02 table names. Click the table name *tblBroker* in the list of tables. Click the New Object button list arrow (see Figure 2.26) on the toolbar, and then click AutoForm from the drop-down list. (Clicking the New Object button instead of the list arrow is a shortcut to create an AutoForm.) A Form window appears containing your newly created form (see Figure 2.33). The Form window Title bar contains the table name by default. You can change it later if you want. Leave the Form window open, because you will save the form in a few moments. That's all there is to creating a form from a table. You probably agree with us that the form is attractive and functional. We show you how to modify and enhance a form in Chapter 5. For now, simply save the new form on your copy of the database.

Saving a Form

You can save a form design by executing either Save or Save As from the File menu. Then you supply the form's name.

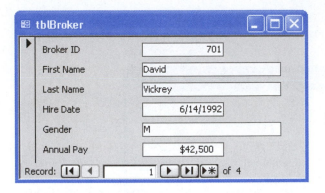

Figure 2.33   Broker form.

 TRY IT

With the newly created Broker form still displayed, select Save in the File menu. Type the name **frmBrokerAutoForm** in the Form Name text box of the Save As dialog box. Click OK to complete the form save operation. Click the form's Title bar Close button to close the form.

The form is saved in your database, Ch02. We have also saved the form in the Ch02 database on your Companion CD. It is called *frmBroker*.

Editing Data with a Form

It is often easier to alter data in a table using a form. Because only one table row is usually displayed on the form, you are less likely to make mistakes. Editing table data through a form is simple. While looking at a form in Form view (not Design view), you click the field that you want to change and make any needed changes. Try editing a record in the Broker table through the form.

EXERCISE 2.13: EDITING DATA WITH A FORM

1. Double-click the form name *frmBrokerAutoForm* to open it, if necessary.
2. Move to the record for David Vickrey (press PgUp or PgDn or use the navigation buttons if necessary).
3. Press Tab repeatedly to move to the Hire Date field. (The entire value is highlighted if you use Tab or the arrow keys to move to the selected fields instead of the mouse.)
4. Type the correct hire date, **7/5/1990**
5. Click the Form window's Close button to close the form.
6. Click the Next Record navigation button to cause Access to post the change to the underlying table. Then, click the Previous Record navigation button to verify the change you made.
7. Close the form.

Changes to a particular record are not posted (saved) to the table until you move to another record or close the database. Keep in mind that the form merely displays table data. The form itself is not changed. Only the table data are actually changed. Changed data are automatically saved for you, and you need not save a form again unless you change its design.

Querying a Database with a Form

When you are looking for a particular record in a table containing many records, there's no better way to locate it than by using a form. You can load a form and then use the command Filter By Form or Filter By Selection. Additionally, you can create a more complex search using the Advanced Filter/Sort tool. To illustrate this process, let's use the Filter By Form command to locate all the stocks purchased by client 1013. You can imagine how daunting this task would be if you had to visually examine every row in the *tblStock* table looking for all of a given client's transactions. Naturally, you wouldn't do it that way. Instead, you would request Access to apply a filter—another term for applying selection criteria so that only a subset of records is displayed—and retrieve only records of interest.

EXERCISE 2.14: FILTERING DATA THROUGH A FORM

1. Click Forms in the Objects bar of the Database window to display the existing form names.
2. Double-click *frmStockValue* to open that form.
3. Click the Records menu, point to Filter, and then click Filter By Form. Notice that a down-pointing arrow appears on the ClientID data field and that the menu bar has changed. The ClientID is a drop-down list box from which you can choose one of the unique ClientID values retrieved from the *tblStock* table ClientID column.
4. Click the ClientID drop-down list box arrow to reveal the collection of ClientID values (see Figure 2.34).
5. Click 1013 from the list box. The ClientID field displays the value 1013.
6. Click Filter on the menu bar, and then click Apply Filter/Sort. The first of several client 1013 records is displayed in the form. Notice that the indicator (filtered) appears just to the right of the navigation buttons. (Drag the right border of the form to the right, if necessary, to reveal the indicator.) This indicates the form is displaying a subset of the underlying table, not all the records.
7. Click the navigation buttons to scroll through a few of the records corresponding to client 1013's holdings.
8. When you are done, click Records on the menu bar, and then click Remove Filter/Sort. Alternatively, you can click the Remove Filter button (the funnel in Figure 2.34) found on the toolbar. The Remove Filter toolbar button is renamed Apply Filter when not engaged. You can toggle the filter on and off by clicking the button on and off.
9. Close the form.

You can filter by any form field. Repeat steps 1 through 3, and select the field by which you want to filter. Then, clear the other fields; otherwise, other field values will further restrict the records that are retrieved. Try it yourself. See if you can display in the *frmStock* form information about clients who own Microsoft stock.

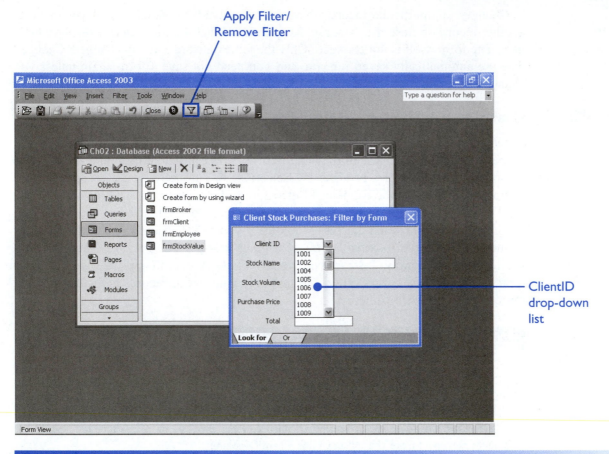

Figure 2.34   Filter By Form example.

Using Filter By Selection works almost the same way. When you choose Filter By Selection, it filters records shown in the form based on the currently selected data. To Filter By Selection, select a field or part of a field in a form and then click Filter By Selection. Only records matching the selected value are displayed in the form.

Printing a Form

Though forms are best suited for onscreen work, you can print them too. To print one record, open the form, locate the record, and click the File menu Print command. (If you click the toolbar Print button, all forms begin printing—something you probably do not want to do.) When the Print dialog box appears, click the Selected Record(s) option button, and then click OK. You will notice that neither the form's Title bar nor its navigation buttons appear on the printout.

Printing a range of records is an equally straightforward process. Select Print from the File menu, click the Pages option button, enter the beginning and ending page numbers in the page range boxes, and click OK. Access prints table rows in the format of the displayed form. However, you probably will not want to print more than a few records this way. There is a better way to print larger amounts of information from tables. An Access report is the most efficient way to design and produce tabular output of the records in a table or a query result. Access reports are introduced next.

DESIGNING REPORTS

Frequently, you will want either to preview a report onscreen or to produce a printed report, which you can pass around at a meeting or keep as a permanent record. Access reports are just that—reports. You cannot enter data or edit data in a report. Reports range from simple, utilitarian designs to professional-looking reports replete with attractive typefaces, drop shadows, and graphics.

Previewing a Report

Reports typically display information from a table, a collection of related tables, or a query. We have created a report from the query you examined earlier (Figure 2.26). Though a lot can be gained from looking at the query's results onscreen, it is even more useful to have a printed report. The report you are about to preview and then print has some added features that make the information delivered by the query *qryStockValue* (Figure 2.26) more understandable and useful. First, let's learn how to open a stored report definition and preview the report prior to actually printing it.

EXERCISE 2.15: LOADING AND PREVIEWING A REPORT

1. Open the Database window, and then click Reports in the Objects bar of the Database window. A list of available reports appears.
2. Click the report named *rptClientStocks*, and click the Preview button. A preview of the report appears in the Print Preview window.
3. Click the Maximize button to display the whole window, and click the mouse over the report preview to alternately zoom in and zoom out. Use the scroll bars to pan the report. Figure 2.35 shows the report preview.
4. Close the report if you wish, or continue examining the report by following the directions in the paragraph that follows.

Use the Report window's scroll bars to move around the displayed page. To move to another page, use the navigation buttons in the lower left corner of the Print Preview window. You can also use the arrow keys and the PgUp and PgDn keys to move around the report. Take a few moments to try out the page navigation buttons. Go to the last report page, and then go back to the first. There is a brief pause as Access moves to a particular page and repaints the Print Preview window. Experiment with printing a report page. Select Print from the File menu, click the Pages option, enter a page range to print, and click OK to start the printing process. Close the report by clicking the Close button in the upper right corner of the Print Preview window. The Database window for Ch02 reappears.

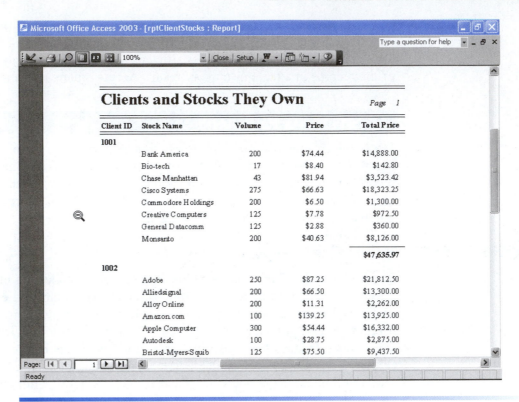

Figure 2.35   Previewing a report.

Now that you have seen an example of a report based on a query and how to preview and print it, let's create a simple report. It is based on the *tblClient* table.

Creating a Report Quickly

Creating a report from a table is similar to creating a form from a table. You select a table name in the Database window, click the New Object toolbar button, and select AutoReport from the drop-down list. A default-format report appears. In the following exercise you will create an AutoReport based on the *tblClient* table.

EXERCISE 2.16: CREATING A REPORT QUICKLY

1. Close any open windows except the Database window. Click Tables in the Objects bar of the Ch02 Database window.
2. Click *tblClient* in the list of tables (highlight its name, but do not open the table).
3. Click Insert on the menu bar, and then click AutoReport. Access creates a default style report and displays it in the Print Preview window (see Figure 2.36).

By default, an AutoReport-generated report displays each table field arranged vertically, one above the other, with the numeric data fields right aligned and the character fields left aligned. You can easily change any of these elements or remove them.

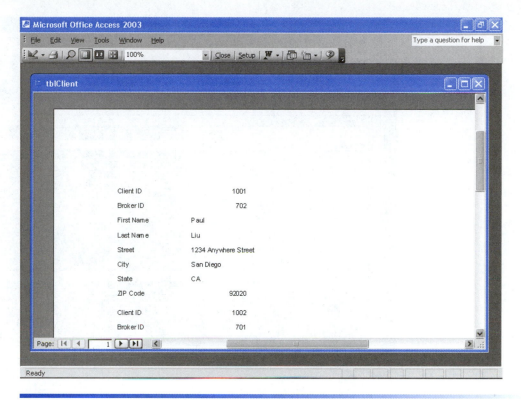

Figure 2.36 Typical AutoReport-style report.

However, you must display the report in Design view to make structural changes to any report.

Click the Close button located on the Print Preview toolbar (or select Design View from the View menu). The report's design is displayed in the Design view window. Figure 2.37 shows the Client report's design.

In the Design window, you can change a report in many ways. For instance, you can remove a report field by selecting it with the mouse and then pressing the Delete key after the square selection handles appear surrounding the field. If you make a mistake, remember you can use the Undo command (Undo Delete in this case) in the Edit menu.

Saving a Report

Reports are saved like any other objects described in this text—by selecting the Save or Save As command from the File menu.

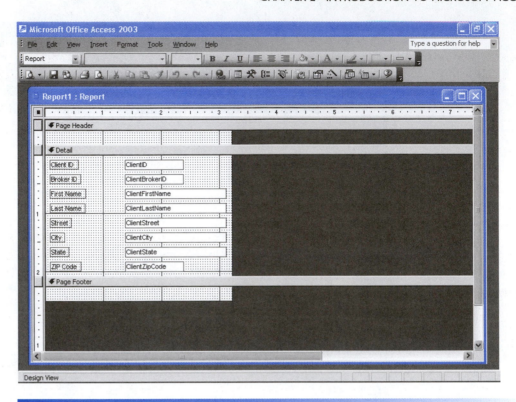

Figure 2.37   Report design.

EXERCISE 2.17: SAVING A REPORT

1. With the previously generated report open in either Design view or Print Preview, click File on the menu bar and then click Save As. The Save As dialog box appears.
2. Type **rptClientTest** in the upper text box, labeled *Save Report 'Report1' To:* Report1 is the report's name default name (or Report2, etc.). You are changing it to a more meaningful name, and it is listed along with the other Report objects in the database.
3. Click OK to complete the save operation.
4. Click the Close button on the (Design or Print Preview) Report window title bar to close the report.
5. Click File on the Access menu bar, and then click Exit to close Access and the database simultaneously.

Go to **http://perry.swlearning.com** for an in-depth tutorial.

SUMMARY

You have learned a great deal about database systems in general and the Access database system in particular. You understand what a relational database is and why it is the best choice for dealing with related sets of information.

Tables are the building blocks of a database system and consist of columns and rows. You can manipulate tables in several ways to produce the result you want. Access maintains table rows in order when a table has a primary key. The navigation buttons in the Table window facilitate moving to various rows in a table. You can move a column in a table to another position by dragging its heading left or right. This alters the table's display characteristics but does not actually alter a column's position in the stored table.

In addition to tables, Access contains other objects including queries, forms, and reports. Queries, or questions, use the Query by Example method to pose questions about the data stored in one or more tables. Able to retrieve a subset of rows or columns, queries narrow the search for relevant information to just those elements of interest. You learned how to create queries using simple criteria as well as more complex expressions involving comparison operators. You created AND criteria in which two or more conditions must be simultaneously true. You saw that OR criteria are created by placing conditions on two or more rows of the query model. Besides selection queries, you learned how to create a variety of action queries, which alter the database's tables.

Forms provide a simpler interface to tables, because only one row at a time is displayed. You used a form and created a quick form from a table. Forms can be made to look like paper forms encountered in a business. When a form resembles an existing paper—one already in use—the computer form is rather intuitive and easy to use. You learned that by merely clicking a form entry and typing, you can change a table's data. When you move to a new record, the change is then posted to the table. And you learned that you can filter data through a table, thereby restricting which table rows are shown in a form.

Finally, you got a brief look at the hard copy output facility of Access: the report. First, you previewed an existing report. Then, you created an AutoReport for a table. Reports provide a way to print and summarize information from one or more tables in a pleasant-looking format. Reports are output only. You cannot change a table's contents with a report.

This chapter has given you the fundamental tools to begin using Access to build systems. In Chapter 3, we introduce more formal foundations of relational database management systems. In that chapter you will learn about some rules and techniques that will help you design and build accounting information systems using tables, which are well-suited for the purpose.

QUESTIONS AND PROBLEMS FOR REVIEW

Multiple-Choice Questions

1. Access is a _____ database management system.
   a. hierarchical
   b. helical
   c. relational
   d. rational

2. When you launch Microsoft Access and open a database, the _____ window is the first to appear.
   a. Access
   b. form
   c. table
   d. database

3. The View menu lets you display different types of objects including forms, reports, pages, macros, _____, and modules.
   a. favorites
   b. groups
   c. design
   d. tables

4. Only one object actually holds database data. This is the database's _____(s).
   a. table
   b. query
   c. database engine
   d. form

5. You can place selection criterion into a _____ to produce a dynaset, which is a subset of a table's rows.
   a. form
   b. view
   c. query
   d. attribute

6. When you hover the mouse over a toolbar button or icon, _____ appears.
   a. its name
   b. its toolbar name
   c. ToolTip
   d. help
   e. Both a and c are correct.

7. A(n) _____ query can change the contents of a table. A selection query cannot.
   a. advanced
   b. action
   c. redirected
   d. select

8. Every row in a table should have a special field called a(n) (two words) _____ _____, which ensures each row is uniquely identifiable.
   a. address link
   b. hyperlink address
   c. reserved number
   d. primary key

9. You should never store in a table any value that is functionally _____ two or more fields in the same record.
   a. preceding
   b. dependent on
   c. opposed to
   d. linked with

10. To increase the SalesPrice field by 15 percent in a table called *tblSales*, you would write an update query on the *tblSales* table and include what expression in the "Update To" row?
    a. 0.15*[SalesPrice]
    b. [tblSales]*1.15
    c. 1.15*[SalesPrice]
    d. None of the preceding is correct.

Discussion Questions

1. Describe the Access work surface icons, discuss their uses, and tell how they differ from the menu commands.

2. Discuss when it is advantageous to view your data in a Table window and when a Form window is better. Explain your reasons.

3. List the steps necessary to open and display database tables.

4. Discuss why you would use database queries to retrieve information.

5. Describe the different ways to design a database report, and discuss the possible situations where you might use these different designs.

Practice Exercises

Note: Before doing any of the following exercises, first copy *Ch02.mdb* from your Companion CD to the hard drive of the computer on which you are working. Then, clear the copied database's Read-only file attribute (see Chapter 1, Exercise 1.14, Clearing a File's Read-Only Property). Having done that, you can complete each exercise using the copy of the Companion CD database.

1. Sort the *tblClient* table on the ClientState and ClientCity fields so that the rows are in order first by state (A to Z) and then city (A to Z) within each state. Print the sorted table directly from the Table window.

2. Create and execute a query based on the *tblClient* table that displays which clients are assigned broker 702. Display only the columns ClientFirstName, ClientLastName,

ClientID, and ClientBrokerID (in that order, left to right). The query should sort the rows into descending order by the clients' names (like a telephone book listing does). Print the resulting dynaset.

3. Use a Make-Table Query to create a new table from *tblEmployee* that identifies all the employees who were hired before January 1, 1999. Save your new query as *qryServiceAward* and your new table as *tblServiceAward*. Print your results.

4. Use an Update Query to adjust the existing table called *tblSubscriptionData*. Vince Magmer has just won an additional three months ("Length") at no charge to his current subscription. Save the query as *qryUpdateMagmer*, and print both the new query and revised table.

5. Use a Delete Query to remove Penny Cheap from the *tblSubscriptionData* for not having paid her bill. Save the query as *qryDeleteCheap*, and print both the query and revised table.

Problems

Note: Before doing any of the following exercises, first copy *Ch02.mdb* from your Companion CD to the hard drive of the computer on which you are working. Then, ensure that the database is not read-only by clearing, if necessary, the copied database's Read-only file attribute (see Chapter 1, Exercise 1.14). Having done that, you can complete each exercise using the copy of the Companion CD database.

1. Run the query *qryClient1015Stock* found in the query list for the Ch02 database. It produces a list of client 1015's stock purchases in ascending order by transaction identification number. Change the sort order of the rows so that the query returns rows in Price order (low to high). Print the dynaset. Then modify the sort order so that the dynaset is sorted in descending order (high to low) by the Volume column. Print the dynaset. Can you combine these sort criteria so that the dynaset is sorted first in descending order by Volume and then in ascending order by Price within matching volumes? Try it. Print the third dynaset. Remember to write your name on all three printed dynasets.

2. You can create an AutoForm from a query in exactly the same way you do from a table. Create an AutoForm for the query called *qryStockValue* in the query list for the database Ch02. Begin by selecting the query from the list. Click the AutoForm button. When you are done, save the form design under the name *frmAutoForm*. Turn in a printed copy of the first two pages of the form. Remember to write your name on the output.

3. Create an AutoReport report for the *tblStock* table found in the Ch02 database. Print only the first two pages of the report. Print your name on the report. If you feel adventuresome, try adding a label containing your name in the report in either the report header or the page header.

CHAPTER 3
Databases and Accounting Systems

OBJECTIVES

This chapter introduces database accounting systems and compares them to the double-entry book-keeping systems with which you are already familiar. It also explains how accountants break down business activities into transaction cycles and how database accounting systems use those transaction cycles as organizing themes. This chapter covers the theoretical foundations for database accounting systems and contains practical examples of applying database theory. You will learn about the connection between accounting systems and database systems, why a relational database system is the best choice for capturing accounting information, and some of the theory and history of relational database management systems. Just enough theory is provided to aid you in creating efficient, optimal database objects, but the discussion avoids presenting more database theory than you need. In this chapter, you will learn about:

- Differences between double-entry bookkeeping and database accounting systems.
- Advantages and disadvantages of database accounting systems.
- Business activity classifications.
- Transaction cycles.
- The relationship between accounting systems and database systems.
- A brief history leading to the development of database management systems.
- Functions of database management systems.
- Theory and application of relational database management systems.
- The structure of database objects that store accounting events.
- The importance of normalizing tables.
- Performing database selections, projections, and joins.
- How accountants use the REA model when designing accounting databases.

This chapter will help you understand the differences between double-entry bookkeeping and database accounting. The information about business activity classifications and transaction cycles will provide a framework that will help you apply your knowledge of Microsoft Access to the task of building accounting database components.

This chapter uses an accounting application—processing and maintaining invoice data—to illustrate the use of databases in accounting. The company used in our example, a coffee bean and tea wholesaler called The Coffee Merchant, purchases whole-bean coffees and teas at international auctions and sells the coffees and teas to a variety of coffee roasters. To begin, we will briefly examine the connection between accounting and database systems and explore how accounting came to use relational database management systems.

INTRODUCTION

Most accounting students learn the mechanics of accounting for economic transactions using the tools of manual double-entry bookkeeping such as journals and ledgers. This chapter begins with a discussion of the differences between database accounting systems and manual double-entry bookkeeping systems. We then explain the advantages and disadvantages of using a database approach to building accounting systems.

The chapter's discussion of business activity classifications then introduces three levels of complexity that accountants use to classify firms. These classifications will help you understand when to incorporate particular database features into your accounting database system designs. Finally, the chapter describes transaction cycles, which provide a way for accountants and others to classify economic events into related categories.

Many students have learned how to use Microsoft Access as a software application but have not learned much of the database theory that is essential for creating complex applications such as accounting systems. Chapters 4 and 5 describe how to use database software to build accounting system elements for a specific transaction cycle. In these chapters, you will learn how to create forms, queries, and reports to accomplish accounting tasks in all of the major transaction cycles.

DATABASE ACCOUNTING SYSTEMS

Much of the current interest in using databases for accounting systems arose out of businesses realizing the advantages of relational databases, such as Microsoft Access, for all their information processing needs. Rather than maintain separate files and programs for each business function, companies are trying to consolidate their data and data-handling operations. Some firms have created enterprise-wide databases that store all of the firm's information in one system.

Events-Based Theories of Accounting

Over the past forty years, accounting researchers such as William McCarthy, Eric Denna, and George Sorter have developed and refined various events-based approaches to accounting theory. Their work provides a solid theoretical underpinning for accountants' increasing use of relational databases to perform accounting tasks. These events-based approaches argue that accountants should strive to store all relevant attributes of economic events in a readily accessible form. Relational database software products, such as Microsoft Access, provide tools that accountants can use to accomplish that objective. Events theories of accounting offer an alternative to the commonly used double-entry bookkeeping approaches that have been a part of accounting for more than five centuries. Although events approaches to accounting have been discussed for many years, few accounting systems were constructed using events principles until quite recently. Beginning in the early 1990s, advances in information technologies, especially in database management software and disk storage, allowed companies to start building accounting systems based on events theories of accounting.

Double-Entry Bookkeeping Versus Database Accounting

For the better part of five hundred years, double-entry bookkeeping provided an excellent method for recording transactions. It satisfied accountants' need to capture the essence of each transaction. When double-entry bookkeeping was first developed over five hundred years ago, the costs of gathering and storing information were very high. Recording transactions with pen and paper was a time-consuming task. Double-entry bookkeeping gave accountants a valuable tool that quickly identified essential elements of transactions. Therefore, double-entry bookkeeping let businesspersons capture and store key attributes of transactions in a highly aggregated form. This helped keep the cost of information gathering and storage at affordable levels. Also, the debit-credit balancing check provided an important internal control feature in manual accounting systems.

TRY IT

If you would like to see how far we have come in replacing manual accounting systems with database systems, go to your local office supplies store and try to find a pad of two-column accounting paper. If you have trouble finding it, ask a salesperson for help. He or she will probably look up the product's location—in the store's computerized inventory database.

Computerized transaction processing has released accountants from the limitations and drudgery of manual accounting systems. Using computers, we can now quite easily capture a wide variety of information about each transaction. For example, supermarkets and other retail stores routinely read bar codes at checkout stations to capture the date and time of purchase, the identity of the item purchased, the store location, the checkout station number, and the cashier number. Even more important is that they obtain all of this information with one quick swipe!

Technologies such as bar code readers and optical scanners have played a major role in reducing the cost of acquiring and storing multiple attributes of each economic event. To see more clearly how double-entry bookkeeping and database accounting differ, let's consider a simple sales transaction. Most sales transactions begin when a customer sends a purchase order. If the firm receiving the purchase order has the goods in stock and finds the customer's credit to be acceptable, the firm ships the ordered goods and invoices the customer. A double-entry bookkeeping system would record this transaction for the selling firm with the following journal entry:

Date	**Account**	**Debit**	**Credit**
Date	*Accounts Receivable*	*Amount*	
	Sales		*Amount*
	Explanation		

Note that this journal entry includes five items of information:

- Transaction date
- Names of the accounts debited
- Names of the accounts credited
- Transaction amount
- Explanation of the transaction

In a general journal entry such as the one shown above, the explanation might contain the name of the customer. Firms that use specialized journals and subsidiary ledgers can store one additional information item: the customer's name or account code. For example, if the above journal entry had been posted to a subsidiary ledger, the record-keeping process would store the customer's name or account code in the subsidiary ledger. If the sale had been recorded in a specialized sales journal instead of in a general journal as shown above, the format would differ. For example, the account names might be implied by the transaction appearing in the sales journal rather than being explicitly stated; the information recorded would be the same in both cases. To summarize, a double-entry bookkeeping system records five or six transaction attributes and records one of them, the amount, twice.

Now consider how a relational database accounting system might handle the same transaction. A database accounting system would record the transaction in a set of database tables similar to those that appear in Figure 3.1.

The database system shown in Figure 3.1 stores some attributes of the sales transaction in the Sales table, which appears in the figure as *tblSales*. We use the "tbl" prefix in this book to indicate that the Access object is a table. We use similar prefixes for other Access objects, including "frm" for forms, "rpt" for reports, and "qry" for queries.

Note, however, that many other attributes of the sales transaction are stored in the eight other tables that appear in Figure 3.1. A database accounting system can store many more attributes of the sales transaction than a journal entry can store. Note that this database accounting system for sales information stores these attributes in an atomic form, scattered throughout the tables. In Chapter 2 you learned a number of rules for designing effective database tables that store information attributes in multiple tables, yet allow the information to be pulled back together when needed. One of these rules requires you to establish a primary key for each table. The primary key consists of one or more fields in each table that provides a unique identifier for each row in the table. The primary key fields of the tables in Figure 3.1 are shown in bold type.

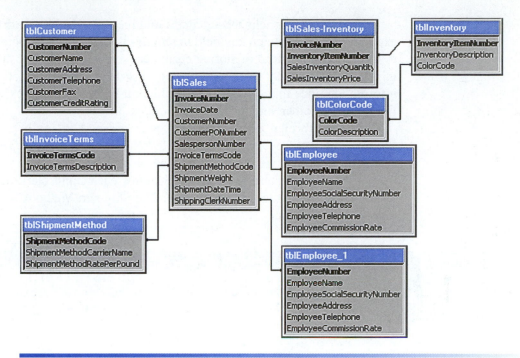

Figure 3.1 Sales transactions stored in a database accounting system.

The database system shown in Figure 3.1 stores 10 transaction attributes in the *tblSales* table and a virtually unlimited number of attributes in the other tables. For example, if the invoice included 20 items, the *tblSales-Inventory* table would store 40 attributes (20 item quantities and 20 item prices) for the transaction. Contrast this with the information stored in the double-entry bookkeeping journal entry. The journal entry does not even tell you how many items were on the invoice, much less tell you anything about those items.

Not only does the database accounting system store many more attributes than the double-entry bookkeeping system, it stores them more efficiently. A key feature of relational database software such as Microsoft Access is that it allows table designs that reduce or eliminate the storage of redundant information. For the sales information database in Figure 3.1, let's examine what is stored in each table, how the tables are linked, and how we might extract information from this sales system.

The primary key of *tblSales* is the InvoiceNumber field. The other attributes of the sale that are stored exclusively in this table include the invoice date, the customer's purchase order number, the shipping weight of the items sold, and a shipping date-time stamp. The other five fields in *tblSales* are foreign key fields. Access, like many other relational database software packages, uses links between primary key fields and corresponding foreign key fields in other tables to maintain the connections among information attributes. The foreign keys in Figure 3.1 show the links from *tblSales* to other tables that contain information about sales.

Foreign key links help accountants avoid recording information more than once. For example, the first foreign key field in *tblSales* is CustomerNumber, which links *tblSales* to *tblCustomer*. Instead of storing customers' names, addresses, and other information in *tblSales* repeatedly for every invoice, this database design lets you store customer information once for each customer and link it to individual sales by including just one field, the CustomerNumber field, in *tblSales*.

The other foreign keys in *tblSales* are SalespersonNumber, InvoiceTermsCode, ShipmentMethodCode, and ShippingClerkNumber. The InvoiceTermsCode links each sale to a table of invoice terms, such as cash, 2/10 net 30, 1/15 net 30, or net 30. If these terms were entered directly in *tblSales*, each input clerk might enter them differently and corrupt the sales database. The ShipmentMethodCode performs a similar error-control function.

TRY IT

With several other members of your class, see how many different logical ways you can record the names of the shipping firms with which you are familiar. You might be surprised at how many variations you can create.

The SalespersonNumber and the ShippingClerkNumber foreign key fields contain the identification numbers for these two employee participants in sales transactions. Although Figure 3.1 shows *tblEmployee* twice to accommodate these two links, the firm has only one Employee table.

The primary key of *tblSales,* InvoiceNumber, participates in a link to *tblInventory* as part of the primary key in *tblSales-Inventory*. Since this primary key includes two fields, it is called a composite primary key. As you may know from your previous work with Microsoft Access, the only way to link two tables that have a many-to-many relationship is through a relationship table. In a sales transaction, each invoice can have many inventory items. Also, each inventory item can appear on many different invoices. In this sales system, *tblSales-Inventory* is the relationship table that models the many-to-many relationship between *tblSales* and *tblInventory*. Its composite primary key includes two fields that link to the primary keys of the two tables that participate in the relationship.

Note that the database system directly records only some of the items that the double-entry bookkeeping system records. The database system records directly the date of the sale, the customer number, and the nature of the transaction as a sale. The database system does not record directly the transaction as an element of accounts receivable. Since sales transactions constitute the left side of the accounts receivable account, storing information about sales in the tables that appear in Figure 3.1 is sufficient in a database accounting system.

To calculate the amount of a particular invoice—the amount that the double-entry bookkeeping system recorded twice in the journal entry—an accountant using a database system would run a query that links *tblSales* with *tblSales-Inventory* and *tblShipment-Method*. The query would obtain the SalesInventoryQuantity and SalesInventoryPrice for each InventoryItemNumber in *tblSales-Inventory* for the InvoiceNumber. The query would also obtain the ShipmentMethodRatePerPound from *tblShipmentMethod* and the ShipmentWeight from *tblSales*. The query would then multiply the SalesInventoryQuantity by the SalesInventoryPrice for each InventoryItemNumber and multiply the invoice's ShipmentWeight by the ShipmentMethodRatePerPound for the ShipmentMethodCode on the invoice. Finally, the query would sum these products to determine the amount of the invoice.

Although database theory argues against storing calculated fields in relational databases, accounting databases sometimes store intermediate calculation results such as this invoice amount calculation. Accountants intentionally violate the strict database rules to increase processing efficiency in databases that store large amounts of transaction data. However, accountants do this reluctantly and avoid storing calculated fields when possible.

Accounting systems that use the database approach can do everything that double-entry bookkeeping does and more. Accountants can use the database tables in Figure 3.1 to calculate invoice amounts and generate the same accounts receivable records and financial statement amounts provided by journals and ledgers. However, the real power of using relational databases to store accounting information arises when managers need specific information that they did not know they would need when the system was created. For example, if a manager wanted to know how many green-colored inventory items were sold during March of last year, the journals and ledgers of double-entry bookkeeping would be virtually useless. Using a database accounting system for sales, however, accountants could quickly provide the manager with an answer that includes number of items and sales in dollars. The database system could even generate subtotals by customer or geographic location for both number of items and sales in dollars.

TRY IT

Examine Figure 3.1 carefully. Identify interesting facts about the firm's sales and sales-related activities that you might find or calculate by searching the database tables and combining the information attributes they contain.

As you can see, relational databases record far more information for each transaction than a traditional double-entry bookkeeping system can record. A database accounting system also provides a flexible web of information relating a firm's economic events to each other. In the next two sections, we discuss some of the advantages and disadvantages of using database management systems in accounting applications.

Advantages of Database Accounting Systems

Manual double-entry bookkeeping systems can be very efficient; however, computer implementations of double-entry bookkeeping use a flat file processing design. In manual systems, the dual nature of the accounting debit and credit model provides a built-in error correction mechanism. In automated systems, this same duality is inefficient and serves no real control purpose.

Database accounting systems store data only once. This feature leads to a number of advantages over flat file double-entry accounting systems. A database accounting system can:

- Reduce data storage costs.
- Eliminate data redundancy.
- Eliminate data inconsistencies.
- Avoid duplicate processing.
- Facilitate the add, delete, and update data maintenance tasks.
- Make data independent of applications.
- Centralize data management.
- Centralize data security.

Database accounting systems offer greater flexibility in extracting data than flat file double-entry accounting systems. This flexibility leads to other advantages. For example, a database accounting system can:

- Make report modifications and updates easier.
- Provide *ad hoc* query capabilities.
- Facilitate cross-functional data analysis.
- Permit multiple users simultaneous data access.

Database accounting systems also provide data entry and integrity controls as part of the database management system. Accounting systems designers can embed these controls into the structure of the tables as they create them, which eliminates the need to program controls into every application that uses the tables' data.

Because a database stores data only once, the storage costs will be lower than for a flat file system that requires redundant storage. By avoiding the need to store data in multiple locations throughout the system, a database accounting system prevents users from creating data inconsistencies. For example, when a customer address changes, a database accounting system needs to make the change only once, in the Customer table. Every application that uses customer addresses—which may include invoicing, billing, sales promotions, marketing surveys, and sales summaries—automatically begins using the updated address from the Customer table as soon as it is entered. Data inconsistencies can be a source of many potentially embarrassing problems for businesses. Since data are entered only once, the tasks of adding, deleting, and updating records can be accomplished more efficiently. By avoiding data redundancy, a database approach also ensures that the data items used in accounting applications will have the same field names, field lengths, and data types as other applications.

Centralizing data management and security lets businesses fix responsibility for these functions on one person or group. By concentrating this activity, a database approach enables the person or persons responsible for data management and security to develop valuable expertise in this function. When a firm adopts a database approach to manage its data, it usually hires a database administrator. The database administrator holds ultimate responsibility for the specifications and structure of all database tables in the information system. The database administrator is also responsible for enforcing security, making backups, and coordinating contingency plans for emergency situations.

Having the best collection of data in the world will not do managers any good if they cannot access it. A major advantage of database accounting systems is that they facilitate users' access to accounting data. By providing intuitive, graphically based report generators, database management software such as Microsoft Access allows accountants to easily change the structure and format of their reports.

One of the most difficult challenges of designing any accounting system has always been the task of creating reports. Designers found it very hard to anticipate every report that accountants and managers using the system might ever want because they had to do it before the system even existed. The powerful query languages built into Access and other database management systems make this task much easier. Queries let users ask database accounting systems for information by combining data tables and performing calculations in ways the systems' designers never imagined. Further, these user-designed queries and reports can access more than accounting data. For example, tables containing marketing and production information can be combined with accounting information tables to create truly cross-functional reports. This *ad hoc* querying and report-generating capability is one of the key advantages of using an accounting system built with relational database software.

Finally, database accounting systems implement many important data input and data integrity controls at the database level. In Chapter 4 you will learn how to include some of these controls in accounting data tables. By implementing these controls as part of the database, you avoid the need to include the controls in every application that uses the data.

Disadvantages of Database Accounting Systems

Despite the long list of advantages outlined in the previous section, database accounting systems do have some disadvantages. The increased functionality of a database system does not come free—the higher price tag for a database system can include costs for items such as:

- Greater hardware requirements
- The database software itself
- Employing a database administrator

Although centralizing management and security control functions in a firm can be advantageous, such centralization can create drawbacks such as:

- The system operation becomes critical.

- Incorrect data entry corrupts many users' work.
- Territorial disputes over data ownership may arise.

One last disadvantage that accountants occasionally note—a disadvantage that is more psychological than real—is accountants' distrust of single-entry accounting systems in general. Double-entry bookkeeping is so pervasive in accounting education and practice that most accountants automatically question and fear anything else.

The increased cost of a database accounting system is often offset by reduced needs for data storage and reduced programming costs. The elimination of data redundancy in a database system reduces the data storage capacity required. Since the data table structures can include many data entry and integrity controls, application programming is simplified—and simpler programming takes less time and costs less money.

The centralization of data and security control is a double-edged sword. Centralization puts all of a firm's information eggs in one basket, and that increases risk. However, it also allows a focusing of resources on contingency planning, security, backup, and recovery that can actually reduce risk levels.

Many firms have decided that the advantages offered by database accounting systems outweigh the disadvantages. Most new accounting system implementations are built using relational database systems. We expect this trend to continue as database management software becomes less expensive, more capable, and easier to use.

BUSINESS ACTIVITY CLASSIFICATIONS

Different businesses require different kinds of accounting information systems. The size of a business determines part of its accounting information requirements. Larger businesses process more transactions and require greater computing capacity than smaller businesses. However, dollar volume alone is not always a good indicator of the kind of information systems a firm needs. The complexity of a firm's business activities also has a significant effect on its accounting system design. Accountants classify the complexity of firms' business activities using three broad categories: service, merchandising, and manufacturing. Not all businesses fit neatly into one of these categories, but the categories provide a good beginning reference point when considering accounting information system options.

Service Firms

Service firms comprise the simplest form of business activity. They provide their customers or clients a service for which they charge a fee. Service firms' accounting information systems track revenues and expenses only; they do not need to track inventory information because service firms do not have inventory. Examples of service firms include:

- Accounting firms
- Advertising agencies
- Barbershops
- Entertainers

- Interior decorators
- Law firms
- Management consulting firms
- Physicians
- Realtors
- Trucking companies

You can see the simplicity of service firm accounting system requirements by examining the income statement in Figure 3.2.

This income statement shows revenues and expenses. The expenses are shown in one list; they are not broken down into categories of expenses. The most important information that most service firms must track is information about revenues. Some service firms also need detailed information about their expenses, including salaries paid to employees.

Merchandising Firms

Merchandising firms are the next step up in complexity from service firms. The goal of merchandising firms is to buy goods at a low enough cost and sell those goods at a high enough price to earn a margin that will cover other expenses and yield a profit. Examples of merchandising firms include:

- Computer stores
- Department stores
- Discount merchandise chains
- Food markets

Example Service Firm
Income Statement
Year Ended December 31, 2005

Revenue		$ 353,150
Expenses:		
Advertising	$ 42,170	
Depreciation	27,640	
Insurance	9,420	
Salaries	94,210	
Rent	106,400	
Other	62,180	342,020
Net income		$ 11,130

Figure 3.2 Example Service Firm income statement.

- Hardware stores
- Health food stores
- Mail-order merchandisers
- Office supply stores
- Shoe stores
- Wholesalers

Merchandising firms' accounting information systems must track revenues and expenses, just like service firms' systems. However, the single largest expense for merchandising firms is the cost of goods that they have sold. A merchandising firm's income statement devotes a separate section to the cost of goods sold calculation. Because firms often buy goods in one period and sell those goods in the next period, their accounting systems must also track inventory. Figure 3.3 contains an example of a merchandising firm's income statement.

Note how the merchandising firm's income statement uses beginning and ending inventory in the cost of goods sold calculation. You should recall from your earlier accounting courses that the purchases amount shown on this income statement is net of

---

Example Merchandising Firm
Income Statement
Year Ended December 31, 2005

Sales		$ 822,370
Cost of goods sold:		
Beginning finished goods inventory	$ 59,530	
Purchases	472,930	
Less: Ending finished goods inventory	(63,240)	469,220
Gross profit		$ 353,150
Selling and adminstrative expenses:		
Advertising	$ 42,170	
Depreciation	27,640	
Insurance	9,420	
Salaries	94,210	
Rent	106,400	
Other	62,180	342,020
Net income		$ 11,130

Figure 3.3   Example Merchandising Firm income statement.

purchase returns and allowances and includes freight on incoming inventory shipments. Merchandising firms track detailed information about their sales and expenses. Many merchandising firms maintain comprehensive records of which products were sold along with the locations and dates of the sales. Some merchandising firms even record the times at which products were ordered and shipped.

Manufacturing Firms

The most structurally complex type of firm is the manufacturing firm. In addition to the activities that merchandising firms undertake, manufacturing firms produce the goods that they sell. Examples of manufacturing firms include:

- Automobile manufacturers
- Canneries
- Construction firms
- Farmers
- Machine tool manufacturers
- Meat packers
- Oil refineries
- Pharmaceutical firms
- Restaurants
- Steel mills

All manufacturing firms engage in similar types of activities even though they create and sell a wide variety of products. Manufacturing firms must engage in activities such as:

- Purchasing raw materials and labor
- Incurring other manufacturing costs
- Processing the raw materials, labor, and other manufacturing costs into finished goods
- Selling the finished goods

A manufacturing firm's accounting information system must track information about all four of these activities. Therefore, a manufacturing firm's system must track the service and merchandising firm activities of purchasing and selling and must bear the additional burden of tracking acquisition costs through the production activity. Figure 3.4 contains an example of a manufacturing firm's income statement.

The manufacturing firm's income statement reflects the increased complexity of its activities. The merchandising firm's cost of goods sold section has expanded to include the three manufacturing costs: direct materials, direct labor, and manufacturing overhead. These costs, adjusted by beginning and ending work-in-process inventories, are shown on the income statement in Figure 3.4 as the cost of goods manufactured. The cost of goods manufactured was $472,930. The cost of goods manufactured is analogous to purchases on a merchandising firm's income statement.

Manufacturing firms are not the only firms using manufacturing accounting systems today. Many service and merchandising firms now use accounting systems based on the

Example Manufacturing Firm
Income Statement
Year Ended December 31, 2005

Sales				$ 822,370
Cost of goods sold:				
Beginning finished goods inventory			$ 59,530	
Cost of goods manufactured:				
Beginning work-in-process inventory		$ 44,900		
Direct materials:				
Beginning inventory	$ 26,270			
Purchases	98,910			
Less: Ending inventory	(28,360)	96,820		
Direct labor		153,460		
Manufacturing overhead		210,600		
Less: Ending work-in-process inventory		(32,850)	472,930	
Less: Ending finished goods inventory			(63,240)	469,220
Gross profit				$ 353,150
Selling and adminstrative expenses:				
Advertising			$ 42,170	
Depreciation			27,640	
Insurance			9,420	
Salaries			94,210	
Rent			106,400	
Other			62,180	342,020
Net income				$ 11,130

Figure 3.4   Example Manufacturing Firm income statement.

manufacturing systems model. For example, many law firms now use a manufacturing-style job-order cost accounting system that treats each case as a separate job. Service firms have found it useful to track details about key business processes using accounting systems that were originally designed for manufacturing applications.

Now that we have seen how the different levels of complexity in the three business activity categories affect a firm's income statements and cost-accumulation procedures, we can discuss accounting information system requirements for each category. These accounting information system requirements are often expressed in terms of transaction cycles.

TRANSACTION CYCLES

Most accounting information systems and auditing textbooks are organized around business cycles. Some authors refer to these cycles as transaction cycles or accounting cycles. This framework, in which accounting systems are viewed in terms of cycles rather than financial statement accounts, is consistent with a database approach to accounting systems. A diagram of commonly used transaction cycles appears in Figure 3.5.

You can see how the transaction cycles relate to each other in Figure 3.5. In the revenue cycle, firms sell finished goods for cash or the promise to pay cash. This cash enters the financial cycle. In the financial cycle, firms obtain cash by issuing equity and debt securities. They also pay dividends on the equity securities and the interest and principal repayments on debt securities in the financial cycle. Cash flows out of the financial cycle and into the purchase and payroll cycles. In the purchase cycle, the firm exchanges cash for materials, supplies, and other expenses related to providing products or services to its customers. In the payroll cycle, the firm exchanges cash for salaries and related labor costs. The production cycle converts materials, labor, and other acquired resources into finished goods, completing the cycle.

Although most accountants use the cycle definitions shown in Figure 3.5, these exact definitions are not universally accepted. Some accountants and systems designers include payroll activities in the purchase cycle since both payroll and purchase cycles culminate in writing a check. However, most accounting information systems texts treat payroll separately because payroll transaction processing is more complex and requires

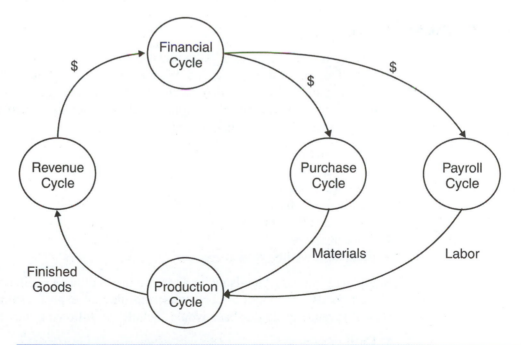

Figure 3.5 Transaction cycles.

tables and calculations that the purchase cycle does not require. You may also see the revenue cycle divided into separate sales and cash receipts cycles. Similarly, the purchase cycle can be divided into separate purchase and cash disbursement cycles.

A firm may not have all of the transaction cycles depicted in Figure 3.5. For example, service and merchandising firms usually do not have a production cycle. The purchase cycle in a merchandising firm acquires finished goods for resale; the purchase cycle in a manufacturing firm acquires raw materials and other resources for production. In many service firms, the purchase cycle is relatively unimportant, since the dollar amounts of materials and supplies purchased are small.

Most accounting information systems courses avoid extensive treatment of the transactions specific to the financial cycle because these transactions are few in number. However, auditing classes do spend significant time on financial cycle transactions because they are unusual and often involve large dollar amounts. The transactions that occur only in the financial cycle, such as stock issuances and large borrowings, are interesting but do not require highly complex information processing systems in most firms because of their infrequent occurrence.

Some accounting systems books describe a general ledger or financial reporting transaction cycle. When a firm uses database accounting, its financial reporting activities do not require it to record a separate set of transactions. Accountants can accomplish these reporting activities by querying and summarizing the data that the firm stores as it conducts its revenue, purchase, payroll, and production activities. Therefore, we do not treat financial reporting as a separate cycle in this book. The remainder of this chapter provides a brief introduction to the revenue, purchase, payroll, and production cycles.

Revenue Cycle

The revenue cycle includes all sales and cash collection activities. The three main transactions that we must record in the revenue cycle are customer orders, sales, and customer payments. We must also record the shipment of goods if it occurs separately from the sales transaction. The revenue cycle accounting system must be able to generate documents and reports that include:

- Sales order reports
- Invoices
- Shipping documents
- Remittance advices
- Cash receipts summaries
- Sales analyses
- Balances owed by customers

Manufacturing, merchandising, and service firms all have similar revenue cycles. They all sell goods or services to customers, and they all expect customers to pay them. A typical revenue cycle database would include the following data tables:

- Cash receipt
- Customer

- Finished goods inventory
- Sales
- Sales order
- Salesperson

The database design should also include relationship tables, such as a Sales-Finished Goods Inventory table.

Purchase Cycle

A manufacturing firm's purchase cycle includes all activities related to ordering raw materials from vendors, receiving the materials ordered, and paying for the materials. A merchandising firm's purchase cycle includes the activities related to ordering, receiving, and paying for goods acquired for resale. If a service firm has a purchase cycle system, it will record the purchase of materials incidental to providing services, such as office supplies. The main transactions that we must record in the purchase cycle are purchase orders, receipt of goods ordered, and payments to vendors. The purchase cycle accounting system must generate documents and reports that include:

- Backorder reports
- Balances owed to vendors
- Checks
- Goods received summaries
- Purchase orders
- Purchase summaries
- Receiving reports

The details included in the purchase cycle tables will vary depending on whether the firm is service, merchandising, or manufacturing. A typical purchase cycle database would include the following data tables:

- Cash disbursement
- Purchase order
- Raw materials inventory
- Raw materials inventory receipt
- Vendor

The database design would also include necessary relationship tables, such as a Purchase Order-Raw Materials Inventory table.

Payroll Cycle

The payroll cycle includes the system elements needed to calculate employees' gross pay, deductions, and net pay. The payroll cycle must comply with a complex set of government regulations. The payroll cycle is closely related to the human resources management system in all firms—many firms have even integrated the two systems. The main transactions that occur in the payroll cycle are employees earning pay, employer making payments to employees, and the employer making payments of payroll taxes and taxes withheld from employees' pay to various governmental entities. The payroll cycle must generate documents and reports that include:

- Checks
- Employee commission reports
- Employee earnings records
- Employee time reports
- Payroll registers

Manufacturing, merchandising, and service firms all have similar payroll cycles since they all have employees. A typical payroll cycle database would include the following data tables:

- Cash disbursement
- Employee
- Time worked

Production Cycle

A manufacturing firm's production cycle converts raw materials and labor into finished goods. The production cycle accounting database must record the use of materials and labor in production and record the allocation of manufacturing overhead costs to units produced. Merchandising and service firms do not usually have a production cycle. The production cycle's main transactions are all internal cost flows and include:

- Materials inventory costs flowing into production
- Labor costs flowing into production
- Overhead costs being allocated to production
- Total production costs flowing into finished goods inventory

The production cycle accounting system must generate documents and reports that include, for example, bills of materials and job cost reports. A typical production cycle database for a job-order manufacturing system might include the following data tables:

- Finished goods inventory
- Job
- Raw materials inventory
- Time worked

ACCOUNTING INFORMATION SYSTEMS AND DATABASE SYSTEMS

Historically, accounting information has been captured in ledgers and journals. Information about credit sales, for instance, would be recorded in a sales journal. Each month, accountants would create financial statements such as income statements and balance sheets from the information in the ledgers. If a manager needed information about the firm's activities in the middle of the month, that manager had to wait until the books were closed at the end of the next month to obtain that information. In today's fast-paced and highly competitive business world, however, managers need more than the standard periodic accounting reports. Some information cannot be obtained easily, if at all, using traditional double-entry accounting software. For example, it would be difficult for a manufacturing manager to obtain data about total monthly inventory spoilage from a traditional accounting system. Other valuable aggregations of data that provide pictures of a company's current financial or labor situation are hard to obtain from traditional accounting systems. Conventional aggregation methods provided by accounting systems have buried valuable information.

Today's accounting systems use a different approach. Customized reports based on database queries are increasingly replacing traditional accounting reports. The advent of both inexpensive and widely available computer hardware and database management software has accelerated the move toward capturing accounting information in database systems. *Events accounting* consists of storing data about an economic event, such as a cash sale or receipt of a purchase order, in one or more database tables. Events accounting goes beyond merely recording the aggregate numbers associated with the event. Information recorded about an economic event can include who was involved (i.e., the customer's name), why the event occurred, when the event occurred, and what resources were affected by the event.

Events-based accounting systems are not bound by accountants' assumptions about how the information captured is to be aggregated, output, or used. Rather, the managers who will be making decisions based on the information are empowered to extract that information from the accounting events database. An inventory manager, for example, can create (or request the creation of) a report to display current stock levels and the percentage change in stock levels from the previous month.

This is a significant change from accounting information systems that made use of the debit and credit method of recording transactions in a highly aggregated form. If managers need information from the accounting system to help make crucial decisions, they simply request the data they need and then review the resultant report. Managers and other decision makers need no longer rely exclusively on the standard financial statements and other reports produced by traditional accounting systems. Although some of the standard financial statements can help managers make enterprise-wide decisions, much information is lost during the aggregation that takes place in traditional accounting systems when those systems generate financial statements.

In this book, you are learning about accounting information systems implemented using database management systems. Because database management systems can store anything an organization wants to record, they provide a wealth of information. Much useful business information can be generated from the data stored in a database's tables. As an emerging accounting information systems expert, you are on the leading edge of this significant shift to more useful accounting systems.

Next, you will learn about the evolution of database management systems and some advantages and disadvantages of using database systems. We begin with a brief look at what software business tools were available before the advent of database systems.

DATABASE MANAGEMENT SYSTEMS

Database management systems (DBMSs) are valuable to business enterprises because they provide a way to store, retrieve, and modify crucial business data. DBMSs can be very cost effective, even though the software can be quite expensive. The next section briefly describes data management and reporting before the advent of database management systems. Subsequent sections describe the general capabilities of database management systems—what core services they typically provide—and the advantages and disadvantages of using database management systems.

Pre-DBMS Data Acquisition and Reporting

Before the availability of modern database management systems, corporate data acquisition and reporting were far different from today. Assume that it is the late 1960s and you are responsible for maintaining customer information for The Coffee Merchant, a small coffee wholesaler, on its medium-sized minicomputer. The data processing department has a staff of computer programmers and support personnel to supply all the company's data processing needs.

Flat files are data files containing information that is not explicitly linked to other information files. Flat files were an important part of business information processing in the early days of computerization. For instance, the accounts receivable department kept customer names and addresses in one file. When purchase orders were received, someone entered the coffee and tea order information into other flat files kept on disk. An orders file contained purchase order data such as the items ordered, quantity requested of each item, and whether the purchase was subject to tax—goods acquired for resale are not taxable until they are sold to a retail customer. Accounts payable kept its own set of files, which contained the names and addresses of vendors to which they owed money, invoice numbers, purchase order numbers, and similar information items.

Standard, frequently requested reports were readily available. These reports summarized data held in the files. When a manager wanted to see the latest sales figures for the previous month, he could place a request with the data processing department. The requested report would be on his desk by the next morning. Finding the current stock levels on all coffees and teas was a typical request that could be easily satisfied. Again, the data processing department would process the management request, run a program that accessed the appropriate files, and produce the report. This was typically how reports were generated for standard, traditional requests.

Requests for custom or unusual reports were a different matter. Although standard reports could be produced by scheduling and running programs written for that purpose, unusual report requests had to be custom-designed and written. For example, suppose the purchasing manager wanted to compare the inventory levels of the 20 most popular coffees and teas with the same period in the previous year. Such a report would require programmers to design and write a custom program. When a special request was received, a system analyst determined what files contained the information used in the report. The analyst would also provide a program design. After the design was approved by the user(s), one or more programmers wrote the program that would read the files, manipulate and summarize the data, and print a report. It was not unusual for a requested custom report to take several weeks before it was delivered to the requesting manager! Keeping a large pool of systems analysts and programmers on staff to supply the data processing needs of the company was expensive. Time is money, and managers could ill afford to wait weeks for critical reports.

Other problems existed in pre-DBMS days. Those problems included the creation of outdated and redundant data. Many departments and individuals created and maintained their own computer files, which resulted in the entry and storage of duplicated information. They would do this so they could access and examine data with their own programs quickly, rather than waiting for the overworked data processing department to respond to their requests. Duplicate data files led to occurrences of data redundancy and data inconsistency.

In many firms, the marketing department kept its own files of information about large customers so they could send out advertising and promotional mailings. The marketing department would hire a bright young programmer to maintain the files and write programs to produce mailing labels from them. Problems occurred when the independently maintained customer list fell out of date. Although the master list of customers was kept current by the data processing department using purchase orders received from customers each month, the marketing department did not have access to the updated data. As existing customers moved and new customers were added, the marketing department's customer list became outdated and, eventually, useless.

You can begin to see the types of problems that arose when businesses used separate information systems. A wall existed between the information consumers and the information itself. That wall was the data processing department, a necessary element in the information request and receipt cycle. Departments coped with unresponsive data processing departments by spawning separate islands of information that were independently maintained. These separate information islands created data redundancy and data inconsistency. In short, much time and money was expended to store and retrieve business data on computers before the arrival of database management systems and accounting information systems based on them.

Functions of a Database Management System

A database management system is a file management system that can store and manage different types of records within one integrated system. Using a database management system's tools, a database administrator can create a sophisticated system that maintains company records, generates invoices, and in general keeps track of all a company's transactions. A *database* is the physical implementation of a particular set of records, and the database management system controls access to those records. A *relational* database management system, one of three classical models of database management systems, consists of tables containing data whose contents are related to one another through the data content of the tables. The capabilities that a database management system provides in development of an information system are the following:

- Efficient data maintenance: storage, update, and retrieval
- User-accessible catalog
- Concurrency control
- Transaction support
- Recovery services
- Security and authorization services
- Integrity facilities

One of the most important abilities of a database management system is its capacity to store, update, and retrieve data. Unlike a flat file system, you need not write and run a special program to store new data in a database. Likewise, when you want to extract information from various data files that are maintained by the DBMS, you can formulate a relatively simple report request in the database system's language. You need not enlist the support of a programmer to write lengthy and complicated programs to extract information. Besides, the DBMS hides all the file storage details from the user. Instead, the user is presented with an uncomplicated view of the data that the DBMS maintains.

Advantages of Database Management Systems

Some of the advantages that a database management system provides should be clear from the preceding material. DBMSs have other advantages over the old file and programmatic access methods. Many larger database systems provide each user with an individual view of the database. Also known as a *subschema*, a view appears to the user to be the real table. It is a definition stored in the database that can extract information from one or more tables and exclude selected rows and columns from being displayed. For instance, a manager might have a view of the database that displays employee data for the employees who report to the requesting manager, but no others. Views are implemented by database systems and provide a measure of security.

Data independence is another advantage of a database management system. The term *data independence* refers to a database management system's ability to hide the details of the physical storage of information from application programs that use the data. To extract information from a database, you merely request information by name and supply conditions that limit which rows are selected. The database system is responsible for translating the information request into data access statements that the database system can understand.

Changes to the structure of a database can be made transparent to the users. This is important because table designs can change over time and it becomes necessary to make changes to the internal structure of one or more tables. Frequently, table structure changes are made to provide significantly shorter database access times. When structure changes occur, using database *views* can mask those changes, since database views restrict what various users can retrieve from the database. The views mimic users' old perceptions of the affected tables' contents, and the database structure change causes no changes to users' access techniques or methods. On the other hand, imagine the degree to which programs would be affected in a flat file system if just a few changes were made to the structure of the files they access. Programmers would have to spend a great deal of time changing all the programs that reference the files whose structure was changed. In large systems it can be very difficult to find all programs that reference a particular file or set of files.

Finally, database systems help users share data with each other. Because corporate data are centrally stored, everyone has access to the same information and that information is always current and consistent, because there is only one copy of it. There are no duplicate versions of inconsistent data, as was often the case in the years prior to the advent of database management systems.

Disadvantages of Database Management Systems

The main disadvantage of a database management system is that it can occupy a large amount of expensive disk storage space. You should consider the cost of disk storage when determining whether a database system is cost effective. Though database systems can occupy more than ten times the space required to hold the same data in flat files, DBMSs can still be a good value. Disk storage costs are much lower than the cost of maintaining data in flat files. Programming costs have gone up rapidly in the last 15 years, but prices of hardware such as disk drives have dropped sharply.

Large database systems often require additional people such as a database administrator to keep the system running smoothly. Other database experts may be hired to handle the information needs of the company. With few exceptions, these added costs are far less than the cost of not using a database management system. Of course, smaller businesses using PC-based database management packages such as Microsoft Access can often avoid these additional personnel costs. In such cases, only the additional disk space cost is a factor in the decision.

RELATIONAL DATABASE MANAGEMENT SYSTEMS

Database management systems can be implemented by following one of three data models in widespread use today. A *data model* is an abstract representation of a database system providing a description of the data and methods for accessing the data managed by the database. The three models in use are the *hierarchical model*, the *network model*, and the *relational model*. Throughout most of the late 1960s and early 1970s, most databases used the hierarchical or network model. IBM's IMS database system, which was widely used in the 1970s, is one example of a hierarchical database management system. Cullinet's IDMS/R is a database built on the network model that was also popular in the 1970s. However, things changed rapidly during that decade. E. F. Codd, working in an IBM research laboratory, developed the relational model for database systems. Since that time, the relational model has evolved and the number of database systems based on the relational model has exploded. Today, the relational model is the overwhelming choice for database systems running on all kinds and sizes of computers.

The relational model provides several significant advantages over the hierarchical and network models. In the relational model, the logical and physical characteristics of the database are distinct; this provides users with a more intuitive view of the data. Using the relational model requires very little training. The relational model includes more powerful retrieval and update operators that allow complex operations to be executed with concise commands. Perhaps most importantly, the relational model provides powerful tools to let analysts know when a database has inherent design flaws.

The advantages of the relational model overwhelm the disadvantages of using database systems. From this point on in the text, when we refer to a database management system, we specifically mean a *relational database management system*, or *RDBMS*.

Database Objects

The relational model is based in mathematical set theory, the theory of relations, and first-order predicate logic. The model defines the conceptual view that the user has all of the objects contained by the database system. Both the data objects and the relationships between them are represented as a collection of tables. All data in a relational database, including the database table definitions and information about database objects such as forms and reports, exist only in tables. This provides a simple and consistent view of the database.

A relational database is a collection of relations. The primary structure in a relational model database is a relation. A table is an example of a relation. For that reason, you will often see the terms *relation* and *table* used interchangeably. A table, or relation, consists of rows and columns, similar to a matrix or spreadsheet. The formal term for row is *tuple*, but most database experts use the less formal term *row*. The formal term for column is *attribute*, but most database experts use the term *column*. Alternative common terms used for relation, tuple, and attribute are *file*, *record*, and *field*, respectively. Figure 3.6 summarizes these three sets of terms.

Formal Term	Common Term	Alternative Common Term
relation	table	file
tuple	row	record
attribute	column	field

Figure 3.6   Three sets of database terms.

You might have used spreadsheet software in some of your other accounting courses. A spreadsheet page resembles a database table in several ways. For example, a spreadsheet page has columns and rows. The columns in a spreadsheet page often have titles that describe the content of the columns. You might want to think of database tables as a special form of spreadsheet pages. The difference is that database tables must comply with very strict rules about what can be included in each row and column. The most important properties of database tables include the following:

- The entries in each column of any row must be single valued.
- Each attribute (column) in a table has a distinct name, called the *attribute name*.
- Every entry in a column contains a value for that column only, and the values are of the same data type.
- The order of the rows is unimportant.
- The order (position) of the columns in relation to each other is unimportant.
- Each row is unique (i.e., it differs from all other rows in the table).

The preceding table properties are very important. Later in this chapter, you will learn about each of these properties in detail. Figure 3.7 shows an example relation that is one of the tables included in the The Coffee Merchant's database. Only the first 20 rows and the first seven columns are shown in the figure.

The Customer table contains hundreds of rows, in no particular order, one for each of The Coffee Merchant's customers. Because the row order is unimportant in a RDBMS, there is no implied meaning that one customer is more important than another. All you can tell from the row order is that the identification number field, called CustomerID, is in ascending order. In relational databases, a row's identity is determined by its content, not by its location within a table.

Primary and Foreign Key Attributes

The table that appears in Figure 3.7 contains ten columns, but only six of these attributes appear in Figure 3.7: CustomerID, CompanyName, Contact, Address, City, and State. However, there is no theoretical reason to list the columns in that order. We have chosen to place the primary key column, CustomerID, as the first table column. Although Access does not require the primary key column to be first, most database designers follow this convention. We could, for example, place the Contact column in the second column, followed by the State and City columns.

Within each column you can see the attribute values for each row. For instance, the row identified as CustomerID 30121 contains "Fairfield Communities Inc." in its CompanyName value and "Best, F. Stanley" in its Contact value. Each row may store a different value for each attribute. In particular, the CustomerID value is unique for each row. This satisfies the rule that each row must be unique. A row is unique if any one of its columns is unique.

Every relation must have a primary key that uniquely identifies each row in the table. The primary key can include one or more columns. When the primary key includes more than one column, the individual column values need not be unique, but the combined column values must be unique.

Every row in a RDBMS must be distinct from all other rows in that table, or else it cannot be retrieved easily. This is one of the fundamental rules of a relational database management system. To ensure uniqueness, a primary key is designated for a table. A primary key, as mentioned previously, is a column (or group of columns) that uniquely identifies a given row. Therefore, the system can distinguish one record (row) of a table

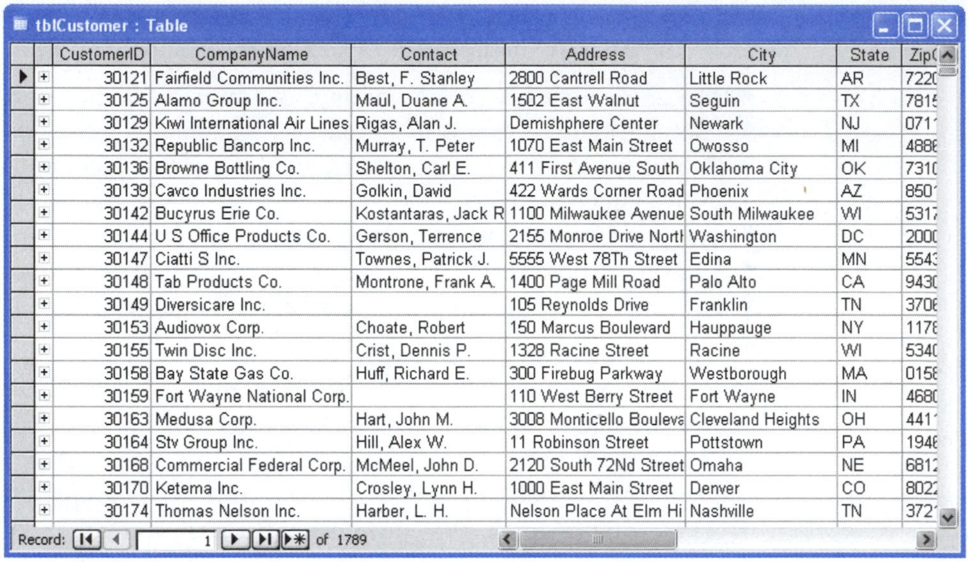

tblCustomer : Table						
CustomerID	CompanyName	Contact	Address	City	State	Zip
30121	Fairfield Communities Inc.	Best, F. Stanley	2800 Cantrell Road	Little Rock	AR	7220
30125	Alamo Group Inc.	Maul, Duane A.	1502 East Walnut	Seguin	TX	7815
30129	Kiwi International Air Lines	Rigas, Alan J.	Demishphere Center	Newark	NJ	0711
30132	Republic Bancorp Inc.	Murray, T. Peter	1070 East Main Street	Owosso	MI	4886
30136	Browne Bottling Co.	Shelton, Carl E.	411 First Avenue South	Oklahoma City	OK	7310
30139	Cavco Industries Inc.	Golkin, David	422 Wards Corner Road	Phoenix	AZ	8501
30142	Bucyrus Erie Co.	Kostantaras, Jack R	1100 Milwaukee Avenue	South Milwaukee	WI	5317
30144	U S Office Products Co.	Gerson, Terrence	2155 Monroe Drive North	Washington	DC	2000
30147	Ciatti S Inc.	Townes, Patrick J.	5555 West 78Th Street	Edina	MN	5543
30148	Tab Products Co.	Montrone, Frank A.	1400 Page Mill Road	Palo Alto	CA	9430
30149	Diversicare Inc.		105 Reynolds Drive	Franklin	TN	3706
30153	Audiovox Corp.	Choate, Robert	150 Marcus Boulevard	Hauppauge	NY	1178
30155	Twin Disc Inc.	Crist, Dennis P.	1328 Racine Street	Racine	WI	5340
30158	Bay State Gas Co.	Huff, Richard E.	300 Firebug Parkway	Westborough	MA	0158
30159	Fort Wayne National Corp.		110 West Berry Street	Fort Wayne	IN	4680
30163	Medusa Corp.	Hart, John M.	3008 Monticello Bouleva	Cleveland Heights	OH	4411
30164	Stv Group Inc.	Hill, Alex W.	11 Robinson Street	Pottstown	PA	1946
30168	Commercial Federal Corp.	McMeel, John D.	2120 South 72Nd Street	Omaha	NE	6812
30170	Ketema Inc.	Crosley, Lynn H.	1000 East Main Street	Denver	CO	8022
30174	Thomas Nelson Inc.	Harber, L. H.	Nelson Place At Elm Hi	Nashville	TN	3721

Record: ◄◄ ◄ 1 ► ►► ►* of 1789

Figure 3.7 The Customer relation, *tblCustomer*.

from another. In the *tblCustomer* table, for instance, the CustomerID column—the customer's identification number—uniquely identifies a row. Thus, CustomerID is the primary key for the *tblCustomer* table.

Another important table field is a foreign key. A *foreign key* is an attribute in one table that matches the primary key field of another table. Figure 3.8 shows two of The Coffee Merchant tables used to retrieve invoice data from the set of tables constituting the database. Many database designers use the same field name for related primary key and foreign key columns to indicate the two columns tie together two tables. For example, the foreign key CustomerID in the table *tblInvoice* is related to the identically named field in the table *tblCustomer*. Although many database designers do follow this naming practice, Microsoft Access and other database management software packages do not require it.

The CustomerID column in the Invoice (*tblInvoice*) table is a foreign key, because it references a primary key found in one row of the *tblCustomer* table. The associations between foreign keys and primary keys are important because relational databases use them to establish connections between related tables.

Schema of a Relation

The schema of a relation is a set of information that includes the name of a relation and its attributes. Some database designers also call this set of information a *table structure*. A compact representation of the schema for the *tblCustomer* table, using the reduced number of columns in this illustration, is:

Customer(<u>CustomerID</u>, CompanyName, Contact, Address, City, State)

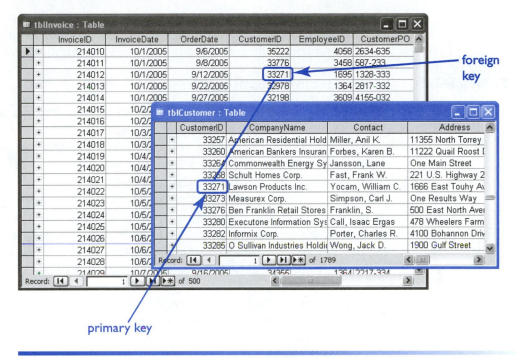

Figure 3.8 Primary key and foreign key relationship.

The table's attributes are enclosed in parentheses following the table name. In this notation, an underline indicates the primary key column(s). This is not the only way to write this schema, but it is one you will find in common use in many books on database design and in many accounting information systems textbooks. Though not shown here, a double underline or a line appearing over one or more fields indicates the field is a foreign key. Another common notation system uses bold type to indicate a primary key and italics to indicate a foreign key.

Data Dictionary

Relational database systems have a data dictionary. A data dictionary is a collection of tables containing the definition, characteristics, structure, and description of all data maintained by the RDBMS.

In addition to table descriptions, the data dictionary can store view definitions, database object owner names, database login names, and passwords. Fields in the data dictionary are automatically changed whenever an object's structure is changed. For example, if you delete a column from a table and rename another table, both operations cause changes to the data dictionary entries. A row in a table holding other tables' column names is deleted when you delete a column, and a row containing table names is updated when you rename a table. Having a data dictionary makes the job of the database management system and the database administrator easier, because all information needed about the system is contained in one place.

Unfortunately, Microsoft Access does not include a facility that automatically creates a data dictionary. You can create a data dictionary in a separate Access file, but it will not automatically update itself when you change the elements of the database.

The Coffee Merchant Tables

To understand how accounting information can be organized in a database system, let's look at an example. Several of the tables contained in the *Ch03.mdb* database, which is stored in the Ch03 folder on your Companion CD, include invoice data for customers of The Coffee Merchant. Figure 3.9 shows schema for each table used in the invoicing subsystem of The Coffee Merchant's database.

When bits of data from each of these tables are combined in the proper way, you can build and print an invoice. The *tblCustomer* table contains information about each customer. Each customer is assigned a primary key—a sequence of integers beginning with any number is sufficient—so that a customer can be uniquely identified. The Invoice table, *tblInvoice*, contains a history of invoices sent out by The Coffee Merchant. Each row is identified by the primary key, InvoiceID, and it holds each customer's invoice date (InvoiceDate), order date (OrderDate), customer identification number (CustomerID), identification number of the associated salesperson (EmployeeID), and the customer's original purchase order number (CustomerPO). Of course, an invoice shows more details than these held in the Invoice table *tblInvoice*, but those additional details (such as the customer's address) are contained in *tblCustomer*, which is linked to the Invoice table on the CustomerID attribute—the primary key in *tblCustomer* and a foreign key in *tblInvoice*. Figure 3.10 shows a Datasheet view of some *tblInvoice* rows.

Order lines contain details about individual items ordered by the customer and included on the current invoice such as quantity ordered, unit price, and discount. These order line details are not stored in the Invoice table. Instead, those details are stored in

tblCountryName	(<u>CountryID</u>, CountryName, ExportCoffeeBags, ExportTeaPounds)
tblCustomer	(<u>CustomerID</u>, CompanyName, Contact, Address, City, State, ZipCode, PhoneNumber, FaxNumber, CreditLimit)
tblEmployee	(<u>EmployeeID</u>, EmployeeFirstName, EmployeeLastName, EmployeeWorkPhone, EmployeeTitleID, EmployeeCommRate, EmployeeHireDate, EmployeeDOB, EmployeeGender, EmployeeNotes)
tblEmployeeTitle	(<u>TitleID</u>, Title)
tblInventory	(<u>InventoryID</u>, ItemID, Caffeinated, Price, OnHand)
tblInventoryDescription	(<u>ItemID</u>, Name, BeverageType, Flavored, CountryID, Comments)
tblInvoice	(<u>InvoiceID</u>, InvoiceDate, OrderDate, CustomerID, EmployeeID, CustomerPO)
tblInvoiceLine	(<u>InvoiceID</u>, <u>InventoryID</u>, Quantity, UnitPrice, Discount)
tblSalesTaxRate	(<u>StateAbbreviation</u>, StateName, TaxRate, Population, LandArea)

Figure 3.9 Schemas of tables in the invoicing system.

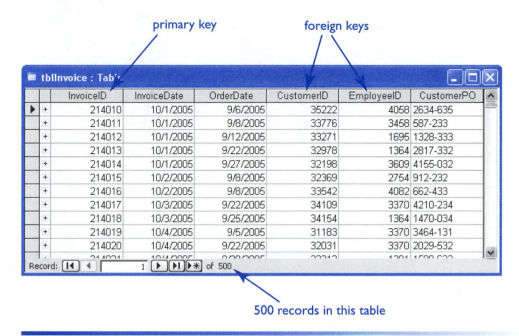

primary key   foreign keys

500 records in this table

Figure 3.10 Example rows in the Invoice table, *tblInvoice*.

three other tables: *tblInvoiceLine*, *tblInventory*, and *tblInventoryDescription*. Figures 3.11, 3.12, and 3.13 show sample rows from each of these tables. The *tblInvoiceLine* table may appear to be a bit unusual at first glance. It contains only five attributes: two fields that make up its composite primary key and three other fields that contain information about the items on each invoice. These information items include the quantity ordered, the quoted unit price (which can vary for a given product depending on the customer), and the discount percentage for each item on each invoice. A composite primary key consists of more than one attribute. In this table, InvoiceID and InventoryID combine to form the composite primary key. These two attributes identify the invoice and each inventory item number that will appear on a line of that invoice. The *tblInventory* and *tblInventoryDescription* tables store information about the coffees and teas available from The Coffee Merchant. Only a few of the over 100 items stored in the inventory tables appear in Figure 3.12. InventoryID identifies each inventory item uniquely, and other characteristics about the inventory item are stored in the *tblInventory* and *tblInventoryDescription* tables.

These tables do not store the extended price, subtotal, and other information that normally appears on an invoice. The way to obtain these information items is to have Access calculate them when it prints invoices. Calculated values need not be stored in tables, because they can be obtained by multiplying each invoice line's quantity and price attributes. It is undesirable to store values in a table that can be calculated from other table fields. Thus, the data in these four tables plus the Customer table, *tblCustomer*, contain all of the information needed to produce invoices for The Coffee Merchant.

primary key foreign key

tblInvoiceLine : Table

InvoiceID	InventoryID	Quantity	UnitPrice	Discount
214010	1184	18	$6.90	0.05
214010	1192	17	$13.30	10%
214010	1195	17	$3.90	0%
214010	1209	14	$6.20	15%
214010	1237	17	$10.90	5%
214011	1104	19	$5.30	5%
214011	1133	8	$7.90	0%
214011	1137	15	$7.00	15%
214011	1197	2	$7.10	0%
214011	1211	10	$14.70	15%

Record: 1 of 2192

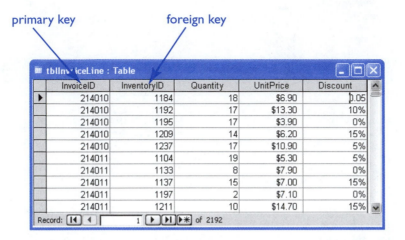

Figure 3.11 Example rows in the Invoice Line table, *tblInvoiceLine*.

primary key foreign key

tblInventory : Table

InventoryID	ItemID	Caffeinated	Price	OnHand
1101	116	☑	$8.10	512
1102	422	☐	$5.30	3,190
1103	440	☐	$7.70	-130
1104	455	☐	$5.30	3,380
1105	449	☐	$7.60	3,300
1106	224	☑	$7.40	1,130
1107	113	☑	$8.80	315
1108	134	☑	$10.30	443
1109	275	☑	$8.00	354
1110	353	☐	$13.70	354

Record: 1 of 154

Figure 3.12 Example rows in the primary Inventory table, *tblInventory*.

Now that you understand the details of The Coffee Merchant's database tables, you can learn about normalization. We will use The Coffee Merchant tables to illustrate the reasons for and the definitions of normalized tables.

Normalization

In a relational table design, it is important to think carefully about where individual pieces of data are stored. The process of determining the correct location for each attribute is called *normalization*. Another way of thinking about normalization is this: normalizing a database is storing data where it uniquely belongs. Unnormalized databases can lead to redundant, inconsistent, or incorrect information being stored in tables.

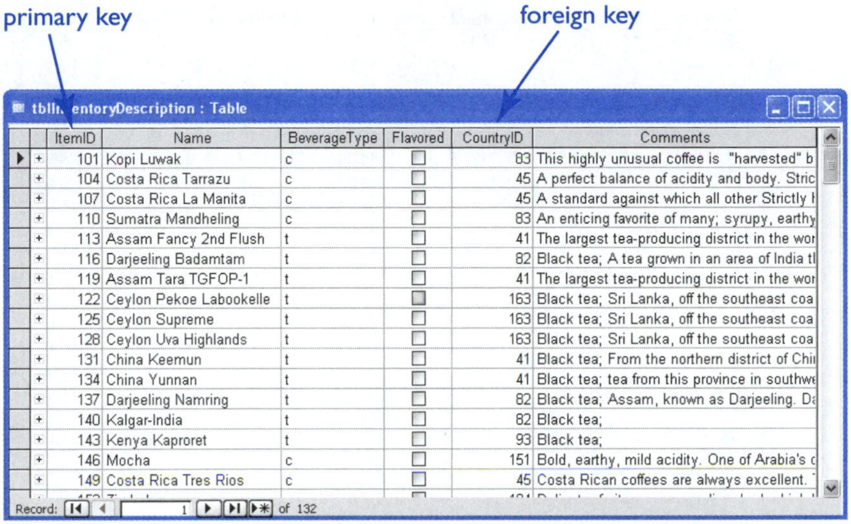

primary key

foreign key

Figure 3.13 Example rows in the secondary Inventory table, *tblInventoryDescription*.

There are many ways to arrange the invoice system attributes in sets of tables. Some arrangements are better than others. A particular subset of the ways that attributes can be organized into tables is called a *normal form*, and the basis of this arrangement is called *normalization theory*.

Database theorists have identified seven normal forms. Like layers of an onion, each normal form includes compliance with the rules of all lower normal forms. For example, a table that is in third normal form is automatically in first and second normal forms and complies with the rules for those three normal forms. The rules applied to achieve each normal form are successively more stringent. The least restrictive is called the *first normal form*, which is abbreviated as 1NF. Following that form are the *second*, *third*, *Boyce-Codd*, *fourth*, *fifth*, and *Domain-Key* normal forms. Most accounting systems require use of only the first three normal forms. Tables in third normal form are better than tables in second normal form. Likewise, tables in second normal form are better than tables in first normal form. The goal of the normalization process is to start with a collection of tables (or relations), apply normalization, and arrive at an equivalent collection of tables in a higher normal form. The process is repeated until all tables are in third normal form (3NF).

FIRST NORMAL FORM. A table that contains a repeating group is called an unnormalized table. The relational model requires that all tables be in first normal form. To achieve this, repeating data must be removed from the table and stored elsewhere. For example, suppose that an invoice table held each invoice line for all invoices in the arrangement shown in Figure 3.14.

Notice that for each invoice in the Invoice table, there are several inventory item numbers, quantities, unit prices, and discounts. For instance, invoice number 214010

InvoiceID	InvoiceDate	CustomerID	InventoryID	Quantity	UnitPrice	Discount
214010	10/1/2005	35222	1184	18	$6.90	5%
			1192	17	$13.30	10%
			1195	17	$3.90	0%
			1209	14	$6.20	15%
			1237	17	$10.90	5%
214011	10/1/2005	33776	1104	19	$5.30	5%
			1133	8	$7.90	0%
			1137	15	$7.00	15%
			1197	2	$7.10	0%
			1211	10	$14.70	15%
214012	10/1/2005	33271	1127	17	$4.50	0%
			1129	5	$8.40	0%
			1189	14	$5.30	15%
			1203	12	$8.10	15%
			1249	2	$11.90	0%
214013	10/1/2005	32978	1139	10	$5.30	15%
			1198	17	$8.10	5%
			1208	14	$4.50	15%
			1216	19	$7.20	5%
			1229	5	$12.90	0%
			1249	5	$11.90	0%
214014	10/1/2005	32198	1170	6	$44.50	10%

(repeating group annotations shown for InvoiceID groups 214010, 214011, 214012, and 214013)

Figure 3.14   Example table containing repeating groups.

contains five items; each item corresponds to an invoice detail item on a printed invoice. The schema for this table is:

tblInvoice (InvoiceID, InvoiceDate, CustomerID,
    InventoryID, Quantity, UnitPrice, Discount,
    InventoryID, Quantity, UnitPrice, Discount, . . .)

where the ellipsis indicates that InventoryID, Quantity, UnitPrice, and Discount can repeat any number of times—as many times as there are items listed on a single invoice.

To be in first normal form, a table cannot store repeating groups (multiple values) in one table column, nor can it store a variable number of {InventoryID, Quantity, UnitPrice, Discount} sets in each row. To convert the table shown in Figure 3.14 into first normal form, you can remove the repeating groups from the existing Invoice table and place them into a new table. However, you must add an additional column to the new table linking the rows of the newly formed table with the original Invoice table. An example of the structure of the two tables conforming to first normal form is this:

tblInvoice(InvoiceID, InvoiceDate, OrderDate, CustomerID, EmployeeID,
    CustomerPO)
tblInvoiceLine(InvoiceID, InventoryID, Quantity, UnitPrice, Discount)

The new table, *tblInvoiceLine*, contains five columns. The first two columns, InvoiceID and InventoryID, combine to form the new table's primary key. This is a *composite primary key* because the primary key includes two attributes.

SECOND NORMAL FORM. Tables in first normal form can be placed into a relational database system, but in many cases first normal form is not sufficient to prevent problems. For example, Figure 3.15 shows an example of some rows of a Customer table in first normal form. The schema for this table is:

tblCustomer(<u>CustomerID</u>, CompanyName, PhoneNumber, Contact, <u>InvoiceID</u>, Total)

The Customer table contains customer information including the customer identification number, company name, telephone, and contact person. The last two columns indicate the customer's invoice number and amount. The two table columns, CustomerID and InvoiceID, form the table's primary key. Both are needed to access a row.

Several potential problems exist with the proposed 1NF Customer table. Suppose that the Customer table is the only place in which customer information such as address or name is stored. Further, suppose that a new customer has paid for an order in advance. The design would not allow such a customer to be added, because the InvoiceID value would be empty. When an attribute is empty, or has no value, it is *null*. The InvoiceID attribute cannot be null, because the primary key cannot be null or include a null attribute if it is a composite primary key. The inability to add a record is called an *insertion anomaly*.

Consider this scenario. Cavco Industries pays for its two invoices, numbers 214123 and 214460 (see Figure 3.15, second and third rows), bringing its amount due to zero. The two rows corresponding to Cavco Industries are removed from *tblCustomer*. Not only are the two invoices removed, but the customer's identification number, name, phone, and contact person are deleted as well. So the deletion has a wider effect than desired; you lose knowledge of the customer entirely. Your mailing list is being destroyed! This predicament is known as a *deletion anomaly*.

Finally, the *tblCustomer* table shown in Figure 3.15 contains much redundant information. For instance, the company identification number, name, phone number, and contact person are repeated for each new invoice that is issued for a particular customer. The customer name *Cavco Industries Inc.* is entered twice, as is *Golkin, David,* the contact person. It is pure luck that both the company name and contact person's name have been spelled correctly both times. To change the company name, you must

CustomerID	CompanyName	PhoneNumber	Contact	InvoiceID	Total
30125	Alamo Group Inc.	(210) 555-1483	Maul, Duane A.	214480	306.80
30139	Cavco Industries Inc.	(602) 555-6141	Golkin, David	214123	225.11
30139	Cavco Industries Inc.	(602) 555-6141	Golkin, David	214460	315.10
30174	Thomas Nelson Inc.	(615) 555-9079	Harber, L. H.	214390	491.96
30174	Thomas Nelson Inc.	(615) 555-9079	Harber, L. H.	214418	185.95
30206	Matlack Systems Inc.	(302) 555-2760	Gordon, W. Phil	214334	218.39
30212	Lilly Industries Inc.	(317) 555-6762	Choong, Jerry	214117	152.20
30221	Mcdonald & Co. Investments Inc.	(216) 555-2368	Bianco, Andrew R.	214249	297.34
30225	Krause S Furniture Inc.	(510) 555-6208	Woltz, Neil G.	214087	260.15
30228	F N B Corp. Pa	(412) 555-6028	Fancher, William R.	214284	98.35
30231	Everest & Jennings Internation	(314) 555-7041	Gray, Robert R.	214036	270.60
30231	Everest & Jennings Internation	(314) 555-7041	Gray, Robert R.	214256	165.96
30258	Lcs Industries Inc.	(201) 555-5666	Lebuhn, Eugene	214230	895.25
30258	Lcs Industries Inc.	(201) 555-5666	Lebuhn, Eugene	214308	541.97

Figure 3.15 Example rows of the Customer table in first normal form (1NF).

find all occurrences of the name in the database and change each one. What a time-consuming task that could be! This small example illustrates that tables in first normal form can contain redundant data.

Altering a table's structure and changing it into second normal form can prevent these anomalies. A table (relation) is in *second normal form* (2NF) if it is in first normal form and none of the nonkey attributes depend on only one portion of the primary key. That is, second normal form requires that each nonkey attribute depend on the entire primary key, not just part of it. This rule applies only when you have a composite primary key—one consisting of more than one table column.

The attribute Total in the Customer table in Figure 3.15 violates the 2NF definition. The value of Total is determined by the partial primary key InvoiceID. We say that Total is *functionally dependent* on InvoiceID, because a particular value of InvoiceID determines a single value of Total. On the other hand, Total does not depend on the attribute and partial primary key CustomerID, because the total invoice amount varies from invoice to invoice; no relationship exists between Total and a particular customer. On the other hand, the attributes CompanyName, PhoneNumber, and Contact each functionally depend on the partial primary key CustomerID. These two sets of functional dependencies are shown in Figure 3.16.

The arrows lead from a primary key to another attribute. For instance, the arrow leading from CustomerID to CompanyName means that CustomerID *determines* CompanyName (or CustomerID is a *determinant* of CompanyName). It is clear that we can correct this problem by breaking *tblCustomer* into two tables. Of course, we must note the relationship between these two tables by including an extra attribute—a foreign key—that links both tables on the CustomerID key. You can restructure *tblCustomer* and the related table *tblInvoice* so they are in second normal form by using a design such as this:

> tblCustomer(<u>CustomerID</u>, CompanyName, PhoneNumber, Contact)
> tblInvoice(<u>InvoiceID</u>, <u>CustomerID</u>, Total)

In this design, the CustomerID field in *tblInvoice* is a foreign key to *tblCustomer*. The double underline below CustomerID in *tblInvoice* indicates that it is a foreign key.

THIRD NORMAL FORM. The design goal for relational databases is to create tables that are in third normal form. A table is in *third normal form* (3NF) if it is in

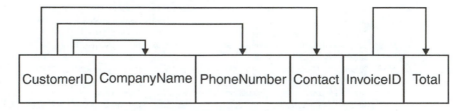

Figure 3.16 Functional dependencies in the Customer table.

second normal form and all transitive dependencies have been eliminated. A *transitive dependency* exists in a table if attribute B determines attribute C, and attribute C determines attribute D.

You have probably heard an expression that can help you understand and remember the difference between 2NF and 3NF. Part of the phrase used to swear in witnesses who are about to take the stand in a trial is: "... to tell the truth, the whole truth, and nothing but the truth." The second normal form is analogous to "the whole truth" part of the phrase—each attribute depends on the *whole* primary key. Similarly, the third normal form is analogous to "and nothing but the truth." Each attribute depends *only* on the primary key and on no other attribute in the relation. For example, consider the Invoice table shown in Figure 3.17.

The Invoice table's primary key is InvoiceID. Because only one customer may be assigned a particular invoice number (the value in the InvoiceID field), the invoice number uniquely determines the invoice date, order date, customer identification number, employee identification number, and company contact person. There are no repeating groups in the table. Therefore, it is in first normal form. Furthermore, it is in second normal form because all attributes depend on the single-attribute primary key. However, it is not in third normal form, because all attributes are not functionally dependent on only the InvoiceID attribute. There is a transitive dependency in this design. The InvoiceID determines the CustomerID value, and CustomerID, in turn, determines the Contact column. Figure 3.18 shows the dependency in the Invoice table.

The arrows above the attribute boxes show the dependencies that exist between attributes and the table's primary key. Those relationships are fine. However, the arrow below the boxes shows a transitive dependency between CustomerID (the determinant attribute) and Contact. The easiest way to remove the transitive dependency is to create another table containing at least the determinant attribute and all attributes that are dependent on that determinant attribute. Once the transitive dependency is removed,

tblInvoice : Table					
InvoiceID	InvoiceDate	OrderDate	CustomerID	EmployeeID	CustomerPO
214010	10/1/2005	9/6/2005	35222	4058	2634-635
214011	10/1/2005	9/8/2005	33776	3458	587-233
214012	10/1/2005	9/12/2005	33271	1695	1328-333
214013	10/1/2005	9/22/2005	32978	1364	2817-332
214014	10/1/2005	9/27/2005	32198	3609	4155-032
214015	10/2/2005	9/8/2005	32369	2754	912-232
214016	10/2/2005	9/8/2005	33542	4082	662-433
214017	10/3/2005	9/22/2005	34109	3370	4210-234
214018	10/3/2005	9/25/2005	34154	1364	1470-034
214019	10/4/2005	9/5/2005	31183	3370	3464-131

Record: 21 of 500

Figure 3.17 Invoice table in second normal form (2NF).

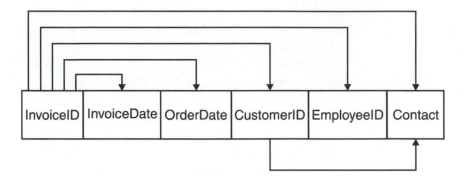

Figure 3.18   Transitive dependencies in the Invoice table shown in Figure 3.17.

the table will be in 3NF. The CustomerID field becomes a foreign key to link the invoice to individual customer information. The new tables could be structured as follows to bring them in compliance with 3NF:

tblInvoice(InvoiceID, InvoiceDate, OrderDate, CustomerID, EmployeeID)
tblCustomer(CustomerID, Contact)

Third normal form enforces an informal rule stating that a table should store one fact and one fact only. Prior to decomposing *tblInvoice* into two separate tables, it housed two facts: one fact about invoices (InvoiceDate, OrderDate, etc.) and one fact about customers (Contact). After two tables are created from a single table, each new table's structure (shown previously) holds only one fact.

TABLE RELATIONSHIPS.   You have learned that the process of normalizing a database's tables usually produces several additional tables. Yet, the relationships between associated tables are maintained by the foreign key to primary key links. There are three fundamental types of relationships between related tables: one-to-one (1–1), one-to-many (1–M), and many-to-many (M–M). The capital letter *M* indicates *many* records. Knowing about these three is important in understanding how to reconstruct information from data stored in constituent tables. Recall that rows from two tables are joined when the foreign key in one table's row matches the primary key in another table.

One-to-one relationships usually indicate unnecessary tables in the database design. You can usually combine tables with a one-to-one relationship into one table. Exceptions to this general rule can occur. For instance, the Customer table could have a one-to-one relationship with *tblCustomerNotes*, which might hold supplementary information about a few of The Coffee Merchant's customers. Because only a few customers have notes in the *tblCustomerNotes* table, you do not want to allocate an additional column for an occasional note. This would waste storage space. So, *tblCustomerNotes* would contain the foreign key CustomerID and a Notes column. CustomerID would serve both as the primary key for the *tblCustomerNotes* table and as a foreign key into the parent *tblCustomer* table. The following notation shows this relationship conveniently:

tblCustomer ^{1}————>^{1} tblCustomerNotes

Databases often contain tables that have one-to-many relationships with each other. There are several examples in The Coffee Merchant's database. Look again at Figure 3.8. Consider the relationship between the *tblCustomer* table and the *tblInvoice* table. Each customer can have as many unpaid invoices as The Coffee Merchant permits (or none). On the other hand, an invoice row in the *tblInvoice* table can be associated with one and only one customer in the *tblCustomer* table. The relationship between the *tblCustomer* table and the *tblInvoice* table is said to be a one-to-many relationship (in that direction—customer to invoice). Although it is technically correct to talk about "many-to-one" relationships, most database designers indicate the "one" side of the relationship first and use the "one-to-many" phrasing. A one-to-many relationship is shown this way:

tblCustomer ^{1}————>^{M} tblInvoice

Finally, consider the relationship between invoices and the coffee and tea items found on individual invoice lines. Various coffees and teas can appear on the many lines of a single invoice. An invoice might contain a line for 10 pounds of Kona coffee and another line for 5 pounds of Zimbabwe. Similarly, the coffee and tea items in The Coffee Merchant's inventory can appear in several invoices. For example, many different invoices might include Kona coffee. This type of relationship between the Invoice table and Inventory table is called a many-to-many relationship. We depict this type of relationship as follows:

tblInvoice ^{M}————>^{M} tblInventory

Many-to-many relationships can be difficult to represent and maintain in a relational database system. Most database designers create a new table to represent the M–M relationship. This table is called a *relationship* table or a *junction* table, and it combines attributes from the tables that participate in the M–M relationship. The relationship table makes the connection between the two tables by converting the M–M relationship into two 1–M relationships. The relationship table in The Coffee Merchant's database is called Invoice Line (*tblInvoiceLine*); it preserves the relationship between invoices (*tblInvoice*) and inventory (*tblInventory*). You can represent this three-table relationship for the M–M relationship as:

tblInvoice ^{1}————>^{M} tblInvoiceLine ^{M}<————^{1} tblInventory

Thus, it is always possible to break a many-to-many relationship between two tables into two one-to-many relationships by using an intermediate relationship table. The following are some general rules governing relationships among tables.

1. Primary keys must not be null.
2. Create a foreign key from the primary key on the one side of the 1–M relationship.

3. Many-to-many relationships are handled by creating an additional table—the relationship table—that consists entirely of the parent tables' primary keys. (The relationship table can contain other columns as well.)
4. Most one-to-one relationships indicate unnecessary tables in the database design. In most cases, if your analysis results in a one-to-one relationship between two tables, you should merge the two tables into one table. The one-to-one relationship means that each row in the first table has one and only one row in the second table that is related to it. Thus, combining the tables makes sense. In some cases, however, such as when one group of fields is used more frequently than other fields or when some fields need a greater degree of security, keeping the fields in separate tables is better.

Fundamental Relational Database Operations

Relational database management systems provide several important and fundamental retrieval operations. Among the most significant are select, project, and join.

SELECT. The select operator chooses a set of rows from a table. Rows are selected based on a set of qualifying factors, often called *selection criteria*. A new, virtual table is created by the select operation. There are several ways to implement a select operation. Some RDBMSs, such as Access, provide a Query by Example (QBE) graphical interface, in which you can choose example elements to specify selection criteria and check the attributes to be displayed.

Figure 3.19 shows a select operation and the resulting dynaset, another table. The query selects rows from a smaller version of an Employee table. Rows are selected in which the HireDate is after a particular date. Notice that the result returns all columns of the original table satisfying the selection criterion. The result is a table, because queries in relational database systems always deliver answers in table form.

PROJECT. The project operator returns a subset of columns from one or more tables. Columns retrieved are a result of the user indicating them, not a result of specifying a selection criterion. Figure 3.20 shows an example of a projection of the Name and Gender columns of our example Employee table shown previously in Figure 3.19. Notice that a project operation does not specify which *rows* are retrieved. Projections indicate only which *columns* are retrieved in the result. Of course, you can combine the selection and project operations in one query to produce both a row and column subset of a table.

JOIN. The most important relational database operation is the *join operation*. It provides the ability to pull together data from associated tables into a single, virtual table. Usually, you join two tables together using a common attribute found in both tables. This is the role of the foreign and primary keys. In the most common form of the join operation, one table's foreign key value is used to locate a matching primary key in another table. Then, the selected data from the matching rows in both tables are

Employee table:

ID	Name	Comm	HireDate	BirthDate	Gender
1301	Stonesifer	5%	07/06/96	03/10/66	F
1364	Pruski	4%	12/01/00	01/26/79	M
1528	Pacioli	6%	08/26/95	05/06/50	M
1695	Nagasaki	4%	01/28/00	04/10/77	M
2240	Stonely	15%	11/05/88	05/03/61	F
2318	Hunter	8%	11/16/93	01/26/54	F
2754	Kahn	5%	05/14/97	05/29/61	M
3370	Kole	9%	02/08/92	03/23/63	M
3432	English	8%	10/01/93	02/14/56	F
3436	Gates	6%	04/11/95	03/09/54	M
3458	Morrison	15%	12/13/89	07/04/56	F
3609	Chang	5%	09/16/97	03/30/77	F
. . .	. . .	. . .	. . .	. . .	. . .
4112	Goldman	11%	12/24/90	03/05/62	M

Result of selection operation: HireDate > 1/1/97

ID	Name	Comm	HireDate	BirthDate	Gender
1364	Pruski	4%	12/01/00	01/26/79	M
1695	Nagasaki	4%	01/28/00	04/10/77	M
2754	Kahn	5%	05/14/97	05/29/61	M
3609	Chang	5%	09/16/97	03/30/77	F

Figure 3.19 Select operation.

combined. That is, rows of one table are concatenated with (placed next to) rows of the second table for which the common attribute matches.

For instance, suppose we want to join a slightly altered Employee table with the employee title information found in a table on your Companion CD called *tblEmployee Title*. In the Employee table is a number, which stands in place of an actual job title. The number is used so that the title is not misspelled when it is entered over and over in the Employee table. *tblEmployeeTitle* contains the numbers and actual job titles associated with the numbers. Normalization has produced the two tables rather than a single table with repeating job titles, which would violate 3NF rules. The tables are joined on title number columns found in both tables. In the Employee table, this column is called *EmployeeTitleID*, although the Caption property setting for that field has been shortened to *TitleID*. The *EmployeeTitleID* column in *tblEmployeeTitle* is the primary key and contains a corresponding title field, *Title*. Joining the two tables in TitleID produces the result shown in Figure 3.21. Note that the join column does

Employee table: **Projection:**

ID	Name	Comm	HireDate	BirthDate	Gender	Name	Gender
1301	Stonesifer	5%	07/06/96	03/10/66	F	Stonesifer	F
1364	Pruski	4%	12/01/00	01/26/79	M	Pruski	M
1528	Pacioli	6%	08/26/95	05/06/50	M	Pacioli	M
. . .	. . .	. . .	. . .	. . .	. . .	. . .	. . .
4057	Bateman	9%	02/16/92	05/01/58	M	Bateman	M
4058	Halstead	5%	06/16/96	12/22/73	F	Halstead	F
4082	Flintsteel	11%	03/21/90	08/22/58	F	Flintsteel	F
4112	Goldman	11%	12/24/90	03/05/62	M	Goldman	M

Figure 3.20   Project operation.

not have to have the same name in both tables. In the illustration, TitleID is a foreign key in the *tblEmployee* table, whereas TitleID is the primary key in the *tblEmployee Title* table. Joining is a matter of matching foreign key and primary key values. The join illustration in Figure 3.21 is an example of the most common type of join. It is called an *equijoin*, because rows from the two tables are placed next to each other (concatenated) on matching join column values, and the join column appears only once in the result.

Another join operation type combines rows from two or more tables on the join column, but rows that do not match on the join column are included in the result. This type of join is called an *outer join*. Outer joins are useful for creating reports that show information such as employees who have made no sales or students who have not signed up for a particular class.

There is no theoretical limit to the number of tables that may be joined. For instance, one of the results we can produce with a join operation are invoices. An invoice is created by a query that joins five of The Coffee Merchant's tables whose schemas are shown in Figure 3.9. Tables joined to form an invoice are connected in pairs on common columns, but not all on the same columns. For instance, the *tblCustomer* table can be joined to the *tblInvoice* table via their common column, CustomerID. Continuing, the *tblInvoice* table can be joined to the *tblInvoiceLine* table (individual invoice lines) over the join column InvoiceID, an attribute found in both tables. The Inventory table, *tblInventory*, is joined to *tblInventoryDescription* to link the names of each invoiced item. *tblInventory* is joined to *tblInvoiceLine* on the common column InventoryID. Figure 3.22 illustrates how the join columns of all involved tables are connected to form the single result. All of the joins shown in Figure 3.22 are equijoins.

tblEmployee

ID	Name	TitleID	HireDate	Gender
1301	Stonesifer	2	07/06/96	F
1364	Pruski	1	12/01/00	M
1528	Pacioli	2	08/26/95	M
1695	Nagasaki	1	01/28/00	M
2240	Stonely	3	11/05/88	F
2318	Hunter	2	11/16/93	F
2754	Kahn	2	05/14/97	M
3370	Kole	2	02/08/92	M
3432	English	2	10/01/93	F
3436	Gates	2	04/11/95	M
. . .	. . .	. . .	. . .	. . .
4082	Flintsteel	3	03/21/90	F
4112	Goldman	3	12/24/90	M

tblEmployeeTitle

TitleID	Title
1	Sales Trainee
2	Sales Associate
3	Senior Sales Associate
4	Sales Manager
5	Senior Sales Manager
6	Division Sales Manager
7	Regional Manager
8	Division Manager
9	National Sales Manager

Result of join operation:

ID	Name	TitleID	HireDate	Gender	Title
1301	Stonesifer	2	07/06/96	F	Sales Associate
1364	Pruski	1	12/01/00	M	Sales Trainee
1528	Pacioli	2	08/26/95	M	Sales Associate
1695	Nagasaki	1	01/28/00	M	Sales Trainee
2240	Stonely	3	11/05/886	F	Senior Sales Associate
2318	Hunter	2	11/16/93	F	Sales Associate
2754	Kahn	2	05/14/97	M	Sales Associate
3370	Kole	2	02/08/92	M	Sales Associate
3432	English	2	10/01/93	F	Sales Associate
3436	Gates	2	04/11/95	M	Sales Associate
. . .	. . .	. . .	. . .	. . .	. . .
4082	Flintsteel	3	03/21/90	F	Senior Sales Associate
4112	Goldman	3	12/24/90	M	Senior Sales Associate

Figure 3.21 Join operation.

INTRODUCTION TO DATABASE DESIGN

A well-designed database that accurately models an enterprise's operations is crucial to the success of any database system designed to maintain accounting information. A badly designed database can be worse than using no system at all; information can be misrepresented, difficult to find, or completely lost.

One important aspect of database design is carefully choosing the rows and attributes that you want to include in each table. This activity, often referred to as *modeling*, can be accomplished using any of several methods. We introduce you to two

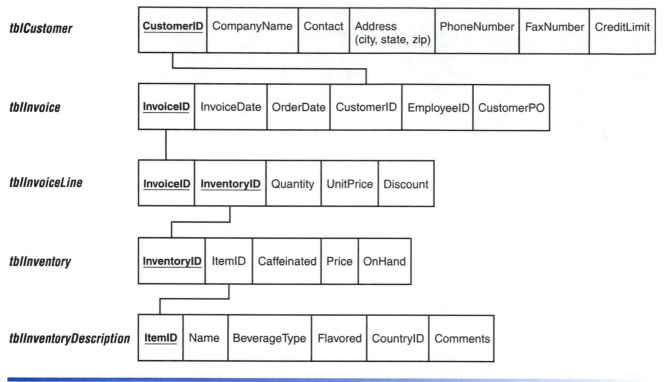

Figure 3.22   Joining tables with primary key/foreign key relationships.

of these methods in this section. The first method draws information from existing business documents. The other method, called *entity-relationship* (abbreviated *E-R*) *modeling*, is described in the context of The Coffee Merchant's invoice system.

Bottom-Up Database Design

One way to approach designing database objects is to use existing documents as a starting point. For instance, you can use a customer invoice form used in an existing manual accounting system as the basis for the design of the database tables that will be included in the database system. The first step in designing database objects to replace paper forms is to list all the information found on the document and to assign names to the attributes. Next, you should identify functional dependencies, if any. Then, you can create the entities (tables) by selecting which attributes belong in which tables. Finally, you apply normalization rules to the tables to ensure that all tables (entities) conform to third normal form. This approach is often called a *bottom-up* approach because the designer begins with a list of the fields that will be included in the tables and then collects the individual fields into tables.

The first step is to list potential attributes from an existing document. Attribute names may not be exactly right the first time, but they provide a starting point. Figure 3.23

CustomerContactPerson   ItemExtendedPrice
CustomerName   ItemName
CustomerNumber   ItemNumber
CustomerPhone   ItemPrice
CustomerAddress   ItemQuantity
InvoiceDate   OrderDate
InvoiceNumber   OrderNumber
InvoiceTotalAmount   SalesTax
ItemDescription   ShippingCharges

Figure 3.23 A list of possible attribute names.

shows a list of possible attribute names. To keep the example simple yet sufficient to illustrate the modeling process, other possible attributes have been omitted from the list such as Ship Date, Item Quantity Backordered, and Item Quantity Shipped.

The next step is to identify functional dependencies. You can make a good guess as to which attributes determine the value of other attributes. Do not worry about making a mistake. Any errors will be uncovered when you show your design to the people who will be using the system. Figure 3.24 shows an example of a dependency list. Dependent attributes are listed below the attributes that determine them.

CustomerNumber:
    CustomerName
    CustomerPhone
    CustomerContactPerson
    CustomerAddress

InvoiceNumber:
    InvoiceDate
    CustomerNumber
    OrderDate
    OrderNumber
    ShippingCharges
    InvoiceTotalAmount
    SalesTax

InvoiceNumber, ItemNumber:
    ItemQuantity
    ItemExtendedPrice

ItemNumber:
    ItemDescription
    ItemPrice
    ItemName

Figure 3.24 Tentative dependency list.

After making initial assignments of attributes, you might discover that you need to change these assignments. For example, you might determine that the price charged to a customer depends on the CustomerNumber and the ItemNumber. This can happen when particular customers are given price reductions based on volume or other factors. Finally, attributes that are calculated from other database fields should not be stored in the database at all. Examples of such calculated fields in this example would include InvoiceTotalAmount, SalesTax, and ShippingCharges. SalesTax, for instance, depends on additional attributes besides InvoiceNumber. A change in the unit price of an item would not automatically be reflected in SalesTax.

As the last step in this process, you develop a revised list of attributes that conform to third normal form. The attributes upon which each group depends constitute the relation's primary key, and each table's attributes are the primary key and the attributes listed below the primary key. The list of corrected dependencies is left as an exercise for the student (Hint: See Figure 3.9).

DEVELOPING ENTITY-RELATIONSHIP MODELS

Another popular modeling technique is called *entity-relationship (E-R) modeling*. Introduced by Peter Chen in 1976, E-R modeling has gained wide acceptance as a graphical approach to database design.

Database designers often use three terms to describe a company's information: entities, relationships, and attributes. *Entities* are objects (people or things) that are important to the company (nouns such as customer, inventory, employee, or vendor) or important activities (nouns such as sale, purchase, or cash disbursement). *Relationships* describe the way in which entities interact or are related to one another. For example, the entity customer is related to the entity sale when the company sells something to a customer. *Attributes* describe the characteristics of entities and relationships.

In the E-R model, diagrams represent entities and relationships. The diagrams contain three symbols: rectangles, diamonds, and lines. Rectangles represent entities, and diamonds represent relationships. Lines are the connections between the two. A digit or letter above the line indicates the degree of the relationship: one-to-one, one-to-many, or many-to-many. Figure 3.25 shows an example of an E-R diagram for The Coffee Merchant's invoice system.

At first, the E-R model allowed both entities and relationships to have attributes. In an E-R diagram, attributes are often shown as a list near the relationship or entity to which they belong. Another way to show attributes is to have an attribute name attached to a line leading from the entity or relationship to the attribute. Chen later suggested a slight change to the E-R approach. The altered E-R model allowed only entities to have attributes, not relationships.

A problem arises with the refined E-R methodology when a database includes many-to-many relationships. In this case, a new entity—shown with a diamond within a rectangle—is used to redraw two entities as three. The new entity reduces the many-to-many relationship to two relationships: a 1–M degree relationship on one side and an M–1 degree relationship on the other side (see Figure 3.26). 1–M signifies that one

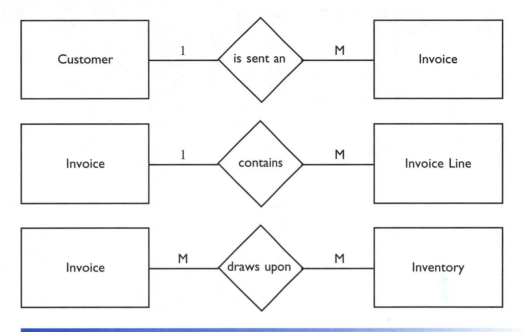

Figure 3.25 Entity-relationship diagram.

record from the table on one side may have many related records in the table on the other side of the relationship. For instance, an invoice can have a 1–M relationship to the items on the invoice: one invoice has many possible invoice lines.

The newly created entity in the middle is implemented in a database as a *relationship table*, which includes the primary keys of the two joined entities as two elements in its composite primary key. A relationship table is sometimes called a *junction table* or a *bridge table*.

After the E-R diagrams are complete, they can be combined into a single E-R diagram. This process is called *view integration*. For larger systems, the process is started by placing the most often used entity in the center of the diagram. Then, lines connect the related entities as in the original diagrams. From these entities, you can identify tables. One table is created for each entity. Primary keys for each table must be identified next. The relationships between entities, exemplified by lines connecting the entities, are maintained by foreign key/primary key linkages between tables. That is, a line from one entity to another is implemented by a key in one table (a foreign key) that matches one or more primary keys in the other table. In the case of a 1–M relationship, the "one" side of the relationship has a foreign key matching possibly several rows on the "many" side of the relationship.

When a many-to-many relationship exists in the E-R diagram, such as the relationship between *tblInvoice* and *tblInventory*, a relationship table is created. The InvoiceInven table in Figure 3.26 contains the primary key from the *tblInvoice* table and the primary key from the *tblInventory* table. Once the relationship table is created, the three tables have a pair of one-to-many relationships.

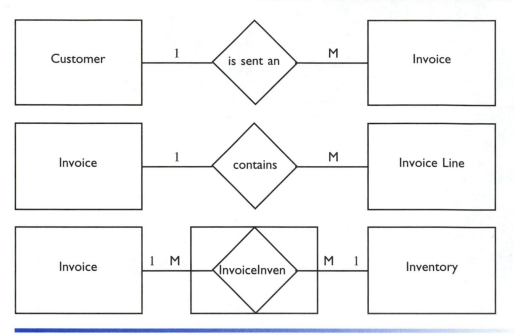

Figure 3.26   Revised entity-relationship diagram.

A table can also be related to itself in a special case in which rows of a table are related to other row(s) in the same table. A typical example is an employee table in which the primary key identifies employees and a Supervisor column contains foreign keys pointing to each employee's supervisor. Supervisors are in the same table because they are themselves employees. A parts inventory is another example. Some parts are made from several other parts, all of which are stored in the same inventory table. When rows of a table are related to rows in the same table, the relationship is called *recursive*.

The last step in view integration is to normalize the individual tables. For best results, all tables should be at least in third normal form.

RESOURCES, EVENTS, AGENTS (REA) MODELING

William McCarthy drew upon the principles of relational database theory developed by E. F. Codd and the entity-relationship modeling principles of Peter Chen to create a modeling approach specifically designed for accounting systems. In the late 1970s, McCarthy proposed an entity classification system that would allow accountants to use relational databases to handle accounting information efficiently and effectively.

McCarthy's approach, called the *REA (Resources, Events, Agents) model*, provides categories of entities that accountants can use to classify the entities that appear in accounting systems. In the REA model, resources are assets such as cash, inventory, and fixed assets. Events are transactions or other occurrences that have accounting effects and include things such as purchases and sales. Events can also be more subtle occurrences, such as the passage of time that causes interest to accrue on a loan or depreciation

Resources	Events	Agents
Cash	Purchase Order	Vendor
Materials Inventory	Receipt of Goods	Receiving Clerk
	Cash Disbursement	Purchasing Agent

Figure 3.27 Purchase cycle entities organized using the REA model.

of a fixed asset to occur. Agents are humans or organizations that interact with resources and events. Agent entities commonly found in accounting systems include customers, suppliers, and employees.

A number of researchers have proposed extensions to McCarthy's basic model since it was first introduced more than twenty years ago. For example, Eric Denna devised a *REAL model*, which added an entity classification for location to McCarthy's REA model. Although these extensions and the application of the REA model itself have been discussed in the academic accounting literature for many years, most accounting researchers agree that the REA model has considerable value as an approach to the design of accounting information systems. Figure 3.27 shows a list of entities for a purchase cycle accounting system that have been classified using the REA model.

Go to http://perry.swlearning.com for an in-depth tutorial.

SUMMARY

In this chapter, you have learned about database accounting systems, business activity classifications, transaction cycles, database management systems, database tables, relationships between tables, and database design. You learned why double-entry bookkeeping was an excellent system for organizing manual data gathering and storage tasks for many years but that database accounting systems can now offer significant advantages over computerized double-entry bookkeeping systems. Most firms today have concluded that the advantages of database accounting systems outweigh their disadvantages.

The discussion of business activity classifications showed you how to categorize firms as manufacturing, merchandising, and service businesses. You then learned how these classifications can help you match particular database features to accounting applications. The chapter discussed transaction cycles and the characteristics of database accounting systems for the revenue, purchase, payroll, and production cycles.

This chapter also introduced database management systems and their application to accounting information. Database management systems are the basis of many accounting systems and provide several advantages over nondatabase approaches to managing data. High on the list of advantages are cost savings resulting from the centralization of all data management functions and the enforcement of data integrity and consistency by the database system. Relational database management systems provide the needed capabilities to represent accounting information. Data maintenance in a relational database management system does not require a programmer's help. Usually, people can learn to insert and delete database records and to query database systems. Valuable accounting information can be retrieved in a variety of formats and aggregation levels; information retrieval is not limited to a standard set of accounting reports.

The chapter also emphasized the importance of representing table objects in normalized form. First, second, and third normal forms have been described. First normal form precludes repeating groups; second normal form requires that all table attributes be dependent on the table's entire primary key, not just part of it. Third normal form includes all the characteristics of first and second normal forms. In addition, tables in third normal form do not contain attributes that depend on other nonkey attributes. Tables in third normal form avoid problems that can impair the integrity of accounting information.

The chapter closed with a brief overview of the REA model developed by William McCarthy. The REA model specifies three or more categories of entities that commonly occur in accounting information systems. The REA model helps accountants identify the entities that should be included in the E-R models for accounting databases.

QUESTIONS AND PROBLEMS FOR REVIEW

Multiple-Choice Questions

1. Bar code scanners are useful elements in accounting database systems because they can quite easily
   a. post journal entries to the general ledger.
   b. capture a wide variety of information about each transaction.
   c. prevent or detect cashier fraud.
   d. identify pricing errors in the database.

2. The events-based approach to accounting theory
   a. classifies businesses in terms of their complexity.
   b. requires the use of the REA model to classify entities.
   c. supports the use of double-entry bookkeeping systems.
   d. supports the use of relational database accounting systems.

3. A double-entry bookkeeping system records each transaction
   a. twice.
   b. as an abstraction.
   c. in a relational database.
   d. on the day it occurs.

4. Computerized accounting systems
   a. can be used to implement either a double-entry bookkeeping model or a database accounting model.
   b. always require the installation of expensive database management software.
   c. must be certified by the Internal Revenue Service and the American Institute of Certified Public Accountants before being sold.
   d. record all transactions in a general journal before posting them to special journals.

5. Database systems store data only once. This feature
   a. allows multiple users to have simultaneous data access.
   b. facilitates cross-functional data analysis.
   c. greatly reduces data inconsistencies within the system.
   d. makes it easier for managers to create their own customized reports.

6. The term *cost of goods manufactured* on a manufacturing firm's income statement is analogous to
   a. cost of goods sold on a merchandising firm's income statement.
   b. revenue on a service firm's income statement.
   c. purchases on a merchandising firm's income statement.
   d. gross profit on a merchandising firm's income statement.

7. The purchase cycle includes
   a. manufacturers' ordering and receipt of raw materials.
   b. merchandisers' ordering and receipt of goods for resale.
   c. both a and b.
   d. none of the above.

8. A collection of tables that contain information about a database, including the database table structures and a list of all fields included in each table, is called a
   a. data dictionary.   c. database index.
   b. master data file.   d. database summary.

9. *Select* and *project* are two fundamental data retrieval operations that you can use in a relational database. Which of the following is a true statement regarding these operations?
   a. The select operation selects columns from a table.
   b. The project operation selects columns from a table.
   c. The project operation moves data from one table to another table.
   d. You must join two tables before using either the select or project operations.

10. A table that does not include any transitive dependencies
    a. cannot be in any normal form; all normal forms require at least one transitive dependency.
    b. is in first normal form or higher.
    c. is in second normal form or higher.
    d. is in third normal form or higher.

11. To represent a many-to-many relationship in a relational database, the designer must
    a. create four tables, each having a one-to-one relationship with the other three tables.
    b. create three tables, one for each of the entities and a third relationship table that includes the primary keys of the two entity tables.
    c. combine the two entity tables that share the many-to-many relationship into a single table.
    d. eliminate the many-to-many relationship; such relationships are not permitted.

Discussion Questions

1. Why is double-entry bookkeeping better suited to manual accounting systems than to computerized accounting systems?

2. What prevents accountants from using a database model to automate a double-entry bookkeeping system?

3. In which of the business activity classifications described in this chapter would you include a hospital? Why?

4. Discuss the problems that can arise from storing data in two different places.

5. What is a primary key, and why is it so important in a relational database management system?

Practice Exercises

Note: Before doing any of the following practice exercises, first copy *Ch03.mdb* from your Companion CD to the hard drive of the computer on which you are working. Then, clear the copied database's Read-only file attribute (see Chapter 1, Exercise 1.14, Clearing a File's Read-Only Property). Having done that, you can complete each exercise using the copy of the Companion CD database.

1. Create a query for *tblInventory* in the *Ch03.mdb* file that combines three project operations and a select operation as follows: project the attributes InventoryID, Price, and OnHand; select rows in which the value for the Price attribute is between $4.00 and $5.00 per pound. Print your resulting datasheet.

2. Describe the tables that a grocery store would use in its revenue cycle. Be sure to include all necessary relationship tables and foreign keys.

3. Assume you are working for a manufacturing firm that operates 14 factories, each with 16 departments. What tables would you add to those listed in this chapter for the payroll cycle to track employee time worked by factory and department?

4. Redraw Figure 3.5 for a merchandising firm.

5. Discuss the inherent problems of storing an employee's age as one of the attributes of a table. Discuss alternative solutions that would not cause inaccuracies in the database.

Problems

Note: Before doing any of the following problems, first copy *Ch03.mdb* from your Companion CD to the hard drive of the computer on which you are working. Then, clear the copied database's Read-only file attribute (see Chapter 1, Exercise 1.14, Clearing a File's Read-Only Property). Having done that, you can complete each exercise using the copy of the Companion CD database.

1. Create a query for *tblInventoryDescription* in the *Ch03.mdb* file that combines four project operations and two select operations as follows: project the attributes ItemID, Name, Flavored, and BeverageType; select rows in which the value for the Flavored attribute is Yes and for which the BeverageType attribute is "c" (these are the expressions you should place in the Criteria cells for those two attributes, respectively). Examine your results to ensure that they do not contain any rows with tea products, only coffee products. Print your resulting datasheet.

2. Carefully examine *tblInvoiceLine* in the *Ch03.mdb* database and answer the following questions: What type of table is *tblInvoiceLine*? What is the primary key of *tblInvoiceLine*? Unlike most printed invoices, which include quantity, the unit price, and an extension (quantity multiplied by unit price) for each inventory item, this table does not include an extension. Why not?

3. Suppose you are designing a database that contains information about university classes, students enrolled in classes, and instructors teaching various classes. The Catalog table lists all the courses that the university offers. The Classes table describes the classes offered during the semester and includes names of students currently enrolled in each class. The Students table contains one record for each student enrolled in the university. The Instructor table contains information about instructors including their names, phone numbers, and office telephone numbers. Discuss the relationship between the Instructor table and the Classes table. Is the relationship 1–1, 1–M, or M–M? Describe the relationship between the Students table and the Classes table. Finally, draw a diagram showing the tables Catalog, Classes, Instructor, and Students and how they might be linked. Use Figure 3.22 as a model of how to represent the tables. Include only the primary and foreign key fields in each table's representation.

CHAPTER 4
Tables and Queries

OBJECTIVES

This chapter extends the knowledge that you gained in Chapters 2 and 3 with detailed information about Microsoft Access. You will learn about creating and altering tables and queries. Exercises throughout this chapter emphasize Microsoft Access techniques critical to building accounting information systems. Like Chapter 2, this chapter is application-oriented and contains very little theory; however, we emphasize employing the theory we presented earlier. In this chapter you will learn how to use two important types of Access objects: tables and queries. In particular, you will learn how to:

- Reset the Tables and Queries toolbars to their original configuration.
- Define a table's structure.
- Enter data into a table.
- Alter a table's structure.
- Set a table's field properties.
- Join tables and establish referential integrity checks between them.
- Create queries involving a single table.
- Create queries for tables with a many-to-many relationship.
- Create queries involving multiple tables, derived column values, and expressions.
- Create queries with an outer join relationship to reveal hidden information.
- Create parameter queries.

We continue using The Coffee Merchant's tables as the backdrop application in this chapter. All the tables and queries mentioned in Chapter 3 have been copied to the Ch04 folder on the Companion CD. For all exercises and examples in this chapter, we assume that you have inserted the Companion CD into your CD drive, copied the database *Ch04.mdb* to your hard disk, turned off the database file's read-only attribute, started Microsoft Access, and opened the Ch04 database. If not, then please be sure to do so before doing the exercises in this chapter.

ACCESS OBJECTS

The term *Access objects* refers to several ways you can store and display information in your tables. Like most database systems, Access provides a rich variety of objects

157

for your use. Beginning with the most fundamental, objects include tables, queries, forms, reports, pages, macros, and modules.

Tables

All database information is stored in one or more tables comprised of rows and columns. A row contains all the information about a particular item in the table. Also called a *record*, a row's columns contain individual values for each attribute that characterizes the row. For instance, The Coffee Merchant's *tblCustomer* table contains a row for each current or potential customer. Columns in the Customer table hold information about ten different attributes of a customer record.

Each column can contain only one data type. Though the exact names of these data types vary from one RDBMS to another, they are all drawn from a small, common set. Data types constrain the type of information that can be entered into a column. Access supports the data types listed in Figure 4.1. Of the listed types, you will probably use the AutoNumber, Currency, Date/Time, Text, and Number data types most frequently.

Data Type	Description and Use
Text	Holds up to 255 characters consisting of anything you can type on the keyboard. Data cannot be used in calculations.
Memo	Lengthy, variable-length text and numbers for comments or explanations. A memo field can contain up to 65,535 characters.
Number	Numeric data used in calculations. Set the Field Size property to define the specific number type including byte, integer, long integer, single, double, replication ID, and decimal.
Date/Time	Holds date or time information. Several formats are available, or you can establish a custom format.
Currency	Holds monetary data of up to 19 significant digits (15 to the left of the decimal point and 4 to the right). Currency fields are formatted to display a currency symbol and two decimal places. Use currency to avoid rounding errors in financial calculations.
AutoNumber	A unique sequential number that Access automatically generates. This data type is often used for primary keys, because it guarantees unique values.
Yes/No	Yes/No, True/False, or On/Off are all examples of legitimate field values. Choose the Yes/No data type when only two values are possible (gender or invoice paid, for example).
OLE Object	Contains objects from another Windows application such as a picture, graph, or spreadsheet. When you double-click an OLE object, the program that created the object is launched so you can modify or view the OLE object.
Hyperlink	Text or combinations of text and numbers constituting a World Wide Web hyperlink address.
Lookup Wizard	A field that provides the mechanism to automatically look up a value from another table or list of fields by using a combo box or list box control.

Figure 4.1   Access data types.

Queries

A query is a question that you ask about one or more tables in your database. You use queries to locate and display a subset of the rows of a table, combine information from several tables into a single result, or perform calculations on fields. You can also use queries to make massive changes to a table, delete data from a table, or insert rows into a table. These latter queries are known as *action queries*.

Access uses the popular Query by Example (QBE) method in which you select one or more tables to query and then check off the columns you would like to see. By placing values or expressions below particular column names, you can limit the rows that are retrieved. These values or expressions are called *selection criteria*. By using the appropriate selection criteria, you can, for instance, list all customers who live in the Midwest. Or, you can compute the total value of all outstanding invoices based on an invoice table or tables. Queries are used to reduce the amount of information that is displayed, summarizing it and giving it meaning.

Forms

Forms provide a simpler way of examining data in a table one row at a time. You can look at a great deal of information or only a small amount. Data displayed in a form are exactly the same data found in its underlying table. One huge difference between data displayed in a form and data displayed in a table is that you can format and enhance the data's appearance in a form. Figure 4.2 shows a form displaying data from The Coffee Merchant's Employee table.

A form is especially useful for people not familiar with the Access database software and who must enter or change data in tables. Data entry is also much easier when using a well-designed form. A forms designer can supply helpful form controls and

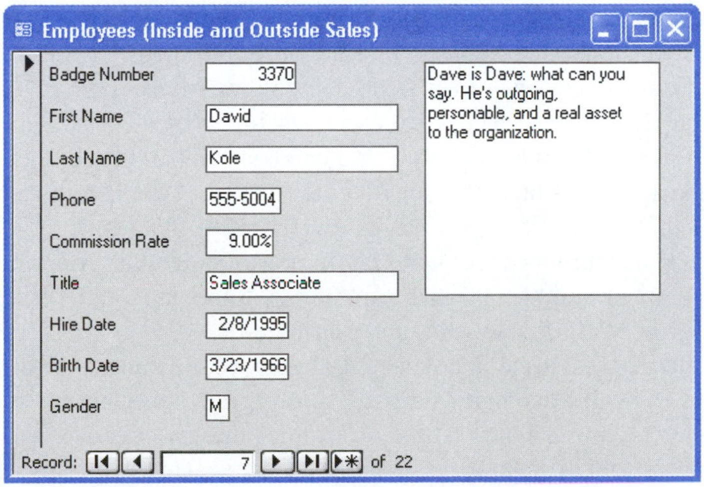

Figure 4.2   Example form.

other objects, such as drop-down lists or radio buttons, to create an easy-to-use form. For example, drop-down lists (also called *list boxes*) are helpful when you encounter an entry whose possible values are limited but not known to the user. By making a list available, your database form user can choose one of a select set of values by simply clicking a list member. When a form user moves to another row, Access automatically posts any changed information to the underlying table.

Form navigation buttons make moving the data around easy. You can move to the first or last row in a table, up or down one row at a time, or to a particular row. Access provides tools allowing you to customize a form so that it precisely matches an existing paper form. Electronic forms that match paper ones make the computerized version less intimidating—especially to new database users. You will learn about forms in Chapter 5.

Reports

While forms provide an excellent way to view and alter data in one or more tables, *reports* are superb for providing boardroom-quality printed information. You can sort, group, and summarize results with reports. Reports can contain subtotals, totals, averages, and counts, all attractively printed. Like other reporting tools, you can include report headers and footers and page headers and footers. You can also create mailing labels using the Access report facility.

Like forms, reports can take advantage of Access' many design tools, including graphic import, lines, boxes, and text, to name a few. Data can be drawn from several tables and combined in one report. Figure 4.3 shows an example of a simple report that can be quickly and easily produced with Access. You will learn about reports in Chapter 5.

Pages

A data access *page* is a special Web page designed to allow you to view and work with Access databases through the Internet or an intranet. Any data access page can contain data from sources other than Access, including Microsoft Excel worksheets or text files.

You design data access pages in Design view. The collection of page designs is found in the Pages collection of the database. When you design a data access page, the page is actually stored as a separate file outside Access, and Access automatically adds a shortcut to the file in the Pages collection of objects in the Database window. Data access pages are a convenient way to consolidate and group information that is stored in a database and then publish summaries of the data on the Internet. Data access pages also allow you to view, add, and edit records.

A data access page is connected directly to a database. When users display the data access page in Microsoft Internet Explorer, they are viewing their own copy of a page. Thus, if each user filters, sorts, or changes the way the database is displayed, just their own copy of the data access page is affected. However, any change a user makes to the database—by deleting records, editing fields, or adding data—does affect the database. The changes are available to anyone viewing the database through Access or

Employees Grouped by Title

Title	Name	ID	Hire Date	Birth Date	Gender
Sales Trainee					
	Nagasaki, Ted	1695	1/28/2003	4/10/1980	M
	Pruski, Kevin	1364	12/1/2003	1/26/1982	M
Count: 2					
Sales Associate					
	Bateman, Giles	4057	2/16/1995	5/1/1961	M
	Chang, Annie	3609	9/16/2000	3/30/1980	F
	Ellison, Larry	3700	4/18/1997	12/12/1957	M
	English, Melinda	3432	10/1/1996	2/14/1959	F
	Gates, William	3436	4/11/1998	3/9/1957	M
	Halstead, Whitney	4058	6/16/1999	12/22/1976	F
	Hunter, Helen	2318	11/16/1996	1/26/1957	F
	Kahn, Phillipe	2754	5/14/2000	5/29/1964	M
	Kole, David	3370	2/8/1995	3/23/1966	M
	Pacioli, Luca	1528	8/26/1998	5/6/1953	M
	Stonesifer, Patti	1301	7/6/1999	3/10/1969	F
	Watterson, Barbara	3943	10/10/1996	5/1/1964	F
Count: 12					
Senior Sales Associate					
	Ballmer, Steve	3692	5/16/1988	7/13/1947	M
	Flintsteel, Hillary	4082	3/21/1993	8/22/1961	F
	Goldman, Ted	4112	12/24/1993	3/5/1965	M
	Manispour, Sharad	4029	12/18/1993	2/4/1972	M
	Minsky, Barbara	4012	10/13/1993	4/12/1962	F
	Morrison, Alanis	3458	12/13/1992	7/4/1959	F
	Shoenstein, Brad	3892	9/5/1993	3/6/1958	M
	Stonely, Sharon	2240	11/5/1991	5/3/1964	F
Count: 8					

Figure 4.3 Example report.

through data access pages on the Web. A clear advantage of data access pages is that remote users with an Internet connection can view and (optionally) manipulate an Access database without having Microsoft Access installed, though they must have a Microsoft Office license to do so. Figure 4.4 shows a page generated from Access. It behaves just like an Access form (discussed in Chapter 5).

Macros and Modules

Macros are Visual Basic codes that can be executed at the click of a button or when a form is opened. They define one or more actions that you want Access to perform in response to a particular event. Macros are frequently attached to objects located on a form, but you can write stand-alone code segments that can be invoked by a wide variety of objects in your applications. For example, you can write a small macro to check the value of an entry after the user moves to the next form field. If the field fails a value range test performed by the macro, then the macro can display an error message and move back to the erroneous field.

A *module* is an object containing custom procedures that you code using Visual Basic. Modules provide a finer degree of control and flow that allow you to write a code that recognizes and traps errors—something macros cannot do. Modules are stand-alone, global objects that can be called into action from anywhere within your Access

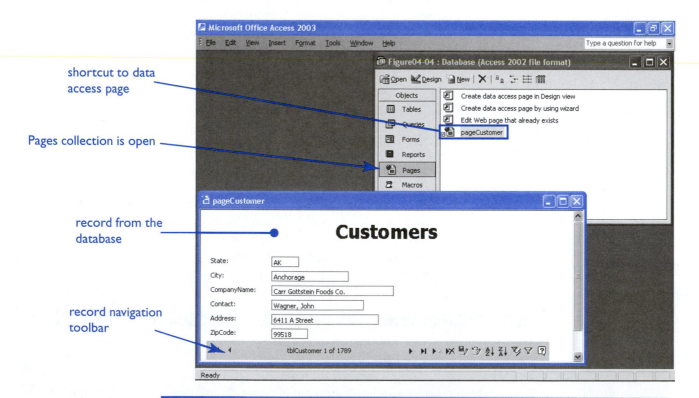

Figure 4.4 Viewing a database record with Internet Explorer.

application. Defining modules means the code can be reused by all of your forms, scripts, and other libraries.

Separating Tables from Other Objects

Whether or not you are developing an application for a client server environment, you may find it convenient to separate an application's tables from queries, forms, reports, and other database objects. Doing so allows you to store tables in one database and other related objects in another database. You can then create queries, forms, reports, macros, and modules based on linked tables. A *linked table* is stored in a file outside the open database from which Microsoft Access can access records. You can perform all the normal database operations on linked tables except altering their structure. That is, you can insert, delete, update, and view records in linked tables.

Why would you bother to separate tables—the only database objects storing data— from other database objects? The most important reason is to provide application development independence. As a developer, you can continue to improve and develop the queries, forms, and reports embedded in one of the two application database files. Then, when you replace a client's application with the newest version of the database application you have been independently developing, you simply replace all the objects in the database containing the queries, forms, reports, macros, and modules with the new ones. The database containing tables with the latest information remains unchanged. This way, your client's ever-changing tables are not affected, and the client can continue processing using the database. This method allows you to transparently update software without affecting the firm using your database software. Figure 4.5 shows a graphical representation of table/object separation.

WORKING WITH TABLES

We described tables in Chapters 2 and 3. In this chapter, you learn how to alter an existing table's structure and how to modify a table whose rows are related to another table. Prohibiting removal of a parent table row until all the rows in another table referring to the parent table are first removed is called *referential integrity*. This is an important feature provided by most relational database management systems. Referential integrity can be enforced, and we will show you how on one of the existing tables for The Coffee Merchant. In this section we show you how to add and delete columns from a table and how to forge a permanent link between related tables. First, let's see how to add and delete table columns.

One of the important tables in the evolving invoice subsystem contains customer names, addresses, and telephone numbers (and other fields) collected from both customers and people who merely expressed an interest in receiving a catalog. Besides periodically sending out promotional material to selected members of the customer "list," customer information appears in the "Ship to," "Sold to," or "Bill to" areas of invoices. The Coffee Merchant sample Customer table is somewhat large (over 1,700 rows), but it is small when compared to the customer database of a company such as Microsoft.

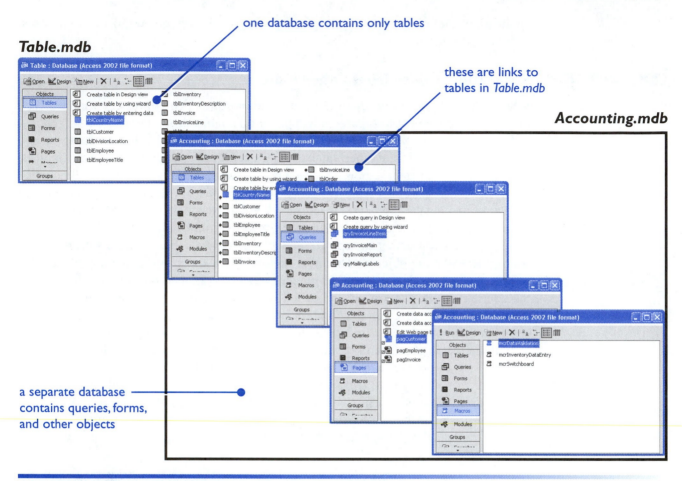

Figure 4.5   Separating tables from other database objects.

The Coffee Merchant Customer table, called *tblCustomer*, is stored in the database called *Ch04.mdb*. The database is found on your Companion CD in the Ch04 folder. We have loaded *tblCustomer* with several rows so you can experience manipulating a nontrivial table. All of the data are real, including company names and addresses. The telephone numbers and contact persons have been randomized to protect the privacy of individuals. You will notice that the telephone area codes are correct and correspond to the city in which the business is located.

In the next several sections we want you to create a table from scratch and enter data into it. Rather than have you be mere observers of our data, you will be involved with the entire process, from start to finish, of designing your own table. Doing so prepares you to create quality databases after you finish reading this book and working its exercises. That's why it is instructive for you to build and fill at least one of the tables so that you experience the process. If you have trouble, the Companion CD contains all the tables and other objects for The Coffee Merchant. The next section begins the process by describing how to create a mini-version of the Customer table. The section afterward describes the step-by-step process of filling (*populating*) your table.

DEFINING A TABLE'S STRUCTURE

From here on in the chapter, you will be doing a lot of work with the Ch04 database. If you have not already done so, copy the database from your Companion CD to the hard drive on your computer. Every change you make to the database occurs on the copy of the database you just created on your hard disk.

Prepare for the first exercise by launching Access. Follow the steps in the next exercise to create an example Customer table that is a much smaller version of the *tblCustomer* table already stored in the Chapter 4 database.

EXERCISE 4.1: STARTING TO CREATE THE CUSTOMER TABLE STRUCTURE

1. With Access open, click File, click Open, and then use the Look in list box to locate *Ch04.mdb* in the Open dialog box. Double-click *Ch04.mdb* to open the database.
2. Click Tables in the Objects bar, if necessary, and click the New button on the Database toolbar.
3. Click Design View from the list of choices, and click OK to get started.

Next, you will define the names, data types, and descriptions for each field in your table. When you complete Exercise 4.2, you will have a new table structure into which you can place data.

EXERCISE 4.2: DEFINING THE TABLE'S NAME, DATA TYPE, AND DESCRIPTION FIELDS

1. With the empty table design grid open, type **CustomerID** in the first row of the Field Name column in the Table dialog box. Press Tab, type **N** in the Data Type column, press Tab to move to the Description field, and type the description **Customer identification number**
2. Click the Primary Key button on the toolbar. (The Primary Key toolbar button displays a small key. Move the mouse over it, pause, and the ToolTip "Primary Key" appears, confirming you have selected the correct button.) Access places a small key symbol to the left of the field name indicating that CustomerID is the table's primary key.
3. Type **CompanyName** in the Field Name column, press Tab, double-click the Field Size property in the Field Properties list found in the lower half of the dialog box (or press F6), type **25** in the Field Size cell, click the Description column in the CompanyName field row, type **Company name**, and press Tab to move to the next row in the Table dialog box.
4. Type **PhoneNumber**, press Tab, click the Text data type, change the default data length (Field Size property, lower panel) to **8**, click the Description column in the PhoneNumber field row, type **Telephone number**, and press Tab to move to the next row.
5. Type **LastContactDate**, press Tab, type **D** to select the Date/Time data type, press Tab, type the description **Date of last contact**, and press Tab to move to a new row.

6. Type **CreditLimit**, press Tab, type **N** to select the Number data type, press Tab, type the description **Credit limit**, and press Tab.

7. Type **Notes**, press Tab, type **M** to select the Memo data type, press Tab, and then type **Miscellaneous notes** in the Description field.

8. Click File, and then click Save to save the newly defined table structure. The Save As dialog box appears (see Figure 4.6).

9. Type **tblMyCustomer** in the Table Name text box, and then click OK. Access saves your newly created Customer table, *tblMyCustomer*, in the Ch04 database.

10. Click Close in the File menu to close the table. (Alternatively, you can click the Close button on the table's Title bar to close its Design view.)

Be sure that you save your new table with the name *tblMyCustomer*, not *tblCustomer*. This is a safety feature. This way you still have the original table *tblCustomer*, which is on the Companion CD, for use in the textbook's exercises.

Populating a Table

When you *populate a table*, you are simply placing data into a table whose structure already exists. Entering data into a table is straightforward. First, ensure that *Ch04.mdb* is open. Then, locate *tblMyCustomer* in the Tables objects of the Database window. Double-click the *tblMyCustomer* table name to open it in Datasheet view. Maximize the Table window so that you can see the full table.

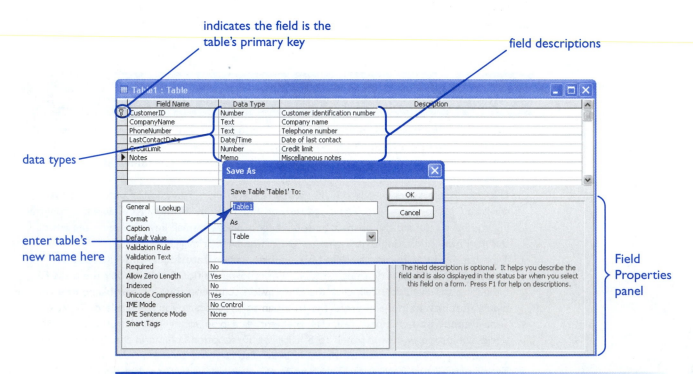

Figure 4.6 Defining a table's structure and saving it.

In Exercise 4.3, you will use three different methods to move from one field to the next one: pressing Tab, clicking the next field, and pressing Enter. That way you can decide which method you prefer.

EXERCISE 4.3: ENTERING A RECORD INTO A TABLE

1. In the CustomerID field, type **3101** and press Tab to move to the CompanyName field.
2. Type **Experience Coffee** in the CompanyName field. Move to the PhoneNumber field by clicking the cell just under the PhoneNumber field name.
3. Type **555-1233** in the PhoneNumber field. Press Enter to move to the next column, LastContactDate.
4. Type **5/23/2004** in the LastContactDate field. Press Tab to move to the CreditLimit column.
5. Type **4000** and press Tab to move to the last column, Notes.
6. Type **This is a good customer** in the memo field.

Don't press any keys for a moment. Do you notice the small pencil symbol in the row selector button of the table? This indicates that a record's contents have been changed but not yet posted to the table. You post changes to a table simply by moving to another table record. You will do that in a moment.

If you make a mistake anywhere while entering data, simply use the arrow keys to move left or right in the field, or use the Backspace or Delete keys to delete information. Pressing a key inserts the letter into the field at the insertion point indicated by the cursor. To correct a value in a field to the left of the current field, press Shift+Tab repeatedly until the cursor arrives at the field to be changed. To display the blinking insertion point, simply press F2. Then you can use the arrow keys to move the insertion point within a field. Pressing Tab or Shift+Tab moves to another cell and selects the entire value.

Next, enter the remaining *tblMyCustomer* table data by completing Exercise 4.3. When you move to a new row, the previous row is stored on disk. The last record you enter in a table is saved when you close the table or you close the entire database. Alternatively, you can simply press the up arrow key to move to a previous record to save the latest record.

EXERCISE 4.4: ENTER THE REMAINING *TBLMYCUSTOMER* TABLE DATA

1. With the *tblMyCustomer* table still displayed, click in the CustomerID column of the second table row.
2. Enter the remaining table rows. Figure 4.7 shows all customer table rows. Refer to it as you enter the remaining customer records. You can enter anything you like (or nothing) in the Notes field of each customer record. That's entirely up to you.
3. After you enter the last customer's information, click the Table window Close button to close the table. The last row of the *tblMyCustomer* table will be posted automatically to the database.

CustomerID	CompanyName	PhoneNumber	LastContactDate	CreditLimit
3101	Experience Coffee	555-1233	5/23/2004	4000
3122	Gourmet Grinder	555-7826	9/14/2003	1000
3245	La Jolla Expresso	555-3919	7/9/2004	5500
3658	Starbucks Coffee	555-5561	9/14/2003	15000
3702	Kensington Coffee Company	555-6153	12/16/2003	1000
3824	Intermezzo Espresso Bar	555-8282	8/5/2004	7500
3961	Just Bean Counters	555-9646	3/15/2004	2500

Figure 4.7   Contents of the example customer table, *tblMyCustomer*.

Adding a Column to a Table

If you create and use a table and later—perhaps much later—discover you have left out an important column or two, you can add new columns to tables at any time. You can add a column to a table either in Datasheet view or Design view. Adding a column in Design view is the best way, because you can add a column and define all of its characteristics in one window—the Design view window. On the other hand, you can add a column more quickly in Datasheet view.

The Coffee Merchant's Division Location table (*tblDivisionLocation*) contains the city and state in which each of The Coffee Merchant's divisions is located. It is useful to place often-repeated character strings such as cities or organization names in their own table along with a unique identification number. Then, you can refer to the cities with a number in place of the long string in the original table. Among other advantages, this prevents you from misspelling "Cincinnati" or other city names when they occur frequently in a table's columns. This is the purpose of the *tblDivisionLocation* table. A related column, yet to be placed in the *tblEmployee* table, will contain a number that is related to the company division number found in the *tblDivisionLocation* table. Your next job will be to add a new table column to *tblEmployee*—a division number column—which is a foreign key field linked to the primary key of the *tblDivisionLocation* table. A foreign key is a column whose values match similar values in another table's primary key column. A foreign key column in one table always corresponds to a primary key column in another table. Once the *tblEmployee* and *tblDivisionLocation* tables are linked together through their primary key/foreign key pairs, you will be able to determine the city and state in which each employee and each employee's division are located.

Each employee row should have an entry indicating which division the employee works for. Adding or deleting a column in a table is called altering the table's structure. Do not confuse this activity with adding or deleting data in a table's columns.

The next exercise shows you how to add a column to a table. In particular, you will add a column called EmployeeDivisionID to the *tblEmployee* table. This column is a foreign key to the *tblDivisionLocation* table.

EXERCISE 4.5: ADDING A COLUMN TO THE EMPLOYEE TABLE

1. Click Tables in the Database Objects bar if necessary, select *tblEmployee*, click the Design button, and maximize the Table window.
2. Click the EmployeeTitleID row selector button to select the entire row, click Insert on the menu bar, and then click Rows. A new, empty row is added to the table's structure above the EmployeeTitleID row.
3. In the new row, click the Field Name cell, type **EmployeeDivisionID**, and press Tab to move to the Data Type column.
4. Type **N** because the EmployeeDivisionID field will hold a number and then press Tab to move to the Description field.
5. In the Description field, type **Identification of the division for which this employee works** to document the field's use.
6. In the Field Properties panel, click the Caption property box and then type **Division ID** (with an embedded space). The Caption property text appears in place of the column's actual name in forms, reports, and Datasheet views of tables.
7. Click File on the menu bar, and then click Save to save the newly altered table structure.

To complete this operation, you need to place data in the newly created EmployeeDivisionID column. This is relatively easy because the table is small. Make sure you fill in the field for each employee row, because the next exercise will use the EmployeeDivisionID column values to establish a connection to the *tblDivisionLocation* table.

EXERCISE 4.6: PLACE VALUES IN THE EMPLOYEEDIVISIONID COLUMN

1. Click the Datasheet View button to display the table's contents (not its structure), and then click any entry in the EmployeeWorkPhone column.
2. Click Records in the menu bar, point to Sort, and click Sort Ascending to sort the table from low to high on the telephone numbers.
3. Select the topmost Division ID cell corresponding to employee David Kole and type **101** into the cell.
4. Repeat step 3 for the next five employees. The first six employees all work in division 101.
5. Type the value **102** in the next six Division ID cells, indicating that employees Sharad Manispour through Whitney Halstead work in Division 102. (Hint: After entering the value 102 once, use Copy/Paste to rapidly paste the next five entries.)
6. Type **103** for the next six employees' Division ID attributes—employees whose names are Kevin Pruski through Luca Pacioli. (Remember to speed up data entry by pasting—Ctrl+V—copies of the same field into successive rows' cells.)
7. Finally, type **104** for the remaining four employees—Ellison through Flintsteel.

8. Close the table (click the Datasheet view Close button), and click No when asked if you want to save changes to the design of the table. (We are not interested in preserving the view of the table in sorted order, even though the table is not actually sorted.)

Keep the following distinction in mind. A table's design has to do with its structure—the number of columns and their characteristics. A table's design has nothing to do with the data stored in its columns—its contents. You have changed the table's contents just now, and those changes are automatically posted to the table. Remember to save any table structural changes by executing the Save command in the File menu.

Deleting or Renaming a Table Column

It is easy to remove unwanted columns from any table or to give one or more columns a new name. Though you don't need to delete table columns right now, you should learn how to do it. You can delete a column while viewing a table in either Datasheet view or Design view. It is equally easy to delete a column in either view. To delete a table's column in Design view, click Tables in the Database Objects bar, select a table, and open it in Design view. Click the row selector to the left of the column you want to delete, and then click the Delete button. Remember to click the Save button (or File, Save) to post the changed table structure to your database. To delete a table column in Datasheet view, right-click the column's field selector, select Delete Column from the pop-up menu, and click Yes when a dialog box asks if you want to permanently delete the column. In Design view, any attribute rows that are below the deleted field are moved up to close the gap. In Datasheet view, any columns to the right of the deleted column move left to close the gap left by the deleted column.

You may decide that a column name no longer makes sense or is otherwise inappropriate. Renaming a column is straightforward. You can change a table column's name either in Datasheet view or Design view. In Datasheet view, simply double-click the column's selector, type a new name, and press Enter. The new name replaces the name originally assigned. Also, the renamed field's Caption property is deleted. (You will learn about field properties later in this chapter.) To rename a table column in Design view, first display the table in Design view. Next, click the Field Name cell that you want to change, and type over the old name with its replacement. Finally, click Save in the File menu to store the altered table.

Moving a Table Column

Although the order of columns in a table has no importance whatsoever, you can rearrange table columns so they appear in a different order in Datasheet view. Just like other table structure alteration operations mentioned here, you can rearrange table columns either in Datasheet view or Design view. To move a column or a group of contiguous columns while in Datasheet view, you begin by selecting the columns. Click the field selector of the column you want to move. To select adjacent columns, click a column field selector, and move the mouse to adjacent columns without releasing the mouse. In either case, one or more columns is selected. Click and hold the mouse in the field selector again, and drag the column(s) to their new location. Release the mouse button to "drop" the selected columns into their new locations. Click Save in the File menu to save the altered table structure in the database.

Establishing Referential Integrity

Access provides a way to enforce *referential integrity* whereby defined relationships between tables are maintained permanently and automatically. For example, referential integrity rules prevent you from adding a record to a related table if there is no associated record in the primary table. Additionally, the rules prevent deleting or changing records in a primary table that would result in orphan records in a related table. Suppose you want to enforce referential integrity between the Invoice table (*tblInvoice*) and the related Invoice Line table (*tblInvoiceLine*). Once you tell Access to enforce referential integrity rules between two tables, you cannot delete an invoice from the parent Invoice table unless there are no related invoice line items in the Invoice Line table. As you work more with Access, you will gain a deeper understanding of how referential integrity works to preserve a kind of "parent/child" relationship between tables falling under the integrity protection rules.

In the next exercise, you will do your work in the Relationships window, a window that displays linkages between tables for a given database. You define permanent linkages—primary key to foreign key relationships—to make forming multiple-table queries easier. You can also choose whether or not the Relationships window displays none, some, or all intertable relationships. To illustrate just how this works, you will establish referential integrity between the Employee table (*tblEmployee*) and the Division Location table (*tblDivisionLocation*). This will ensure that a division in the table *tblDivisionLocation* cannot be deleted until all employees (*tblEmployee*) have been reassigned to a new division or first removed completely.

EXERCISE 4.7: ESTABLISHING REFERENTIAL INTEGRITY

1. Close all windows except the Database window.
2. Click Tools on the menu bar, and then click Relationships. The Relationships window opens. It may appear empty initially.
3. Click Relationships on the menu bar, and then click Show Table (or click the Show Table button on the toolbar). A Show Table dialog box opens.
4. Click the Tables tab in the Show Table dialog box, if necessary.
5. Double-click the *tblEmployee* table to add it to the Relationships window (see Figure 4.8).
6. Click *tblDivisionLocation*, click the Add button to display that table's field roster in the Relationships window, and then click the Close button in the Show Table dialog box to close it. (You may want to drag the bottom border of *tblEmployee* to reveal all of its attributes. Drag the right border of *tblEmployee* to reveal the longer field names.)
7. In the Relationships window, click the DivisionID field in *tblDivisionLocation*, and drag and drop the field onto the EmployeeDivisionID field in *tblEmployee* (see Figure 4.9).

Tables tab

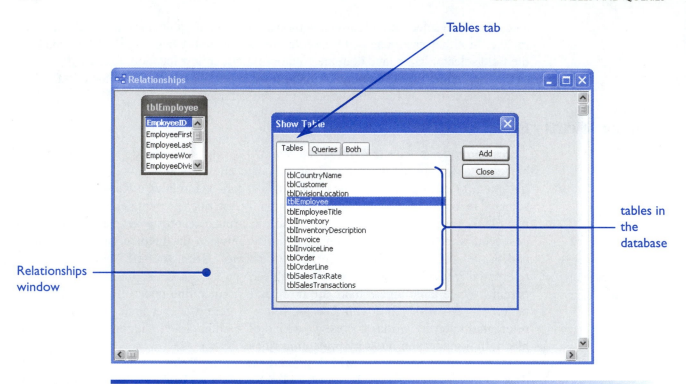

Relationships window

tables in the database

Figure 4.8 Show Table dialog box.

8. Click the Enforce Referential Integrity check box to place a check mark in the check box (see Figure 4.10).
9. Click the Create button to establish referential integrity between the two tables.
10. Finally, click the Relationships window Close button, and click Yes when asked "Do you want to save changes to the layout of 'Relationships'?" This preserves the newly established relationship and the referential integrity constraint.

Figure 4.11 shows the Relationships dialog box before you close it. On one end of the line connecting the two tables' field rosters is the number *1*, which indicates the primary key side of the relationship. On the other end of the line is the infinity symbol, which indicates the foreign key side of the relationship. The infinity symbol means that several records can be related to a single record in the "parent" table.

When you join two tables in the Relationships window as illustrated here, their Datasheet view is slightly different from the way it appears before the tables are joined. A new column called the *expand indicator* appears in the first column of each table that is explicitly linked to another table. The indicator displays either a plus sign (+) or minus sign (-). When viewing a linked table in Datasheet view, you can click the expand indicator attached to any row to view any related records. The next exercise illustrates how to view related records in the *tblEmployee* and *tblDivisionLocation* tables.

click and drag the DivisionID field
to the foreign key in *tblEmployee*

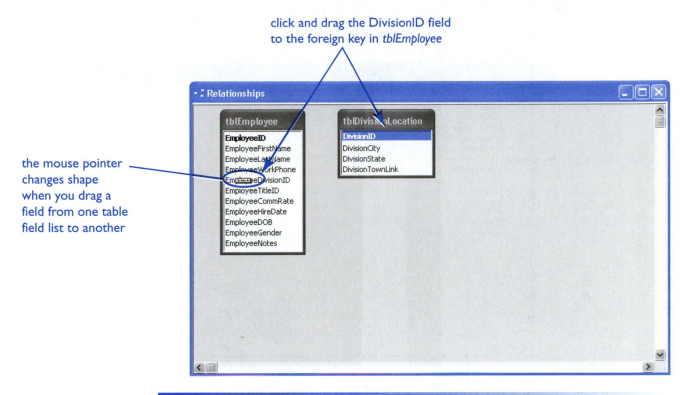

the mouse pointer
changes shape
when you drag a
field from one table
field list to another

Figure 4.9 Establishing a link between related tables.

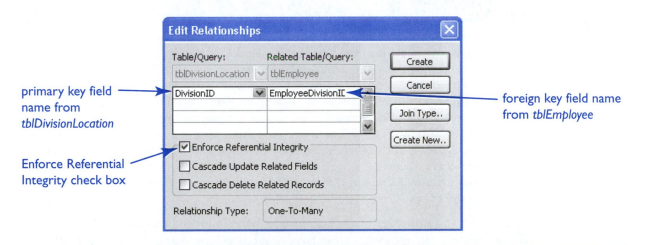

primary key field
name from
tblDivisionLocation

foreign key field name
from *tblEmployee*

Enforce Referential
Integrity check box

Figure 4.10 Enforcing Referential Integrity.

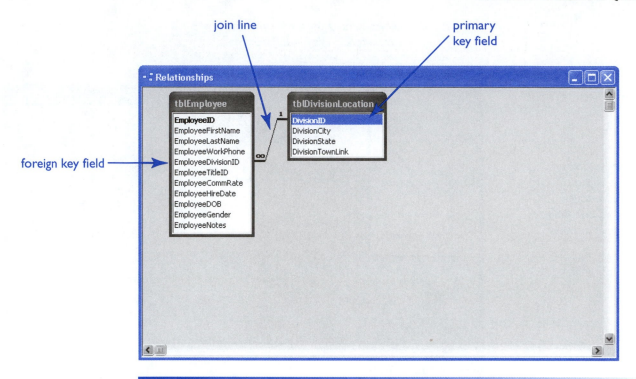

Figure 4.11   A join line connects two tables.

EXERCISE 4.8: DISPLAYING RELATED TABLES WITH THE EXPAND INDICATOR

1. With the *Ch04.mdb* open, close all windows except the Database window.
2. Select Tables from the Database Objects bar, and double-click *tblDivisionLocation* to open it. The table opens in Datasheet view (the default view when you double-click a table name).
3. Click the expand indicator of the first *tblDivisionLocation* row, which corresponds to DivisionID 101. A portion of the Employee table opens, revealing which employees work in that division (see Figure 4.12). Notice that the expand indicator, normally a plus sign, changes to a minus sign. The minus sign indicates that the related table rows are open. Of course, if no rows are related to the row whose expand indicator you clicked, then no related *tblEmployee* rows are displayed.
4. After you examine the results, click the *tblDivisionLocation* expand indicator to close the rows of *tblEmployee*.

Any table rows revealed after clicking an expand indicator are called a *subdatasheet*. Not all rows in *tblDivisionLocation* have a subdatasheet. For example, no employees are currently working at the Knoxville, Tennessee, plant. You can add rows to subdatasheets that are open by simply entering data in the open row at the end of the table—next to the new row indicator. If you add a row to the *tblEmployee* table subdatasheet, Access automatically fills in the foreign key field value for EmployeeDivisionID—the value that corresponds to that group of related rows.

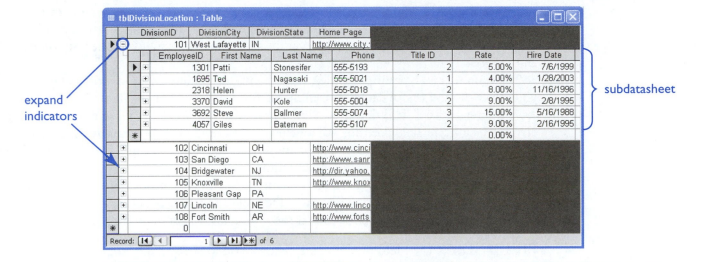

Figure 4.12 Clicking the expand indicator reveals related records.

TRY IT

Click the expand indicator corresponding to Knoxville in *tblDivisionLocation*. An empty row appears. This indicates that no employee currently is assigned to that location.

Editing and Removing Intertable Relationships

You can remove or edit an existing relationship between pairs of tables by following a procedure similar to the preceding one. For example, you can remove referential integrity checks between *tblEmployee* and *tblDivisionLocation* by opening the Relationships window, right-clicking the line connecting the two tables, selecting Edit Relationship, and clearing the Enforce Referential Integrity check box. This modifies the relationship between the tables but does not remove it. To remove a relationship, open the Relationships window (choose Relationships from the Tools menu), click the line that connects the two tables, and then press the Delete key. Similarly, you can right-click the line connecting the tables and select Delete from the pop-up menu that appears. In either case, the connecting line disappears along with the explicit relationship definition. Whenever you change a relationship by editing or removing it, be sure to select Save from the File menu to preserve the relationship changes.

Setting Field Properties

You can customize each field of a table by setting its specific properties. Each field has property settings that affect the way the field looks and behaves—in the table and in other classes of objects such as queries, forms and reports. These property settings appear in the Field Properties panel, which is visible when you display a table in Design view (see Figure 4.6). When you set one or more properties for a particular field, Access enforces those properties wherever the field appears—including queries, forms, and reports.

The number and type of properties vary slightly depending on the field's data type you select. A field whose data type is numeric, for instance, has a Decimal Places property, whereas a Text field does not. Similarly, a text type field has a Field Size property, but a data type field does not. All together, there are 45 distinct properties available. We will discuss a few of the most important properties here. You can learn about other field properties by pressing F1 to obtain online help.

Next, you will learn about several important properties. We present these in the same order as they appear from top to bottom in the Field Properties panel. After we explain key properties, we present exercises that show you how to set Field Properties values.

FIELD SIZE. The Field Size property allows you to specify the length of text and number fields. Text fields can be from 0 through 255 characters long. The default Field Size for text fields is 50. Number fields have sizes varying from a single-byte integer (Byte) to two integer sizes (Integer or Long Integer) and have two floating point number sizes (Single or Double). The size of a text field limits how much information you can enter. Specifying a numeric field size restricts fields to a particular magnitude and to either integer numbers or real numbers (numbers containing decimal places). Data sizes that exceed the maximum length of any data in the column do not waste space. Access does not keep unused space in the database. For example, you can set the Field Size of a text field to 20 characters to limit how much a user can type. If the longest value in that text field is, in fact, only 12 characters, Access compresses the text column so it has no extra, unused spaces—eight spaces in this example.

FORMAT. You can use the Format property to customize the way numbers, dates, times, and text appear when they are printed or displayed. For example, you can set the EmployeeCommRate (employees' commission rates) Format property to percent and the Decimal Places property to 2 so that a value such as 0.057 will be displayed as 5.70% in the tables, queries, forms, or reports—wherever the field is referenced. The Format property uses different settings for different data types. Consult Access help for details about the several format choices.

INPUT MASK. The Input Mask property makes data entry easier and allows you to control the values that users can enter. For example, an Input Mask for a date field can indicate exactly what you expect the user to enter and prevent all keystrokes except digits: __/__/__. It is frequently easier to use the Input Mask Wizard to help you create an Input Mask.

CAPTION. The Caption property provides an alternative field name—an alias—that appears in various views. Field captions specify the heading for the field in a table's Datasheet view or a query's Datasheet view. When a field appears in a report or form, the table's caption appears as the field's label. The Caption property is a string expression that can contain up to 2,048 characters. If you do not specify the Caption property value, then the table's Field Name appears wherever the field is referenced.

DEFAULT VALUE. The Default Value property specifies a value that is automatically entered in a field when you create a new record. For example, if you are entering the names and addresses of members of your Chicago area club or organization, you can set the default value for the City field to Chicago. When anyone adds a new record to the table, "Chicago" automatically appears in the City field. You can either accept this value or enter the name of a different city. Set the Default Value property whenever you can identify a field whose contents are often a particular value.

VALIDATION RULE AND VALIDATION TEXT. The Indexed property has the value of Yes or No. When a field's Index property is Yes, Access performs a special operation on that field—called *generating an index*—to speed up searches on the field. Fields that have an Index property value of No do not have associated indexes. While access can search any nonindexed field, search operations on indexed fields are much faster. Primary key fields are always indexed. You might want to index a Last-Name field of a table if you anticipate frequent searches by last name. In a small table, there is no noticeable difference between indexed and nonindexed field searches. In large tables—tables with 50,000 rows for instance—the search times between indexed and nonindexed fields is significant.

To illustrate how to set properties, you will set the field properties of two fields of the *tblEmployee* table. The fields are EmployeeWorkPhone and EmployeeCommRate. The employee phone numbers should be restricted to seven digits (assume the phones are all on a corporate system in which you can call any division without first entering a telephone area code). Furthermore, you want the hyphen between the first three digits and the last four digits inserted automatically. That will save time whenever anyone enters a telephone number and will ensure that the hyphen is placed in the correct position. The caption "Phone" is better than the default column name that is displayed: "EmployeeWorkPhone." So you will set the EmployeeWorkPhone field Caption property to display a more concise field name.

You will make several property changes to the commission rate field, which is called EmployeeCommRate. The commission rate is a small number, so you will indicate that its field size is single to accommodate small numbers with decimal places. Set the format so that the commission rate is displayed in percentage format with two decimal places. For example, the value 0.0895 displays as 8.95% in Datasheet view. You will change the Caption property so that the commission rate column displays the heading "Rate" instead of the default and awkward heading "EmployeeCommRate," the column's field name. New employees and management personnel earn no commission, so you want to set the default value for the commission field to zero percent. Lastly, you will establish a valid range of commission rates so that no one can mistakenly enter an unreasonable commission rate such as 45 percent. A Validation Rule will validate all newly entered commission rates, and an appropriate Validation Text message will display when the commission rate is invalid.

EXERCISE 4.9: SETTING FIELD PROPERTIES FOR THE EMPLOYEEWORKPHONE FIELD

1. Ensure that *Ch04.mdb* is open, and close all windows except the Database window. Open the table *tblEmployee* in Design view.
2. Click anywhere in the EmployeeWorkPhone row, and then press F6 (a shortcut) to move to the Field Size property in the Field Properties panel.
3. Type **7** in the Field Size property.
4. Click in the Input Mask field, and type **000\-0000;1;_** (three zeroes, a backslash, a hyphen, four zeroes, a semicolon, the digit 1, another semicolon, and an underline character). We explain these symbols following the exercise.
5. Click in the Caption property, and type **Phone**
6. Click File on the menu bar, and then click Save (or click the Save button on the Table Design toolbar). A warning dialog box opens and displays the ominous message "Some data may be lost."
7. Click the Yes button in the dialog box. No data will be lost.
8. Close the Design view window.

The Input Mask property symbols require some explanation. The zeroes in the Input Mask mean that a digit is required in the given mask-digit position. A backslash indicates that the character that follows the backslash, a hyphen in this case, is a literal character and not an operator such as subtraction. The first semicolon ends the first part of the Input Mask. The value 1 between the semicolons indicates that the hyphen in any phone number a user may enter will not be stored in the field—only the seven digits of the phone number. The second semicolon ends the second part of the Input Mask. Finally, the third part of the Input Mask, the underline character, specifies the character that Access displays for the location where an end user should type a character. In other words, an underline appears in the Phone field wherever no digits appear.

TRY IT

To see how the Phone field mask operates, open *tblEmployee* in Datasheet view. Then, drag across the digits of the Phone field of any employee, and press Delete to erase the current phone number. Notice that the Phone field displays a series of underlines separated by a hyphen. Next, type **5557777** (without entering a hyphen). Notice that the digits 555 are placed before the hyphen and the remaining four digits are placed after the hyphen. Close the Datasheet view window.

EXERCISE 4.10: SETTING FIELD PROPERTIES FOR THE EMPLOYEE COMMISSION FIELD

1. Open *tblEmployee* in Design view, and click in any column of the EmployeeCommRate row.
2. Press F6 to move to the Field Size property in the Field Properties panel.
3. Click the Field Size drop-down list arrow, and click Single.

4. Click the Format property, then click its drop-down list arrow, and click Percent.
5. Click the Decimal Places property, drag the mouse to select the current entry, and type **2** to designate two decimal places.
6. Click the Caption property, and type **Rate**. Observe the comment in the right portion of the Field Properties panel. It has helpful information about the selected property.
7. Click the Default Value property, and type **0**
8. Click the Validation Rule property, and type **between 0 and 0.15** to specify the (inclusive) range of valid commission rates. Be sure the second value is 0.15, not 15. A value of 15 means 1500 percent.
9. Click the Validation Text property, and type **Commission rates range from 0% to 15%**, the message that is displayed when a new, invalid commission rate is entered. Figure 4.13 shows *tblEmployee* in Design view and the new properties you set in this exercise.
10. Click File, and then click Save. A dialog box opens and displays a warning indicating that data integrity rules have been changed and that existing data may not be valid. Click No to by-pass the validity check for existing data. The warning occurs because you have established criteria for the commission rate field—criteria that were not in place when some records were entered. Access recognizes that existing commission data may fall outside the accept-able range. We know the data are fine.
11. Click View on the menu bar, and then click Datasheet View. Notice the Rate caption, ap-pearing in place of the field name EmployeeCommRate. Observe that the commissions are formatted with a percentage sign and two decimal places.
12. Close the Datasheet View window.

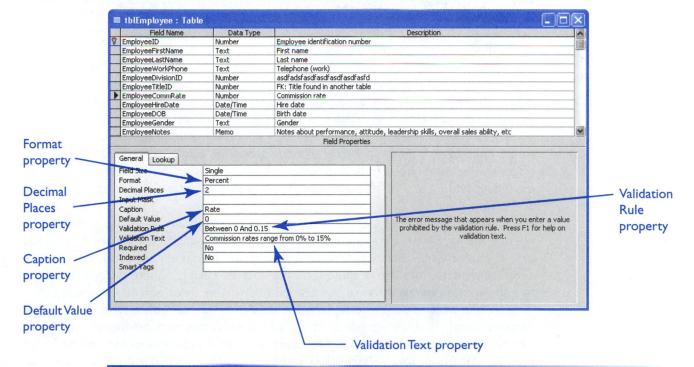

Figure 4.13 Setting *tblEmployee* field properties.

TRY IT

Open *tblEmployee* in Datasheet view. Go to the bottom of *tblEmployee* in Datasheet view, and enter the new EmployeeID number, **4567**, in the empty row, and press Tab to move to the next column. Continue entering information in the column and pressing Tab to move to a new column of the row. When you reach the Rate column, type **0.55** and press Tab. What happens? Type the valid commission rate, **12%**. Move to a new row to post the new employee row to the table. Then, click in any field in the row you just added, and press the Delete Record button on the Table Datasheet toolbar. Click Yes when the dialog box appears to confirm the record-delete operation. Close the Datasheet view window.

Be careful whenever you set both a field's Default and Validation Rule properties. They can come into conflict with each other if you aren't careful. For instance, suppose you set the default value of a field to 2 and subsequently type the Validation Rule Between 3 And 25. Clearly, the default value is not in the range of allowed values set forth by the Validation Rule property. That conflict can occur inadvertently when you skip the field and Access attempts to insert the default value, 2, into the field—violating the Validation Rule.

CREATING AND USING QUERIES

A database's ability to retrieve selected rows and columns from tables lies at the heart of its information retrieval ability. Managers seeking information about employees can retrieve rows and columns from an employee table, but information gathering would be limited if retrieval was restricted to a single table. Without the ability to select which rows are retrieved and without the ability to select information from multiple, related tables, a database's retrieval capabilities would be no better than those of a flat file system. Further, suppose someone wants to display an entire customer table in an attempt to locate all customers from Idaho, or inventory items supplied by manufacturers from California or Oregon. Manually scanning a list for candidate table rows satisfying those criteria would be time-consuming, frustrating, and error-prone.

There are two general classes of queries you can use: action queries and selection queries. *Action queries* are queries that allow you to change, insert, create, or delete sets of data in your database. *Selection queries* are queries that allow you to retrieve and display data from one or more tables or queries. Chapter 2 introduced you briefly to both of these query types. In this section, we will focus on selection queries.

Selection queries pose questions to the database. Unlike tables, which hold information, queries actively search specified tables and return answers to your questions. For instance, you can use a query to return a list of all employees in the San Diego branch office in order by department and last name within department. A query can be used to list all invoices that are over 30 days past due. Although you can accomplish a lot with datasheets—including sorting, updating, filtering, and printing—you will quickly find that manually manipulating a table's Datasheet view is restrictive.

Queries provide you with a convenient way to filter, sort, and manipulate data. Furthermore, you can store the query so that you can repeat the operations on one or more tables. For instance, you can create a query to examine an airline reservation system's database and return the names of passengers on TWA Flight 711 from Memphis to Los Angeles. By creating a query to perform the actions of searching the flight data, extracting passengers' names for a particular flight, and sorting them in name order, you automate the multistep information retrieval process. When you run the stored query next week, the same query (a stored definition) returns a completely new result. The result is called a *dynaset*, which is a temporary table. Called a *closed set,* relational database queries examine, on input, tables and then produce, as output, a table-structured result.

Relational database systems differ in how they deliver a query facility to users. Some systems use a widely accepted RDBMS interface language called *Structured Query Language (SQL)*. Other systems use an interface called *Query by Example (QBE)*. Microsoft Access provides both, but most people use QBE because it is both easier to learn and straightforward to use.

Perhaps the most important feature of queries is their ability to join tables together. Related tables can be linked in a query. Then, you can apply selection criteria to eliminate unwanted data and sort it on any number of fields. For example, suppose you wanted to query The Coffee Merchant tables. You might write a query to list the names and addresses of all customers whose invoices are more than 30 days past due. Two tables, *tblCustomer* and *tblInvoice*, are joined on their linking fields—their CustomerID column. The query's selection criteria limit retrieved rows to those whose InvoiceDate value is more than 30 days ago.

Building queries is not difficult. Here is an overview of the steps. This chapter provides you with a lot of practice using these steps to build actual queries to retrieve information. The steps to creating and saving a database query are:

- Click Queries in the Objects bar of the Database window, and then click New.
- Click Design view from the list, and then click OK.
- Add the table(s) to be included in the query.
- Drag the fields you want returned in the dynaset to the QBE grid.
- Enter selection criteria so that Access returns only rows that match the criteria.
- Open the query in Datasheet view to see the query's results.
- Select Design view, if necessary, to revise the query to achieve the results you want.
- Save the query if you want to rerun it later.

When you build queries involving more than one table, you follow the same basic steps outlined above except that you select additional tables for the query design. You cannot select arbitrary tables to form a query. Selected tables must be related to one another. You can either indicate the relation of one table to another as you design the query, or you can establish a more permanent relationship between tables in the Relationships window.

Before continuing, look at all the table relationships already established for your Ch04 database. Figure 4.14 shows nearly all the tables in your database and the relationship between each pair. Take a moment to study the figure.

Tables related to one another contain a line that connects the primary key of one table to a foreign key of the related table. For all tables in *Ch04.mdb,* the relationships are one-to-many (1–M). For example, *tblCustomer* (upper left corner of Figure 4.14) is on the "one side" of a one-to-many relationship with *tblInvoice*. That means that for each customer record in the Customer table, there may be zero, one, or several related customer invoice records. The line connecting the tables indicates the "one" side of the relationship with the digit 1 above the line next to the primary key. Similarly, Access displays the symbol for infinity to indicate the "many" side of the relationship next to the table's foreign key. Of course, any given table may be related to several other tables in the database. For example, *tblEmployee* has established relationships with four other tables, including *tblDivisionLocation* and *tblEmployeeTitle*. You must explicitly establish any relationships between tables yourself. You must either create a relationship in the Relationships window where relationships persist when you create new queries, or you must create the relationship each time you create a query. Unless the name of a primary key in one table is spelled the same as the foreign key of another, Access will not automatically forge a relationship between table pairs.

We introduce queries by starting with a single-table query—a query whose data are retrieved from one table. Then, you will build more complex queries involving some

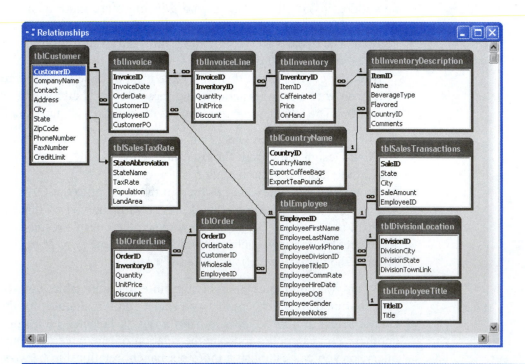

Figure 4.14 Relationships among tables.

rows and some columns of a single table. Finally, you will build queries that draw data from many related tables.

Retrieving Selected Rows from a Table

A query is the best way to extract a select group of records from a large table. A one-table query is easy to construct, and it reduces the list you look at to a manageable size. We will illustrate a one-table query with the *tblInventoryDescription* table. It contains several important product descriptors including the beverage type (the allowed values are only *c* or *t*, which stand for coffee and tea) and whether or not the coffee or tea is flavored (yes/no). Other descriptors include the country of origin (an identification number pointing to the *tblCountryName* table) and lively comments about the particular coffee bean or tea leaf. Figure 4.15 shows some of the rows of the Inventory Description table.

Inventories without quantity or back-order values for each inventory item are not very helpful. A related table, *tblInventory*, holds additional inventory information such as unit price and quantity in stock (see Figure 4.14). Together, the *tblInventory* and *tblInventoryDescription* tables supply all the inventory information for our small example. The two tables have a one-to-many relationship because each coffee listed in the *tblInventoryDescription* (for example, Jamaican Blue Mountain) can have both decaffeinated and caffeinated choices. In reality, the "many" side of the relationship,

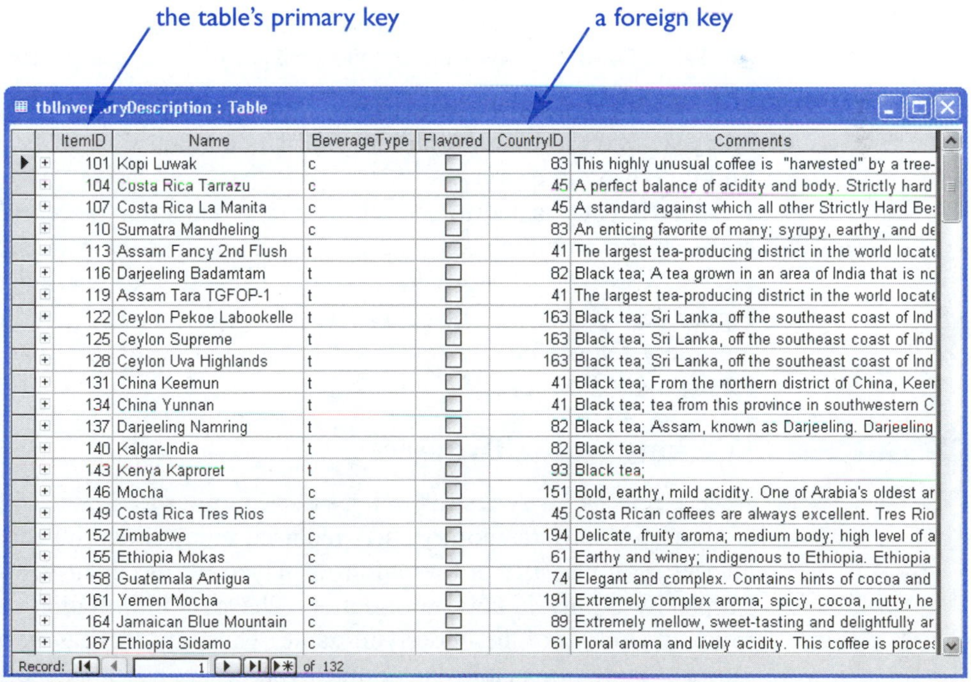

	ItemID	Name	BeverageType	Flavored	CountryID	Comments
+	101	Kopi Luwak	c	☐	83	This highly unusual coffee is "harvested" by a tree-
+	104	Costa Rica Tarrazu	c	☐	45	A perfect balance of acidity and body. Strictly hard
+	107	Costa Rica La Manita	c	☐	45	A standard against which all other Strictly Hard Be:
+	110	Sumatra Mandheling	c	☐	83	An enticing favorite of many; syrupy, earthy, and de
+	113	Assam Fancy 2nd Flush	t	☐	41	The largest tea-producing district in the world locate
+	116	Darjeeling Badamtam	t	☐	82	Black tea; A tea grown in an area of India that is nc
+	119	Assam Tara TGFOP-1	t	☐	41	The largest tea-producing district in the world locate
+	122	Ceylon Pekoe Labookelle	t	☐	163	Black tea; Sri Lanka, off the southeast coast of Ind
+	125	Ceylon Supreme	t	☐	163	Black tea; Sri Lanka, off the southeast coast of Ind
+	128	Ceylon Uva Highlands	t	☐	163	Black tea; Sri Lanka, off the southeast coast of Ind
+	131	China Keemun	t	☐	41	Black tea; From the northern district of China, Keer
+	134	China Yunnan	t	☐	41	Black tea; tea from this province in southwestern C
+	137	Darjeeling Namring	t	☐	82	Black tea; Assam, known as Darjeeling. Darjeeling
+	140	Kalgar-India	t	☐	82	Black tea;
+	143	Kenya Kaproret	t	☐	93	Black tea;
+	146	Mocha	c	☐	151	Bold, earthy, mild acidity. One of Arabia's oldest ar
+	149	Costa Rica Tres Rios	c	☐	45	Costa Rican coffees are always excellent. Tres Rio
+	152	Zimbabwe	c	☐	194	Delicate, fruity aroma; medium body; high level of a
+	155	Ethiopia Mokas	c	☐	61	Earthy and winey; indigenous to Ethiopia. Ethiopia
+	158	Guatemala Antigua	c	☐	74	Elegant and complex. Contains hints of cocoa and
+	161	Yemen Mocha	c	☐	191	Extremely complex aroma; spicy, cocoa, nutty, he
+	164	Jamaican Blue Mountain	c	☐	89	Extremely mellow, sweet-tasting and delightfully ar
+	167	Ethiopia Sidamo	c	☐	61	Floral aroma and lively acidity. This coffee is proce:

Figure 4.15 Some rows of the *tblInventoryDescription* table.

tblInventory, has at most two entries for every named coffee or tea. When necessary, we join the two tables on their common fields—both named ItemID in this case.

Next, you will create a simple query to locate and display all unflavored coffees whose beans are described as "hard bean" in the inventory. Hard bean coffees are grown at higher altitudes than others and generally yield a better coffee.

EXERCISE 4.11: CREATING A ONE-TABLE QUERY

1. Close all open windows except the Database window. In the Database window, click Queries in the Objects bar, and then click the New button on the Database window.
2. Select Design View from the list, and then click OK. (It is often easier to create queries without the Query Wizard.)
3. Double-click the *tblInventoryDescription* table from the list presented in the Show Table dialog box, and click the Close button.
4. Drag the fields ItemID, Name, Comments, BeverageType, and Flavored from the *tblInventory Description* field roster to the first through fifth cells in the Field row of the QBE grid.
5. Clear the Show check boxes under BeverageType and Flavored in the QBE grid, because you do not want to display these fields in the result—they are in the query so we can use them to specify criteria.
6. Enter three selection criteria in the Criteria row:
   - under the Comments column, type **Like "*hard bean*"** (including the quotation marks and asterisks at both ends of the string),
   - under the BeverageType column, type **"c"** (with the quotation marks),
   - and under the Flavored column, type **no** (letter case does not matter, but do not place quotation marks around this criterion or any other Yes/No criterion).
7. Select Datasheet view from the View menu to see the query results (dynaset).

Your dynaset should look like the one shown in Figure 4.16. We have saved this query as *qryHardBeanCoffee* on your Companion CD, so you need not save yours. Simply close the query.

What if you wanted to see all inventory items that were either not flavored or are coffees? We would place one criterion on one Criteria row and the other criterion on the "or" row below the previous criteria. (This type of query is a classic OR question.) Figure 4.17 shows the OR query and part of the result. As indicated in the status line, the query returned many rows—all unflavored beverages (tea or coffee) and all coffees (flavored or not).

Working with a Dynaset

Access returns query results in a dynaset. Similar to a table in behavior and structure, a dynaset is only temporary. It is replaced every time you rerun the query. For most queries, you can alter information displayed by the dynaset while in Datasheet view simply by typing in new information. The new information replaces the appropriate row and column of the underlying table. Thus, most dynasets present live, updateable views of underlying table data. Some dynasets are not updateable, and Access will warn you when you attempt to update data through one of the nonupdateable dynasets. Most of the dynasets presented in this textbook are updateable.

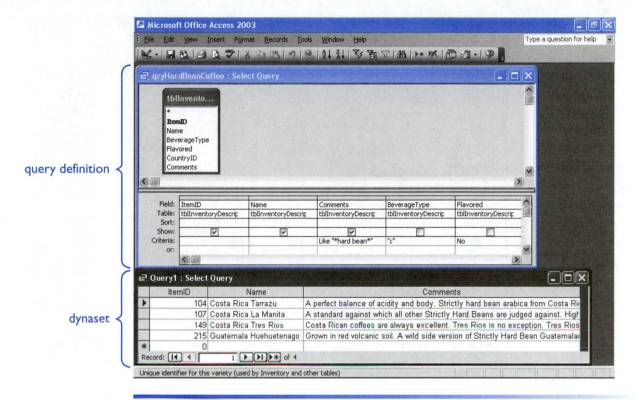

Figure 4.16 One-table query and dynaset.

You can alter the appearance of the dynaset so that the rows are arranged differently, the columns are displayed in a different order, or the columns are formatted in a special way. The next section illustrates how easy it is to make changes to the dynaset.

PRODUCING SORTED QUERY RESULTS. Suppose you want to rearrange dynaset rows so they are displayed in a more useful form. For instance, the list of coffees and teas shown in Figure 4.15 would be easier to use if it appeared in name order. Sorting dynasets is easy. Normally, Access displays dynaset records in ascending order on the table's primary key, if it has one, whether or not the primary key is displayed in the dynaset. Creating a query to sort data in other ways is particularly useful. For example, a list of employees in order by their last and first names is particularly handy when you want to look up someone on a printed list. For example, suppose you want to list all flavored teas in stock in order by their names. First, you would construct a one-table query based on the *tblInventoryDescription* table. In the QBE Field row, you might include the fields ItemID, Name, Flavored, and BeverageType. Only ItemID and Name would have their Show check boxes marked. Flavored and BeverageType would contain the criteria values *Yes* and *t*, respectively, to retrieve only flavored teas (both criteria must be met). How about the sorting part of it? Follow along in the Try It that follows to find out.

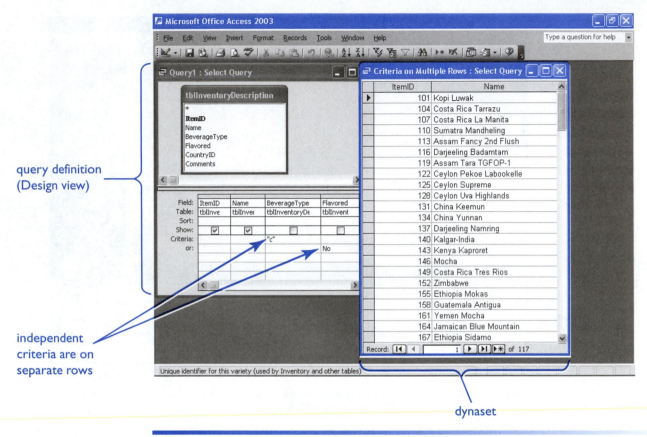

query definition (Design view)

independent criteria are on separate rows

dynaset

Figure 4.17   Query with multiple, independent criteria.

TRY IT

Open in Design view the query *qryFlavoredTea*, which selects flavored teas and displays them in a dynaset. To sort the dynaset results by Name, click the Sort row under the Name column—the attribute by which you want the rows sorted—and click Ascending from the drop-down list. Select Datasheet view from the View menu to see the dynaset. Notice that the rows are in Name order beginning with Apricot and ending with Vanilla with Vanilla Bean. Close the query, but do not save changes to it when prompted.

You can specify a sort order for more than one column. Access sorts by the leftmost field first, followed by the next sort field to the right, and so on. Therefore, you should arrange the columns you want to sort, relative each other, from left to right in the QBE grid. Note that the sort columns do not have to be the first group of columns in the QBE grid. You can sort by fields whose Show check box is cleared and thus does not appear, though the reasons may seem obscure at this point. We will explain later why this may be necessary.

ALTERING THE ORDER AND SIZE OF COLUMNS. You can alter the order of the dynaset columns. The dynaset columns' order is established by the query. For instance, the first field whose Show box is checked in the QBE grid is the first column in the dynaset, but you can alter the dynaset's column order either by altering the query's design or by altering the dynaset's column ordering after Access displays the dynaset. The former method is the best way.

To rearrange query columns, display the query in Design view and move the mouse pointer to the column selector of the field to be moved. (The column selector is the area just above the field name.) When the mouse pointer is on the column selector, it turns to a down-pointing arrow. Click the column. The entire column is darkened, indicating you have selected it. (Be careful not to move the mouse.) Release the mouse but keep it poised over the column selector. Next, click and drag the highlighted column to its new location. A rectangle appears below the pointer, indicating you are about to move the column, and a vertical bar appears as you drag the column, indicating where the column would reside if you were to release the mouse. Release the mouse when the column is in its new location. Columns to the right of the vertical bar move to the right, making room for the new column to be dropped in place.

You can enlarge individual columns by moving to the column selector area of a column and hover the mouse over the right side of the column selector. When the mouse changes from a down-pointing arrow to a double-headed arrow, click and drag the right edge to the right to enlarge the column, or drag it to the left to shrink the column.

You can change both column order and column size in the dynaset—after Access executes a query. When the query results appear, you can move columns or change their size following the procedures outlined in the preceding paragraphs. You can move the cursor to a dynaset column, select Format on the menu bar, and then click Column Width. The Column Width dialog box appears (see Figure 4.18). Click the Best Fit

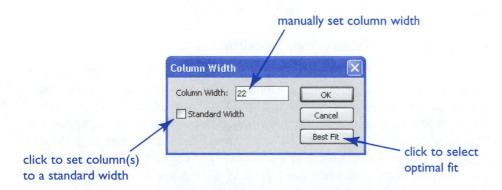

Figure 4.18 Column Width dialog box.

button to size the column so it is just wide enough for the widest entry. (The shortcut for Best Fit is to move the cursor to the right edge of the column selector and then double-click the pointer after it changes to a double-headed arrow.) You can also size multiple columns at once. Drag the mouse across all the column selectors to select multiple contiguous columns. Move the mouse to the right column line of any one of the selected columns. When it changes to a double-headed arrow, double-click the pointer to optimize the column width.

ALTERING COLUMN DISPLAY PROPERTIES. Like other dynaset characteristics, column display formats can also be changed. First, display the query in Design view. Then, move the mouse to the Field row in the QBE grid of the column whose format you want to change. When you right-click a column, a pop-up menu displays several choices. Click the Properties selection to open the Field Properties dialog box. You can experiment with changing characteristics such as format. For instance, try changing the format of the ItemID dynaset column so that the data are displayed in Currency format. After you are done experimenting, there is no need to save the altered query.

Saving a Query and Printing Dynasets

SAVING A QUERY. You should save queries that you anticipate using again. Save a query by clicking File and then clicking Save in either Design or Datasheet view. Access saves the query design in the database with the name you type in the Query Name text box. If you saved your query earlier, then Access saves it under its original name, replacing the older copy with the new one.

PRINTING DYNASETS. Printing query results simply means that you print the dynaset displayed in the Datasheet view. You can select the stored query name and print it, or you can open the query, view it, and print it. In either case, you click File and then click Print to print the dynaset. When the Print dialog box appears, make any adjustments to the page range, and then click OK. Note that you do not have any control over the page headers or footers. Printing tables and dynasets provide a quick and dirty output without any of the fancy features available in Access reports.

Dealing with Many-to-Many Relationships

The relationship between the *tblInvoice* and *tblInventory* tables is many-to-many (M–M). That is, any particular invoice can contain several items drawn from inventory, and any particular inventory item may be found in any number of invoices. Whenever an M–M relationship exists between two tables, you must create a relationship table. Minimally, the relationship table contains primary keys from both the *tblInvoice* and *tblInventory* tables for every item on a particular invoice and all invoices.

There are as many rows in the relationship table as there are invoice line items for all invoices. We have placed invoice lines in the *tblInvoiceLine* table (see Figure 4.14). Matching the invoice number with the InvoiceID attribute of *tblInvoiceLine* can retrieve all the items of a particular invoice. InvoiceID is the primary key of the *tblInvoice* table, whereas the attribute InventoryID in *tblInvoiceLine* is the primary key in *tblInventory*. Thus, InventoryID in *tblInvoiceLine* is a foreign key. The other attributes in the relationship table are Quantity, UnitPrice, and Discount. Quantity is the amount invoiced for a particular item on a given invoice line. UnitPrice is the price charged for this item. It can differ from the Price column stored in the *tblInventory* table. The Discount field holds the percentage discount for a line item on a particular invoice. Discounts vary from customer to customer and from one time of the year to another. The two *tblInvoiceLine* table attributes, InvoiceID and InventoryID, form a composite primary key, because they are both required to form a primary key for the relationship table called *tblInvoiceLine*.

If you encounter other tables having a many-to-many relationship, which cannot be handled easily by a RDBMS, the remedy is simple. Create a relationship table containing a composite primary key that is formed from the primary keys of the two tables having the M–M relationship—just as we have done with the *tblInvoiceLine* table. Once a relationship table is in place, then both of the original tables have a 1–M relationship with the relationship table. In other words, the relationship table provides the "glue" connecting two tables in a one-to-many relationship.

Producing Queries Involving Multiple Tables

The Coffee Merchant contains a number of normalized tables in order to avoid problems such as data redundancy and data inconsistency that occur when unnormalized tables are used. Data appear in several related tables, and the database must connect related tables to retrieve information not found in a single table. When you connect related tables, you are *joining* them. Join related tables by indicating which columns are common to the table pairs. For instance, you could join the *tblCustomer* and *tblInvoice* tables on the common column CustomerID found in each table. Although these columns have the same name, it is not necessary for a table's primary key to be named identically to another table's related foreign key. However, it is often simpler to remember the join columns by naming them identically.

JOINING RELATED TABLES. Linking two or more tables is not difficult. You connect a table's primary key to another's foreign key to explicitly indicate how tables are linked. In many cases, Access can automatically determine how tables are linked when tables to be linked (*joined* is the preferred term) have identically named fields or they have been joined permanently via the Relationships window. If Microsoft Access does not automatically create join lines for you, you can join tables manually.

You join tables manually by creating a query and adding all the related tables to the query in the Show Table dialog box. Then, you can create a join line between each table pair by selecting the primary key field in one table and dragging it to the equivalent foreign key field in the other table. Of course, you can join tables by performing the preceding actions in the Relationships window. Once you join tables in the Relationships window, you never need to do so inside individual queries. Access remembers table-to-table relationships that you create in the Relationships window until you explicitly delete them.

CREATING CONDITIONAL QUERIES. Queries containing conditions are very useful. A condition provides a way for you to specify a range of values, or minimum and maximum values, for a field. For example, suppose you would like to locate all inventory items that are back-ordered. The coffee buyer is preparing to order more coffee and tea from the ranches around the world. One of the important questions that the buyer must answer is which products are back-ordered. In The Coffee Merchant system of tables, a product is back-ordered when the OnHand field in *tblInventory* is negative. In order to make intelligent product buying decisions, the buyer needs to know the product identification number, product name, and back-order volume column values. From that listing, he or she can order the correct quantity and types of products from the various suppliers.

To answer the buyer's question, we must construct a query involving two tables that are to be joined. The tables are *tblInventory*—the Inventory master table—and *tblInventoryDescription*. We will use a special operator called a *comparison operator* to create the selection criterion in a new query. A comparison operator is a special symbol that compares one value to another. The comparison operators are shown in Figure 4.19.

Operator	Meaning
<	Less than
<=	Less than or equal to
>	Greater than
>=	Greater than or equal to
=	Equal to
<>	Not equal to
Between	Test for a range of values where two extreme values are separated by the And operator
In	Test for "equal to" any member in a list
Like	Test a text or memo field to match a pattern string

Figure 4.19 Comparison operators.

EXERCISE 4.12: CREATING A TWO-TABLE QUERY THAT USES A COMPARISON OPERATOR

1. To create a new query joining the tables *tblInventoryDescription* and *tblInventory*, click Queries on the Database window Objects bar, click New, click Design view, click OK, double-click *tblInventoryDescription*, double-click *tblInventory*, and close the Show Table dialog box. Access automatically links the tables on their common field, ItemID, because we previously defined the relationship between them in the Relationships window.

2. Drag the columns ItemID (from *tblInventory*), Name, BeverageType, and OnHand to the Field row of the QBE grid. (You can double-click field names in the field roster to automatically place them in the next available column of the Field row.)
3. Click in the Criteria row of the OnHand column and type <0 (the less than symbol followed by zero).
4. Click View, and then click Datasheet View to display the dynaset. Figure 4.20 shows both the query design and the resulting dynaset. Your screen may be arranged differently, but the dynaset should show the same rows as the figure. (This query is named *qryStockOut* on your Companion CD.)
5. After observing the result, click the Datasheet view Close button, and click No when asked if you want to save changes to the query.

USING WILDCARDS IN CRITERIA. A wildcard character allows you to find information when you are unsure of the complete spelling of an alphanumeric field. Used with the *Like* operator (see Figure 4.19), the wildcard characters define positions that can contain any single character, a single number, or zero or more characters in a

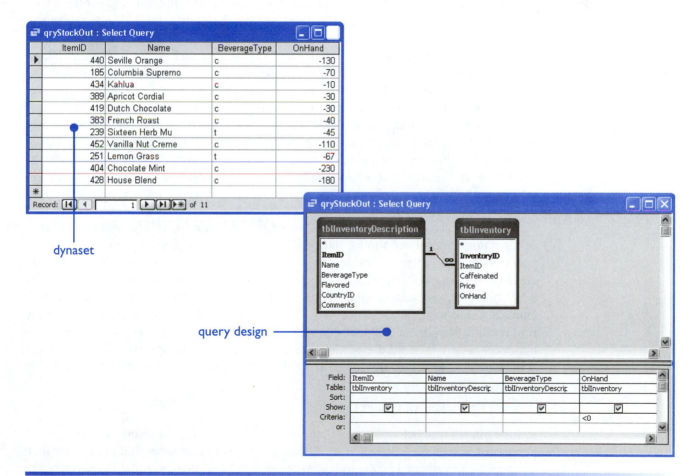

Figure 4.20 Two-table query using a comparison operator.

Wildcard Character	Meaning	Example Pattern Matches
?	Any single character	*b?lk* matches balk or bulk
*	Zero or more characters	*or* matches door, floor, and matador *or** matches ordinary, order, and organize **or** matches bored, category, and fluoride
#	Any single digit	*6#4* matches 604, 644, and 664

Figure 4.21 LIKE wildcard characters.

text string match pattern. Figure 4.21 shows the three wildcard characters available in Access. Here's an example of how you can use them. Suppose you want to check The Coffee Merchant's stock for any beverages whose name contains the word *chocolate* (for example, Dutch Chocolate). You are interested in how much is available, if any. You can use the * (asterisk) wildcard character and the partial word *choc* to return any beverages whose Name field contains *choc* anywhere within it.

The preceding query involves two tables, *tblInventory* and *tblInventoryDescription*. The key search criterion is the wildcard expression *choc*. Place this criterion in the Criteria row just below the *Name* column in the QBE grid. (After you type the preceding expression, Access automatically surrounds it with double quotation marks and precedes the entire phrase with *Like*.) The asterisk preceding *choc* indicates that any word, phrase, or character string can appear before the word—or none at all. Similarly, the asterisk following *choc* indicates that any characters may follow the word—or none at all. That is, the search criterion requests any rows in which the partial word *choc* appears anywhere within the name. Figure 4.22 shows a query and the resulting dynaset.

USING LOGICAL OPERATORS IN QUERY CRITERIA. Some other useful operators helpful in forming selection criteria are called *logical operators*. Logical operators provide a way of bonding two comparison or wildcard criteria. There are several logical operators, but the ones used most often are AND, OR, and NOT. Using the AND operator, you can specify a condition in which two criteria must be true simultaneously. For example, suppose you want to examine the invoices issued during the first week in November 2004. A temporary employee was used to process the invoices that week, and you heard that some invoices were handled incorrectly. You can use the AND operator to bound the range of invoice dates you want to inspect. Specifically, you write the criterion expression

>=#11/1/2004# And <=#11/6/2004#

in the Criteria row below InvoiceDate in the QBE grid. This selection criterion states a range of acceptable invoice dates. The range encompasses dates that are greater than or equal to November 1, 2004 *and* (simultaneously) less than or equal to November 6, 2004. (The # characters always surround dates so that Access doesn't confuse dates

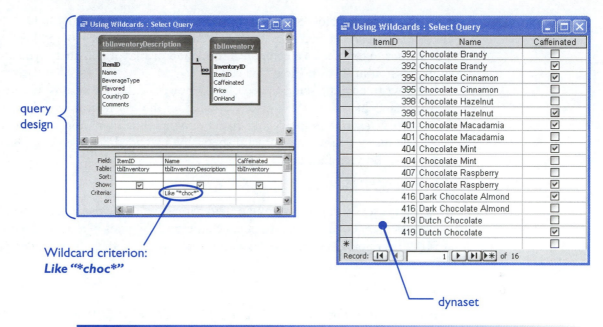

query design

Wildcard criterion:
Like "*choc*"

dynaset

Figure 4.22 Query using a wildcard in its criteria.

with arithmetic expressions.) Thus, the criterion limits rows from the Invoice table to invoices issued during the first week. An equivalent and simpler way of writing the preceding criterion using the Between comparison operator is

Between #11/1/2004# And #11/6/2004#

Any dates between or matching the two dates satisfy the criteria.

Performing Calculations with Queries

Recall that in Chapter 3 we emphasized the importance of omitting from a table any information that can be calculated or derived from other columns in the table. For instance, good database design and normalization rules preclude the inclusion of a column of extended prices in any of The Coffee Merchant's invoice tables. Because the extended price is calculated from the fields Quantity, UnitPrice, and Discount stored in *tblInvoiceLine*, it should not be stored in the table. Why? Suppose the extended price is stored in *tblInvoiceLine* along with Quantity, UnitPrice, and Discount. What if someone discovers a mistake in the Quantity or UnitPrice values in one or more invoices? Changing either renders the extended price value inaccurate. Database experts would say that the database is inconsistent.

That leads us to this question: How do you produce the extended price and other useful calculated results? One answer is that you include any calculations in a query. Access allows you to write expressions that sum, average, and count values as well as write expressions that involve the arithmetic operators, fields, summary operators (we will discuss these in the next section), numeric constants, and comparison operators.

The arithmetic operators are the familiar ones: +, -, *, and /, and you have been introduced to comparison operators. You reference other query or table fields by enclosing their names in brackets. To compute a result and display it in a query, you simply write an expression in its own Field row cell.

Let's write an expression to see exactly how to calculate results and display them in a dynaset. In the next exercise, we will join the *tblInvoiceLine*, *tblInventory*, and *tblInventoryDescription* tables and display invoice line items for invoices in the database. The query you will construct displays the extended price, among other columns, using the following formula:

[Quantity]*[UnitPrice]*(1–[Discount])

(It is always a good idea to surround field names with brackets when you include them in expressions.) For example, if someone ordered 20 pounds of a particular coffee priced at $10.00 per pound and received a discount of 5 percent, then the extended price would be:

20*10*(1–0.05)

Though the Inventory table, *tblInventory*, contains a price field, Price, for each item carried, customers may or may not be charged that suggested price. The actual price charged is stored in UnitPrice, an invoice line field (found in *tblInvoiceLine*), and may vary from one customer to the next.

EXERCISE 4.13: WRITING EXPRESSIONS IN QUERIES

1. Close all windows except the Database window.
2. Create a new query, adding the tables *tblInvoiceLine*, *tblInventory*, and *tblInventoryDescription* to it. Access will draw join lines connecting the three tables on their respective primary and foreign keys. Close the Show Table dialog box.
3. Drag the fields InvoiceID, ItemID, Name, UnitPrice, Quantity, and Discount to the first six Field row cells in the QBE grid (in the order listed).
4. Click in the Sort cell beneath the InvoiceID column in the QBE grid, click the drop-down list box arrow, and select Ascending from the drop-down list box. This will list the invoices in ascending order by invoice number.
5. Click in the seventh cell in the Field row, the first empty cell in the Field row of the QBE grid, and press Shift+F2 to open a Zoom dialog box. (A Zoom dialog box opens a larger area in which you can see the entire expression as you type it.)
6. Type the expression below. When you are done, click OK to close the Zoom dialog box, and then press Enter. Make sure that the Show check box contains a check mark.

Extended Price: [Quantity]*[UnitPrice]*(1–[Discount])

7. Right-click the cell containing the preceding expression and select Properties from the pop-up menu that appears.
8. Click Format, click the list box arrow, and then click Currency from the drop-down list (see Figure 4.23). Doing this formats the calculated expression to display the result rounded to two decimal places and includes a currency symbol and any necessary commas. Click the Format dialog box Close button to close the dialog box.

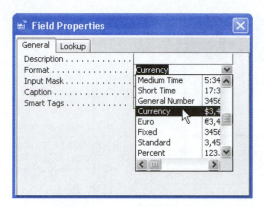

Figure 4.23 Formatting a query's calculated column.

9. Click View, and then click Datasheet View to display the dynaset (see Figure 4.24). We have saved the query as *qryExtendedPrice* on the Companion CD.

10. Close the query without saving it once you are finished examining the results.

Step 6 of Exercise 4.13 illustrates how to write a typical expression in Access. Whenever you refer to Access table field names, always enclose them in brackets to avoid confusion. *Extended Price* is an *alias* for the field. It precedes the expression and assigns it a name. To rename any column in a query, begin with the new name (it can be several words) followed by a colon and a space. Then, write the expression. If you omit an alias in an expression, Access assigns a unique, default field name such as *Expr1* or *Expr38*. Access-assigned field names are neither attractive nor informative.

Grouping and Summarizing Data

Summary information can reveal situations that are not obvious from examining detailed data. Access provides several functions that aggregate information for data groups or an entire table. Figure 4.25 lists seven of the most popular aggregate functions along with a brief description of what each function does. Of the listed functions, the most useful to anyone in the accounting profession are Avg, Count, Max, Min, and Sum.

Sometimes you will want statistics for all rows of a table or joined set of tables. At other times, however, you will need summary statistics on smaller groups of records. For instance, it may be revealing to know the total number of pounds of each type of coffee and tea ordered each month. This would disclose the more popular choices. Or, the accounts receivable department might be interested in a statistic such as the average elapsed days, by customer, between the time invoices are sent and their corresponding payments are received. When Access summarizes information for several sets of rows, that calculation involves grouping. *Grouping* information simply means forming groups of rows that share some common characteristic such as having identical values for a client name, customer identification number, invoice number, or other attribute.

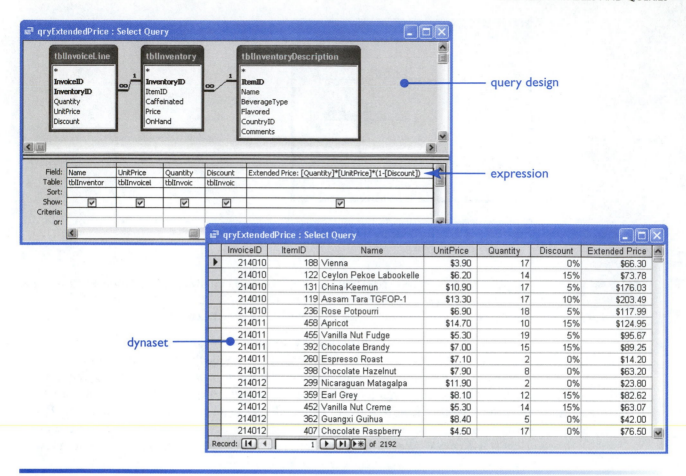

Figure 4.24 Query design and dynaset with calculated column.

The summary functions are often used in queries (but they can also be used in forms and reports). To compute an average of a numeric field in a query, simply click the Totals toolbar button. Access adds a new row to the QBE grid, called the *Total* row. When the row appears, type *Avg* in the Total row beneath the field whose values you want to average. Then, run the query. You can compute multiple summary statistics on a particular field as long as you include multiple copies of the field name in the QBE grid Field row.

In the next exercise, you will try out a summary function and learn how to meld two character fields into one field by concatenating them. Let's try some of the summary functions. You will join together three tables so that you can compute and display the total sales grouped by salespersons' names. In other words, you want to know how much each salesperson sold. The three tables involved in the query are *tblEmployee*, *tblInvoice*, and *tblInvoiceLine*. The fields required to form the query summarizing sales

Function	Meaning
Avg	Computes a field's average value (ignores null fields)
Count	Counts the number of non-null (empty) items in a field
Max	Computes largest value in a field
Min	Computes smallest non-null value in a field
Sum	Computes the total of all items in a field
StDev	Computes the standard deviation of non-null values in a field
Var	Determines the variance of non-null values in a field

Figure 4.25   Access aggregate functions.

are all found in just two tables—*tblEmployee* and *tblInvoiceLine*. However, the relationship between *tblEmployee* and *tblInvoiceLine* is many-to-many. Because Access cannot link many-to-many tables together directly, the *tblInvoice* table serves as a "bridge" table that restructures the M–M relationship into two 1–M relationships.

Whenever you want to combine text fields from a table into a single field, you simply write an expression containing the two fields separated by the symbol for ampersand, &. Suppose you want to produce a listing of employees for a telephone book listing their last name, a comma, a blank, and their first name. Combine text fields in a single cell of the Field row in a query to get the desired result. For instance, the following expression provides the required single text field:

Name: [LastName] & ", " & [FirstName]

The ampersand adds one string onto another. In this case, the previous expression is "adding" three text strings together, back to back. This is a handy tool to keep in mind whenever you need to combine disparate fields from a table into a single field in a query, report, form, or Web page.

EXERCISE 4.14: USING SUMMARY FUNCTIONS IN A QUERY

1. Click Queries on the Objects bar, and then create a new query (click Design view from the New Query dialog box), add the three tables *tblEmployee*, *tblInvoice*, and *tblInvoiceLine* to the query, and close the Show Table dialog box.
2. Select Totals from the View menu to insert in the QBE grid a new row called Total. (You can also click the Totals button on the Design view toolbar.)
3. In the first cell in the Field row enter the following expression, which combines the two name fields together, separated by a blank. Be sure to place a space between the two quotation marks.

Name: [EmployeeFirstName] & " " & [EmployeeLastName]

(You can place a blank on either side of the two ampersand symbols, but you don't have to. Access will do that for you automatically after you move to another cell in the QBE grid.)

4. Click the Show box in the first column so that a check mark appears in it. This causes the employee name you created with the preceding expression to display when you run the query.

5. In the second cell in the Field row enter the following expression to compute and display sales totals, including any discount applied for each customer.

Sales: [quantity]*[unitprice]*(1–[discount])

You may want to press Shift+F2 to produce a larger view of the cell in the Zoom dialog box. The larger display makes it easier to see the whole expression. When you are finished writing the expression in the Zoom dialog box, click OK to close the Zoom dialog box.

6. Click in the QBE grid Total row beneath the second cell—the expression you just typed— and select the Sum function from the drop-down list (click the list box to display the list of summary functions).

7. Click in the QBE grid Sort row beneath the second cell, and select Descending from the drop-down list. You want to see the sales summary sorted from highest sales total to lowest.

8. Set the format of the second cell to Currency by right-clicking the Field row cell containing the expression, clicking Properties, and then clicking Currency from the drop-down list in the Format box of the Field Properties dialog box.

9. Close the Field Properties dialog box, and select Datasheet View from the View menu to see the results. Figure 4.26 shows both the query design and its dynaset.

10. Click File, click Save, and then type **qryTotalSales** to name the new query. Click OK to complete the query save operation. Do not close the query just yet.

The dynaset calculates total sales for 19 salespersons. Switch back to the query Design view in preparation for a little experiment. Notice that Access has changed the expression in the summed column to *Sales: Sum([Quantity]*[UnitPrice]*(1–[Discount]))* and placed the word *Expression* in the Total column. Can Microsoft Access compute the grand total of all invoices that are in the database? Yes. As a matter of fact, you can make a simple change to the query you created in the preceding exercise to yield the grand total.

TRY IT

Display the previous query in Design view. Move the mouse pointer just above the Field row of the Name field (an expression) in the QBE grid. When the pointer changes to a solid, dark, down-pointing arrow, click it to select the entire Name column. Press the Delete key to delete that column. Select Datasheet View from the View menu to see the grand total of all invoices in the database. Your altered query should display a single row with the value of $176,729.37—the current total of all invoices stored in the system. Close the Datasheet view window. Click No when the dialog box displays a message asking if you want to save the query's design, because you want to preserve the original query you created above.

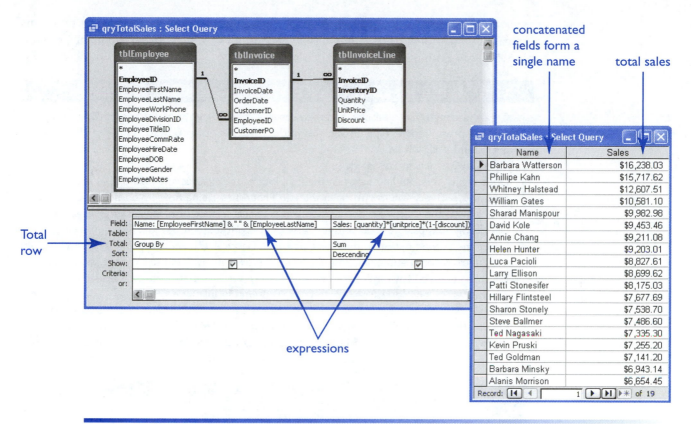

Figure 4.26 Sorted sales totals for each employee created with the Sum aggregate function.

Remember the following when using aggregate (summary) functions. Place the aggregate function in the field you want to summarize (beneath an expression in our previous example). Rename a summary column when desired by typing the new name, a colon, a space, and then the alias (name).

Using an Outer Join in a Query

When you join two tables, you may find that one or more rows in one table do not have matching rows in the other table. Revealing rows that don't match can be important. For example, a sales manager might want to know if there are any salespersons who have sold nothing during a particular period. There are other examples of hidden information in your databases. In your *Ch04.mdb* database, for example, you cannot glean which cities have no employees simply by performing a standard join of the *tblEmployee* and *tblDivisionLocation* tables on matching primary and foreign keys. Instead, you produce this kind of information by using a query that joins tables with an *outer join*, which lists *all* rows from one table and only matching rows from another table.

The next exercise shows you how to create an outer join. It uses as its starting point the query you created in Exercise 4.14 called *qryTotalSales*. You will modify the join properties for both of the existing joins to form an outer join. (The query's two joins are called *inner joins*.) The new query, when completed, will reveal the names of people who sold nothing in addition to those who did.

EXERCISE 4.15: CREATING AN OUTER JOIN QUERY

1. Create a copy of *qryTotalSales*, and then rename it by doing this: Click *qryTotalSales*, press Ctrl+C, press Ctrl+V, type *qryOuterJoin* in the Paste As dialog box to name the cloned query, and click OK.
2. Open *qryOuterJoin* in Design view.
3. Double-click the join line between the field lists of *tblEmployee* and *tblInvoice* in the upper part of the Query window to open the Join Properties dialog box. If you double-click in the wrong area, the Query Properties dialog box opens. In that case, close the Query Properties dialog box, place the tip of the mouse pointer directly on the join line, and try again.
4. Select the second option in the dialog box (see Figure 4.27), and click OK. You should now see an arrow on the join line pointing from the *tblEmployee* field list to the *tblInvoice* field list, indicating you have asked for an outer join with all records from *tblEmployee* regardless of whether or not corresponding records are found in *tblInvoice*.
5. Repeat steps 2 and 3 for the join line between the field lists of *tblInvoice* and *tblInvoiceLine*.
6. Display the query in Datasheet view, and scroll the display so you can see dynaset rows 20 through 22. Notice that the Sales column is empty for Melinda English, Giles Bateman, and

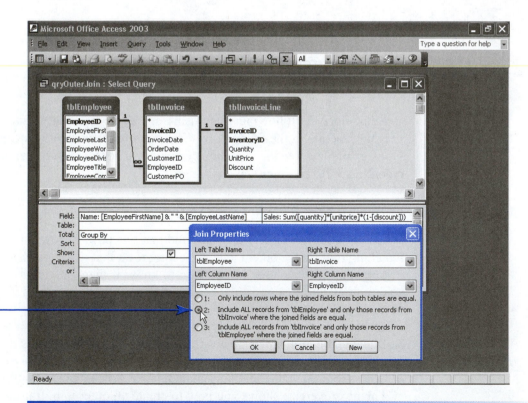

Figure 4.27 Creating an outer join.

Brad Shoenstein. That means that they have no records in the *tblInvoiceLine* table and therefore no sales for the period.

In the next step, you will tell Access to display only the rows whose total sales values are empty.

7. Display the query in Design view, move to the criteria row beneath the Sales (summed sales) column, and type **Is Null** into the Criteria cell. Display the query in Datasheet view. It displays only those employees who did not report sales for the period. Figure 4.28 shows both the query design and its dynaset.

8. Save and close the query.

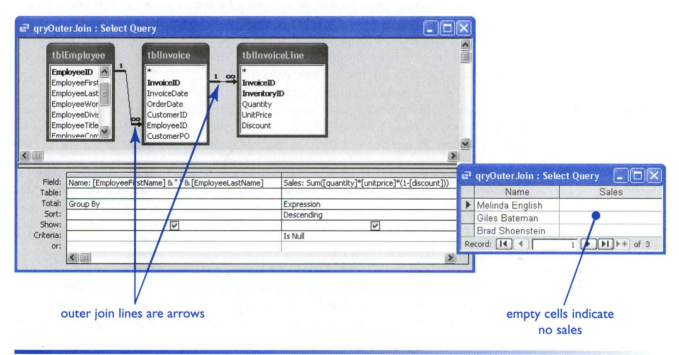

outer join lines are arrows

empty cells indicate
no sales

Figure 4.28   Using "Is Null" to display rows with empty fields.

Designing and Using a Parameter Query

So far you have examined and created queries with selection criteria directly in the design grid of the Query window. However, you can create a special type of query that allows you to specify selection criteria when you run the query. Known as a *parameter query*, it prompts you to enter the selection criteria just before running the query. The advantage of a parameter query over conventional queries is versatility. For example, you could create and run a query that lists all customers who live in Minnesota. Using the query to pass information to a report (Chapter 5), Access could create a form letter that you mail to all Minnesota residents. When the northwest sales region decides to run a similar promotion, it can revise the Minnesota query, substituting "Oregon" for "Minnesota" in the criteria row to extract those residents. Imagine creating 50 such queries simply to generate a listing for each state. Creating those queries would be time-consuming, and your database would be filled with 50 copies of a query whose basic forms are identical except for the criteria each contains.

You can create a single parameter query to replace all of the 50 individual queries. The only action required by a user running the query is to type the state name or abbreviation when prompted by Access. One query does the work of many. You can extend the use of parameter queries to an unlimited number of other accounting applications. A parameter query provides a perfect way to extract a group of invoices for varying time periods. Simply create a parameter query with two parameters—the beginning and ending dates for the billing period—and anyone can retrieve invoices from the date ranges a user enters when the query begins execution. Further, you can imagine a simple search engine query that retrieves a sales tax rate from a table when a user types the state name or state abbreviation. Simply enter the state name, and the query returns the sales tax rate for that state.

The best way to understand parameter queries is to build one. You will create a parameter query that displays a list of customers for any state that the user wishes. When anyone runs the query, he or she is prompted to enter a two-character state abbreviation. The query then retrieves addresses for customers in that state.

EXERCISE 4.16: CREATING A PARAMETER QUERY

1. With *Ch04.mdb* open, close all windows except the Database window. Click Queries in the Objects bar, click New, click Design View from the list in the New Query dialog box, Click OK, double-click *tblCustomer* to add its field roster to the query, and close the Show Table dialog box.
2. Double-click the following fields found in the field roster in this order: CompanyName, Address, City, State, and ZipCode. Access places each field in the Fields row of the QBE grid.
3. Type **[Enter a two-character state abbreviation:]** into the Criteria row in the State column. This sequence of characters, enclosed in beginning and ending brackets, defines a parameter.
4. Click View, and then click Datasheet View to test your new parameter query before you save it. An Enter Parameter Value dialog box appears.
5. Type **NE** (either upper- or lowercase is fine) in the *Enter Parameter Value* text box. This indicates you want to display addresses for Nebraska customers (see Figure 4.29). Recall that the capitalization of search strings doesn't matter. Uppercase "NE" will match table entries such as "Ne" or "nE."
6. Click OK in the Enter Parameter Value dialog box to test the query. If you constructed the query correctly, Access will display a list of 11 companies—all from Nebraska, of course (see Figure 4.30).
7. Select Save from the File menu and type *qryParameter*; then, click OK to save the query under the name you entered.
8. Close the Datasheet view window.

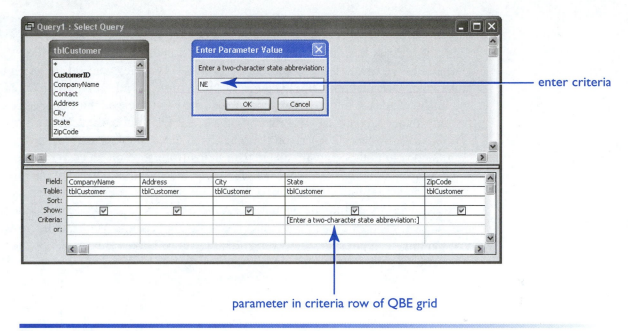

enter criteria

parameter in criteria row of QBE grid

Figure 4.29 A parameter query design and run-time prompt.

Figure 4.30 A parameter query dynaset.

Go to **http://perry.swlearning.com** for an in-depth tutorial.

SUMMARY

This chapter has described how to use Access to create tables and queries. You have learned how to create table structures, enter data into tables, and set limits on the type and size of information that one can enter into a table. In addition, you learned how to establish referential integrity between tables. We have stressed the importance of specifying primary keys when constructing tables. Tables, you learned, hold all of the data in a database system. Queries, on the other hand, access one or more tables to produce combined results that display related data fields from several tables. You know how to write and save queries that involve both single and multiple tables coupled using both equijoin and outer join connections. Queries can contain expressions comprised of comparison operators, arithmetic operators, example elements, and wildcard characters. Using queries, you can focus on the data elements important to you. Finally, you learned that parameter queries are quite versatile and can provide varied results depending on what criteria you enter when you run queries.

QUESTIONS AND PROBLEMS FOR REVIEW

Multiple-Choice Questions

1. Data are posted to a table the moment you
   a. type new data into the appropriate empty field.
   b. type data over the existing data in a field.
   c. move to another table record.
   d. none of the above.

2. The expand indicator is used to
   a. open the Field Properties panel.
   b. expand a field when editing so all the data are visible.
   c. enlarge the current window.
   d. display any related records to the current row.

3. What are the key differences between action queries and selection queries?
   a. Action queries allow you to change data, whereas selection queries allow you to view data from multiple tables or queries.
   b. Selection queries allow you to select and change data, whereas action queries allow you to only look at data.
   c. Action queries allow you to retrieve and display data from multiple tables, whereas selection queries allow you to select, create, and delete data.
   d. All of the above.

4. To build a query in Design view, you need to
   a. add the tables to be included in the query and drag the fields to be returned to the QEB.
   b. enter your selection criteria.
   c. open the query in Datasheet view to see the results.
   d. do all of the above.

5. What field property allows you to control what values users enter?
   a. Caption
   b. Default Value
   c. Indexed
   d. Input Mask

6. The results of a query are returned in what is uniquely called a
   a. datasheet.
   b. table.
   c. dynaset.
   d. page.

7. When writing expressions to perform calculations, table fields are referenced by enclosing the field name in
   a. parenthesis ().
   b. brackets [].
   c. quotes "".
   d. pound signs ##.

8. Using an _____ will list all rows from one table and only matching rows from another table.
   a. inter join
   b. intra join
   c. outer join
   d. in line join

9. What does an ampersand do in an expression?
   a. It inserts a blank.
   b. It inserts a comma.
   c. It multiplies one string with another.
   d. It adds one string to another.

10. What is the advantage of using a parameter query over conventional queries?
   a. It is more versatile.
   b. Selection criteria is specified when the query is run.
   c. It provides varied results based on criteria entered.
   d. All of the above.

Discussion Questions

1. Discuss the advantage(s) of providing a data validity check in the Validation Rule field property. What might happen if you omitted validation rules from text fields, and how could that affect the integrity of your database tables?

2. Explain why referential integrity is so important when dealing with a database, such as The Coffee Merchant's, involving several related tables. Present a scenario in which the lack of referential integrity could cause problems. Be specific.

3. Discuss the problem with storing an extended price (an invoice item quantity multiplied by an item's wholesale or retail price) in the *tblInvoiceLine* table. Why could you not simply add a column called ExtendedPrice to the Invoice Line table?

4. Discuss the advantages of an outer join query. Give an example, different from the one used in the textbook, of using an outer join to display information from two tables related in a query with an outer join. What role does the expression "Is Null" play in outer join queries?

5. Suppose the table *tblStudents* contains the first and last names of students and that *tblClassRosters* contains the list of students enrolled in each class in the university. Discuss the relationship between *tblStudents* and *tblClassRosters*. Is it 1–1, 1–M (or vice versa), or M–M? Are there any problems representing the relationship of these two tables to one another?

Practice Exercises

1. Create a query that lists all inventory items on hand that have a price greater than $15.00. Make sure the dynaset includes ItemID, Name, Price, and OnHand. Sort the results in descending order by Price. Print and write your name at the top of the dynaset.

2. Add a column representing the employee's last name to the Order table (*tblOrder*) just left of the column titled Sales Rep. No (EmployeeID). Name the column Sales Rep. Name (use the Caption property). Create a query to see if the company with CustomerID 35494 has ordered any products. Display the CustomerID, Order ID, Order Date, Sales Rep. Name, and Sales Rep. No. Print the dynaset and write your name at the top.

3. Create a query joining tables, *tblInventoryDescription* and *tblCountryName*. Display Name, BeverageType, CountryName, and Comments. Include only the countries of Brazil and Colombia. Sort by CountryName in descending order. Print the dynaset. Does either country produce a tea?

4. List all products with a negative on-hand inventory by creating a query that displays ItemID, Name, and OnHand. Make sure the results are sorted in ascending order by the OnHand value. Print the dynaset results and write your name at the top.

5. Create a query using the Customer table (*tblCustomer*) that returns the CustomerID, Contact, City, and PhoneNumber for all customers located in Birmingham, Alabama. Sort CustomerID in ascending order, save as *qryBirmingham*, and print the dynaset. Write your name at the top of the results.

Problems

1. Create and run a query that displays all employees from the Employee table (*tblEmployee*) who have the title Senior Sales Associate (*tblEmployeeTitle*). In the dynaset display only each qualifying employee's last name and gender (in that order). Sort the dynaset by gender and then by last name within gender groups. (The sort will group females and then males and then sort them by last names within each group.) Print the resulting dynaset. Remember to write your name on the output.

2. You want to examine the invoices issued in November 2003 in order by date. You are interested only in general information. To answer this question, form a query that joins The Coffee Merchant tables *tblInvoice* and *tblCustomer*. Display the company names, invoice dates, and invoice numbers (InvoiceID) for invoices issued only during the period 11/1/03 through and including 11/30/03. Sort the dynaset in ascending order by invoice date and then by company name among the same invoice dates. Print all pages. Save the query. (Figure 4.14 contains the schemas of all tables for The Coffee Merchant.)

3. Write a query that displays the five most densely populated states in the United States. Use criteria to eliminate the District of Columbia. Include in the dynaset the full state name, the abbreviated state name, and the calculated field, density. Assign the column alias Density to the population density column. Format the Density column so that it displays two decimal places. Sort the dynaset in descending order by Density. (Hints: *tblSalesTaxRate* contains state names, populations, and area—in square miles—of each state. Density is, of course, the measure of the number of people per square mile. Right-click the blank area above the QBE grid to locate and set the Top Values property of the Query Properties so that only the top five results are displayed.)

4. Create a query that produces invoice information from The Coffee Merchant's tables: *tblInvoice*, *tblInvoiceLine*, *tblEmployee*, *tblCustomer*, *tblInventory*, and *tblInventoryDescription*. Display the following columns: InvoiceID, ItemID, Quantity, UnitPrice, Discount, InvoiceDate, OrderDate, CustomerID, EmployeeLastName, CompanyName, and PhoneNumber. Write the expression for extended price, Quantity*Price*(1–Discount), and rename the resulting column Extended Price. Format the Extended Price column to display a dollar sign and two decimal places—the Currency format. After you have completed the query's design, run it. Use Page Setup to print in landscape instead of the default, portrait. The output is very long, so print only the first three pages. Write your name on the first page of the output.

5. The boss has decided to split the table *tblInventoryDescription* into teas and coffees, dropping the "beverage" field in the process. Write two make-table queries to split the table, making a coffee-only table called *tblCoffee* and a tea-only table called *tblTea*. Run the make-table queries, and then print the two tables.

CHAPTER 5
Forms and Reports

OBJECTIVES

This chapter extends your Access knowledge by providing detailed information about Microsoft Access forms and reports. You will learn about the advantages of using forms and reports and about defining and using accounting forms and reports. Throughout this chapter, exercises emphasize Microsoft Access techniques critical to building accounting information systems. Like the chapters before it, this chapter is application-oriented and contains very little theory. Exercises actively engage you in using the theory you learned earlier to create typical accounting forms and reports. In particular, you will learn how to:

- Put forms to work in a variety of accounting applications.
- Create a form with formatted fields and aesthetic enhancements.
- Add controls including a label, text box, and drop-down list box to a form.
- Build forms and associated subforms from queries and tables.
- Examine the details of a report's structure.
- Produce a grouped data report.
- Design and print reports ranging from one-table reports to more complex multiple-table reports employing summary information.

We continue using The Coffee Merchant's database system as the backdrop application in this chapter. All the tables, but no queries, that you used in Chapter 4 have been carried over to the *Ch05.mdb* database found in the Ch05 folder on your Companion CD. For all exercises and examples in this chapter, we assume that you have inserted the Companion CD into the CD-ROM drive, copied the database *Ch05.mdb* to your hard disk, and (if necessary) removed the database's read-only protection. In addition, be sure to start Microsoft Access and open the Ch05 database.

CREATING AND USING FORMS

A form displays information from one or more tables in an easily understood, attractive format on a computer screen. Unlike a Table window, a Form window can show one row of a table at a time. One advantage of a form over a Datasheet view of a table is that you can design a database form to resemble any of a company's paper forms.

When database forms match paper forms, the computer forms are almost always intuitive and familiar to those using them. And because the computer forms look familiar, they are not intimidating to new computer users. Forms are the primary interface between users and database applications. As far as your users know, forms are the application—not the tables and other objects that are behind the scenes. Forms can be used to store information and pass it from one form to another or from one phase of your application to the next.

Forms can have a plain but functional design, or they can be elaborate, with drop-down lists, built-in help, attractive field designs, graphics, and buttons that activate predefined activities when users click them. Forms, like queries, do not store any information. They simply display information retrieved from one or more tables. Data exhibited in a form can be retrieved from a single table or from multiple tables joined on a common key field. Forms can also display data directly from a query of arbitrary complexity. Any of the queries we created in the previous chapter could be the basis of a form.

Putting Forms to Work

Forms provide a convenient way to control application flow and organize your database application. Using command buttons on a form, you can create macros or code (VBA) that automate all major database procedures. When a user clicks one of the buttons, it activates a procedure such as producing a report or displaying invoices. Forms can contain a special code that runs when a specific event occurs. For example, you can easily create a code, stored with one of your forms, that performs a specific action when someone clicks a button, opens a form, or moves to a particular text box on a form.

Forms are a particularly attractive and effective way to control the data users enter into a database. For example, you could create a special form for entering new information into an invoice table. The new form contains control information that prevents a user from entering an already-assigned invoice ID number or entering an unreasonable value for a unit cost field. You can provide these types of data consistency checks as part of the logic of a form. Such checks are far more versatile and robust than the elementary table property checks. Figure 5.1 shows an example of an inventory input form.

Forms are by far the most widely used interface for entering, editing, and checking database information. You can use forms to add, change, or delete information from one or several tables at once. Forms allow you to lock selected table fields to prevent their alteration. Other options allow forms to fill in values with default and calculated values based on other entries the user makes.

Creating forms that display the progress of a database application is an effective way to communicate with the user. During a particularly lengthy database update process, for example, you can display a form that contains a progress chart indicating how far along the update operation is. Forms are the favored way to display informative messages such as warnings or error conditions in various parts of the database. For exam-

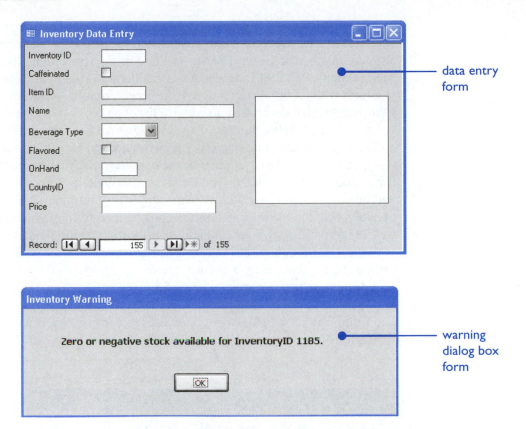

Figure 5.1 Example of two ways to use forms.

ple, a form can simply display the message "Ordered item, ID number 123445, is now out of stock." when you ship the last of an inventory item. Figure 5.1 shows a sample warning dialog box—a form. Notice the warning dialog box has no close button and no control menu.

Although forms are designed primarily for viewing on a screen, you can print them. An invoice form can serve the dual role of input and output. Data entry personnel can use a form to enter invoice information, and accounts receivable personnel can use the same form to generate individual invoices to mail to customers. The differences between the input form and the printed form may be slight. An input form may have different headers and footers—one for the customers and one for the company's data entry personnel.

Viewing Form Types

You can create several different types of forms either manually or by using the Form Wizard. Normally, the Form Wizard is your best choice for creating most forms—at least until you become comfortable with creating forms.

A form can contain several sections, or subdivisions. These include the Page Header and Page Footer sections, Form Header and Form Footer sections, the Detail section, and any number of Group Header and Group Footer sections. Headers or footers for each section can be set independent of each other. That is, a Page Header may appear in a form without its corresponding Page Footer. Similarly, a form may contain a Group Header listing the department to which a list of employees belongs but no Group Footer. As you have probably guessed, Page Headers and Footers occur at the beginning and ending of each page, respectively. Likewise, a Form Header appears at the top of each form, and a Form Footer appears at the bottom of each form—regardless of whether a form is displayed or printed. The Detail section contains information from the database and labels to identify individual items. Typically, information in the Detail section is variable, because the information there is obtained from queries and tables in the database. Figure 5.2 shows an example of a form containing Header, Detail, and Footer sections. Unless you view a multipage printout of forms, it is difficult to distinguish a form's Page Header from a Form Header.

A form type that is particularly useful for browsing through several records at once is a *continuous form*. A continuous form displays several records simultaneously on one form. The form resembles a spreadsheet, because labels appear at the top of each field and row selectors appear on the left side of each record. Figure 5.2 is an exam-

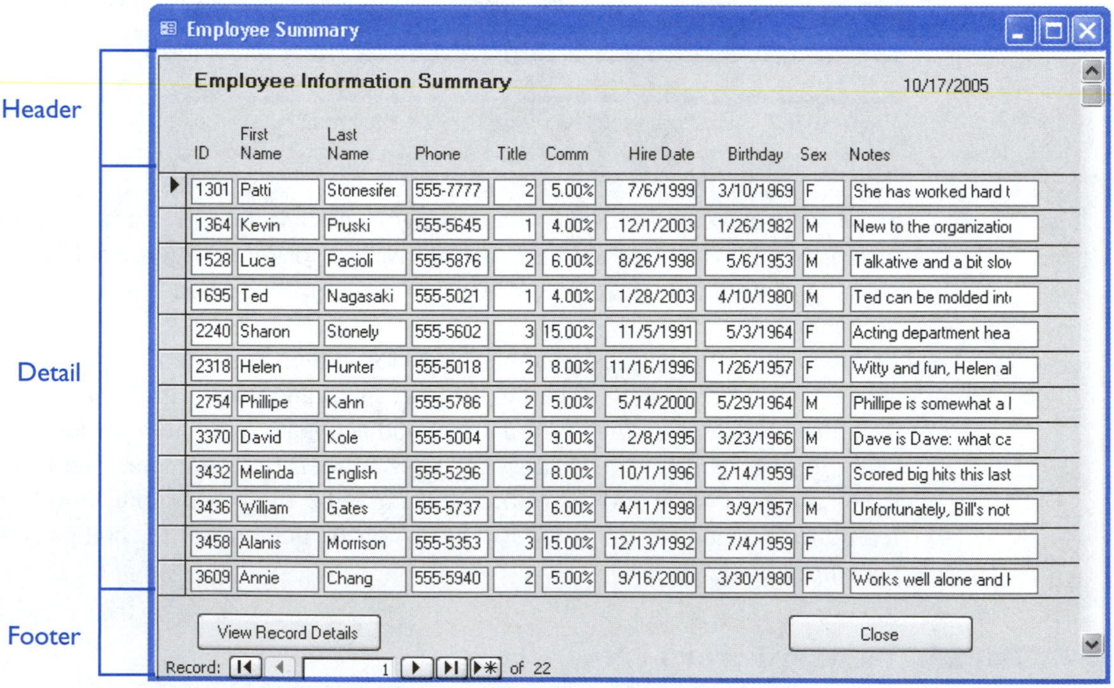

Figure 5.2 Example form with Page Header, Detail, and Page Footer sections.

ple of a continuous form showing all of the fields of several employee records. To view the remaining records, you click the scroll bar on the right side of the form or you can click the record number box and navigation buttons in the lower left portion of the form.

Forms designed to display a lot of information are usually designed as multiple-page forms. *Multiple-page forms* contain too much information to be displayed on a single screen. Thus, they group information into page-sized pieces. A user simply scrolls down the form to view its other parts. There are many examples of multiple-page forms in use. An employee form might contain many text boxes with name, address, date of birth, and similar information in the first screen-sized form piece. Lower in the form could be a large text box containing the employee's resume, a salary history, and other longer text passages.

Periodically in a database application it is helpful to have a window that remains the topmost window on the Windows desktop. Known as a pop-up form, the form might display an opening statement the first time you open a database file, or the pop-up form might provide users with information about the person who developed the database application. Unlike most windows, a pop-up window remains the topmost window, regardless of which other windows you activate on your desktop. This is especially useful to ensure that the database user reads the important information found in the pop-up form. Pop-up forms always contain a button—usually labeled OK—that closes the window. A special version of a pop-up form is called a modal form. A modal form is one that requires a response before the user can continue working on any other part of the application. A *modal form* might provide a stern warning about some action that is about to occur, or it may simply list critical information. In either case, a modal window will not let you click and activate any other window in the database application. Modal windows really get your full attention, and you should use them sparingly. Figure 5.3 shows an example of a pop-up form. (Of course, it would be impossible for you to determine if a form is modal simply by examining a textbook figure.)

A *subform* is especially useful when you want to display information on the "many" side of a one-to-many relationship. For example, a subform is a perfect way to display invoice lines that make up a larger form that is the entire invoice. An invoice's main form displays customer information, while a subform displays details about the line items. You will see several examples of this form/subform relationship in this chapter—particularly when you create invoice forms by following this chapter's exercises. Figure 5.3 shows a form and subform example.

We begin our exploration of forms and their utility by creating a rather simple form from a single table. Then we will create a form whose data are derived from multiple related tables. The last form will be created from a query.

Building a Simple Form

It is much easier to enter data and alter data in the Customer table using a form. The next exercise shows you how to create an *AutoForm* from the Table window.

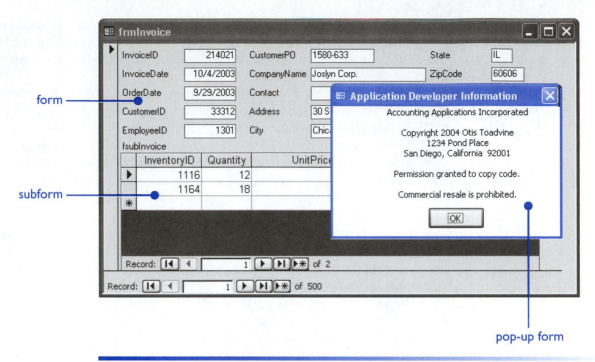

Figure 5.3   A pop-up form displays information about an application's developer.

Subsequent exercises will enhance the form's appearance. First, start with a clean slate. Launch Access, if necessary, and open your copy of *Ch05.mdb*. Close any open windows except the Database window. Then, create a form by doing the steps in the following exercise.

EXERCISE 5.1: CREATING A FORM FROM A TABLE

1. Click Tables in the Objects bar of the Database window, and select the table *tblCustomer*. You do not need to open it to perform the remaining steps in this exercise, but you can if you wish.
2. Click Insert on the menu bar, and then click AutoForm. Access quickly builds a form and a related subform.
3. Click the form's maximize button to reveal two sets of navigation buttons (see Figure 5.4).
4. To save the newly created form, click File on the menu bar, click Save, and then type **frmMyCustomer** in the Form Name text box of the Save As dialog box. Click OK to store the form in the database. (The *frm* is the customary form name prefix.)

Notice that the first row of *tblCustomer* is displayed along with an empty row in the subform beneath the main customer record. Two rows of navigation buttons appear. The top row of navigation buttons moves the record pointer through invoices that are stored in *tblInvoice* and are related to the *tblCustomer* table. The lower row of navigation buttons moves from one customer record to another. Whenever you move to a new customer, the associated invoice rows change to those of the new customer.

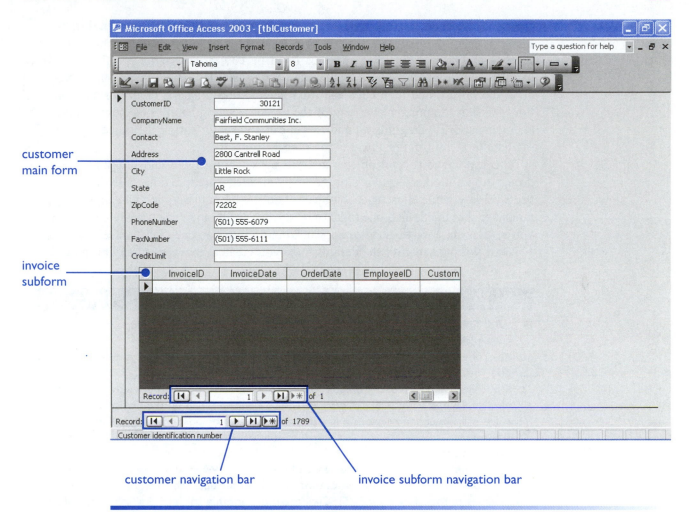

customer main form

invoice subform

customer navigation bar

invoice subform navigation bar

Figure 5.4   AutoForm generated for the table *tblCustomer*.

TRY IT

Click the next record navigation button for the customer—the lower set of navigation buttons—and view different customers' information and invoice records. Click the Last Record navigation button to view the last customer's information. Click the form's Restore Window button to reduce the size of the form. Click the toolbar Design View button to examine the form's *design*. Close the form. Click Forms on the Database Objects bar to see the new form's name, *frmMyCustomer*.

Whenever you want to create a form to enter or examine data in a table, the easiest way is to first create an AutoForm-style form for a table. You can subsequently alter the default form to suit your needs, making it more attractive and functional.

One of the fundamental operations you will use in the Form design window is moving and sizing fields and other form objects. When you select an object, one larger and several small square handles appear around it. The larger handle is called the *Move* handle. The smaller handles are called the *Sizing* handles. To move an object, you first click the object, and then click its Move handle and drag the object to its new location. Passing the pointer over any of the object's Sizing handles causes the pointer to change shape. By dragging a handle, you can enlarge or shrink the object by dragging the handle away from or towards the object, respectively.

You can move several objects at once by selecting them and dragging the entire group. As with other Windows programs, you select multiple objects by holding down the Shift key while clicking each object in turn. Alternatively, you can simply drag the mouse so that the dashed line touches or surrounds all objects you wish to select. When you release the mouse, handles appear around all the objects that you selected.

Next, you will modify the default form you created above by changing its title.

EXERCISE 5.2: ALTERING A FORM'S TITLE

1. Click *frmMyCustomer*, click the Design View button on the Database window toolbar, and then click the form's Maximize button.
2. Click View on the menu bar, and then click Form Header/Footer. Access adds Form Header and Form Footer sections to your form.
3. Click View, and then click Toolbox to display the toolbox on the work surface. You can also display the toolbox by clicking the Toolbox button found on the Design View toolbar—it has a hammer and wrench on it. You can move the toolbox anywhere on the screen by dragging its Title bar, or you can drag it to the top, left, right, or bottom of the screen to dock it there.
4. Hover the mouse over the lower edge of the toolbox. When the mouse pointer changes to a double-headed arrow, drag downward on the border until the toolbox displays two columns of tools (see Figure 5.5). Click the toolbox's title bar, and drag it to the right so you can see all the form's controls.
5. Click the toolbox Label button, move the mouse to the upper left corner of the form header, drag it down and to the right until the outline is approximately 0.25″ by 2.0″, and release the mouse. An empty label appears in the Form Header section of the form. If your form does not display vertical and horizontal rulers, then click View and then Ruler.
6. Type **Coffee Merchant Customers** in the label box. Click outside the label box to see the text.
7. Click the toolbox's Close button to remove the toolbox from the screen.
8. Right-click the label box in the Form Header, and select Properties from the shortcut menu to open the *property sheet*. (Alternatively, you can click the Properties button on the Design View toolbar.)
9. Click the Format tab, scroll to the Text Align property, near the end of the list of properties, click the Text Align property text box, click the list arrow, and click Center from the drop-down list.
10. Scroll to the Font Size property, click the Font Size list box, select the current value shown, and type **14** to indicate you want a point size of 14. Close the property sheet by clicking its Close button.

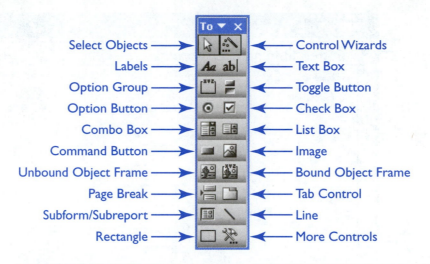

Figure 5.5 Access Toolbox.

11. If the title is not entirely visible in its text box, move the mouse to the label's center, right sizing handle. When the pointer turns to a double-headed arrow pointing left and right, drag the sizing handle to the right until the entire title is visible. (This will require you to drag and release the handle to review your progress and perhaps drag and release again.)
12. Click View on the menu bar, and then click Form View to see the altered form. If the label is not tall enough to display the name, then return to design view, use the mouse to drag the Detail bar down, click the label, and drag the lower, center sizing handle down enough to reveal the entire label.
13. Close and save your form.

Your revised form, called *frmMyCustomer*, should resemble the one shown in Figure 5.6. We have saved it as *frmCustomer* on your Companion CD.

Using a Form

By using a form-based interface to a database and its tables, you will realize that data entry with a form is more intuitive and easier than entering data directly into a table. In your database is a simple form called *frmOrder* (remember to use the prefix *frm* for all your form names) that will introduce you to the look and feel of a typical form. The form *frmOrder* found on the Companion CD provides a convenient work surface to enter new orders into the tables comprising the order database. The form provides all the requisite mechanisms to automatically place order information into two tables called *tblOrder* and *tblOrderLine*. Furthermore, the form supplies a helpful table lookup feature in two key locations: the Customer No. (customer identification number) field and the Sales Rep. (sales representative) field.

A table lookup field is helpful to anyone entering information with which he or she is unfamiliar. For instance, if you do not know a customer's number—a typical situation—you can click the combo box (a combination of a text box and a list box) to

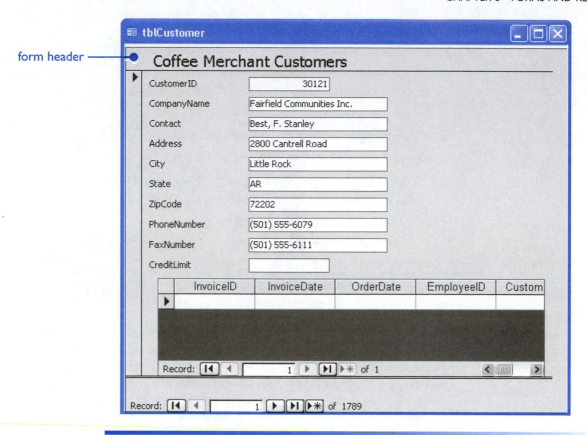

form header

Figure 5.6   Customer form with a form header.

display customer names. When the cursor is on the customer number entry, you can click the down-pointing arrow to peruse the list of existing customer numbers and names. Similarly, you can look up a sales representative's name by clicking the list box arrows associated with the field. Let's enter one order into the system using the order form.

Prepare for the next exercise by launching Access, if necessary, and closing all windows except the Database window. Follow the steps in this exercise to enter and save information in an existing order entry table.

EXERCISE 5.3: USING THE ORDER ENTRY FORM

1. Click Forms on the Objects bar, and double-click *frmOrder* found in the list of forms. The Order Entry form opens.
2. Type **5678** into the Order Number field. Press Tab to move to the next field.
3. Enter a date in the form *mmddyy* (for example, type **031504**) into the Order Date field. (Access will automatically supply the / separator between the month and day and between the day and year.) Press Tab to move to the next field.

4. With the cursor in the Customer field, click the combo box arrow on the right side of the field to display a list of customer numbers and names.

5. Scroll through the list of customers until the company name *Cheesecake Factory Inc.* appears (see Figure 5.7). Click that name. After you select the name, its corresponding customer number is inserted into the field and thus the underlying table.

6. Click the list arrow on the Salesperson combo box and select (click) the name *English, Melinda.*

7. Press Tab to move to the Sale Type option group. Click the Retail option button. (Option buttons within a group are mutually exclusive: clicking one button deselects any other previously selected option button in the group.)

8. Click the Inventory column in the first row of the subform. This is another way to move the focus in a form. (The *focus* is the active field on a form into which you can type or press the spacebar.)

9. Type **1128**, press Tab, and type **20** in the Quantity column. Press Tab to move to Unit-Price.

10. Type **8.5**, and press Tab twice. The cursor moves to the next row in the subform. Notice that Access automatically inserts the ItemID, Name, and Price into the form. Access also calculates and inserts the extended price. Discount takes on its default value, 0.00, because you do not enter a value.

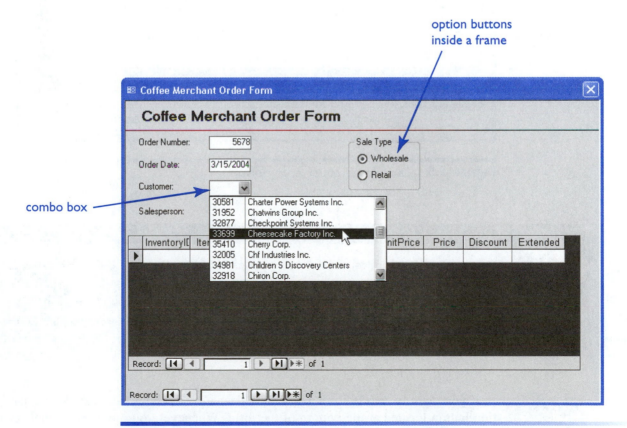

Figure 5.7 Using a combo box to select a customer.

11. Continue entering values into the subform, using Figure 5.8 as a guide. In addition to entering InventoryID, Quantity, and UnitPrice values for each row, remember to type **5%** and **15%** (type the percent sign) in the Discount column for the last two entries, respectively. (What happens if you type 15 in the Discount column—without typing a trailing percent sign—and then press Enter? Try it. It won't hurt anything.)

12. Click the Form view Close button to cease entering values, or continue on with the Try It examples.

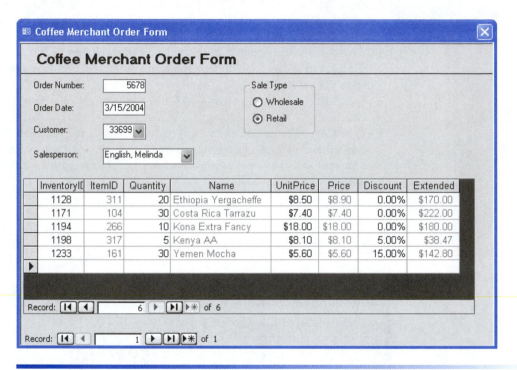

Figure 5.8 Completed order entry form.

TRY IT

You may not have noticed that there are helpful hints available called *ControlTips* that display when you hover the cursor over a field in the form. *Hovering* simply means that you move the mouse pointer over a control and pause (but do not click the mouse). After a brief pause, a tip displayed in a yellow box appears. Hover over the Order Number, Order Date, and Customer fields, in turn, and observe their ControlTips.

If you want to try the form again, first clear it by clicking the Next Record navigation button located at the bottom of the form. Whenever you move to another record, Access automatically posts the current data to various tables. Then, Access clears the form to make way for new data. When you are done entering information, click the form's Close button. Don't be concerned that you might lose data. Microsoft Access automatically posts any newly entered data to the database when you move off the current record or close the form.

You have used a Table window's navigation buttons to view the data in a table. Similarly, you can examine all the data in the Order form—from multiple tables—through a form. Assuming you have entered additional orders, you can click the First Record button to go to the first order you entered, or click the Last Record button to go to the last order entered in the system. Other navigation buttons work in a familiar way.

Editing data couldn't be simpler. In a Form view window, click on any field you would like to change, and type the change. For form fields using lookup tables (fields having list boxes or combo boxes), click the arrow near the field to display the list of values; then enter a new value or select one of the displayed entries. It is best to use a lookup table when available, especially for noncontiguous values such as sales representative identification numbers. As budding form designers, you should incorporate lookup tables for fields whose values are limited to a specific and small list of acceptable values. This saves much frustration and confusion on the part of form users.

With forms, you can view particular records or groups of records using either the Filter By Form or Filter By Selection techniques. When you filter objects, you are restricting what is displayed to some subset of the total objects available. Filtering records being viewed through a form is no different. You simply specify the criteria—similar to query criteria—that are used to restrict your view of the records and then select Apply Filter/Sort from the Filter menu. Records are displayed in the usual way in the form, but you will notice that only a select group of records is available. The total number of records in the filtered set is indicated to the right of the navigation buttons at the bottom of the form. Try it yourself.

TRY IT

Display, in Form view, the form *frmCustomer* found on your Companion CD. Notice that there are 1,789 customer records. All are available for viewing. Next, click the Records menu, point to Filter, and click Filter By Form. Let's see how many customers from California there are in the database—and who they are. Click the Clear Grid button on the Filter/Sort toolbar. Click the State form field and type **CA** in either uppercase or lowercase letters. Click Filter in the menu bar, and then click Apply Filter/Sort. (Be careful not to click Advanced Filter/Sort. That will yield a different result.) Access reveals that there are 196 customers in California (see Figure 5.9). Use the navigation buttons to go to the next record and the last record. Select Remove Filter/Sort from the Records menu. The form indicates all records in the table are available again. Close the form, *frmCustomer*. If a Save dialog box appears, click the *No to All* button.

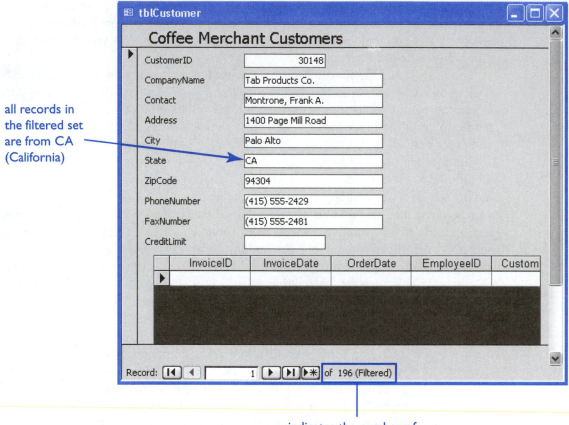

all records in
the filtered set
are from CA
(California)

indicates the number of
records in the filtered set

Figure 5.9   Filter By Form example.

Filter By Selection works in almost the same way as Filter By Form. You select a field, such as City, which has an entry by which you would like to filter, and then choose Filter By Selection from the Records menu. Access displays only records whose fields match that of the selected field.

TRY IT

Display in Form view the form *frmCustomer*. Move to the first customer in the Customer table, Fairfield Communities Inc. Click the City form field, and drag the cursor across the entire city name to select it. Let's see how many other customers we have in the selected city of Little Rock. Click the Records menu, point to Filter, and click Filter By Selection. Access indicates that there are currently six customers in Little Rock. Click Records in the menu bar, and then click Remove Filter/Sort. The form indicates all (1,789) records in the table are available again. Close the *frmCustomer* form.

Creating a Multitable Form and Subform

Many forms display data from more than one table. The Coffee Merchant's Order form is an example of a multitable form, because data such as the order number, order date, and sales representative number are stored in a table called *tblOrder*. Details about the items ordered (item ID and quantity ordered) are stored in another table called *tblOrderLine*. The Coffee Merchant's Order form also references the Inventory table, *tblInventory*, although no new inventory items can be entered via the form. Finally, you can locate and display customer numbers in the Customer field through the *tblCustomer* table. Four tables are joined and referenced by The Coffee Merchant's Order form.

Although using The Coffee Merchant's Order form is an informative exercise, you will benefit much more from building a form from scratch. Once you create a form, it is only a short time until you will be designing elaborate forms for your own applications. Figure 5.10 shows you an example of a multitable invoice review and data entry form that displays data from several of The Coffee Merchant's tables. That form has the look of the finished form we are striving for in this section. When finished, your form should start to resemble the one in Figure 5.10.

The invoice form that you will build in this section is actually two forms: a main form and a subform. The main form displays one record from the *tblInvoice* table. Simultaneously, the subform displays several related records that are line items in the invoice. Information on the subform includes item number, item name, quantity ordered, unit price, discount, and extended price. Access synthesizes the subform from data supplied by the query called *qryInvoiceLineItem* found on your Companion CD.

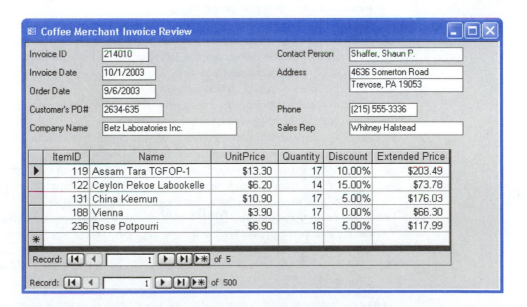

Figure 5.10 Example invoice review and data entry form.

Creating a Form Containing a Subform

Access allows you to create forms and reports that use data found in more than one table or query. The best way to create a main form and its subform is to use a Form Wizard. The following exercise outlines how to create an invoice form. Prepare for the next exercise by closing all open windows except the Database.

EXERCISE 5.4: CREATING AN INVOICE FORM AND SUBFORM

1. Click Forms in the Objects bar, and then click the New button on the Forms collection of the Database window. Access displays the New Form dialog box.
2. Select Form Wizard from the list of form choices, click the list box arrow in the lower portion of the window, and select *qryInvoiceMain* from the list. (When creating forms with subforms, it is usually best to use the Form Wizard.) You base the top half of the form on the table or query that contains the data to appear on the main form (the data on the "one" side of the one-to-many relationship). In this case the main form will contain customer invoice information. The subform will contain invoice detail lines with products, quantities, prices, etc.
3. Click OK to begin the form-building process. The first of several Form Wizard dialog boxes appears.
4. Click the >> button to move all fields on the Available Fields list entries onto the Selected Fields list. The latter list contains the fields that Access will display on the completed form.
5. Click the list arrow beneath the Tables/Queries list box to display the queries and tables in the database, allowing you to add subform fields to the form.
6. Locate *qryInvoiceLineItem* in the list, and click it. The query-supplied fields appear in the Available Fields list (see Figure 5.11).
7. Click the >> button to move all the subform fields onto the Selected Fields list.
8. In the Selected Fields list, locate and select the field called *qryInvoiceLineItem.InvoiceID*.
9. Click the "<" button to remove the extra InvoiceID field, moving it from the Selected Fields list back onto the Available Fields list.
10. Click the Next button to proceed to the next step.
11. When the dialog box appears asking how you want to view your data, click the Next button to accept the suggested default.
12. Select the suggested Datasheet layout for your subform by clicking the Datasheet option button, if necessary. Click Next to go to the next step.
13. Accept the suggested "Standard" style by clicking the Next button. Be careful on the last Form Wizard dialog box: change the form and subform names by altering them in the text boxes. If you do not do it here, it is more difficult to do later.
14. In the Form text box, type **frmInvoice2** and in the Subform text box, type **fsubInvoice2** (Be sure to enter the prefix *fsub* for the subform. This prefix indicates a form is a subform and is the accepted standard for naming subforms.)
15. Click the *Open the form to view or enter information* option button, if necessary.
16. Click the Finish button to conclude the form-building process.

Access takes a few moments to build both the form and subform and then opens it for your use (see Figure 5.12). Scroll through the records to experience how the form

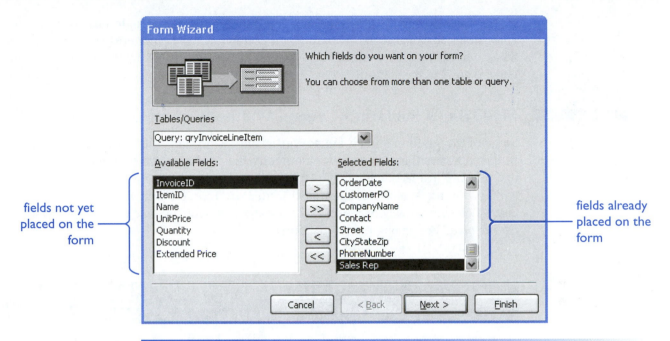

Figure 5.11 Selecting main form and subform fields.

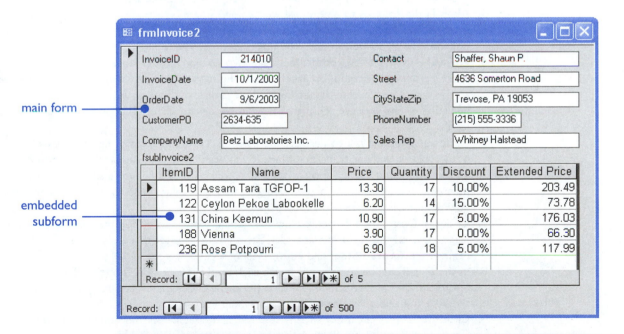

Figure 5.12 Main form and embedded subform created by the Form Wizard.

works. Occasionally, you may want to scroll through the subform to display all the invoice items for a particular invoice. Keep in mind that the outermost set of navigation buttons pages through whole invoices, while the inner set skips from line to line on invoice details in the subform.

Modifying a Subform's Column Widths and Labels

Some of the subform's fields are not sufficiently wide, and others are not visible at all. In the exercises that follow, you will modify the widths of some subform columns so that they are just large enough to display their information but not too large. Then, you will change the subform column label from *UnitPrice* to *Price*. Prepare for this exercise by closing all windows except the Database window. Notice that *frmInvoice2* and *fsubInvoice2* are among the list of forms.

EXERCISE 5.5: MODIFYING A SUBFORM'S COLUMN WIDTHS AND LABELS

1. If necessary, click Forms on the Database window Objects bar to display the list of forms in your database.
2. Double-click the subform *fsubInvoice2* to open it. If necessary, select Datasheet View from the View menu so the information is displayed as a datasheet, not a form.
3. Alter all the columns to an optimal width: hover the mouse pointer over the leftmost column label, ItemID. When it turns to a down-pointing arrow, drag it to the right until all columns are highlighted—displayed in black. Release the mouse.
4. Move the mouse to any border between two columns in the label area or to the rightmost border of the rightmost label. When the mouse pointer changes to a double-headed arrow with a vertical line dissecting it, double-click the mouse. All columns change size, adjusting to the smallest width that is wide enough to display the largest values or column labels.
5. Click any datasheet cell to deselect the columns. Now the columns display the widest values in the column without truncating them. If you wish to further customize individual column widths, you can do so by dragging the line to the right of a column's label when the mouse pointer is a double-headed arrow. Dragging the right column line to the right widens the column; dragging to the left narrows the column.
6. Click the Design View button on the Formatting toolbar to display the form in Design view.
7. Click View on the menu bar, and click Form Header/Footer to deselect the menu item and remove the form's Header and Footer sections.
8. In the Detail section, locate and double-click the UnitPrice label (not the UnitPrice text box) field. The property sheet appears. (If double-clicking is difficult for you, then right-click the field and select Properties from the pop-up list.)
9. Click the Format tab, if not already selected, and double-click the value displayed in the Caption property. Type **Price** to replace the caption.
10. Click the property sheet Close button.
11. Click the *fsubInvoice2* subform's Close button, and click Yes when asked if you want to save the changed design.

What you have learned here is that to resize subform fields displayed as a datasheet, you simply resize the table fields. This automatically causes the fields to be displayed in their new widths in any subforms constructed from the changed subform design.

You will do additional work on this form, but it is always a good idea to preserve the partially completed work. This way, you don't risk losing a large amount of work if something should happen to your computer.

There are several controls on the forms with which you are working. *Controls* are all the objects that appear on forms or reports. For example, the label *InvoiceID* is a control, as is the InvoiceID field displaying the value 214010. There are three types of controls in Access forms: bound controls, unbound controls, and calculated controls. A *bound control* has as its data source a field in a table. The invoice date field in Figure 5.12 is a bound control. An *unbound control* has no data source and is used to display a title or label on forms and reports. It does not change from one record to the next. The invoice date label (InvoiceDate) in Figure 5.12 is an example of an unbound label. A *calculated control* has as its data source an expression rather than a table field. The Extended Price field is an example of a calculated control. Access database users and developers use the term control frequently when referring to objects on forms or reports.

Altering a Subform's Column Formatting

When you want to alter one or more of an object's properties such as its display format, you open its property sheet and make the necessary changes. You use the property sheet to set, view, or change the properties of a table, query, form, report, or controls on forms and reports. Available in the Design view of a Table, Query, Form, or Report window, the property sheet appears whenever you click the Properties button on the toolbar. The property sheet remains on the work surface, even when you select other controls or objects, until you explicitly close it. You can also display the property sheet for a selected object by right-clicking the mouse and then choosing Properties from the pop-up menu.

The next exercise illustrates how to change the display properties of two numeric values found in *fsubInvoice2*. Currently, the Price and Extended Price columns display their values in currency format. This may not be desirable in some situations. You will change the display format for the columns to eliminate the currency symbols.

EXERCISE 5.6: CHANGING A COLUMN'S DISPLAY CHARACTERISTICS

1. Open the subform, *fsubInvoice2*, in Design view.
2. Press and hold the Shift key, click the UnitPrice control (not the label), click the Extended Price control, and release the Shift key.
3. Click the Properties button on the Form Design toolbar. The property sheet appears with the Title bar displaying *Multiple selection*, which indicates more than one object is selected and will be affected.
4. Click the Format tab, if necessary. (The group of properties associated with the way data appears when displayed are called Format properties.)

selected objects have sizing
handles around them

the Format
property

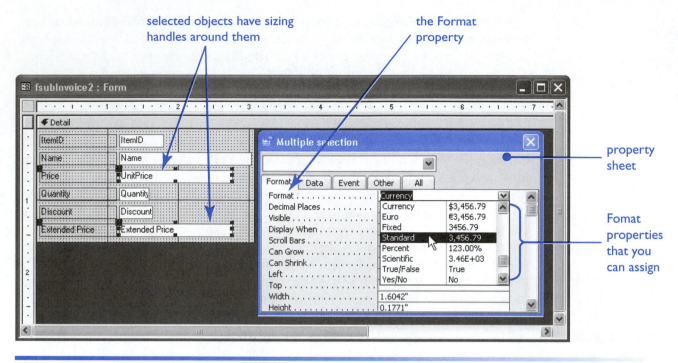

property
sheet

Fomat
properties
that you
can assign

Figure 5.13 Changing objects' properties.

5. Click the Format property text box, click its list box arrow, and locate and then click Standard (see Figure 5.13).
6. Close the property sheet.
7. Click the subform's Close button, and click Yes to save the changed subform.

If you want to verify the property changes you have just made, simply open the form *frmInvoice2* in Form view. Observe that currency symbols no longer appear in either the Price or the Extended Price fields. Figure 5.14 shows the altered invoice form and subform.

Rearranging Form Fields

You can easily rearrange controls on a form by selecting them and then dragging them to a new location. For example, you can move the CompanyName control closer to the customer's address controls on the right side of the form. You move controls by displaying the form or subform in Design view. Then, after you click the bound control, you can move the mouse over the selected control. When the mouse pointer changes to a small hand, click and drag the bound control and its attached unbound control (its label) to a new location. If you want to move a group of controls, simply Shift-click each of them and then move them as a group. To deselect controls, simply click outside the selected control or group of controls.

If a subform's data are not fully visible because the form is not wide enough (a likely case), click the View button, select Design View, click the subform frame to select it,

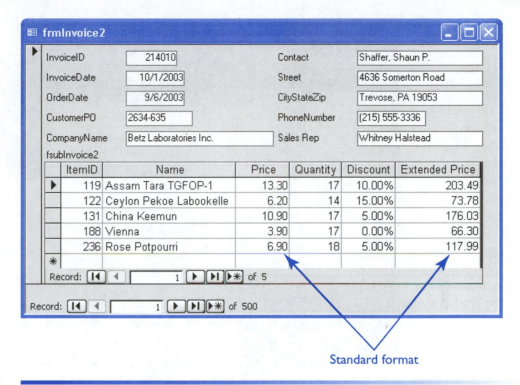

Figure 5.14 Altered invoice form and subform.

and drag the right border handle to the right to widen the entire frame. (You may have to switch back and forth between Design view and Form view until you have adjusted the subform frame to your satisfaction.) Though your form does not exactly match our Invoice form, it is very close. Only a few embellishments remain to make them identical. You can do that on your own, if you want to practice the techniques.

Printing a Form

Usually, you do not print forms. However, printing one page of a form is a good way to keep track of all the forms you have developed for any accounting system. Printing a form is a straightforward task. First, select and open in Form view the form you want to print from the list on the Forms sheet of the Database window. Optionally, you can use the form navigation buttons to display a particular record, or you can simply print the first record that appears in a form. In either case, click File, and then click Print. When the Print dialog box opens, click the "Selected Record(s)" option button so that Access prints only one form (see Figure 5.15). Click OK to start the print process. If your form is wider than can be accommodated by the current print setup, you will receive a warning similar to the one shown in Figure 5.16. In that case, click the Cancel button to close the warning dialog box and click Page Setup in the File menu. Next, click the Page tab and click the Landscape option button. That should fix the print problem.

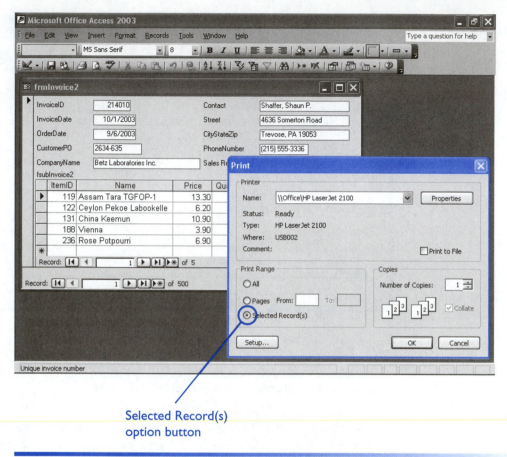

Selected Record(s)
option button

Figure 5.15   Printing a single form.

You can print properties, permissions, and design information for database objects, including your forms' designs. Printing the design characteristics of your database objects helps you document your database's design and the accounting application you develop. Click Tools on the menu bar, point to Analyze, and then click Documenter. Then, check the objects for which you want printed definition information. Click OK,

Figure 5.16   Print width warning dialog box.

and Access will create the report and display it in the Object Definition window. If you decide to print the report, simply click the Print button on the toolbar. If not, click the Close button on the toolbar to discard the report and return to the Database window.

TRY IT

Close all windows except the Database window. Click Tools, point to Analyze, and then click Documenter. Click the Forms tab of the Documenter dialog box, and click the check box to the left of the form *frmInvoice2*. Click OK. Access takes a second or two to construct a report and display it in the Object Definition window. Examine the report. Click the Zoom button on the toolbar, and click inside the Object Definition window to alternately zoom in and zoom out. Close the Object Definition window after you are done, and close the *Ch05.mdb* database. Take a break if you wish.

When you want to see a comprehensive list of information from one or more tables, then printing forms is not adequate. Instead, you need a report. Reports and how to produce them are described next.

BUILDING AND PRINTING REPORTS

Reports provide the mechanism to produce high-quality printed database information. While you can use a form for viewing or altering information in the database, you cannot enter or alter information in a report. Reports are strictly for output. Like forms, reports are based on information found in tables or supplied by queries. Unlike forms, reports allow you to group information from one table. With forms, you must join two or more tables to group information by using a form/subform combination.

Using Reports

Reports are used in accounting database applications to provide hard copy output that compares, summarizes, and subtotals data found in customer and billing data. An Access report can produce printed shipping labels, purchase orders, bill of materials lists, or invoices that mimic paper-only forms used by businesses. Producing mailing labels from database customer records using Access reports can save money for larger mailings because Access can presort the information into zip code order prior to producing a report. When you group mail by zip code, the U.S. Postal Service provides lower postage rates.

Using Report Wizards

Microsoft Access provides two ways to create reports. You can create a report from scratch, starting with a blank form, or you can use a Report Wizard. You will probably prefer using Report Wizards because the process is easier and faster than creating reports from scratch.

Report Wizards offer several styles of reports, including Columnar AutoReport, Tabular AutoReport, Chart Wizard, and Labels Wizard. The AutoReport Wizards create preformatted, single-column (Columnar) or multicolumn (Tabular) reports with very little involvement from you.

You invoke a Report Wizard from the Database window after clicking Reports on the Objects bar and then clicking the New button on the Reports page. Of course, reports get their data from tables or queries. So, you must designate the table or query that produces the data that are placed in the report. Next, you select one of the report types, such as Report Wizard, from the list displayed in the New Report dialog box. Once you click OK, an Access Wizard guides you step by step through the process of creating a report. Simply follow the Report Wizard's dialog boxes, and respond to its questions. When you click the Finish button in the last step of the Wizard-guided report creation process, Access quickly builds an attractive report that it displays in the Print Preview window.

Examining a Report's Structure

The Report window has three views: Design, Print Preview, and Layout Preview. You change the layout and design of a report in Design view. You use Print Preview to check all the data and its appearance in the report. In Layout Preview, you can review the general layout and appearance of a report. Design view is where you will spend most of your time, because you create and modify report layouts in that view.

An Access report is divided into sections, which appear at prescribed locations on the report. There are seven different types of sections, but a report does not have to include all seven sections. Each section appears once in Design view. When you print a report, some sections are repeated as needed. Figure 5.17 shows an example of a report's design with the seven sections.

The Detail section is required in each report; all other sections are optional. Beginning at the very top of the report is the Report Header section. It appears once at the beginning of the report. Access prints the Page Header's contents at the top of every page. A Group Header's contents appear every time a grouping field value changes. Access prints one line in the Detail section for each record selected from the underlying table(s) or queries. The Group Footer prints at the end of each group. The Page Footer prints at the bottom of each page. The Report Footer prints on a page at the end of the report.

Creating a Tabular-Style Report with a Report Wizard

In many ways, creating a report resembles creating a form. You design a report, including its field layouts, headings, and other details, in the report Design view window. At any stage in your design, you can see the report replete with data by clicking the Print Preview button on the toolbar.

Experiment building a report by using the Employee table. Suppose you want a printed list of employee names and other information sorted by the employees' last names. All the requisite information is found in one table, *tblEmployee*. Follow the steps in the next exercise to create a report with the help of the Access Report Wizard.

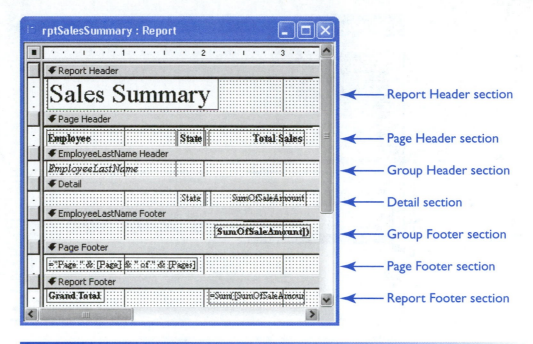

Figure 5.17 Report sections.

EXERCISE 5.7: CREATING A REPORT

1. Close all open windows except the Database window, click Reports in the Objects bar, and then click the New button.
2. Click Report Wizard, an entry appearing in the right panel of the New Report dialog box.
3. Click the list box arrow to display all the database's tables and queries, click *tblEmployee* in the list of tables and queries, and click OK to start the Report Wizard. A new dialog box is displayed in which you choose which fields will appear on the report.
4. From the Available Fields list, double-click the following fields, one at a time, to move them onto the Selected Fields list: EmployeeID, EmployeeLastName, EmployeeHireDate, EmployeeDOB, and EmployeeGender (see Figure 5.18). Click the Next button when you have entered all the preceding fields. (You can also select a field and press the "<" button to move a field onto the Selected Fields list, but it is faster to double-click field names.)
5. The Report Wizard displays a dialog box asking if you want to create a grouping level. Because you do not want to do so for this report, click Next without making any changes.
6. The next dialog box asks if you want to sort the report records. Because we want the report to display the employee information in name order, click the list box arrow next to the first sort box, and select EmployeeLastName from the list of report fields. Click the Next button to proceed.
    Note: If you discover you have made a mistake on an earlier Report Wizard dialog box, you can simply click the Back button repeatedly until you reach the dialog box containing the mistake. Make any changes, and then click the Next button to return to where you left off.

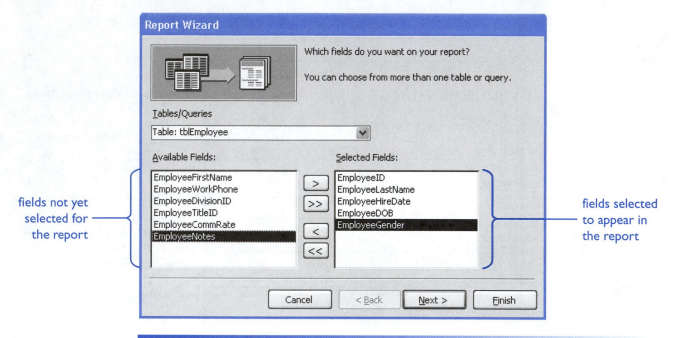

Figure 5.18   Selecting fields for a report.

7. Ensure that the Tabular option (in the Layout option group) and the Portrait option (in the Orientation option group) are selected. Also ensure that the "Adjust the field width so all fields fit on a page" check box is checked. Click the Next button.
8. Select the Formal report style and press the Next button.
9. Type **Coffee Merchant Employees** in the text box. Click the Finish button to finalize your choices and generate your report.
10. After reviewing the report preview, click the Design View button on the Report Design toolbar to view the report's design. Finally, click the Design View Close button to close and save the report.

Access also uses the report title that you entered in step 9 to name the report. That is not a good feature of Access reports. You should rename the report *rptMyEmployee* immediately after you save it. To rename a report, select the report from the list of reports in the Database window, press F2, type **rptMyEmployee**, and press Enter. You can rename any object that way. We have saved this report as *rptEmployee* on your Companion CD.

Access creates the report and displays it in Print Preview (see Figure 5.19). The report lists employee records in name order. Did you notice that some report column labels such as Last Name, Hire Date, and Birth Date are different from their source table column names? The reason for this is that we included less cryptic names for them in the Caption property of the table design when we created the *tblEmployee* table. To verify this, examine the Employee table in Design view, and pay particular attention to the Caption property as you select field names in the upper portion of the Design view. Print the report, if you wish, by selecting Print from the File menu.

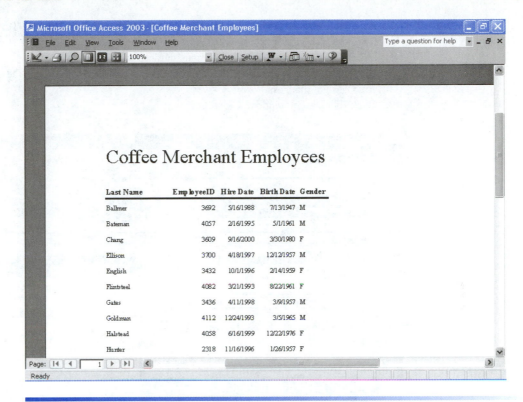

Figure 5.19 Print Preview window showing a tabular-style report.

Modifying a Report Field's Data Alignment

You can enhance the appearance of a control's data or label by adjusting its alignment (its Text Align property). Some of the data columns in the Employee report do not line up well with their column labels. For example, the column label EmployeeID is far to the left of the actual identification number column values. Similarly, the Gender data values appear misaligned when compared to their column label. You can alter the alignment of labels (unbound controls) or data (bound controls) to achieve the effect you want. We briefly illustrate how to alter the data alignment in the next exercise.

EXERCISE 5.8: ALTERING REPORT CONTROLS' DATA ALIGNMENT

1. Display in Design view your newly minted Employee report, *rptMyEmployee*.
2. In the Detail section, press and hold the Shift key, click EmployeeID, click EmployeeGender control (the right-most control in the Detail section), and release the Shift key. Be very careful not to move the controls when you select them.
3. Click View on the menu bar, and then click Properties to display the property sheet.
4. Click the Format tab, if necessary, to reveal that collection of format related properties.

5. Scroll the property list to locate the Text Align property. Click the Text Align property text box, and click the Text Align list box arrow to reveal the alignment choices.
6. Select Center from the five alignment choices (see Figure 5.20).
7. Close the property sheet, and click the Save button on the Report Design toolbar to save your design changes.
8. Click the Design window Close button.

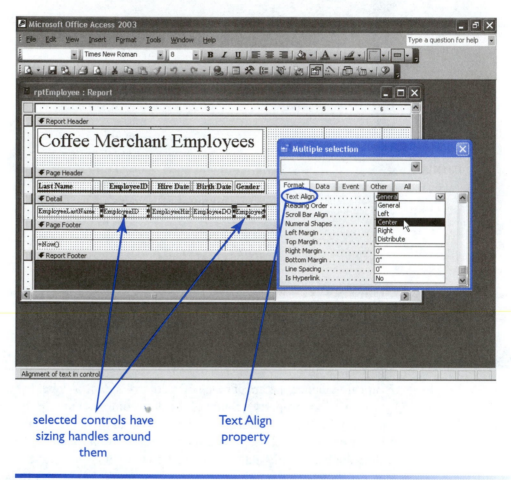

selected controls have sizing handles around them

Text Align property

Figure 5.20   Altering the alignment property of multiple controls.

Deleting Controls and Report Sections

Because the *rptMyEmployee* report is short, there is no need for a Page Footer section. Currently, the Page Footer section contains a single control that displays the current page number, which is unnecessary in a one-page report. Deleting a report section—the Page Footer section in this case—is straightforward, so we will skip a formal exercise and simply describe the steps in the following Try It paragraph. Before eliminating the Page Footer section, you must first remove all its controls. There are three controls in the Page Footer section: two calculated controls and an unbound control.

TRY IT

Display *rptMyEmployee* in Design view. Using the horizontal scroll bar, move to the left edge of the report, and locate the control in the Page Footer section containing the Access function =Now(). Click it (selection handles appear around it), and press the Delete key to remove it. In a similar way, remove the second control that resides in the Page Footer. Move to the right edge of the report, and locate the Page Footer control containing the expression =" *Page* " & *[Page]* & " *of* " & *[Pages]*. Select the control, and press Delete to remove it. Finally, select the thin line (the unbound control) that appears near the top of the Page Footer section. Press Delete to remove it. Once you have removed all controls in a section, you delete the section by dragging up the bar below the section. To eliminate the Page Footer section, move the mouse to the bottom of the Page Footer section until it turns into a double-headed arrow pointing up and down. Then, drag the arrow up until the Page Footer section is eliminated. Release the mouse button. Click the Save button on the Report Design toolbar to save the altered report. Then, close the Design view window.

In the Try It steps you executed above prior to saving the report, you reduced the height of the Page Footer section to zero. That removes it. Removing the Page Header section and the Page Footer section *simultaneously* is even simpler. Click View in the menu bar, and then click Page Header/Footer to remove the check mark to its left. Access removes the two sections as well as any controls they contain simultaneously.

Saving and Printing a Report

You should save any reports that you anticipate running periodically. On the other hand, you need not save any reports that are used only once. You can save a report in Design view or Print Preview. For new reports, you must supply a name before Access will save the report definition in the database.

Reports exist to be printed, so let's print this report. You can print a report from either the Design view window or the Print Preview window. Before actually printing a report, you may want to modify some global report settings such as margins, page orientation (portrait or landscape), or paper size. You alter any of those settings by clicking the Setup button in the Print dialog box or by clicking Page Setup in the File menu. You should print the report *rptMyEmployee* so you have a copy of its final form. We will not be using this report further, so you can either save it or delete it from the database.

Is it possible to produce a report similar to *rptEmployee* or *rptMyEmployee* but sort the rows into order by division location and by employee names within each division? Yes—by using the Report Wizard to add report groups to your report. You learn how to do this next.

Producing a Grouped Data Report

You learned that either tables or queries can be the basis of any forms you create. The same is true for reports. When you base a report on a query, you can alter the query's selection criteria, save the query, run another report, and produce different report results. For example, you could create a query that selects invoices that are 30 days past due, base a report on that query, and then run and print the report. Printing a list of invoices that are 31 to 60 days past due would then be easy. Simply modify the existing query to select rows whose invoice date is 31 to 60 days ago, save the modified query, and rerun the report. Alternatively, you could create a parameter query that prompts you for the value of "days past due" and run the report after the query processes your input.

Building a report that lists employees and their division locations involves information from at least two tables: *tblEmployee* and *tblDivisionLocation*. There are two general approaches to producing the report. One way is to first create a query that joins the two tables and then create a report based on the query. The other way is to create a report, with the help of a Report Wizard, by including all the tables involved and let the Report Wizard join the tables. The latter approach produces a report through the use of a "behind the report" query. A behind the report query is one that is stored inside the report's definition but is not available for general use in the Queries collection. When you create a specialized report whose query will not have widespread use, the latter report method is preferable.

EXERCISE 5.9: CREATING A GROUPED DATA REPORT WITH A REPORT WIZARD

1. Click Reports on the Database window Objects bar, click the New button on the Database window toolbar, and click Report Wizard in the New Report dialog box.
2. Click the list box arrow to display all the database's tables and queries, click *tblEmployee* in the list of tables and queries, and click OK to start the Report Wizard. A new dialog box is displayed in which you choose which fields will appear on the report.
3. From the Available Fields list, double-click the following fields, one at a time, to move them onto the Selected Fields list: EmployeeLastName, EmployeeID, EmployeeHireDate, EmployeeDOB, and EmployeeGender.
4. Click the Tables/Queries list box arrow to display the database's tables and queries once again, and then click the entry Table: *tblDivisionLocation*. You may have to use the scroll bar to locate the table, which is just above the entry *tblEmployee* in the drop-down list.
5. From the Available Fields list, double-click DivisionCity, and then click the Next button to move to the next step in the report-building process.
6. The Report Wizard asks how you want to view your data. Click the choice by *tblDivisionLocation* listed in the left panel. That causes Access to group the report's rows by city (see Figure 5.21). Click the Next button to move to the next step.
7. The dialog box requests whether or not you want additional grouping levels. Because you do not, click the Next button to move to the next step.

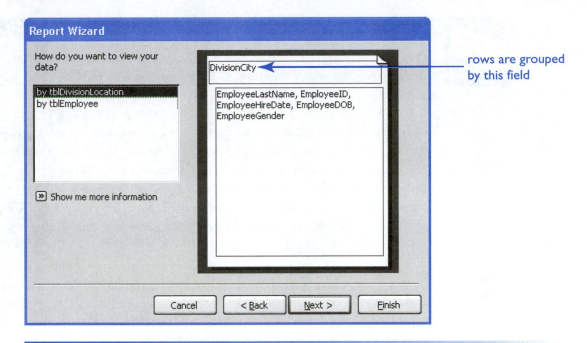

Figure 5.21 Selecting a grouping field.

8. The next dialog box asks if you want to sort the detail records. Click the list box arrow next to the first sort box, and select EmployeeLastName from the list of report fields. Click the Next button to proceed.
9. Ensure that the Stepped option (in the Layout option group) and the Portrait option (in the Orientation option group) are selected. Also ensure that the "Adjust the field width so all fields fit on a page" check box is checked. Click the Next button.
10. Select the Formal report style, and press the Next button.
11. Type **Employees by Location** in the report title text box. Click the Finish button to finalize your choices and generate a preview of your report.
12. After reviewing the report preview, click the Design View button on the toolbar (not the Close window button) to view the report's design. Finally, click the Design View Close button to close and save the report.

Remember that the report is saved under the name you typed for the report title—a nonconforming database object name. Be sure to rename the report *rptEmpLoc*. For your convenience, we have placed the report on your Companion CD. It is called *rptEmployeesByLocation*. Examine that report, or print it if you wish.

A Group Footer prints in the report just after the grouping element changes. Currently, our report does not have a Group Footer because the report contains no numeric fields whose sums or averages need to be displayed after a complete group is printed. Let's add a Group Footer to see how it's done.

TRY IT

Open the *rptEmployeesByLocation* report in Design view. Drag the window's borders to widen and lengthen the report if necessary. Click View on the menu bar, and then click Sorting and Grouping. When the Sorting and Grouping dialog box appears, click under the heading Field/Expression in the DivisionID row, and then click the list box arrow to the right of the DivisionID row. Click DivisionCity from the drop-down list. (This will group and sort entries by city name rather than city identification number.) Click the row selector to the left of the entry DivisionCity to select it. Then, double-click the Group Footer list box located below in the Group Properties panel. This will change the value from "No" to "Yes," which means that a Group Footer will appear in the report (see Figure 5.22). Close the Sorting and Grouping dialog box. Notice the new Group Footer section in the report.

When you place a page break in a report, it causes the printer to skip to the top of a new page. You can place a page break in any section of a report. For instance, you can place a page break in the Group Footer section. That way, Access prints each city and the employees located in it on a separate page.

TRY IT

Place a page break in the *rptEmployeesByLocation* report so that each group prints on a new page. First, display *rptEmployeesByLocation* in Design view. Display the toolbox (click the Toolbox toolbar button if needed), click the Page Break button, and move the mouse to the left side of the report within the Group Footer section. Click the mouse to drop the page break into the report's Page Footer section (see Figure 5.23). Close the toolbox. Save the report again, and print the first two pages to examine the changes you made to the report. Close the report, but leave the Database window open. We are done changing the design of the *rptEmployeesByLocation* report.

Building Reports with Queries and Expressions

Next, we will design a report that produces invoices. You will participate in building the invoice report, and we will help. We merely outline some of the easier procedures, however. You are familiar with all of the steps needed to build the Invoice report except for a few. We will explain these carefully in individual exercise steps. We begin with the query—one that you have not seen before—that joins six tables to assemble all the fields we need for an industrial strength invoice.

Figure 5.24 shows the query that will produce the fields needed for each invoice. The QBE grid columns are narrow so that you can see several of the Field row entries, though most fields are out of view. Before continuing, please open the query, which is

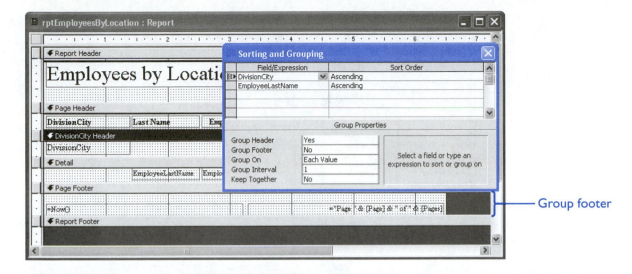

Figure 5.22 Inserting a Group Footer into a report.

the foundation of our Invoice report, and study it briefly. The query is saved on your Companion CD as *qryInvoiceReport*. Observe how the tables are joined.

The *tblCustomer* and *tblInvoice* tables are joined on the column CustomerID. The table *tblInvoice* is joined to the table *tblInvoiceLine* on the column InvoiceID found in both tables. Other joined tables are *tblInvoice* to *tblEmployee* on the column

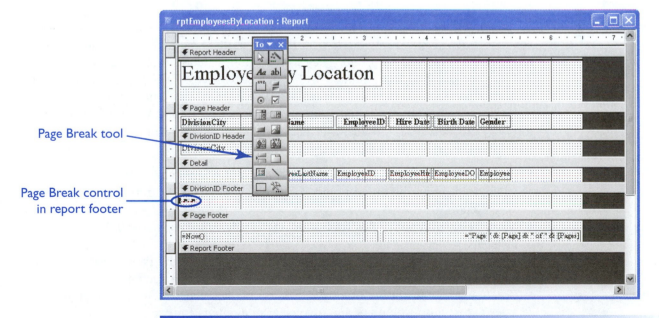

Figure 5.23 Report design containing a Page Break control.

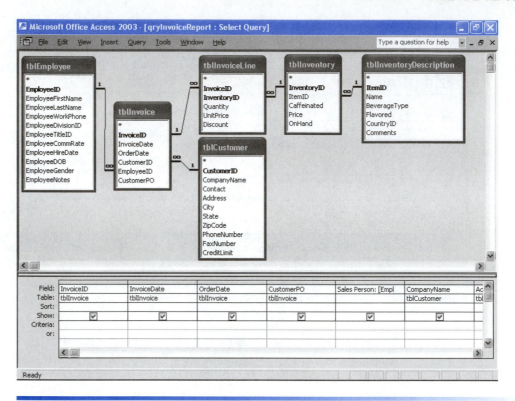

Figure 5.24   Query to select fields for an invoice report.

EmployeeID, *tblInvoiceLine* to *tblInventory* on the column InventoryID, and *tblInventory* to *tblInventoryDescription* on the key column ItemID. Thus, the six tables are joined by five sets of primary key to foreign key pairs. Figure 5.25 shows a typical invoice that you can produce with Microsoft Access. The report produces one customer invoice per page and is ready to be mailed to customers.

Begin by generating the initial report using the Access Report Wizard. However, before you proceed, examine this brief list of the steps needed to create the Invoice report from the *qryInvoiceReport* query:

- Use the Report Wizard, which will automatically group data on the InvoiceID value, to produce the initial report with data supplied solely from the query qryInvoiceReport.
- Move selected report fields from the Page Header into the InvoiceID Group Header.
- Move selected report fields from the Report Header into the Page Header.
- Delete the Report Header, Report Footer, and Page Footer sections.
- Create expressions in the InvoiceID Footer that calculate the invoice subtotal, sales tax (if any), shipping, and invoice total amounts for each invoice.
- Add miscellaneous graphics and other labels as needed to embellish the invoice.

Invoice

Invoice Number: 214010
Invoice Date: 10/1/2003
Order Date: 9/6/2003
Customer PO #: 2634-635
Sales Person: Whitney Halstead

The Coffee Merchant
5998 Alcala Park
San Diego, CA 92110

Sold to: Betz Laboratories Inc.
4636 Somerton Road
Trevose, PA 19053

Item #	Qty	Description	Price	Discount	Extended
119	17	Assam Tara TGFOP-1	$13.30	10%	203.49
122	14	Ceylon Pekoe Labookelle	$6.20	15%	73.78
131	17	China Keemun	$10.90	5%	176.03
188	17	Vienna	$3.90	0%	66.30
236	18	Rose Potpourri	$6.90	5%	117.99

				Subtotal:	$637.59
				Sales Tax:	0.00
				Shipping:	20.75
				Invoice Total:	$658.34

Figure 5.25 First page of the invoice report.

Creating the Report's First Draft

It is almost always best to create the first draft of a report with the Report Wizard. Creating a report with no help is difficult work, and the Report Wizard is sophisticated and resourceful. The Wizard determines that we need a report with groups because the data is produced from a query whose tables are joined in a chain of several one-to-many relationships. That's just what we want. In particular, we want all the invoice detail lines—the item name, quantity, price, discount, and total price—in any given invoice grouped by invoice number.

EXERCISE 5.10: USING THE REPORT WIZARD

1. Click Reports in the Database window Objects bar, click the New button on the Database window, select Report Wizard, and click the drop-down arrow on the list box to display the names of tables and queries in your database. Click *qryInvoiceReport*, and then click OK.
2. Make these choices (and click the Next button as needed) as you go through the remaining Report Wizard steps:
   - Select all available fields from the query to appear on the report.

- Choose to view data with the "by tblInvoice" group.
- Select no other grouping levels.
- Sort your records in ascending order by the ItemID field. On the sort field step, click the Summary Options button, and check the box under the Sum column of the Extended row to sum that field for both detailed and summary fields (see Figure 5.26). Click OK to confirm your choices.
- Accept the Stepped report layout in Portrait orientation.
- Select the Formal report style.
- Type the report title **Invoice** in the text box on the last dialog box.

3. After reviewing the draft report, close it and its Design window.
4. Rename the report by selecting Invoice from the list of reports, pressing F2, and typing **rptInvoiceCut1**. This name allows you to keep each successive, improved version so you can compare and contrast them.
5. Reopen the *rptInvoiceCut1* report in Design view.

Figure 5.27 shows the initial report in Design view. Notice that we have removed the rulers and grid lines. While viewing a report in Design view, you can remove the rulers or the grid lines by clicking Ruler or Grid, respectively, in the View menu. Access removes the check mark beside the Ruler choice or the Grid choice, indicating

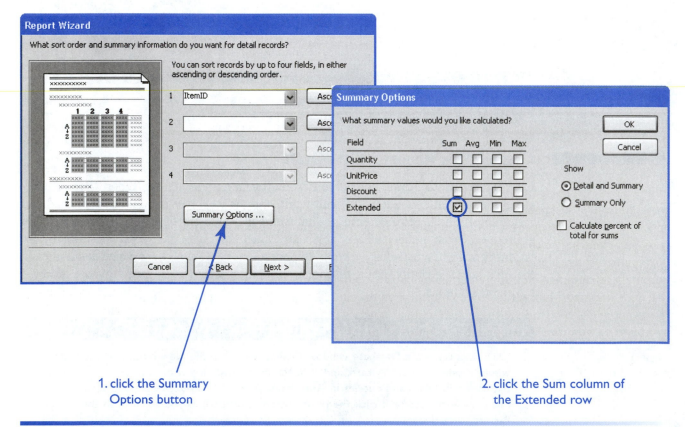

1. click the Summary Options button

2. click the Sum column of the Extended row

Figure 5.26   Report Wizard Summary Options choices.

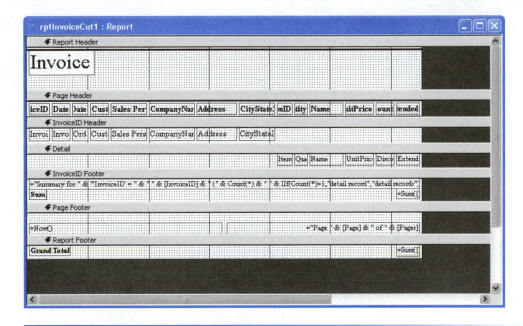

Figure 5.27 Initial invoice report layout.

they won't display. Because check mark menu items are toggle commands, you can select either one again to reestablish them.

Rearranging and Deleting Report Fields

The next step is to move selected text fields from the Page Header section to the InvoiceID Header section. Follow the discussion as we outline how to rearrange fields. All the fields in the Page Header will be either moved or eliminated.

First, you must make room in the InvoiceID Header section. Drag the bottom of the InvoiceID Header section—just above the Detail bar—down until the InvoiceID Header section is about two inches tall. Then, select all fields in the Page Header section (they are all labels). Remember that you first press and hold the Shift key and then click each field in turn to select all of them. (Be careful not to accidentally move them as you click.) Drag the selected fields down into the InvoiceID Header area, and release the mouse. Click anywhere to deselect the items. In the Page Header, delete the two horizontal lines (select each and press Delete). Move the large label *Invoice* and its attendant horizontal line from the Report Header section to the Page Header section.

Move the ItemID, Quantity, Name, UnitPrice, Discount, and Extended text labels down so that they are just above the bar labeled Detail and about one inch in from the left edge of the report border. With those six controls still selected, move the pointer to the right side of any one object and double-click its side handle to enlarge all labels so that their full names are visible. (Label controls are bold, whereas bound controls displaying field values are not bold.) In a similar way, select the Detail section bound controls, and spread them out from one another a bit. With all Detail section controls selected, drag any one of the bound controls' right selection handles to enlarge all selected controls. Delete the labels *CompanyName*, *Address*, and *CityStateZip*. Be careful to not delete the bound controls of the same name, because the bound controls display the actual customer information.

Continue to rearrange bound and unbound controls. Do not worry when the labels and associated bound controls do not line up horizontally or vertically. You can fix that later. For now, simply rearrange objects so that their approximate location matches Figure 5.25. Eliminate the very long character string in the InvoiceID Footer and the label Sum, leaving in place only the expression *=Sum([Extended])*. (The expression sums the extended prices from each invoice line's extended price, yielding the subtotal.) Using Figure 5.25 as a guideline, rearrange each of the Group Header labels and bound controls so they resemble the layout shown. Switch to Print Preview view periodically to see how the data and labels line up and to ensure bound controls are wide enough to display the data.

The Coffee Merchant's name and address shown in Figure 5.25 are bold, 12 point, Times New Roman typeface. Create them by opening the toolbox and dragging three labels to the Group Header section; change the Format properties of all three using the property sheet; and type the name and address information you see. Below The Coffee Merchant's address is the customer's address. It consists of four bound controls referring to the fields CompanyName, Address, and CityStateZip, which are all supplied by the query. The latter is a concatenation of the three tblCustomer fields City, State, and Zip Code. The expression found in the query that "glues" these three fields together is:

[City] & ", " & [State] & " " & [ZipCode]

The ampersands are character string operators that "add" one group of characters to the end of another. Once your design is fairly close to Figure 5.25, click Save As in the File menu, type **rptInvoiceCut2**, and click OK to save your new report design.

Next, you can simplify the report by eliminating the Report Header, Report Footer, and Page Footer. These contain unnecessary lines and summary information—information that is unsuitable for our Invoice report. It is simple to eliminate entire report sections, and you don't need to remove any fields from the sections beforehand. Remove the Report Header and Footer first by clicking the Report Header/Footer selection in the View menu. Click Yes when the warning dialog box appears. Because you want to retain the Page Header, you cannot use the same technique to eliminate the Page Footer. Instead, simply delete all controls in the Page Footer. This removes the Page Footer itself because nothing prints there or below that band.

MODIFYING EXISTING LABELS

Notice in Figure 5.25 that the label to the left of the invoice number is *Invoice Number:* (with a colon), not the original label taken from the field name, *InvoiceID*. To alter labels, click the label you wish to change once, and the entire label is selected. Then, click the label a second time (do not double-click the label). A vertical I-beam (insertion point) style cursor appears in the label so you can add and delete characters. If you find the activity of slowly clicking twice difficult, you can use an alternate technique: Double-click the label to bring up its property sheet. Then click the property sheet's Format tab, and type in the Caption property text box the corrected label. You can close the property sheet or leave it open. Leaving it open makes it simpler to change other labels' Caption properties. Change all labels in the InvoiceID header to match Figure 5.25. Now is a good time to save your design. A lot of work has gone into the invoice since you last saved it. Select Save As from the File menu, and type **rptInvoiceCut3**. The name indicates that this is version three of the report design.

Creating Calculated Fields

Writing an expression involving arithmetic operators, numeric or character constants, table field names, and report objects creates a calculated control. For example, the query *qryInvoiceLineItem*, which supplies information to a form, contains an expression that forms the product of the Quantity, UnitPrice, and Discount fields. You can create calculated controls, or expressions, in forms and reports also. For example, Subtotal, Sales Tax, Shipping, and Invoice Total in Figure 5.25 are calculated fields. They are not values stored in tables, because that would violate normalization rules and quickly lead to inconsistent data.

Because the Subtotal, Sales Tax, Shipping, and Invoice Total fields are calculated, their values change with each invoice printed or displayed on the console. The Report Wizard automatically created the Subtotal report field in the InvoiceID Footer when you selected Summary Options and checked Sum for the Extended field. The calculated control computes the sum of the Extended Price fields for every invoice. Next, you will rename the Subtotal calculated control so you can refer to it by an appropriate name in subsequent calculated controls, such as the Invoice Total control's expression. Other fields such as Sales Tax and Invoice Total will reference the field holding the summation of Extended Price. Here is how you rename an existing control—assigning it a new internal name that other controls can reference.

TRY IT

With *rptInvoiceCut3* open in Design view, click the field in the InvoiceID Footer that subtotals the Extended Price field. Click View, and then click Properties to display the property sheet. Select the tab labeled *Other*. Type **ctlSubtotal** in the Name property text box, replacing the current entry. Close the property sheet. That assigns the control a new and meaningful name.

Prefixes such as *ctl* identify the source of the value, a report control. Assigning objects names such as *ctlSubtotal* or *ctlSalesTax* accomplishes two important things. First, the names document the meaning of the fields you create on a design document (report or form). Second, names are mnemonic and easy to remember when you construct other calculated expressions.

Creating a new field that contains an expression is straightforward. The next two exercises explain how to create the *ctlSalesTax* and *ctlShipping* calculated controls that are placed just below the Subtotal field in the InvoiceID Footer. First, create more room in the InvoiceID Footer so that it can accommodate the additional fields. Move the mouse to the bottom edge of the footer. When the pointer changes to a double-headed arrow, drag the bottom edge of the InvoiceID Footer down so that it is approximately two inches high.

EXERCISE 5.11: CREATING A SALES TAX CALCULATED CONTROL

1. Display *rptInvoiceCut3* in Design view, open the toolbox, and click the toolbox Text Box tool. (Hover the mouse pointer over a tool for a moment, and a ToolTip displaying the tool's name will appear.)
2. Move the mouse to a position just below the subtotal control in the InvoiceID Footer, and drag the mouse to create a control that is the same size as the *ctlSubtotal* control. When you release the mouse, an unbound text box control appears on the form.
3. Display the new control's property sheet, and change the control's name: type **ctlSalesTax** in the Name property. (Remember to click the Other tab to locate the Name property.)
4. Click the property sheet Format tab, select the Format property, and select *Standard* from the down list.
5. Click the Data tab in the property sheet.
6. Click anywhere inside the Control Source text box, and then click the Build button that appears at the right side of the Control Source property. (The Build button has three dots, called an ellipsis, on it.) The Expression Builder dialog box opens.
7. Because our customers are wholesale customers, we will not charge sales tax (a simplifying assumption). In the Expression Builder box, type **=0** and then click OK to close the dialog box. (Notice that Access expressions resemble Excel spreadsheet expressions. They begin with an equal sign and are followed by an arbitrarily complex expression, though just a constant in our example here.)
8. Edit the label control to the left of the sales tax control: click it twice, and type **Sales Tax:**
9. Click outside the sales tax label, and then click the label to reselect it.
10. Click the Format tab, and change the label's Text Align property to Right. (The Text Align property is far down in the list of Format properties. Use the scroll bar to locate it.) Click outside the label to deselect it.

Leave the property sheet and toolbox open for the expression you will build in the next exercise. Next, let's construct the expression to calculate the shipping cost. To keep things relatively uncomplicated, assume that it costs $0.25 per pound to ship everything, regardless of the size of an order. The number of pounds is determined by summing the Quantity bound control (Quantity is recorded in pounds). The next exercise builds the shipping cost control expression.

EXERCISE 5.12: CREATING A SHIPPING CALCULATED CONTROL

1. With the report displayed in Design view, click the Text Box tool in the toolbox.
2. Move the mouse to a position just below the sales tax control, *ctlSalesTax*, in the InvoiceID Footer, and drag and release the mouse to create a control that is approximately the same size as the *ctlSubtotal* control.
3. Click the property sheet's Other tab, and type **ctlShipping** in the Name property to change the control's name.
4. Click the property sheet Format tab, select the Format property, and click *Standard*.
5. Click the property sheet Data tab, click inside the Control Source property text box, and click the Build button (labeled with the ellipsis).
6. Type the expression **=0.25*Sum([Quantity])** to calculate shipping costs (see Figure 5.28).
7. Click OK to close the dialog box.
8. Type the text **Shipping:** into the label control, and right-align it. Place the label control to the left of the calculated control, *ctlShipping*.

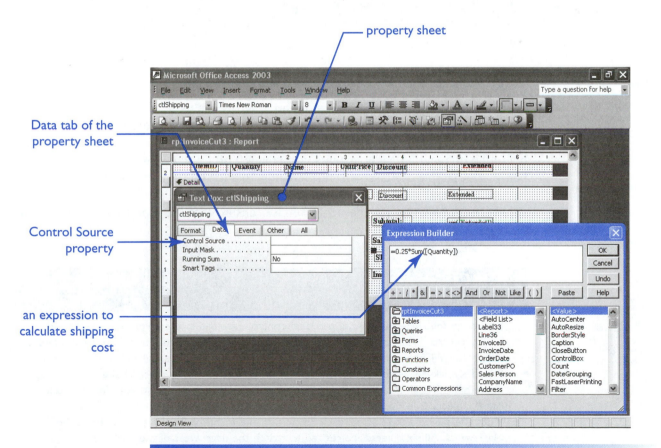

Figure 5.28 Writing an expression for a calculated control.

Click the Print Preview button to verify that the subtotal, sales tax, and shipping values are correct. Click any of the navigation buttons to verify that other invoices display correct values for the three controls you have created so far. Switch back to Design view to complete the remaining work on your report. If you haven't already, create a label to the left of the subtotal calculated control and type the text **Subtotal:** in the label.

Following the two previous exercise examples, create the Invoice Total calculated control. Name it **ctlInvoiceTotal**, and type the expression

=[ctlSubtotal]+[ctlSalesTax]+[ctlShipping]

for the Control Source. Choose the Currency format. Edit and right-align the label to the left of the Invoice Total control, typing **Invoice Total:** for its Caption property. Though labels attached to text boxes are bold by default, you can put other controls' contents in bold by selecting the control(s) (shift-click if more than one) and then changing the Font Weight property (found on the Format sheet) to Bold. Save the report as *rptInvoiceCut3*, and then save it again as *rptInvoiceCut4* to preserve your work and provide a new report name for the work you are about to complete in the following paragraphs.

Aligning and Sizing Fields

It is important to know how to align report controls (fields) and size them so that your report looks professional. Up to this point you have not been concerned with how labels and data are aligned. For instance, we have ignored the fact that the Extended label in the InvoiceID Header appears far to the left of the actual prices in the detail lines below it. A simple exercise will illustrate how to align one column of values. Once you have aligned and sized one column, you can repeat the same steps for other labels and values. In preparation for the next exercise, ensure that the report *rptInvoiceCut4* is open in Design view.

EXERCISE 5.13: ALIGNING AND SIZING MULTIPLE FIELDS

1. Select the following six objects: the label control *Extended* in the InvoiceID Header, the bound control Extended in the Detail section, and the four calculated controls *ctlSubtotal*, *ctlSalesTax*, *ctlShipping*, and *ctlInvoiceTotal*. Release the mouse when all six objects are selected. Quick tip: Select all the objects by clicking above the topmost label and then drag down and through the objects. Keep the rectangle outline narrow so you do not "touch" other objects (see Figure 5.29.)
2. With the six objects selected, click Format on the menu bar, point to Size, and click To Narrowest. All six objects are resized to match the narrowest of them all.
3. Click Format on the menu bar, point to Align, and click Right. All objects snap into vertical alignment on the rightmost object of the six.
4. Click outside the objects to deselect them.

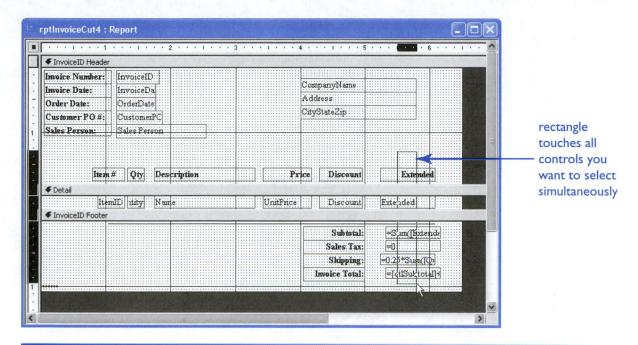

Figure 5.29   Selecting multiple objects in different report sections.

Repeat the preceding four steps for the label control/bound control pairs ItemID, Quantity, UnitPrice, and Discount. However, do not narrow the Name column, so that lengthy names of coffees and teas can be displayed. Instead, size the Name label and value controls by executing Format, pointing to Size, and clicking To Widest. The Name label in the header widens to match the values in the Detail section. If necessary, you can widen both controls later to accommodate long descriptions.

Finally, place a Page Break control near the bottom of the InvoiceID Footer, below all existing InvoiceID Footer controls. Be sure to place the page break far enough down so that it will fall below the Shipping and Invoice Total controls. Save your report one more time.

Preview your Invoice report in the Report window. Your screen should resemble the one shown in Figure 5.25. There are several small embellishments you need to add to spruce it up, but you can fine-tune your invoice any time you wish. So that you will have a good base from which to understand this report, we have saved the complete Invoice report and named it *rptInvoiceReport* on your Companion CD. You can improve on your design, or you can study ours.

 Go to http://perry.swlearning.com for an in-depth tutorial.

SUMMARY

This chapter has emphasized using Access to create and modify forms and reports. You crafted forms for several tables that display a friendlier, more intuitive interface between the form user and the database. You learned how to add columns to forms and how to change the properties of fields on the form.

You have gained a lot of knowledge about Access reports in this chapter. You built a tabular-style report using a Report Wizard. You learned that reports can receive their data from both tables and queries. One of the reports you built contained a query. You also created an invoice report that tied together six of The Coffee Merchant's tables with a query. Various report headers and footers were described, including Group Headers and Footers, and you added calculated controls to the Group Footer that computed invoice subtotals, sales tax, shipping, and total invoice values. Having read this chapter, you can design and use Access forms and reports. Now that you have read the first five chapters, you are ready to apply your knowledge to build richly featured accounting database systems that serve the needs of your users.

QUESTIONS AND PROBLEMS FOR REVIEW

Multiple-Choice Questions

1. Which type of form requires a response before the user can continue working?
   a. Continuous form
   b. Subform
   c. Multiple-page form
   d. Modal form

2. The active field on a form into which you can type or press the spacebar is called
   a. the hub.
   b. the focus.
   c. the domain.
   d. the center.

3. When using Form Wizard, clicking the >> button will
   a. move all fields from Available to Selected fields.
   b. move only the highlight field from Available to Selected fields.
   c. move all fields from Selected to Available fields.
   d. move only the highlighted field from Selected to Available fields.

4. Which type of control has an expression as its data source?
   a. Bound
   b. Unbound
   c. Calculated
   d. Processed

5. What view do you use to move controls on a form or subform?
   a. Datasheet
   b. Design
   c. Form
   d. Properties

6. Which section of a report is required?
   a. Report Header
   b. Report Footer
   c. Page Header
   d. Detail

7. When using Report Wizard to create a new report, the fields you want on the report are first selected. From where can these fields be selected?
   a. Any table in the database
   b. Any query in the database
   c. One table or query in the database
   d. More than one table or query in the database

8. Which view do you use to change the layout of a report?
   a. Design View
   b. Print Preview
   c. Layout Preview
   d. None of the above

9. You apply a more meaningful name to an existing control in Design view by
   a. selecting Properties from View, then Other, and typing in the Name text box.
   b. double-clicking on the control, selecting Other, and typing in the Name text box.
   c. pressing F4, selecting Other, and typing in the Name text box.
   d. All of the above.

10. To resize multiple fields in a report as well as realign, which menu do you select?
    a. Tools
    b. View
    c. Format
    d. Edit

Discussion Questions

1. Discuss the advantage(s) of providing a list box or a combo box in a form. How does it help a user? What possible disadvantages are present when using a list box control?

2. What are the advantages of using a form to view or update data in a table? Are there any disadvantages to using a form rather than viewing the table directly?

3. Explain why you might want to use a form to search a database. Can you change values in underlying tables through a form? Explain.

4. Discuss the differences in use between a form and a report. Where is each one best used? What advantages does a form provide when compared to a report?

5. Explain, or speculate, when it is best to use a query as the basis of a report and when it is better to use a Report Wizard and select multiple, related tables.

Practice Exercises

1. Create and print a form that displays all the information from *tblInventory*. Include the title *Inventory Records By ID Number* as well as your name in each form. Print the first page of the form.

2. Create a form from *qryInventory*. Save as *frmNewInventoryItem*. Determine next InventoryID available and add a new record for ItemID 458 that is caffeinated, cost is $8.50, and a quantity of 500. Include the title Inventory Item Form in the header along with your name. Print the new form. Go to *tblInventory*, and sort by *ItemID* in descending order. Print page 1 (see your new item listed), and write your name at the top.

3. Create a form that uses *tblInventoryDescription* as the main form and *tblInventory* as the subform. Alter all the columns in the subform to their optimal width. Alter the main so that CountryID and its value fall under Comments. Include the title *Inventory Details Form* as well as your name. Print any record from your new form.

4. Create a report named *Inventory On Hand* using *qryInventory* that includes all the fields from the query and views the data with Name in its own grouping level at the top. The other records need to be in ascending order by ItemID and by InventoryID, and then OnHand in descending order. Sum the OnHand inventory values. Delete the long character string associated with the summary for Name. Print the first page, and include your name.

5. Modify the report named *Inventory Value By Product Name*. Change the label Sum in the Name Footer to Summary of Product Inventory. Add a column called *Extended* to the left of Price that will calculate the value of each ItemID row (Price times OnHand). Use meaningful control names. Then, sum Extended in the Name Footer to obtain a total value of each product on hand. Rename the labels appropriately. Print a page of the report. Include your name on the report.

Problems

1. Create and print the form shown in Figure 5.2. The form displays information from several rows of the table *tblEmployee*. Include a title at the top of each form, and include your name, course number, and section in each form. Print only the first page of the form.

2. Create a report that lists employees' last names, employees' first names, and their sales in order of each employee's last name. Employee sales data are stored in the table *tblSalesTransactions*. The foreign key in that table linking it to employees is EmployeeID. Once you get the query right, produce a report showing all sales transactions for the employees whose last names are Pacioli, Hunter, or Ellison. Include an unbound control containing your name. If your instructor requests it, include other unbound controls (labels) indicating other identification information such as the course name and section number.

3. Create a form that resembles the Inventory Data Entry form shown in Figure 5.1, except that your form has a record selector—a standard form item. In addition to the fields you see in Figure 5.1, add an unbound control labeled "Country of Origin" and an associated bound control that displays each coffee's country of origin. Use the Form Wizard, and base the form on tables that you specify using the Form Wizard. There is no need to first build a query and then link together the appropriate tables. The tables that you need to build the form are *tblCountryName*, *tblInventory*, and *tblInventoryDescription*. Add an unbound control with your first and last name. When the Form Wizard asks about grouping, select "view by tblInventory." Use the Filter command to locate any single coffee produced by the country of Zimbabwe. Print the form showing the Zimbabwe coffee displayed by the form. Extra credit: Remove from the form the record selector, the Minimize button, and the Maximize button.

4. Create a columnar form displaying all the fields from the table *tblSalesTaxRate*. Fields in the table include StateAbbreviation, StateName, TaxRate, Population, and LandArea. Once you or a Form Wizard creates the basic form, add a calculated control that computes and displays the population density. (Population density is the population divided by the land area and is measured, in this case, in people per square mile.) Format the calculated control Fixed with two decimal places. Change any unbound controls (labels) such as "StateName" to "State Name" so that no label is two or more words back to back. Align all unbound controls so that they line up on their right sides. Align all bound controls (text boxes showing database values) so that their values display in the left side of their respective text boxes. This is not the same as using the Format menu Align command. You must set a particular property of the control. Ensure that there is an equal amount of vertical space between all bound/unbound control pairs. Create a Form Header, and place an unbound control with your first and last name. Print a form showing only one record, not several, from the database.

5. You want to mail out a large number of flyers to all your current customers. Use the Access Label Wizard to create a report. The report is, in fact, a set of Avery labels. Create a new report based on the table *tblCustomer*. Select Label Wizard from the list of report types. Then, make the following choices: Click "English Unit of Measure" and select Avery 5160 labels. Place the following fields on your mailing labels: Contact, Address, City, State, and ZipCode. Arrange the fields on the

label with the Contact on line 1, Address on line 2, and City, State, and ZipCode on line 3. Place a comma between the City and State. Ensure there is at least one blank following the comma and between State and ZipCode. Sort the mailing labels by State and then by City within state. Name your report "Mailing Labels" (without the double quotation marks). Print only the first page of the report. Be careful in making your Print dialog box choices—the report is almost 60 pages long. Write your name and any other identification required by your instructor on the printed, single-page report.

CHAPTER 6
Revenue Cycle

OBJECTIVES

Revenue cycle activities include accepting orders from customers, recording sales, invoicing customers, recording cash received from customers, and maintaining records of these events. In this chapter, you will learn how to use Microsoft Access to design tables, queries, forms, and reports that can help you:

- Create and maintain customer records.
- Create and maintain finished goods inventory records.
- Record sales orders.
- Record sales/shipment information.
- Print invoices.
- Record payments received from customers.
- Summarize and report cash receipts information.

INTRODUCTION

This chapter describes the revenue cycle elements of accounting information systems. We illustrate many of these components using example data for the Pipefitters Supply Company, a merchandising firm. The revenue cycle includes those activities related to the sale of goods or services. Whether firms are manufacturers, merchandisers, or service businesses, their revenue cycles are similar. For example, manufacturing and merchandising firms sell products to customers; service firms perform services for customers. In both cases, customers place orders for the product or service that they are purchasing. The selling firm then ships the product or performs the service. At this point, the selling firm will send the customer an invoice that shows details of the sale. Customers then, pursuant to the terms stated on the invoice, usually pay the amount due shown on the invoice. Some customers will pay on receipt of a monthly statement that lists all of the invoices for that month. The practice of paying the statement amount once each month is a holdover from the days when running batch computer processes or manually writing checks was a cumbersome ordeal. Most businesses now find it more convenient to print checks daily and, therefore, pay from invoices rather than from monthly statements.

In addition to handling orders, invoices, and incoming payments, the revenue cycle accounting system must maintain a permanent record of customer information and provide tools for updating and revising that customer information. As you learned in Chapter 1, a key feature of database accounting systems is their ability to store much more information about each transaction than a traditional double-entry system. To take full advantage of this feature, users must be able to access the revenue cycle information stored in the system to perform sales and cash flow analyses. Users must also be able to perform update and maintenance tasks on finished goods inventory information. Finally, the revenue cycle system should give financial accountants the information they need to create ledgers, journals, and financial statements.

Copies of all tables, forms, queries, and reports that appear in this chapter are included in the *Ch06.mdb* database on your Companion CD. Feel free to copy that file to your hard drive and experiment with it as you work through this chapter. Remember to remove the read-only attribute from the file after you have copied it, as you learned in Exercise 1.14. Note, however, that the step-by-step instructions for this chapter assume you are working in your own Access file. For example, if you follow our instructions to save the Customer table and you are working in the *Ch06.mdb* file, Access will display a message asking if you want to replace the existing Customer table with the new one you have created.

PIPEFITTERS SUPPLY COMPANY REVENUE CYCLE INFORMATION

Pipefitters Supply Company accepts orders over the telephone, via fax, and by mail. When an order arrives, one of the salespersons enters it as a sales order. The sales order includes the customer's name and a list of the inventory items that the customer wishes to purchase. This inventory list includes the quantity of each inventory item and the price at which Pipefitters is currently selling the item. When the order is ready to ship, Pipefitters completes an invoice and records the sale. Sometimes, some of the inventory items a customer has ordered are not in stock. In those cases, Pipefitters will ship partial orders. Customers are expected to pay their invoices within 30 days. Most customers do pay on time; however, some customers make partial payments over two or more months.

The data model for Pipefitters includes five entities: customer, sales order, sale, inventory, and cash receipt. Each customer may have many sales orders, many sales, and many cash receipts. Sales orders, sales, and cash receipts, however, can each have only one customer. Sales orders and sales can each have many inventory items, and each inventory item can appear on many sales orders and many sales. The data model for Pipefitters, showing these five entities and the one-to-many and many-to-many relationships among them, appears in Figure 6.1.

This chapter will show you how to build elements of the accounting system for Pipefitters' revenue cycle. The design will include five tables for the entities and two

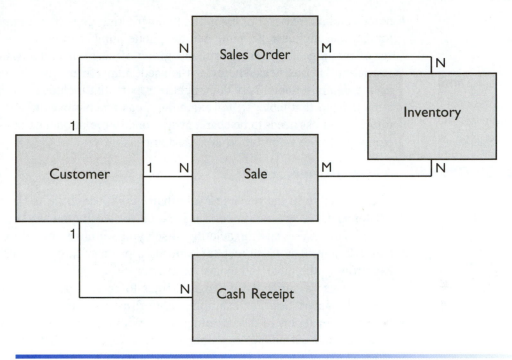

Figure 6.1 Pipefitters Supply Company revenue cycle data model.

additional tables to model the many-to-many relationships. You will learn how to create forms to enter data into these tables efficiently. You will also learn how to create queries and reports that extract information about revenue cycle activities.

CUSTOMER INFORMATION

Customers are the lifeblood of any business; therefore, accounting system database tables must include many details about each customer. At a minimum, firms want to know where their customers are located, what they have purchased, and when they purchased it. Businesses also want to track when their customers pay and the amounts of the individual payments. Some businesses do not record information about their customers' identities. For example, businesses such as retail stores, fast-food restaurants, and amusement parks seldom record individual customers' names and addresses. Customers of these businesses pay cash and would not tolerate the time it would take to record their identities. These businesses do, however, keep careful records of customer traffic by day, hour, and location. Increasingly, these types of firms are developing ways to obtain information about their customers' identities. Many supermarket chains now offer their customers an identification card that gives them a discount on merchandise. The discount is the price that these supermarket chains are willing to pay to obtain customer identity information.

Customer information appears on many documents that businesses create and use. Invoices, shipping documents, and end of month account statements require customer names and addresses. For example, the marketing department might want a list of customers that includes the name and telephone number of customer contact persons or a set of mailing labels for a particular group of customers. To ensure that customer information is consistent wherever it is used, many firms keep all customer information in one database table. Any document or report that includes customer information obtains it from that table. If, for example, a customer moves to a new location, the customer's address needs to be changed only once. A relational database accounting system stores customer information in a Customer table.

The Customer Table

The first table in the revenue cycle that we will describe is the *Customer table*. The Customer table provides a central location for storing all information about each customer. This makes adding, deleting, displaying, or changing customer information easy and efficient. The Customer table needs a primary key field that uniquely identifies each row in the table and exists for every row.

Firms use a variety of coding schemes to create customer numbers that will have these characteristics. For example, some firms use alphanumeric codes that combine the first four letters of the customer name with the first four digits of the customer address to create a unique customer number. To ensure that each CustomerNumber is unique, many firms assign a sequential number to each new customer. A sequential number scheme gives each new customer a number that is one greater than the largest customer number that currently exists. In Exercise 6.1, you will begin creating a Customer table, called *tblCustomer*. In this exercise, you will open a new table and create its primary key field, CustomerNumber. Pipefitters uses a five-digit sequential numbering scheme for its customer numbers that they have designed to start with a customer number of 10001 and to accommodate up to 89,999 customers.

EXERCISE 6.1: CREATING *TBLCUSTOMER* AND THE CUSTOMERNUMBER FIELD

1. Start Microsoft Access, select the File, New menu command, and then click the Blank Database icon in the task pane at the right side of the screen. In the File New Database dialog box, select the folder in which you want to save your Pipefitters revenue cycle database, type the name you want to give your database in the File name box, and click the Create button.

2. Double-click the Create table in Design View icon in the Database window.

3. Type the name of *tblCustomer's* first field, **CustomerNumber**, and press Enter. When you press Enter, the first row in the Data Type column changes into a combo box, and the Field Properties list appears in the bottom pane of the Table window.

4. Click the Primary Key button on the toolbar to make the CustomerNumber field the primary key for *tblCustomer*. A small key symbol appears in the row selector box to the left of the first row in the Field Name column, and the Indexed property sets itself to Yes (No Duplicates).

5. Since you will not be using the CustomerNumber field in any calculations, you can set its data type to Text. The Data Type combo box contains Text as its default selection.

6. Press Tab to accept the Text default selection. You can use the Description column to store a description of the CustomerNumber field if you wish. The Description column is a built-in documentation tool that is especially useful for storing explanations of complex or potentially confusing fields.

7. Press F6 to switch to the Field Properties pane. The cursor will highlight the default Field Size value of 50. Type **5** in the Field Size column to replace the default selection.

8. Press the Tab key three times, and type **Customer Number** (including the space between words) as the field's Caption property.

This Caption property setting will cause *Customer Number*, rather than the field's name, *CustomerNumber*, to appear as the default text for form and report controls that reference the field. Creating a useful Caption property setting can be a real time saver when you are building reports and forms that use table fields.

The panel on the right side of the Field Properties pane provides detailed instructions for each step in the property-setting process. Figure 6.2 shows the new Customer table with the CustomerNumber primary key field and the caption setting in Design view.

Another important table property is the Validation Rule property. The Validation Rule property provides a useful internal control feature at the table level. You can use this property to limit the values that a user can enter for a table field. This feature can help prevent data entry errors. For example, CustomerNumber is a five-digit field. The Validation Rule property lets you limit data entered into the field to numbers that are

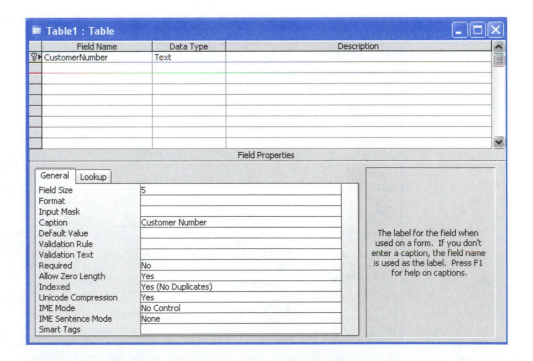

Figure 6.2 The CustomerNumber field in *tblCustomer*.

exactly five digits long. In the next exercise, you will set the validation properties for the Customer table.

EXERCISE 6.2: SETTING THE VALIDATION PROPERTIES FOR *TBLCUSTOMER*

1. Press the Tab key twice or click the Validation Rule property box to select it.
2. Type the expression **Like "#####"** in the Validation Rule box to prevent a user from entering anything other than exactly five digits in the CustomerNumber field. For example, this Validation Rule would prevent a user from entering JTP46 (which contains nondigit characters) or 9244 (which contains four, not five, digits) in the CustomerNumber field. You can make this data input internal control feature even more useful by entering Validation Text to accompany the Validation Rule.
3. Press Tab to move the cursor to the Validation Text property box.
4. Type **Invalid entry. You must enter a Customer Number of exactly five digits.**

The text you enter as a field's Validation Text property will appear in an error message dialog box whenever a user attempts to enter a CustomerNumber value that violates the Validation Rule. Figure 6.3 shows the Table window with all of the property settings you have created for the CustomerNumber field.

Since the CustomerNumber field is the primary key of *tblCustomer*, Access will require that a unique value be entered for each record before saving it. Therefore, you

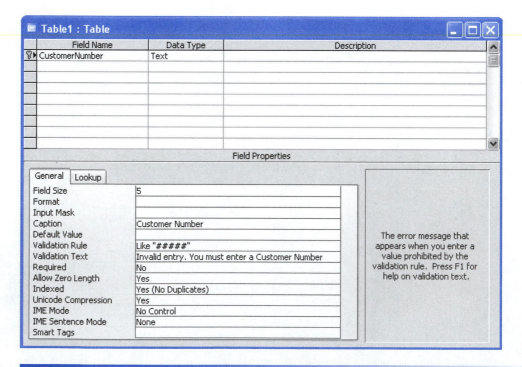

Figure 6.3 Property settings for the CustomerNumber field.

do not need to specify a value in the Required property. Setting the Required property to Yes for a primary key field does not alter the database's behavior. The Validation Rule property setting will override the Allow Zero Length property.

The Indexed property was automatically set to Yes (No Duplicates) when you made CustomerNumber the table's primary key in Exercise 6.1. Access automatically sets the Unicode Compression property to Yes. Unicode compression reduces the amount of disk space that text and memo fields require for storage, so most database designers leave the property set to the default setting.

In Exercise 6.3 you will create the remaining nine fields in the Customer table. These fields will store customer names, addresses, telephone numbers, and other valuable information about customers. Note that the address is stored in multiple fields. Placing customer city, state, and zip code information in separate fields helps users more easily search and select records from the database on values of those specific address elements.

EXERCISE 6.3: CREATING THE REMAINING FIELDS IN *TBLCUSTOMER*

1. Type **CustomerName** in the second row of the Field Name column, and leave its Data Type set to Text. The appropriate size for CustomerName will vary from firm to firm, but you should set it to accommodate the longest customer name you anticipate. For this example, set the CustomerName Field Size property to **25**. When you use the CustomerName field in forms and reports, the context will usually indicate that you are referring to a customer name. Select the Caption property, and set it to **Name**. Of course, the Caption property sets only the default, so if you need to clarify the label in a particular form or report, you can change the control's text in that form or report. Note that this firm's customers are business entities. If the customers had been individuals, you might have stored the customer name by creating separate fields for CustomerFirstName, CustomerMiddleInitial, and CustomerLastName.

2. Enter **CustomerAddress1** and **CustomerAddress2** fields with property settings that are similar to those of the CustomerName field. The CustomerAddress2 field lets the table accommodate customers with a second address line, such as a suite or office number. In the sample form, we set the Caption property to **Address** for both of these fields.

3. Enter **CustomerCity** as a Text Data Type with a Field Size property of **25**, and then set its Caption property to **City**.

4. Enter **CustomerState** as a Text Data Type with a Field Size property of **2**, and then set its Caption property to **State**.

5. Enter **CustomerZipCode** as a Text Data Type with a Field Size property of **10** to accommodate the U.S. Postal Service's five-digits-plus-four ZIP Code format, and then set its Caption property to **Zip Code**.

6. Enter **CustomerTelephone** as a Text Data Type and a Field Size property setting of **14**, and then set its Caption property to **Telephone**.

7. Enter **CustomerCreditLimit** in the next open row of the Field Name column. Type **Currency** over the default Data Type setting of Text. Currency is a number Data Type that displays dollar signs automatically. Selecting a Currency Data Type automatically sets the Format property to Currency and the Decimal Places property to Auto. You will not

see these settings until you press F6 or click in the Field Properties pane of the Design view window. To restrict credit limit amounts to integer values, change the Decimal Places property to **0**. Set the Caption property to **Credit Limit**

8. Enter **CustomerPrimaryContact**. Use your own judgment in setting the Data Type, Field Size, and Caption properties for this field.

TRY IT

Another way to choose a field's Data Type is to click the combo box button and select one of the choices that appear in the drop-down list. For example, you could have chosen Currency in step 7 of the previous exercise by clicking the Data Type cell and selecting Currency from the list.

You now have a complete set of fields in *tblCustomer* that Pipefitters can use to store its customer data. Recall that you used the validation properties to control data entry in the CustomerNumber field. The validation properties check the entire contents of a field when it is entered. Access provides another tool for controlling data entry, the Input Mask property. This property checks each character as a user enters it. An input mask will not permit a user to enter any character that violates the input mask rules for a field. Unfortunately, the Input Mask property does not allow you to customize the error message that appears when an entry is incorrect. You should carefully consider whether to use the Input Mask property or the Validation Rule property for a particular field.

The CustomerState field is an excellent candidate for an input mask, since all U.S. state abbreviations are two capital letters. In the following exercise, you will create an input mask that controls the data entered into the CustomerState field so that it conforms to the U.S. Postal Service's abbreviation convention.

EXERCISE 6.4: CREATING A CUSTOM INPUT MASK FOR CUSTOMERSTATE

1. Select the CustomerState field by clicking it in the Field Name column that appears in the top pane of the Table window.
2. Type **>LL** in the Input Mask property box.

The > symbol converts lowercase letters to uppercase letters. For example, if a user enters the letters *oh*, the input mask converts them to *OH*. The LL placeholders in the expression limit the entry to two letters. Entering any other value, a number or punctuation symbol for example, will generate an error message.

Using an Input Mask property setting for the CustomerZipCode field also works well. The CustomerZipCode Field Size property setting of 10 provides enough characters to use the U.S. Postal Service's five-digits-plus-four Zip Code format. This format is so common that Access includes an Input Mask Wizard that can create an appropriate input mask for you. When you select the Input Mask property box, a button with an ellipsis (three periods) label, called the *Build button*, appears to the right of the Input Mask box. Clicking the Build button starts the Input Mask Wizard, which can create input mask templates for zip codes and other commonly used fields.

EXERCISE 6.5: USING THE INPUT MASK WIZARD FOR CUSTOMERZIPCODE

1. Select the CustomerZipCode field by clicking it in the Field Name column that appears in the top pane of the Table window.
2. Click the Input Mask property box.
3. Click the property's Build button to open the Input Mask Wizard. A Microsoft Access dialog box appears informing you that you must save the table before proceeding. Save the table with the name *tblCustomer*, and open the Input Mask Wizard dialog box, which appears in Figure 6.4.
4. Select Zip Code from the list of Input Mask names, and click the Next button.
5. Click the Next button to accept the default placeholder character, the underscore.
6. Click the Option button to indicate that you want to store the field with the symbols in the mask (this changes the data storage default of not storing the hyphen so that Access does store the hyphen as part of the field contents), and then click the Next button.
7. Click the Finish button to return to the Table window. The Wizard will create the Input Mask property setting of 00000\ -9999;0;_ for the CustomerZipCode field.

Input Mask property settings includes three parts; each part is separated by a semicolon. The first part contains the template. The Zip Code template includes the placeholder *00000*, which requires the user to enter five digits in this field. The backslash

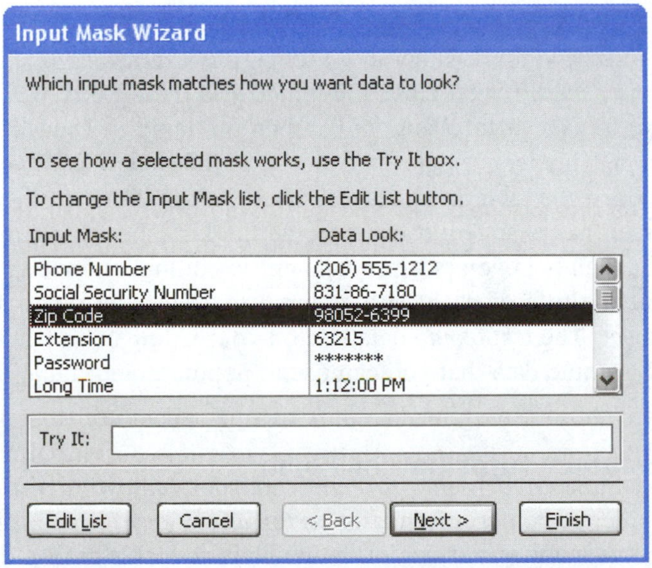

Figure 6.4 Using the Input Mask Wizard to select a Zip Code setting.

character tells Access to recognize the next character, a hyphen, as itself. When a character that has a special meaning in an expression is used as itself, it is called a *literal*. The *9999* placeholder permits, but does not require, the user to enter another four digits. The *0* in the second part of the setting, between the first and second semicolon, tells Access to store the hyphen along with the digits in the CustomerZipCode field. The third part of the setting makes the underscore character the default placeholder that will appear in CustomerZipCode field controls on data entry forms.

You can use the Input Mask Wizard to set the CustomerTelephone field's Input Mask property to the predefined Phone Number setting that appears at the top of the list in the Input Mask Wizard dialog box shown in Figure 6.4. In our example database on the Companion CD, we elected to store the telephone numbers with the Input Mask characters (the parentheses, space, and hyphen that are used in U.S. telephone numbers and area codes).

TRY IT

Note that we used a number of different characters in the Input Mask properties of the fields in *tblCustomer*. To see a complete list of characters that you can use in customizing Input Mask properties, consult the Microsoft Access online help feature. Select Help, Microsoft Access Help from the menu, click the Index tab, and type **InputMask**. Click the Search button, and double-click the words "InputMask Property" that appear in the Choose a Topic dialog box. This help topic includes a complete list of available characters and explains how to use them in the Input Mask property's syntax. Click the Close button to close the Microsoft Access Help dialog box.

At this point, you can either close the Table window or open the table in Datasheet view to enter data. If you close the window, a dialog box will appear and ask if you would like to save your changes. To open the table in Datasheet view, click the first toolbar icon. This icon toggles between Datasheet view and Design view for tables.

If you open the table in Datasheet view, you may notice that the toolbar at the top of the screen has changed; it has become the Datasheet toolbar. This toolbar provides buttons that can help you perform data entry, editing, and viewing tasks. You may also notice that the title of each table column in Datasheet view is the Caption property value you set. The *Ch06.mdb* database on your Companion CD includes a *tblCustomer* table with sample data that you can use to populate your table instead of entering data yourself.

The Customer Information Form

You can enter customer information in *tblCustomer* while it is open in Datasheet view. However, the number and size of the fields in the table makes this a difficult task. Depending on your screen resolution, only six or seven of the table's ten fields will be displayed in the Datasheet view window. Entering customer information in Datasheet view requires that you scroll back and forth to enter all ten field values for each record. In this section, you will learn how to create a form for *tblCustomer* that will make entering, changing, and deleting customer information much easier.

You can create a form for *tblCustomer* by using the AutoForm tool. Access offers several ways to activate AutoForm; perhaps the easiest is the Insert menu. First, make sure you have selected Tables objects in the Database window and have selected *tblCustomer*. Then, choose Insert, AutoForm from the menu, as shown in Figure 6.5.

AutoForm examines the selected table and creates a form that accommodates many of the table's field characteristics. AutoForm is quick, easy to run, and often creates a usable form. Even when it does not create an ideal form, it creates a form that you can edit to meet your specific needs. The results of the AutoForm action appear in Figure 6.6. Note that the form shown in the figure is bound to the version of *tblCustomer* included on the Companion CD that contains a number of customer records. Your form will not show any data unless you have entered or copied data into your Customer table object.

Figure 6.5 Selecting AutoForm from the menu for *tblCustomer*.

Figure 6.6   The AutoForm-generated Customer Data Entry form.

Although AutoForm did a good job of creating a usable form, you can improve the appearance of the form and enhance its usefulness. You will learn how to do this in the next exercise. As you follow these instructions, remember that you should try to develop your own sense of what makes a form useful. Your forms do not need to look exactly like the forms we show in this book.

EXERCISE 6.6: IMPROVING THE CUSTOMER DATA ENTRY FORM

1. To modify the form, you will need to work in Design view. To enter Design view while the new form is displayed, click the Design View toolbar button or select View, Design View from the menu. You can click and drag the edges of the form to make all of the form's controls visible.
2. Select the CustomerNumber label by clicking the box in its upper-left corner—the mouse cursor will change to a hand with a pointing index finger—and carefully drag the label toward the CustomerNumber text box control to its right. Leave only one or two grid dots exposed between the label and the text box control.
3. Select all of the label controls. You can do this by holding down the Shift key as you click each control, or you can click and drag a marquee around the controls. Select the menu command Format, Align, Right to right-justify the label controls.
4. Click the Align Right text formatting toolbar button to align the label text within the controls.
5. Click the Bold text formatting toolbar button to format the labels as bold text.
6. Drag the left edge of the CustomerNumber control label (it is the widest label) far enough to the left to expose all of its text.
7. Right-click the CustomerCreditLimit control, and select Properties. In the Properties sheet, click the Format tab, and change the Text Align value from General to Left. (You may have to scroll the properties to expose the Text Align property.)
8. With the Properties sheet still open, select the form by choosing Edit, Select Form from the menu or clicking the small gray box in the upper-left corner of the form.

9. Click the Format tab in the Properties sheet, and change the value of the Caption property from *tblCustomer* to **Customer Information**. You can also change the value of the Record Selectors property from Yes to **No**, the value of the Dividing Lines property from Yes to **No**, and the value of the Scroll Bars property from Both to **Neither**. Close the Properties sheet.

10. Adjust the widths of the bound controls to accommodate the longest possible field contents.

This last step may require some trial and error adjusting. You can use the Form View and Design View toolbar buttons to switch between the two views. Note that as you switch back and forth, the form changes size because the Design View rulers and the Detail section indicator bar disappear when you open the form in Form View.

TRY IT

Many people new to Access find that the additional elements that appear when the form is open in Design view—the Detail section bar and the rulers at the top and left side—are confusing. You cannot eliminate the Detail section bar from the Design View window, but you can remove the rulers. Select View, Ruler from the menu. Note that this action operates as a toggle; if you repeat the action, the rulers will reappear. This little trick works in the Design View window for reports, too.

You can make additional adjustments to the form's look to satisfy your own sense of aesthetics. Figure 6.7 shows a finished version of the Customer Information form. To save the Customer Information form, select File, Save As from the menu, or press Ctrl+S and enter **frmCustomer** as the new name for the form in the Save As dialog box. Click OK to save it. You can close your Customer Information form with the menu command File, Close. The form is saved in the Forms section of the database. To see the form, click the Forms tab.

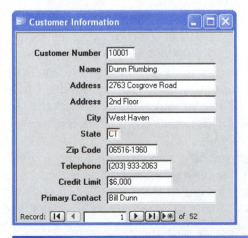

Figure 6.7   The finished Customer Information form in Form view.

Maintaining Customer Records

Now that you have created a Customer table to store customer information and a form that makes using that table easy, you can efficiently and effectively maintain customer records. First, you will want to create records for new customers. Second, you will occasionally delete customer records you no longer need. Third, you will need to update the table as customers move, get new telephone numbers, and change other information that you have entered in *tblCustomer*.

You will want to keep your file of customer information current. Remember, one advantage of using a relational database model for an accounting system is that you only need to add, delete, or change information in one place. For customer information, *tblCustomer* is that place.

To use *frmCustomer* to add customers to *tblCustomer*, open the form by clicking the Forms tab in the Database window and double-clicking *frmCustomer*. To enter customer information, just begin typing. Press Enter after typing the information into each control field. Notice how the Input Mask and Validation Rule properties that you set for *tblCustomer* help you avoid data entry errors in the CustomerNumber, CustomerState, CustomerZipCode, and CustomerTelephone fields.

After entering all of the information for a customer, press Enter to go to the next record. After you have entered a number of customers, you can move backward and forward through the table using the PgUp and PgDn keys or the navigation buttons at the bottom of the form.

Deleting records from *tblCustomer* is a dangerously easy operation. Open the Customer Information form by clicking the Forms tab in the Database window and double-clicking *frmCustomer*. To delete a record, move to that record by using the navigation buttons at the bottom of the form; then choose Edit, Select Record from the menu. Press the Delete key to delete the record (if you are using the database supplied on the Companion CD, it will not permit you to delete customer records because of integrity constraints that we have built into that database). Microsoft Access gives you a warning message that asks you to confirm the deletion. The deletion is not reversible, because Access does not store table records in a buffer when it deletes them.

You can delete individual fields in a record using the Delete key while you are in Form view. Individual field deletions are reversible by selecting Edit, Undo Delete before you move to another field. After you move to another field, you can reverse all field deletions in the current record by selecting Edit, Undo Current Field/Record from the menu or pressing Esc. If you want to reverse changes you have made to a field and changes to other fields in the record, press Esc twice. All other deletions are permanent.

Deleting records in accounting databases is an action you will always want to consider carefully. Data in accounting tables is usually related to data in other tables. For example, if you examine a record in a Sales Order table, it will contain a customer number. The only place you will find that customer's name and address is in the related Customer table. If someone deletes that customer's record in the Customer table, you might never find out who the customer was!

Keeping existing customer records current to reflect address changes, new telephone numbers, and other changes is an easy and straightforward task using *frmCustomer*. Open the Customer Information form by clicking the Forms tab in the Database window and double-clicking *frmCustomer*. Use the navigation buttons at the bottom of the form to move to the customer record that you want to change. The Input Mask and Validation Rule property settings for *tblCustomer* will limit any changes you make to field contents, just as though you were entering data for the first time.

TRY IT

You can move through the individual fields of the displayed record by using the Enter or Tab keys. The Shift+Tab key moves backward through the record. The up and down arrow keys also move the cursor through the form.

Useful Variations on the Customer Information Form

The Customer Information form that you just created is an attractive, functional data entry screen. However, you can improve its usefulness by adding more features to the form. For example, you could use the Command Button tool in the Toolbox to create buttons on the form that would make it easier to use.

TRY IT

Open *frmCustomer* in Design view. Click the Toolbox toolbar button, and ensure that the Control Wizards Toolbox tool is depressed. Then, click the Command Button tool. Draw a new command button on the form to open the Command Button Wizard. The first Command Button Wizard dialog box provides three categories of buttons that might be useful on this form. The Record Navigation category includes buttons that can help users navigate the table more easily. The Record Operations category includes buttons that can help users add, delete, and undo changes to records more easily. The Form Operations category includes buttons that perform other form operations and filter database records. Click Cancel to close the Command Button Wizard dialog box. Select and delete the command button.

In accounting databases, you will often want to create separate forms for entering and modifying different portions of each record. By restricting users' access to particular fields, you can increase the internal control strength of your system. For example, you may want only the credit department to be able to set and modify customers' credit limits. You could then create two versions of the Customer Information form, one for general data entry and the other for the credit department.

In the general data entry version of the form, you can prevent access to the CustomerCreditLimit control by changing its properties. You can remove a control from the form's tabbing sequence and prevent it from being selected or edited. To indicate to users that they cannot change the field, you can modify the control's appearance by changing its Back Color property to the light gray color of the form background. In Exercise 6.7 you will learn how to modify the CustomerCreditLimit control's properties to accomplish these objectives.

EXERCISE 6.7: PREVENTING EDITS OF THE CUSTOMERCREDITLIMIT FIELD

1. Open the Customer Information form in Design view by clicking the Forms object button in the Database window, selecting *frmCustomer*, and clicking the Design button.
2. Right-click the CustomerCreditLimit control, and choose Properties to open its Properties sheet.
3. Click the Data tab, and change the Enabled property to **No**; then, change the Locked property to **Yes**
4. Click the Other tab, and change the Tab Stop property to **No**
5. Click the Properties sheet's Format tab, and change the Back Style property to **Transparent**. Type the number of the form's background color, which is **-2147483633**
6. Change the Special Effect property to **Flat** and the Border Style property to **Transparent**
7. Close the Properties sheet, and display the form in Form view.

The CustomerCreditLimit control now blends in with the form's background, suggesting to users that they will not be able to select or change a customer's credit limit. Try to enter the field you have protected. You will find that you cannot select the field by clicking it, tabbing into it, or using the arrow keys to move to it. You can save this form in the current database by switching to Design view, selecting File, Save As, and entering **frmCustomerGeneral** as the new name for the form in the Save As dialog box. Click OK to save the form.

Just as you do not want the persons who enter and edit customer information to be able to access the credit limit field, you also want to prevent persons in the credit department from changing customer attributes such as name and phone number. To create a version of this form for the credit department, you can change the properties of every control on the form except CustomerCreditLimit. To do so, complete Exercise 6.8.

EXERCISE 6.8: CREATING A CREDIT DEPARTMENT VERSION OF THE CUSTOMER FORM

1. Open the Customer Information form in Design view by clicking the Forms tab in the Database window, selecting *frmCustomer*, and clicking the Design button.
2. While holding down the Shift key, click each control except CustomerCreditLimit; then click the Properties toolbar button to open a Properties sheet for all the selected controls.
3. Click the Data tab, and change the Enabled property to **No**; then, change the Locked property to **Yes**

4. Click the Other tab, and change the Tab Stop property to **No**
5. Click the Properties sheet's Format tab, and change the Back Style property to **Transparent**
6. Change the Special Effect property to **Flat** and the Border Style property to **Transparent**
7. Choose Edit, Select Form from the menu. Click the Format tab on the Properties sheet, and change the form's Caption property to **Customer Information - Credit Department**
8. Close the Properties sheet.
9. You can save this form in Design view by selecting File, Save As and entering **frmCustomerCreditDepartment** as the new name for the form in the Save As dialog box. Click OK to save the form.
10. Switch to Form view to see the effects of your changes.

Now you have a Customer table that contains information about customers. The table relates each piece of information to a particular customer through the CustomerNumber primary key field. All information about a particular customer appears in one row of the Customer table. You also have built two versions of a form that facilitate entering, deleting, and changing customer information.

INVENTORY INFORMATION

Customer information is very important to any business, but potential customers will become actual customers only if a firm has something to sell them. *Inventory* is a generic term for what firms sell to their customers. Inventory, broadly defined, may include products, services, or both. For example, a hardware store sells products, an accounting firm sells services, and an auto repair shop sells both products and services.

In this revenue cycle discussion of inventory, we are interested only in the goods or services available for sale to customers. You will learn how to create databases to track the acquisition of inventory or inventory components in Chapter 7. Firms need information about the inventory they have for sale in the revenue cycle because they must track which inventory items they sell, at what price they sell them, when they sell them, and to whom they sell them.

To ensure that inventory information is consistent wherever they use it, firms try to keep all inventory information in one database table. Any document, report, or transaction that needs inventory information must obtain it from that one inventory table.

The Inventory Table

The revenue cycle requires an inventory table that contains at least two fields. The first field should be the primary key, a number or code that uniquely identifies the product or service. For products, this field might contain an item number, item code, part number, catalog number, UPC (universal product code), or SKU (stock-keeping unit) number. For services, this field might contain a labor code, task code, or service number. The second field should contain a description of the product or service.

Some firms use a third field to store inventory selling prices in the inventory table. If a firm has fixed selling prices for each inventory item, it can store those selling prices in the inventory table. Firms that sell the same product or service at different prices to different customers must store selling prices in a sales-inventory relationship table.

Firms that offer discounts from the list price to certain customers or classes of customers can store the list price in an inventory table and store the discount percentage in their Customer table.

One problem that firms face when they store their inventory prices in the inventory table occurs when they change their prices. For example, if a firm recalculates and prints an invoice from last year with this year's prices, it will obtain an incorrect result. Possible solutions to this problem include storing the selling price in a sales-inventory relationship table or creating aggregate records of invoices that include the inventory prices in effect at the time of the transaction. Some firms store prices in an inventory table and copy them to the sales-inventory relationship table when a sale occurs.

Before accounting and inventory control systems were automated, the primary key often contained encoded descriptive information about the inventory item. For example, a women's clothing retailer might have used the mnemonic code *WSk-10-Br-HM* to identify a size 10 brown wool skirt supplied by Hometown Mills. A salesclerk could easily become familiar with many of the codes and not need to look up item descriptions—often a time-consuming task in a manual system. Some firms now assign sequential numbers to their inventory items. However, if employees without easy access to the automated system perform warehousing or shipping tasks, coding inventory items according to some logical mnemonic plan still makes sense.

Now we can consider some alternatives for creating a simple inventory coding and description scheme for our example Pipefitters Supply Company, which is a plumbing supply business that sells pipe and fittings. To keep the database simple, we will assume that it sells only copper and brass pipe and offers a limited number of pipe lengths, diameters, and types of fittings. The table in Figure 6.8 shows the composition, type, and diameter of the inventory items. The table also shows mnemonic codes that might be used for each inventory attribute.

Note that even this fairly simple inventory will fill 60 rows (2 compositions × 5 types × 6 diameters) in a database table. Therefore, each alternative you consider should accommodate these 60 inventory items and logical additions. For example, Pipefitters might decide to carry plastic pipe and fittings in all types and diameters that it currently sells. This would add another 30 records to the Inventory table.

Composition	Code	Type	Code	Diameter (Inches)	Code
Brass	B	4-foot pipe	4	0.25	025
Copper	C	8-foot pipe	8	0.50	050
		Cap fitting	C	1.00	100
		Elbow	L	2.00	200
		T-connector	T	3.00	300
				4.00	400

Figure 6.8 Inventory items.

One coding scheme that might work for the Pipefitters inventory is to assign sequential numbers to the inventory items. For example, using a sequential code with a size of three characters and starting with 101 would accommodate up to 899 inventory items. An alternative is to create a code that uses letters and numbers in a systematic way. For example, we could create a coding scheme that would assign *BT-200* to the 2-inch Brass T-connector shown in Figure 6.8. This second coding scheme would help warehouse and shipping employees identify inventory items even if they do not have ready access to the computer system on the warehouse floor or the shipping dock.

Once you have decided on a coding scheme, you must determine how best to store the inventory descriptions in the table. One alternative would be to use one field for the entire inventory description. This field would contain, for example, *2-inch Brass T-connector*. This alternative requires strictly enforced standards for entering the descriptions. For example, you would not want to have one description entered as *2-inch Brass T-connector* and another description entered as *Elbow, 1-inch Copper*. In practice, such standards can be difficult to monitor. A better alternative uses separate fields for each description element. Using separate fields makes it easier to create effective input validity checks. Using separate fields also lets users search, query, and generate reports from the table more easily. In the following exercises, you will learn how to create an inventory table for the Pipefitters data that demonstrates a mnemonic coding scheme and separate description fields.

EXERCISE 6.9: CREATING AN INVENTORY TABLE AND ITS PRIMARY KEY

1. Click the Tables object button in the Database window, click the New button, and then double-click Design View in the New Table dialog box.
2. To create the item code field, type **InventoryItemCode** in the first row of the Field Name column. Leave its Data Type set to Text.
3. Click the Primary Key toolbar button.
4. Press F6 to move the cursor to the Field Properties pane of the Table window, set the Field Size to **6**, and then press the Tab key twice to move the cursor to the Input Mask property line.
5. Type **>LA\ -000;0;_** in the Input Mask property box.
6. Set the InventoryItemCode Caption property to **Item Code**

The Pipefitters mnemonic coding scheme uses the first character to indicate product composition, the second character to indicate product type, and a string of three characters to indicate product diameter. To implement this coding scheme, you can use an Input Mask property that requires the first character to be a letter, capitalizes the first two characters, inserts a hyphen automatically, and requires the last three characters to be numbers.

The > in the input mask converts all subsequent characters to uppercase, the L requires entry of a letter in the first position, the A requires entry of either a letter or a digit in the second position, the \ - automatically inserts a literal hyphen, and the 000 requires entry of three digits following the hyphen. The ;0 tells Access to store the hyphen in the Inventory table, and the ;_ makes the underscore character the place-holder on input forms.

In Exercise 6.10, you will enter the InventoryComposition field. This is the first of three inventory element description fields. All of Pipefitters' current inventory items are either *Brass* or *Copper*. You can prevent errors and ease data entry by creating a field that accepts only these two field values. Another thing you can do to make data entry easier is to have the form automatically capitalize the first character.

EXERCISE 6.10: CREATING THE INVENTORYCOMPOSITION FIELD

1. Enter a Field Name of **InventoryComposition**, and leave its Data Type set to Text.
2. Press F6, and change the default Field Size to **6**
3. Press Tab twice, and set the Input Mask property to **>?<?????**
4. Press Tab, and set the Caption property to **Composition**
5. Press Tab twice, and set the Validation Rule property to **="Brass" Or ="Copper"**
6. Press Tab, and set the Validation Text property to **You must enter either Brass or Copper in this field**

Thus, the InventoryComposition field uses a combination of Input Mask and Validation properties to control user data entry and reduce errors. The next inventory description field is InventoryType.

EXERCISE 6.11: CREATING THE INVENTORYTYPE FIELD

1. Enter a Field Name of **InventoryType**, and leave its Data Type set to Text.
2. Press F6 and change the Field Size to **11** to accommodate the longest type names that Pipefitters currently has for this field.
3. Enter a Caption property of **Type**
4. Press Tab twice, and set the Validation Rule property to **="Cap fitting" Or ="Elbow" Or ="T-connector" Or ="4-foot pipe" Or ="8-foot pipe"**
5. Press Tab, and set the Validation Text property to **You must enter one of the following in this field: Cap fitting, Elbow, T-connector, 4-foot pipe, or 8-foot pipe**

Note that Pipefitters will need to change the validation properties of this field if it adds a new type of inventory. Companies that have frequent changes in their inventory must store the inventory descriptions in tables rather than as part of the validation properties. The last element of the inventory description is the InventoryDiameter field.

EXERCISE 6.12: CREATING THE INVENTORYDIAMETER FIELD

1. Enter a Field Name of **InventoryDiameter**, and leave its Data Type set to Text.
2. Press F6, and change the Field Size to **8**
3. Press Tab twice, and set the Input Mask property to **&&&"-inch";0;_**
4. Press Tab, and set the Caption property to **Diameter**

5. Press Tab twice, and set the Validation Rule property to **Like ".25-inch" Or Like ".50-inch" Or Like "1.0-inch" Or Like "2.0-inch" Or Like "3.0-inch" Or Like "4.0-inch"** to limit the field so that it accepts only correct values.

6. Press Tab, and set the Validation Text property to **You must enter one of the following values in this field: .25-inch, .50-inch, 1.0-inch, 2.0-inch, 3.0-inch, or 4.0-inch**

Once again, Pipefitters will need to change the validation properties of this field if it adds new diameters of pipe stock to its inventory. The Inventory table's structure is now completely defined, so you can save the file by selecting File, Save As and entering a new name for the table of **tblInventory**. Click OK to save the table definition. Close the table for now. Figure 6.9 shows the populated *tblInventory* that is included in the *Ch06.mdb* database on your Companion CD.

To enter data into *tblInventory*, click the Tables object in the Database window and double-click *tblInventory*. The table will open in Datasheet view, ready to accept data. As you enter data, notice how the Validation Rule properties you incorporated in this table make the job easier. You should also try to enter some invalid data. See what types of errors your data input controls detect—and which errors slip through.

The Inventory Form

Although you can enter data directly into *tblInventory* more easily than you could enter data into *tblCustomer*, you can make data entry and update tasks easier and less error-prone by creating a Data Entry form for *tblInventory*. In our example firm, we restricted the inventory composition, type, and diameter. Although this is somewhat

Item Code	Composition	Type	Diameter
B4-025	Brass	4-foot pipe	.25-inch
B4-050	Brass	4-foot pipe	.50-inch
B4-100	Brass	4-foot pipe	1.0-inch
B4-200	Brass	4-foot pipe	2.0-inch
B4-300	Brass	4-foot pipe	3.0-inch
B4-400	Brass	4-foot pipe	4.0-inch
B8-025	Brass	8-foot pipe	.25-inch
B8-050	Brass	8-foot pipe	.50-inch
B8-100	Brass	8-foot pipe	1.0-inch
B8-200	Brass	8-foot pipe	2.0-inch
B8-300	Brass	8-foot pipe	3.0-inch
B8-400	Brass	8-foot pipe	4.0-inch
BC-025	Brass	Cap fitting	.25-inch
BC-050	Brass	Cap fitting	.50-inch
BC-100	Brass	Cap fitting	1.0-inch
BC-200	Brass	Cap fitting	2.0-inch
BC-300	Brass	Cap fitting	3.0-inch
BC-400	Brass	Cap fitting	4.0-inch
BL-025	Brass	Elbow	.25-inch
BL-050	Brass	Elbow	.50-inch
BL-100	Brass	Elbow	1.0-inch

Record: 1 of 60

Figure 6.9 The populated Inventory table in Datasheet view.

unrealistic for our example firm, it did give us an opportunity to illustrate table-level controls. It also let us illustrate some form design techniques that you will find useful in many different accounting applications.

In Exercise 6.13 you will create an Inventory Data Entry form. Pipefitters employees can use this form to enter new inventory items into their accounting system. Since *tblInventory* has only four small fields, you do not need to use a columnar form layout to fit the fields into view on the form. You can display a number of records at one time by using a tabular form layout.

EXERCISE 6.13: CREATING THE INVENTORY DATA ENTRY FORM

1. Click the Forms object in the Database window, and click the New button.
2. Select *tblInventory* in the combo box near the bottom of the New Form dialog box; then, double-click AutoForm: Tabular in the list above the combo box.
3. Select File, Close from the menu; then, enter a Form Name of **frmInventory**, and click the OK button.

The Access AutoForm tool creates a fairly good-looking form that you can modify to meet Pipefitters' specific needs for entering inventory data efficiently and effectively. This version of the form is included as *frmInventory1* in the *Ch06.mdb* database on your Companion CD.

Of course, we can improve the usefulness of this form. In this section we will provide several exercises that you can follow to improve the appearance and functioning of the form. You can use these techniques in many applications other than inventory forms. Our first exercise includes some general improvements to the form. The results of this exercise, in Form view, appear in Figure 6.10. You can use this figure as a guide while you work through the steps in the next exercise.

EXERCISE 6.14: MAKING GENERAL IMPROVEMENTS TO THE INVENTORY FORM

1. Open your *frmInventory* form in Design view.
2. Select the label controls in the Form Header, and click the Bold button on the formatting toolbar.
3. Increase the horizontal spacing between the fields. You can do this by selecting Format, Horizontal Spacing, Increase from the menu with all of the fields selected or by clicking and dragging each control separately.
4. Resize the label controls in the Form Header section to display the larger, bold text. You can do this manually or use the Format, Size, to Fit menu command.
5. Resize the text box controls in the Detail section to display the full contents of the fields. This will require that you toggle back and forth between Design view and Form view. Be sure to scroll down through all of the table records when checking the width of the controls. You can match the width of the text box controls to the label controls. Click each control while holding down the Shift key; then, select the Format, Size, to Widest menu command.

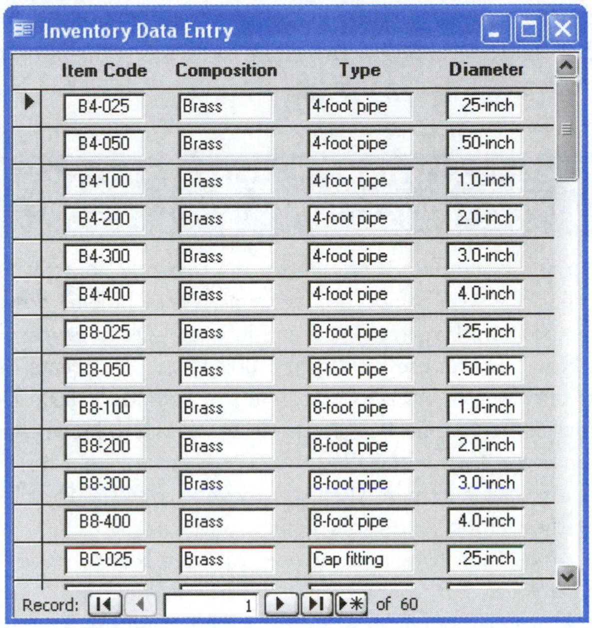

Figure 6.10 The improved Inventory Data Entry form in Form view.

6. Use the toolbar text align buttons to align the headings and column contents as you see fit. We centered the Item Code and Diameter fields and left-justified the other fields in the example form that appears in Figure 6.10.
7. Choose Edit, Select Form from the menu; then, click the Properties toolbar button to open the Properties sheet for the form. Click the Format tab, and change the Caption property to Inventory Data Entry. Click the Properties toolbar button to close the Properties sheet.
8. To prepare for the next exercise, open the toolbox by clicking the Toolbox button on the toolbar. Because the toolbox will open in whatever position it was last closed, you may need to drag it to a more useful position and shape.

You can save your partially completed design by selecting File, Save As, typing a name for the form, such as *frmInventoryImproved*, and then clicking OK. Our results for Exercise 6.14 appear in Figure 6.10 and are included as *frmInventory2* in the *Ch06.mdb* database on your Companion CD.

Recall that a combo box control is a combination of a text box and a list box. In the next exercise, you will learn how to make the form a more efficient data entry device that also helps prevent input errors by replacing three of the text box controls with combo box controls. You will learn two ways to specify the list of acceptable values for a combo box control. For the InventoryComposition and InventoryType controls, you will build the acceptable values list directly into each control. In the InventoryDiameter control, you will have the control look up values in another table. Each of these methods has its place in accounting database design.

Entering values into controls works best when the list of acceptable values is short and will not change frequently. When the values list is long, or if the values that are acceptable change frequently, most systems designers find it easier to store the values list in a separate table. To begin the next exercise, you should have your Inventory Data Entry form open in Design view.

EXERCISE 6.15: ADDING A COMBO BOX CONTROL FOR INVENTORYCOMPOSITION

1. The first step in this exercise is to remove the text box controls for the three fields that you will be replacing with combo box controls. While holding down the Shift key, click the InventoryComposition, InventoryType, and InventoryDiameter text boxes. Then, press the Delete key. Now you can use the Combo Box Wizard to create new controls.

2. Be sure that the Control Wizards button in the Toolbox is highlighted (if it is not, click it once); then, click the Combo Box button in the toolbox. Move the mouse cursor into the Detail section of the form just below the Composition label (the mouse cursor will become a cross with a combo box icon when you move it over the Detail section); then, double-click to start the Combo Box Wizard.

3. In the first Combo Box Wizard dialog box, click the second option button with the caption *I will type in the values that I want;* then, click the Next button.

4. Enter **1** in the Number of columns box, and then press the Tab key.

5. Type **Brass** in the first row, press Tab, and then type **Copper** in the second row.

6. Move the mouse cursor to the right edge of the Col1 column header. When the cursor becomes a thick vertical bar with a horizontal double-arrow, click and drag the right edge of the column to the left. Decrease the column's width so that it accommodates the widest text in the values list, Copper. Click the Next button to open the next dialog box.

7. Click the second option button with the caption *Store that value in this field;* then, click the combo box arrow button, and select the InventoryComposition field. Click the Next button to open the last dialog box, enter **cboInventoryComposition** as the control's label, and then click the Finish button. The Wizard creates a combo box control according to your specifications and places it on the Inventory form.

8. To test the new control, click the Form View button. Then, click the InventoryComposition combo box arrow button to display the two choices, Brass and Copper. Return to Design view by clicking the Design View toolbar button. The new combo box control should still be selected. Select the combo box label (and only the label) by clicking and dragging a marquee through it. You may want to click the label's handle in its upper left corner and drag it away from other controls if it is overlaying them. Press the Delete key. You can then adjust the size and position of the combo box control to match the text box control it replaced.

TRY IT

When you are adding new controls to a form that already has one or more controls, and the controls already on the form are the right size and in the right location, you can use this trick to make sizing and locating the new controls easier. When you create the new control, be sure it is shorter and narrower than the existing control or controls. You can then select both the new and old control (click on each while holding down the Shift key) and use the Format, Size, To Tallest and the Format, Size, To Widest menu commands to match the new control's size to the existing controls. Similarly, you can place the new control a little below or to one side of the existing control and then use the Format, Align menu commands to line up the new control with the existing control or controls.

In the next exercise, you will create a combo box control for the InventoryType field. You could use the Combo Box Wizard to create the control, but an alternative is to make a copy of the existing combo box, then modify the new control to suit the requirements of its field.

EXERCISE 6.16: ADDING A COMBO BOX CONTROL FOR INVENTORYTYPE

1. Select the InventoryComposition combo box, press Ctrl+C, and then press Ctrl+V.
2. Drag the new combo box into its correct position in the Detail section of the Inventory form.
3. With the new InventoryType combo box selected, click the Properties toolbar button to open the control's Properties sheet, and then click the Data tab.
4. Change the Control Source property to **InventoryType** and the Row Source property to **"4-foot pipe"; "8-foot pipe"; "Cap fitting"; "Elbow"; "T-Connector"**. Click the Other tab in the Properties sheet, and change the Name setting to **cboInventoryType**. Close the Properties sheet, and switch to Form view to test your new InventoryType combo box.

The InventoryDiameter combo box will provide a list of acceptable values by looking up those values in a separate table, which you must first create. You can take a break from your form-building task—you may close or minimize the Inventory form—and create a simple table that contains the InventoryDiameter values by following the steps in the next exercise.

EXERCISE 6.17: CREATING AN INVENTORY DIAMETER LOOKUP TABLE

1. Click the Tables object in the Database window, and click the New button. Double-click Design View in the list that appears in the New Table dialog box.
2. Enter a Field Name of **InventoryDiameter** in the first row, and click the Primary Key toolbar button. Change the Field Size to **8**, and select View, Datasheet from the menu.
3. Save the table as **tlkpInventoryDiameter** ("tlkp" is the prefix we use for a lookup table).
4. Enter the six valid values in the InventoryDiameter column as shown in Figure 6.11. You can return to the Inventory form by selecting File, Close from the menu.

To continue with the next exercise, reopen *frmInventory2* in Design view. Now you can connect the values in the lookup table to a new combo box control for InventoryDiameter.

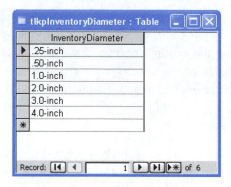

Figure 6.11   Entering values in the Inventory Diameter Lookup table.

EXERCISE 6.18: CREATING AN INVENTORYDIAMETER COMBO BOX

1. Select the InventoryComposition combo box, press Ctrl+C, and then press Ctrl+V.
2. Drag the new combo box into its correct position in the Detail section of the Inventory form.
3. With the new InventoryDiameter combo box selected, click the Properties toolbar button to open the control's Properties sheet and change the combo box Control Source property to **InventoryDiameter**, its Row Source Type property to **Table/Query**, and its Row Source property to **tlkpInventoryDiameter**
4. Click on the Properties sheet's Other tab, and change the control's name to **cboInventoryDiameter**

At this point, the Inventory Data Entry form should include three functional combo box controls for the three fields that contain the elements of the inventory description. The form should look like the one in Figure 6.12.

You can switch to Form view and test the operation of the Inventory Data Entry form. This version of the form is provided as *frmInventory3* in the *Ch06.mdb* database on your Companion CD. When you are finished viewing the form, close it and save the changes.

Note that the Validation Rules you built into the underlying *tblInventory* still operate in the form, no matter how you change the controls. You should always be careful not to create rules in your forms or form controls that conflict with the rules you built into the underlying tables. If you are not paying close attention to these details, it is possible to create a table-form combination that will prevent you from entering any data at all!

SALES ORDERS

When customers decide to buy products or services, they communicate this desire by sending a purchase order form, sending a letter, making a phone call, or telling a salesperson. Each of these actions is a type of *purchase order*. The firm that receives the purchase order often records it in its own records as a *sales order*.

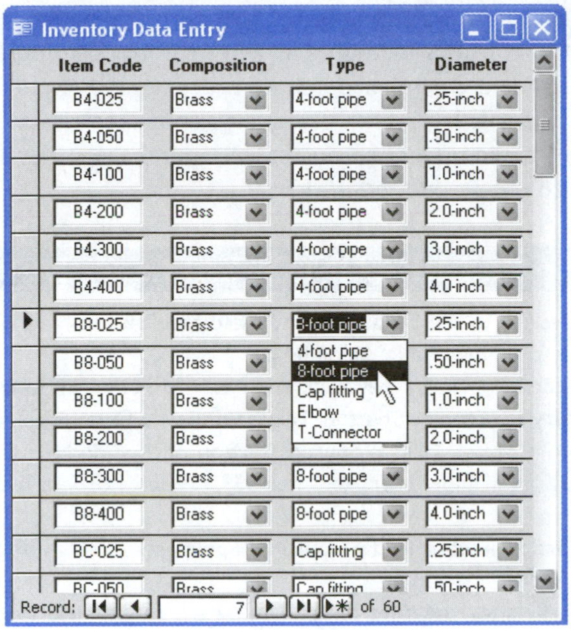

Figure 6.12 Testing the InventoryType combo box control in Form view.

No matter whether the order arrives as printed paper in the mail, a verbal order over the telephone, or a digital signal through a telecommunications link, all sales orders contain common components that identify when the sales order occurred, which customer placed the order, and which inventory item(s) the customer wishes to purchase.

To record these sales orders for Pipefitters Supply Company, you will need a Sales Order table, *tblSalesOrder*. To identify which customer placed each order, you can include a customer number field in *tblSalesOrder* that is linked to the *tblCustomer* table that you created earlier in this chapter. To track the individual inventory items that the customer has ordered, you can create a link to *tblInventory*. The link between *tblSalesOrder* and *tblInventory* is a many-to-many link since each sales order may contain many items and each inventory item may appear on many different sales orders. Therefore, you cannot use a foreign key link to join the tables. As you learned in Chapter 3, you must create a separate relationship table to model this link. You will learn how to create a relationship table, *tblSalesOrder-Inventory*, that will do just that.

The Sales Order Table

Since each sales order comes from only one customer, and a sales order needs a customer to exist, you can build the customer-sales order link into the Sales Order table. The primary key in *tblCustomer*, CustomerNumber, will become a foreign key in *tblSalesOrder*. Of course, the Sales Order table will need its own primary key and a field for the date of the sales order.

Since customers often send purchase order forms to indicate what items they want to buy, you should consider including a field to store customers' purchase order numbers. We will include a customer purchase order number field in our example. Therefore, *tblSalesOrder* will have four fields: a primary key, a date, a foreign key link to *tblCustomer*, and a record of the customer's purchase order number. Exercise 6.19 shows you how to create this *tblSalesOrder*.

EXERCISE 6.19: CREATING A SALES ORDER TABLE

1. Click the Tables tab in the Database window; then click the New button. Double-click Design View in the New Table dialog box.
2. To create the table's primary key field, enter a Field Name of **SalesOrderNumber**, and click the Primary Key toolbar button. Leave the field's Data Type set to Text.
3. Press F6 to move to the Field Properties section of the window, and change the Field Size to **6**. This setting will allow users to enter 899,999 sales orders if they use a starting number of 100001.
4. Set the SalesOrderNumber field's Input Mask property to **000000;;_** and its Caption property to **Sales Order Number**
5. Next, create a field for the sales order date by entering a Field Name of **SalesOrderDate** and a Data Type of **Date/Time**
6. Set its Format property to **Short Date** and its Input Mask property to **99/99/0000**. If you prefer, you can use the Input Mask Wizard by clicking the Build button that appears to the right of the Input Mask property box. If you use the Wizard, select the Short Date option. Set its Caption property to **Date**
7. Enter a Field Name of **CustomerNumber**, and leave the Data Type set to Text. Set the Field Size to **5**, the Input Mask to **00000**, and the Caption property to **Customer Number**. This field is the foreign key link to *tblCustomer*. Although the field's name in this table need not match its name in *tblCustomer*, it is a good idea to use the same name. We follow this convention in our examples here and on your Companion CD. More importantly, the Data Types of these two fields must be compatible. The easiest way to ensure Data Type compatibility is to make the fields an exact match. The primary key in *tblCustomer* is Customer-Number, a Text field with a Field Size of 5.
8. Enter **CustomerPONumber** as the next Field Name, leave its Data Type set to Text, and set its Field Size property to **15**. Set the Caption property to **Customer PO Number**. This field must allow any combination of numbers, letters, and symbols that customers might decide to use in identifying their purchase orders. Since you cannot anticipate the characteristics of this field, you cannot build any data entry internal controls into the table for this field.

This completes the basic design of *tblSalesOrder*. You will learn how to create the foreign key's referential integrity link to *tblCustomer* later in this chapter. To save your work, select File, Save As from the menu, and enter **tblSalesOrder** as the table's name. Click OK to save the table. The table that appears in Datasheet view in Figure 6.13 is included as *tblSalesOrder* in the *Ch06.mdb* database on your Companion CD. Close the table.

The Sales Order table identifies when an order was received, records which customer placed the order, and assigns the sales order a unique identifying number as its primary key. You can enter only part of the sales order information in this table, since *tblSalesOrder* does not store information about which inventory items customers have tblSalesOrder : Table

Sales Order Number	Date	Customer Number	Customer PO Number
100001	1/14/2005	10001	101-PR-753979
100002	1/16/2005	10003	26754
100003	1/16/2005	10007	BP-8666789
100004	1/17/2005	10005	276-555438
100005	1/17/2005	10010	985553
100006	1/18/2005	10005	276-555497
100007	1/18/2005	10006	DD-78725-NC3
100008	1/18/2005	10001	101-PR-754007
100009	1/19/2005	10002	8779465QW
100010	1/20/2005	10004	B-462-121894
100011	1/20/2005	10024	8675309
100012	1/22/2005	10035	ACR-1501
100013	1/22/2005	10016	Q-54-2743
100014	1/23/2005	10017	97613
100015	1/23/2005	10029	PBR-6905
100016	1/24/2005	10031	HZ-37-PZR
100017	1/24/2005	10048	5790-808
100018	1/25/2005	10050	212-35P
100019	1/26/2005	10046	84-PB-634
100020	1/26/2005	10012	2112-3

Record: 1 of 100

Figure 6.13 The Sales Order table in Datasheet view.

ordered on specific sales orders. This would require *tblSalesOrder* to have repeating fields, a violation of the normalization rules you learned in Chapter 3. To store this additional information, the database needs a relationship table to link *tblSalesOrder* and *tblInventory*.

The Sales Order-Inventory Table

If Pipefitters Supply Company accepted orders for only one inventory item at a time, it would not need this table. We could add fields for inventory item code and quantity ordered to *tblSalesOrder*. Most businesses would find this policy too restrictive, since it would require their customers to send a separate sales order for each item they wanted to buy.

The Sales Order-Inventory table is a relationship table that records the many-to-many link between *tblSalesOrder* and *tblInventory*. Therefore, the Sales Order-Inventory table needs four fields to store:

- The primary key of *tblSalesOrder*
- The primary key of *tblInventory*
- The quantity of each inventory item that appears on each sales order
- The price of each inventory item that appears on each sales order

The primary keys from *tblSalesOrder* and *tblInventory* will combine to form the composite primary key in the *tblSalesOrder-Inventory* relationship table. In Microsoft Access, you create a composite primary key by creating two separate fields, one for each entity table's primary key, and then designating both fields as primary keys. If you are using the Microsoft Access help screens, you may notice that Microsoft uses the term *junction table* instead of *relationship table* in its online help and other documentation. Before you begin the next exercise, close any open tables or forms.

EXERCISE 6.20: CREATING THE *TBLSALESORDER-INVENTORY* RELATIONSHIP TABLE

1. Click the Tables object in the Database window, click the New button, and then double-click Design View.
2. Enter a Field Name of **SalesOrderNumber**, and leave its Data Type set to Text.
3. Press F6, and change the Field Size property to **6**
4. Set the Input Mask property to **000000;;_**
5. Set the Caption property to **Sales Order Number**, the Required property to **Yes**, and the Indexed property to **Yes (Duplicates OK)**. The Indexed property setting must allow duplicates because a field that is part of a composite primary key may contain duplicate values. Remember that the entity table primary keys that form the composite primary key in a relationship table must always match exactly on Type and Size. These matched fields will allow the database to store values simultaneously in the SalesOrderNumber fields in this table and *tblSalesOrder*. The other half of the composite primary key is the primary key of *tblInventory*, InventoryItemCode.
6. In the second Field Name row, enter **InventoryItemCode**, and leave its Data Type set to Text. Press F6, and change the Field Size property to **6**. Set the Input Mask property to **>LA\ -000;0;_**, the Caption property to **Item Number**, the Required property to **Yes**, and the Indexed property to **Yes (Duplicates OK)**
7. The next field in *tblSalesOrder-Inventory* will store the quantity of each inventory item a customer orders on a particular sales order. Enter a Field Name of **SOInvQuantity**, and set its Data Type to **Number**
8. Set the Field Size property to **Long Integer**, the Decimal Places property to **0**, and the Caption property to **Quantity**. The integer property setting assumes that Pipefitters Supply Company does not accept orders for fractional units. The long integer property setting will allow the company to record a quantity of up to 2 billion units for any one inventory item on any one sales order.
9. The last field in *tblSalesOrder-Inventory* will store the price that the customer agrees to pay for each inventory item on each sales order. To create this field, enter Field Name of **SOInvPrice**, set its Data Type to **Currency**, leave its Field Size property set to Currency, set its Decimal Places property to **2**, and set its Caption property to **Price**

If you followed the steps in Exercise 6.20 carefully, you will have created most of the structure for *tblSalesOrder-Inventory*. The next step is to set the table's composite primary key. To begin this exercise, you should have *tblSalesOrder-Inventory* open in Design view.

EXERCISE 6.21: CREATING A COMPOSITE PRIMARY KEY FOR *TBLSALESORDER-INVENTORY*

1. While pressing the Ctrl key, click the row selectors for SalesOrderNumber and for InventoryItemCode.

2. With both fields selected, click the Primary Key toolbar button. The primary key symbol should appear in the row selectors of both fields, as shown in Figure 6.14.

This completes the basic design of *tblSalesOrder-Inventory*. To save your work, select File, Save As from the menu and type **tblSalesOrder-Inventory** as the New Name in the Save As dialog box. Close the table. A version of this table that includes data for the Pipefitters Supply Company is included in the *Ch06.mdb* database on your Companion CD.

You have learned how to create *tblCustomer*, *tblInventory*, *tblSalesOrder*, and *tblSalesOrder-Inventory*. Now you are ready to model the relationships among these tables. In Exercise 6.22, you will establish relationships among these four tables. If your tables do not contain any data, you should not have any problems as you follow the steps. If you have entered data in the tables, you must make sure that the data in key fields are compatible before you begin the exercise. For example, if you have entered any CustomerNumber values in *tblSalesOrder*, those exact values must exist in the CustomerNumber field in *tblCustomer*. Similarly, any values you have entered in the SalesOrderNumber or InventoryItemCode fields in *tblSalesOrder-Inventory* must exist in the corresponding fields of *tblSalesOrder* and *tblInventory*, respectively. If corresponding values do not exist in these fields, Access will not permit you to establish referential integrity on those links.

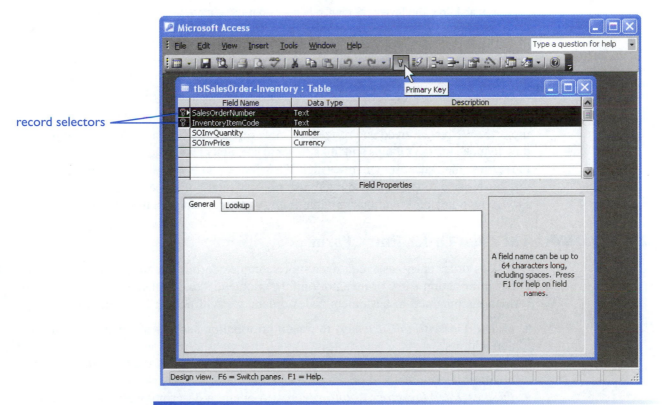

Figure 6.14 Creating a composite primary key for *tblSalesOrder-Inventory*.

EXERCISE 6.22: CREATING RELATIONSHIPS AMONG *TBLCUSTOMER, TBLINVENTORY, TBLSALESORDER,* AND *TBLSALESORDER-INVENTORY*

1. Close any tables or forms that are open on the desktop, and then select the menu command Tools, Relationships.
2. In the Show Table dialog box, select *tblCustomer, tblInventory, tblSalesOrder,* and *tblSalesOrder-Inventory* by clicking their names while holding down the Ctrl key.
3. Click the Add button to place the tables you have selected into the Relationships window; then click the Close button.
4. The tables you have chosen should appear in the Relationships window. You may wish to resize and rearrange the tables in the Relationships window using Figure 6.15 as a guide.
5. Click and drag the CustomerNumber field from *tblCustomer* to the CustomerNumber field in *tblSalesOrder*.
6. In the Relationships dialog box that appears, click the Enforce Referential Integrity check box, and then click the Create button. Establishing the referential integrity option provides an internal control on the CustomerNumber field in *tblSalesOrder*. This referential integrity link will prevent users from entering customer numbers in *tblSalesOrder* that do not already exist in *tblCustomer*. The nature of the one-to-many link is denoted in the Relationships window by the number 1 that appears on the "one" side of the link and the infinity symbol that appears on the "many" side of the link.
7. Click and drag the InventoryItemCode field from *tblInventory*, and drop it on the InventoryItemCode field in *tblSalesOrder-Inventory*. In the Relationships dialog box that appears, click the Enforce Referential Integrity check box, and then click the Create button.
8. Click and drag the SalesOrderNumber field from *tblSalesOrder*, and drop it on the SalesOrderNumber field in *tblSalesOrder-Inventory*. In the Relationships dialog box that appears, click the Enforce Referential Integrity check box; then click the Create button.

The Relationships window showing all of the links you have created appears in Figure 6.15. We have moved and resized the table representations in the Relationships window to make the table fields and links easier to see. Select the File, Close menu command to return to the Database window. Click Yes when asked if you want to save the changes you have made to the database relationships. Now that you have established the necessary foreign key and relationship table links, you can create a Sales Order Entry form.

The Sales Order Entry Form

The sales order entry task requires a more complex form than either the tasks of customer information entry or inventory information entry required. To enter all of the information contained in customers' sales orders, we will need a form that links:

- *tblSalesOrder* to *tblCustomer*, to obtain information such as the customer's name and address.
- *tblSalesOrder* to *tblSalesOrder-Inventory*, to obtain a list of the inventory item numbers, quantities, and prices for each item on each sales order.
- *tblSalesOrder-Inventory* to *tblInventory*, to obtain a description for each item on each sales order.

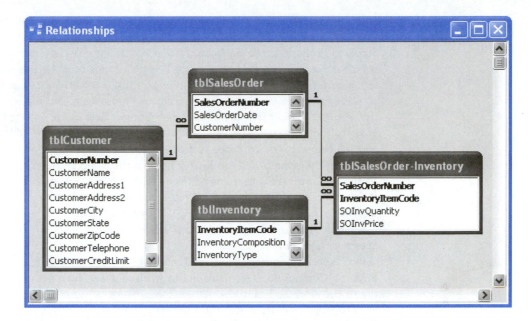

Figure 6.15 Relationships among *tblCustomer*, *tblInventory*, *tblSalesOrder*, and *tblSalesOrder-Inventory*.

A sales order entry form that meets these objectives will use four tables. The form must read from *tblCustomer* and *tblInventory* and write to *tblSalesOrder* and *tblSalesOrder-Inventory*. Since this form will read data from *tblCustomer* and tblInventory, you must have data entered in these tables. The *Ch06.mdb* database on your Companion CD includes populated versions of these tables. If you have not entered data in the tables you have created, you can import the *Ch06.mdb* tables into your database file. Alternatively, you can copy some or all of the individual records from the *Ch06.mdb* and paste them into your database tables. Either of these procedures will save you the time and trouble of entering large amounts of data into tables and will help speed you along to the form-building exercises that follow.

EXERCISE 6.23: CREATING A SALES ORDER ENTRY FORM

1. Be sure that you have closed all tables and forms. Click the Forms object in the Database window; then click the New button.
2. Double-click Form Wizard in the New Form dialog box. Since some of the fields have the same name but appear in different tables, you must be careful to select each field from the correct table. For the Sales Order Entry form, you will want to select the SalesOrderNumber and CustomerNumber fields from *tblSalesOrder* and the InventoryItemCode field from *tblSalesOrder-Inventory*.
3. Select Table: tblSalesOrder from the Tables/Queries combo box in the Form Wizard dialog box, and click the >> button to move all of the *tblSalesOrder* fields to the Selected Fields box.

4. Select Table: tblCustomer from the Tables/Queries combo box, and click the >> button to move all of the *tblCustomer* fields to the Selected Fields box.

5. Scroll up in the Selected Fields box, and select *tblCustomer.CustomerNumber*. Click the < button to move that one field back to the Available Fields box. An alternative method is to select each field in the Available Fields box except CustomerNumber and click the >> button to place each field into the Selected Fields box individually. No matter which method you use, you must select the CustomerPrimaryContact field in the Selected Fields box before going to the next step. This will ensure that the next field will be added after these fields and will help the Wizard properly create the form. The Wizard places fields on the form it creates in the same order you list the fields in the Selected Fields box here.

6. With the CustomerPrimaryContact field selected in the Selected Fields box, select Table: tblSalesOrder-Inventory from the Tables/Queries combo box. Select the InventoryItemCode field name in the Available Fields box, and click the > button to place it into the Selected Fields box. Repeat this procedure to place the SOInvQuantity and SOInvPrice fields into the Selected Fields box.

7. Select Table: tblInventory from the Tables/Queries combo box. Select the InventoryComposition field name in the Available Fields box, and click the button to place it into the Selected Fields box. Repeat this procedure to place the InventoryType and InventoryDiameter fields into the Selected Fields box.

8. Now that you have selected the fields that will appear on the form, you can give the Form Wizard further instructions that it can use to create the form. Click the Next button. The Form Wizard should indicate that it has chosen to view data by *tblSalesOrder*, to create a Form with subform(s), and to arrange the fields as shown in Figure 6.16. Click the Next button to accept the Form Wizard's proposed design.

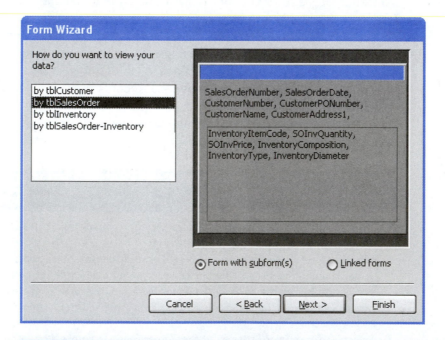

Figure 6.16   The Form Wizard's proposed design for the Sales Order Entry form.

9. Move through the next two dialog boxes, selecting the Tabular option in the first and the Standard style in the second.

10. Enter **frmSalesOrder** and **fsubSalesOrder** as the Form and Subform titles, respectively. Click the Finish button to have the Form Wizard create the Sales Order Entry form-subform combination you have specified.

The Form Wizard may take some time—more than a minute on slower computers—to generate the forms. When it has completed its work, it will display the finished Sales Order Entry form as shown in Figure 6.17. This figure shows the form connected to tables that are populated with data to show the operation of the form better. Your form will not show any data unless you have populated your tables. Remember that this form is actually two forms, a subform nested inside a form. The Form Wizard has already saved these objects under the names you assigned them in the preceding exercise.

Although this Wizard-generated form is certainly usable and includes all of the controls needed to enter, delete, and modify sales order information, you can probably see some ways to improve it. The next two exercises show you how to make improvements that will make the form and subform more effective and easier to use. You might identify other improvements or alternative ways of making the improvements we suggest. We encourage you to experiment, since form design is as much an art as a science. Just remember that you are designing a form for an input clerk to use many hours each day, so avoid bright colors and other design features that might irritate the user.

Whether you have created the Sales Order Entry form using tables that contain data or you have entered data into the form after you created it, you may notice that the form does not scroll through the sales orders in numeric order. The Form Wizard did not include a sorting rule in the query it built behind *frmSalesOrder*. Fortunately, this is fairly easy to change.

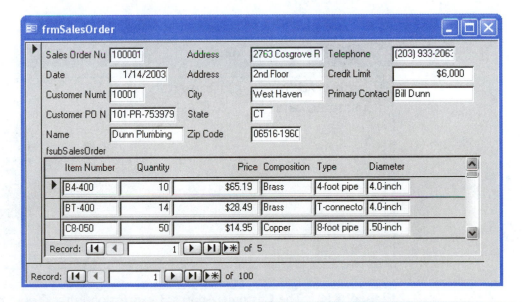

Figure 6.17   The Sales Order Entry form generated by the Form Wizard.

EXERCISE 6.24: CHANGING THE SORT ORDER IN *FRMSALESORDER*

1. Open *frmSalesOrder* in Design view.
2. Click the Properties toolbar button to open the form's Properties sheet if it is not already open on the Access desktop.
3. Click the Properties sheet's Data tab, and then click the Record Source property's Build button to open the Query Builder window for the query behind the form.
4. Type **Ascending** in the SalesOrderNumber field's Sort cell in the QBE grid.

While the Query Builder window is open from the previous exercise, you can create a new field, CustomerAddress3, that combines the CustomerCity, CustomerState, and CustomerZipCode fields. Often, combined fields such as this are easier to position on forms because you need not align the individual controls. Follow the steps in Exercise 6.25 to create this combined address field.

EXERCISE 6.25: CREATING THE CUSTOMERADDRESS3 FIELD IN *FRMSALESORDER*

1. Use the scrollbar at the bottom of the QBE grid to move to the next open grid column, and press Shift+F2 to open the Zoom box.
2. Type **CustomerAddress3: [CustomerCity] & ", " & [CustomerState] & " " & [CustomerZipCode]** in the Zoom box. Then, click the OK button to close the Zoom box. Figure 6.18 shows this expression in the Zoom box where you can more easily see the required spacing in the expression (we increased the font size in the Zoom box for this screen capture).

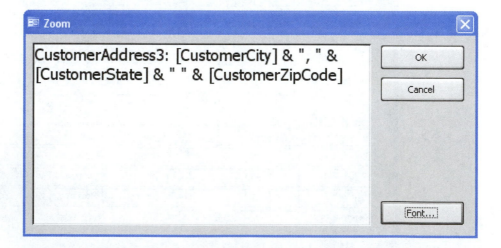

Figure 6.18 The CustomerAddress3 expression in the Zoom box.

TRY IT

To check your work, click the Run toolbar button (it is the button with the exclamation point), and scroll to the far right of the resulting dynaset. Examine the new field you have created, CustomerAddress3. The new field should show the city name, a comma, a space, the state abbreviation, a space, and the zip code.

Exercise 6.26 offers you steps that make cosmetic changes to the form's layout. These improvements can make the form easier to use. These changes are only recommendations; feel free to use your own judgment as you improve the form. You may find it helpful to refer to Figure 6.19, which shows the form modified using the steps in this exercise. You may either close the Properties sheet or drag it to the bottom of the screen so it is out of your way while you perform the steps below.

EXERCISE 6.26: IMPROVING *FRMSALESORDER*

1. Select the CustomerCity text box control with the Properties sheet open. Click the Data label, and change the Control Source property to **CustomerAddress3**
2. Delete the CustomerState and CustomerZipCode label and text box controls.
3. Delete the fsubSalesOrder label on the Subform/Subreport object. Consider deleting the labels for those text box controls that are self-explanatory and in which you will not be entering data on this form. We chose to delete labels for CustomerName, all of the customer address fields, and CustomerTelephone.
4. You can set the properties of the controls that the form will use to display information (rather than allow the user to enter information) so that they blend in with the background of the form. In addition to changing the appearance of these information display controls, you can set their properties to prevent data entry persons from using them to change data in *tblCustomer*. Locking controls to prevent data entry is an important internal control feature that you can build into Access forms. This internal control feature is especially useful in preventing data entry clerks from introducing unintentional errors into the database. With the Properties sheet open, hold down the Shift key, and click on the information display text box controls (CustomerName, CustomerAddress1, CustomerAddress2, CustomerAddress3, CustomerTelephone, CustomerCreditLimit, and Customer PrimaryContact) and the CustomerCreditLimit and CustomerPrimaryContact label controls to select them.
5. Click the Properties sheet's Format tab, and change the Back Style property to **Transparent**, the Special Effect property to **Flat**, and the Border Style property to **Transparent**
6. Hold down the Shift key, and click on the two information display label controls (CustomerCreditLimit and CustomerPrimaryContact) to deselect them. Click the Data tab, and change the Enabled property to **No** and the Locked property to **Yes**
7. Click the Other tab, and change the Tab Stop property to **No**

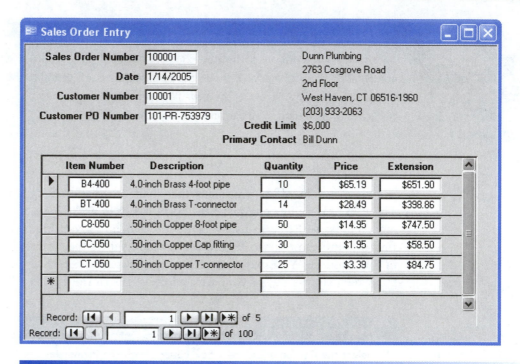

Figure 6.19   The modified *frmSalesOrder* in Form view.

TRY IT

You can make the following appearance adjustments using Figure 6.19 as a guide. As you fine-tune the form, you will find the Format menu commands (Align, Size, Horizontal Spacing, and Vertical Spacing) to be quite helpful. For making small adjustments to form controls, the Ctrl+arrow keys and Shift+arrow keys are also useful. The Ctrl+arrow keys move the selected object(s), and the Shift+arrow keys change the size of the selected object(s).

8. Resize and rearrange the controls so that the data entry controls (SalesOrderNumber, SalesOrderDate, CustomerNumber, and CustomerPONumber) are separated from the information display controls. Use the tools on the Formatting toolbar to set the labels' typefaces to Bold. You can also use the Formatting toolbar tools to change the justification of the text box control contents.
9. Choose Edit, Select Form from the menu, click the Format tab, and change the Caption property to **Sales Order Entry** and the Record Selectors property to **No**

The results of these modifications to *frmSalesOrder* appear in Figure 6.19. This form is included as *frmSalesOrder* in the *Ch06.mdb* database on your Companion CD. Close the form, and save your changes.

In the next exercise, you will make similar modifications to the subform, *fsubSalesOrder*. These modifications appear in the subform control portion of the Sales

Order form in Figure 6.19. The modified subform itself appears in Figure 6.20. You can use both figures for guidance as you work through Exercise 6.27. Be sure you have closed all tables and forms before beginning this exercise.

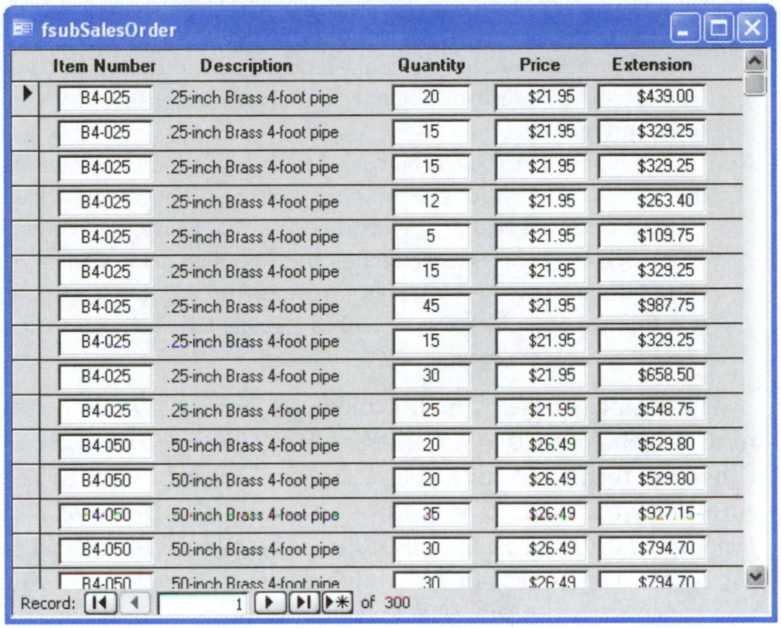

Figure 6.20 The modified *fsubSalesOrder* in Form view.

EXERCISE 6.27: IMPROVING *FSUBSALESORDER*

1. Click the Forms tab in the Database window, select *fsubSalesOrder*, and then click the Design button.
2. Delete the InventoryType and InventoryDiameter text box controls (in the Detail section) and the InventoryType and InventoryDiameter label controls (in the Form Header section).
3. Arrange the remaining text box controls and labels in the following left-to-right order on the form: InventoryItemNumber, InventoryComposition, SOInvQuantity, and SOInvPrice.
4. If the Properties sheet is not already open, click the Properties toolbar button. Select the InventoryComposition text box control. Change its properties as follows: click the Format tab, and set the Back Style property to **Transparent**, the Special Effect property to **Flat**, and the Border Style property to **Transparent**; click the Data tab, and set the Enabled property to **No** and the Locked property to **Yes**; then click the Other tab, and set the Tab Stop property to **No**. Next, we will show you how to open the query behind the form and create two new calculated fields that you can use on this form.
5. Choose Edit, Select Form from the menu. Click the Properties sheet's Data tab, select the Record Source property, and then click its Build button to open the Query Builder window.
6. Scroll right in the QBE grid, select the first open Field cell, and press Shift+F2 to open the Zoom box. Type **Description: [InventoryDiameter] & " " & [InventoryComposition] & " " & [InventoryType]** in the Zoom box, and click the OK button.

7. Click in the next open Field cell in the QBE grid, and press Shift+F2. Type **Extension: [SOInvPrice] * [SOInvQuantity]** in the Zoom box, and click the OK button. Close the Query Builder window, and save your changes.

8. Select the InventoryComposition text box control with the Properties sheet open. Click the Data tab, and change the Control Source property to **Description**. Under the Other tab, make the same change to the control's Name property.

9. Select the InventoryComposition label control, and change its Caption property under the Format tab to **Description**. Under the Other tab, change the Name property to **Description Label**

10. Click the Field List toolbar button, click and drag the Extension field to the Detail section of the form to the right of the other controls, and then click the Field List toolbar button again to close the field list. Select the Extension field's label control, press Ctrl+X to cut the label, click the Form Header section bar, and then press Ctrl+V to paste the label in the Form Header. Use the Ctrl+right arrow key to align the label control over the Extension text box control. Using Figure 6.20 as a guide, adjust the font characteristics and alignment of the fields on the form.

The results of these modifications to *fsubSalesOrder* appear in Figure 6.20. This form is included as *fsubSalesOrder* in the *Ch06.mdb* database on your Companion CD. Close the form, and save your changes. You should open *frmSalesOrder* and make sure that your revised subform still fits in the *fsubSalesOrder* subform object on *frmSalesOrder*. You can modify either or both forms to obtain a precise fit. Unfortunately, Microsoft Access has not automated this task, so you must do some trial-and-error fitting to get a good result. The Sales Order form in Figure 6.20 has been adjusted to fit the modified *fsubSalesOrder*. We encourage you to experiment and enhance this form and other sales order forms that you create for your own projects or client applications.

RECORDING SALES

After the credit department approves the sales order and the goods are ready to be shipped, the system must create an invoice and shipping documents. Shipping documents, such as bills of lading or packing slips, vary greatly in appearance and design. However, they always contain a subset of the information that appears on the invoice.

In this section we will show you how to create an invoice report. You can easily modify this invoice to create shipping documents that suit a particular application. The invoice is a very important record in the revenue cycle; it summarizes each sales transaction for accounting and includes valuable marketing information. To create an invoice, you will need two new tables: a Sales table and a Sales-Inventory relationship table. You will also use the *tblCustomer* and *tblInventory* tables that you have already created.

The Sales Table

Since Pipefitters conducts each sales transaction with only one customer, and the sales transaction needs a customer to exist, you can build the customer-sales link into the Sales table by putting a foreign key field into *tblSales* that corresponds with the primary key field of *tblCustomer*. The Sales table will need fields to store its own primary key and the date the items were shipped. We will also include a SalesOrder-Number field in our example. Therefore, *tblSales* will have four fields: a primary key, a shipment date, a foreign key link to *tblCustomer*, and SalesOrderNumber. In Exercise 6.28 you will create this Sales table.

EXERCISE 6.28: CREATING A SALES TABLE

1. Click the Tables object in the Database window, and then click the New button. Double-click Design view in the New Table dialog box.
2. To create the primary key field, enter a Field Name of **InvoiceNumber**, and click the Primary Key toolbar button. Leave the field's Data Type set to Text.
3. Set the Field Size property to **6**, the Input Mask property to **000000;;_**, and the Caption property to **Invoice Number**
4. To create a field for the invoice date, enter a Field Name of **InvoiceDate** and a Data Type of **Date/Time**. Set the Format property to **Short Date**
5. Set the Input Mask property to **99/99/0000**. If you prefer, you can use the Input Mask Wizard by clicking the Build button that appears to the right of the Input Mask property box. If you use the Wizard, select the Short Date option.
6. Set the Caption property to **Date**
7. Next, enter a Field Name of **CustomerNumber**, leave the Data Type set to Text, set the Field Size to **5**, set the Input Mask to **00000**, and set the Caption property to **Customer Number**
8. Enter **SalesOrderNumber** as the next Field Name, leave its Data Type set to Text, set its Field Size property to **6**, set its Input Mask property to **000000;;_**, and set its Caption property to **Sales Order Number**

This completes the design of *tblSales*. You will add referential integrity links from this table to *tblCustomer* and to the relationship table that connects *tblSales* to *tblInventory* after you create that relationship table in the next exercise. To save your work on the Sales table, select File, Save As from the menu, and type **tblSales** as its new name. Click OK to complete the table-save operation. An example *tblSales* is included in the *Ch06.mdb* database on your Companion CD.

The Sales-Inventory Table

The design and structure of this table are very similar to the design and structure of the *tblSalesOrder-Inventory* table you created earlier in this chapter. The Sales-Inventory table provides the many-to-many link between *tblSales* and *tblInventory* and stores the quantity and price of each inventory item on each invoice. In Exercise 6.29 you will create *tblSales-Inventory* with four fields: InvoiceNumber, InventoryItemNumber, SInvQuantity, and SInvPrice. Before you begin, close all tables, and open the Database window.

EXERCISE 6.29: CREATING THE *TBLSALES-INVENTORY* RELATIONSHIP TABLE

1. Click the Tables object in the Database window, click the New button, and then double-click Design View.

2. To create the first half of the composite primary key, enter a Field Name of **InvoiceNumber**, and leave its Data Type set to Text. Set the Field Size property to **6**, the Input Mask property to **000000;;_**, the Caption property to **Invoice Number**, and the Indexed property to **Yes (Duplicates OK)**

3. To create the second half of the primary key, enter a Field Name of **InventoryItemCode**, and leave its Data Type set to Text. Set its Field Size property to **6**, its Input Mask property to **>LA\ -000;0;_**, its Caption property to **Item Number**, and its Indexed property to **Yes (Duplicates OK)**

4. While pressing the Ctrl key, click the row selector for InvoiceNumber, and then click the row selector for InventoryItemNumber. With both fields selected, click the Primary Key toolbar button. The primary key symbol should appear in the row selectors of both fields.

5. Next, enter a Field Name of **SInvQuantity** and set its Data Type to **Number**

6. Set the Field Size property to **Long Integer**, the Decimal Places property to **0**, and the Caption property to **Quantity**

7. Enter the last Field Name of **SInvPrice** and set its Data Type to **Currency**

8. Leave its Format property set to Currency, set its Decimal Places property to **2**, and set its Caption property to **Price**

This completes *tblSales-Inventory*. To save your work, select File, Save As from the menu, and type **tblSales-Inventory** as the table's new name. Click OK to complete the table-save operation. A version of this table that includes data for the Pipefitters Supply Company is included in the *Ch06.mdb* database on your Companion CD for your reference.

In Exercise 6.30 you will model the relationships needed to record sales for the Pipefitters Supply Company. These relationships link *tblCustomer*, *tblInventory*, *tblSales*, and *tblSales-Inventory*. If you have entered data in the tables, be sure that the data in the tables' key fields are compatible; otherwise, Access will not permit you to establish referential integrity links on those fields.

EXERCISE 6.30: CREATING RELATIONSHIPS AMONG *TBLCUSTOMER*, *TBLINVENTORY*, *TBLSALES*, AND *TBLSALES-INVENTORY*

1. Close any tables or forms you have open on the desktop.

2. Select the menu command Tools, Relationships. The Relationships window will appear and display the relationships you established in Exercise 6.22. Since you are going to add more tables to the window in the exercise, you may want to click and drag the edges of the window to make it larger.

3. Select the menu command Relationships, Show Table. Select *tblSales* and *tblSales-Inventory* by clicking their names in the Show Table dialog box while holding down the Ctrl key.

4. Click the Add button, and then click the Close button in the Show Table dialog box. The tables you have chosen will appear in the Relationships window. You may wish to resize and rearrange the tables in the Relationships window using Figure 6.21 as a guide.

5. Click and drag the CustomerNumber field from *tblCustomer* to the CustomerNumber field in *tblSales*. In the Relationships dialog box that appears, click the Enforce Referential Integrity check box, and then click the Create button.

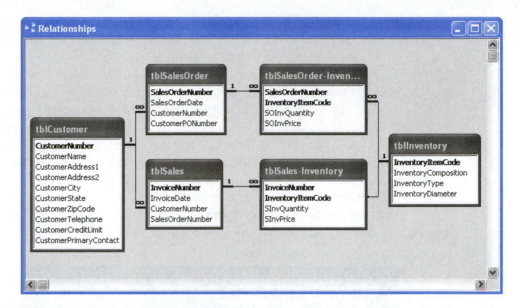

Figure 6.21   Relationships among *tblCustomer*, *tblInventory*, *tblSales*, and *tblSales-Inventory*.

6. Click and drag InventoryItemCode from *tblInventory* to the InventoryItemCode field in *tblSales-Inventory*. In the Relationships dialog box, click the Enforce Referential Integrity check box, and then click the Create button.

7. Click and drag InvoiceNumber from *tblSales* to the InvoiceNumber field in *tblSales-Inventory*. In the Relationships dialog box, click the Enforce Referential Integrity check box, and then click the Create button.

The Relationships window showing these links, along with the links you created earlier, appears in Figure 6.21. We have moved and resized the table representations in the Relationships window to make the table fields and the links easier to see.

Close the Relationship window, and save your changes. Now that you have established the necessary links, you can create a form in which you can enter sales information.

The Sales Entry Form

The Sales Entry form closely resembles the Sales Order Entry form that you created earlier in this chapter. The Sales Order Entry form lets Pipefitters Supply Company enter the items that its customers order. The Sales Entry form lets Pipefitters enter the items it actually shipped to its customers. If Pipefitters were certain that it would have all inventory items in stock at all times, it could generate invoices directly from information in the Sales Order table. Unfortunately, this assumption is unrealistic for most companies.

To enter sales information for Pipefitters, you will need a separate form that reads from *tblCustomer* and *tblInventory* and writes to *tblSales* and *tblSales-Inventory*. Since the Sales Entry form will read data from *tblCustomer* and *tblInventory*, you must have data in these tables before you can build and test the Sales Entry form.

Since the Sales Entry form is so much like the Sales Order Entry form you created earlier in this chapter, you can adapt that form to become the Sales Entry form instead of starting all over. The next two exercises show you how to edit the objects in *frmSalesOrder* and *fsubSalesOrder* to create a sales entry form-subform combination, *frmSales* and *fsubSales*. You will also learn more about how to construct Access forms in general by working through these exercises. The Form Wizard, when it created *frmSalesOrder* and *fsubSalesOrder* for you, hid some of the more interesting details of Access form creation from you.

Whenever you work with form-subform combinations in Access, you should start with the innermost subform and work out from that to the main form. Therefore, you will modify *fsubSalesOrder* in the first of these two exercises.

EXERCISE 6.31: MODIFYING *FSUBSALESORDER* TO CREATE *FSUBSALES*

1. Click the Forms tab in the Database window, and select *fsubSalesOrder*. Press Ctrl+C to copy the form object, and then press Ctrl+V to paste it back into the Database window. Type **fsubSales** in the Paste As dialog box, and click the OK button. Select the new form object, and click the Design button to open the form in Design view.

2. To make this form work as a Sales Entry subform, you must replace *tblSalesOrder-Inventory* with *tblSales-Inventory* in the query behind the form and change the query's field references. Click the Properties toolbar button to open the Properties sheet for the form, and then click the Data tab.

3. Select the Record Source property, and click its Build button to open the form's query. Then, select Query, Show Table from the menu. Double-click *tblSales-Inventory*, and then close the Show Table dialog box.

4. Click anywhere in the *tblSalesOrder-Inventory* object to select it, and press the Delete key.

5. Click and drag InvoiceNumber from *tblSales-Inventory* to the first Field cell in the QBE grid. All of the existing columns will move to the right when you release the mouse button. Set the InvoiceNumber field's Sort order to **Ascending**

6. Click and drag InventoryItemCode from *tblSales-Inventory* to the second Field cell in the QBE grid. Once again, all of the existing columns will move to the right when you release the mouse button. Be careful to select this field from *tblSales-Inventory* and not from *tblInventory*. If you select the InventoryItemCode field from *tblInventory*, the form will not work properly.

7. Repeat this procedure by clicking and dragging SInvQuantity and SInvPrice to the third and fourth Field cells, respectively.

8. Using the scroll bar at the bottom of the QBE grid, move the grid so that the Extension field is visible (it should be the last Field cell that contains an entry). Select the Extension field and press Shift+F2 to open the Zoom box. Edit the expression to read **Extension: [SInvPrice]*[SInvQuantity]**, and click OK. Close the Query Builder window, and save your changes.

9. Because you changed the underlying query of the form, you must change the Control Source properties of the text box controls on the form that are bound to fields that you

have removed from the query. Select the SOInvQuantity text box control. If the Properties sheet is not open, click the Properties toolbar button. Click the Data tab, and change the Control Source property to **SInvQuantity**

10. Select the SOInvPrice text box control. Click the Properties sheet Data tab, and change the Control Source property to **SInvPrice**. Close and save the form.

In the next exercise, you will turn *frmSalesOrder* into the main form component of a working Sales Entry form. Be sure you have closed all forms and tables before proceeding.

EXERCISE 6.32: MODIFYING *FRMSALESORDER* TO CREATE *FRMSALES*

1. Click the Forms tab in the Database window and select *frmSalesOrder*. Press Ctrl+C to copy the form object, and then press Ctrl+V to paste it back into the Database window. Type **frmSales** in the Paste As dialog box, and click the OK button. With the new form object selected, click the Design button to open the form in Design view.

2. To make this form work as a Sales Entry subform, you must replace *tblSalesOrder-Inventory* with *tblSales-Inventory* and change the query's field references. Open the form in Design view. Then, open the form's Properties sheet, and click its Data tab. Select the Record Source property, and click its Build button to open the query behind the form.

3. Select the Query, Show Table menu command, and then double-click *tblSales*. Click the Show Table dialog box Close button. Click anywhere in the *tblSales-Order* object to select it, and press the Delete key.

4. Click and drag InvoiceNumber from *tblSales* to the first Field cell in the QBE grid. The existing columns will move to the right when you release the mouse button. Set the InvoiceNumber field's Sort order to **Ascending**

5. Click and drag InvoiceDate, CustomerNumber, and SalesOrderNumber from *tblSales* to the second, third, and fourth Field cells in the QBE grid, respectively. As in the previous step, the existing columns will move to the right when you release the mouse button.

6. Close the Query Builder window, and save your changes.

7. Because you changed the underlying query of the form, you must change the Control Source properties of the text box controls that are bound to fields that you have removed from the query. Either by typing directly in the text box controls on the form or by editing the Control Source properties in each control's Properties sheet, change SalesOrderNumber to **InvoiceNumber**, SalesOrderDate to **InvoiceDate**, and CustomerPONumber to **SalesOrderNumber**

8. Change the Caption properties of the accompanying labels for these controls to match. You may want to refer to Figure 6.22 as a guide. You should change the Name properties (under the Other tab) for both the text box and label controls, too.

9. Click the *fsubSalesOrder* Subform/Subreport object at the bottom of the form, and click the Data tab on the Properties sheet. Change the Source object to **fsubSales**. Change both the Link Child Fields and the Link Master Fields properties to **InvoiceNumber**. You should also change the Subform/Subreport object's Name property to **InvoiceNumber**

You can save your modified *frmSales* form by clicking File, Save. The completed form, showing *fsubSales* nested within *frmSales*, appears in Figure 6.22 in Form view.

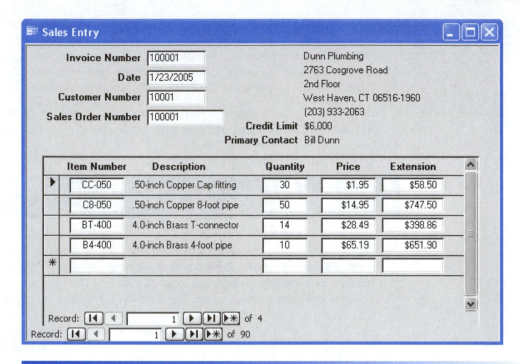

Figure 6.22   The completed Sales Entry form in Form view.

The Invoice Report

The Sales Entry form you just created facilitates the entry of information about sales into the Pipefitters Supply Company revenue cycle accounting system. When Pipefitters ships a customer order, it will want to send an invoice. Although more firms are using electronic data interchange every day, many customers still want an invoice printed on paper. The Access report objects help you provide nicely formatted printed output. In this section, you will create a printed invoice. The first step in generating an invoice report is to build a query that will gather the information we have stored about the sales transaction in *tblSales*, *tblCustomer*, *tblInventory*, and *tblSales-Inventory*. In Exercise 6.33, you will build just such an invoice query.

EXERCISE 6.33: BUILDING AN INVOICE QUERY

1. In the Database window, click the Queries object, click the New button to open the New Query dialog box, and then double-click Simple Query Wizard.
2. Select Table: tblSales in the Tables/Queries combo box, and click the > button to move all of that table's fields to the Selected Fields box.
3. Select Table: tblCustomer, and use the >> button to move the CustomerName, Customer-Address1, CustomerAddress2, CustomerCity, CustomerState, and CustomerZipCode fields to the Selected Fields box.
4. Select Table: tblSales-Inventory, and move the InventoryItemCode, SInvQuantity, and SInvPrice fields to the Selected Fields box.

5. Select Table: tblInventory, and move the InventoryComposition field to the Selected Fields box.

6. Click the Next button to move to the next Query Wizard dialog box, and then click the Next button in that dialog box to accept the Detail query default.

7. Name the query **qryInvoice**, click the option button to select Modify the query design, and click the Finish button. The new query will open in Design view.

8. Set the QBE grid Sort cells for InvoiceNumber and InventoryItemCode to **Ascending**.

9. Scroll to the first open column in the QBE grid, select the Field cell, press Shift+F2 to open the Zoom box, type **Description: [InventoryDiameter] & " " & [InventoryComposition] & " " & [InventoryType]**, and then click OK.

TRY IT

Note that this is the same expression we used in *fsubSalesOrder* and *fsubSales*. If you prefer, you can copy and paste this expression from one of those forms' queries instead of typing it again. The next two expressions are the same as those we used in *frmSalesOrder* and *frmSales*, so you can copy and paste instead of typing them, too.

10. In the next QBE grid Field cell, open the Zoom box, and type **Extension: [SInvPrice]*[SInvQuantity]**, and click OK.

11. In the next QBE grid Field cell, open the Zoom box, and type **CustomerAddress3: [CustomerCity] & ", " & [CustomerState] & " " & [CustomerZipCode]**, and then click OK.

You can click the Run toolbar button to run the query. Examine the dynaset it produces to check whether you entered the expressions correctly. Close the Query Builder window, and save your changes to *qryInvoice*. Next, you will use this query as the basis for the Invoice report.

EXERCISE 6.34: CREATING AN INVOICE REPORT

1. In the Database window, click the Reports tab, and then click the New button. In the New Report dialog box, select Report Wizard, and choose *qryInvoice* in the combo box. Click the OK button to proceed.

2. Click the >> button to move all of the query's fields from the Available Fields box to the Selected Fields box. Click the Next button to continue.

3. In the next dialog box, click the Next button to accept the default view, by *tblSales*.

4. Click the Next button since you do not need to specify any additional grouping levels for this report.

5. Enter **InventoryItemCode** in the first sorting box, and then click the Summary Options button. Click the check box to Sum the Extension field, click OK to return to the previous dialog box, and then click the Next button.

6. The next dialog box gives you a choice of Layout options. We used Align Left 1, but you can choose any of the options that you prefer for the look of the printed invoice. Click the

Next button to open the styles dialog box. Again, you may choose any one that you prefer. Our choice was the Formal style. Click the Next button to continue.

7. Type **rptInvoice** in the title box, and click the option button to select *Modify the report's design*. Click the Finish button to generate the report.

The report generated by the Report Wizard is fairly close to being a usable document. We have made a number of adjustments to the report's appearance. One page of the finished Invoice report appears in Figure 6.23.

The design elements appear in the partial image of *rptInvoice* in Report Design view shown in Figure 6.24. We suggest several changes to *rptInvoice* in the next exercise, but we encourage you to use Figure 6.23, Figure 6.24, and your own judgment to create an attractive and useful Invoice report for Pipefitters Supply Company.

EXERCISE 6.35: IMPROVING THE INVOICE REPORT

1. Select all of the controls in the InvoiceNumber Header section, and then press the Ctrl-down arrow repeatedly to move the controls down and expand the open space at the top of the Header.

2. Move the label control that includes the text *rptInvoice* and the line object from the Report Header section to the InvoiceNumber Header section.

Invoice

Pipefitters Supply Company
5998 Alcala Park
San Diego, CA 92110

Invoice Number 100001   Sold to: Dunn Plumbing
                                           2763 Cosgrove Road
         Date 1/23/2005   2nd Floor
                                           West Haven, CT 06516-1960
Sales Order Number 100001
                                           Customer Number 10001

Item Number	Quantity	Price	Description	Extension
B4-400	10	$65.19	4.0-inch Brass 4-foot pipe	$651.90
BT-400	14	$28.49	4.0-inch Brass T-connector	$398.86
C8-050	50	$14.95	.50-inch Copper 8-foot pipe	$747.50
CC-050	30	$1.95	.50-inch Copper Cap fitting	$58.50
			Invoice Total	$1,856.76

Figure 6.23   A printout from the Invoice report.

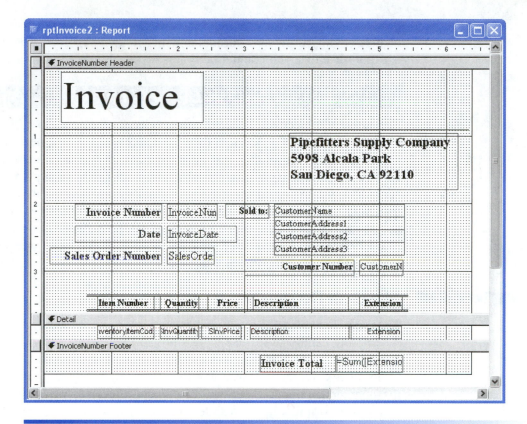

Figure 6.24 The Invoice report in Report Design view.

3. Select View, Report Header/Footer from the menu to delete these sections. Click the Yes button to confirm this deletion. Delete the Page Header/Footer using the same procedure.
4. To print one invoice per page, click the InvoiceNumber Footer, and click the Properties toolbar button to open its Properties sheet. Click the Format tab, and set its Force New Page property to After Section.
5. Click the Toolbox button to open the toolbox. You can use the Label tool to create a label control for Pipefitters Supply Company's name and address.

TRY IT

When you are typing text in a label control, you will find that the Enter key does not create a carriage return; it just accepts the changes you have made to the control. To place a carriage return in a label control, you must use either Shift+Enter or Ctrl+Enter.

Your Companion CD includes two Invoice report objects in the *Ch06.mdb* file, *rptInvoice1*, which is the report that the Wizard generated, and *rptInvoice2*, which is the report shown in Figures 6.23 and 6.24. These invoices are only two of many possible designs. Different businesses and other organizations use other document designs and include slightly different information items on their invoices. Note that, with a few minor modifications, you could modify this Invoice report for use as a shipping document.

RECORDING CASH RECEIVED FROM CUSTOMERS

The ultimate objective of the revenue cycle is, of course, to receive customers' payments for the goods or services they have purchased. Firms need to record the amount and date of each incoming customer payment. In this section, you will learn how to construct a simple cash receipts table that tracks cash receipts by customer. A more elaborate system would track cash receipts by invoice number and permit an exact matching of customer payments to specific invoices. Since customers sometimes do not pay by invoice, this matching process can be difficult to design and execute. You can satisfy many business information needs with the basic customer payment tracking procedure described in this section.

The Cash Receipts Table

The Cash Receipts table includes information about payments received from customers. A tempting candidate for this table's primary key is the preprinted check number that appears on checks that Pipefitters receives from its customers. Unfortunately, this customer check number is not a good primary key because you cannot be certain that the number is unique. Pipefitters could easily receive two different checks from two different customers that have identical preprinted check numbers. Most firms use a *remittance advice number* as the primary key for their Cash Receipts tables. You have probably seen remittance advices but might not have known what they were called. For example, the portion of a credit card statement that you tear off and return with your payment is a remittance advice. Businesses usually prepare remittance advices for, or assign remittance advice numbers to, every check they receive.

In addition to the remittance advice number primary key, you will want to include fields for the date that the check was received, the check number, the amount of the check, and the customer number. CustomerNumber will be the foreign key that will link the Cash Receipts table to the Customer table. In this exercise you will build a Cash Receipts table for Pipefitters.

EXERCISE 6.36: BUILDING A CASH RECEIPTS TABLE

1. Click the Tables object in the Database window, and then click the New button. Double-click Design View in the New Table dialog box.
2. Enter **RemittanceAdviceNumber** as the first Field Name. Click the Primary Key toolbar button to make this field the table's primary key. Leave the Data Type set to Text, but set the Field Size property to **6**
3. Set the Input Mask property to **000000** and the Caption property to **RA #**
4. Enter **CashReceiptDate** as the next Field Name. Set its Data Type to **Date/Time**. Set its Input Mask property to **99/99/0000** and its Caption property to **Date**

5. The next field in the Cash Receipts table will store the customer check number. Although most firms use only numeric characters in their check numbers, some may include other characters. Therefore, this field must allow any combination of numbers, letters, and symbols that might appear on a customer check. Since you cannot anticipate the characteristics of this field, you cannot build any input mask or validation rule data input controls for this field into the Cash Receipts table. Enter **CustomerCheckNumber** as the next Field Name, leave its Data Type set to Text, set its Field Size property to **15**, and set its Caption property to **Customer Check #**

6. To create the foreign key field, enter **CustomerNumber** as the next Field Name with a Text Data Type, a Field Size of **5**, and an Input Mask property of **00000**. Set its Caption property to **Customer Number** and its Required property to **Yes**

7. Enter **CashReceiptAmount** as the last Field Name, set its Data Type to **Currency**, its Decimal Places property to **2**, and its Caption property to **Amount**

8. Save the table you have created by selecting File, Save As from the menu and typing **tblCashReceipts** as the table's new name. Click OK, and close the Design View window.

Your Companion CD includes *tblCashReceipts* in the *Ch06.mdb* database. Figure 6.25 shows the Cash Receipts table in Datasheet view. Note that the column titles show the text you entered in the Caption properties for each field.

The final step in creating *tblCashReceipts* is to establish a referential integrity link to *tblCustomer* on the foreign key, CustomerNumber. In the next exercise, you add the Cash Receipts table to the Relationships window and connect it to the Customer table.

RA #	Date	Customer Check #	Customer Number	Amount
100001	1/28/2005	10207	10010	$2,000.00
100002	1/28/2005	33256	10005	$631.20
100003	1/28/2005	4927	10001	$1,856.76
100004	1/29/2005	108755	10007	$781.00
100005	1/30/2005	10256	10010	$122.50
100006	1/30/2005	4952	10001	$84.75
100007	1/30/2005	652	10006	$4,519.80
100008	1/31/2005	33402	10005	$825.76
100009	2/1/2005	5751	10003	$2,000.00
100010	2/2/2005	1041	10004	$1,417.40
100011	2/4/2005	4970	10001	$641.55
100012	2/4/2005	20122	10002	$739.40
100013	2/5/2005	273255	10024	$1,116.25
100014	2/7/2005	1097	10004	$24.90
100015	2/7/2005	267	10050	$736.07
100016	2/10/2005	4462	10029	$825.05
100017	2/10/2005	309152	10035	$708.75
100018	2/12/2005	991	10016	$485.70
100019	2/13/2005	8679	10048	$303.90
100020	2/13/2005	97362	10031	$476.00

Record: 1 of 80

Figure 6.25 The Cash Receipts table in Datasheet view.

EXERCISE 6.37: LINKING THE CASH RECEIPTS TABLE TO THE CUSTOMER TABLE

1. Click the Relationships toolbar button to open the Relationships window. Click the Show Table toolbar button, select *tblCashReceipts*, click the Add button, and then click the Close button.
2. Click and drag CustomerNumber from *tblCustomer* to CustomerNumber in *tblCashReceipts*.
3. Click the Enforce Referential Integrity check box, and then click the Create button.
4. Close the Relationships window, and save your changes.

The Cash Receipts table, linked to *tblCustomer* on CustomerNumber, is included in the Relationships window that appears in Figure 6.26. The Cash Receipts table is the last table we will include in this chapter's revenue cycle accounting system. Therefore, Figure 6.26 shows a complete picture of the relationships among all revenue cycle tables.

You may want to compare the tables and relationships that appear in Figure 6.26 with the data model in Figure 6.1. You can see by comparing these two figures how the data model is the backbone of database design.

The Cash Receipts Entry Form

The construction of the Cash Receipts form is simple and straightforward. The form works with only one table, *tblCashReceipts*, and that table has few fields. Exercise 6.38 shows you how to create the Cash Receipts form, *frmCashReceipts*.

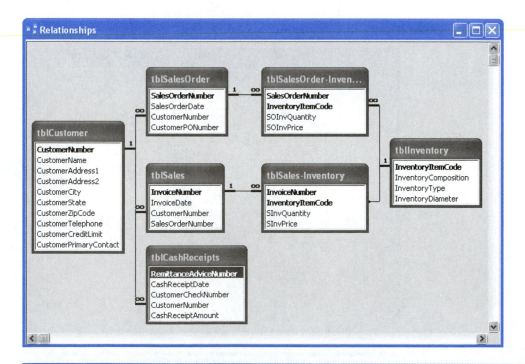

Figure 6.26 Relationships among the revenue cycle tables.

EXERCISE 6.38: BUILDING A CASH RECEIPTS FORM

1. Click the Forms object in the Database window, and click the New button. In the New Form dialog box, select Form Wizard, and choose *tblCashReceipts* in the combo box. Click OK to proceed.
2. Click the >> button to move all of the *tblCashReceipts* fields to the Selected Fields box, and then click the Next button.
3. Click the Tabular option button, and then click the Next button.
4. In the next dialog box, select the Standard style; then click the Next button.
5. Enter the form name, **frmCashReceipts**, click the Modify the form's design option button, and then click the Finish button to have the Form Wizard generate the form.
6. With the form in Design view, you can make a few minor adjustments to the form's appearance, such as boldfacing the titles, increasing the horizontal spacing between the fields, changing the alignment properties of the text box and label controls, typing **Cash Receipts Entry Form** in the form's Caption property, and changing the form's Scroll Bar property to Vertical Only.

The completed *frmCashReceipts* in Form view appears in Figure 6.27. You can use this figure as a guide to fine-tuning your form. Close the form, and save your changes.

Cash Receipts Reports

Standard reporting forms for cash receipts do not exist; so, you may create your own report designs to meet the needs of your or your clients' specific businesses. Some firms may want reports of cash receipts by customer, by date, or by geographic region. Although aggregate cash receipts information is important, the details are seldom as interesting as, for example, details of sales transactions.

Cash Receipts Entry Form

RA #	Date	Customer Check #	Customer Number	Amount
100001	1/28/2005	10207	10010	$2,000.00
100002	1/28/2005	33256	10005	$631.20
100003	1/28/2005	4927	10001	$1,856.76
100004	1/29/2005	108755	10007	$781.00
100005	1/30/2005	10256	10010	$122.50
100006	1/30/2005	4952	10001	$84.75
100007	1/30/2005	652	10006	$4,519.80
100008	1/31/2005	33402	10005	$825.76
100009	2/1/2005	5751	10003	$2,000.00
100010	2/2/2005	1041	10004	$1,417.40
100011	2/4/2005	4970	10001	$641.55

Record: 1 of 80

Figure 6.27 Completed *frmCashReceipts* in Form view.

One useful cash receipts report is the Daily Cash report that you can create by following the steps in the next exercise. Many businesses follow the internal control procedure of depositing all cash receipts intact each day. The Daily Cash report provides the check figures for the bank deposit.

EXERCISE 6.39: CREATING A DAILY CASH REPORT

1. In the Database window, click the Reports object, and then click the New button. In the New Report dialog box that appears, select Report Wizard and enter **tblCashReceipts** in the combo box. Click the OK button to continue.
2. Click the >> button to move all of the *tblCashReceipts* fields to the Selected Fields box. Click the Next button to continue.
3. Click CashReceiptDate in the list of fields on the left side of the dialog box, and then click the > button. The Wizard will insert a second grouping level, titled CashReceiptDate by Month, in the report template. Click the up-arrow button above the word Priority to move the new grouping to the top of the template.
4. Click CustomerNumber in the report template window, and then click the < button to remove CustomerNumber as a grouping level.
5. Click the Grouping Options button. Enter **Day** in the Grouping intervals combo box, and click the OK button. The Wizard changes the grouping level CashReceiptDate by Month to CashReceiptDate by Day. Click the Next button to continue.
6. Enter **CustomerNumber** in the first sort order box, and then click the Summary Options button. Click the Sum check box for the CashReceiptAmount field, click the OK button, and then click the Next button to continue.
7. Select the Align Left 1 Layout, and click the Next button.
8. Select the Corporate style, and click the Next button.
9. Enter a report title of **Pipefitters Supply Company Daily Cash Report**, click the option button to Modify the report's design, and then click the Finish button.
10. Using Figure 6.28 as a guide, make any appearance modifications you would like to see on the form. Select Save As from the menu, enter **rptDailyCash** as its name, and then click the OK button. Close the report window.

We have included two Daily Cash report objects on your Companion CD. The *rptDailyCash1* object is the report that the Wizard generated; the *rptDailyCash2* object includes a few modifications to make the report easier to read. We used *rptDailyCash2* to print the report page shown in Figure 6.28.

OTHER REVENUE CYCLE COMPONENTS

In this chapter, you have created sales order reports, invoice reports, and cash receipts reports. Our purpose was to demonstrate how to generate useful reports from revenue cycle accounting data tables. This section discusses some other revenue cycle reports that you might want to create or adapt to specific business needs.

Customer Statements

Many firms send their customers a statement of account activity at the end of each month. The statement shows a beginning balance, lists each sale and cash receipt, and

Pipefitters Supply Company Daily Cash Report

For Internal Use Only

Cash Receipts for: *Friday, January 28, 2005*

Customer Number	RA #	Date	Customer Check #	Amount
10001	100003	1/28/2005	4927	$1,856.76
10005	100002	1/28/2005	33256	$631.20
10010	100001	1/28/2005	10207	$2,000.00
			Total	*$4,487.96*

Cash Receipts for: *Saturday, January 29, 2005*

Customer Number	RA #	Date	Customer Check #	Amount
10007	100004	1/29/2005	108755	$781.00
			Total	*$781.00*

Cash Receipts for: *Sunday, January 30, 2005*

Customer Number	RA #	Date	Customer Check #	Amount
10001	100006	1/30/2005	4952	$84.75
10006	100007	1/30/2005	652	$4,519.80
10010	100005	1/30/2005	10256	$122.50
			Total	*$4,727.05*

Cash Receipts for: *Monday, January 31, 2005*

Customer Number	RA #	Date	Customer Check #	Amount
10005	100008	1/31/2005	33402	$825.76
			Total	*$825.76*

Cash Receipts for: *Tuesday, February 01, 2005*

Customer Number	RA #	Date	Customer Check #	Amount
10003	100009	2/1/2005	5751	$2,000.00
			Total	*$2,000.00*

Figure 6.28 First page of the Daily Cash report.

calculates an ending balance. This statement lets customers regularly review their purchases and payments. It also lets customers reconcile their accounts payable records with the statement. As we noted earlier in the chapter, many firms now pay from invoices rather than from monthly statements.

Systems designers use two general approaches for combining sales and cash receipts tables in one monthly statement report. One approach requires the use of a common field, such as a sequential transaction number. You can easily modify the *tblSales* and *tblCashReceipts* tables we created in this chapter to include a transaction number field for this purpose. This will, however, denormalize both tables. A second approach uses queries to summarize and place sales and cash receipts data into an accounts receivable table that has no primary key. This second approach also violates the normalization rules; however, it does so in an aggregate table, rather than in the tables that store the originally entered transaction data.

Sales Analysis

Database accounting information systems include much information that is useful to nonaccountants. Traditional accounting records contained only the date and dollar amount of each sale and cash receipt. A database accounting system contains much more information about each sale and cash receipt. The sales, sales order, inventory, and Customer tables we described in this chapter can be combined in many ways to provide useful information to the marketing and strategic management functions.

For example, you could combine our Customer, Sales, and Inventory tables to generate reports that show sales by customer, inventory item code, customer city, time period, or any combination of these. If Pipefitters' sales manager wanted to know what dollar amount of brass fittings the company sold in North Dakota during last December, you could easily create a query that would provide the answer.

Sales and Accounts Receivable on the Financial Statements

The traditional function of accounting systems has been to capture and store the information needed to prepare financial statements in accordance with GAAP. You learned a database approach to developing a revenue cycle accounting system that provides much more than the highly aggregated information contained in financial statements.

The database approach also provides basic debit-and-credit accounting information. For example, to obtain the general ledger entry credit to Sales and debit to Accounts Receivable, you can simply add a control to *rptInvoice* that sums the sales totals in its Report Footer. You can create subsidiary ledger debits and credits by adding a CustomerNumber grouping level to *rptInvoice* and including a control that sums the sales totals in the CustomerNumber Footer.

You can follow similar procedures to obtain the general ledger debit to Cash and credit to Accounts Receivable using the numbers generated by the *rptDailyCash* report we illustrated earlier in this chapter.

Go to http://perry.swlearning.com for an in-depth tutorial.

SUMMARY

In this chapter you learned how to construct the tables, forms, queries, and reports commonly used in the revenue cycle of accounting information systems. Tables are the basic building blocks of the revenue cycle. Forms make data entry, editing, and deletion easier. Queries can extract data from several tables at once to help answer complex questions about revenue cycle activities. Reports include invoices and shipping documents; they also may contain summaries of revenue cycle activities for internal management use.

The revenue cycle begins with customer records and finished goods inventory records. As sales orders arrive, we must record information about which customers want to buy which inventory items. When goods are shipped to customers, we create invoices and shipping documents. We record customer payments when we receive them. Finally, we summarize all of these activities and create reports and journal entries that allow the preparation of financial statements.

QUESTIONS AND PROBLEMS FOR REVIEW

Multiple-Choice Questions

1. The revenue cycle includes all of the following except
   a. keeping customer information current.
   b. recording the cost of merchandise purchased.
   c. recording payments received from customers.
   d. summarizing sales information.

2. The revenue cycle could use a shipments table to provide
   a. a record of sales.
   b. a record of shipment department employee names.
   c. names of vendors that supplied the products sold.
   d. quantity of products purchased.

3. The InventoryItemCode field in *tblInventory* is a
   a. composite primary key.
   b. foreign key.
   c. primary key.
   d. relationship key.

4. A good policy would be to delete a record in a Customer table only when that customer
   a. files for bankruptcy court protection from creditors.
   b. moves its offices out of the country permanently.
   c. has not made a purchase within the past 12 months.
   d. is no longer related to any other database tables.

5. Data entry form text box controls that allow editing of their bound table fields should have their Locked and Tab Stop properties set as
   a. Locked = Yes, Tab Stop = Yes.
   b. Locked = Yes, Tab Stop = No.
   c. Locked = No, Tab Stop = Yes.
   d. Locked = No, Tab Stop = No.

6. If you wanted to help experienceed employees identify inventory items in a warehouse where those items were labeled with the primary key of the inventory table, you would use a coding scheme that is
   a. sequential.
   b. mnemonic.
   c. hierarchical.
   d. randomly generated.

7. A sales order-shipments table would most likely be
   a. an entity table.
   b. a referential integrity table.
   c. a query table.
   d. a relationship table.

8. The link from *tblSalesOrder-Inventory* to *tblInventory* on the InventoryItemCode field is a
   a. one-to-one relationship.
   b. one-to-many relationship.
   c. many-to-one relationship.
   d. many-to-many relationship.

9. Some companies use several fields in their inventory tables for the item description, others use one field. An advantage of using multiple description fields is that it
   a. makes changing the descriptions easier because the fields are smaller.
   b. allows users to query by inventory category more easily.
   c. provides a way to calculate a self-checking digit for the primary key of the table.
   d. saves users the trouble of concatenating multiple fields to obtain a complete description of the inventory items.

10. To create a sales analysis report that would show sales of specific products by customer and by time period, you would need to begin with a query that includes
    a. *tblCustomer*, *tblSales*, *tblSales-Inventory*, and *tblInventory*.
    b. *tblCustomer*, *tblInventory*, and *tblCashReceipts*.
    c. *tblCustomer*, *tblTimePeriod*, *tblSales*, and *tblSales-Inventory*.
    d. *tblCustomer*, *tblInventory*, *tblSalesOrder*, and *tblSalesOrder-Inventory*.

Discussion Questions

1. The examples in this chapter assumed that Pipefitters Supply Company was doing business only in the United States. What changes would you make if Pipefitters had many customers from other countries?

2. Service businesses, such as real estate agents, law firms, and accounting firms, do not have inventory. What table would a service business have instead of *tblInventory*?

3. Restaurants do not usually record customers' names and addresses or send out invoices. What tables, forms, queries, and reports might you use in the accounting information system for a restaurant's revenue cycle?

4. How would you decide whether to enforce referential integrity for a foreign key link?

5. Describe how you might create a customer statement that showed sales and cash receipts from customers on one report.

Practice Exercises

Note: Before doing any of the following practice exercises, first copy *Ch06.mdb* from your Companion CD to the hard drive of the computer on which you are working. Then, clear the copied database's Read-only file attribute (see Chapter 1, Exercise 1.14, Clearing a File's Read-Only Property). Having done that, you can complete each exercise using the copy of the Companion CD database.

1. Change *tblCustomer* so that the CustomerState field will accept only legal state abbreviations. Hint: You should consider adding another table to the revenue cycle system to accomplish this task.

2. Many firms keep track of which salespersons handle particular sales. Modify the revenue cycle system in this chapter to include a salesperson entity.

3. Create a report that shows sales by customer with sales by product grouped under each customer.

4. Modify the revenue cycle system presented in this chapter to include a ship-to address on the invoice.

5. Create a report that shows the month-end general ledger entries for sales and cash receipts.

Problems

Note: Before doing any of the following problems, first copy *Ch06.mdb* from your Companion CD to the hard drive of the computer on which you are working. Then, clear the copied database's Read-only file attribute (see Chapter 1, Exercise 1.14,

Clearing a File's Read-Only Property). Having done that, you can complete each exercise using the copy of the Companion CD database.

1. Green, Prakash, and Singh, LLP (GPS) is a law firm that has asked for your help in developing a billing and revenue collection database. The three partners perform several types of legal services for corporations (the firm does no work for unincorporated individuals or partnerships), including general litigation, insurance defense, general corporate, and tax planning. Each partner has a different billing rate. The partners keep track of the time they work on cases by client and by type of services. They record time in six-minute (one-tenth of an hour) intervals. GPS sends bills to clients every Friday for the services rendered during the week ended on that Friday. Most clients pay at the end of each month, but some pay every week and others run an unpaid balance from month to month and pay what they can when they are able. List the entities that exist in the GPS sales cycle. State any assumptions you needed to make.

2. Refer to the GPS case described in Problem 1 and create a diagram similar to that shown in Figure 6.1 for the GPS law firm. The diagram should show the entities you identified in Problem 1 along with the relationships between those entities and their cardinalities.

3. Refer to the GPS case described in Problem 1 and the work you did in Problem 2. Use Access to build the tables and create the relationships you have defined. Populate the tables with sample data that you create, and test the tables to make certain that the relationships operate to enforce referential integrity as appropriate. You can import the records from *tblCustomer* in the *Ch06.mdb* database to the appropriate table in your database to save data entry time and effort.

4. Refer to the work you have done in the preceding three problems. Create data entry forms for the GPS sales database that allow you to enter data into every table without opening the table itself. Use the forms in the *Ch06.mdb* database as guides.

5. Refer to the work you have done in the preceding four problems. Create reports for the GPS sales database as follows:
   a. Create a weekly report that shows services provided by partner and then by client.
   b. Create a weekly report that shows cash receipts by client.
   c. Create a client list that shows the types of legal services that the firm has provided to each client.
   d. Create any additional specific reports your instructor might have assigned.

CHAPTER 7
Purchase Cycle

OBJECTIVES

A company's purchase cycle activities include placing orders with vendors, recording purchases, recording payments made to vendors, and maintaining records of these activities. In this chapter, you will learn how to design Microsoft Access tables, queries, forms, and reports that can help you:

- Create and maintain vendor records.
- Create and maintain materials inventory records.
- Print purchase orders.
- Summarize and report purchase order information.
- Record the receipt of ordered materials.
- Print checks and record disbursements to vendors.
- Summarize purchases and accounts payable information.

INTRODUCTION

In this chapter you will learn how to use Microsoft Access to build the purchase cycle components of accounting information systems. We define the purchase cycle to include acquisition of goods and services and payment for those goods and services. We cover payroll accounting systems, which accountants sometimes consider to be part of the purchase cycle, in Chapter 8. Payroll record-keeping calculations and record keeping can be quite complex and are, we believe, deserving of a separate chapter.

In manufacturing firms, the main focus of the purchase cycle is ordering, receiving, and paying for materials—including both direct and indirect materials. In a merchandising firm, the main focus of the purchase cycle is the acquisition of goods for resale. Since materials acquisition is not a major concern for service firms, their purchase cycle is somewhat less important to them than it is to manufacturing and merchandising firms. However, all businesses—even service firms—must acquire goods and services that support their selling and administrative functions. This acquisition activity takes place within the purchase cycle. Therefore, all three types of firms need accounting systems that can record purchase cycle activities.

In a manufacturing firm, the purchase cycle process begins when one of the production departments prepares a materials requisition document. In some manufacturing systems, this document is automatically generated by the computer when materials inventory falls below a predetermined reorder point. For example, in a *materials requirement planning (MRP) system*, the computer can use the master schedule to generate timely materials requisitions without human intervention. In a *just-in-time (JIT) production control system*, materials requisitions are generated frequently—often daily or weekly. The materials requisition document goes to the purchasing department as its authorization to prepare a purchase order. In many automated MRP and JIT systems, the computer generates the purchase order directly.

Many merchandising firms, particularly retailers, find that the demand for their goods is highly unpredictable. Manufacturers often have the luxury of planning production; retailers must react quickly to shifts in consumer demand. Ability to accommodate this rapidly fluctuating demand is often the difference between success and failure for a retailer. Therefore, retail merchandisers delegate purchasing decisions to highly skilled buyers who have authority, within a predetermined dollar budget, for purchasing a particular category of merchandise. These buyers use daily sales reports, inventory reports, market research, and their intuitions to make inventory purchase decisions. To record their purchase decisions, buyers create either purchase requisition documents or purchase orders.

All three types of firms must acquire and pay for goods and services that fall into the category that accountants call selling and administrative expenses. For example, merchandising, manufacturing, and service firms all purchase office supplies, pay for advertising, and reimburse employees for travel expenses. An office manager, department head, or other responsible manager creates the purchase requisition document that authorizes purchase of and payment for such items.

In all three types of firms, the purchasing department uses materials or purchase requisitions as authorization to place purchase orders. Purchasing agents try to find the best prices, terms, and delivery dates offered by approved vendors. In some industries the purchasing agent is a skilled negotiator with considerable latitude in making decisions. Whether it is the result of spirited deal making or is generated automatically, the purchase order is sent to the vendor by the purchasing department. In the past, purchase orders were always printed paper forms; however, many firms now use e-mail, electronic data interchange (EDI), or other electronic transmission methods to send purchase orders to vendors.

The purchasing department sends a copy of the purchase order, with quantities omitted, to the receiving department or makes similar information available electronically. When shipments of ordered goods arrive, the receiving department completes a receiving report. The accounting department must compare the receiving report, the purchase order, and the vendor's invoice. If the details on all these documents match, accounting prepares a check for the amount due. The check is then forwarded to the treasurer with supporting documentation. This documentation typically includes the purchase order, the receiving report, and the vendor's invoice. The package of supporting documents is often called a *voucher*. The treasurer signs the check, marks or mutilates the voucher and the supporting documents so they cannot be used to authorize a second payment for the same purchase, and sends the check to the vendor.

The purchase cycle system must generate summary reports of purchase and cash disbursement activities for management's use. The system should also generate information that financial accountants can use instead of their traditional double-entry bookkeeping debits and credits to create ledgers, journals, and financial statements.

ELECTRIC CONTROLS COMPANY PURCHASE CYCLE INFORMATION

In this chapter, you will learn how to build the components of a purchase cycle system for Electric Controls Company, a firm that manufactures custom electrical control panels for industrial customers. Electrical control panels are larger and more complex versions of the metal box that contains the circuit breakers at your house or apartment. Electric Controls buys components such as switches, circuit breakers, and relays to assemble these control panels from a number of different suppliers.

Electric Controls Company contacts vendors to place purchase orders. Each purchase order can include many inventory items. When a shipment arrives at the receiving dock, a receiving clerk counts the inventory items and records which items were received and their quantities as an inventory receipt. The inventory receipt record also includes a notation of the purchaser order on which the inventory items were ordered. Periodically, the accounting department pays for inventory received by writing a check to the vendor. Although Electric Controls Company usually pays for all inventory receipts at the end of each month, it sometimes will pay only part of a large inventory receipt that occurs near the end of the month and pay the balance when it becomes due in the next month, 30 days after the inventory receipt.

The data model for the Electric Controls Company includes five entities: vendor, purchase order, inventory receipt, inventory, and cash disbursement. Each vendor can have many purchase orders. A purchase order can have many inventory items. Because vendors can ship inventory items that appear on one purchase order in many shipments, Electric Controls must be able to record many inventory receipts for a single purchase order. Sometimes vendors will ship inventory from several purchase orders together, but Electric Controls receiving clerks use a separate receiving report for each purchase order to record those inventory receipts. An inventory receipt usually has only one cash disbursement, but it may have more than one if it is large and occurs near month-end. A cash disbursement can be in payment of many inventory receipts. The data model for Electric Controls Company's purchase cycle, showing these five entities and the one-to-many and many-to-many relationships among them, appears in Figure 7.1.

In this chapter, you will learn how to build elements of the accounting system for Electric Controls' purchase cycle. The design will include five tables for the entities and three additional tables to model the many-to-many relationships. You will learn how to create forms to enter data efficiently, queries that extract information about purchase cycle activities, and reports that Electric Controls can use to print purchase orders, checks, and summary purchase cycle information.

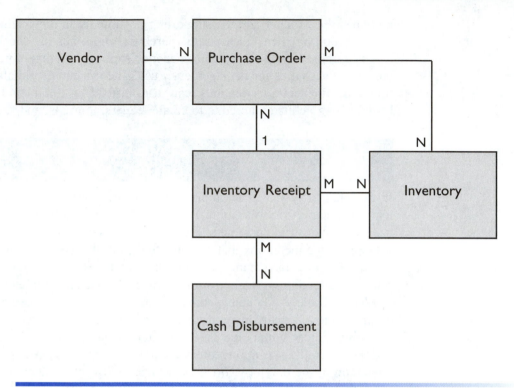

Figure 7.1 Electric Controls Company purchase cycle data model.

VENDOR INFORMATION

Firms need easy and quick access to information about their vendors. Purchasing agents need vendor names, addresses, and telephone numbers. They also need to know for which inventory items a particular vendor has been approved. Vendor information appears on many business documents such as purchase orders and checks. To ensure that vendor information is consistent wherever it is used, firms keep all vendor information in one database table. Any document that needs vendor information obtains it from that one table. If, for example, a vendor moves to a new location, the vendor's address needs changed only once. In a relational database accounting information system, vendor information resides in a vendor table.

The Vendor Table

The first purchase cycle table that you will build is the vendor table, which will provide a central location for storing all information about each vendor. This makes adding, deleting, or changing vendor information easy and efficient. Many firms also include information about potential vendors—firms they might buy from in the future—in their vendor tables.

Remember that examples of all the tables, forms, queries, and reports that we use in this chapter are included in the *Ch07.mdb* database on your Companion CD. When you are finished with Exercise 7.1, you might want to open this *Ch07.mdb* database and compare your work with the Vendor table we have provided in that database. You can import some or all of the vendor information from that table to save you the time of creating your own vendor data.

EXERCISE 7.1: CREATING A VENDOR TABLE AND ITS PRIMARY KEY FIELD

1. Start Microsoft Access, click the Tables tab in the Objects bar, and then click the New button near the top of the Database window. Double-click Design View in the New Table dialog box.
2. Enter **VendorNumber** as the first Field Name, leave its Data Type set to Text, and click the Primary Key toolbar button to make this field the Vendor table's primary key.
3. Press F6 to switch to the Field Properties pane of the Table window, and then set the Field Size property to **4** and the Caption property to **Vendor Number**. Using a sequential number scheme starting with 1001 lets the Electric Controls Company store information for up to 8,999 vendors in the table.
4. Set the Validation Rule property to the expression **Like "####"**. Set the Validation Text property to **Invalid entry. You must enter a Vendor number of exactly four digits**

Figure 7.2 shows the Table window displaying the VendorNumber field's property settings at this point.

The Validation Rule property setting will prevent a user from entering anything other than four digits in the VendorNumber field. The Validation Text property makes this internal control feature even more useful. It lets us customize the error message that

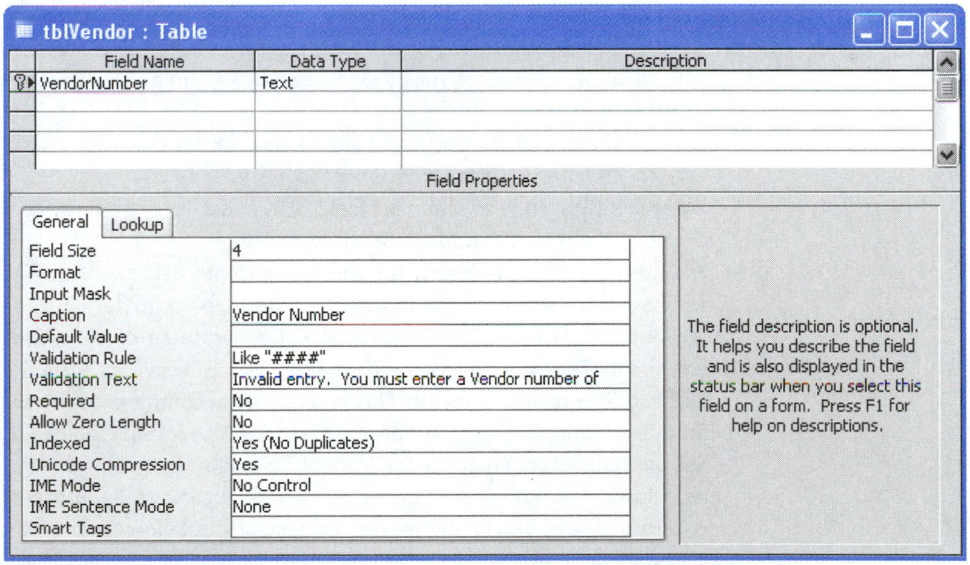

Figure 7.2 The VendorNumber field property settings.

will appear in a dialog box whenever a user enters a VendorNumber value of anything other than four digits.

Recall that you can use either an Input Mask property setting or a Validation Rule property setting to control data input. Each method has its strengths and weaknesses. The Input Mask property operates on each character as it is entered but issues only a standard error message. The Validation Rule property operates on the field as a whole and thus does not warn users of errors until they try to exit the field. A Validation Rule does, however, allow us to customize the error message.

TRY IT

You can obtain more information about the Like operator and its syntax by selecting Help, Microsoft Access Help Topics from the menu, and then clicking the Index tab and entering **like operator** as the search term. You can also learn more by entering **ValidationRule Property** or **ValidationText Property** in the Help Index window.

The next exercise provides steps you can follow to add fields for vendor address, telephone, and primary contact information. These fields will complete the Vendor table.

EXERCISE 7.2: COMPLETING THE VENDOR TABLE

1. Enter **VendorName** as the next Field Name. Leave its Data Type set to Text, and set its Field Size property to **25**. Set the VendorName field's Caption property to **Name**, since it will usually be obvious from the context on forms and reports that we are referring to a vendor's name.

2. Create **VendorAddress1** and **VendorAddress2** fields to store vendors' street addresses and office or suite numbers, respectively. Use your own judgment in setting the properties of these two fields.

3. Enter **VendorCity** as the next Field Name. Set its Data Type to Text, its Field Size property to **25**, and its Caption property to **City**

4. Enter **VendorState** as the next Field Name. Set its Data Type to Text, its Field Size property to **2**, and its Caption property to **State**

5. Set the Input Mask property for the VendorState field to **>LL**. The > symbol converts lowercase letters to uppercase letters, and the LL placeholders in the expression limit entry to two letters. Any other value entered will generate an error message.

6. Enter **VendorZipCode** as the next Field Name. Leave its Data Type set to Text, and set its Field Size property to **10**. This setting will accommodate the U.S. Postal Service five-plus-four Zip Code. Set the Caption property for VendorZipCode to **Zip Code**

7. Set an Input Mask property for VendorZipCode of **00000-9999;0;_**. This requires five digits, allows the extra four digits as an option, automatically inserts the hyphen as the user enters the data, stores the hyphen as part of the field contents, and uses the underscore character as a placeholder.

8. Enter **VendorTelephone** as the next Field Name. Leave its Data Type set to Text. Set its Field Size property to **14** (this will provide enough space to store the seven-digit number, a

tblVendor : Table

Vendor Number	Name	Address1	Address2	City	State	Zip Code	Telephone
1001	Square P Corporation	14532 Electron Way		Middletown	OH	45061-2079	(513) 688-2795
1002	Bolden Wire and Cable Co.	2798 Larsen Road	Suite 400	Flint	MI	48502-2966	(313) 762-7486
1003	Witchita Relays, Inc.	5764 Dawkins Drive		Witchita Falls	TX	76308-4711	(817) 689-4280
1004	Allied Electrical Supply	58927 South Wacker Drive	2nd Floor	Chicago	IL	60627-9811	(312) 702-8041
1005	Bomac Sheet Metal Co.	2788 Waterson Parkway		Long Beach	CA	90840-3762	(310) 985-7721
1006	Billiter Extrusions, Inc.	7076 Sherwood Road		Carson	CA	90747-1076	(310) 516-6405
1007	US Electrical Controls	14878 Freemont Avenue	Suite 1800	St. Louis	MO	63127-5588	(314) 527-6420
1008	Mayberry Switch & Control	1946 Mabry Hood Road		Knoxville	TN	37927-6449	(615) 271-9946
1009	Haskins Hardware Co.	9478 Jackson Drive		Chester	PA	19013-3215	(215) 499-2888
1010	Pirozolli Supply, Inc.	1746 Hurley Place		Rock Hill	SC	29733-2100	(803) 750-2344
1011	Delray Supply Company	2953 Dawson Road		Olmstead	IL	62971-2265	(618) 694-7231
1012	Century Cable Co.	891 Industrial Way		Florissant	MO	63033-7784	(314) 273-6884
1013	Haywood Metals, Inc.	6199 Denton Hills Place	N416	Omak	WA	98841-2073	(509) 714-3291
1014	Tanner Castings Co.	12779 Detras Street		Ridgely	MD	21682-1429	(410) 685-2779

Record: 1 of 14

Figure 7.3 The Vendor table, *tblVendor*, in Datasheet view.

three-digit area code, the two parentheses, one hyphen, and a space) and its Caption property to **Telephone**. Click the Input Mask property Build button to have the Input Mask Wizard create an input mask of **!(999)000-0000;0;_** for this field as shown in Figure 7.3. Access will require that you save the table before using the Wizard. You can save it with the name **tblVendor** when prompted. Be sure to choose the option of storing the literal characters (the hyphen and the parentheses) with the number.

9. Enter **VendorPrimaryContact** as the last Field Name for *tblVendor*. Leave its Data Type set to Text, and set its Field Size property to **25** and its Caption property to **Primary Contact**

This completes our *tblVendor* design. At this point, you can either close the Table window or open the table in Datasheet view to enter data. If you close the window, a dialog box will appear asking if you would like to save your changes. To open the table in Datasheet view, click the first toolbar icon. This icon toggles between Datasheet view and Design view for tables.

If you open the table in Datasheet view, you may notice that the title of each table column is the Caption property value you set. The *Ch07.mdb* database on your Companion CD includes a Vendor table, *tblVendor*, that includes sample data for Electric Controls Company. This table appears in Datasheet view in Figure 7.3.

Users could enter records directly into *tblVendor* in Datasheet view, but as you can see in Figure 7.3, the *tblVendor* fields do not all appear on the screen at once, even if the display is set to a a very small font size. Entering data could quickly become a tiresome task, requiring the user to scroll back and forth to view and enter the values in each record. You can make data entry and data viewing tasks much easier by creating a form for *tblVendor*.

The Vendor Information Form

Creating a form for the Vendor table will make entering, changing, and deleting customer information much easier than using *tblVendor* in Datasheet view. You can use the Access AutoForm tool to create a form and then modify that form to make it more useful. First, close all open windows except the Database window.

EXERCISE 7.3: CREATING A VENDOR INFORMATION FORM WITH THE AUTOFORM TOOL

1. Click Tables in the Objects bar, and select *tblVendor*.
2. Choose Insert, AutoForm from the menu.

The AutoForm tool's result appears in Figure 7.4. This compact form is quite usable. Note that AutoForm examined the fields and determined that a columnar presentation would be necessary for this form. This form is included as *frmVendor1* in the *Ch07.mdb* database on your Companion CD.

Although the AutoForm tool is a handy and quick way to produce a form, some of the form's shortcomings are easy to overcome. The next exercise guides you through some changes that will make the form easier to use. To begin the exercise, have the AutoForm-generated Vendor Information form open on the Access desktop.

EXERCISE 7.4: MODIFYING THE VENDOR INFORMATION FORM

1. Select the View, Design View command from the menu to open the form in Design view, and then click and drag its lower-right corner to make it larger in both dimensions. Click and drag the right edge of the gray Detail section background to fill the now-available space.
2. Click and drag a marquee (selection rectangle) around the label controls (and only the label controls) to select them. Click the Bold button on the Formatting toolbar, and then click the Align Right button on the Formatting toolbar. Select the Format, Align, Right menu command.

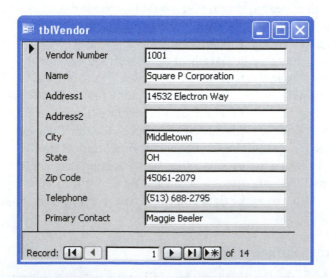

Figure 7.4 The Vendor Information form created by the AutoForm tool.

3. Change the text in the VendorAddress1 label control to **Address**, and delete the text in the VendorAddress2 label control.

4. Because the form displays one record at a time, the record selector on the left side of the form serves no useful function. To delete it, choose Edit, Select Form from the menu, click the Properties toolbar button to open the form's property sheet, click the Format tab, and change the Record Selectors property to **No**. You can also change the Dividing Lines property to **No**

5. While the property sheet is open for the form, change its Caption property to **Vendor Information Form**

6. Reduce the size of the VendorState text box control, since it only needs to display two letters.

You can make other adjustments to the form's appearance using the completed form shown in Figure 7.5 as a guide. The form displays information for vendor number 1001, the Square P Corporation. To save the form while in Design view, select File, Save As from the menu, and enter **frmVendor** in the Save As dialog box. Click OK to complete the save operation. This form is included as *frmVendor2* in the *Ch07.mdb* database on your Companion CD. Close your newly created form.

Maintaining Vendor Records

You have now built a Vendor table to store vendor information and a Vendor Information form that makes it easy to enter and view data in that table. With the Vendor Information form, you can:

- Create records for new vendors.
- Delete records for vendors that have become inactive or have gone out of business.
- Update Vendor table records as vendors move, get new telephone numbers, and change other items of information you have stored in the Vendor table.

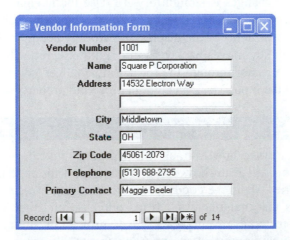

Figure 7.5 The improved Vendor Information form, *frmVendor*.

You will want to keep your file of vendor information current. A key advantage of the relational database model is that you add, delete, or change information in only one table. To use the Vendor Information form to add vendors to *tblVendor*, open *frmVendor*. As you enter values, notice how the Input Mask and Validation Rule properties you set in *tblVendor* limit the values you can enter in the VendorNumber, VendorState, VendorZipCode, and VendorTelephone controls. Try entering out-of-range values in these fields to test the internal controls you built into the table.

TRY IT

Deleting records from the Vendor table is easy. Open the Vendor Information form by clicking the Forms tab in the Database window and double-clicking *frmVendor*. To delete a record, move to that record using the navigation buttons at the bottom of the form, and then choose Edit, Delete Record from the menu. Access gives you a warning message that asks you to confirm the deletion. This deletion is not reversible. You can delete individual fields in a record using the Delete key in Form view. Individual field deletions are reversible by selecting Edit, Undo delete before you move to another field. After you move to another field, you can reverse field deletions in the current record by selecting Edit, Undo Current Field/Record. You can also press Esc repeatedly to reverse deletions.

Be careful when deleting records in accounting databases. Data in one accounting table are usually related to data in other tables. For example, if you examine a record in a purchase order table, it will contain a vendor number. The only place that vendor's name and address is stored is in the related vendor table. If someone deletes that vendor's record in the vendor table, you may never be able to identify the vendor.

Keeping existing vendor records current to reflect address changes, new telephone numbers, and other changes is straightforward. Use the navigation buttons at the bottom of the form to move to the vendor record that you want to change. You can move through the individual fields of the displayed record by using the Enter key or the Tab key. The Shift+Tab key moves backward through the record. The up and down arrow keys also move the cursor through the form. Any changes you make to field contents will be limited by the Input Mask and Validation Rule property settings for *tblVendor*.

MATERIALS INVENTORY

In Chapter 6 you learned how to track finished goods inventory in the revenue cycle. In this section, you will learn how to build tables and forms that can help you track materials inventories—both the goods that merchandising firms purchase for resale and the raw materials that manufacturing firms purchase and then convert into finished goods. Firms use materials inventory records to provide inventory descriptions on purchase orders, receiving reports, and other documents. To ensure that materials inventory information is consistent wherever it is used, firms keep all materials inventory information in one database table. Any document, report, or transaction that needs inventory information obtains it from that table.

The Materials Inventory Table

The purchase cycle requires a materials inventory table that includes at least two fields. The first field must contain the primary key, a number or code that uniquely identifies the inventory item. This primary key field might contain an item number, item code, part number, or catalog number. In some industries, these inventory item identifiers are standardized; for example, some firms use UPC (universal product code) or SKU (stock-keeping unit) numbers as the primary keys in their materials inventory tables. The second field should contain a description of each inventory item. The description may include information about an item's size, weight, shape, color, hardness, or other qualities. A firm may decide to store these inventory item attributes in separate fields.

Electric Controls Company has decided to use a two-field description scheme in its materials inventory table. Electric Controls classifies the parts it uses to build control panels into six categories: circuit breakers, connectors, relays, sheet metal, switches, and wire.

Few firms can store inventory purchase prices in the materials inventory table—that would require the firm to know, in advance, exactly what price it will pay for each item. Thus, Electric Controls Company does not store the prices in its materials inventory table. Each vendor is likely to have its own inventory part number. Since vendors might change their part numbers from time to time, Electric Controls stores the vendor part number for each item as it orders the items instead of in the materials inventory table.

Electric Controls Company's materials inventory description will include two fields. One field will identify an item's category; the second field will store details about the particular item. The purchasing department personnel who will be using materials inventory information have ready access to Electric Controls Company's computer system. This reduces the benefit of using a mnemonic coding scheme such as the one you created for Pipefitters Supply in Chapter 6. Therefore, you can use a sequential number scheme for the primary key field in the Materials Inventory table for Electric Controls. A three-digit field will allow Electric Controls to maintain records on as many as 899 different materials inventory items. In Exercise 7.5 you will build this table.

EXERCISE 7.5: BUILDING A MATERIALS INVENTORY TABLE

1. In the Database window, click the Tables tab, click the New button, and then double-click Design View in the New Table dialog box.
2. Enter **MaterialsInventoryStockNumber** as the first Field Name, and click the Primary Key toolbar button. Leave its Data Type set to Text. Set its Field Size property to **3**, its Input Mask property to **000**, and its Caption property to **Stock Number**.
3. Enter a Field Name of **MaterialsInventoryCategory** for the first description field. Leave its Data Type set to Text. Set its Field Size property to **16** to match the number of characters in the longest inventory category name.

4. Set its Input Mask property to **>L<CCCCCCCCCCCCCCC**. This setting will automatically capitalize the first letter entered in the field, thus making data entry easier, and will ensure that any other characters entered are either lowercase letters or spaces.
5. Set the Caption property to **Category**
6. Enter **MaterialsInventoryDescription** as the third Field Name. Leave its Data Type set to Text. Set its Field Size property to **25** and its Caption property to **Description**
7. Save the table, entering **tblMaterialsInventory** in the Save As dialog box. Click OK, and then close the table.

Figure 7.6 shows *tblMaterialsInventory* in Datasheet view displaying the data for Electric Controls Company. These data are included in *tblMaterialsInventory* in the *Ch07.mdb* database on your Companion CD.

Stock Number	Category	Description
101	Sheet metal	1/8" Steel 4x4 sheet
102	Switch	DPDT 240v 100a
103	Wire	500' Copper #22AWG
104	Sheet metal	1/4" Steel 4x4 sheet
105	Switch	SPDT 240v 100a
106	Relay	SPDT 120v 40a Silver
107	Circuit breaker	240v 40a
108	Relay	TPST 240v 100a Mercury
109	Sheet metal	1/8" Aluminum 4x4 sheet
110	Wire	500' Copper Twin #18AWG
111	Connector	F 240v 100a solderless
112	Switch	DPST 240v 50a
113	Connector	M 120v 40a clip
114	Sheet metal	1/4" Aluminum 4x4 sheet
115	Circuit breaker	120v 40a

Record: 1 of 15

Figure 7.6   The Electric Controls Company *tblMaterialsInventory* in Datasheet view.

The Category Table

The Input Mask property setting for the MaterialsInventoryCategory field in *tblMaterialsInventory* capitalizes the first letter and limits the field to 16 characters. However, this setting does not limit the values entered to the six specific categories. As you learned in Chapter 6, a Validation Rule property setting can restrict values entered to the six categories.

An alternative to creating a Validation Rule property that enforces rules about the field's characteristics is to build a separate table that contains the permitted values. You can then enforce referential integrity on a link between the category field in *tblMaterialsInventory* and the category field in the new table. When more than four or five permitted values exist, this separate-table technique can be much more efficient than setting a Validation Rule property. By storing the permitted values in a separate table, the tasks of adding, altering, and deleting values become much easier than if the values are buried in a Validation Rule property setting. In the next two exercises, you will create a category table and enforce referential integrity on a link from that table to *tblMaterialsInventory*.

EXERCISE 7.6: BUILDING A MATERIALS INVENTORY CATEGORY TABLE

1. In the Database window, click the Tables tab, click the New button, and then double-click Design View in the New Table dialog box that appears.
2. Enter **Category** in the first row of the Field Name column, and click the Primary Key toolbar button to make this field the primary key.
3. Leave its Data Type set to Text, and enter a Field Size property of **16**
4. Select Save As from the menu, and enter **tblCategory** as the table's name; then click OK.
5. Select View, Datasheet View from the menu to open the table, and then enter the six category values shown in Figure 7.7. When you are finished, close the table.

Figure 7.7 shows *tblCategory* in Datasheet view displaying the six categories that Electric Controls Company uses to classify its materials inventory. This table is included in the *Ch07.mdb* database on your Companion CD. Tables like *tblCategory* are sometimes called *lookup tables* because the main table field looks up entered values to determine their validity. You may recall that we used a lookup table in Chapter 6 to store inventory diameter values for use in a combo box control on *frmInventory*. In the next exercise, you will create a lookup link in the Relationships window for the Category table and enforce referential integrity on that link.

EXERCISE 7.7: ENFORCING REFERENTIAL INTEGRITY ON THE CATEGORY LINK

1. Close all open tables. With the Database window displayed, choose the Tools, Relationships menu command.
2. Click the Tables tab in the Show Table dialog box, and then select (click while holding down the Ctrl key) *tblCategory and tblMaterialsInventory*.

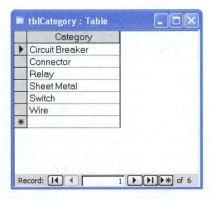

Figure 7.7 The Category table in Datasheet view.

3. Click the Add button, and then click the Close button. You can adjust the size and location of the tables displayed in the Relationships window using Figure 7.8 as a guide.

4. Click and drag the Category field from *tblCategory* to the MaterialsInventoryCategory field in *tblMaterialsInventory*. When the Relationships dialog box appears, check it carefully to make certain that you did drag the field to its proper destination.

5. Click the Enforce Referential Integrity check box, and then click the Create button.

The Relationships window showing the two linked tables appears in Figure 7.8. To return to the Database window, close the Relationships window and save your changes.

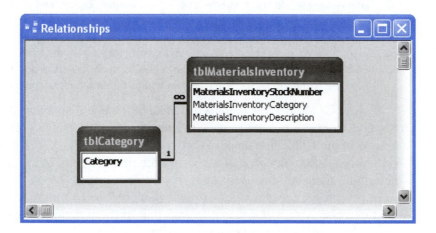

Figure 7.8 Linking *tblCategory* and *tblMaterialsInventory*.

The Materials Inventory Form

The materials inventory form will help users enter inventory records easily and accurately. The form will also provide a convenient way for users to view, update, or delete existing inventory records. In Exercise 7.8 you will create *frmMaterialsInventory*, a materials inventory form.

EXERCISE 7.8: USING AUTOFORM TO CREATE A MATERIALS INVENTORY FORM

1. Click the Forms object in the Database window, and then click the New button. Since *tblMaterialsInventory* has only three short fields, you do not need to use a columnar form. You can display a number of records at one time by using a tabular form. Select *tblMaterialsInventory* from the drop-down list in the New Form dialog box.

2. Double-click AutoForm: Tabular in the New Form dialog box.

3. To save the form, press Ctrl+W, click the Yes button to confirm that you want to save changes to the form's design, and enter a Form Name of **frmMaterialsInventory** in the Save As dialog box.

4. Click OK to save the form. Leave the form open, because you will modify it in the next exercise.

As you can see in Figure 7.9, AutoForm creates a fairly good-looking form that you can modify to meet Electric Controls' specific needs efficiently and effectively. Note how the tabular format lets users view more than one record at a time. This version of the form is included as *frmMaterialsInventory1* in the *Ch07.mdb* database on your Companion CD. This file also includes *tblMaterialsInventory*, which includes the records displayed in Figure 7.9. Your form will show the records, if any, that you entered in your Materials Inventory table.

Although the AutoForm tool has made a good start toward creating a usable form, you can improve the appearance and usefulness of the form considerably. To make the design tools more accessible, you can click the Toolbox toolbar button.

TRY IT

You can click and drag the toolbox around the Design window as you work, but you might find it useful to move the toolbox to the top of the Design window. When you do this, the toolbox icons become slightly larger and arrange themselves across the top of the work area just below the toolbar. You can see this in Figure 7.10, which shows the Materials Inventory form in Design view with the toolbox moved to the top of the Design window, just under the Formatting toolbar. We usually work with the property sheet open, too. To open the property sheet, click the Properties toolbar button. As you can see in Figure 7.10, we often keep the property sheet just partially exposed on the desktop, off to one side or below the form on which we are working.

You can try doing the next two exercises with the toolbox and property sheet open if you wish. In Exercise 7.9 you will improve the design and appearance of *frmMaterialsInventory*.

EXERCISE 7.9: IMPROVING THE MATERIALS INVENTORY FORM

1. Click the Design View toolbar button.
2. Choose Edit, Select Form from the menu, click the Format tab in the property sheet, and change the form's Caption property to **Materials Inventory**
3. Click and drag the right edge of the form to make it wider; then click and drag the edges of the gray Detail section background to fit the enlarged frame.
4. Select the label controls in the Form Header section, and click the Bold button on the Formatting toolbar. You may also want to click the Center button on the Formatting toolbar to center-align the labels and use the Shift+right arrow key to make the labels a little wider to expose all of the labels' text.
5. Click and drag a marquee around all of the controls (in both sections of the form), and repeatedly select Format, Horizontal Spacing, Increase from the menu to increase the space

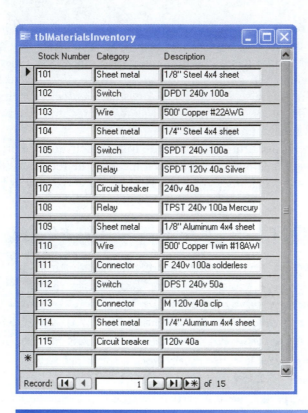

Figure 7.9   The Materials Inventory form created by the AutoForm tool.

between the controls. You can use Figure 7.11 as a guide. Remember, you may need to switch back and forth between Form view and Design view to obtain your desired results.

In the next exercise, you will replace the text box control for the category field with a combo box. By linking this combo box control to *tblCategory*, you can make data entry easier for the employees of Electric Controls Company. You should have the form open in Design view after completing the previous exercise.

EXERCISE 7.10: ADDING A COMBO BOX TO THE MATERIALS INVENTORY FORM

1. Select the MaterialsInventoryCategory text box control in the Detail section, and press the Del key.
2. Make sure that the Control Wizards button toolbox tool is highlighted.
3. Click the Combo Box tool button in the toolbox, and draw a combo box control in the Detail section to replace the MaterialsInventoryCategory text box you just deleted. This will start the Combo Box Wizard.
4. In the first Combo Box Wizard dialog box, click the Next button to accept the default of linking the combo box to a table or query.
5. Double-click *tblCategory* in the list box. This action also moves the Wizard to its next dialog box.

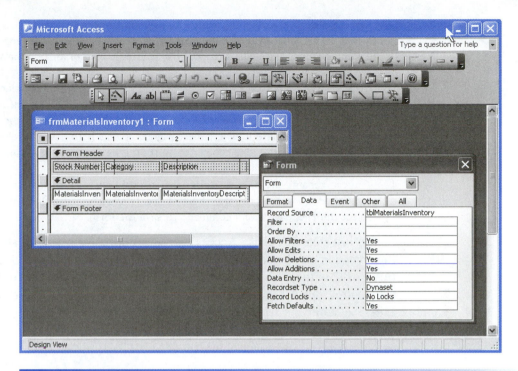

Figure 7.10 The Materials Inventory form in Design view with the toolbox and property sheet opened.

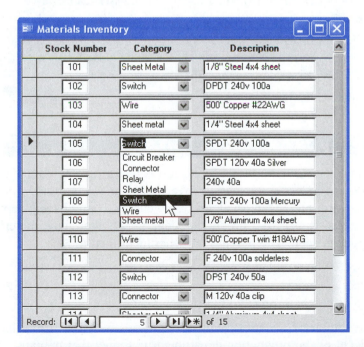

Figure 7.11 The operation of the *cboMaterialsInventoryCategory* combo box control.

6. Double-click Category, and then click the Next button.
7. In the next Combo Box Wizard dialog box, double-click the right edge of the Category column header. This adjusts the column so that it accommodates the widest text, Circuit breaker. Click the Next button.
8. Click the option button to Store that value in this field, and then select MaterialsInventoryCategory in the combo box. Click the Next button, and then click the Finish button.
9. When the Wizard returns you to the Design view desktop, select the new combo box control's label, and delete it. The easiest way to do this is to use the Select Object combo box control on the Formatting toolbar to select the new combo box label (it will have a suffix of _Label) and press the Del key.
10. You can rename the control (select the control first) by changing its Name property under the Other tab in the property sheet to *cboMaterialsInventoryCategory*.
11. Select the File, Save menu command to save the form.

The last step will cause Access to overwrite the form you created earlier. This modified version of the form with the combo box control is included as *frmMaterialsInventory2* in the *Ch07.mdb* database on your Companion CD. To test your new combo box control, select View, Form from the menu, and then click the *cboMaterialsInventoryCategory* control's arrow button. The combo box should display the six choices from *tblCategory* as shown in Figure 7.11.

TRY IT

The Combo Box Wizard writes a query that accesses *tblCategory* and inserts the six values from the Category field in that table. To examine this query, click the MaterialsInventory Category combo box in Design view with the property sheet open, click the Data tab, select the Row Source property, and click its Build button. It is a simple query, but it does the job. Close all windows except the Database window.

PURCHASE ORDERS

Now that you have built tables and forms that a firm could use to enter and maintain records of vendors and materials inventory, you can build the system components that facilitate ordering inventory items from vendors. A purchasing department receives materials requisitions from production departments that show materials descriptions and quantities needed. The purchasing department then must:

• Identify vendors that provide these materials.
• Select a vendor.
• Send a purchase order to the chosen vendor.

The format of materials requisitions varies with the firm's industry, size, and the skill level of the production department personnel that prepare materials requisitions. The format also depends on the nature of the firm's production cycle. The form of purchase orders also varies from firm to firm; however, all purchase orders must contain the following:

- Order date.
- Vendor name and address.
- Identification of the inventory item(s) to be purchased.
- Quantities and prices of the inventory item(s) to be purchased.

The purchase order also frequently contains shipping information, including an expected shipping date. You can identify vendors with purchase orders by linking the Vendor table to a new table, the Purchase Order table, because there will be only one vendor for each purchase order. However, connecting purchase orders to the specific inventory items listed on each purchase order requires a separate relationship table to model the many-to-many nature of that link.

The Purchase Order Table

In this section, you will learn how to create a purchase order table, *tblPurchaseOrder*. Since only one vendor will be associated with any specific purchase order, you can include the table's primary key, VendorNumber, as a foreign key in *tblPurchaseOrder* to establish the needed link. Of course, *tblPurchaseOrder* will need its own primary key and a field for the order date.

To keep this example simple, you can omit specific shipping data and just record an expected shipping date. The expected shipping date is the date on which the vendor agrees to ship the items listed on the purchase order. Therefore, *tblPurchaseOrder* needs four fields: a primary key, an order date, a foreign key link to *tblVendor*, and an expected vendor ship date. Exercise 7.11 provides step-by-step procedures you can follow to create a purchase order table for Electric Controls Company.

EXERCISE 7.11: BUILDING A PURCHASE ORDER TABLE

1. In the Database window, click the Tables tab, click the New button, and then double-click Design View in the New Table dialog box that appears.
2. Type **PurchaseOrderNumber** as the first Field Name. Leave its Data Type set to Text, and click the Primary Key toolbar button.
3. Set PurchaseOrderNumber's Field Size property to **6** and its Input Mask property to ######, which will accommodate 899,999 purchase orders with a starting number of 100001. Set its Caption property to **P.O. Number**
4. Enter a Field Name of **PurchaseOrderDate**, and set its Data Type to **Date/Time**. Set the Input Mask property to **99/99/0000;0;_** and the Caption property to **P.O. Date**
5. The next field is the foreign key link to *tblVendor*. In the next exercise, you will establish a referential integrity link on this field to *tblVendor*. Therefore, this field must match the VendorNumber field in *tblVendor*. Enter **VendorNumber** as the Field Name, and leave its Data Type set to Text. Set the Field Size property to **4** and the Caption property to **Vendor Number**. You do not need an Input Mask property for VendorNumber because the link to *tblVendor* will ensure that values entered already exist in *tblVendor*.

6. Enter a Field Name of **PurchaseOrderExpectedShipDate**, and set its Data Type to **Date/Time**. Set this field's Input Mask property to **99/99/0000;0;_** and its Caption property to **Expected Ship Date**

7. Close and save the table as *tblPurchaseOrder*.

In the next exercise, you will connect the Purchase Order table to the Vendor table on the VendorNumber field. Be sure that all tables are closed and the Database window is open on the Access desktop.

EXERCISE 7.12: LINKING THE PURCHASE ORDER TABLE TO THE VENDOR TABLE

1. Click the Relationships toolbar button.
2. Click the Show Table toolbar button, double-click *tblPurchaseOrder*, double-click *tblVendor*, and then click the Close button in the Show Table dialog box.
3. Click and drag the VendorNumber field from *tblVendor* to the VendorNumber field in *tblPurchaseOrder*.
4. Click the Enforce Referential Integrity check box, and then click the Create button.
5. Close the Relationships window, and save the changes you have made.

A copy of *tblPurchaseOrder* is in the *Ch07.mdb* database on your Companion CD. This completes the job of building *tblPurchaseOrder*; however, you cannot enter purchase orders in this table yet. The Purchase Order table does not identify which inventory items are ordered, nor does it identify the quantities and prices of items ordered. In the next section, you will learn how to create a purchase order-materials inventory relationship table to properly store this information.

The Purchase Order-Materials Inventory Table

If Electric Controls Company ordered only one inventory item on each purchase order, it would not need this table. It could add fields for the inventory item, its quantity, and its price to *tblPurchaseOrder*. Unfortunately, Electric Controls and most other businesses would find themselves drowning in purchase orders if they adopted this approach. The purchase order-materials inventory table is a relationship table that models the many-to-many link between *tblPurchaseOrder* and *tblMaterialsInventory*. That is, each purchase order may have many materials inventory items, and each materials inventory item may appear on many purchase orders. The purchase order-materials inventory table needs five fields to store the following values:

- Primary key of *tblPurchaseOrder*
- Primary key of *tblMaterialsInventory*
- Quantity of specific materials inventory items that appear on specific purchase orders
- Price of specific materials inventory items that appear on specific purchase orders
- Vendor inventory stock number for each materials inventory item at the time of a specific purchase order

In the next exercise, you will learn how to create *tblPurchaseOrder-Materials Inventory*, a relationship table for Electric Controls Company that will provide these two links and store these five fields. To begin the exercise, close any tables or forms you have open on the desktop and open the Database window.

EXERCISE 7.13: BUILDING A PURCHASE ORDER-MATERIALS INVENTORY TABLE

1. In the Database window, click the Tables object, click the New button, and double-click Design View in the New Table dialog box that appears.
2. Type **PurchaseOrderNumber** as the first Field Name. Leave its Data Type set to Text.
3. Set PurchaseOrderNumber's Field Size property to **6**, its Input Mask property to **######**, its Caption property to **P.O. Number**, and its Indexed property to **Yes (Duplicates OK)**
4. Type **MaterialsInventoryStockNumber** as the next Field Name. Leave its Data Type set to Text. Set its Field Size property to **3** and its Caption property to **Item Number**. Set its Indexed property to **Yes (Duplicates OK)**
5. While holding down the Ctrl key, click the row selectors of the PurchaseOrderNumber field and the MaterialsInventoryStockNumber field. Click the Primary Key toolbar button. The primary key symbol should appear in the row selectors of both fields, indicating that you have created a composite primary key for the table.
6. Enter a Field Name of **PurchaseOrder-MaterialsInventoryQuantity**, and set its Data Type to **Number**. Set PurchaseOrder-MaterialsInventoryQuantity's Field Size property to **Long Integer**, its Decimal Places property to **0**, and its Caption property to **Quantity**
7. Enter a Field Name of **PurchaseOrder-MaterialsInventoryPrice**, set its Data Type to **Currency**, and set its Caption property to **Price**
8. Enter a Field Name of **PurchaseOrder-MaterialsInventoryVendorStockNumber**, leave its Data Type set to Text, set its Field Size property to **20**, and its Caption Property to **Vendor Stock Number**
9. Save the table as *tblPurchaseOrder-MaterialsInventory*, and then close the table.

We have included a *tblPurchaseOrder-MaterialsInventory* object in the *Ch07.mdb* database on your Companion CD for your reference. Now that the table design is complete, you can create the links to *tblMaterialsInventory* and *tblPurchaseOrder*. The next exercise shows you how. Begin with all tables and forms closed and the Database window open on the Access desktop.

EXERCISE 7.14: LINKING THE PURCHASE ORDER-MATERIALS INVENTORY TABLE

1. Click the Relationships toolbar button.
2. Click the Show Table toolbar button, double-click *tblPurchaseOrder-MaterialsInventory*, and then click the Close button.
3. Click and drag the MaterialsInventoryStockNumber field from *tblMaterialsInventory* to the MaterialsInventoryStockNumber field in *tblPurchaseOrder-MaterialsInventory*.
4. Click the Enforce Referential Integrity check box, and then click the Create button.
5. Click and drag the PurchaseOrderNumber field from *tblPurchaseOrder* to the PurchaseOrderNumber field in *tblPurchaseOrder-MaterialsInventory*.

6. Click the Enforce Referential Integrity check box, and then click the Create button.
7. Close the Relationships window, and save your changes.

Figure 7.12 shows the relationships you have created thus far in this chapter. These relationships link Purchase Order to Vendor and to Materials Inventory through the relationship table, *tblPurchaseOrder-MaterialsInventory*.

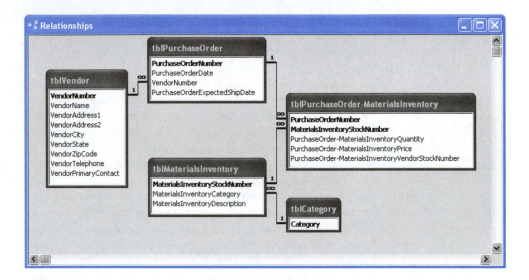

Figure 7.12   Relationships between the Purchase Order, Vendor, and Materials Inventory tables.

Now that you have built the necessary tables and linked them, you can create a form that Electric Controls Company can use to enter its purchase orders. The next section shows you how to create such a form.

The Purchase Order Entry Form

The purchase order entry form is fairly complex. To enter purchase orders, you will create a form that links:

- The Purchase Order table to the Vendor table, to provide the vendor name.
- The Purchase Order table to the Purchase Order-Materials Inventory table, to provide a list of inventory stock numbers, quantities, prices, and vendor stock numbers for each item on each purchase order.
- The Purchase Order-Materials Inventory table to the Materials Inventory table, to provide a description for each item on each purchase order.

A purchase order entry form that meets these objectives will use four tables. The form must read from *tblVendor* and *tblMaterialsInventory* and will write to *tblPurchaseOrder* and *tblPurchaseOrder-MaterialsInventory*. Since the form will read data from *tblVendor* and *tblMaterialsInventory*, you will need to have data in these tables to test the form's operation as you build it. The versions of these two tables that we have included in the *Ch07.mdb* database on your Companion CD contain data. You can use these tables or copy the data from them to your own tables.

The Purchase Order Entry form will allow Electric Controls Company to enter purchase order information simultaneously in *tblPurchaseOrder* and *tblPurchaseOrder-MaterialsInventory*. Microsoft Access handles this simultaneous data entry task best with a form-subform design. This design links *tblPurchaseOrder* to *tblVendor* in the main form and links *tblPurchaseOrder-MaterialsInventory* to *tblMaterialsInventory* in the subform. In Exercise 7.15 you will use the Access Form Wizard to create these two forms.

EXERCISE 7.15: BUILDING THE PURCHASE ORDER ENTRY FORMS

1. Click the Forms object in the Database window, and click the New button to open the New Form dialog box. Select *tblPurchaseOrder* in the source table combo box, and then double-click Form Wizard in the list box.
2. The Form Wizard dialog box should display Table: tblPurchaseOrder in its Tables/Queries combo box. Click the > button to move all of the fields from the Available Fields list box to the Selected Fields list box.
3. Select Table: tblVendor in the Tables/Queries combo box. Select VendorName in the Available Fields list box, and click the > button to move it to the Selected Fields list box.
4. Select Table: tblPurchaseOrder-MaterialsInventory in the Tables/Queries combo box. Using the > button, move the following fields to the Selected Fields list box: MaterialsInventoryStockNumber, PurchaseOrder-MaterialsInventoryQuantity, PurchaseOrder-MaterialsInventoryPrice, and PurchaseOrder-MaterialsInventoryVendorStockNumber.
5. Select Table: tblMaterialsInventory in the Tables/Queries combo box. Using the > button, move the MaterialsInventoryCategory and MaterialsInventoryDescription fields to the Selected Fields list box.
6. Click the Next button to continue. The Form Wizard presents a template of the form-subform design and main sort order in its next dialog box as shown in Figure 7.13.
7. Click the Next button to accept the Form Wizard's design template and continue.
8. Click the Tabular layout option button, and then click the Next button.
9. Select the Standard style, and then click the Next button.
10. Enter a Form title of **frmPurchaseOrder** and a Subform title of **fsubPurchaseOrder** Click the Finish button to have the Form Wizard create the two forms.

The Purchase Order Entry form generated by the Form Wizard appears in Figure 7.14 in Form view. We have included the main form and subform that comprise this form in the *Ch07.mdb* database on your Companion CD as *frmPurchaseOrder1* and *fsubPurchaseOrder1*.

Although this design is a good start, you can enhance the form to make it more useful. For example, the first record that appears in the form is purchase order number 100008, not 100001, and the MaterialsInventoryDescription field does not show on the

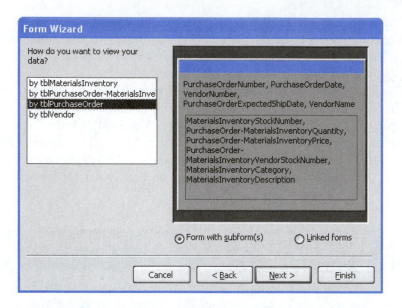

Figure 7.13 The Form Wizard's proposed template for the Purchase Order Entry form.

subform because the subform object the Form Wizard created in the purchase order form is not wide enough. You will learn how to fix these problems and identify other ways to improve the form in the next three exercises. Exercise 7.16 shows you how to make some changes to queries behind the form and subform.

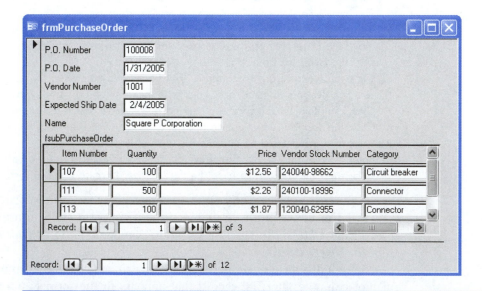

Figure 7.14 The Form Wizard-generated Purchase Order Entry form.

EXERCISE 7.16: EDITING THE PURCHASE ORDER ENTRY FORM AND SUBFORM QUERIES

1. Open *frmPurchaseOrder* in Design view by selecting the form and clicking the Design button; then click the Properties toolbar button to open the property sheet. We will assume that you have the property sheet open and available in Form Design view throughout this exercise.

2. Select Edit, Select Form from the menu, and then click the Data tab in the property sheet. Select the form's Record Source property, and click its Build button to open the query that the Form Wizard built behind the form.

3. The form opened with PurchaseOrderNumber 100006, and not PurchaseOrderNumber 100001, because the Form Wizard did not set any sorting options in the query behind *frmPurchaseOrder*. Enter **Ascending** in the PurchaseOrderNumber field's Sort cell in the first QBE grid column to fix this problem. Close the Query Builder window, and save your changes.

4. Close *frmPurchaseOrder*, and save your changes. Access will display the Database window. Open *fsubPurchaseOrder* in Design view.

5. Click the Data tab in the property sheet, select the Record Source property, and then click its Build button to open the query behind the form. Enter **Ascending** in the MaterialsInventoryStockNumber field's Sort cell in the first QBE grid column.

6. Scroll the QBE grid to expose the first open Field cell, select it, and then press Shift+F2 to open the Zoom box. Enter **Description: [MaterialsInventoryCategory] & ", " & [MaterialsInventoryDescription]** in the Zoom box, and then click the OK button. Close the Query Builder window, and save your changes.

In the next exercise, you will make some changes that improve the appearance of the Purchase Order subform. You can use Figure 7.15, which shows the finished subform in Form view, as a guide. Make sure that *fsubPurchaseOrder* is open in Design view before you begin this exercise.

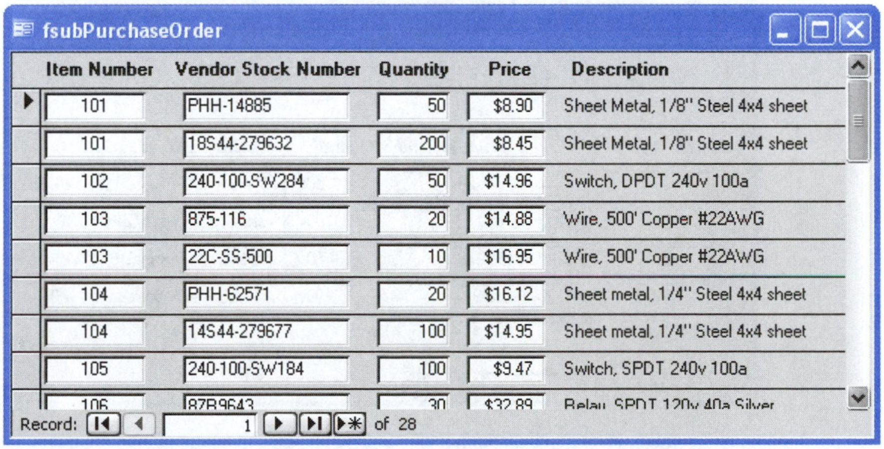

Figure 7.15 The enhanced version of *fsubPurchaseOrder*.

EXERCISE 7.17: ENHANCING THE APPEARANCE OF THE PURCHASE ORDER SUBFORM

1. Select the MaterialsInventoryCategory text box control and label. Press the Del key to remove them from the form.
2. Move the PurchaseOrder-MaterialsInventoryVendorStockNumber text box control and label to the right of the MaterialsInventoryStockNumber controls. You will need to move the other controls on the form to the right to make room for this adjustment. See Figure 7.15 for guidance.
3. Select the MaterialsInventoryDescription text box control, click the Data tab in its property sheet, and then change its Control Source property to **Description**. Change the Enabled property to **No** and the Locked property to **Yes**
4. Click on the property sheet Format tab, and set the control's Back Style to **Transparent**, its Special Effect property to **Flat**, and its Border Style property to **Transparent**. Click the Other tab, and enter a Name property of **Description**
5. Select the label controls in the Form Header, and then click the Bold button on the Formatting toolbar. Change the size, alignment, and arrangement of the text box and label controls using Figure 7.15 as a guide.
6. Close *fsubPurchaseOrder*, and save your changes.

Notice that the enhanced version of the subform makes it easy for users to tell which fields require an entry and which do not. In fact, the Description control is locked so that users cannot accidentally change data in the underlying fields. In Exercise 7.18, you will make changes to the main Purchase Order form that will improve its usefulness. You can use Figure 7.16, which shows the finished Purchase Order form, as a guide while you are making these changes.

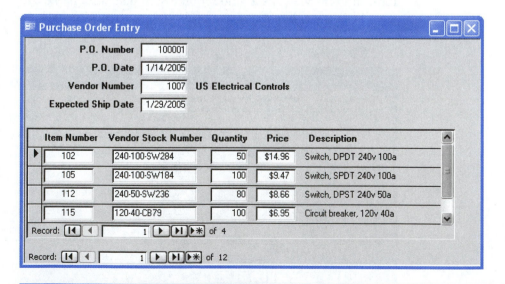

Figure 7.16   The completed Purchase Order Entry form.

EXERCISE 7.18: ENHANCING THE APPEARANCE OF THE PURCHASE ORDER FORM

1. Open *frmPurchaseOrder* in Design view.
2. Select the Subform object label that appears just above the subform, and press Ctrl+X to delete it.
3. Select the VendorName label, and press Ctrl+X to delete it; then click and drag the VendorName text box control to a position to the right of the VendorNumber text box control. You may wish to use the Format, Align menu commands to ensure a precise alignment.
4. With the VendorName text box control still selected, click the Data tab in its property sheet; then change its Enabled property to **No** and its Locked property to **Yes**. Click on the property sheet Format tab, and set the control's Back Style to **Transparent**, its Special Effect property to **Flat**, and its Border Style property to **Transparent**
5. Select the VendorName text box control and all of the label controls—you can do this by holding down the Shift key as you click each one—and click the Bold button on the Formatting toolbar.
6. Choose the Edit, Select Form command from the menu, click on the form's property sheet Format tab, change its Caption property to **Purchase Order Entry**, and set the Record Selectors property to **No**
7. Using Figure 7.16 as a guide, make any other changes you wish to the form's appearance; then, close the form and save your changes.

The Purchase Order form and subform that appear in Figure 7.16 are included in the *Ch07.mdb* database on your Companion CD as *frmPurchaseOrder2* and *fsubPurchaseOrder2*, respectively.

Printing Purchase Orders

In this section, you will learn how to retrieve and print the purchase cycle information that Electric Controls Company will gather through the forms and store in the tables that you have created. Entering purchase order information is an important step, but sending the printed purchase orders to vendors is an important function of the purchase cycle. In Exercise 7.19, you will use the Report Wizard to generate printed purchase orders.

EXERCISE 7.19: BUILDING A PURCHASE ORDER REPORT

1. Click the Reports object in the Database window, and then click the New button to open the New Report dialog box. Enter **tblPurchaseOrder** in the source table combo box, and then double-click Report Wizard in the list box.
2. The next Report Wizard dialog box should display Table: tblPurchaseOrder in its Tables/Queries combo box. Click the > button to move all of the fields from the Available Fields list box to the Selected Fields list box.
3. Select Table: tblVendor in the Tables/Queries combo box. Using the > button, move the following fields to the Selected Fields list box: VendorName, VendorAddress1, VendorAddress2, VendorCity, VendorState, and VendorZipCode.

4. Select Table: tblPurchaseOrder-MaterialsInventory in the Tables/Queries combo box. Using the > button, move the following fields to the Selected Fields list box: MaterialsInventoryStockNumber, PurchaseOrder-MaterialsInventoryQuantity, Purchase-Order-MaterialsInventoryPrice, and PurchaseOrder-MaterialsInventoryVendorStockNumber.

5. Select Table: tblMaterialsInventory in the Tables/Queries combo box. Using the > button, move the MaterialsInventoryCategory and MaterialsInventoryDescription fields to the Selected Fields list box. Click the Next button to continue. The Report Wizard presents a template of the report-subreport design and main sort order in its next dialog box as shown in Figure 7.17.

6. To accept the Report Wizard's proposed design, click the Next button. Click the Next button in the dialog box that appears to accept the Report Wizard's grouping on PurchaseOrderNumber.

7. Select MaterialsInventoryStockNumber in the first sort order combo box, and then click the Next button.

8. Click the Outline 1 Layout option button; then click the Next button.

9. Select the Bold style; then click the Next button.

10. Enter **rptPurchaseOrder** as the report title; then click the Finish button.

11. Close the report's preview window.

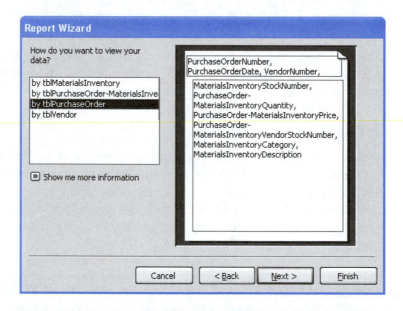

Figure 7.17 The Report Wizard's proposed report template for *rptPurchaseOrder*.

The report generated by the Report Wizard is in very rough form. It does not have a page break at the end of each purchase order and does not include Electric Controls Company's name or address. In the next three exercises, you will take this report, which is on your Companion CD in the *Ch07.mdb* database as *rptPurchaseOrderCreated ByReportWizard*, and transform it into a useful purchase order report. In Exercise 7.20, you will make changes to the query behind the Purchase Order report.

EXERCISE 7.20: MODIFYING THE QUERY BEHIND THE PURCHASE ORDER REPORT

1. Open the report you just created (or *rptPurchaseOrderCreatedByReportWizard* on your Companion CD) in Design view. Click the Properties toolbar button to open the property sheet. We will assume that you have the property sheet open throughout this exercise.
2. Click the property sheet Data tab, select the Record Source property, and click on its Build button to open the query behind the report. Type **Ascending** in the first Sort cell in the QBE grid, under the PurchaseOrderNumber Field name.
3. Scroll to the last column in the QBE grid, and then choose Insert, Columns from the menu. Select the new column's Field cell, and press Shift+F2 to open the Zoom box. Enter **Description: [MaterialsInventoryCategory] & ", " & [MaterialsInventoryDescription]** in the Zoom box, and then click the OK button.
4. Use the procedure in the preceding step to insert another column in the QBE grid, select the new column's Field cell, and press Shift+F2 to open the Zoom box. Enter **Extension: [PurchaseOrder-MaterialsInventoryQuantity]*[PurchaseOrder-MaterialsInventoryPrice]**, and click the OK button. This expression calculates the quantity ∞ price extension for each item on the purchase order.
5. Insert another column in the QBE grid, select the new column's Field cell, and press Shift+F2 to open the Zoom box. Enter **VendorNameAndAddress: [VendorName] & Chr(13) & Chr(10) & [VendorAddress1] & Chr(13) & Chr(10) & IIf(IsNull([VendorAddress2]), "",([VendorAddress2] & Chr(13) & Chr(10))) & [VendorCity] & ", " & [VendorState] & " " & [VendorZipCode]** in the Zoom box; then click the OK button.
6. Close the Query Builder window, and save your changes.

You may wish to move the property sheet to an unobtrusive location before proceeding. The expression you created for VendorNameAndAddress combines the components of the vendor address into one field that you can print on the purchase order. The expression includes two interesting components. First, the expression uses the Chr() function with the values of 13 and 10 to insert a carriage return and line feeds. Second, the expression uses an IsNull() function nested inside an IIF() function to test whether the VendorAddress2 field contains data. If it does, the expression prints it as the third line of the field.

TRY IT

You can learn more about these two functions in Microsoft Access online help. You may recall that you used four separate lines for customer name and address information in the Chapter 6 Invoice report. When you print that report, you can see that invoices for customers that did not have second address line information included a blank line in the address. Now that you have seen how to use the Chr(), IsNull(), and IIF() functions, you might want to go back and incorporate these functions into *rptInvoice*.

In Exercise 7.21 you will modify the report's appearance to accommodate the changes you made to its underlying query in Exercise 7.20. As you work through Exercise 7.21, you may want to use the Design view of the finished report, shown in Figure 7.18, and the printout of the finished report, shown in Figure 7.19, as guides to help you with control placement and appearance adjustments. You should have the Purchase Order report open in Design view to begin this exercise.

EXERCISE 7.21: MODIFYING THE PURCHASE ORDER REPORT'S APPEARANCE

1. Click and drag the top of the Detail section bar down to make room in the PurchaseOrderNumber Header for a title and Electric Controls Company's name and address. Select all of the objects in the PurchaseOrderNumber Header; then, click and drag the selected objects down to make room at the top of the section. You may find it easier to use the Ctrl+down arrow key to move the objects straight down.

2. Change the label control text in the Page Header to **Purchase Order**, and then select all three objects (the label control and the two line graphics) in the Page Header. The easiest way to select all three objects is to click and drag in the left ruler space from the top of the Page Header section to its bottom. Press Ctrl+X to cut these objects. If any objects remain visible in the Page Header, press Ctrl+Z to undo the cut and try again.

3. Select the PurchaseOrderNumber Header by clicking its Title bar; then press Ctrl+V to paste the objects from the Report Header.

4. Select View, Report Header/Footer from the menu to delete the report's header and footer sections. Select View, Page Header/Footer from the menu to delete the page header and footer. Click the Yes button to confirm that you want to delete the controls in the Page Footer section.

5. Click the Toolbox button on the toolbar, and then select the Label tool. Use it to draw a new label control near the top of the PurchaseOrderNumber Header. Enter Electric Controls Company name and address in that label. Remember to use Ctrl+Enter to insert line breaks when you are typing inside the label control.

6. Select the PurchaseOrderNumber, PurchaseOrderDate, VendorNumber, and PurchaseOrderExpectedShipDate fields; click on the Format tab in the property sheet and change the controls' Border Style to **Transparent**. Select the PurchaseOrderDate and PurchaseOrderExpectedShipDate fields, click the Format tab in the property sheet, and enter a Format property value of **mmmm d ", " yyyy**

7. Change the text of the labels, and arrange these controls as they appear in Figures 7.18 and 7.19. You can use the Toolbox label control to create the label with the text **Please include this number on all invoices and shipping documents.**

8. Select and delete the six vendor name and address fields. Click the Field List toolbar button to open the Field List; then, click and drag VendorNameAndAddress to the PurchaseOrderNumber Header section. Change the label control's text to To: and expand the text box control to accommodate the full vendor name and address. We used a 12-point bold Arial font for this text box in our version of the report.

9. Delete the MaterialsInventoryCategory text box control and its label. Select the MaterialsInventoryDescription text box control in the Detail section, click on the Data tab in the property sheet, and change the Control Source property to **Description**

10. Copy and paste the PurchaseOrder-MaterialsInventoryPrice text box control and label. Change the new text box control's Control Source property to **Extension**, and then change the new label's Caption property to match. Using Figures 7.18 and 7.19 as guides, arrange and set the Text Align properties of the report's text box and label controls.

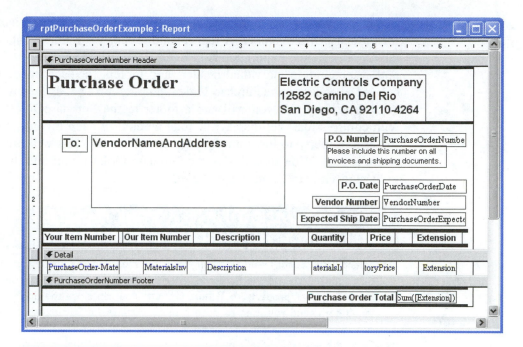

Figure 7.18 The Purchase Order report in Design view.

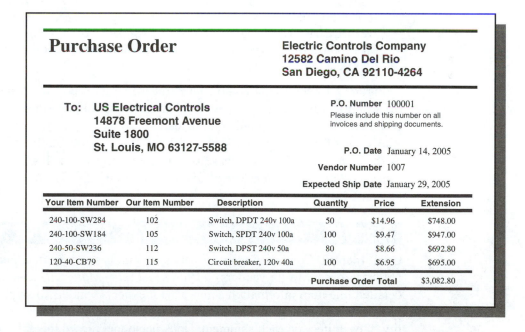

Figure 7.19 The purchase order number 100001 printout generated by *rptPurchaseOrderExample*.

When the Report Wizard created the Purchase Order form, it included a report band for PurchaseOrderNumber. A report band groups the report's data by values in one of the report's fields. Report bands in Access can include a variety of sorting and display options, including individual headers and footers for each band. The Report Wizard created a header for the PurchaseOrderNumber report band, but it did not create a footer.

In Exercise 7.22, you will add a footer to the PurchaseOrderNumber report band with controls that will display the total amount of each invoice. You will also set the footer's property to force a new page after it prints. This will print each invoice on a separate page. You should have the Purchase Order report and its property sheet open in Design view to begin this exercise.

EXERCISE 7.22: ADDING A PURCHASEORDERNUMBER FOOTER TO THE PURCHASE ORDER REPORT

1. Select View, Sorting And Grouping from the menu. In the Sorting and Grouping dialog box that appears, change the PurchaseOrderNumber's Group Footer property to **Yes** and its Keep Together property to **Whole Group**. You can close the dialog box by repeating the menu command you used to open it or by clicking the Sorting And Grouping toolbar button.
2. Click the new PurchaseOrderNumber Footer bar, and then click the Format tab in the property sheet. Set the Force New Page property to **After Section**
3. You can copy the line objects from the PurchaseOrderNumber Header section, or create your own footer design. The Footer needs only two controls, a text box control to total the Extension field and an accompanying label control. Copy the Extension text box to this section using the Ctrl+C and Ctrl+V cut-and-paste procedure. Click the Data tab in the property sheet, and change the Control Source property to **=Sum([Extension])**. Add a label control with the text **Purchase Order Total** to the Footer section.
4. Close the form, and save your changes.

Figure 7.18 shows the completed Purchase Order report in Design view. We turned off the grid (by selecting View, Grid from the menu) for this screen picture so you could see the report's details more clearly.

A copy of purchase order number 100001 for Electric Controls Company, generated as the first page of our Purchase Order report, appears in Figure 7.19. This purchase order, *rptPurchaseOrderExample*, is included in the *Ch07.mdb* database on your Companion CD.

RECORDING MATERIALS INVENTORY RECEIPTS

Once Electric Controls Company enters its purchase order data and mails the printed purchase orders to its vendors, *tblPurchaseOrder-MaterialsInventory* will contain the detailed line item information about what it expects vendors to ship. When materials arrive on the receiving dock, Electric Controls will want to record the quantity and identity of each item on each shipment. Dock personnel record this information on receiving reports. In the past, the receiving report was a paper form on which the dock worker wrote the information about items received. Today, dock workers can enter the receiving information directly into the firm's accounting database using a database form. This electronic receiving report enters data directly into the Inventory Receipt table.

One advantage of direct data entry into the Inventory Receipt table is that we can assign each item a unique receipt number. Many firms use bar code scanners that read inventory identification codes on inventory packages. These scanners also can date- and time-stamp the inventory receipt record. The accounts payable department collects other information about inventory received, including vendor invoice number and each item's price, from vendor invoices and can enter that information directly into the Inventory Receipt table.

The Inventory Receipt Table

An inventory receipt table for Electric Controls Company will require seven fields. They store the following information attributes: a primary key for each receipt, the date of the receipt, Electric Control's materials inventory stock number, Electric Control's purchase order number, the vendor's invoice number, the quantity of the item received, and the price billed on the vendor's invoice for the item. In Exercise 7.23, you will create *tblInventoryReceipt*, an inventory receipt table for the Electric Controls Company that meets these data storage requirements.

EXERCISE 7.23: BUILDING AN INVENTORY RECEIPT TABLE

1. In the Database window, click the Tables object, click the New button, and then double-click Design View in the New Table dialog box that appears.
2. Enter the first Field Name, **InventoryReceiptNumber**, and leave its Data Type set to Text. Click on the Primary Key toolbar button to make this field the table's primary key. Set its Field Size property to **6**, its Input Mask property to **######;;_** and its Caption property to **Inventory Receipt Number**
3. In the next row, enter a Field Name of **InventoryReceiptDate**, set its Data Type to **Date/Time**, its Format property to **Short Date**, its Input Mask property to **99/99/0000;;_**, and its Caption property to **Date Received**
4. To create the table's first foreign key field, enter a Field Name of **PurchaseOrderNumber**, and leave its Data Type set to Text. Set its Field Size to **6**, its Input Mask property to **000000;;_**, and its Caption property to **Purchase Order Number**
5. To create the table's second foreign key field, enter a Field Name of **MaterialsInventoryStockNumber**, and leave its Data Type set to Text. Set its Field Size to **3**, its Input Mask property to **000;;_**, and its Caption property to **Stock Number**
6. In the next row, enter a Field Name of **InventoryReceiptVendorInvoiceNumber**, and leave its Data Type set to Text. Set its Field Size to **20** and its Caption property to **Vendor Invoice Number**. Since Electric Controls Company cannot control the nature or length of the invoice numbers that their vendors might choose, you must provide sufficient space to hold the longest number a vendor might use.
7. In the next row, enter a Field Name of **InventoryReceiptQuantity** for the next field. Set its Data Type to **Number**, its Field Size property to **Long Integer**, its Decimal Places property to **0**, and its Caption property to **Quantity**

8. In the next row, enter a Field Name of **InventoryReceiptPrice** for the last field. Set its Data Type to **Currency**, its Decimal Places property to **2**, and its Caption property to **Price**

9. Click File, Save As to save your work and close the table. Enter **tblInventoryReceipt** as the Table Name in the Save As dialog box. Click OK, and then close the Table window.

In the next exercise, you integrate the Inventory Receipt table with the other purchase cycle tables. You can do this by creating links to the new table and setting referential integrity constraints on those links. Enforcing referential integrity on the links from *tblInventoryReceipt* to the primary keys of *tblPurchaseOrder* and *tblMaterialsInventory* improves internal control in Electric Controls Company's purchasing system. The link to *tblPurchaseOrder* will prevent dock workers from erroneously entering nonexistent purchase order numbers. The link to *tblMaterialsInventory* will prevent entry of nonexistent MaterialsInventoryStockNumbers. To begin the exercise, be sure that all tables, forms, and reports are closed and that the Database window is open on the Access desktop.

EXERCISE 7.24: LINKING THE INVENTORY RECEIPT TABLE TO EXISTING TABLES

1. Select Tools, Relationships from the menu. The relationships window will appear with a display of the relationships you created earlier in this chapter.
2. Click the Show Table toolbar button.
3. Double-click *tblInventoryReceipt*, and then click the Show Table dialog box Close button. You may want to resize and rearrange the tables in the Relationships window using Figure 7.20 as a guide.
4. Click and drag the PurchaseOrderNumber field from *tblPurchaseOrder* to the corresponding field in *tblInventoryReceipt*. Click the Enforce Referential Integrity check box, and then click the Create button.
5. Click and drag the MaterialsInventoryStockNumber field from *tblMaterialsInventory* to the corresponding field in *tblInventoryReceipt*. Click the Enforce Referential Integrity check box, and then click the Create button. The completed set of relationships appears in Figure 7.20.
6. Close the Relationships window, and save your changes.

Figure 7.20 shows the updated relationships among the purchase cycle tables. A copy of the *tblInventoryReceipt* table is included in the *Ch07.mdb* database on your Companion CD. Now that you have a table in which to store information about inventory receipts, your next task is to build a form that will make entering data into the table easy and effective.

An Inventory Receipt Form

The inventory receipt form is simple and straightforward. Since you can rely on the referential integrity links to existing values in *tblPurchaseOrder* and *tblMaterials-Inventory* for the foreign key fields, PurchaseOrderNumber and MaterialsInventoryStockNumber, you can build the form based on *tblInventoryReceipt* alone. You do not need a complex form design, nor do you need an underlying query. Exercise 7.25 shows you how to create an inventory receipt data entry form for Electric Controls Company.

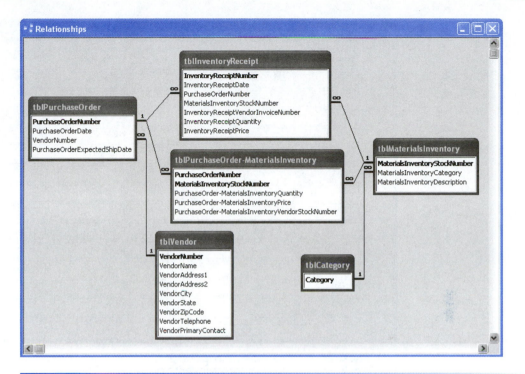

Figure 7.20 Connecting *tblInventoryReceipt* with existing purchase cycle tables.

EXERCISE 7.25: BUILDING AN INVENTORY RECEIPT FORM

1. In the Database window, click the Forms object, and then click the New button.
2. Type **tblInventoryReceipt** in the table box or select it from the drop-down list in the New Form dialog box.
3. Double-click AutoForm: Tabular in the New Form dialog box. This AutoForm tool generates a simple tabular form. With a few minor changes, this form will work quite well as Electric Controls Company's Inventory Receipt form.
4. Select View, Design View from the menu; then, click the Properties toolbar button to open the property sheet.
5. Select Edit, Select Form from the menu; then, click the Format tab in the form's property sheet and enter a Caption property of **Inventory Receipts Data Entry Form**
6. Select all of the label controls in the Form Header. Then, click the Bold button on the Formatting toolbar.
7. Select the label controls in the Form Header. Then, press the Shift+down arrow repeatedly to increase the height of the controls enough that two lines of text appear in the controls.
8. Using Figure 7.21 as a guide, adjust the arrangement, size, and alignment of the controls on the form. Remember, you can force a line break in a label control by pressing Ctrl+Enter.
9. Close the Inventory Receipt form, and save your changes.

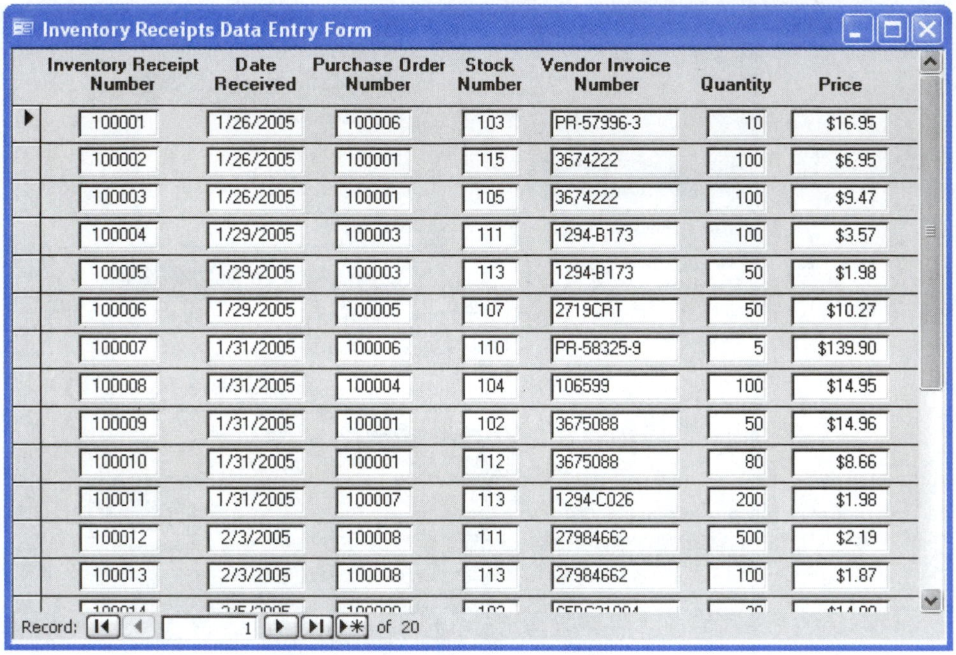

Inventory Receipts Data Entry Form

Inventory Receipt Number	Date Received	Purchase Order Number	Stock Number	Vendor Invoice Number	Quantity	Price
100001	1/26/2005	100006	103	PR-57996-3	10	$16.95
100002	1/26/2005	100001	115	3674222	100	$6.95
100003	1/26/2005	100001	105	3674222	100	$9.47
100004	1/29/2005	100003	111	1294-B173	100	$3.57
100005	1/29/2005	100003	113	1294-B173	50	$1.98
100006	1/29/2005	100005	107	2719CRT	50	$10.27
100007	1/31/2005	100006	110	PR-58325-9	5	$139.90
100008	1/31/2005	100004	104	106599	100	$14.95
100009	1/31/2005	100001	102	3675088	50	$14.96
100010	1/31/2005	100001	112	3675088	80	$8.66
100011	1/31/2005	100007	113	1294-C026	200	$1.98
100012	2/3/2005	100008	111	27984662	500	$2.19
100013	2/3/2005	100008	113	27984662	100	$1.87

Record: 1 of 20

Figure 7.21 The completed Inventory Receipt form.

The completed form appears in Figure 7.21 in Form view displaying Electric Controls Company's sample data. This Inventory Receipt data entry form is included in the *Ch07.mdb* database on your Companion CD as *frmInventoryReceiptExample*.

If you test the form, you will find that the foreign key links to *tblPurchaseOrder* and *tblMaterialsInventory* prevent you from entering a value for a purchase order number or stock number that does not already exist in the underlying entity table. Note that Electric Controls Company assigns a unique inventory receipt number to each individual stock number received on a purchase order. Many firms still use a receiving report format in which they assign one receiving report number to an entire shipment—a practice that is a holdover from manual record-keeping systems. As computer facilities become increasingly available, even on receiving docks, workers gain the ability to enter atomic-level data directly into the system. In the next section, you will learn how to present some of these inventory receipts data.

Inventory Receipt Reports

Businesses do not use standard reporting forms for inventory receipts; so, you may create your own report designs to meet your needs or those of your clients. In this section you will learn how to build an inventory receipt report that calculates the price × quantity extensions for inventory received by the Electric Controls Company.

The report groups inventory receipts by vendor to show what Electric Controls owes its vendors for materials it has received. To be even more useful, the report groups receipts by purchase order number within vendor. Exercise 7.26 shows you how to use the Report Wizard to select fields from Electric Control's Inventory Receipt, Purchase Order, and Vendor tables. You will also learn how to modify the Report Wizard-generated report to calculate price × quantity extensions for each materials inventory receipt.

EXERCISE 7.26: BUILDING AN INVENTORY RECEIPT REPORT

1. Click the Reports tab in the Database window, and then click the New button to open the New Report dialog box. Enter **tblInventoryReceipt** in the source table combo box; then, double-click Report Wizard in the list box. The first Report Wizard dialog box should display Table: tblInventoryReceipt in its Tables/Queries combo box. Click the > button to move all of the fields from the Available Fields list box to the Selected Fields list box.
2. Select Table: tblPurchaseOrder in the Tables/Queries combo box. Using the > button, move the VendorNumber field to the Selected Fields list box.
3. Enter Table: tblVendor in the Tables/Queries combo box. Using the > button, move the VendorName field to the Selected Fields list box. Click the Next button to continue.
4. Since you are going to create your own grouping design for this report, you do not need to give the Report Wizard any instructions about how to view the data. To accept the default design, data organized by *tblInventoryReceipt*, click the Next button.
5. We want the report to group the inventory receipts data by vendor and, within each vendor, by purchase order number. Select VendorName in the grouping levels list box; then, click the > button to modify the Report Wizard's template. Next, select PurchaseOrderNumber, and click the > button. The Wizard will make the changes to the report design template shown in Figure 7.22.
6. To accept the modified design, click the Next button.
7. Select InventoryReceiptNumber in the first sort order combo box.

TRY IT

At this point, you are going to play a little trick on the Report Wizard. You want to multiply the price by the quantity to obtain an extension value to include in this report. Because the Report Wizard does not offer this option, you will need to add the extension field after the Report Wizard has created the report. You also will want footers in the report that include text box controls with Sum() functions that subtotal the extension amounts for each purchase order and each vendor. To trick the Wizard into generating the footers and text box controls with Sum() functions, you can instruct it to sum the Inventory ReceiptPrice fields. You will still need to edit the controls to change InventoryReceiptPrice to Extension, but the Report Wizard will do most of the work for you.

8. Click on the Summary Options button. In the next dialog box, click the Sum check box for InventoryReceiptPrice. Be sure that the Show Detail and Summary option button has been selected. Click the OK button to return to the previous dialog box; then click the Next button to proceed.

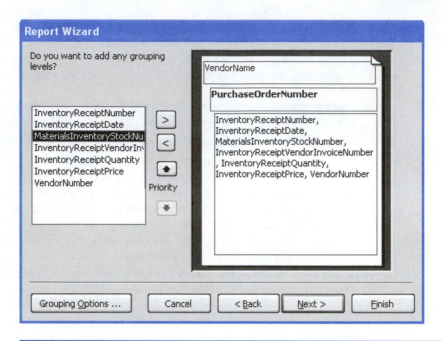

Figure 7.22   The Report Wizard's modified template for *rptInventoryReceipt*.

9. Select the Outline 1 Layout and the Corporate style in the next two dialog boxes, respectively; then, enter a report title of **rptInventoryReceipt**. Click the Finish button to generate the report.

10. Open your new form in Design view. Click the Properties toolbar button to open the property sheet.

11. Click the property sheet Data tab, select the Record Source property, and click on its Build button to open the query behind the report.

12. Select the first open Field cell in the QBE grid, and press Shift+F2 to open the Zoom box. Enter **Extension: [InventoryReceiptQuantity] * [InventoryReceiptPrice]**, and click the OK button. This expression calculates the quantity × price extension for each item received. Close the Query Builder window, and save your changes.

13. Make a copy of the InventoryReceiptPrice text box control in the Detail section and its accompanying label control in the PurchaseOrderNumber Header section. Place these new controls, which will contain the Extension field, to the right of the original controls (see Figure 7.23). Change the text box control's Control Source property to Extension. Select the text in the label control, press Ctrl+Enter, and then type **Extension**

14. Enter **=Sum(Extension)** in the Control Source property of the controls in the PurchaseOrderNumber Footer, the VendorNumber Footer, and the Report Footer, and then change the labels for those controls to match those shown in Figure 7.23.

15. Using Figure 7.23 as a guide, adjust the placement and appearance of the report's controls. Save your new report, and close the Report window.

An Inventory Receipt report, *rptInventoryReceiptExample*, is included in the *Ch07.mdb* database on your Companion CD. We encourage you to use Figure 7.23 and the example report on the CD as springboards for experimenting with your own report design ideas.

Inventory Receipts
By Vendor and by Purchase Order   *Electric Controls Company*

for internal use only

VendorNumber 1001   Square P Corporation

Purchase Order Number 100008

Inventory Receipt Number	Date Received	Stock Number	Vendor Invoice Number	Quantity	Price	Extension
100012	2/3/2005	111	27984662	500	$2.19	$1,095.00
100013	2/3/2005	113	27984662	100	$1.87	$187.00

Total for this Purchase Order $1,282.00
Total for this Vendor $1,282.00

VendorNumber 1002   Bolden Wire and Cable Co.

Purchase Order Number 100006

Inventory Receipt Number	Date Received	Stock Number	Vendor Invoice Number	Quantity	Price	Extension
100001	1/26/2005	103	PR-57996-3	10	$16.95	$169.50
100007	1/31/2005	110	PR-58325-9	5	$139.90	$699.50

Total for this Purchase Order $869.00
Total for this Vendor $869.00

VendorNumber 1003   Witchita Relays, Inc.

Purchase Order Number 100002

Inventory Receipt Number	Date Received	Stock Number	Vendor Invoice Number	Quantity	Price	Extension
100016	2/10/2005	106	779462887	30	$34.75	$1,042.50

Total for this Purchase Order $1,042.50
Total for this Vendor $1,042.50

VendorNumber 1005   Bomac Sheet Metal Co.

Purchase Order Number 100004

Inventory Receipt Number	Date Received	Stock Number	Vendor Invoice Number	Quantity	Price	Extension
100008	1/31/2005	104	106599	100	$14.95	$1,495.00

Total for this Purchase Order $1,495.00
Total for this Vendor $1,495.00

Page 1 of 3

Figure 7.23 The completed Inventory Receipt report, *rptInventoryReceipt*.

CASH DISBURSEMENTS

Thus far in this chapter, you have learned how Electric Controls Company can maintain vendor records, maintain materials inventory records, prepare purchase orders, and record receipts of ordered inventory items. Once the company receives materials inventory items, its vendors would like it to pay for those items. This section describes one way to use the information you have gathered in your purchase cycle tables to write checks. The approach is just one of many possible ways to do this. Since you have a record of materials received in the Inventory Receipts table, you can use that table as a basis for payments.

More elaborate systems might compare purchase order terms to vendor invoice terms before payment. One way to do this is with a voucher system, in which accounting personnel compare purchase orders with vendor invoices, shipping documents, and receiving reports before authorizing payment. You can build on the tables and forms described in this section to create such a system; however, the details of a full voucher system are beyond the scope of this book.

The Cash Disbursements Table

The cash disbursements table must include fields that store the check number and date of each check. In Exercise 7.27, you will create a cash disbursements table with these fields.

EXERCISE 7.27: BUILDING A CASH DISBURSEMENTS TABLE

1. Open a new table in Design view.
2. Enter **CheckNumber** as the first Field Name, and click the Primary Key toolbar button. Leave its Data Type set to Text and set its Field Size property to **5**, its Input Mask property to **#####;;_**, and its Caption property to **Check Number**
3. Next, enter a Field Name of **CashDisbursementDate**, set its Data Type to **Date/Time**, its Format property to **Short Date**, its Input Mask property to **99/99/0000;;_**, and its Caption property to **Date**
4. Save the table as **tblCashDisbursement**, and then close the table.
5. Since *tblCashDisbursement* needs a foreign key link to *tblVendor*, you must establish that link in the Relationships window. You should also enforce referential integrity on the link to ensure that Electric Controls does not erroneously write a check to a supplier that is not in its Vendor table. Select Tools, Relationships from the menu.
6. The Relationships window will appear with a display of the relationships we have already created for the purchase cycle tables. Click the Show Table toolbar button.
7. Double-click *tblCashDisbursement*, and then click the Close button.
8. Close the Relationships window, and save your changes.

Your Companion CD includes, in its *Ch07.mdb* database, a table object, *tblCashDisbursement*, that we constructed using the steps listed in Exercise 7.27. The last table you need to complete the purchase cycle for the Electric Controls Company is a relationship table that will connect the inventory receipts with the checks written to pay for those inventory receipts, the Cash Disbursements-Inventory Receipts table.

The Cash Disbursements-Inventory Receipts Table

Since Electric Controls Company often pays for more than one materials inventory receipt with each check and sometimes pays for one materials receipt with two or more checks, you need a relationship table to model the many-to-many link between the Cash Disbursements table and the Inventory Receipts table. Exercise 7.28 shows you how to build this Cash Disbursements-Inventory Receipts table. This table contains only two fields, the primary keys of *tblCashDisbursement* and *tblInventoryReceipt*, which combine to form this table's composite primary key.

EXERCISE 7.28: BUILDING A CASH DISBURSEMENTS-INVENTORY RECEIPTS TABLE

1. Open a new table in Design view.
2. Enter a Field Name of **CheckNumber**, and leave its Data Type set to Text. Set its Field Size property to **5**, its Input Mask property to **#####;;_**, its Caption property to **Check Number**, and its Indexed property to **Yes (Duplicates OK)**
3. Enter a second Field Name of **InventoryReceiptNumber**, and leave its Data Type set to Text. Set its Field Size property to **6**, its Caption property to **Inventory Receipt Number**, and its Indexed property to **Yes (Duplicates OK)**
4. While pressing the Ctrl key, click the row selectors for each of the two fields. While the two rows are selected, click the Primary Key toolbar button. The primary key symbol should appear in both row selectors.
5. Close and save the table, entering **tblCashDisbursement-InventoryReceipt** as the table name in the Save As dialog box. Click OK to complete the table-save operation.

The *Ch07.mdb* database on your Companion CD includes a table named *tblCashDisbursementInventoryReceipt* table. This table contains Electric Controls Company's cash disbursements-inventory receipts information. In the next exercise you will create links back to the entity tables joined by *tblCashDisbursement-InventoryReceipt* and enforce referential integrity on those links. Be sure that all tables, forms, and reports are closed and that the Database window is open on the Access desktop before you begin Exercise 7.29.

EXERCISE 7.29: LINKING THE CASH DISBURSEMENTS-INVENTORY RECEIPTS TABLE

1. Select Tools, Relationships from the menu.
2. Click the Show Table toolbar button. Double-click *tblCashDisbursement-InventoryReceipt*, and then click the Close button. You may want to resize and rearrange the tables in the Relationships window using Figure 7.24 as a guide.
3. Click and drag the CheckNumber field from *tblCashDisbursement* to the corresponding field in *tblCashDisbursement-InventoryReceipt*. Click the Enforce Referential Integrity check box, and then click the Create button.
4. Click and drag the InventoryReceiptNumber from *tblInventoryReceipt* to the corresponding field in *tblCashDisbursement-InventoryReceipt*. Click the Enforce Referential Integrity check

box, and then click the Create button. The completed set of relationships appears in Figure 7.24.

5. Close the Relationships window, and save your changes.

Figure 7.24 shows all of the tables for Electric Controls Company's purchase cycle. Compare this figure to the data model for this cycle that appears in Figure 7.1. You can see how the model provides the basis for the relational tables you created. The five entities and their many-to-many relationships each have a table in the Access implementation. The need for the Category table, which does not appear in the data model, became apparent as you constructed the tables.

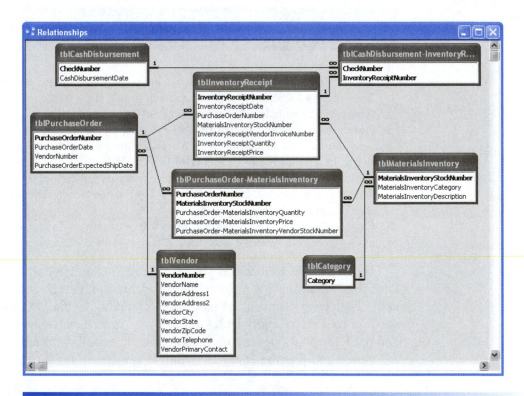

Figure 7.24   The complete purchase cycle Relationships window.

Printing Checks

You can use the cash disbursement information that you have stored to build a report that can print checks. Of course, the report formatting details will vary with the type of check used. Rather than focus your efforts on these formatting details, you will learn how to extract the essential information from the purchase cycle tables that a firm would need no matter what its check format was. In the next exercise, you will learn how to get the data out of the tables and onto paper instead of trying to match a specific check format.

EXERCISE 7.30: EXTRACTING THE INFORMATION NEEDED TO PRINT A CHECK

1. In the Database window, click the Reports object, and then click the New button. In the New Report dialog box, select Report Wizard, and choose *tblCashDisbursement* in the combo box. Click the OK button to proceed.

2. The Tables/Queries combo box should be displaying Table: tblCashDisbursement. Click the > button to move both of the table's fields from the Available Fields box to the Selected Fields box.

3. Select Table: tblCashDisbursement-InventoryReceipt in the Tables/Queries combo box. Select InventoryReceiptNumber in the Available Fields list box; then, click the > button to move that field to the Selected Fields list box.

4. Select Table: tblInventoryReceipt in the Tables/Queries combo box. Select and use the > button to move the following fields to the Selected Fields list box: PurchaseOrderNumber, MaterialsInventoryStockNumber, InventoryReceiptVendorInvoiceNumber, InventoryReceiptQuantity, and InventoryReceiptPrice.

5. Select Table: tblVendor in the Tables/Queries combo box. Using the > button, move the following fields to the Selected Fields list box: VendorName, VendorAddress1, VendorAddress2, VendorCity, VendorState, and VendorZipCode. Click the Next button to continue.

6. The Report Wizard design template for the report appears in the next dialog box. It bases this template on the fields selected and the existing relationships among the tables included in earlier Wizard steps. The Wizard placed the PurchaseOrderNumber field in the detail section because Electric Controls Company may write one check for items from several different purchase orders. Click the Next button to continue. Click Next again to accept the grouping levels.

7. Enter or select InventoryReceiptNumber in the first sort order combo box; then, click the Next button to continue.

8. Select the Outline 1 Layout and the Corporate style in the next two dialog boxes, respectively. Enter a title of **rptCheck** in the last dialog box, and then click the Finish button.

The Report Wizard creates a report that contains most information items that would appear on a check. In the next exercise, you will learn about some modifications that you can make to the form. Remember, each firm will have specific formatting requirements so that the information will appear correctly on its printed checks.

Our main goal here is to show you how to extract the information attributes from the four tables. Other than the information that appears on the Wizard-generated report, Electric Controls Company will need a total dollar amount to print on the check. This amount does not exist in any of our tables because it is a calculation result. Recall that a good database design avoids storing calculation results in relational tables.

In the next exercise you will modify the query behind the report to calculate the check amount and add it to the report. You will also create a single vendor name and address field for use on the printed check. To begin Exercise 7.31, have *rptCheck* open in Design view.

EXERCISE 7.31: CALCULATING THE CHECK AMOUNT

1. Open the property sheet if necessary by clicking the Properties toolbar button.
2. Click the property sheet Data tab, select the Record Source property, and click on its Build button to open the query behind the report.
3. Select the next open Field cell in the QBE grid, and press Shift+F2 to open the Zoom box. You will need to scroll right in the QBE grid to find the next open column.
4. Enter **Extension: [InventoryReceiptQuantity] * [InventoryReceiptPrice]**, and click the OK button. This expression calculates the quantity × price extension for each inventory receipt.
5. Insert an additional column in the QBE grid, select the new column's Field cell, and press Shift+F2 to open the Zoom box. Enter **VendorNameAndAddress: [VendorName] & Chr(13) & Chr(10) & [VendorAddress1] & Chr(13) & Chr(10) & IIf(IsNull([VendorAddress2]),"",([VendorAddress2] & Chr(13) & Chr(10))) & [VendorCity] & ", " & [VendorState] & " " & [VendorZipCode]** in the Zoom box; then, click the OK button. Close the Query Builder window, and save your changes.

This expression combines the separately stored elements of the vendor address into one field that you can print on the check. This expression is identical to the one you created for the Purchase Order report earlier in this chapter; thus, you could open that report's query and copy the text of the expression instead of typing it again.

TRY IT

As you work with Access, you will develop a number of expressions that you use frequently. Since these expressions are all just plain text, you can store them in a word processor file or a text file. Whenever you need one of these expressions, you can simply open your word processor or text editor, make any changes to the expression, and then copy and paste the expression into an Access control or property.

The next exercise gives you some general formatting guidelines for improving the check report. You can use the printed check report that appears in Figure 7.25 as you work through Exercise 7.32. You should have *rptCheck* open in Design view as you begin.

EXERCISE 7.32: IMPROVING THE CHECK REPORT

1. Click and drag the top of the Detail section bar down to make room in the CheckNumber Header for the title and Electric Controls Company's name and address. Click and drag a marquee around all of the objects in the CheckNumber Header; then, drag the selected objects down.
2. Change the label control text in the Report Header to **Check Report**. Select that label control and the two graphic line objects in the Report Header; then, press Ctrl+X to cut these objects. Select the CheckNumber Header by clicking on its Title bar, and then press Ctrl+V to paste the three objects you cut from the Report Header.

Check Report

Electric Controls Company
12582 Camino Del Rio
San Diego, CA 92110-4264

Check Number 10001

Date January 31, 2005

Pay to the Order of Bolden Wire and Cable Co.

In the Amount of $869.00

Mail Check to:
Bolden Wire and Cable Co.
2798 Larsen Road
Suite 400
Flint, MI 48502-2966

Inventory Receipt Number	Purchase Order Number	Stock Number	Vendor Invoice Number	Quantity	Price	Extension
100001	100006	103	PR-57996-3	10	$16.95	$169.50
100007	100006	110	PR-58325-9	5	$139.90	$699.50

Figure 7.25 The Check report for check number 10001.

3. Select View, Report Header/Footer from the menu to delete the Report Header and Report Footer sections of the report. Select View, Page Header/Footer from the menu to delete the page header and footer. Click the Yes button to confirm that you want to delete the controls in the Page Footer section.
4. Click the Toolbox button on the toolbar, and then select the Label tool. Use it to draw a new label control for the Electric Controls Company name and address. Enter the name and address in the new label control.
5. Select the CashDisbursementDate text box control, click the Format tab in its property sheet, and enter a Format property value of **mmmm d ", " yyyy**
6. While holding down the Shift key, select the five vendor address text box controls in the Detail section and the five related label controls in the CheckNumber Header; then, press Del.
7. Click the Field List toolbar button to open the Field List. Then, click and drag VendorNameAndAddress to the PurchaseOrderNumber Header section. Change the label control's text to **Mail Check to:**, and expand the text box control to accommodate the full vendor name and address. Click the Field List toolbar button to close the Field List.
8. Move the VendorName text box control to the CheckNumber Header, and change the VendorName label control text to **Pay to the Order of**
9. Select the InventoryReceiptPrice text box control in the Detail section, and press Ctrl+C to copy the control. We chose to copy this control because it has the currency format settings that we would like to use for our Extension fields.
10. Press Ctrl+V to make a copy of the control in the Detail section. Align the new control as shown in Figure 7.25. Click the Data tab in the property sheet for the control, and change its Control Source property to **Extension**. Use the same procedure to make a copy of the label control in the CheckNumber Header section.
11. Create a second copy of the new Extension control using the same procedure; however, this time paste the control into the CheckNumber Header.

12. With the new Extension control selected, click the Data tab in its property sheet and change the Control Source property to =Sum([Extension]). This control will calculate and display the total amount of the check. Add a label control with the text **In the Amount of** to the CheckNumber Header section.

13. Click the CheckNumber Header bar and then click the Format tab in its property sheet. Set the Force New Page property to **Before Section**. This will put each check on a new page.

14. Arrange the report's controls as shown in Figure 7.25 or create your own design. Close the report and save your changes.

A printout generated by the Check report providing sufficient information to permit Electric Controls Company to write check number 10001 appears in Figure 7.25. This report is provided on your Companion CD in the *Ch07.mdb* database as *rptCheckExample*.

PURCHASE CYCLE INFORMATION ON THE FINANCIAL STATEMENTS

In this chapter, you have learned how to use purchase cycle data to create purchase orders, checks, and other useful reports. This section discusses how accountants can extract the purchase cycle information for presentation on financial statements. The two main financial statement items that use purchase cycle information are the purchases account on the income statement and the accounts payable account on the balance sheet.

Purchases and Accounts Payable on the Financial Statements

The traditional function of an accounting system was to capture and store the information needed to prepare financial statements and tax returns. The database approach to developing the purchase cycle accounting system that we presented in this chapter provides much more than that minimal level of information. However, the database approach does include the basic debit and credit accounting information that we need to prepare financial statements.

You can calculate the amount of the general ledger debit to Purchases, which is also the amount of the credit to Accounts Payable, by adding one text box control to the Report Footer section of *rptPurchaseOrder*. Set the control's Control Source property to the expression **Sum([Extension])**. A Sum() function in a report footer will provide a grand total for the entire report. To obtain the amount for a particular period, you need to limit the purchase orders included to those that occurred in that period. You can do this in the query behind *rptPurchaseOrder* by setting the Criteria cell value in the QBE grid for the PurchaseOrderDate to a limited set of dates. To obtain the purchases general ledger debit for the year 2005, you would enter an expression of **>=#1/1/05** And **<=12/31/05** in the Criteria cell.

You can also generate the amounts to debit the individual vendor accounts in the subsidiary accounts payable ledger. Simply add another grouping level, on VendorNumber to *rptPurchaseOrder*, and copy the **Sum([Extension])** control we described in the preceding paragraph to the new VendorNumber Footer. The value in that control will be the debit to the subsidiary account for each vendor. Of course, you would not really need to maintain a subsidiary accounts payable ledger if you had a relational database purchase cycle system such as the one we described in this chapter, but we have seen old accounting habits linger before!

The general ledger and accounts payable subsidiary ledger account credits to Cash and debits to Accounts Payable are just as easy to extract from our purchase cycle relational database tables. Simply add a report footer to *rptCheck*, and include a **Sum ([Extension])** control in it to calculate the general ledger amounts. To obtain the subsidiary account entry amounts, add a new grouping level on VendorNumber to *rptCheck* and copy the **Sum([Extension])** control to the new VendorNumber Footer.

Go to http://perry.swlearning.com for an in-depth tutorial.

SUMMARY

In this chapter, you learned how to construct tables, forms, queries, and reports to use in the purchase cycle of an accounting information system. Tables are the basic building blocks of the purchase cycle and store information about vendors, materials inventories, and purchase cycle transactions. Forms make entering, editing, and deleting transaction information easier. Queries can simultaneously extract data from multiple tables to help answer complex questions about materials inventory, vendors, payments to vendors, and receipts of inventory. Queries also provide a basic building block on which you can construct purchase cycle reports. You learned how to create typical purchase cycle printed outputs such as purchase orders and checks.

The purchase cycle begins with vendor records and materials inventory records. Production departments send materials requisitions to the purchasing department. Using these requisitions, purchasing agents negotiate price and delivery terms, and then issue purchase orders to vendors. When materials inventory arrives at the receiving dock, dock workers enter inventory receipts information. Based on this receipts information and its agreement with purchase orders issued and invoices received from vendors, the accounting department prints checks that the treasurer will sign and mail to vendors. Finally, you can summarize all of this activity and create reports and journal entries that facilitate financial statement preparation.

QUESTIONS AND PROBLEMS FOR REVIEW

Multiple-Choice Questions

1. The Purchase Order table is
   a. a referential integrity table.
   b. a query table.
   c. a relationship table.
   d. an entity table.

2. A good primary key for a Materials Inventory Receipts table would be a
   a. remittance advice number.
   b. receiving report number.
   c. vendor invoice number.
   d. purchase order number.

3. The Vendor table described in this chapter, *tblVendor*, is not in third normal form because
   a. its primary key, VendorNumber, is not unique.
   b. it contains VendorAddress1 and VendorAddress2, which are repeating fields.
   c. the VendorState field is transitively dependent on the VendorZipCode field.
   d. the VendorCity field is functionally dependent on the VendorState field.

4. Purchase cycle activities include all of the following except
   a. keeping vendor information current.
   b. recording the cost of materials purchased.
   c. recording payments received from customers.
   d. printing purchase orders.

5. The Electric Controls Company database described in this chapter uses a Category table to enforce a business rule instead of using
   a. a Validation Rule property in the Materials Inventory table.
   b. an Input Mask property in the Materials Inventory table.
   c. a combo box control on the Purchase Order Data Entry form.
   d. referential integrity on the MaterialsInventoryCategory field.

6. In a MS Access report, the value that results from a function (such as Sum or Count) in a text box control will
   a. return an error if the text box control is attached to a label control.
   b. vary depending on the report section in which the control is placed.
   c. be correct only if the report is set to recalculate automatically.
   d. be incorrect if the control is placed in the report's detail section.

7. In a materials requirements planning system,
   a. the master schedule replaces materials requisitions.
   b. inventory receipts are not recorded.
   c. the computer can generate materials requisitions.
   d. materials requisitions are generated daily.

8. Enforcing referential integrity on VendorNumber from *tblVendor* to *tblPurchaseOrder* is a good way to ensure that
   a. the VendorNumber in *tblVendor* is valid.
   b. the VendorNumber in *tblPurchaseOrder* is valid.
   c. the VendorNumber in both tables contains the right number of characters.
   d. both a and c are correct.

9. The list of materials that production sends to purchasing is called a
   a. request for quote.
   b. purchase order.
   c. bill of materials.
   d. materials requisition.

10. On an Access form or report, a designer can create a concatenated expression using the IIF function and the IsNull function in a text box control to
   a. suppress the display of a blank line when a field contains no value.
   b. display a warning message when a value is incorrect.
   c. display negative and positive calculation results in different font colors.
   d. insert a period after a middle initial if it was omitted when the value was entered.

Discussion Questions

1. In the Materials Inventory table for Electric Controls Company, you used a Validation Rule property to control input to the MaterialsInventoryCategory field. In the Purchase Orders-Materials Inventory relationship table, you used a foreign key link with referential integrity on the MaterialsInventoryStockNumber field to the Materials Inventory table to accomplish a similar objective. Discuss the advantages and disadvantages of each approach.

2. Describe how you would design the Cash Disbursements Entry form mentioned in the chapter.

3. How would you modify the purchase cycle accounting system described in this chapter if you wished to include vouchers in the system?

4. How could you use the tables in this chapter to measure vendor price and delivery performance? What additional information would you like to add to the system design to make these measurements more effectively?

5. How would you add quality measurements to the purchase cycle system described in the chapter?

Practice Exercises

Note: Before doing any of the following practice exercises, first copy *Ch07.mdb* from your Companion CD to the hard drive of the computer on which you are working. Then, clear the copied database's Read-only file attribute (see Chapter 1, Exercise 1.14, Clearing a File's Read-Only Property). Having done that, you can complete each exercise using the copy of the Companion CD database.

1. Using the database file provided for this chapter, create a query that identifies those vendors from whom Electric Controls Company has purchased sheet metal products.

2. Using the database file provided for this chapter, create a Check Register report. Include check number, check date, payee, and check amount in your report.

3. Using the database file provided for this chapter, create a report that lists materials inventory items sorted by category.

4. Modify the purchase cycle system presented in this chapter to include shipping information and freight costs on the Purchase Order form and report.

5. Using the database file provided for this chapter, create a query that will find items on purchase orders that vendors should have shipped seven days before today but that you have not received as of today. Hint: Microsoft Access includes a Date() function that you might find helpful.

Problems

Note: Before doing any of the following problems, first copy *Ch07.mdb* from your Companion CD to the hard drive of the computer on which you are working. Then, clear the copied database's Read-only file attribute (see Chapter 1, Exercise 1.14, Clearing a File's Read-Only Property). Having done that, you can complete each exercise using the copy of the Companion CD database.

1. The Bayside Falafel Hut (BFH) is a restaurant owned by Dima Jhari that specializes in Middle Eastern cuisine. BFH has grown rapidly and has found that managing its purchasing function is essential to controlling costs and operating profitably. BFH has asked you to design a database that will help it control its purchasing operation. BFH buys ingredients and supplies from several different food products wholesalers. Amit Kamir is the restaurant's executive chef and functions as its purchasing agent. All orders with vendors are placed by Amit and are confirmed with a written purchase order. When the shipments arrive, one of three or four kitchen staff members counts the items and fills out a receiving report. These staff members sign each report at the bottom on the "receiving clerk" line. Vendors mail invoices within a few days of shipping the orders to BFH. At the end of each month, Dima matches copies of the purchase orders, receiving reports, the invoices received from the vendors and writes checks for the amounts due. Dima always pays the outstanding balances at the end of each month, even if she has to borrow money to do so. She always pays each vendor with one check, even if that vendor has sent multiple shipments during the month. List the entities that exist in the BFH purchases cycle. State any assumptions you believe are necessary.

2. Refer to the BFH case described in Problem 1 and create a diagram similar to that shown in Figure 7.1 for the restaurant. The diagram should show the entities you identified in Problem 1 along with the relationships between those entities and their cardinalities.

3. Refer to the BFH case described in Problem 1 and the work you did in Problem 2. Use Access to build the tables and create the relationships you have defined. Pop-

ulate the tables with sample data that you create and test the tables to make certain that the relationships operate to enforce referential integrity as appropriate.

4. Refer to the work you have done in the preceding three problems. Create data entry forms for the BFH purchases cycle database that allow you to enter data into every table without opening the table itself. Use the forms in the *Ch07.mdb* database as guides.

5. Refer to the work you have done in the preceding four problems. Create reports for the BFH purchase cycle database as follows:

   a. Create a monthly report that shows purchases by vendor and, within vendor, by product.

   b. Create a monthly report that shows items received organized by receiving clerk (that is, your report will have a Receiving Clerk header section).

   c. Create a monthly Purchases Summary report that lists all items purchased, sorted by total quantity purchased.

   d. Create any additional specific reports that your instructor assigns.

CHAPTER 8
Payroll Cycle

OBJECTIVES

The payroll cycle system calculates employee earnings, records payments to employees, and maintains payroll records. These records must satisfy a complex array of government regulations pertaining to time and pay records. Firms also use payroll cycle information to create management reports and financial statements. This chapter shows you how to use Microsoft Access tables, queries, forms, and reports to:

- Create and maintain employee records.
- Create and maintain records of time worked.
- Calculate gross and net pay.
- Prepare payroll registers.
- Prepare employee earnings reports.
- Print payroll check information.
- Calculate payroll expense and accruals.
- Calculate payroll tax expense and accruals.

The payroll cycle offers more opportunities to include internal control features than either the revenue cycle or the purchase cycle. Therefore, we will use the payroll cycle system components in this chapter to illustrate a number of data input and review procedure internal controls.

INTRODUCTION

In this chapter you will learn how to use Access to create the payroll cycle elements of accounting information systems. Many firms chose the payroll cycle to be the first part of their accounting information systems that they automated. The payroll cycle was an ideal first candidate for computerization because it involves complex, yet repetitive, calculations.

Accountants sometimes consider the payroll cycle to be a part of the purchase cycle. The payroll cycle can also be integrated into the production cycle in manufacturing

369

firms. However, treating the payroll cycle as separate from both purchasing and production cycles helps highlight some of its interesting and unique characteristics. Designing and implementing an integrated human resources management and payroll system is a complex undertaking. You will learn the fundamental payroll cycle system components in this chapter. These fundamental elements form the basis of even the most complex integrated accounting and human resources management systems.

All but the very smallest manufacturing, merchandising, and service firms have payroll cycle activity. In this chapter you will learn about payroll activities that virtually all firms undertake. In service and merchandising firms, payroll cost appears as an expense item on the income statement. In manufacturing firms, the portion of payroll expenditures that is related to manufacturing activities becomes a part of the cost of goods manufactured. This cost appears on the financial statements in the cost of goods sold and in the cost of finished goods and work in progress inventories.

GREENWOOD LUMBER COMPANY PAYROLL CYCLE INFORMATION

In this chapter, you will learn how to build the components of a payroll cycle system for Greenwood Lumber Company. Greenwood is a seller of lumber and related products. It sells primarily to the local construction industry but in recent years has been increasing its retail sales to homeowners and amateur woodworkers. Because its operations have become more complex, Greenwood is increasingly interested in tracking its payroll costs by department.

Greenwood employs 50 people in nine departments, including four sales departments, three operations departments, and two business management departments. The largest departments are inside sales. Persons in these departments—one for commercial sales and another for retail sales—sell to customers who visit Greenwood's lumberyard or call in their orders. The commercial and retail outside sales staff members travel to customer locations. The three lumberyard operations departments are purchasing, materials handling, and maintenance. The two business management departments are accounting and administration. The administration department handles general management and human resources functions. Greenwood employees are permanently assigned to work for one department.

Greenwood calculates employee pay by the hour and pays employees on the last day of each month for all hours worked during that month. No employees are on a fixed salary. The normal work week at Greenwood is 40 hours, and employees earn overtime at 1.5 times their normal pay rate for any hours they work beyond the normal work week. All employees are paid at the end of each month based on time cards that they submit.

The data model for Greenwood Lumber includes only two entities, Employee and Time Worked. A diagram of the data model, showing the two entities and the one-to-many relationship, appears in Figure 8.1.

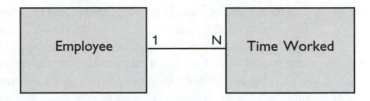

Figure 8.1   Greenwood Lumber Company payroll cycle data model.

EMPLOYEE INFORMATION

The basic building block for any payroll system is employee information. At a minimum, Greenwood will need employee names, social security numbers, and pay rates. To calculate net pay amounts, it will need number of exemptions and marital status information. Greenwood will also need employee addresses for mailing paychecks and employee start dates for determining eligibility for pension and other benefit plans. These are only a few examples of the types of employee information stored in payroll databases. Indeed, some firms track hundreds of individual data items for each employee!

Integrated human resources management systems are the end product of an evolutionary process. Originally, human resources systems and payroll systems were separate in most companies. When firms began adopting database approaches to reduce data redundancy in their information processing activities, these two systems were ideal targets for integration. However, to enhance internal control, even today's integrated human resources management systems limit accounting personnel's access to employee data—additions, deletions, and changes to employee records are typically handled by the human resources department.

The Employee Table

The first payroll cycle table that we will describe is the Employee table. The Employee table provides a central location for storing all information about each employee. This makes the human resources job of adding, deleting, and updating employee information easy and efficient. It also eliminates data redundancy; human resources creates and maintains data in this table, yet the accounting department can use information stored in the table to calculate payroll and print paychecks. The Employee table will include a fairly large number of fields. You will need to identify a good primary key field and then add fields to store employee names, addresses, social security numbers, pay rates, and start dates. You will also need to store other information in the Employee table, such as marital status and number of exemptions, that Greenwood will need to use when it calculates withholding tax amounts.

The first field you will include in the Employee table is its primary key, the employee number. Recall that a table's primary key must be a unique identifier that exists for every record in the table. One tempting primary key candidate for the Employee table is the employee social security number; however, privacy laws discourage firms from using social security numbers to identify employees. Also, large companies have found that the Social Security Administration occasionally assigns the same number to more than one person and sometimes assigns a person more than one number. By creating its own employee numbering scheme, Greenwood can maintain complete control over the integrity of its Employee table's primary key.

Some firms use the employee number to store information implicitly. For example, a firm could make all managers' numbers begin with the digit 4. This approach breaks down, however, if employees can be promoted or demoted from one job to another. Greenwood has decided to use a simple sequential numbering scheme to ensure that each employee number is unique and that the number contains no implicit information about an employee that might change. In a sequential number scheme, you assign each new employee a number that is one greater than the largest employee number already assigned. You do not reuse old employee numbers after employees leave because the employee number provides a permanent access path to past employees' records. Although specific rules and practices vary from state to state, employers often are required to keep data about past employees for many years.

As you design the fields that will store employee names, keep in mind what you have learned in earlier chapters about good database design practices. For example, you will store the employee name data in the most atomic form possible; that is, in the smallest possible logical chunks. Greenwood has decided to break employee names into three logical pieces: first name, middle initial, and last name. Other firms might also include separate fields to store titles, such as Mr. and Ms., or surname suffixes, such as Sr., Jr., and III.

The next set of fields in Greenwood's Employee table are the address and telephone number fields. Designing these fields should be a familiar task for you by now, since you have already created address and telephone number fields for customers and vendors in Chapters 6 and 7, respectively. The address and telephone number fields for the Employee table and their properties are similar to those of the Customer and Vendor tables you have already built.

The final group of fields will store information that Greenwood Lumber needs to calculate employees' gross and net pay. This information includes employees' pay rates, number of exemptions claimed, and marital status. You also will need a field to store employees' start dates. Greenwood Lumber organizes its management and supervision by department, so we will include a department identifier in the Employee table. Note that storing the department number in the Employee table works only because Greenwood permanently assigns employees to departments and employees do not work in more than one department. Other companies that do not have such a policy must store the employee-department link in a relationship table to accommodate the many-to-many relationships that can arise.

In the first exercise, you will create an Employee table for Greenwood Lumber Company. Have the Database window for a new database open on the Access desktop to begin this exercise.

EXERCISE 8.1: BUILDING AN EMPLOYEE TABLE

1. Click the Tables object in the Database window, and then click the New button. Double-click Design View in the New Table dialog box that appears.

2. To create the employee number field, type **EmployeeNumber** in the first row of the Field Name column. Since you will not be using EmployeeNumber in any calculations, we can leave its Data type set to Text. Click the Primary Key toolbar button to make this field the table's primary key. When you use a sequential number coding scheme, the size of the EmployeeNumber field will depend on how many employees we expect the business will have. Set the Field Size property to **3**. This will let Greenwood have up to 899 employees if it starts with an EmployeeNumber value of 101. Set the Input Mask property to **000** to limit EmployeeNumber entries to numbers and require an entry of exactly three digits. Set the Caption property to **Employee #**

3. Enter **EmployeeLastName** in the second row of the Field Name column, and leave its Data Type set to Text. Set its Field Size property to **30** to accommodate the longest employee surname we expect to include in the table, and set its Caption property to **Last Name**

4. Enter **EmployeeFirstName** in the next row of the Field Name column, and leave its Data Type set to Text. Set its Field Size property to **15** to accommodate the longest first name we expect to include in the table, and set its Caption property to **First Name**

5. Enter **EmployeeMiddleInitial** in the next row of the Field Name column, and leave its Data Type set to Text. Set its Field Size property to **1** and its Input Mask property to **>L**. This will permit a one-letter middle initial and force it to be capitalized, even if a user enters it in lower case. Set this field's Caption property to **MI**

6. Enter a Field Name of **EmployeeSSN** for the social security number field, and leave its Data Type set to Text. Set its Field Size property to **11** to store nine digits and two hyphens for each social security number. Set its Input Mask property to **000\ -00\ -0000;0;_** to help users enter the field values in the U.S. Social Security System's format, and set its Caption property to **SSN**

7. Enter **EmployeeAddress** in the next row of the Field Name column, and leave its Data Type set to Text. Set its Field Size property to **40** and set its Caption property to **Address**

8. Enter **EmployeeCity** in the next row of the Field Name column, and leave its Data Type set to Text. Set its Field Size property to **20** and set its Caption property to **City**

9. Enter **EmployeeState** in the next row of the Field Name column, and leave its Data Type set to Text. Set its Field Size property to **2**, its Input Mask property to **>LL**, and its Caption property to **State**

10. Enter **EmployeeZipCode** in the next row of the Field Name column, and leave its Data Type set to Text. Set its Field Size property to **10**, its Input Mask property to **00000\ -9999;0;_**, and its Caption property to **Zip Code**

11. Enter **EmployeeTelephone** in the next row of the Field Name column, and leave its Data Type set to Text. Set its Field Size property to **14**, its Input Mask property to **!\ (999")** **"000\ -0000;0;_**, and its Caption property to **Phone**. This Input Mask property lets the user enter an area code but does not require that an area code be entered. Remember, you can easily create these complex input masks by using the Build button to invoke the Input Mask Wizard.

12. Enter **EmployeeMaritalStatus** as the next Field Name. Leave its Data Type set to Text, set its Field Size property to **1**, its Input Mask property to **>L**, and its Caption property to **Marital Status**. If an employee does not declare a marital status, U.S. law requires employers to withhold at the single person rate. Therefore, we can set the Default Value property to

S. Note that Access automatically encloses the value with quotation marks when you leave the Default Value property.

13. Since an employee must be either single or married, the only permissible values for this field are M and S. You can use the Validation properties to limit data entry to these values. Set the Validation Rule property for the EmployeeMaritalStatus field to **=M Or S**. Once again, quotation marks automatically enclose the stated values when you leave the property box.

14. Set the Validation Text property to **Please enter an M for Married or an S for Single**

15. Another information item that Greenwood needs to calculate its employees' federal income tax withholding amounts is the number of exemptions each employee claims. In the next open row of the Field Name column, type **EmployeeExemptions**

16. Since Greenwood will use the EmployeeExemptions value in calculating net pay, you must store it as a number. The value for this field will always be a whole number (an integer) and will never exceed 255. Set the EmployeeExemptions Data Type to **Number**, its Field Size property to **Byte**, and its Decimal Places property to **0**. Set the field's Input Mask property to **0** and its Caption property to **Exempts**

TRY IT

To save storage space and increase database access speed, you should try to use the smallest storage space on the disk for number fields. In this case, a Byte field size is the most efficient. To learn more about the Field Size property settings that Microsoft Access provides for Number fields, select Help, Microsoft Access Help Topics from the menu, click the Index tab, enter **FieldSize Property**, double-click on the selection, and then double-click on FieldSize Property in the Topics Found dialog box. This Help Topic provides detailed information about the available Field Size property settings including range, decimal precision, and storage requirements.

17. If an employee does not specify a number of exemptions, U.S. tax law requires withholding at the rate for zero exemptions; therefore, set the EmployeeExemptions Default Value property to **0**. Note that Microsoft Access does not automatically enclose the 0 in quotation marks, because it is a Number Data Type, not a Text Data Type. The quotation marks are necessary only for character values, not number values. When you set the Default Value property for a field with a Number Data Type, Microsoft Access knows to store the default value as a number.

18. To calculate employees' gross pay, we must know what their pay rates are. Greenwood Lumber Company pays all of its employees by the hour; so, we can store each employee's pay rate in a field in an EmployeePayRate field. In the next open row of the Field Name column, type **EmployeePayRate**. Set its Data Type to **Currency**, its Decimal Places property to **2**, and its Caption property to **Pay Rate**

19. The U.S. government and many states have established minimum hourly wages. You can use the Validation Rule property to prevent entry of a value in the EmployeePayRate field that is less than the minimum wage. Using the Validation Rule property this way is an example of a limit check, an internal control procedure that limits the range of values that a field will accept. You can also use the Validation Rule property to set a maximum value on the field.

One way that a data entry person can perpetrate payroll fraud is to change an accomplice's pay rate to a large number and issue him or her one paycheck. The accomplice then quits and disappears. A data entry person could also commit an unintentional error that overpays an employee. Although you cannot completely prevent this type of fraud or error, you can reduce the impact by setting a maximum limit on the EmployeePayRate value. If you assume that the legal minimum wage is $6.20 per hour and the highest wage Greenwood expects to pay is $40.00 per hour, you can set minimum and maximum limits on the EmployeePayRate field. Set the EmployeePayRate Validation Rule property to **> 6.19 And < 40.01**, and set its Validation Text property to **The Pay Rate you have entered is not within the allowed range of Pay Rate values**. This Validation Rule property requires that any EmployeePayRate value be within the limit check values. The Validation Text property includes the error message that will appear in a dialog box if a user attempts to enter an out-of-range value.

20. Enter a Field Name of **EmployeeDepartment** and leave its Data Type set to Text. Set its Field Size property to **2**, its Input Mask property to **00**, and its Caption property to **Dept**

21. The last field will store the date each employee began work. Enter a Field Name of **EmployeeStartDate**, set its Data Type to **Date/Time**, its Input Mask property to **99/99/0000;0;_**, and its Caption property to **Start Date**

22. To save the Employee table, select the File, Save As menu command and enter **tblEmployee** as the New Name in the Save As dialog box. Close the table.

The *Ch08.mdb* file on your Companion CD includes an Employee table, *tblEmployee*, that includes sample records for the 50 Greenwood Lumber Company employees. This table appears in Figure 8.2 in Datasheet view in a maximized window. This window displays a partial view of the first few Greenwood employee records.

Employee #	Last Name	First Name	MI	SSN	Address	City	State	Zip Code	Phone	Marital Status
101	Greenwood	Artemis	Q	195-61-5487	5793 Bucolic Drive	San Diego	CA	92177-4264	(619) 195-5487	M
102	Greenwood	Ethel	Z	432-48-8079	5793 Bucolic Drive	San Diego	CA	92177-4264	(619) 432-8079	M
103	Baron	Ethel	P	338-81-6808	115 Park Avenue	San Diego	CA	92123-2269	(858) 338-6808	S
104	Oppenheim	Cecelia	J	596-83-1255	3221 Lila Avenue	Escondido	CA	92647-1073	(760) 596-1255	M
105	Washington	Ronald	D	314-52-5791	7599 Wakeman Street	San Diego	CA	92107-4870	(619) 314-5791	M
106	Wheeler	Henry	X	158-52-8275	2424 Greenleaf Drive	San Diego	CA	92164-1951	(619) 158-8275	M
107	Surkamp	Elizabeth	T	733-27-4571	79844 Waxwing Lane	La Jolla	CA	92019-1866	(858) 733-1463	S
108	Diamond	Timothy	Y	571-26-3070	7176 Sierra Ridge Road	San Diego	CA	92109-1066	(619) 571-3070	M
109	Roche	Max	E	090-41-2930	6768 Vista Circle	San Diego	CA	92135-5243	(619) 823-1195	M
110	Badillo	Lucille	B	693-03-5280	1899 Laurel Drive	San Ysidro	CA	92015-9119	(619) 693-5528	S
111	Ballenger	Judith	F	239-49-9808	19945 Stevens Avenue	Solana Beach	CA	92036-1074	(858) 239-9808	S
112	Dewar	Melanie	C	217-53-8989	4517 Manchester Street	San Diego	CA	92125-6425	(619) 217-8989	M
113	Brown	Alicia	K	383-81-6589	8983 Purchase Street	San Diego	CA	92151-8077	(619) 383-6589	S
114	Klusky	Irene	R	478-45-7684	5125 Redbird Lane	San Diego	CA	92132-6284	(619) 478-7684	M
115	Tufts	Esther	L	284-61-6492	1776 Potomic Boulevard	San Diego	CA	92119-3416	(619) 284-6492	S
116	Thurgood	Margaret	S	377-08-4315	11426 Suffolk Street	Descanso	CA	92265-1006	(619) 377-4315	M
117	Boldway	Michael	B	381-41-3013	9400 Easterly Court	San Diego	CA	92143-0865	(619) 381-3013	S
118	Fenster	Janice	S	758-36-6061	9009 Via Rosa	Escondido	CA	92608-7905	(760) 758-6061	S
119	Sherwood	Natalie	R	339-66-3999	6710 Darbydale Drive	Chula Vista	CA	92017-3342	(619) 339-3999	M
120	Simon	Arlene	P	911-44-5115	4510 Fryman Street	San Diego	CA	92129-2151	(619) 911-5115	S
121	Morris	Anne	F	819-49-5513	97006 Redondo Street	San Diego	CA	92132-6649	(619) 819-5513	S
122	Clark	Carol	C	437-12-8878	579 Wandering Road	San Diego	CA	92163-0875	(619) 437-8878	M
123	Smith	Dierdre	R	417-81-6871	94 Linwood Road	El Cajon	CA	92246-7395	(619) 417-6871	M
124	Young	Louise	K	326-39-2303	844 Via La Jolla	San Diego	CA	92117-3466	(619) 326-2303	M
125	Studd	Chester	V	422-10-6356	490911 Martindale Lane	San Diego	CA	92109-0742	(619) 422-6356	S
126	Ward	Colleen	H	484-26-2878	4002 Vista Way	Oceanside	CA	92346-6871	(760) 484-2878	S
127	Johnson	Travis	D	210-18-5662	3540 Mendicino Way	San Diego	CA	92111-0446	(858) 210-5662	S
128	Gonzales	David	G	173-65-1574	4510 Bridges Road	San Diego	CA	92136-2175	(858) 173-1574	S
129	Quinn	Charles	H	631-43-2925	32 Hope Court	San Diego	CA	92155-8165	(619) 631-2925	M
130	Flores	Hector	L	343-87-4781	89555 Glen Helen Court	San Diego	CA	92122-7194	(619) 343-4781	S

Figure 8.2 Greenwood Lumber Company's *tblEmployee* in Datasheet view.

Although the Employee table you just built includes 15 fields, it is actually less complex than the employee tables you will encounter in practice. In addition to the information included in this example, employee tables often include fields that store title, job skill, education level, insurance and pension plan participation codes, direct-deposit bank account information, and even the name of a person to call in case of an emergency.

Many firms associate particular employees with jobs, projects, or departments. For example, Greenwood Lumber Company assigns employees to departments. In the preceding exercise, you avoided wasting storage space by using a field to store the department number rather than the department name. Using a department number makes data entry easier and less error-prone. The next section describes a department table in which you can store department names.

The Department Table

The Greenwood Lumber Company Department table needs to include two fields. The first field will store a two-digit identifying number for each department. The second field will store the department descriptions. Exercise 8.2 provides step-by-step instructions for building this table.

EXERCISE 8.2: BUILDING A DEPARTMENT TABLE

1. Click the Tables object in the Database window, and then click the New button. Double-click Design View in the New Table dialog box.
2. Enter **DepartmentNumber** as the first Field Name, and leave its Data Type set to Text.
3. Click the Primary Key toolbar button, and then enter the following property values: Field Size, **2**; Input Mask, **00**; and Caption, **Dept #**
4. Enter **DepartmentDescription** as the second Field Name, and leave its Data Type set to Text. Enter a Field Size property of **40** and a Caption property of **Description**
5. Select the File, Save As menu command, and type **tblDepartment** as the Table Name in the Save As dialog box.
6. Select View, Datasheet to open *tblDepartment* in Datasheet view.

The table shown in Datasheet view in Figure 8.3 is included as *tblDepartment* in the *Ch08.mdb* file on your Companion CD. With the table open in Datasheet view, you can enter Greenwood's department numbers and names. After entering the permitted values, you can follow the steps in Exercise 8.3 to create the link between *tblEmployee* and *tblDepartment*.

EXERCISE 8.3: LINKING *TBLEMPLOYEE* AND *TBLDEPARTMENT*

1. Close *tblEmployee* and *tblDepartment* to return to the Database window.
2. Select the Tools, Relationships menu command to open the Relationships window and the Show Table dialog box.
3. Double-click *tblDepartment* and *tblEmployee* to place them in the Relationships window; then click the Close button.

Figure 8.3 The Department table in Datasheet view.

4. Click and drag the DepartmentNumber field in *tblDepartment* to the EmployeeDepartment field in *tblEmployee*.
5. Click the Enforce Referential Integrity check box, and then click the Create button.
6. The Relationships window showing the link appears in Figure 8.4. To return to the Database window, select the File, Close menu command, and then click the Yes button to save the changes you have made to the table relationships.

Now that you have completed the brief detour to build *tblDepartment* and link it to *tblEmployee*, you can turn your attention to designing a data entry form for Greenwood's employee information.

Figure 8.4 Linking the Employee table and the Department table.

The Employee Information Entry Form

The number and size of the fields in the Employee table make the task of entering data directly into the table in Datasheet view cumbersome. In this section, you will learn how to build a form for the Employee table that will make entering, changing, and deleting employee information much easier.

The Employee Information Entry form must include controls for the 15 fields in *tblEmployee*. One way to make data entry easier in a form with so many fields is to reduce visual clutter. You can do that on this form by grouping related fields into separate sections of the form. Greenwood's Employee table includes information that you can sort into four logical groups: employee identification fields, employee name fields, employee address fields, and payroll calculation information fields.

The employee identification fields are EmployeeNumber, EmployeeDepartment, and EmployeeStartDate. The employee name fields are EmployeeLastName, EmployeeFirstName, and EmployeeMiddleInitial. The employee address fields are EmployeeAddress, EmployeeCity, EmployeeState, EmployeeZipCode, and Employee Telephone. The payroll calculation fields are EmployeeSSN, EmployeeMaritalStatus, EmployeeExemptions, and EmployeePayRate.

You will learn how to arrange controls in logical sections for this employee information form in the next three exercises. These exercises will also give you valuable practice in creating a form from scratch; that is, starting with a blank form. You will construct all of the form elements without using the Form Wizard. You can use Figures 8.5 and 8.6 as guides for placing the graphics objects, labels, and controls on the form as you complete the next three exercises. We have also provided two forms in the *Ch08.mdb* file on your Companion CD to which you can refer as you build the form. These forms, *frmEmployeeInformation-InProgress-01* and *frmEmployeeInformation-InProgress-02*, show the form at two different stages in the building process. Close all tables, and have the Database window open on the Access desktop to begin this exercise.

EXERCISE 8.4: CREATING THE EMPLOYEE INFORMATION ENTRY FORM

1. Click the Forms object in the Database window, and then click the New button. Select *tblEmployee* in the combo box control, and double-click Design View in the New Form dialog box to open a blank form.
2. Open the toolbox by clicking the Toolbox toolbar button, and then open the property sheet by clicking the Properties toolbar button. You should keep the toolbox and the property sheet open on the desktop throughout this exercise.
3. Use the Rectangle toolbox tool to draw a box for the identification fields.
4. Use the Label toolbox tool to create a label for the box and enter the text **Identification** in the label. Set the label's Text Align property to **Center**, its Font Size property to **10**, and its Font Weight to **Bold**
5. Select the box and the label (press the Shift key while clicking each object in succession), click the property sheet Format tab, and then set both objects' Special Effect properties to **Raised**

6. Draw a marquee (selection rectangle) around both objects, press Ctrl+C to copy the object group, and then press Ctrl+V three times to paste three copies of the object group to the form.

7. Change the label text in the three new groups to **Payroll Calculation**, **Name**, and **Address** as shown in Figure 8.5.

Note that Figure 8.5 shows the property sheet and the toolbox open. Now that you have a rough layout for the overall form, you can complete the design of each individual section.

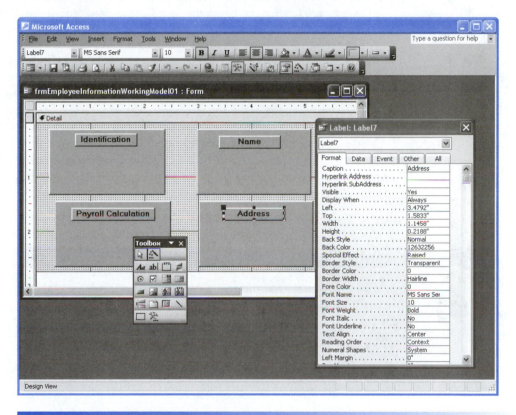

Figure 8.5 The Employee Information form under construction.

EXERCISE 8.5: ADDING FIELDS TO THE EMPLOYEE INFORMATION ENTRY FORM

1. Click the Field List toolbar button to open the *tblEmployee* field list.

2. Click and drag the EmployeeNumber and EmployeeStartDate fields to the first box you created.

3. Use the Combo Box tool from the toolbox to draw a field in the Identification section between the EmployeeNumber and EmployeeStartDate fields. After you draw the combo box control on the form, the first Combo Box Wizard dialog box appears.

4. Click the Next button to accept the default option since you want the combo box control to look up the values for this field in the Department table.

5. Select *tblDepartment* from the list box control, and then click the Next button.

6. Click the >> button to move both DepartmentNumber and DepartmentDescription from the Available Fields list box to the Selected Fields list box; then click the Next button.

7. Click the *Hide key column (recommended)* check box to remove the check mark. In this form, we do want to display *tblDepartment*'s key field.

8. Reduce the first column's width and increase the second column's width so that the field values are displayed without extra unused space. Then, click the Next button.

9. Double-click the DepartmentNumber field name in the Available Fields list box. This selects DepartmentNumber and opens the next Combo Box Wizard dialog box.

10. Click the *Store that value in this field* option button, enter **EmployeeDepartment** in the combo box control, and then click the Next button.

11. Enter **Department Number** as the combo box label name, and click the Finish button.

12. Using Figure 8.6 as a guide, adjust the size and spacing of the three controls in the Identification Box. You can also set the controls' Font Size, Font Weight, Special Effect, and other properties using Figure 8.6 and your own judgment.

You can follow the same general procedure to click and drag the other *tblEmployee* fields to the appropriate sections of the form, set their properties, and adjust their sizes and spacing. As you refine the appearance of the form, you may find it helpful to toggle between Design and Form view.

TRY IT

You can move between the two view options for forms using the view menu command or the first button on the Form Design toolbar. This button has a drop button to its right, which makes it work much like a combo box control. Clicking on the drop button presents you with a choice of Design view, Form view, and Datasheet view.

EXERCISE 8.6: COMPLETING THE EMPLOYEE INFORMATION ENTRY FORM

1. Choose the Edit, Select Form menu command to select the form. Click the property sheet Format tab and change the form's Caption property to **Employee Information Entry**, its Scroll Bars property to **Neither**, and its Record Selectors property to **No**

2. Click the Detail section bar at the top of the form. Then, click the property sheet Format tab and change the Detail section's Back Color property to a color that contrasts with the rectangles that contain the text box controls.

3. Select File, Save As from the menu, and enter **frmEmployeeInformation** as the form's new name.

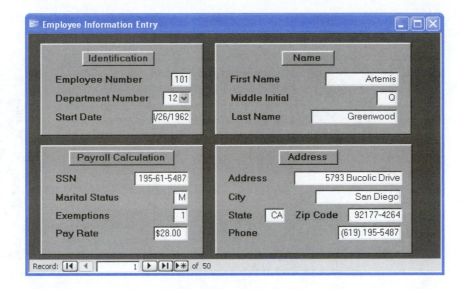

Figure 8.6 The completed Employee Information Entry form.

TRY IT

When you select any Color property for a form object, a Build button appears to the right of the property box. You can click on this Build button to open a Color palette that offers you a choice of 48 colors and gives you the option of creating your own custom colors. After you choose a color and click the OK button, the number of the color you chose appears as the new property setting. We find this to be much easier than remembering that, for example, maroon is 4194432.

The form shown in Figure 8.6 is included as *frmEmployeeInformationExample* in the *Ch08.mdb* file on your Companion CD. In Figure 8.6, the form is displaying the first record of Greenwood Lumber Company sample data. In addition to learning more about the payroll cycle in this exercise, you learned how to use color, control properties, and object grouping to create a form that contains many fields but is still easy to read and to use for data entry and editing tasks.

Maintaining Employee Records

Now that you have an Employee table and a form that makes using that table easy, you can efficiently and effectively maintain employee information. With the Employee Information Entry form, Greenwood can enter new employee information easily and update records as employees move, change their number of exemptions or marital status, get new telephone numbers, and change other information items they have entered in the Employee table.

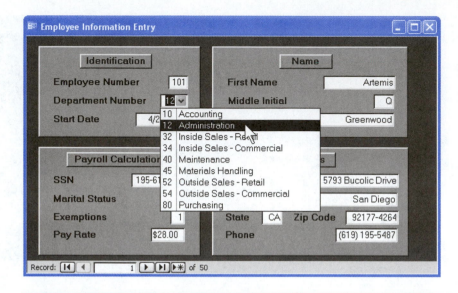

Figure 8.7 Using the combo box control to enter a department number.

Notice how the combo box control for the EmployeeDepartment field makes data entry easier. When you click the combo box button, a list of all the DepartmentNumber and DepartmentDescription values that are in the Department table appears as shown in Figure 8.7.

When a user selects a particular DepartmentDescription value, the combo box control enters the related DepartmentNumber value into the EmployeeDepartment field of the Employee table. The advantages of using a combo box control here include:

- Data entry clerks do not need to memorize lists of department numbers.
- Only valid department numbers can be entered in the Employee table.
- It reduces storage needs in the Employee table by storing department numbers instead of descriptions.
- New departments can be added easily to the Department table, and they will automatically appear in the Employee Information Entry form combo box.

Note how the Default Value property settings you incorporated into the Employee table operate in the form. For example, immediately after you create a new record by entering a new EmployeeNumber, the EmployeeMaritalStatus value becomes *S* and the EmployeeExemptions value becomes *0*.

TRY IT

You can test the operation of the other internal control features you built into the table's design. For example, try entering illegal values in the EmployeePayRate field. If you attempt to enter a value less than 6.2 or greater than 40 in the field, a dialog box appears with the error message we entered as the Validation Text property. Note that the form will not permit you to leave the record until you enter an acceptable value in the EmployeePayRate field.

Updating existing employee records to reflect pay rate changes, new addresses, new telephone numbers, and other changes is straightforward. The navigation buttons at the bottom of the form make it easy to find and display any employee record we want to change. The form will let a user move through the individual fields in the displayed record using the Up and Down arrow keys, the Tab and Shift+Tab keys, or the Enter key. Also, remember that any internal control features that you built into the table's structure will limit changes to existing field values. That is, the changes you make cannot result in a value that would violate any of the controls.

To summarize, you now have a table that contains information about Greenwood Lumber Company's employees. The table relates each piece of information to a particular employee through the employee number—a primary key that uniquely identifies each employee. All information about a particular employee appears in one row of *tblEmployee* and depends on the primary key value for that row. You also have a form that facilitates entering, deleting, and changing employee information. You can use the information in this Employee table to construct payroll cycle forms, queries, and reports for Greenwood Lumber Company.

Employee Information Reports

You can build a variety of reports using information in *tblEmployee*. The example report that you will build in the next exercise shows one possibility. This example Employee Pay report will list employee names, start dates, and pay rates. The report will group employee records by department and show the average pay rate for each department.

EXERCISE 8.7: BUILDING AN EMPLOYEE PAY REPORT

1. Click the Reports object in the Database window, and then click the New button. Select *tblEmployee* in the combo box control, and double-click Design View in the list box control. The report must obtain department names from the Department table. To add the Department table to the report, you must change the report's Record Source property from *tblEmployee* to a query. You can build this query by opening and editing a query behind the report.
2. Select Edit, Select Report from the menu, click the Properties toolbar button, click the Data tab, select the Record Source property, and then click the Build button. Click Yes to open the Query Builder window.
3. Add the Department table using the Show Table toolbar button.

4. Click and drag the DepartmentNumber field from *tblDepartment* to the first Field cell in the QBE grid, and enter **Ascending** in its Sort cell.
5. Click and drag the DepartmentDescription field from *tblDepartment* to the second Field cell in the QBE grid.
6. Click and drag the EmployeeNumber field from *tblEmployee* to the third QBE grid Field cell, and enter **Ascending** in its Sort cell.
7. Click and drag the asterisk from the Employee table box to the fourth QBE grid Field cell.
8. Click in the fifth QBE grid Field cell, and enter **EmployeeName: EmployeeFirstName & " " & EmployeeMiddleInitial & ". " & EmployeeLastName**
9. Return to the Design view window, and save your changes when prompted.

Now that you have built the query, you can refine the layout of the report. You will begin by setting up a department group section on the report.

EXERCISE 8.8: REFINING THE LAYOUT OF THE EMPLOYEE PAY REPORT

1. Click the Sorting and Grouping toolbar button, and enter **EmployeeDepartment** in the first Field/Expression cell in the Sorting and Grouping dialog box. Press F6, and enter a Group Header property of **Yes**. Enter a Keep Together property of **Whole Group**; then, press Alt+F4 to close the dialog box.
2. You should now have four sections on the report: Page Header, EmployeeDepartment Header, Detail, and Page Footer. You can click and drag the bottom edges of these sections to change the size of each. This will give you room to include all of the controls that the report requires. You can refer to Figures 8.8 and 8.9 as you place controls, text boxes, and graphic objects on the report.

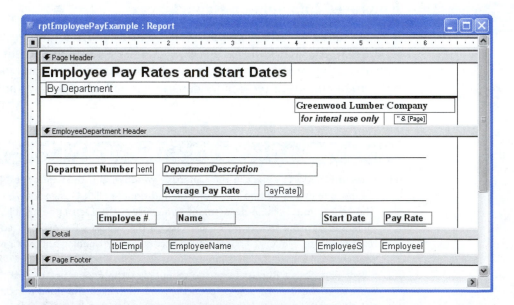

Figure 8.8   The Employee Pay report in Design view.

Employee Pay Rates and Start Dates
By Department

Department Number   40   *Maintenance*

Average Pay Rate $16.73

Employee #	Name	Start Date	Pay Rate
111	Judith F. Ballenger	1/21/1968	$18.00
124	Louise K. Young	7/15/1996	$14.20
142	Karl S. Smothers	6/15/2001	$18.00

Department Number   45   *Materials Handling*

Average Pay Rate $14.07

Employee #	Name	Start Date	Pay Rate
143	Byron D. White	8/2/2001	$9.10
106	Henry X. Wheeler	8/3/1964	$15.40
115	Esther L. Tufts	10/31/1980	$16.60
126	Colleen H. Ward	4/15/1997	$12.20
132	James R. Foster	12/1/1998	$14.90
139	Edward G. Perciavalle	2/2/2001	$16.20

Department Number   52   *Outside Sales - Retail*

Average Pay Rate $9.45

Employee #	Name	Start Date	Pay Rate
149	Donald T. Forrest	12/17/2001	$6.80
146	Joel B. Blum	11/1/2001	$6.70
119	Natalie R. Sherwood	9/21/1991	$12.80
131	Antonio N. Pelligrini	10/15/1998	$11.50

Figure 8.9   Page 3 of the Employee Pay report.

3. Click the Field List toolbar button, and then click and drag the following fields to the Detail section: tblEmployee.EmployeeNumber, EmployeeName, EmployeeStartDate, and EmployeePayRate. Each of these fields will become a control on the report.
4. Draw a selection rectangle around the control labels, and press Ctrl+X. This will cut the labels from the text box portion of the control. Click the EmployeeDepartment Header bar,

and then press Ctrl+V to place the labels in that section. Using Figure 8.8 as a guide, align the labels and controls in two rows.

5. Click and drag the EmployeeDepartment and DepartmentDescription fields to the EmployeeDepartment Header section.

6. To report an average pay rate for each department, you can add a calculating control to the EmployeeDepartment Header. Open the toolbox, and then use the Text Box tool to draw a new control in the EmployeeDepartment Header.

7. Change the new control's Name property to **Average Pay Rate**, its Control Source property to **=Avg([EmployeePayRate])**, its Format property to **Fixed**, and its Decimal Places property to **2**

8. Arrange the controls and add label controls and line objects to the Page Header section using Figures 8.8 and 8.9 to guide your judgment. Figure 8.9 shows a printed page from the Employee Pay report for the Greenwood Lumber Company sample data.

TRY IT

As you make fine adjustments to objects' placement on the report, you may find it easier to work with Snap to Grid turned off. You can toggle this desktop setting by selecting Format, Snap to Grid from the menu. You may also find that you have more room to work if you turn the ruler off. You can do this by choosing View, Ruler from the menu.

Save the Employee Pay report by selecting File, Save As from the Design view menu and entering a name of *rptEmployeePay* for the report. The Employee Pay report shown in Figures 8.8 and 8.9 is included in the *Ch08.mdb* file on your Companion CD as *rptEmployeePayExample*.

RECORDING TIME WORKED

The second main entity in the payroll cycle is an event that measures the work of each employee. Often this measure is the time that employees have worked. Greenwood Lumber pays employees by the hour, as many companies do. However, not all organizations pay their employees on the basis of time worked. For example, firms may pay salespersons a percentage of their sales as a commission. Similarly, companies sometimes pay their managers bonuses based on their departments' profit, production, or efficiency. Even when firms calculate pay using time worked, the methods they use to capture time data vary tremendously. Some have their workers punch a time clock, others use automated bar code scanners that read employee badges, and still others have workers fill out time sheets using pen and paper. Regardless of how firms capture time worked data, they must store the data by employee and by pay period before calculating payroll. In the Greenwood Lumber Company payroll database, you will store this information in a time worked table.

The Time Worked Table

In this section, you will learn how to build a time worked table that stores regular and overtime hours worked by each employee for each pay period. We have made two key simplifying assumptions: that Greenwood calculates all pay on an hourly basis, and that Greenwood pays all of its employees once each month.

You will need a primary key that uniquely identifies each employee's time worked in each pay period. You could create a sequential number for each employee-pay period combination; however, Greenwood already has an employee number for each employee. If you add a field that identifies the pay period for each record, you can build a composite primary key that includes the employee number field and the pay period field that uniquely identifies each pay record.

The Time Worked table will also include two fields that will store the hours employees have worked—one field for regular hours, the other field for overtime hours. Greenwood uses only one overtime pay rate and that rate is one and one-half times the regular pay rate. Further, you can assume that when Greenwood's accounting personnel enter the time worked data in this table, they have already calculated regular and overtime hours from workers' time sheets.

In Exercise 8.9 you will create a Time Worked table for Greenwood Lumber Company that accomplishes the necessary data storage objectives. The Time Worked table also illustrates some internal control features that can help reduce potential losses from errors or irregularities as Greenwood processes its payroll. You should have the Database window open on the Access desktop to begin this exercise.

EXERCISE 8.9: BUILDING A TIME WORKED TABLE

1. Click the Tables object in the Database window, and then click the New button. Double-click Design View in the New Table dialog box that appears.
2. Enter a Field Name of **EmployeeNumber**, leave its Data Type set to Text, and set its Field Size to **3**. Enter an Input Mask property of **000**, a Caption property of **Employee #**, and an Indexed property of **Yes (Duplicates OK)**
3. The second part of the primary key must identify the pay period. Since Greenwood pays once each month, you can use the last day of each month as the value for this field. Enter **TWPayPeriodEnded** in the second Field Name row, and enter a Data Type of **Date/Time**. Enter an Input Mask property of **99/99/0000;0;_**, a Caption property of **Month Ended**, and an Indexed property of **Yes (Duplicates OK)**
4. To designate these fields as the composite primary key, hold down the Ctrl key and select both fields by clicking their row selectors. With both fields selected, click the Primary Key toolbar button. The primary key symbol should appear in the row selectors of both fields.
5. Enter the next Field Name of **TWRegularTime**. Enter a Data Type of **Number**, a Field Size of **Single**, and a Caption property of **Regular Time**
6. The greatest number of business days that occurs in a calendar month is 23. If Greenwood pays overtime for all hours over eight per day, the TWRegularTime field will never have a legitimate value greater than 184 (23 days $\times$ 8 hours per day). You can use the Validation Rule and Text property settings to enforce a limit check internal control on this field. Enter **<185** as the TWRegularTime field's Validation Rule property.

7. Enter **The number of Regular Hours you have entered is too large.** as the TWRegularTime field's Validation Text property.

8. The second hours field, TWOvertime, will store the overtime hours worked. Enter a Field Name of **TWOvertime**, set its Data Type to **Number**, its Field Size to **Single**, and its Caption property to **Overtime**

9. You can establish a limit check internal control on the TWOvertime field, too. However, selecting the limit value is a bit trickier than it was for the TWRegularTime field. Since a Validation Rule property setting will prohibit any greater value, you must set it to accommodate the largest possible number of overtime hours that any employee might ever work. Enter **<200** as the TWOvertime field's Validation Rule property.

10. Enter **The number of Overtime Hours you have entered is too large.** as the TWOvertime field's Validation Text property.

11. Select File, Save As from the menu, and enter a name of **tblTimeWorked** in the Save As dialog box.

The table shown in Figure 8.10 is included as *tblTimeWorked* in the *Ch08.mdb* file on your Companion CD. The table in this figure displays the example data as we entered it for Greenwood Lumber Company. Your table will not display any data unless you have entered it or copied it from the version of the table that is on the Companion CD.

Employee #	Month Ended	Regular Time	Overtime
101	1 /31/2005	168	0
101	2 /28/2005	160	0
101	3 /31/2005	184	0
101	4 /30/2005	168	0
101	5 /31/2005	176	0
101	6 /30/2005	168	0
101	7 /31/2005	168	0
101	8 /31/2005	184	0
101	9 /30/2005	176	0
101	10/31/2005	168	0
101	11/30/2005	176	0
101	12/31/2005	176	0
102	1 /31/2005	168	0
102	2 /28/2005	160	0
102	3 /31/2005	184	0
102	4 /30/2005	168	0
102	5 /31/2005	176	0
102	6 /30/2005	168	0
102	7 /31/2005	168	0
102	8 /31/2005	184	0
102	9 /30/2005	176	0
102	10/31/2005	168	0
102	11/30/2005	176	0
102	12/31/2005	176	0
103	1 /31/2005	168	0
103	2 /28/2005	160	0
103	3 /31/2005	184	0
103	4 /30/2005	168	0
103	5 /31/2005	174	0

Record: 1 of 600

Figure 8.10   The Time Worked table in Datasheet view.

Greenwood Lumber's Time Worked table should have a link to *tblEmployee* on the EmployeeNumber field in both tables. If you enforce referential integrity on this link, it will prevent users from entering time worked for employee numbers that do not exist in *tblEmployee*. This internal control feature, called an *existence check* or a *validity check*, can reduce the threat of errors and irregularities in payroll processing. Exercise 8.10 shows you how to create this control feature. Be sure you have closed *tblTimeWorked* and have the Database window open on the Access desktop before you begin this exercise.

EXERCISE 8.10: LINKING *TBLTIMEWORKED* TO *TBLEMPLOYEE*

1. Click the Relationships toolbar button to open the Relationships window. The existing relationship between the Department and Employee tables will appear in the Relationships window.
2. Use the Show Table toolbar button to open the Show Table dialog box. Double-click *tblTimeWorked* to add it to the Relationships window. Close the Show Table dialog box.
3. Click and drag the EmployeeNumber field in *tblEmployee* to the EmployeeNumber field in *tblTimeWorked*.
4. Click the Enforce Referential Integrity check box, and then click the Create button. The Relationships window with the new table and link appears in Figure 8.11.

To close the Relationships window and return to the Database window, select the File, Close menu command, and click OK to save your changes. Now you can build a data entry form through which you can enter and edit time worked data.

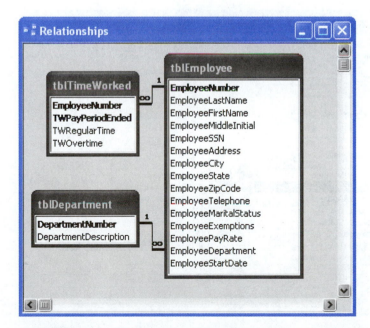

Figure 8.11 Linking the Time Worked table to the Employee table.

The Time Worked Entry Form

You can build a data entry form for the Time Worked table that will ease the task of entering employees' time records. The Time Worked Data Entry form will use the employee name fields in the Employee table to provide another validity check that can help data entry clerks detect errors. You can design the Time Worked Data Entry form so that it displays the employee's name when a user enters an employee number. This lets the user check the displayed name against the employee name on the time sheet source document. In Exercise 8.11 you will create a Time Worked Data Entry form that includes this control feature.

EXERCISE 8.11: BUILDING A DATA ENTRY FORM FOR TIME WORKED

1. In the Database window, click the Forms object, and then click the New button. In the New Forms dialog box, enter **tblTimeWorked** in the combo box control, and double-click Form Wizard in the list box.
2. The Form Wizard dialog box will open with Table: *tblTimeWorked* selected in the Tables/Queries combo box. Click the >> button to move all of the *tblTimeWorked* fields from the Available Fields list box to the Selected Fields list box.
3. Select Table: *tblEmployee* in the Tables/Queries combo box.
4. Use the > button to move EmployeeFirstName, EmployeeMiddleInitial, and EmployeeLast-Name (in that order) from the Available Fields list box to the Selected Fields list box. Figure 8.12 shows the Form Wizard Dialog box at this point. Click the Next button to continue.

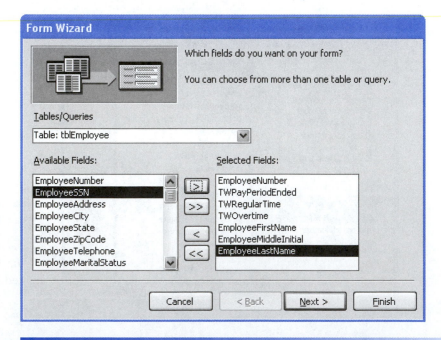

Figure 8.12 Selecting Fields in the Form Wizard dialog box.

5. Click the Next button to accept the default of viewing the data by *tblTimeWorked*.
6. Click the Tabular option button, and then click the Next button to continue.
7. Click the Standard style, and then click the Next button.
8. Enter **frmTimeWorked** as the form title, and then click the Finish button to have the Form Wizard create the form.

The Form Wizard has created a usable form; however, you can make several improvements that will enhance the form's effectiveness and appearance. The next exercise provides steps for doing this. Have the Wizard-generated form open in Design view as you begin this exercise. If the property sheet is not already open on the Access desktop, click the Properties toolbar button to open it.

EXERCISE 8.12: IMPROVING THE WIZARD-GENERATED TIME WORKED DATA ENTRY FORM

1. Delete the EmployeeFirstName and EmployeeMiddleInitial text box controls and their labels.
2. Choose Edit, Select Form from the menu, click the Data tab in the property sheet, and then click the Build button for the form's Record Source property to open the query behind the form.
3. Select the second QBE grid column (the TWPayPeriodEnded field), and press the Delete key.
4. Click and drag the TWPayPeriodEnded field from *tblTimeWorked* to the first QBE grid Field cell, and drop it on the EmployeeNumber field name in that cell. The EmployeeNumber field should move one cell to the right, leaving TWPayPeriodEnded in the first cell.
5. Enter **Ascending** in the first two columns' Sort cells. These Sort cell entries will cause the form to sort first by TWPayPeriodEnded and then by EmployeeNumber. This will allow a data entry clerk to add all of the time records in employee number order for a particular month end.
6. Scroll to the right to find the first open QBE grid column and enter **EmployeeName: EmployeeFirstName & " " & EmployeeMiddleInitial & ". " & EmployeeLastName** in its Field cell.
7. Close the Query Builder window, and save your changes.
8. Select the EmployeeLastName text box control, click on the Data tab in its property sheet, and change its Control Source property to **EmployeeName**. Click on the property sheet Format tab; then change the Back Style property to **Transparent**, the Special Effect property to **Flat**, and the Border Style property to **Transparent**
9. Using Figure 8.13 as a guide, make the final appearance modifications to the form, which include rearranging the controls, bolding the labels, and entering **Time Worked Data Entry** as the form's Caption property. You can also set the EmployeeName control's Enabled, Locked, and Tab Stop properties to prevent a user from entering data in that field.

When you are satisfied with your form, you can save it as *frmTimeWorkedEntry*. A version of this form is included in the *Ch08.mdb* file on your Companion CD as *frmTimeWorkedEntryExample*. Figure 8.13 shows the Time Worked Entry form displaying records from the Greenwood Lumber Company Time Worked and Employee tables.

The Greenwood Lumber example includes some simplifying assumptions. The sample data includes only one year of data for 50 employees. All employees are paid on an hourly basis that includes regular hours and only one class of overtime hours. A

Time Worked Data Entry				
Employee #	**Name**	**Month Ended**	**Regular Hours**	**Overtime Hours**
101	Artemis Q. Greenwood	1/31/2005	168	0
102	Ethel Z. Greenwood	1/31/2005	168	0
103	Ethel P. Baron	1/31/2005	168	0
104	Cecelia J. Oppenheim	1/31/2005	168	4
105	Ronald D. Washington	1/31/2005	168	8
106	Henry X. Wheeler	1/31/2005	168	11
107	Elizabeth T. Surkamp	1/31/2005	168	0
108	Timothy Y. Diamond	1/31/2005	142	0
109	Max E. Roche	1/31/2005	87	0
110	Lucille B. Badillo	1/31/2005	168	0
111	Judith F. Ballenger	1/31/2005	168	7
112	Melanie C. Dewar	1/31/2005	126	0
113	Alicia K. Brown	1/31/2005	147	0
114	Irene R. Klusky	1/31/2005	168	0
115	Esther L. Tufts	1/31/2005	168	3

Record: |◄ ◄ 1 ► ►| ►* of 600

Figure 8.13 The Time Worked Data Entry form displaying sample records in Form view.

more sophisticated payroll system would track accrual and use of vacation time, paid time off, unpaid time off, and sick days. Payroll systems often must track several types of overtime (for example, over eight hours per day, over forty hours per week, hours worked on holidays) and calculate pay using measures other than hours. However, even with the limited example components included in this chapter, you can generate some useful and interesting reports.

Time Reports

Businesses create and use many different reports built on time worked payroll data. The Greenwood Lumber Company example includes only regular and overtime hours in the Time Worked table. However, even in this simple example, the Time Worked table combines with the Employee and Department tables to yield a total of 19 different fields that you can use in queries and reports.

To illustrate how you can use these tables to build payroll cycle reports, this section describes a report that displays total regular and overtime hours worked by department. This kind of report can direct managers' attention to departments that might have staffing or work scheduling problems.

You will build this report in two steps. First, you will design a query that links the Time Worked, Employee, and Department tables. In the second step, you will build a report based on this query. Exercise 8.13 shows you how to build the Time Worked query. You should have closed the Time Worked Data Entry form and have the Database window open on the Access desktop to begin.

EXERCISE 8.13: BUILDING THE TIME WORKED QUERY

1. In the Database window, click the Queries object, and click the New button. Double-click Design View in the New Query dialog box.
2. In the Show Table box, hold down the Ctrl key, and select *tblDepartment*, *tblEmployee*, and *tblTimeWorked*. Click the Add button, and then click the Close button.
3. Click and drag the DepartmentDescription field from *tblDepartment* to the first Field cell in the QBE grid.
4. Double-click the TWRegularTime and TWOvertime fields to copy them to the next two QBE grid Field cells.
5. Click the Run toolbar button to test the query.

The dynaset resulting from this query should include the three fields you selected from *tblDepartment* and *tblTimeWorked*. Notice that you included *tblEmployee* in the Query window but did not use any fields from that table in the query. The Employee table provides the link between *tblDepartment* and *tblTimeWorked*; therefore, you must include it in the query model even though you are not including any Employee table fields in the query.

When you are satisfied that your Time Worked query is operating properly, you can save it as **qryTimeWorked**. Close the query. The *Ch08.mdb* file on your Companion CD includes a *qryTimeWorked* object that you can use as a reference.

Now you can build the Time Worked report using this query. The Time Worked query was a little unusual. The Time Worked report has a twist that makes it interesting, too. To find out more, follow the steps in Exercise 8.14.

EXERCISE 8.14: BUILDING THE TIME WORKED REPORT

1. In the Database window, click the Reports tab, and then click the New button to open the New Report dialog box. Enter or select **qryTimeWorked** in the combo box control, and then double-click Design View.
2. Drag the bottom edge of the Detail section up until the Detail section background grid disappears. The interesting twist to this report is that it contains no detail records! Everything on the form is either a header or a calculated total field.
3. If the form does not open with a Report Header and Footer, use the Format, Report Header/Footer menu command to create them.
4. Click the Sorting and Grouping toolbar button, and enter **DepartmentDescription** in the first Field/Expression cell in the Sorting and Grouping dialog box. Change the Group Header property to **Yes**, and then press Alt+F4 to close the dialog box.
5. Click the Field List toolbar button. Then, click and drag the DepartmentDescription field from the Field List to the DepartmentDescription Header. Delete the new control's label.
6. Open the toolbox, and use the Text Box tool to create two controls in the DepartmentDescription Header section. Delete both new controls' labels.

7. Click the Properties toolbar button, and set the Control Source property of the first control to =Sum([TWRegularTime]). Set the Control Source property of the second control to =Sum([TWOvertime]). These controls calculate subtotals of the TWRegularTime and TWOvertime values for each DepartmentDescription value. Using Figure 8.14 as a guide, you can arrange these controls, add label controls to the Page Header section, and add graphic line objects to the report's design.

8. Close the report, saving it with the name rptTimeWorked

The Time Worked report that appears in Figure 8.14 is included in the *Ch08.mdb* file on your Companion CD as *rptTimeWorkedExample*. This report illustrates how you can use the three payroll cycle tables to obtain some interesting information.

The report also demonstrates how you can build a query that uses one table as a link between two other tables that contain data in which you are interested. The Time Worked report is an interesting example of a report that contains no detail records.

By examining the ratio of overtime hours to regular hours shown in this report, managers at Greenwood Lumber Company can identify departments that are improperly staffed or that have scheduling problems. Your next task is to use the information in the three payroll cycle tables to calculate payroll.

Time Worked in 2005

By Department	Regular Hours	Greenwood Lumber Company
		for internal use only

	Regular Hours	Overtime Hours
Accounting	8,836	24
Administration	5,852	8
Inside Sales - Commercial	10,936	33
Inside Sales - Retail	17,132	14
Maintenance	5,269	88
Materials Handling	11,043	110
Outside Sales - Commercial	8,869	32
Outside Sales - Retail	4,117	11
Purchasing	6,717	1

Figure 8.14   The Time Worked report.

CALCULATING PAYROLL

Thus far in this chapter you have learned how to enter and maintain payroll cycle information. You have used this payroll cycle information to produce two useful reports; however, the main transaction processing objective of the payroll cycle is to calculate payroll and print paychecks.

Queries are useful tools for performing payroll calculations. Indeed, if relational database management software lacked a query language, you could not use it to calculate payroll. Because payroll calculations can be very complex, you will learn how to build several queries that each accomplish a step in calculating payroll. Then you will learn how to use these queries to build payroll register reports, employee earnings record reports, and payroll check reports. You can extend this step-by-step approach to more complex payroll systems as you encounter them in your future studies or in your practice of accounting.

Payroll Calculation Queries

The first payroll calculation is simple: you must compute regular pay. To do this, you need only multiply each employee's pay rate by the number of regular hours he or she worked in the pay period. Since you have pay rates in *tblEmployee* and regular hours by pay period in *tblTimeWorked*, you can query these two tables to calculate regular pay.

You can use the Greenwood Lumber Company sample data to learn how to build these queries. Greenwood's Employee table has 50 employee records, and its Time Worked table includes a full year of monthly pay period time data. You will use the January payroll period for the example calculations in these exercises.

EXERCISE 8.15: CALCULATING GROSS PAY

1. In the Database window, click the Queries object, and then click the New button. Click Design View in the New Query dialog box, and then click the OK button. The Query Builder window will open along with the Show Table dialog box.
2. Double-click *tblEmployee* and *tblTimeWorked* in the Show Table dialog box; then click the Close button.
3. Click and drag the EmployeeNumber field from *tblTimeWorked* to the first QBE Field cell. Set the Sort cell in the first QBE column to **Ascending**
4. Click and drag the TWPayPeriodEnded field from *tblTimeWorked* to the second QBE Field cell.
5. To have the query obtain only the records for the year's first payroll period, you must set a criterion for the TWPayPeriodEnded field that is equal to the date that the first payroll period ended. Enter **=#1/31/2003#** in the second Criteria cell in the QBE grid. The # symbols tell Access to interpret the characters they enclose as a date. To calculate the regular and overtime pay amounts, you can use the pay rate field from *tblEmployee* and the time fields from *tblTimeWorked*.
6. Click in the third QBE Field cell, and press Shift+F2 to open the Zoom box. Enter **RegularPay: TWRegularTime * EmployeePayRate** in the Zoom box, and then click OK.

7. Click in the fourth QBE Field cell, press Shift+F2, enter **OvertimePay: TWOvertime * EmployeePayRate * 1.5** in the Zoom box, and then click OK. These two calculations will compute the amounts of regular pay and overtime pay.

8. To check your work at this point, click the Run toolbar button. The query should produce the dynaset shown in Figure 8.15.

9. Verify that the pay calculations are correct before you continue. The new RegularPay field should be the result of multiplying the TWRegularTime field from *tblTimeWorked* by the EmployeePayRate field from *tblEmployee*. The new OvertimePay field should equal the TWOvertime field times the EmployeePayRate field times 1.5 (to pay the overtime rate of one and one-half times the regular rate). For example, several employees whose gross pay calculations appear in the figure had overtime hours in January. You can use a calculator to check the OvertimePay calculations for those employees. When building complex queries in steps, you should always check results after each step. To create the field that will calculate gross pay, return to the Query window by selecting View, Design View from the menu.

10. Once you have defined a calculated field in a query, Microsoft Access lets you use that new field in further calculations. Click in the fifth QBE grid Field cell, press Shift+F2 to open the Zoom box, enter **GrossPay: RegularPay + OvertimePay**, and click OK.

11. To test the query, click the Run toolbar button. The dynaset resulting from the revised query appears in Figure 8.16.

Once again, you should check the GrossPay field calculations with a calculator before you continue. You can save your query as **qryGrossPay**. The *Ch08.mdb* file on

Employee #	Month Ended	RegularPay	OvertimePay
101	1 /31/2005	4704	0
102	1 /31/2005	4704	0
103	1 /31/2005	1377.6	0
104	1 /31/2005	1579.2	56.4
105	1 /31/2005	2066.4	147.6
106	1 /31/2005	2587.2	254.1
107	1 /31/2005	3763.2	0
108	1 /31/2005	1306.4	0
109	1 /31/2005	652.5	0
110	1 /31/2005	2167.2	0
111	1 /31/2005	3024	189
112	1 /31/2005	1234.8	0
113	1 /31/2005	1558.2	0
114	1 /31/2005	1512	0
115	1 /31/2005	2788.8	74.7
116	1 /31/2005	4032	0
117	1 /31/2005	1489.2	0
118	1 /31/2005	1372	0
119	1 /31/2005	1689.6	0
120	1 /31/2005	3007.2	53.7
121	1 /31/2005	750	0
122	1 /31/2005	1156.2	24.6
123	1 /31/2005	3612	0

qryGrossPay-IntermediateResults : Select Query

Record: 1 of 50

Figure 8.15 The Gross Pay query calculation intermediate results.

Employee #	Month Ended	RegularPay	OvertimePay	GrossPay
101	1 /31/2005	4704	0	4704
102	1 /31/2005	4704	0	4704
103	1 /31/2005	1377.6	0	1377.6
104	1 /31/2005	1579.2	56.4	1635.6
105	1 /31/2005	2066.4	147.6	2214
106	1 /31/2005	2587.2	254.1	2841.3
107	1 /31/2005	3763.2	0	3763.2
108	1 /31/2005	1306.4	0	1306.4
109	1 /31/2005	652.5	0	652.5
110	1 /31/2005	2167.2	0	2167.2
111	1 /31/2005	3024	189	3213
112	1 /31/2005	1234.8	0	1234.8
113	1 /31/2005	1558.2	0	1558.2
114	1 /31/2005	1512	0	1512
115	1 /31/2005	2788.8	74.7	2863.5
116	1 /31/2005	4032	0	4032
117	1 /31/2005	1489.2	0	1489.2
118	1 /31/2005	1372	0	1372
119	1 /31/2005	1689.6	0	1689.6
120	1 /31/2005	3007.2	53.7	3060.9
121	1 /31/2005	750	0	750
122	1 /31/2005	1156.2	24.6	1180.8
123	1 /31/2005	3612	0	3612

Record: 1 of 50

Figure 8.16 The Gross Pay query final calculation results.

your Companion CD includes *qryGrossPay*, which you can examine if you have trouble getting your query to work properly.

Of course, calculating gross pay is only the first half of the payroll calculation. The second half is to calculate the deductions from gross pay that determine net pay. Your next step will be to revise *qryGrossPay* so that it calculates deductions and net pay. Payroll deductions include taxes, insurance, profit-sharing contributions, and many other items. The rules for calculating each of these deductions generally fall into one of four categories:

- *Fixed Amount Deductions.* These deductions are easy to calculate because they are a fixed amount each pay period. Examples of these include deductions for health insurance premiums, group life insurance premiums, and employee-approved donations to charitable organizations such as the United Way.
- *Fixed Percentage Deductions.* These deductions are a fixed percentage of gross income each pay period. Examples of these include deductions for employer-withheld city and county earnings taxes in many parts of the United States. Some state income taxes are also calculated as a fixed percentage of all earned income.
- *Varying Percentage Deductions.* These deductions are similar to the fixed percentage deduction except that the percentage changes with variables such as level of income, marital status, and number of exemptions claimed. The U.S. federal

income tax payments that employers must withhold from employee pay is the most common example of this type of tax. Many states have income tax withholding rules that are similar to the federal rules and, therefore, also fall within this category.

- *Fixed Percentage Deductions Subject to a Ceiling.* These deductions are a fixed percentage of gross income each pay period until a ceiling amount is reached. The most common example of this deduction type is the deductions under the U.S. Federal Insurance Contributions Act (FICA), which is commonly called the *social security tax*. Employers deduct a fixed percentage of gross pay only until the FICA limit for the year is reached. Some states, such as California, require employee contributions to unemployment insurance funds that are calculated this way, too.

The first type of deduction, a fixed amount each pay period, is easy to model. You only need one additional Employee table field, a binary indicator of whether the employee was subject to the deduction, to trigger the calculation. The second type of deduction, a fixed percentage, is even easier to implement. You simply build the fixed percentage into the payroll calculation query. The third type of deduction, a varying percentage, can be difficult to implement because it requires one or more additional tables. These tables contain the various percentages and the points at which they change from one value to another. The fourth type of deduction, a fixed percentage subject to a ceiling, is even more difficult to implement. It requires an additional query to calculate year-to-date totals and compare the calculated totals to the ceiling amounts. The ceiling amounts may be stored in a separate table or included in the query.

The Greenwood Lumber Company example payroll calculation includes the second and third types of deductions. The fixed percentage calculation is the social security, or FICA, tax. A deduction for FICA tax is actually the fourth type, since it is a fixed rate up to a maximum pay amount per year. However, we have designed the Greenwood Lumber Company sample data so that none of the employees exceed the FICA ceiling. Therefore, you can model the FICA tax for Greenwood Lumber Company as a fixed percentage deduction. The deduction for the federal income tax that Greenwood must withhold from its employees' pay shows some of the intricacies of modeling the third type of deduction. This deduction is usually called *federal withholding tax (FWT) or federal income tax (FIT) withheld*.

Please note that the tax deduction calculations we model in this chapter are not intended to be complete or accurate. Employer tax laws change constantly and vary by state. Our purpose here is to give you some practice building tables and queries that you can adapt to specific user needs and to the ever-changing requirements of government regulators.

Before you create the query that will calculate net pay, you will build two tables that contain tax rates and exemption amounts. You could include these rates and amounts in *qryNetPay*, but placing them in separate tables makes updating and modifying the rates and amounts much easier. And remember, tax laws change even more frequently than software versions!

EXERCISE 8.16: BUILDING THE MARITAL STATUS TABLE

1. Click the Tables object in the Database Window, and then click the New button. Double-click Design View in the New Table dialog box.
2. Enter **MSMaritalStatus** in the first row of the Field Name column, and leave the Data Type set to Text. Click the Primary Key toolbar button.
3. Enter a Field Size property of **1**, an Input Mask property of **>L**, and a Caption property of **Marital Status**
4. Enter **="M" Or "S"** as the Validation Rule property.
5. Enter **Please enter an M for Married or an S for Single.** as the Validation Text property.
6. Enter **MSFWTRate** in the second row of the Field Name column.
7. Enter a Data Type of **Number**, a Field Size property of **Double**, and a Caption property of **FWT Rate**
8. Save the Marital Status table with the name **tblMaritalStatus**
9. Click the Datasheet toolbar button to change the Marital Status table to Datasheet view to enter the two tax rates shown in Figure 8.17. After you enter the tax rates, close the table.

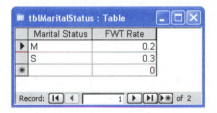

Figure 8.17   The record values in *tblMaritalStatus*.

The table shown in Figure 8.17 is included as *tblMaritalStatus* in the *Ch08.mdb* file on your Companion CD. The Marital Status table stores the percentages that you will use to calculate federal withholding tax for Greenwood Lumber Company. The next exercise shows you how to build a second table that will store the exemption values for the deduction calculation. The exemption values are dollar amounts that the tax withholding calculation will deduct from gross pay before applying the percentages in *tblMaritalStatus*.

EXERCISE 8.17: BUILDING THE EXEMPTION TABLE

1. Click the Tables object in the Database Window, and then click the New button. Double-click Design View in the New Table dialog box.
2. Enter **ExemptionNumber** in the first row of the Field Name column, and set its Data Type to **Number**. Click the Primary Key toolbar button.
3. Set the ExemptionNumber's Field Size property to **Byte**, its Decimal Places property to **0**, its Input Mask property to **99**, and its Caption property to **Number of Exemptions**
4. Enter **ExemptionAmount** in the second row of the Field Name column.
5. Set its Data Type to **Number**, its Decimal Places property to **0**, and its Caption property to **Exemption Amount**
6. Save your new table as **tblExemption**

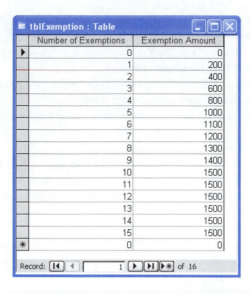

Figure 8.18   The record values in *tblExemption*.

The table shown in Figure 8.18 is included as *tblExemption* in the *Ch08.mdb* file on your Companion CD. You can click the Datasheet toolbar button to open the Exemption table in Datasheet view. Then, you can enter the field values shown in Figure 8.18. The simplified tax rules we have assumed for this example allow $200 per monthly pay period for each of the first five exemptions and $100 for each of the next five. After 10 exemptions are claimed, further exemptions do not yield an allowance. After you enter the exemption values, close the table, and return to the Database window.

Next, you will create a Net Pay query that can calculate the two sample deductions, FICA and FWT, and net pay. The computation rules for the two simplified deductions are:

● FICA: A rate of 7% calculated on gross pay.
● FWT: A rate of 20% if married, 30% if single. FWT is calculated on gross pay less allowable exemptions.

In the Net Pay query, you will link four tables: Employee, Time Worked, Exemption, and Marital Status. An easy way to create this Net Pay query is to modify the Gross Pay query you built earlier. In the next exercise, you learn how to design a Net Pay query that calculates the two deductions and net pay for Greenwood Lumber's December pay period.

EXERCISE 8.18: CALCULATING NET PAY

1. In the Database window, click the Queries object, click *qryGrossPay* to select it, and then click the Design button.

2. Click the Show Table toolbar button, double-click *tblExemption* and *tblMaritalStatus* to add them to the Query Builder window, and then click the Close button in the Show Table dialog box.

3. Note that the two tables you just added to the Query window are not linked to either *tblEmployee* or *tblTimeWorked*. To perform the inner joins required by the payroll deduction calculations, you must create links to *tblEmployee*. Click and drag the MSMaritalStatus field from *tblMaritalStatus* to the EmployeeMaritalStatus field in *tblEmployee*.

4. Click and drag the ExemptionNumber field from *tblExemption* to the EmployeeExemptions field in *tblEmployee*.

5. To perform the calculation for the last pay period of the year, change the TWPayPeriodEnded Criteria cell contents to **#12/31/2005#**

6. Since you have modified the Gross Pay query, you should save it using the File, Save As menu command. Give the new query a name of **qryNetPay**. The query appears at this stage in Figure 8.19.

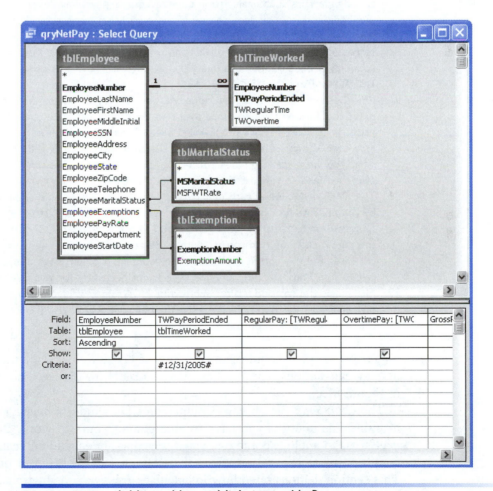

Figure 8.19 Adding tables and links to *qryNetPay*.

TRY IT

When you are modifying an existing query, form, report, or table that you want to keep, it is always a good idea to save the modified object under a new name immediately after making changes to it. Otherwise, you risk accidentally overwriting the existing object with the modified object.

7. Enter **FICA: [GrossPay] * 0.07** in the next open Field cell in the QBE grid.
8. Click the Run toolbar button to test the query.
9. Notice that some of the calculated values for FICA have more than two decimal places. Rounding errors can create many hours of extra work in accounting systems, and payroll calculations are perhaps the most infamous source of those rounding errors. To eliminate rounding errors at the calculation point, accounting systems designers have developed a number of tricks. You can use one of these tricks to make sure FICA values are stored with two decimal places. The trick is to multiply the result by 100, use an integer function to round the value, and then divide the rounded value by 100. You can incorporate this rounding procedure into this query by revising the FICA calculation so that it reads **FICA: Int([GrossPay] * 0.07 * 100) / 100**
10. Run the query to test the revised expression. The FICA column values in the resulting dynaset should now have no more than two decimal places. You could have revised the expression to read: **FICA: Int([GrossPay] * 7)** and it would have worked just as well. However, the expression you used has the advantage of being self-documenting—it reveals what you were thinking when you wrote the expression. This can be important if someone else may need to revise the expression in the future—a likely occurrence in payroll systems!
11. The FWT deduction is each employee's gross pay less allowable exemptions multiplied by the tax rate for his or her marital status. Enter **FWT: ([GrossPay] × [ExemptionAmount]) * [MSFWTRate]** in the next open QBE grid Field cell. To test the query, click the Run toolbar button. Because of the values we assumed for the example tax rates and exemption allowances, the rounding problem does not appear in the FWT calculation. Thus, the Int() function trick is not necessary for this calculation.
12. Net pay is the remainder after subtracting FICA and FWT from gross pay. Enter **NetPay: [GrossPay] × [FICA] × [FWT]** in the next open QBE grid Field cell. To test the query, click the Run toolbar button.

As always, you should use a calculator to check a few of the individual employees' net pay calculations. The Net Pay query's results for the December pay period appear in Figure 8.20.

The *Ch08.mdb* file on your Companion CD includes a *qryNetPay* object. You can examine this query if you have trouble getting yours to work. Both *qryNetPay* and *qryGrossPay* include complex expressions that are easy to enter incorrectly. You can copy and paste expressions from the example queries to your queries if you wish. This section demonstrated how to calculate gross pay, deductions, and net pay using queries. You can use these queries to create useful payroll cycle reports and accounting entries.

qryNetPay : Select Query

Employee #	Month Ended	RegularPay	OvertimePay	GrossPay	FICA	FWT	NetPay
101	12/31/2005	4928	0	4928	344.96	945.6	3637.44
102	12/31/2005	4928	0	4928	344.96	945.6	3637.44
103	12/31/2005	1443.2	0	1443.2	101.02	312.96	1029.22
104	12/31/2005	1654.4	0	1654.4	115.8	210.88	1327.72
105	12/31/2005	2164.8	0	2164.8	151.53	352.96	1660.31
106	12/31/2005	2710.4	0	2710.4	189.72	542.08	1978.6
107	12/31/2005	3942.4	0	3942.4	275.96	1122.72	2543.72
108	12/31/2005	1058	0	1058	74.06	11.6	972.34
109	12/31/2005	615	0	615	43.05	3	568.95
110	12/31/2005	1754.4	0	1754.4	122.8	466.32	1165.28
111	12/31/2005	3168	27	3195	223.65	958.5	2012.85
112	12/31/2005	1019.2	0	1019.2	71.34	43.84	904.02
113	12/31/2005	1431	0	1431	100.17	369.3	961.53
114	12/31/2005	1566	0	1566	109.62	273.2	1183.18
115	12/31/2005	2838.6	24.9	2863.5	200.44	799.05	1864.01
116	12/31/2005	4224	0	4224	295.68	764.8	3163.52
117	12/31/2005	1366.8	0	1366.8	95.67	410.04	861.09
118	12/31/2005	1204	0	1204	84.28	301.2	818.52
119	12/31/2005	1331.2	0	1331.2	93.18	226.24	1011.78
120	12/31/2005	3150.4	0	3150.4	220.52	945.12	1984.76
121	12/31/2005	850	0	850	59.5	195	595.5
122	12/31/2005	1115.2	0	1115.2	78.06	63.04	974.1
123	12/31/2005	3784	0	3784	264.88	676.8	2842.32

Record: 1 of 50

Figure 8.20 The Net Pay query results for the December pay period.

The Payroll Register

The payroll register is a columnar report that lists each employee's gross pay, deductions, and net pay for a particular pay period. Firms use payroll registers to reconcile paycheck totals to net pay and to support the period's payroll journal entries. Firms can also use information in the payroll register to calculate payroll taxes. You can build a Payroll Register report using the payroll calculation queries and tables that you have created.

You can base the Payroll Register report on a query that does the calculations since Access does not support calculation and summing operations on the same fields in reports. You can modify the *qryNetPay* query to build a Payroll Register query that will extract some of the fields you need from tables and calculate the other fields you need. The data you will need to create Greenwood Lumber Company's payroll register are employee number, employee name, regular pay, overtime pay, gross pay, FWT deduction, FICA deduction, net pay, and payroll period. In the next exercise you will modify *qryNetPay* and use it to build a Payroll Register query that will extract the information needed for the Payroll Register report.

EXERCISE 8.19: BUILDING A PAYROLL REGISTER QUERY

1. Click the Queries object in the Database window, select *qryNetPay*, and then click the Design button.
2. The Net Pay query includes all of the fields you need for the Payroll Register report except employee name. Since you stored the employees' names in three separate fields, you can combine them in different orders to suit different purposes. In this report, Greenwood would like the names to appear in a last-name-first order. Click in the next open QBE Field, press Shift+F2, enter **Name: [EmployeeLastName] & ", " & [EmployeeFirstName] & " " & [EmployeeMiddleInitial] & ". "** in the Zoom box, and then click OK.
3. Run the query to test the new field calculation.
4. When you are satisfied that your Payroll Register query operates properly, save it as **qryPayrollRegister**; then close the query.

The *Ch08.mdb* file on your Companion CD includes *qryPayrollRegister* for your reference. The next exercise shows you how to build a Payroll Register report using the Payroll Register query you created in the previous exercise.

EXERCISE 8.20: BUILDING A PAYROLL REGISTER REPORT

1. In the Database window, click the Reports object, and then click the New button. Select *qryPayrollRegister* in the combo box control in the New Report dialog box, and then double-click Design View in the list box control.
2. Use the View, Page Header/Footer and the View, Report Header/Footer menu toggles to include a Report Header and Footer instead of the Page Header or Footer on the blank report.
3. Click and drag the right edge of the report to, but not past, the 6.5 inch mark on the top ruler.
4. Click the Field List toolbar button, and then click and drag the following fields to the Detail section: EmployeeNumber, Name, RegularPay, OvertimePay, GrossPay, FICA, FWT, and NetPay. Each field will become a text box control with an attached label control in the Detail section of the report.
5. Click and drag the TWPayPeriodEnded field to the Report Header section of the report.
6. Draw a marquee (selection rectangle) around the label controls that remain in the Detail section, and press the Delete key.
7. Open the toolbox, and use the Text Box tool to create a control in the Report Footer section. Open the new control's property sheet by clicking the Properties toolbar button, and change its Control Source property to **=Sum([RegularPay])**
8. Create similar total controls for the other five calculated fields in the report.
9. Use Figures 8.21 and 8.22 as guides in adding and arranging labels, line objects, and controls on the report.
10. Save the report with the name **rptPayrollRegister**, and then close the report.

Figure 8.21 shows the Payroll Register report in Report Design view. Unfortunately, Access does not permit you to adjust the size or spacing of report objects while in Print Preview. Therefore, as you refine the design of the Payroll Register report, you will find it helpful to toggle between Print Preview and Design view using the toolbar but-

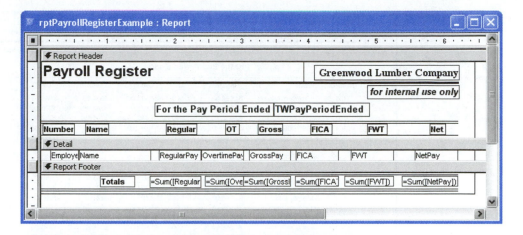

Figure 8.21 The Payroll Register report in Report Design view.

ton or the View menu commands to move between the two views. Of course, the Payroll Register report shown here is only one way to design the report. You can easily customize this report to meet the needs of specific users. The Payroll Register report shown in Figures 8.21 and 8.22 is included in the *Ch08.mdb* file on your Companion CD as *rptPayrollRegisterExample*.

The Employee Earnings Report

The Payroll Register report lists all employees' earnings for one pay period. In contrast, an Employee Earnings report lists one employee's earnings for all pay periods in a year. The Employee Earnings report provides information for unemployment tax calculations and the year-end W-2 form. You will learn how to build an Employee Earnings report for Esther Tufts, who is employee #115 in the Greenwood Lumber Company sample data. You can extend this example to generate similar reports for other employees, for groups of employees, or even for all employees. One way to build the Employee Earnings report is to modify the Payroll Register query and create the Employee Earnings report based on the new query. You will learn how to do the first step, modifying the Payroll Register query, in the next exercise.

EXERCISE 8.21: MODIFYING THE PAYROLL REGISTER TO CREATE AN EMPLOYEE EARNINGS REPORT

1. In the Database window, click the Queries object, click *qryPayrollRegister* to select it, and then click the Design button.
2. To avoid accidentally overwriting your Payroll Register query with the modifications you make here, save the query now under its new name. Select the File, Save As menu command, and enter **qryEmployeeEarnings** as the query's new name; then, click the OK button.

Payroll Register   **Greenwood Lumber Company**

for internal use only

For the Pay Period Ended December 31, 2005

Number	Name	Regular	OT	Gross	FICA	FWT	Net
101	Greenwood, Artemis	$4,928.00	$0.00	$4,928.00	$344.96	$945.60	$3,637.44
102	Greenwood, Ethel Z.	$4,928.00	$0.00	$4,928.00	$344.96	$945.60	$3,637.44
103	Baron, Ethel P.	$1,443.20	$0.00	$1,443.20	$101.02	$312.96	$1,029.22
104	Oppenheim, Cecelia	$1,654.40	$0.00	$1,654.40	$115.80	$210.88	$1,327.72
105	Washington, Ronald	$2,164.80	$0.00	$2,164.80	$151.53	$352.96	$1,660.31
106	Wheeler, Henry X.	$2,710.40	$0.00	$2,710.40	$189.72	$542.08	$1,978.60
107	Surkamp, Elizabeth	$3,942.40	$0.00	$3,942.40	$275.96	$1,122.72	$2,543.72
108	Diamond, Timothy Y	$1,058.00	$0.00	$1,058.00	$74.06	$11.60	$972.34
109	Roche, Max E.	$615.00	$0.00	$615.00	$43.05	$3.00	$568.95
110	Badillo, Lucille B.	$1,754.40	$0.00	$1,754.40	$122.80	$466.32	$1,165.28
111	Ballenger, Judith F.	$3,168.00	$27.00	$3,195.00	$223.65	$958.50	$2,012.85
112	Dewar, Melanie C.	$1,019.20	$0.00	$1,019.20	$71.34	$43.84	$904.02
113	Brown, Alicia K.	$1,431.00	$0.00	$1,431.00	$100.17	$369.30	$961.53
114	Klusky, Irene R.	$1,566.00	$0.00	$1,566.00	$109.62	$273.20	$1,183.18
115	Tufts, Esther L.	$2,838.60	$24.90	$2,863.50	$200.44	$799.05	$1,864.01
116	Thurgood, Margaret	$4,224.00	$0.00	$4,224.00	$295.68	$764.80	$3,163.52
117	Boldway, Michael B.	$1,366.80	$0.00	$1,366.80	$95.67	$410.04	$861.09
118	Fenster, Janice S.	$1,204.00	$0.00	$1,204.00	$84.28	$301.20	$818.52
119	Sherwood, Natalie R	$1,331.20	$0.00	$1,331.20	$93.18	$226.24	$1,011.78
120	Simon, Arlene P.	$3,150.40	$0.00	$3,150.40	$220.52	$945.12	$1,984.76
121	Morris, Anne F.	$850.00	$0.00	$850.00	$59.50	$195.00	$595.50
122	Clark, Carol C.	$1,115.20	$0.00	$1,115.20	$78.06	$63.04	$974.10
123	Smith, Dierdre R.	$3,784.00	$0.00	$3,784.00	$264.88	$676.80	$2,842.32
124	Young, Louise K.	$2,499.20	$0.00	$2,499.20	$174.94	$459.84	$1,864.42
125	Studd, Chester V.	$673.20	$0.00	$673.20	$47.12	$141.96	$484.12
126	Ward, Colleen H.	$2,147.20	$18.30	$2,165.50	$151.58	$649.65	$1,364.27
127	Johnson, Travis D.	$3,168.00	$0.00	$3,168.00	$221.76	$890.40	$2,055.84
128	Gonzales, David G.	$666.00	$0.00	$666.00	$46.62	$19.80	$599.58
129	Quinn, Charles H.	$1,307.20	$0.00	$1,307.20	$91.50	$41.44	$1,174.26
130	Flores, Hector L.	$2,868.80	$0.00	$2,868.80	$200.81	$740.64	$1,927.35
131	Pelligrini, Antonio N.	$2,024.00	$0.00	$2,024.00	$141.68	$324.80	$1,557.52
132	Foster, James R.	$2,622.40	$0.00	$2,622.40	$183.56	$726.72	$1,712.12
133	Schwartz, Harold T.	$4,048.00	$0.00	$4,048.00	$283.36	$1,214.40	$2,550.24
134	Jeffries, Mark T.	$1,276.80	$0.00	$1,276.80	$89.37	$323.04	$864.39
135	Andrej, Arthur R.	$2,851.20	$0.00	$2,851.20	$199.58	$795.36	$1,856.26
136	Klippenger, Steven	$1,584.00	$0.00	$1,584.00	$110.88	$316.80	$1,156.32
137	Beeler, Sheldon O.	$1,734.60	$0.00	$1,734.60	$121.42	$460.38	$1,152.80
138	Patel, Shantu L.	$2,481.60	$0.00	$2,481.60	$173.71	$684.48	$1,623.41
139	Perciavalle, Edward	$2,851.20	$0.00	$2,851.20	$199.58	$330.24	$2,321.38
140	Faumuina, Celestine	$2,205.00	$0.00	$2,205.00	$154.35	$601.50	$1,449.15
141	Ochoa, Raul V.	$4,576.00	$0.00	$4,576.00	$320.32	$1,312.80	$2,942.88
142	Smothers, Karl S.	$3,168.00	$0.00	$3,168.00	$221.76	$950.40	$1,995.84
143	White, Byron D.	$1,601.60	$0.00	$1,601.60	$112.11	$240.32	$1,249.17
144	Chalfonte, Yves M.	$1,708.00	$0.00	$1,708.00	$119.56	$452.40	$1,136.04
145	Applegate, Victor N.	$3,819.20	$0.00	$3,819.20	$267.34	$1,145.76	$2,406.10
146	Blum, Joel B.	$1,179.20	$0.00	$1,179.20	$82.54	$293.76	$802.90
147	Landers, Myra T.	$1,108.80	$0.00	$1,108.80	$77.61	$141.76	$889.43
148	Schumacher, Dirk S.	$1,058.40	$0.00	$1,058.40	$74.08	$257.52	$726.80
149	Forrest, Donald T.	$897.60	$0.00	$897.60	$62.83	$139.52	$695.25
150	Ruvido, Gina C.	$767.00	$0.00	$767.00	$53.69	$110.10	$603.21
	Totals	$109,139.20	$70.20	$109,209.40	$7,644.51	$24,705.64	$76,859.25

Figure 8.22   The printed Payroll Register report.

3. Enter **115** in the first QBE grid Criteria cell to select only the payroll information for that EmployeeNumber record. Access automatically encloses the text in quotation marks when you leave the cell because it examines the underlying table's field properties and finds that the EmployeeNumber field has a Data Type of Text.

4. Delete the #12/31/2005# entry in the second QBE grid Criteria cell. You want to include all of the pay periods in the Employee Earnings report.
5. Enter **Ascending** in the second QBE grid Sort cell.
6. Save your changes, and close the query.

The modified query appears in Figure 8.23. This query will perform the same calculations as the Payroll Register query; however, it will perform the calculations for all of the year's pay periods for one employee. The dynaset that results from running the Employee Earnings query appears in Figure 8.24. The *Ch08.mdb* file included on your Companion CD includes a query object *qryEmployeeEarnings* that you can use as an example to check your work in the preceding exercise.

Now you can build an Employee Earnings report based on *qryEmployeeEarnings*. This report, which you will create in Exercise 8.22, includes a particularly interesting design feature. It uses the Group On property to generate quarterly subtotals.

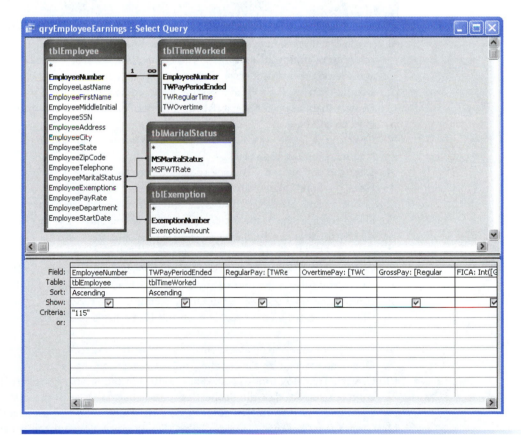

Figure 8.23 Modifying *qryPayrollRegister* to create *qryEmployeeEarnings*.

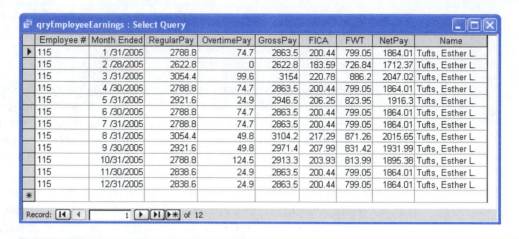

Figure 8.24 The results for the Employee Earnings query.

EXERCISE 8.22: BUILDING *RPTEMPLOYEEEARNINGS* BASED ON *QRYEMPLOYEEEARNINGS*

1. In the Database window, click the Reports object, and then click the New button. Enter or select **qryEmployeeEarnings** in the combo box control in the New Report dialog box, and then double-click Design View in the list box control.
2. Use the Format, Page Header/Footer menu command to delete the Page Header and Footer; then, use the Format, Report Header/Footer menu command to add a Report Header and Footer.
3. Click and drag the right edge of the report's background almost to (but not beyond) the 6.5 inch mark on the top ruler.
4. Click the Sorting and Grouping toolbar button, and enter **TWPayPeriodEnded** as the first Field; the Sort Order will set itself to Ascending. Enter **Yes** for both the Group Header and Group Footer properties, and enter **Qtr** as the Group On property.
5. In the second row of the Field/Expression column, enter **TWPayPeriodEnded** again. Press Alt+F4 to close the Sorting and Grouping dialog box.
6. Click the Field List toolbar button, and then click and drag the following fields to the Detail section: TWPayPeriodEnded, RegularPay, OvertimePay, GrossPay, FICA, FWT, and NetPay. When you release the mouse button, each field will become a text box control with an accompanying label control in the Detail section of the report.
7. Click and drag the EmployeeNumber and Name fields to the Report Header section of the report.
8. Select all of the control labels remaining in the Detail section, and press Ctrl+X to delete them.
9. Open the toolbox by clicking the Toolbox button on the toolbar.
10. Use the Text Box tool to add a new control in the Report Footer section. With the new control selected, click the Properties toolbar button to open the new control's property sheet and enter **=Sum([RegularPay])** as its Control Source property (under the Data tab).
11. Create text box controls with similar =Sum() expressions for the other five calculated fields in the report.

12. Copy and paste the six total-calculating controls from the Report Footer to the TWPayPeriodEnded Footer. When these controls are placed in the group footer, they will compute quarterly subtotals.

Figure 8.25 shows the Employee Earnings report in Report Design view. You can use Figures 8.25 and 8.26 as guides for positioning line objects and arranging controls on the report.

Save the report, entering a name of **rptEmployeeEarnings**, and then close the report. The Employee Earnings report that appears in Figures 8.25 and 8.26 is included in the *Ch08.mdb* file on your Companion CD as *rptEmployeeEarningsExample*. Figure 8.26 shows the Employee Earnings record that *rptEmployeeEarnings* generates for Greenwood Lumber employee Esther Tufts.

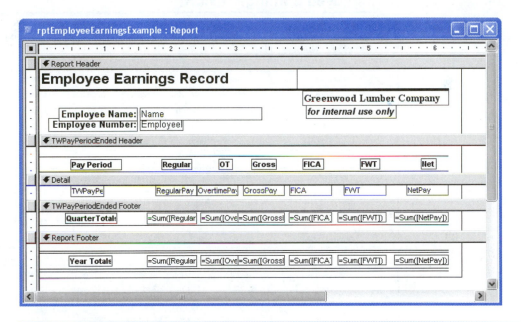

Figure 8.25 The Employee Earnings report in Report Design view.

Printing Payroll Checks

The last payroll cycle report we will discuss in this chapter is the payroll check itself. The payroll check should always include an earnings statement or pay stub that shows how the check was calculated. Payroll registers report payroll details for all employees for one pay period. Employee earnings records show one employee's payroll record for the year. The payroll check is one record from each of these reports.

You can use the same queries you built for the Payroll Register report and the Employee Earnings report to generate payroll checks. For example, you can add employee address fields to the information you already have in the Payroll Register query and build a report based on the query that includes page breaks between each employee record. Such a report would print all of the information Greenwood would need to include on a paycheck. The exact form of payroll checks and earnings statements will vary from firm to firm. Since we have already illustrated many report design techniques in this chapter, you are well equipped to create your own paycheck reports for users or clients.

Employee Earnings Record

Greenwood Lumber Company
for internal use only

Employee Name: Tufts, Esther L.
Employee Number: 115

Pay Period	Regular	OT	Gross	FICA	FWT	Net
1/31/2005	$2,788.80	$74.70	$2,863.50	$200.44	$799.05	$1,864.01
2/28/2005	$2,622.80	$0.00	$2,622.80	$183.59	$726.84	$1,712.37
3/31/2005	$3,054.40	$99.60	$3,154.00	$220.78	$886.20	$2,047.02
QuarterTotals	$8,466.00	$174.30	$8,640.30	$604.81	$2,412.09	$5,623.40

Pay Period	Regular	OT	Gross	FICA	FWT	Net
4/30/2005	$2,788.80	$74.70	$2,863.50	$200.44	$799.05	$1,864.01
5/31/2005	$2,921.60	$24.90	$2,946.50	$206.25	$823.95	$1,916.30
6/30/2005	$2,788.80	$74.70	$2,863.50	$200.44	$799.05	$1,864.01
QuarterTotals	$8,499.20	$174.30	$8,673.50	$607.13	$2,422.05	$5,644.32

Pay Period	Regular	OT	Gross	FICA	FWT	Net
7/31/2005	$2,788.80	$74.70	$2,863.50	$200.44	$799.05	$1,864.01
8/31/2005	$3,054.40	$49.80	$3,104.20	$217.29	$871.26	$2,015.65
9/30/2005	$2,921.60	$49.80	$2,971.40	$207.99	$831.42	$1,931.99
QuarterTotals	$8,764.80	$174.30	$8,939.10	$625.72	$2,501.73	$5,811.65

Pay Period	Regular	OT	Gross	FICA	FWT	Net
0/31/2005	$2,788.80	$124.50	$2,913.30	$203.93	$813.99	$1,895.38
1/30/2005	$2,838.60	$24.90	$2,863.50	$200.44	$799.05	$1,864.01
2/31/2005	$2,838.60	$24.90	$2,863.50	$200.44	$799.05	$1,864.01
QuarterTotals	$8,466.00	$174.30	$8,640.30	$604.81	$2,412.09	$5,623.40

Year Totals	$34,196.00	$697.20	$34,893.20	$2,442.47	$9,747.96	$22,702.77

Figure 8.26 The printed Employee Earnings report.

PAYROLL CYCLE INFORMATION ON THE FINANCIAL STATEMENTS

In this chapter, we have described how to use payroll cycle data to create data tables, track employee and time worked information, calculate payroll, and print a number of useful reports. This section discusses how payroll cycle information appears on firms' financial statements.

Accountants have always tracked the information needed to prepare financial statements and tax returns. Our database approach to developing payroll cycle accounting system elements provides a variety of information that managers can use to make better decisions. However, the database approach also provides everything that accountants need to calculate payroll cycle debits and credits.

Payroll Expense, Accruals, and Payables

The general ledger debit to Payroll Expense is the gross payroll total at the bottom of each payroll period's payroll register. The general ledger credit to Cash is included in the same report. By referring to Figure 8.22, the Payroll Register report for Greenwood Lumber Company, you can prepare the December 31, 2005 journal entry. The necessary numbers appear in that report's totals:

Date	Account	Debit	Credit
Dec. 31, 2005	Payroll Expense	108,886.20	
	FWT Payable		24,617.48
	FICA Payable		7,621.88
	Cash		76,646.84

Since Greenwood Lumber pays on the last day of each month, our example firm conveniently avoids accruing payroll expenses. However, you could calculate Accrued Payroll using the same information you used to calculate payroll in this chapter. For example, if *tblTimeWorked* had included uncompensated time at the end of a reporting period, you could have run *rptPayrollRegister* to obtain the debits and credits for the accrual entry. This entry would be the same as the journal entry to record Payroll Expense except that the last credit in the entry would be to Accrued Payroll Expense or to Payroll Expense Payable instead of to Cash.

Payroll Tax Expense, Accruals, and Payables

Payroll tax calculations all use the current period payroll information included in the payroll register. Many payroll taxes require cumulative information, since the tax is payable only on earnings up to a fixed amount per employee each year. State and federal unemployment taxes are good examples of this type of payroll tax.

Go to http://perry.swlearning.com for an in-depth tutorial.

SUMMARY

In this chapter, you have learned how to use payroll cycle data to track employee and time worked information, calculate payroll, and print employee information reports, time reports, payroll registers, and employee earnings reports. Many of these reports required you to construct queries and use the queries to build reports.

The payroll cycle begins with employee records and time worked records. Periodically, the firm pays employees and calculates payroll. Payroll calculation can be complex; employers must not only multiply pay rate by number of hours worked, but must comply with state and federal withholding regulations. Many firms also arrange to deduct charges for insurance and profit-sharing contributions from employees' pay. Employers must maintain payroll records to comply with numerous government regulations. Finally, accountants prepare financial statements and tax returns from the payroll cycle information.

QUESTIONS AND PROBLEMS FOR REVIEW

Multiple-Choice Questions

1. You can use a report in the payroll cycle to
   a. store time worked data.
   b. store employee pay rates.
   c. calculate payroll deductions.
   d. print a summary of employee earnings.

2. A good primary key for an employee table in a firm that pays fixed monthly salaries would be
   a. employee number.
   b. number of month.
   c. employee number and month.
   d. employee number or month.

3. Payroll cycle activities include all of the following except
   a. keeping employee addresses current.
   b. recording changes in employee pay rates.
   c. calculating overtime pay.
   d. recording employee time billed to clients.

4. To make a data entry form that contains a large number of fields easier to use, a designer might
   a. put the fields in alphabetical or numeric order.
   c. use a sharply contrasting background color.
   c. group related fields together on the form.
   d. specify a tabular form design in the Forms Wizard.

5. To prevent an unintentional violation of state minimum wage laws, a designer who is creating an employee data entry form could
   a. set the Input Mask property of the EmployeePayRate text box control to an appropriate limit.
   b. set the Validation Rule property of the EmployeePayRate text box control to an appropriate limit.
   c. set the OnUpdate property of the EmployeePayRate text box control to an appropriate limit.
   d. any of the above.

6. The EmployeeDepartment field in *tblEmployee* is a
   a. lookup key.
   b. primary key.
   c. foreign key.
   d. relationship key.

7. A payroll register lists
   a. all wages paid to a single employee for the year.
   b. wages paid to all employees in a single pay period.
   c. all employees who received wages within the past year.
   d. accrued vacation time for all employees.

8. The *qryTimeWorked* object that is described in this chapter could be used to identify
   a. employees who worked excessive overtime.
   b. employees who worked no overtime.
   c. employees who are eligible for retirement.
   d. departments that had excessive overtime.

9. A good way to handle multiple calculations in Access reports that are based on queries is to
   a. perform the horizontal calculations in the query and the vertical calculations in the report.
   b. perform the vertical calculations in the query and the horizontal calculations in the report.
   c. perform all calculations in the query and use the report tools to make the report look better.
   d. perform all calculations in the report and use the query to gather the underlying information from the tables.

10. When recording a period's payroll, the debit to Payroll Expense is always
    a. the same as the credit to Cash.
    b. less than the credit to Cash.
    c. greater than the credit to Cash.
    d. equal to the credit to Cash plus the total debits for all payroll taxes (such as state and federal unemployment taxes).

Discussion Questions

1. If you wanted to add employees to whom you pay a percentage commission to the payroll system described in this chapter, you would need to store the commission rate in a table. Discuss which table(s) you might use and why.

2. Describe how you could modify *tblTimeWorked* to include hourly time records. What would be primary key candidates for the modified table?

3. Why are the purchase cycle and the payroll cycle often discussed separately?

4. How could you modify the time worked by department report to make it more useful to Greenwood Lumber managers?

5. Discuss the advantages and disadvantages of storing employee names in *tblEmployee* in three parts.

Practice Exercises

Note: Before doing any of the following practice exercises, first copy *Ch08.mdb* from your Companion CD to the hard drive of the computer on which you are working. Then, clear the copied database's Read-only file attribute (see Chapter 1, Exercise 1.14, Clearing a File's Read-Only Property). Having done that, you can complete each exercise using the copy of the Companion CD database.

1. Write a query that independently verifies the gross pay calculation that *qryGrossPay* performs. You can use the queries in *Ch08.mdb* as a starting point for your query design.

2. Create a report that uses the tables in *Ch08.mdb* to print a payroll check and earnings statement for one employee.

3. Add any necessary tables to *Ch08.mdb* and revise *qryNetPay* to include a deduction for medical insurance. Clearly state any assumptions you must make to accomplish this task.

4. Modify *Ch08.mdb* to include employees that earn a fixed salary each pay period. (Hint: Think of the salary as a pay rate and the pay period as a unit of time worked.)

5. Modify the payroll register report in *Ch08.mdb* so that it displays only the summary information that Greenwood Lumber Company needs to prepare its general ledger entry for payroll each month.

Problems

Note: Before doing any of the following problems, first copy *Ch08.mdb* from your Companion CD to the hard drive of the computer on which you are working. Then, clear the copied database's Read-only file attribute (see Chapter 1, Exercise 1.14, Clearing a File's Read-Only Property). Having done that, you can complete each exercise using the copy of the Companion CD database.

1. Garcia Intermodal Transport (GIT) is a freight and distribution company that operates local delivery trucks and long-distance tractor-trailer rigs from its location in El Paso, Texas. GIT would like you to design an Access database that it can use to manage its payroll function. The company has 30 employees who perform a wide variety of functions. All of GIT's employees are qualified to operate all of the company's vehicles, and all are qualified to drive interstate and international routes. Employees also perform dispatch, truck loading and unloading, and administrative work. GIT pays its employees every week based on the work they have completed through Friday of that week. Because all employees are capable of all job functions in the business, and because the value of the work performed depends on the function performed, GIT pays a rate based on the work performed rather than paying each employee a set pay rate for all work performed. The company has pay rates for local driving, interstate driving, international driving, dispatch, truck loading/unloading, and administrative work. List the entities that exist in the GIT payroll cycle. State any assumptions you believe are necessary.

2. Refer to the GIT case described in Problem 1, and create a diagram similar to that shown in Figure 8.1 for the restaurant. The diagram should show the entities you identified in Problem 1 along with the relationships between those entities and their cardinalities.

3. Refer to the GIT case described in Problem 1 and the work you did in Problem 2. Use Access to build the tables and create the relationships you have defined. Populate the tables with sample data that you create, and test the tables to make certain that the relationships operate to enforce referential integrity as appropriate.

4. Refer to the work you have done in the preceding three problems. Create data entry forms for the GIT payroll cycle database that allow you to enter data into every table without opening the table itself. You can use the forms in the *Ch08.mdb* database as guides.

5. Refer to the work you have done in the preceding four problems. Create reports for the GIT payroll database as follows:
   a. Create queries that calculate gross pay and net pay.
   b. Create a payroll register report.
   c. Create an employee earnings report.
   d. Create any additional reports that your instructor assigns.

CHAPTER 9
Production Cycle

OBJECTIVES

The production cycle includes all activities that convert raw materials, labor, and overhead into finished products. Therefore, some accountants call this cycle the conversion cycle. The production cycle accounting system must trace or allocate manufacturing costs to products produced. It also must provide managers with information they can use to monitor the manufacturing process. It must also provide financial accountants with information they can use to value inventories and determine the cost of goods sold. This chapter will show you how to use Microsoft Access tables, queries, forms, and reports to:

- Track materials cost.
- Track labor cost.
- Allocate manufacturing overhead cost.
- Create a bill of materials.
- Accumulate costs in a job order cost system.
- Summarize and report job costs.

This chapter also explains how you can adapt the job order cost system examples presented here to build process, hybrid, and activity-based cost systems. Our discussion of the production cycle assumes that you have studied the purchase cycle in Chapter 7 and the payroll cycle in Chapter 8. You will learn how to modify some of the tables you created as you worked through those chapters. You can combine those modified tables with new tables, forms, queries, and reports to build the production cycle system components in this chapter.

INTRODUCTION

This chapter shows how to use Microsoft Access to create the elements of production cycle accounting systems. Although many accounting textbooks use manufacturing firms to illustrate the production cycle, a growing number of service firms now examine their business processes using a product costing approach. In this approach, a service firm identifies specific components of the services it offers, then tracks and allocates costs to those service components—just as a manufacturing firm tracks and allocates costs to the products it creates. Some merchandising firms also track and allocate costs to specific product lines or customers. Thus, the techniques you learn in this chapter will help you design accounting systems for all three types of firms, even though we will use a manufacturing company for the example.

In Chapter 7 you learned how to record the cost of materials purchased. In Chapter 8 you learned how to record the cost of paying employees. In this chapter you will learn how to combine materials and labor costs with other manufacturing costs to determine the total cost of manufactured products. You will modify some of the Chapter 7 and 8 database objects as you work through this chapter. First, however, you need to understand the different ways that firms can accumulate costs in the production cycle.

COST ACCUMULATION APPROACHES

The goal of the production cycle accounting system is to assign costs to cost objects. If a firm is manufacturing airplanes, the ultimate cost object is an airplane. If a firm is manufacturing tomato soup, the ultimate cost object is a can of tomato soup. However, most production cost systems do not allocate costs directly to the ultimate cost object. Instead, they use a three-step approach:

1. Assign costs to intermediate-level cost objects.
2. Assign the intermediate-level cost objects to higher-level cost objects.
3. Assign higher-level cost objects to ultimate cost objects.

Logical intermediate-level cost objects for particular industries or product lines fall into two general categories: jobs and departments. The nature of the manufacturing process usually dictates which category of intermediate-level cost object is appropriate. Therefore, the nature of the manufacturing process typically determines which cost accumulation approach a firm will use.

Firms that manufacture different types or quantities of products use a job order cost accumulation system. The intermediate-level cost objects in job order cost systems are jobs. Firms that manufacture one product or similar types of products that require the same processes and the same mix of labor and overhead use process cost accumulation systems. The intermediate-level cost objects in process cost systems are departments.

Job Order Cost Accumulation

Firms that produce many different products use *job* as the intermediate-level cost object in their cost accumulation systems. They break down their production processes into jobs, accumulate costs by job, and then divide each job's cost by the number of units in each job to determine the cost of each unit. A job order system uses job numbers to track direct costs. Each raw materials inventory item that goes into production is assigned a job number. Each hour or other unit of labor is assigned a job number. Indirect manufacturing overhead costs are allocated to jobs using some rational allocation base, such as direct labor hours or machine hours. Figure 9.1 shows the job order approach to cost accumulation.

Note that the ultimate cost object, such as *Unit* in Figure 9.1, can be a direct material item with respect to a subsequent job or process. For example, if the task represented in Figure 9.1 was to manufacture computer keyboards, the cost of each unit would include the direct materials, direct labor, and manufacturing overhead cost of one keyboard. If the firm were to then use these keyboards to build computers, the keyboard units would become a direct material in the computer assembly job.

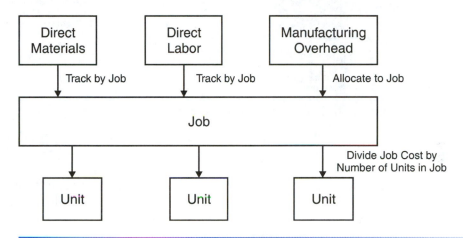

Figure 9.1 Job order cost accumulation.

Process Cost Accumulation

Firms that produce one product or similar products using the same manufacturing processes use *department* as the intermediate-level cost object in their cost accumulation systems. They organize their production processes by departments and accumulate costs by department. To obtain unit cost, they divide each department's monthly total cost by the number of units the department manufactured that month. Therefore, a process cost system uses department numbers to track direct costs. Each raw materials inventory item that enters production is tracked to a specific department.

Some firms assign employees to particular departments. Other firms track each employee-hour worked to a specific department. Firms that use process cost systems allocate indirect manufacturing overhead costs to departments using some rational allocation base. Two common allocation bases are direct labor hours and machine hours. Figure 9.2 describes the process approach to cost accumulation.

The ultimate cost objects in process cost systems, such as *Unit* in Figure 9.2, can be direct materials to a subsequent department. For example, if the job that is diagrammed in Figure 9.2 involved the manufacture of plastic soda bottles, the cost of each unit would include the direct material, direct labor, and manufacturing overhead cost of one bottle. If the firm were to fill these bottles with soda in a subsequent department, the bottles would be accounted for as a direct material in the bottle-filling department.

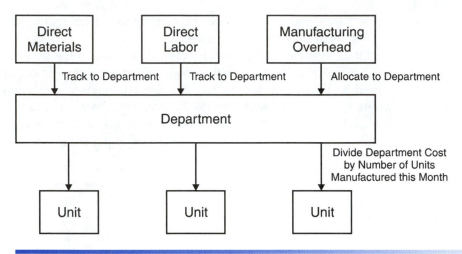

Figure 9.2 Process cost accumulation.

Hybrid Cost Accumulation

Some firms produce similar products using the same manufacturing processes yet different materials in different batches. For example, a clothing manufacturer may make cotton shirts and silk shirts. The manufacturing processes of cutting, sewing, and attaching buttons is similar for both kinds of shirts. However, the cost of cotton and silk differ considerably. *Department* would be an ineffective intermediate-level cost object for accumulating materials costs—since cloth costs would not be traced to specific batches, all shirts manufactured in a month would have the same cost.

The solution to this problem is a *hybrid cost system*. The clothing manufacturer can track the cost of direct materials by batch using a job order approach and can track direct labor and overhead costs by department using a process approach. The job order part of the cost system would track the direct materials cost for each shirt in each batch. The process part of the cost system would track labor and allocate overhead cost for each shirt of either kind manufactured during the month. This particular hybrid system of using a job order approach for direct materials and a process approach for direct labor and manufacturing overhead is called *operation costing*.

Implications for Production Cycle Accounting Systems

Choosing between job order, process, and hybrid cost accumulation systems is an essential part of production cycle system design. The system must match the nature of the manufacturing process.

Firms that produce a variety of products or provide a variety of services use job order costing systems. These firms need a way to track costs as they flow in different amounts to different customized products or services. Examples of firms that typically use job order costing include aircraft manufacturers, auto repair shops, hospitals, and public accounting firms.

Process costing is the choice of firms that make one or only a few different products that are homogeneous in design and resource use. These firms do essentially the same things the same way every month. Examples of firms that typically use process costing include oil refineries, cement manufacturers, and some chemical manufacturers.

Operation costing is a blend of job order and process costing. Firms that use operation costing have some costs that flow evenly and regularly into their products or services and other costs that vary significantly by job, customer, or production batch. Examples of firms that use operation costing include jewelry manufacturers, garment manufacturers, luggage manufacturers, and auto manufacturers.

Although the meaning of information contained in reports and queries will vary with the accumulation system, table and form designs are surprisingly consistent across system types. In a job order system, all costs are traced or allocated using a job number. In a process system, all costs are traced or allocated using a department number. In both systems, tables and data entry forms must accommodate a number, but the design of the tables and forms is the same whether the number is a job number or a department number.

In this chapter, you will work with a job order cost system example to learn about production cycle accounting system elements; however, remember that you can substitute *department number* for *job number* in a production cycle database design to convert a job order accumulation system to a process accumulation system.

COST TRACING VERSUS COST ALLOCATION

Traditionally, accountants have divided manufacturing costs into two categories: direct and indirect. *Direct costs* are costs that accountants can easily track through the manufacturing process to ultimate cost objects. Accountants usually classify raw materials and labor costs of employees that work in the manufacturing process as direct costs—using the terms *direct materials* and *direct labor*, respectively. All other manufacturing costs are classified as *indirect* and referred to as *manufacturing overhead*.

Manufacturing Overhead Allocation

Manufacturing overhead includes all indirect manufacturing costs. Some raw materials costs are not significant enough to warrant the effort and expense of tracking them to jobs or departments. These indirect materials costs are part of manufacturing overhead. The labor costs of employees that do not work directly in the manufacturing process—such as maintenance, materials handling, and supervisory employees—are considered to be indirect labor and included in manufacturing overhead. All other manufacturing costs—for example, insurance, rent, supplies, and utilities—are also included in manufacturing overhead.

To smooth out fluctuations in manufacturing overhead acquisition that might distort product costs, accountants have long followed a practice of normalizing manufacturing overhead costs. The most common normalization procedure is to apply manufacturing overhead costs using a predetermined overhead rate. This normalization procedure requires four steps:

1. Estimate the manufacturing overhead cost for the year.
2. Estimate usage of some activity base that is related to overhead consumption for the year. Common bases include direct labor hours, machine hours, and direct labor cost.
3. Divide the estimated manufacturing overhead cost by an estimate of activity base usage to obtain a predetermined overhead rate.
4. Each period, multiply the predetermined overhead rate by the actual amount of the activity base used in that period by each job or department.

Note that the manufacturing overhead cost for each job or department will vary with the amount of the activity base it consumes during the period. This approach to allocating manufacturing overhead is a *volume-based approach*, since the quantity of the activity base consumed by a particular job or department usually varies with its volume of production.

Activity-Based Costing

The volume-based approach to allocating manufacturing overhead has been criticized because it can lead to product cost distortions. An alternative procedure for allocating manufacturing costs is to measure activities and track costs for those activities. To perform this activity-based costing procedure, a firm follows four steps:

1. Track individual manufacturing process activities.
2. Record the costs of those activities.
3. Divide the activity cost by a physical measure of the activity to obtain the cost per activity unit.
4. Multiply the cost per activity unit times the quantity of the activity used by the job or department.

Note that these four steps are very similar to those in the normalization process we described earlier. In production cycle systems terms, activity-based costing simply adds another intermediate-level cost object to the cost flow. Figure 9.3 shows the job order cost accumulation system modified to include activity-based cost allocation.

The two activities tracked in this system are machine setups and repairs. This system identifies machine setup and repair costs in the manufacturing overhead cost pool. These identified costs are then traced to the specific activity. Finally, using the number of setups and repair hours that each job requires, the activity costs are allocated to specific jobs. Note that other manufacturing overhead costs are still allocated using direct labor hours or machine hours. Even with activity-based costing, firms still have some manufacturing overhead costs that they cannot trace to specific activities.

Implications for Production Cycle Accounting Systems

Normalizing manufacturing overhead requires the accounting system to do double duty. The system must track the actual overhead costs and the applied overhead costs. Fortunately, you have already created a system for recording and paying actual costs in

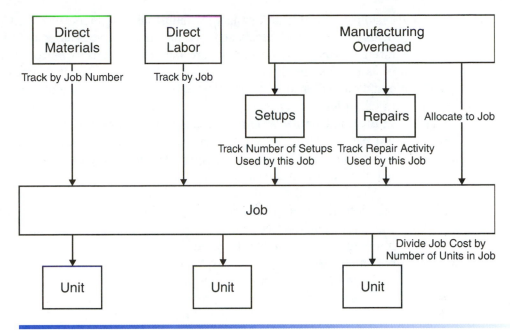

Figure 9.3 Activity-based job order cost system.

Chapter 7. Although you built a direct materials acquisition system in the Chapter 7 purchase cycle example, those system elements require only minor modifications to record actual manufacturing overhead costs. You also built a system to record actual labor costs in Chapter 8. In this chapter, you will learn how to add the overhead allocation element to a database accounting system.

Activity-based costing does not change the nature of cost allocation; it merely adds another layer to the allocation process. Therefore, you can easily extend the examples in this chapter to perform activity-based costing. All you need to do is replicate the cost tracking and allocation systems for each activity center in the system. For example, the cost system you will build in this chapter allocates manufacturing overhead cost using direct labor hours. You could add activity centers for machine setups and repairs to this system by building two additional tables to track machine setups and repair hours by job number. Similarly, you could extend this chapter's job order system to allocate overhead using separate rates for each department instead of one rate for all departments.

ELECTRIC CONTROLS COMPANY PURCHASE CYCLE INFORMATION

In this chapter, you will learn how to build the components of a production cycle system for Electric Controls Company, the firm for which you developed a purchasing cycle system in Chapter 7. As you may recall, Electric Controls Company manufactures custom electric control panels for industrial customers. Electric Controls buys components of the control panels and then has its employees assemble them. In this manufacturing process, overhead costs are incurred. Electric Controls applies these overhead costs to jobs based on direct labor. Thus, Electric Controls tracks the direct materials and direct labor to jobs and allocates overhead to those jobs. This is a typical approach in job order cost systems.

Electric Controls Company creates a job record for each control panel or set of control panels that a customer orders. It uses a bill of materials form to organize the direct materials items that are used on each job. Employees record the number of hours that they work on each job.

The data model for Electric Controls Company production cycle includes six entities: job, finished goods, customer, direct materials, time worked (direct labor), and employee. Each job can have many direct materials items and can have many entries in the time worked table. Each entry in the time worked table only has one employee, but an employee can have many time entries in the time worked table. Each job is dedicated to producing a particular type of finished goods item; however, a particular type of finished goods item can be produced in many different jobs. Similarly, each job creates an item for one customer, but a customer may order items that require many jobs.

Although manufacturing overhead is applied to jobs in this system, it does not need its own table. Once an application rate is calculated, the amount of direct labor a job uses determines the manufacturing overhead that will be applied to that job. You will learn how to do this overhead application using a query later in this chapter. The data model for Electric Controls Company production cycle, showing these six entities and the one-to-many and many-to-many relationships among them, appears in Figure 9.4.

The remainder of this chapter will show you how to build elements of the accounting system for Electric Controls' production cycle. The design will include six tables—one for each entity—and one additional table to model the many-to-many relationship. You will learn how to create forms to enter data efficiently, queries that calculate job costs, and reports that Electric Controls can use to print information about jobs and their costs.

TRACING AND ALLOCATING MANUFACTURING COSTS

Since Electric Controls wants to trace and allocate manufacturing costs to jobs, it will need a table in which to store the individual job records. Each job record will include those direct materials, direct labor, and manufacturing overhead costs that are related to it. Direct materials and direct labor each require a separate table because cost systems track these specific cost flows. Manufacturing overhead does not require its own table, because it is an allocated cost.

Although Electric Controls' system is a job order cost system, you can use the same database components in a process accumulation system. You need only substitute *department number* for *job number*. You can also use these system components to perform activity-based costing by adding an additional table for each activity that the system must track or allocate.

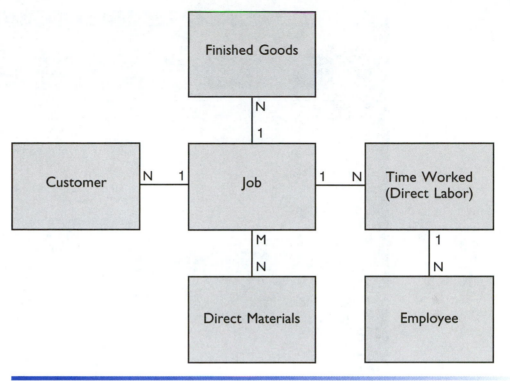

Figure 9.4 Electric Controls Company production cycle data model.

The Job Table

The Job table must have a primary key field that uniquely identifies each job. The Job table must also include fields to store important job dates and foreign key fields that will be different for each firm. For example, one firm may want to relate each job to the customer that ordered the job. You could build such a relationship by including a CustomerNumber foreign key field in the Job table that links to the primary key in the Customer table. Other firms might run jobs as production for inventory rather than for specific customers. These firms would want you to include an InventoryItemCode foreign key field in the Job table that would establish a link to the primary key in the Finished Goods Inventory table. Some firms might use both foreign key links.

Since you have already learned how to build Customer and Inventory tables in Chapter 7, we will not repeat that information here. However, we have included *tblCustomer* and *tblFinishedGoodsInventory* for Electric Controls Company in the *Ch09.mdb* file on your Companion CD. These two tables appear in Datasheet view on the Access desktop in Figure 9.5. They contain sample data that you can use as you create forms, queries, and reports for Electric Controls in this chapter's examples.

In Exercise 9.1 you will build a Job table that will work with the Finished Goods Inventory table and the Customer table in the production cycle. You should have Access running with the Database window open as you begin this exercise.

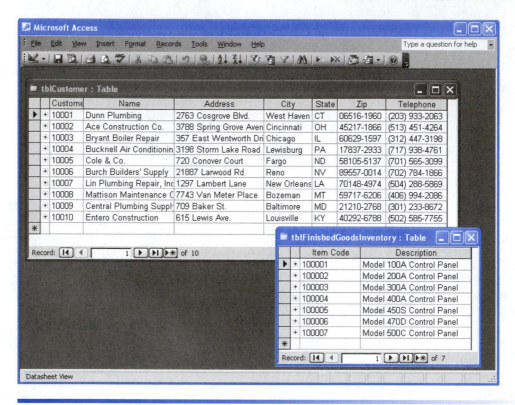

Figure 9.5 The Customer and Finished Goods Inventory tables in Datasheet view.

EXERCISE 9.1: BUILDING A JOB TABLE

1. To build the Job table, select the Insert, Table menu command, and double-click Design View in the New Table dialog box.

2. Enter **JobNumber** in the first row of the Field Name column, and leave its Data Type set to Text. Click the Primary Key toolbar button. Enter a Field Size property of **4**, an Input Mask property of **0000**, and a Caption property of **Job #**

3. Enter **JobOrderDate** in the second row of the Field Name column, and enter a Data Type of **Date/Time**. Enter **99/99/0000;0;_** as the JobOrderDate field's Input Mask property, and enter **Order Date** as its Caption property.

4. Enter **JobCompletionDate** in the third row of the Field Name column, and enter a Data Type of **Date/Time** for that field. Enter **99/99/0000;0;_** as its Input Mask property and **Completion Date** as its Caption property. The JobCompletionDate field will store the expected completion date for each job. Many firms also record an actual completion date to use in generating performance reports.

5. To create the foreign key links to *tblCustomer* and *tblFinishedGoodsInventory*, you can add two fields that match these tables' primary key fields. Enter **CustomerNumber** in the fourth row of the Field Name column, and leave its Data Type set to Text. Set its Field Size property to **5**, its Input Mask property to **00000**, and its Caption property to **Customer #**

6. Enter a Field Name of **InventoryItemCode** in the fifth row, and leave its Data Type set to Text.

tblJob : Table

Job #	Order Date	Completion Date	Customer #	Item Code
1001	12/1 /2005	12/26/2005	10006	100004
1002	12/2 /2005	12/30/2005	10003	100007
1003	12/2 /2005	1 /6 /2006	10002	100003
1004	12/3 /2005	1 /15/2006	10009	100001
1005	12/4 /2005	1 /14/2006	10007	100006

Record: 1 of 5

Figure 9.6 The *tblJob* records.

7. Set the InventoryItemCode Field Size property to **6**, its Input Mask property to **000000**, and its Caption property to **Item Code**

Note that you cannot enforce referential integrity on either of the links from these two foreign key fields to their entity tables unless you know that every job will have a customer and a finished goods inventory item code when the job is entered. Save the Job table you have just completed, entering *tblJob* as the table's name in the Save As dialog box. The *Ch09.mdb* file on your Companion CD contains a version of *tblJob* that includes the job records shown in Figure 9.6.

You will use these sample job records in queries and reports later in this chapter. Note that the five jobs in *tblJob* include two that were completed in December and three that continue into January.

The Direct Materials Inventory Table

To track the cost of direct materials, you will need to build a table much like the Materials Inventory table you created and used in Chapter 7 to record materials purchases. In the Chapter 7 purchase cycle system, you stored the cost of each inventory item in the Purchase Order-Materials Inventory table. This design allowed the system to record different costs for the same inventory items purchased from different vendors, or from the same vendors purchased at different times.

In this chapter, we focus on tracing direct materials costs into production. To simplify our example here, you will include the cost of direct materials in the Direct Materials Inventory table. Although a discussion of standard cost systems is beyond the scope of this book, such systems also store the standard cost of each direct materials item in a Direct Materials Inventory table.

Since the Direct Materials Inventory table is so similar to the Materials Inventory table we created in Chapter 7, you can save some work by modifying that table to make a Direct Materials Inventory table instead of starting all over. You can import a copy of the Materials Inventory table from the *Ch07.mdb* file using the procedure you learned earlier in this book.

After you have imported a copy of *tblMaterialsInventory*, it will appear as a Tables object in the *Ch09.mdb* Database window. In Exercise 9.2, you will modify this table for use in the production cycle.

EXERCISE 9.2: CONVERTING *TBLMATERIALSINVENTORY* TO *TBLDIRECTMATERIALSINVENTORY*

1. In the Database window, click the Tables object, and click *tblMaterialsInventory*. Press Ctrl+C to make a copy of the table.
2. Press Ctrl+V to paste the copy of the table. Enter **tblDirectMaterialsInventory** as the Table Name in the Paste Table As dialog box. Be sure the Structure and Data option button is selected in the Paste Options section, and then click OK.
3. Select *tblDirectMaterialsInventory* in the Database window, and click the Design button to open the table in Design view.
4. Change the names of the three fields to **DMStockNumber**, **DMCategory**, and **DMDescription**, respectively.
5. In the fourth row of the Field Name column, enter **DMCost**
6. Set the new field's Data Type to **Currency**, its Decimal Places property to **2**, and its Caption property to **DM Cost**
7. Select View, Datasheet View to open the table in Datasheet view. Click Yes when prompted to save the changes you have made thus far to the table.
8. In Datasheet view, the table should display values in the first three fields. You can enter the DMCost values using Figure 9.7 as a guide. The *Ch09.mdb* file on your Companion CD includes a version of *tblDirectMaterialsInventory* that includes the sample job records shown in Figure 9.7.
9. Select File, Close to close the table.

Now you have a Job table with a record for each job and a Direct Materials Inventory table with a record for each materials inventory item that Electric Controls Company might use in a particular job. To link these two tables and track the direct materials used on each job, you need a relationship table, the Job-Direct Materials Inventory table.

		Stock #	Category	Description	DM Cost
▶	+	101	Sheet metal	1/8" Steel 4x4 sheet	$8.45
	+	102	Switch	DPDT 240v 100a	$14.96
	+	103	Wire	500' Copper #22AWG	$16.95
	+	104	Sheet metal	1/4" Steel 4x4 sheet	$14.95
	+	105	Switch	SPDT 240v 100a	$9.47
	+	106	Relay	SPDT 120v 40a Silver	$32.89
	+	107	Circuit breaker	240v 40a	$10.27
	+	108	Relay	TPST 240v 100a Mercury	$18.96
	+	109	Sheet metal	1/8" Aluminum 4x4 sheet	$12.68
	+	110	Wire	500' Copper Twin #18AWG	$27.98
	+	111	Connector	F 240v 100a solderless	$3.57
	+	112	Switch	DPST 240v 50a	$8.66
	+	113	Connector	M 120v 40a clip	$1.98
	+	114	Sheet metal	1/4" Aluminum 4x4 sheet	$19.49
	+	115	Circuit breaker	120v 40a	$6.95
*					$0.00

tblDirectMaterialsInventory : Table

Record: 1 of 15

Figure 9.7 The populated Direct Materials Inventory table in Datasheet view.

The Job-Direct Materials Inventory Table

Since each job can include many different direct materials and each direct materials item can be used in many different jobs, the Job table and the Direct Materials Inventory table have a many-to-many relationship. The Job-Direct Materials Inventory table is the relationship table that models this relation. The composite primary key for this relationship table will require two fields, the primary key fields of the two entity tables: the Job table and the Direct Materials Inventory table. The table also needs a field to store the quantity of each inventory item used on each job. In the next exercise you will build the Job-Direct Materials Inventory table for the production cycle.

EXERCISE 9.3: BUILDING A JOB-DIRECT MATERIALS INVENTORY TABLE

1. With the Database window open, select Insert, Table from the menu, and then double-click Design View.
2. Enter the name of *tblJob*'s primary key field, **JobNumber**, as the first Field Name. Leave its Data Type set to Text and set its Field Size to **4**. Remember, when using entity table primary keys as part of the composite primary key in a relationship table, you always want to match Data Type and Field Size exactly.
3. Set JobNumber's Input Mask property to **0000**, its Caption property to **Job #**, and its Indexed property to **Yes (Duplicates OK)**
4. Enter **DMStockNumber** in the second row of the Field Name column. Leave its Data Type set to Text. Set its Field Size property to **3**, its Input Mask property to **000**, its Caption property to **Stock #**, and its Indexed property to **Yes (Duplicates OK)**
5. While pressing the Ctrl key, select both fields by clicking the row selectors for each field. With both fields selected, click the Primary Key toolbar button. The Primary key symbol should appear in the row selectors of both fields.
6. The third field will store the quantity of each materials item used on each job. Enter **JobDMQuantity** on the third Field Name line. Set its Data Type to **Number** and its Caption property to **Quantity**
7. Select the File, Save As menu command. Type **tblJob-DirectMaterialsInventory** as the name for your new table in the Save As dialog box.
8. Select the File, Close menu command to close the table.

A copy of this table that includes the sample records you will use later in this chapter is included as *tblJob-DirectMaterialsInventory* in *Ch09.mdb* on your Companion CD. To ensure that any JobNumber value entered in the Job-Direct Materials Inventory table exists in *tblJob*, you can establish referential integrity between *tblJob-DirectMaterialsInventory* and *tblJob* on the JobNumber field. You can also ensure that each record in *tblJob-DirectMaterialsInventory* refers to an existing materials stock number by establishing referential integrity with *tblDirectMaterialsInventory* on the DMStockNumber field. To create these two links and enforce referential integrity on them, follow the steps in Exercise 9.4. To begin the exercise, you should close all tables and have the Database window open on the desktop.

EXERCISE 9.4: LINKING JOB AND DIRECT MATERIALS RECORDS

1. Click the Relationships toolbar button to open the Relationships window and the Show Table dialog box.
2. Double-click *tblDirectMaterialsInventory*, *tblJob*, and *tblJob-DirectMaterialsInventory* to place them in the Relationships window. Close the Show Table dialog box.
3. Click and drag the JobNumber field in *tblJob* to the JobNumber field in *tblJob-DirectMaterialsInventory*. Click the Enforce Referential Integrity check box, and then click the Create button.
4. Click and drag the DMStockNumber field in *tblDirectMaterialsInventory* to the DMStockNumber field in *tblJob-DirectMaterialsInventory*.
5. Click the Enforce Referential Integrity check box, and then click the Create button.
6. The Relationship window showing these links appears in Figure 9.8. To return to the Database window, select the File, Close menu command. Click the Yes button to save your changes to the Relationships layout.

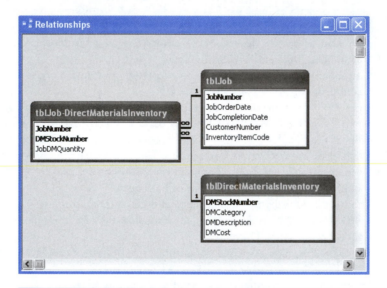

Figure 9.8   Creating referential integrity links for *tblJob-DirectMaterialsInventory*.

The Bill of Materials Form

Many firms use a *bill of materials* to organize the list of direct materials for each job. We can use this idea to create a form that will make entering records into *tblJob-DirectMaterialsInventory* easier and less prone to error. The Bill of Materials form is fairly complex. It must write records to *tblJob-DirectMaterialsInventory* and read records from:

- *tblJob*—to obtain the job order and completion dates.
- *tblDirectMaterialsInventory*—to obtain the category, description, and cost of each materials item.

- *tblCustomer*—to obtain the customer name.
- *tblFinishedGoodsInventory*—to obtain the description of the finished goods inventory item that the job produces.

Since the Bill of Materials form will read data from *tblCustomer* and *tblDirectMaterialsInventory*, it is very important to have data in these tables before you build the form. If you have not entered data in these tables yet, you can copy the sample records from the tables that we have included in the *Ch09.mdb* file on your Companion CD.

You will use the Bill of Materials form to enter job information simultaneously in both *tblJob* and *tblJob-DirectMaterialsInventory*. As you have seen in earlier chapters, Access handles this task best with a form-subform design. In this Bill of Materials form design, you will link *tblJob* to *tblCustomer* in the main form section. The link from *tblJob-DirectMaterialsInventory*, the relationship table, to *tblDirectMaterialsInventory* will occur in the subform section.

Since you have had experience working with complex forms in Chapters 7 and 8, you will not use the Form Wizard to construct this form. Instead, you will learn how to build a form-subform combination from blank forms. When you build complex forms in Access, you should always create the subform first. If you have a multiple subform design, you should start with the most deeply nested subform. In Exercise 9.5, you will create the query behind the Bill of Materials subform.

EXERCISE 9.5: BUILDING THE BILL OF MATERIALS SUBFORM QUERY

1. Click the Forms object in the Database window, and then click the New button. Enter *tblJob-DirectMaterialsInventory* in the combo box control of the New Form dialog box; then double-click Design View in the list box control.
2. Select the View, Form Header/Footer menu command.
3. Select the Edit, Select Form menu command.
4. Click the Properties toolbar button, click the Data tab in the form's property sheet, and then click the Record Source property's Build button. Click Yes to open the form's Query Builder window.
5. Click the Show Table toolbar button, and then double-click *tblDirectMaterialsInventory*. Click the Close button. The Direct Materials Inventory table, linked on DMStockNumber to *tblJob-DirectMaterialsInventory*, should now appear in the top section of the Query Builder window.
6. Click and drag the JobNumber field from *tblJob-DirectMaterialsInventory* to the first QBE grid Field cell; then, set its Sort order to **Ascending**
7. Click and drag the DMStockNumber field from *tblJob-DirectMaterialsInventory* to the second QBE grid Field cell; then, set its Sort order to **Ascending**
8. Click and drag the JobDMQuantity field from *tblJob-DirectMaterialsInventory* to the next open QBE grid Field cell.
9. Enter **Description: [DMCategory] & " - " & [DMDescription]** in the next open QBE grid Field cell (you may want to press Shift+F2 to open the Zoom box to make entering this expression easier).

10. Click and drag the DMCost field from *tblDirectMaterialsInventory* to the next open QBE grid Field cell.

11. Close the Query Builder window, and save your changes.

Figure 9.9 shows the Bill of Materials subform query in the Query Builder window Design view.

The Bill of Materials subform should be open in Design view as you begin the next exercise.

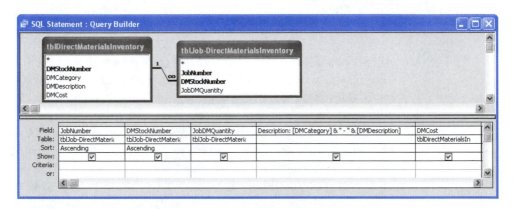

Figure 9.9   The Bill of Materials subform query.

EXERCISE 9.6: COMPLETING THE BILL OF MATERIALS SUBFORM

1. Click the Field List toolbar button; then click and drag the DMStockNumber, JobDMQuantity, Description, and DMCost fields to the Detail section of the form.

2. Using Figure 9.10 as a guide, arrange the controls and labels on the form.

3. You can also change the form and control appearance properties as shown in the figure. Remember to set the Enabled, Locked, and Tab Stop properties for the Description and DMCost controls to prevent users from changing values in those fields.

4. Save the subform by choosing the menu command File, Save As. Enter a name of **fsubBillOfMaterials** for the form.

5. Select File, Close from the menu to close the form.

In the next two exercises, you will build the main part of the Bill of Materials form. Since you have gained considerable experience in designing and building forms as you worked through the exercises in the earlier chapters of this book, we encourage you to use your own ideas as you create this form. We have provided an example form for your reference on the Companion CD, but we do encourage you to use this exercise to practice your form-building skills.

To have the form automatically look up the CustomerName when a user enters a CustomerNumber, you must include *tblCustomer* in the form's design and make the CustomerName field available to the form. You will also need to include

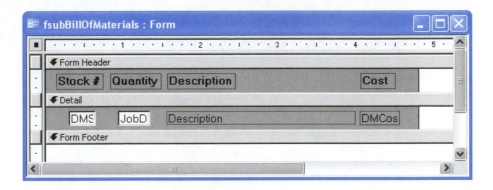

Figure 9.10 The Bill of Materials subform in Design view.

tblFinishedGoodsInventory and make its InventoryDescription field available to the form so the form can display the description of the item being manufactured on the job. The first step in building the main form is to open a new form and create its underlying query.

EXERCISE 9.7: CREATING A QUERY FOR THE BILL OF MATERIALS MAIN FORM

1. Click the Forms object in the Database window, and then click the New button. Enter **tblJob** in the New Form combo box control, and then double-click Design View.
2. Open the form's property sheet by selecting the form and then clicking the Properties toolbar button.
3. Click the form's Record Source property Build button, and then click Yes to open a new query behind the form.
4. Click the Show Table toolbar button, and add *tblCustomer*, *tblJob-DirectMaterialsInventory*, and *tblFinishedGoodsInventory* to the top pane of the Query Builder window. Close the Show Table dialog box.
5. Note that *tblCustomer*, linked on CustomerNumber to *tblJob*, and *tblFinishedGoodsInventory*, linked on InventoryItemCode, now appears in the Query Builder window. Also appearing in the window is *tblJob-DirectMaterialsInventory* with its referential integrity link on JobNumber to *tblJob*. Click and drag the JobNumber field from *tblJob-DirectMaterialsInventory* to the first Field cell in the QBE grid; then, enter **Ascending** in the first Sort cell.
6. Double-click the asterisk in *tblJob* to include all of *tblJob* fields in the next QBE grid Field cell.
7. Double-click the CustomerName field in *tblCustomer*, and then double-click the InventoryDescription field in *tblFinishedGoodsInventory* to include those fields in the next two QBE grid Field cells, respectively.
8. Close the Query Builder window to return to the form, open in Design view. Click the Yes button when prompted to save the query.

Now that you have created the form and built a query behind the form, you can complete the form design. The next exercise provides guidance for that task.

EXERCISE 9.8: COMPLETING THE BILL OF MATERIALS MAIN FORM

1. Click the Field List toolbar button, and then click and drag the following fields to the form: JobNumber, JobOrderDate, InventoryDescription, CustomerName, and JobCompletionDate.
2. If the toolbox is not already open, click the Toolbox toolbar button. If the property sheet is not open, click the Properties toolbar button.
3. Click the Subform/Subreport toolbox button. If the Subform Wizard opens, click the Cancel button.
4. Using Figure 9.11 as a guide, draw the outline of the subform at the bottom of the Detail section.
5. Select the subform's label, and press Ctrl+X to delete it.
6. Click the Data tab in the subform's property sheet. Enter a Source Object property for the subform object of **fsubBillOfMaterials**
7. Enter **JobNumber** in both the Link Child Fields property and the Link Master Fields property.

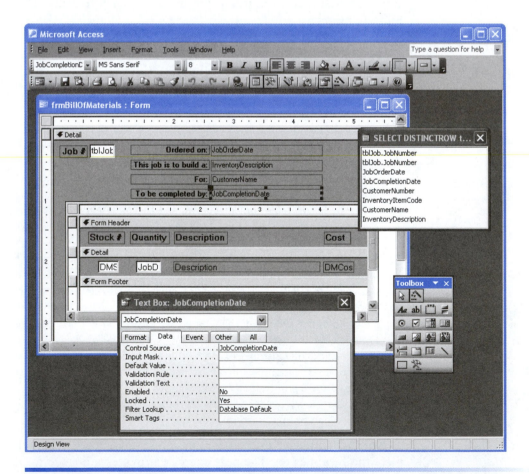

Figure 9.11   The Bill of Materials form in Design view.

8. Using Figures 9.11 and 9.12 as guides, modify the controls' properties and add labels to the Bill of Materials form. Remember to set the Enabled, Locked, and Tab Stop properties for the CustomerName and InventoryDescription controls to prevent users from changing values in those fields.

9. To save your Bill of Materials form, select File, Save As from the menu and enter **frmBillOfMaterials** as the form's new name in the Save As dialog box.

The *Ch09.mdb* file on your Companion CD includes two forms, *frmBillOfMaterials* and *fsubBillOfMaterials*, that you can use as aids in designing your forms. Figure 9.12 shows the Bill of Materials form in Form view after a user has entered the materials for job number 1001 in the sample data. In addition to its role as a data entry tool, this form provides a convenient way for managers to review the materials that have been charged to a job—although most firms would design a report for that purpose.

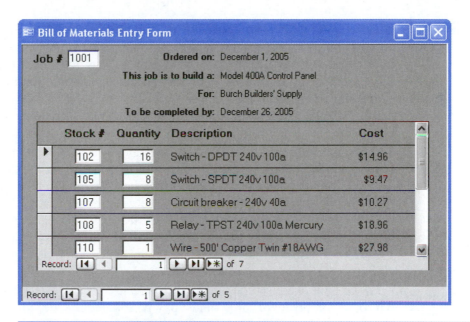

Figure 9.12 The Bill of Materials form in Form view.

The Time Worked Table

To track labor costs into the production process, you need to know the number of hours each employee works on each job. Then, you can multiply the hours by each employee's pay rate to determine the direct labor cost for the job. In Chapter 8, you created two tables that contain most of the information you will need to track direct labor cost in the production cycle. Since you constructed an Employee table in Chapter 8, we will not ask you to recreate your work here. However, we have included an Employee table, *tblEmployee*, in *Ch09.mdb* on your Companion CD. The *tblEmployee* object contains the employee data you will use in this chapter. The Employee table structure appears in Figure 9.13.

tblEmployee : Table

Field Name	Data Type
EmployeeNumber	Text
EmployeeLastName	Text
EmployeeFirstName	Text
EmployeeSSN	Text
EmployeeAddress	Text
EmployeeCity	Text
EmployeeState	Text
EmployeeZipCode	Text
EmployeeTelephone	Text
EmployeePayRate	Currency

Figure 9.13 The Chapter 9 *tblEmployee* structure.

Note that we have simplified the table structure so that you can focus more easily on cost flow issues. For example, we have omitted the EmployeeDepartmentNumber field because Electric Controls is tracking costs by job rather than by department in this chapter. Another simplification is that this Chapter 9 version of *tblEmployee* includes only five employee records.

The Time Worked table requires such substantial modifications that creating a new table is easier than adapting *tblTimeWorked* from Chapter 8. To record time worked on each job in one-hour increments, the table will need a primary key that uniquely identifies each block of time that each employee works on each job—certainly a more difficult challenge than creating a primary key for the Chapter 8 Time Worked table. To avoid the details of time arithmetic, we will assume that each employee completes one time card for each week. Further, we will assume that each time card has preprinted sequential numbers for job time entries. An example of such a time card appears in Figure 9.14. You will use the sequence numbers on the time card as part of the unique identifier for each record in *tblTimeWorked*.

In the next exercise you will create *tblTimeWorked*. The primary key for the table will be a composite of three fields: pay period ended date, time card sequence number, and employee number. The Time Worked table must include these three fields to uniquely identify each bit of time worked by each employee on each job. The table will also need fields for number of hours and job number for each record. The JobNumber field is a foreign key and will link *tblTimeWorked* to *tblJob*. Close all database objects, and have the Database window open to begin the exercise.

EXERCISE 9.9: BUILDING THE PRODUCTION CYCLE TIME WORKED TABLE

1. Select the Insert, Table menu command, and double-click Design View in the New Table dialog box.
2. Enter **EmployeeNumber** as the first Field Name. Leave its Data Type set to Text.
3. Set its Field Size to **3**, its Input Mask property to **000**, its Caption property to **Employee #**, and its Indexed property to **Yes (Duplicates OK)**

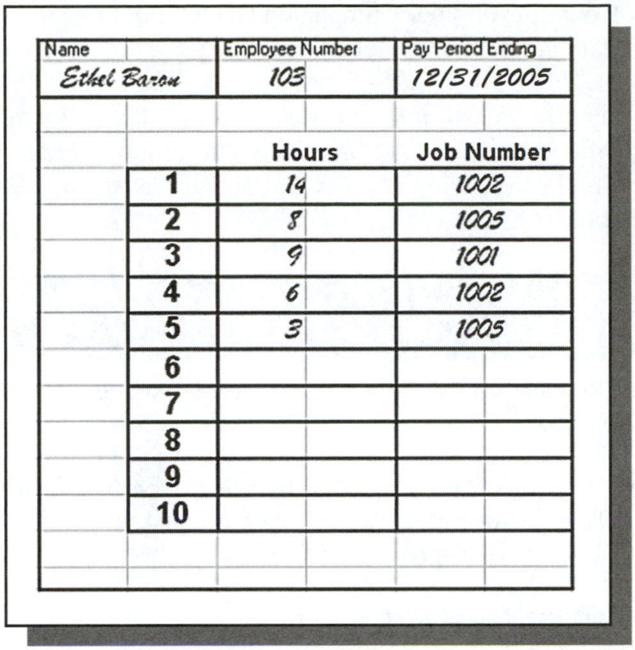

Figure 9.14   A sequentially numbered time card.

4. The second part of the composite primary key must identify the pay period. You can use the last day of each weekly pay period as the value for this field. Enter **TWPayPeriodEnded** in the second row of the Field Name column, and set its Data Type to **Date/Time**

5. Set the field's Input Mask property to **99/99/0000;0;_**, its Caption property to **Week Ended**, and its Indexed property to **Yes (Duplicates OK)**

6. The third part of the composite primary key will identify the line on the time card using the preprinted sequence number. Enter **TWSequenceNumber** in the third row of the Field Name column, and set the Data Type to **Number**. Since the time cards have only ten lines, you can enter a Field Size property of **Byte**

7. Set the field's Decimal Places property to **0**, its Input Mask property to **99**, its Caption property to **Sequence #**, and its Indexed property to **Yes (Duplicates OK)**

8. While pressing the Ctrl key, select all three fields by clicking the row selectors for each field.

9. With the fields selected, click the Primary Key toolbar button. The primary key symbol should appear in the row selectors of all three fields.

10. Next, you can create a field that will store the number of hours recorded on the time card for each sequence number and create the foreign key field for job number. Enter **TWHours** on the fourth row of the Field Name column. Set its Data Type to **Number** and its Caption property to **Hours**

11. Enter **JobNumber** in the Field Name column. Leave its Data Type set to Text. Set its Field Size property to **4**, its Input Mask property to **0000**, and its Caption property to **Job #**

12. To save the table, select the File, Save As menu command, and enter **tblTimeWorked** as the table's new name. Close the table.

The *Ch09.mdb* file on your Companion CD includes *tblTimeWorked*, which contains the sample data you will use later in this chapter. To ensure that each employee number entered in *tblTimeWorked* is for an employee that actually exists, you can build a referential integrity link to *tblEmployee*. You can also enforce referential integrity on the table's foreign key link to *tblJob*. This will ensure that any job number entered in *tblTimeWorked* is a valid job number that already exists in *tblJob*. In the next exercise you will add these links to *tblTimeWorked*.

EXERCISE 9.10: LINKING *TBLTIMEWORKED* TO *TBLJOB* AND *TBLEMPLOYEE*

1. Click the Relationships toolbar button to open the Relationships window, and then click the Show Table toolbar button. Double-click *tblEmployee* and *tblTimeWorked* to add these tables to the Relationships window; then, close the Show Table dialog box.
2. Click and drag the JobNumber field in *tblJob* to the JobNumber field in *tblTimeWorked*.
3. Click the Enforce Referential Integrity check box, and then click the Create button.
4. Click and drag the EmployeeNumber field in *tblEmployee* to the EmployeeNumber field in *tblTimeWorked*.
5. Click the Enforce Referential Integrity check box, and then click the Create button.
6. Select File, Close from the menu to close the Relationships window and return to the Database window. Click the Yes button to save your changes. The Relationships window showing these links added to the existing production cycle system links appears in Figure 9.15.

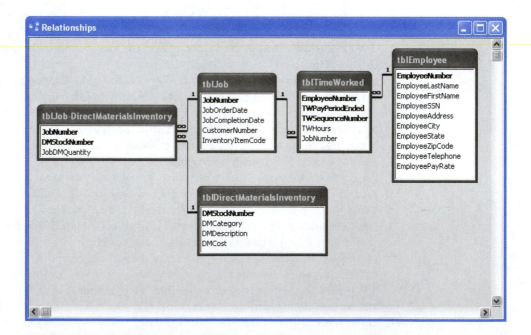

Figure 9.15 Adding referential integrity links to *tblTimeWorked*.

Electric Controls Company can use the records in *tblTimeWorked* in many ways. For example, by multiplying the hours for a particular job from *tblTimeWorked* by the employee pay rates from *tblEmployee* for the employees who worked on that job, the company can calculate the direct labor cost for a particular job. Exercise 9.11 shows you how you can build a query that calculates the direct labor cost for job number 1001 in the sample data.

EXERCISE 9.11: CALCULATING THE DIRECT LABOR COST FOR JOB NUMBER 1001

1. Select the Insert, Query menu command, and then double-click Design View in the New Query dialog box.
2. Double-click *tblEmployee* and *tblTimeWorked* in the Show Table dialog box, and then click the Close button.
3. Click and drag the JobNumber field from *tblTimeWorked* to the first QBE grid Field cell.
4. Enter **1001** in the first QBE grid Criteria cell. Microsoft Access encloses your entry with quotation marks as you leave the cell.
5. Enter **DLCost: [EmployeePayRate]*[TWHours]** in the second QBE grid Field cell. This field multiplies the employee pay rates by the number of hours that employee worked on job number 1001 and places the answer in a new field, DLCost.
6. Click the Run toolbar button to test the query. The result, which shows the direct labor costs for job number 1001, appears in Figure 9.16.

Of course, if a manager at Electric Controls really wanted to know the direct labor cost for job number 1001, the result shown in Figure 9.16 is probably not the best way

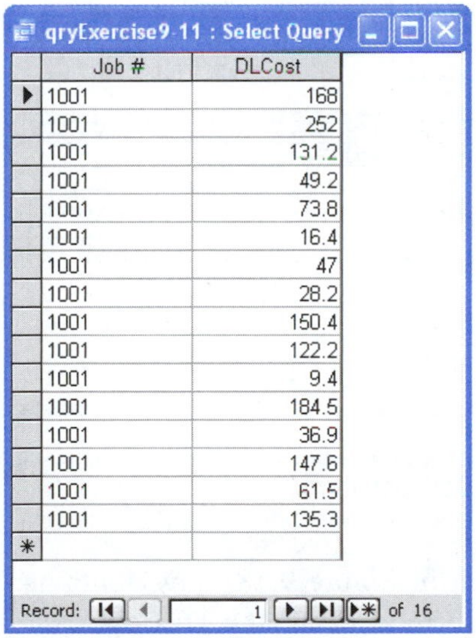

Job #	DLCost
1001	168
1001	252
1001	131.2
1001	49.2
1001	73.8
1001	16.4
1001	47
1001	28.2
1001	150.4
1001	122.2
1001	9.4
1001	184.5
1001	36.9
1001	147.6
1001	61.5
1001	135.3

qryExercise9-11 : Select Query

Record: 1 of 16

Figure 9.16 Direct labor costs for job number 1001.

for you to provide the information. The manager would probably prefer a single dollar amount for the job's total labor costs rather than a column of numbers to enter into a calculator. Fortunately, you can modify the query slightly to get the answer in a more useful form. Follow the steps in the next exercise to learn how.

EXERCISE 9.12: CALCULATING THE TOTAL DIRECT LABOR COST FOR JOB NUMBER 1001

1. Return the desktop to Query Design view. Select View, Totals from the menu or click the Totals toolbar button. This adds a row of Total cells to the QBE grid between the Table cells row and the Sort cells row.
2. Enter **Group By** in the first Total cell, and then enter **Expression** in the second Total cell.
3. In the second QBE grid Field cell, change **DLCost: [EmployeePayRate]*[TWHours]** to **DLCost: Sum([EmployeePayRate]*[TWHours])**. Figure 9.17 shows the Query window with these changes.
4. Click the Run toolbar button to test the modified query.

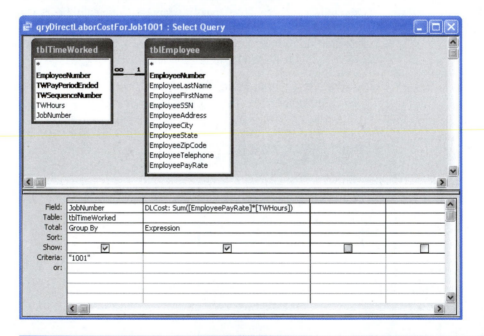

Figure 9.17 Summing the DLCost field.

The query's dynaset, shown in Figure 9.18, now contains only one row with one number, 1613.60, which is the total of all the DLCost calculations for job number 1001 that are displayed in Figure 9.16. This query is included in *Ch09.mdb* on your Companion CD as *qryDirectLaborCostForJob1001*. This query is just one example of how you can use queries on various combinations of the Job, Time Worked, and

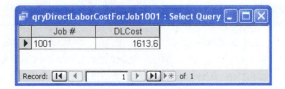

Figure 9.18 The result of summing DLCost field.

Employee tables to answer a variety of questions about the use and cost of direct labor resources.

Allocating Manufacturing Overhead

Cost accounting systems do not track manufacturing overhead costs into production as they track direct materials and direct labor costs. At the beginning of the year, accountants and production managers get together and estimate the total manufacturing overhead costs they expect to incur during the upcoming year. They also estimate the manufacturing activity level for the year. The activity measure is usually volume-based; that is, the activity measure is expected to increase with higher manufacturing volume.

Firms often use direct labor hours, direct labor cost, or machine hours as activity measures. The labor-based activity measures work well for manufacturing operations in which human beings do most of the work. Machine hours work well for manufacturing operations in which machines do most of the work.

Cost accountants divide the estimated manufacturing cost by the estimated activity measure to calculate a predetermined overhead rate. They use this rate to apply overhead to production throughout the year. Assume that Electric Controls' estimates for this year are:

Estimated manufacturing overhead cost	$78,000
Estimated direct labor hours	4,800

The predetermined overhead rate is:

$78,000 ÷ 4,800 direct labor hours = $16.25 per direct labor hour

Therefore, Electric Controls' production cycle accounting system must allocate $16.25 per direct labor hour to each job.

You have already captured the direct labor hours per job in *tblTimeWorked*. Production cycle systems that allocate manufacturing overhead using other allocation bases may need additional tables. For example, a firm that allocates manufacturing overhead using machine hours would need a machine hours table to store the number of machine hours used by each job. The structure of this machine hours table would be very similar to the structure of *tblTimeWorked*.

At this point, you have created tables that will track direct materials and direct labor costs. You have also seen how accountants allocate manufacturing overhead costs. Your next step is to use these tables to calculate job costs.

REPORTING JOB COSTS

The goal of tracking and allocating manufacturing costs is to provide information for calculating job or department costs. Since Electric Controls uses a job order cost accumulation system, you must now calculate job costs. The Job Cost report that you will create in this section summarizes direct materials, direct labor, and manufacturing overhead costs by job.

This task requires a series of four queries and a report. The first three queries calculate and sum the direct materials, direct labor, and manufacturing overhead costs for each job. The fourth query combines these three summation queries and provides a basis for the Job Cost report.

Direct Materials Cost

The first step in building the Job Cost report is to calculate the total direct materials cost for each job. You will perform this calculation with a Direct Materials Cost query in the next exercise.

EXERCISE 9.13: BUILDING THE DIRECT MATERIALS COST QUERY

1. Click the Queries object in the Database window, and then click the New button. Double-click Design View in the New Query dialog box.
2. In the Show Table dialog box, double-click *tblDirectMaterialsInventory*, *tblJob*, and *tblJob-DirectMaterialsInventory* to add these tables to the query. Click the Close button.
3. Click and drag the JobNumber field from *tblJob* to the first QBE grid Field cell.
4. Enter **DM Cost: Sum([DMCost]*[JobDMQuantity])** in the second QBE grid Field cell.
5. Click the Totals toolbar button to open the Total line in the QBE grid.
6. Change the second QBE grid Total cell to **Expression**
7. Select the File, Save As menu command, and enter **qryDirectMaterialsCost** as the query's new name.
8. Close the query. Figure 9.19 shows the query in Design view.

When you run this query, it should return a dynaset with five direct materials cost values, one for each job. The *Ch09.mdb* file on your Companion CD includes this query, named *qryDirectMaterialsCost*, for your reference.

Direct Labor Cost

The second step in building the Job Cost report is to calculate the total direct labor cost for each job. In Exercise 9.14, you will do this with a Direct Labor Cost query.

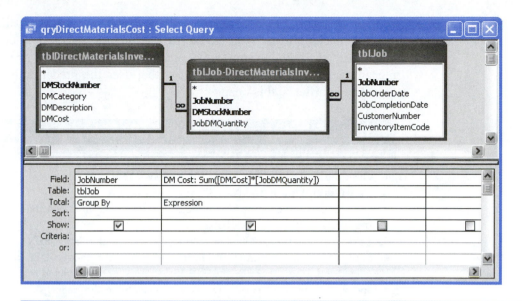

Figure 9.19   The Direct Materials Cost query in Design view.

EXERCISE 9.14: BUILDING THE DIRECT LABOR COST QUERY

1. Click the Queries object in the Database window, and then click the New button. Double-click Design View in the New Query dialog box.
2. In the Show Table dialog box, double-click *tblEmployee*, *tblJob*, and *tblTimeWorked* to add these tables to the query. Click the Close button.
3. Click and drag the JobNumber field from *tblJob* to the first QBE grid Field cell.
4. Enter **DL Cost: Sum([EmployeePayRate]*[TWHours])** in the second QBE grid Field cell.
5. Click the Totals toolbar button to open the Total line in the QBE grid.
6. Change the second QBE grid Total cell to **Expression**
7. Select the File, Save As menu command, and enter **qryDirectLaborCost** as the query's name. Close the query.

When you run the query, it should return a dynaset with direct labor values for the five jobs in *tblJob*. The *Ch09.mdb* file on your Companion CD includes a Direct Labor Cost query, *qryDirectLaborCost*, for your reference.

Manufacturing Overhead Cost

The next step in building the Job Cost report is to calculate the total manufacturing overhead cost for each job. The manufacturing overhead calculation needs the hours worked on each job from *tblTimeWorked* because Electric Controls Company applies overhead using direct labor hours as the activity base. To use a different activity base, such as machine hours, you would need to include a table that contained information about how each job consumed that activity base. In the next exercise, you will create a Manufacturing Overhead Cost query that uses the predetermined overhead rate we calculated earlier in this chapter.

EXERCISE 9.15: BUILDING THE MANUFACTURING OVERHEAD COST QUERY

1. Click the Queries object in the Database window, and then click the New button. Double-click Design View in the New Query dialog box.
2. In the Show Table dialog box, double-click *tblJob* and *tblTimeWorked* to add these tables to the query. Click the Close button.
3. Click and drag the JobNumber field from *tblJob* to the first QBE grid Field cell.
4. Enter **MOH Cost: Sum([TWHours]*16.25)** in the second QBE grid Field cell. This multiplies direct labor hours by the $16.25 per hour predetermined manufacturing overhead rate and then sums these results for all jobs included in the query.
5. Click the Totals toolbar button to open the Total line in the QBE grid.
6. Change the second QBE grid Total cell to **Expression**
7. Select the File, Save As menu command, and enter **qryManufacturingOverheadCost** as the query's name. Close the query.

Figure 9.20 shows the query in Design view. When you run the query, it should return a dynaset with manufacturing overhead values for the five jobs in the Job table. The *Ch09.mdb* file on your Companion CD includes a Manufacturing Overhead Cost query for your reference named *qryManufacturingOverheadCost*.

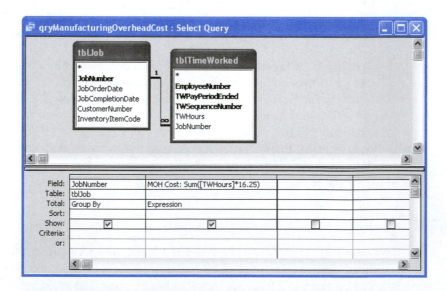

Figure 9.20   The Manufacturing Overhead Cost query in Design view.

Job Cost Allocation

Now you can build the summary query that will combine the results of the direct materials, direct labor, and manufacturing overhead queries. This procedure of using one query to summarize other queries is sometimes called *nesting queries*. In the next exercise you will build a Job Cost query.

EXERCISE 9.16: BUILDING THE JOB COST QUERY

1. Click the Queries object in the Database window, and then click the New button. Double-click Design view in the New Query dialog box.
2. In the Show table dialog box, double-click *tblJob* to add the Job table to the upper pane of the Query Builder window. Click the Queries tab of the Show Table dialog box.
3. Double-click *qryDirectMaterialsCost*, *qryDirectLaborCost*, and *qryManufacturingOverheadCost* to add these queries to the Job Cost query. Close the Show Table dialog box.
4. Click and drag the JobNumber field from *tblJob* to the first QBE grid Field cell.
5. Click and drag the DM Cost, DL Cost, and MOH Cost fields to the next three open QBE grid Field cells.
6. Click the Totals toolbar button to open the Total line in the QBE grid.
7. Enter **Sum** in each of the three QBE grid Total cells for DM Cost, DL Cost, and MOH Cost.
8. Select the File, Save As menu command, and enter **qryJobCost** as the query's name. Figure 9.21 shows the query in Design view. Close the query.

When you run the query, it should return a dynaset with direct materials, direct labor, and manufacturing overhead values for the five jobs in *tblJob*. The query results

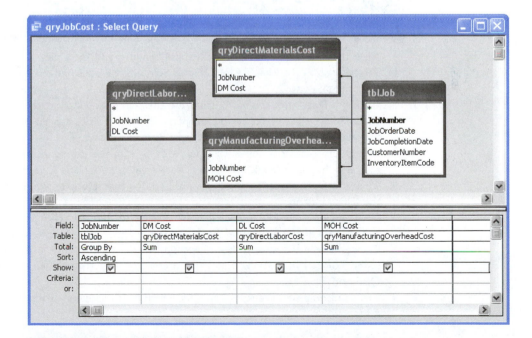

Figure 9.21 The Job Cost query in Design view.

appear in Figure 9.22. The *Ch09.mdb* file on your Companion CD includes *qryJobCost* for your reference.

Job #	SumOfDM Cost	SumOfDL Cost	SumOfMOH Cost
1001	1133.52	1613.6	2145
1002	2055.48	3680.8	4160
1003	884.14	970.5	877.5
1004	335.33	806.4	1170
1005	1158.91	1267.7	2031.25

Figure 9.22 The Job Cost query results in Datasheet view.

The Job Cost Report

The Job Cost query provides useful results, but you can create a better-looking print-out than the Datasheet view results of the query by creating a report in Access. In the next two exercises, you will create a report that uses the *qryJobCost* calculations in a report design. To begin the first exercise, in which you will build the query behind the form, close all tables, forms, and queries, and have the Database window open on the Access desktop.

EXERCISE 9.17: BUILDING THE QUERY BEHIND THE JOB COST REPORT

1. Click the Reports object in the Database window, and then click the New button.
2. Select *tblJob* in the New Report combo box control, and then double-click Design View in the list box control.
3. Click the Properties toolbar button, and then click the Data tab in the form's property sheet. Select the Record Source property, and then click its Build button. Click the Yes button when prompted to open the Query Builder window.
4. The Query Builder window will open with *tblJob* in the top pane. Click the Show Table button, and then double-click *tblFinishedGoodsInventory* to include it in the query.
5. Click the Queries tab on the Show Table dialog box. Double-click *qryJobCost*, and then click the Close button.
6. Click and drag the JobNumber field from *tblJob* to the first QBE grid Field cell. Set the Sort cell to **Ascending**. Click the check box in the Show cell to remove the selection.
7. Click and drag the asterisk from *qryJobCost* to the second QBE grid Field cell.
8. Enter **Total: [SumOfDM Cost]+[SumOfDL Cost]+[SumOfMOH Cost]** in the third QBE grid Field cell.
9. Click and drag the InventoryDescription field from *tblFinishedGoodsInventory* to the fourth QBE grid Field cell.

The Job Cost report's query design appears in the Query Builder window shown in Figure 9.23. Notice that this is a query that includes a query, *qryJobCost*, which in turn

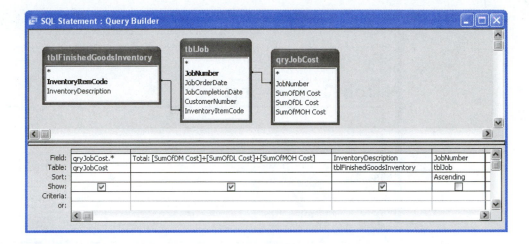

Figure 9.23   The query behind the Job Cost report.

is a query that includes three other queries. This query nesting occurs often in production cycle databases and can be many levels deep. The nesting of queries within queries can become quite complex for systems that calculate costs for manufactured products with many subassemblies and component parts.

You can click the Run toolbar button to test your query. When you are satisfied that the query is operating properly, close the Query Builder window, save your changes, and return to the report in Design view. Next, you will complete the Job Cost report design. You can use Figures 9.24 and 9.25 as guides while you follow the steps in the next exercise.

EXERCISE 9.18: COMPLETING THE JOB COST REPORT

1. Click the Field List toolbar button; then, click and drag all six fields to the Detail Section of the report.
2. Delete the label controls.
3. Use the View menu command to delete the Page Header/Footer and add a Report Header/Footer.
4. Add descriptive labels for the column totals and the report title to the Report Header section.
5. Use the Text Box tool to create controls in the Report Footer.
6. You can use the Sum() function to have these controls in the Report Footer sum the column amounts. For example, the Direct Materials total text box control contains the expression =Sum([SumOfDM Cost]). The square brackets are important here because the field names include a space. Figure 9.24 shows **rptJobCost** in Design view.

We turned off the Design view grid before capturing the screen shown in Figure 9.24 so you can better see the details of the text box controls and the line objects in the report's design. When you are satisfied with your report design, you can save and close the report. The *Ch09.mdb* file on your Companion CD includes *rptJobCost*, which you can examine for details of the report's formatting and layout. A printout of the Job Cost report appears in Figure 9.25.

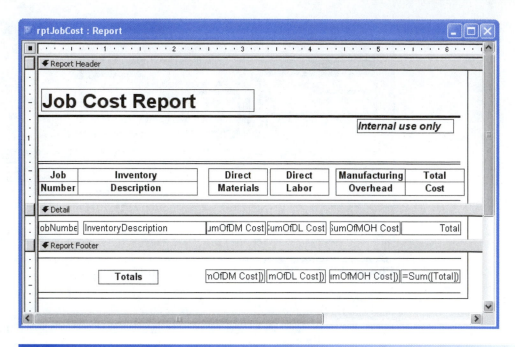

Figure 9.24 The Job Cost report in Design view.

Job Cost Report

Internal use only

Job Number	Inventory Description	Direct Materials	Direct Labor	Manufacturing Overhead	Total Cost
1001	Model 400A Control Panel	$1,133.52	$1,613.60	$2,145.00	$4,892.12
1002	Model 500C Control Panel	$2,055.48	$3,680.80	$4,160.00	$9,896.28
1003	Model 300A Control Panel	$884.14	$970.50	$877.50	$2,732.14
1004	Model 100A Control Panel	$335.33	$806.40	$1,170.00	$2,311.73
1005	Model 470D Control Panel	$1,158.91	$1,267.70	$2,031.25	$4,457.86
Totals		$5,567.38	$8,339.00	$10,383.75	$24,290.13

Figure 9.25 The Job Cost report printout.

Production Cycle Relationships

The production cycle is different from the other three cycles because many of its most useful elements are not stored in tables but are calculated with queries. The Electric Controls Company example you worked through in this chapter is no exception. Although important information is stored in the production cycle tables, the job cost accumulations occur in queries and reports based on those queries. Figure 9.26 shows the complete set of entity tables and their relationships for the production cycle.

Notice that we have added links from the Job table to the Customer table and the Finished Goods table. These links do not have referential integrity constraints because Electric Controls Company wanted to enter jobs that had not yet been associated with either a specific customer or a specific completed part number. You can compare the tables and relationships with the data model for Electric Controls' production cycle that we presented in Figure 9.1 at the beginning of the chapter to see how the implementation follows the model in the production cycle.

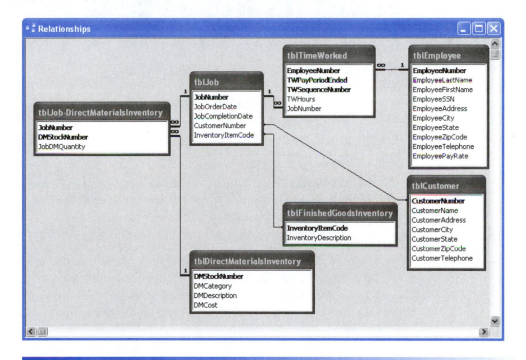

Figure 9.26 Production cycle entity tables and their relationships.

 Go to http://perry.swlearning.com for an in-depth tutorial.

SUMMARY

In this chapter you learned how production cycle activities convert raw materials, labor, and overhead into finished products. You learned how production cycle accounting traces and allocates manufacturing costs to products. The production cycle system elements you built as you worked through this chapter can provide managers with information for monitoring manufacturing processes. The production cycle system also provides financial accountants with information they need to value inventories and determine the cost of goods sold.

Although this chapter explained how to use Access database management software in a manufacturing setting, a growing number of merchandising and service firms are examining their business processes using a product costing approach. Therefore, the techniques you learned in this chapter can help you design accounting systems for all three types of firms: manufacturing, merchandising, and service.

QUESTIONS AND PROBLEMS FOR REVIEW

Multiple-Choice Questions

1. You can use tables in the production cycle to
   a. calculate direct materials cost.
   b. calculate the predetermined overhead rate.
   c. store employee pay rates.
   d. print hours worked by job.

2. Production cycle activities include
   a. allocating manufacturing overhead.
   b. calculating discounts taken on accounts payable.
   c. recording cash received for jobs completed.
   d. all of the above.

3. The production cycle system included in *Ch09.mdb* can track an employee working on more than one job during a single time period because
   a. *tblJob* includes EmployeeNumber as one of its foreign key fields.
   b. *tblTimeWorked* includes EmployeeNumber as part of its composite primary key.
   c. *tblTimeWorked* includes TWSequenceNumber as part of its composite primary key.
   d. *tblTimeWorked* includes JobNumber as one of its foreign key fields.

4. The DMStockNumber field in *tblJob-DirectMaterialsInventory* is a
   a. composite primary key.
   b. foreign key.
   c. primary key.
   d. part of a composite primary key.

5. The database in *Ch09.mdb* could track job completion timeliness if the designer were to add
   a. a time field to the Direct Materials Inventory table.
   b. a Standard Cost table that includes timeliness standards.
   c. a date completed field to *tblJob*.
   d. an estimated time field to *tblJob*.

6. To modify the *Ch09.mdb* database so it would allocate manufacturing overhead cost on a basis of direct labor dollars rather than direct labor hours, you would need to change
   a. the MOHCost Calculation in *qryManufacturingOverheadCost*.
   b. the TWHours field in *tblTimeWorked*.
   c. the MOHRate field in *tblManufacturingOverhead*.
   d. the DLHCost calculation in *qryManufacturingOverheadCost*.

7. The Direct Materials Inventory table includes switches, relays, and connectors rated at 120 and 240 volts. You could improve this table by placing the voltage rating
   a. at the beginning of the description field.
   b. at the end of the description field.
   c. in a separate table.
   d. in a separate field in the same table.

8. The *Ch09.mdb* database does not include a Department table because the Electric Controls Company accumulates costs using a(n)
   a. process cost system.
   b. job order system.
   c. operation cost system.
   d. hybrid cost system.

9. In a process cost accumulation system (as opposed to the job order cost system used in the chapter examples),
   a. direct materials costs are traced to departments.
   b. manufacturing overhead costs are traced to departments.
   c. both a and b.
   d. neither a nor b.

10. In an activity-based job order cost system,
    a. some manufacturing overhead costs are allocated to departments.
    b. all manufacturing overhead costs are traced to departments.
    c. some manufacturing costs are traced to activities and then allocated to departments.
    d. some manufacturing costs are traced to activities and then allocated to jobs.

Discussion Questions

1. Describe the changes you would make to the production cycle system described in this chapter to convert it to a process cost accumulation system.

2. What tables and queries would you add to those described in this chapter to convert it to an activity-based job order cost system?

3. Compare the Employee table in this chapter to the Employee table in Chapter 8. Explain the differences in the tables' structures.

4. Compare the Time Worked table in this chapter to the Time Worked table in Chapter 8. Explain the differences in the tables' structures.

5. Describe the modifications you would make to the production cycle elements described in this chapter to accommodate an operation cost accumulation system.

Practice Exercises

Note: Before doing any of the following practice exercises, first copy *Ch09.mdb* from your Companion CD to the hard drive of the computer on which you are working. Then, clear the copied database's Read-only file attribute (see Chapter 1, Exercise 1.14, Clearing a File's Read-Only Property). Having done that, you can complete each exercise using the copy of the Companion CD database.

1. Open the *Ch09.mdb* database. Add a field to *tblJob* for budgeted cost. Create queries and a report that use this field to compute budget vs. actual differences by job.

2. Open the *Ch09.mdb* database. Create a data entry form that would help persons enter time card data into the Time Worked table. Model the form after the time card shown in Figure 9.14 to make the data entry task easier.

3. Open the *Ch09.mdb* database. Modify *rptJobCost* to display the customer name for each job.

4. Work-in-process inventory includes all jobs that have not been completed at month-end. Open the *Ch09.mdb* database, and modify the Job Cost queries and report to calculate the cost of December's work-in-process inventory.

5. Open the *Ch09.mdb* database, and create a Job Cost Card form that facilitates the input of budgeted direct materials and direct labor cost data into two new fields, Budgeted Direct Materials and Budgeted Time, in *tblJob*. You should add the fields to *tblJob* before you begin building the form.

Problems

Note: Before doing any of the following problems, first copy *Ch09.mdb* from your Companion CD to the hard drive of the computer on which you are working. Then, clear the copied database's Read-only file attribute (see Chapter 1, Exercise 1.14, Clearing a File's Read-Only Property). Having done that, you can complete each exercise using the copy of the Companion CD database.

1. Georgia's Organic Soups (GOS) is a food manufacturing company that specializes in producing and canning organic tomato soup. Georgia has seen the company's tomato soup sales grow and hopes to add more types of soup in the future, but for now, the production and selling of tomato soup is all she has time to manage. She has asked you to design a database that will help her do the company's production accounting. GOS buys ingredients from local farmers and turns those ingredients into soup in three steps. Each production step is accounted for as a department. The three departments are preparation (cleaning and chopping the ingredients), cooking, and packaging. GOS does its production accounting at the end of each month, and it never has any work in process in any of the three departments, because the ingredients, half-cooked soup, and open cans in the packaging department would all just spoil if left uncompleted overnight. GOS uses a process accounting system and takes the total costs in each department at the end of each month and divides those costs by the number of cans of tomato soup produced. GOS allocates manufacturing overhead costs on the basis of direct labor dollars. List the entities that exist in the GOS production cycle. State any assumptions you believe are necessary.

2. Refer to the GOS case described in Problem 1, and create a diagram similar to that shown in Figure 9.4 for GOS. The diagram should show the entities you identified in Problem 1 along with the relationships between those entities and their cardinalities.

3. Refer to the GOS case described in Problem 1 and the work you did in Problem 2. Use Access to build the tables and create the relationships you have defined. Populate the tables with sample data that you create, and test the tables to make certain that the relationships operate to enforce referential integrity as appropriate. You can use data from *tblEmployee* and any other tables in *Ch09.mdb* where possible to save data entry time.

4. Refer to the work you have done in the preceding three problems. Create data entry forms for the GOS production cycle database that allow you to enter data into every table without opening the table itself. Use the forms in the *Ch09.mdb* database as guides.

5. Refer to the work you have done in the preceding four problems. Create reports for the GOS purchase cycle database as follows:
   a. Create queries that calculate the total cost for each of the three departments for each month.
   b. Create a montly report that shows total costs and unit costs (cost per can) for each department.
   c. Create any additional specific reports that your instructor assigns.

CHAPTER 10
Automating Database Procedures

OBJECTIVES

Chapter 10 explains how to automate database procedures with macros and Visual Basic for Applications (VBA) code. You will learn how to write macros and attach them to command buttons. You will learn how to use VBA to create powerful, small code segments to produce database objects that automatically react to changes. Though it sounds like you are in for a lot of programming in this chapter, this is not the case. You will learn to create small code segments that are easy to understand and that provide powerful features. Several of the sub procedures are products of the Access Control Wizard, which helps you create command buttons backed by VBA code and error-checking routines. This chapter teaches you how to create useful and professional-looking enhancements that will make using your forms and reports even easier. In particular, you will learn:

- What events are and how they propagate throughout your application.
- How actions are recognized and triggered by events.
- How to write a macro and attach it to a command button that activates the macro.
- How to write Visual Basic for Applications (VBA) code and attach the code to event procedures.
- How to create form navigation buttons.
- How to incorporate small code segments that reside behind a form and that provide data validity, range, and reasonableness checks on form fields.

MACROS AND VISUAL BASIC FOR APPLICATIONS (VBA)

Access contains two powerful tools that provide you with the capability of taking your database to a full-scale, automated, easy-to-use application. The tools are Access macro programming and Visual Basic for Applications (VBA). Both tools allow you to write code that takes action when selected events occur. Access macros provide simple tools to automate many kinds of tasks. For instance, you can easily create a navigation macro, attached to a button, that goes to the next record in a table when the button is clicked. Clicking a button triggers the click event, one of several events that Access recognizes. This causes the navigation button macro code to execute.

Visual Basic for Applications, while similar to Access macro programming, is a full-featured programming language that extends the macro language and provides tools that are not available in Access macros. For example, VBA handles error conditions, while macros do not. VBA has several looping structures that permit code to be executed repeatedly until the code recognizes some stopping condition. Macros do not provide repetitive processing (looping).

Because macros are easier to write and understand, you will start by writing macros. Then, you will take what you learned about macros and jump into VBA. This chapter is not a substitute for a thorough discussion of either macro programming or VBA programming. The intention here is to give you a good, fundamental understanding of both macros and VBA code. You can extend your knowledge of both by enhancing your database applications and reading books on the topic.

Automating Database Applications

A macro or VBA—known collectively as *code*—is a single action or a series of actions stored with a form or stored independently as an object in the Macros or Modules collection of the Database window. Code automates an application and simplifies the use of tables, queries, forms, and reports. You can automate many database tasks with either a macro or VBA, reducing a task to just a few mouse clicks. Code can be used to create complete turnkey applications, or it can be used to simply enhance an application with small code segments performing specialized duties. Our objective is to introduce you to a few useful language elements that can simplify the use of your applications and automate procedures. Then you can use these representative examples in your applications, applying and extending the techniques you learned in the textbook to specific situations you encounter.

States, Events, and Event Properties

When you click a button on the Access toolbar, you change the state of that button. It changes to *clicked*. Similarly, whenever you use a keyboard or a mouse, you are changing the state of something within the computer. An object's state is its list of characteristics, or properties, and their values. Access keeps track of each object's set of possible states. For instance, you can click a button whenever its enabled state is *true*. Otherwise, a button's enabled state is *false*. Access automatically recognizes that a user cannot click a button (also known as a *command button*) when it is in the disabled state. This is a built-in behavior of a button. Furthermore, Access indicates that a button's state is not enabled by making it appear dim—making the button's label appear light gray instead of black. The importance of knowing that objects have states is that you can take advantage of objects' states by interrupting processing or by taking an alternative action whenever an object is in a certain state. For instance, Access recognizes when a user clicks a button, which triggers a click event. Access automatically transfers execution to the user-written code that is assigned to react to the button click event.

Any change of an object's state is called an *event*. A macro or VBA code can react to an event by performing a series of program steps. Steps of code assigned to react to a button click, for example, are known as *code behind the button*. The code can cause any number of actions to occur and can determine how an object behaves after a triggering event occurs. As a database designer, you indicate which code reacts to which event by naming the code and placing its name in the object's *event property*. Similar to other properties, most objects have several event properties. Each event property is either empty or contains the name of the bit of code that handles that particular event. If an event property is empty, then the event causes nothing to happen—the event goes unnoticed. Otherwise, the code that is named in the event property "listens" for its assigned event to occur on that object and then reacts to the event in a prescribed way.

Figure 10.1 shows the Event tab of a command button's property sheet. Notice the names of the event properties listed. Two event properties have been assigned code to perform prescribed duties when the associated events occur. The On Click event property currently has VBA code assigned to it ("[Event Procedure]" indicates VBA code is assigned). Also called an *event handler*, the assigned event property code responds whenever someone clicks the button to which the property is associated. The only other event handler is a macro named *CheckIt*. A specific name appearing in an event property indicates the assigned code is a macro, not VBA code. Associated with the event "On Dbl Click" (shorthand for "on double click"), the CheckIt macro jumps into action when anyone double-clicks the command button called *cmdExit* (see the property sheet Title bar for an object's type and name).

Here's an example demonstrating how a macro simplifies a process for anyone using a data entry form. You know that in order to delete data stored in the tables constituting the Sales Order system shown in Chapter 5 (Figure 5.8), you must first delete the order lines from the subform. Once you delete the individual order lines, then you can delete the main order record (the main form is shown in Figure 5.8 also). However, someone using your accounting system may not know much about database

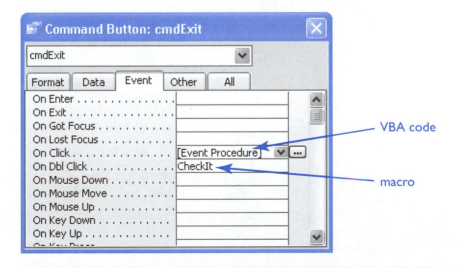

Figure 10.1 A command button's event properties.

systems generally or about referential integrity rules in particular—rules which pre-clude deleting master form records before deleting subform records. Therefore, you cannot expect those using your accounting system to know, for example, which keys to press to delete a record or that they must delete the subform data first.

You can reduce or eliminate these kinds of difficulties by creating intuitively labeled buttons that carry out the required actions in the correct sequence. A button might execute a series of steps to accomplish an activity such as editing a data field or searching a database for a particular item. For instance, you can simplify the process of deleting information by creating a button labeled *Delete Record* and placing it on a form. When a user clicks the command button, it invokes a macro or VBA code. The code automatically selects a complete record, executes the Select Record command, and then executes the Delete command. By automating with buttons frequently used procedures, you minimize users' keystrokes, remove their need to make complicated menu and command choices, and greatly reduce the probability that they will make an error. One button performs a series of steps that accomplish a complete task. Those using your accounting system will be happy that they do not have to study and learn the database commands. Instead, they can concentrate on the accounting task at hand.

Figure 10.2 shows an example of a form containing buttons with code invisibly attached to the buttons. When a user clicks the Save Record button, Access updates the database with the altered record. Similarly, the Cancel Changes button is attached to code that cancels the most recent changes made to the data.

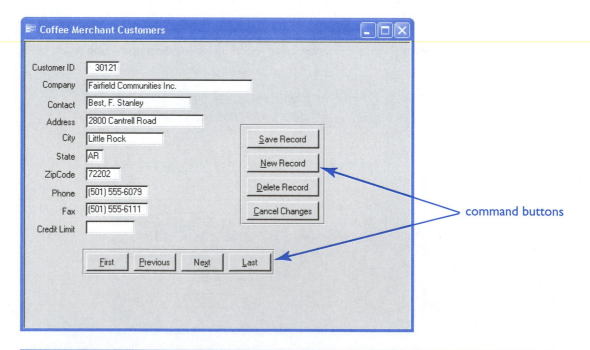

Figure 10.2 Example of a form with command buttons.

An example of the value of a command button and its attached code (a macro in this particular example) is the record navigation button labeled "First" found on The Coffee Merchant's Customer form. The macro that is behind the First button consists of three steps. Figure 10.3 shows the First macro in the Macro design window.

What does the macro accomplish? The Macro window shows three columns: Macro Name, Action, and Comment. The Macro Name column contains the macro's name. The Action column contains one or more steps or actions that the macro performs. In this example, the macro contains three actions: Echo, GoToRecord, and GoToControl. Access executes a macro beginning with the first step, which also contains the macro's name in the Macro Name step of the same row. The Echo command freezes the screen while the macro is running to suppress displaying messages and actions as they occur in quick sequence. The next statement, GoToRecord, moves to the first record in the table. The third statement, GoToControl, moves the focus to the first field in the form, CustomerID. (When an object—a field or button, for example—has the focus, you can affect the object by typing something on the keyboard or by clicking the mouse. Only one object at a time can have the focus.)

Do not be concerned if the meanings of the lines in Figure 10.3 are not apparent to you. You will learn more about these later in this chapter. The example merely illustrates a typical macro.

Macros or VBA code can be attached to objects other than buttons. You can attach code to a form itself. For instance, you can embellish a form with a macro that prompts users for a password whenever the form is opened and before displaying database information. Form fields can have macros attached to them as well. You can modify a form field so its value is validated before the cursor is allowed to pass to the next field.

In the next section, you will learn about how to attach a macro to a button's click event. Following the explanation, you will learn how to create more versatile code to

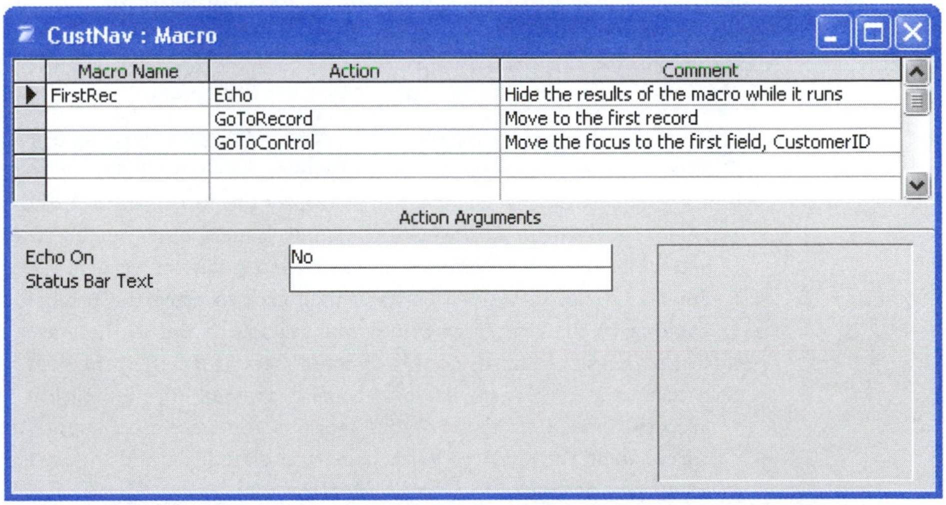

Figure 10.3 The macro that responds when the First command button is clicked.

attach to buttons' events using Visual Basic. Once you see the power of VBA, we think you will agree that VBA is the best and most efficient way to write code to perform tasks in response to events. First, let's look at a simple macro and build a button to launch it.

AUTOMATING FORMS WITH COMMAND BUTTONS

You develop macros and VBA code by planning them, attaching them to the objects whose behaviors are to be affected, and then testing them to ensure that they work correctly. To understand both macros and VBA code and their usefulness, we will add a few command buttons to the Customer form, *frmCustomer*. That form displays The Coffee Merchant customer information and allows you to update customer information. To set the stage for this chapter, first start Windows and copy the database *Ch10.mdb* found in the Ch10 folder on your Companion CD to your hard drive. Remember to clear the Read-only property of the copied database before you attempt to open it. Once the database is copied, open *Ch10.mdb*. When the Security Warning appears, simply click the Open button to proceed.

Creating a Command Button

Let's make things a bit easier for your users by placing database navigation buttons on the form displaying customer information. Though navigation buttons are available in the Form window, the ones we design will be larger and easier to locate. Later, we will add some safeguards that are not available with the Access-supplied, standard navigation buttons. (We have set one of the form properties specifically to *not* display the usual navigation buttons.) First, you will create a button that will move to the first customer record in the database and display it. After you create that button, you will create three other navigation buttons using the first one as a model. The other buttons move to the next record, the previous record, and the last record. In the next steps, you will follow steps to create a button. Then, you will create a macro that causes an action to occur whenever anyone clicks the button. Follow the steps in the next exercise to create a button object and place it on the Customer form, *frmCustomer*.

EXERCISE 10.1: CREATING A COMMAND BUTTON

1. Click Forms on the Objects bar to display the form names in the Database window.
2. Select the form *frmCustomer* and then click the Design button to display the form in Design view. Maximize the form design window so it fills the screen.
3. Select View on the menu bar, and then click to place the toolbox on the screen. Drag the toolbox to the right edge of the window so it is out of the way.
4. If the Control Wizards tool is selected (see Figure 10.4; the tool has a rust-colored background, a dark blue border, and appears pressed in), then click it so that the Control Wizard does not interfere with your work as you build a command button. The dark border surrounding the Control Wizards button disappears and the background becomes blue when you deselect the Control Wizards tool.
5. Click the Command Button tool in the toolbox (see Figure 10.4). Then, move the mouse pointer below the Credit Limit field in an open area, and click the mouse to drop the but-

ton onto the form. If the Command Button Wizard opens, then simply click the Cancel button located near the bottom of the dialog box.

6. Click the newly created button twice slowly until a vertical bar (the insertion point) appears within the button's label.

7. Using the Backspace and Delete keys, remove the command button's current label (*Command25*, for example) and type **&First** in its place. Click outside the button to deselect it.

An ampersand preceding any letter in the command button's label indicates which key is the button's access key. An access key is a keyboard shortcut. Pressing Alt and typing the access key (*f* in this example) is equivalent to clicking the command button with your mouse.

8. Click File on the menu bar, click Save As, and then type **frmCustomer1** in the upper text box of the Save As dialog box.

9. Click OK to save the form under the new name. (Leave the form on your screen because you will continue to make changes to it.)

Figure 10.4 Access Toolbox showing some of its many tools.

With the new button in place, switch to Form view and try it out. Click the First button with your mouse or press Alt+F. Notice that it seems to do nothing except appear sunken when you click it. The sunken appearance is one of a command button's *built-in* behaviors. The reason nothing else happens is that you have not yet associated any code—a macro or VBA code—to the button's *On Click event*. You do that next.

Creating a Macro and Attaching It to a Command Button

To change the way a button behaves when you click it, you can attach a macro to one of the button's event properties (it has several). Because you want the button to do a series of actions when it is clicked, you associate code (a macro in this example) with the button's On Click event. You do this by displaying the command button's property sheet and writing the macro's name into the text of the On Click property. First, though, you must create a macro that performs the duties of going to the first record in the database displayed by the form. Once the macro is created and saved, you can then attach it to an event property.

In the next exercise, you create a macro that is attached to the First navigation button (see Figure 10.2) and executed when the button is clicked. Ensure that the form *frmCustomer1* is still loaded and displayed in Design view.

EXERCISE 10.2: CREATING A DATABASE NAVIGATION MACRO

1. Display the maximized form in Design view, close the toolbox, right-click the First button, and then click Properties from the pop-up menu to display the button's property sheet. Drag the property sheet to a location where you can see both it and the First button.
2. Click the property sheet's Other tab, double-click the Name property text box, and type **cmdFirst** (this changes the button's internal name).
3. Click the property sheet's Event tab, and then click the On Click property text box. An arrow and a Build button (...) appear on the right side of the text box.
4. Click the Build button. When the Choose Builder dialog box appears, double-click the Macro Builder choice. The Save As dialog box opens.
5. Type the macro name **CustNav**, and click OK.
6. Click View in the menu bar, and then click Macro Names to display the Macro Name column in the Design view window.
7. Move the insertion point to the first row (if necessary) and the Macro Name column, and type **FirstRec** to mark the macro's first line of code.
8. Press Tab, click the drop-down list box arrow to display the action list, scroll the list until "Echo" appears, and click Echo. Echo appears in the Action column.
9. Press Tab to move to the comment column (same row), and type the comment **Hide the results of the macro while it runs** in that cell.
10. Double-click the Echo On text box in the Action Arguments panel until its value displays No.
11. Click the cell in the second row of the Action column, click the drop-down list box arrow, scroll the list to locate GoToRecord, and then click GoToRecord.
12. Press Tab, and then type the comment **Move to the first record** in that cell.
13. In the Action Arguments panel, click the Record row in the argument list, click the drop-down list box arrow, and select First from the list. The hint box to the right gives you information on what to specify for the action argument.
14. Click the cell in the third row of the Action column. Click the drop-down list box arrow, scroll the list until the action GoToControl appears, and click GoToControl to place it in the Action column.
15. Press Tab, and type the comment **Move the focus to the first field, CustomerID** in that cell.
16. In the Action Arguments panel, click the Control Name text box, and type **CustomerID**
17. Click the Macro window Close button, and click the Yes button when asked if you want to save the changes.

The completed macro is called *FirstRec*. It appeared previously in Figure 10.3. Your macro should match that one.

You have just created a macro group. A *macro group* is a collection of macros. When you use a macro group, it is easier to keep track of related macros such as the navigation button macros. They are contained in one macro group rather than stored as several separate macros. Over time, creating individual macros causes their numbers to soar and makes them very difficult to manage. Creating macro groups is no different from creating single macros. The advantage of a group is organization. Related macros can be placed under one "roof" so they can be easily located later. This is especially helpful when you have an application with hundreds of macros.

Although you have attached the CustNav macro—a group macro name—to the First button's On Click event, the actual name that appears in the On Click property must be changed to FirstRec before you can execute the macro by clicking the First button. After all, FirstRec is the name appearing in the Macro Name column of the CustNav macro group. FirstRec contains the code to move to the first database record, so let's change the macro name associated with the First button's On Click event. The next exercise shows you how to make this simple change.

EXERCISE 10.3: ATTACHING A MACRO TO A BUTTON'S ON CLICK EVENT

1. With the form displayed in Design view, click the First button, and examine its Event properties in the property sheet.
2. Click the On Click text box, and then click the down arrow that appears on the right side of the text box (see Figure 10.5). Be careful not to click the Build button, because that will display the macro instead of the list of macro names.
3. Click the choice *CustNav.FirstRec* in the selection list. (You refer to a particular macro that is part of a macro group by specifying the macro group name, a dot, followed by the macro name.)
4. Click the property sheet's Close button.
5. Click File on the menu bar, click Save to save your form changes, and click the form's Restore Window button on the right side just below the title bar Restore Window button.
6. Click the form's Close button.

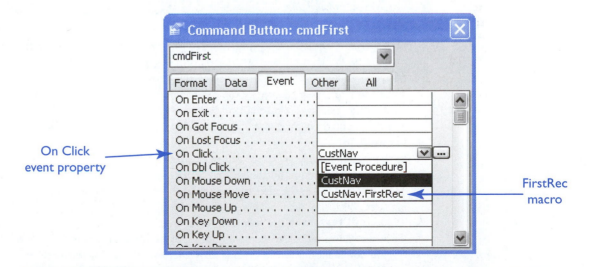

On Click
event property

FirstRec
macro

Figure 10.5 Attaching a macro to the command button's On Click event.

Try out the new button. Double-click the *frmCustomer1* form in the database window to open it in Form view. Then, click Edit on the menu bar, point to GoTo, and click Last to move to the last customer record. Now, click the First button on the form. The form displays the first record in the table.

In the next section, you create the remaining three navigation buttons by building Visual Basic for Applications code and attaching the VBA code to the remaining navigation buttons.

Creating Other Form Navigation Buttons with VBA

Creating the remaining navigation buttons that perform the duties of a form's traditional navigation buttons is relatively simple. You have created the first of these already. The procedure is similar for the *Previous*, *Next*, and *Last* navigation buttons. This time, however, you will use a Wizard to help you build the command buttons and the code that they invoke when they are clicked. Let's create a command button to go to the previous record in the database. In preparation for the exercise, open the *Ch10.mdb* database, click Forms on the Objects bar, and open *frmCustomer1* in Design view. Execute the steps in the following exercise to create a new navigation button backed by VBA code.

EXERCISE 10.4: CREATING A COMMAND BUTTON USING THE CONTROL WIZARDS TOOL

1. Display *frmCustomer1* in Design view. Then, click View in the menu bar, and click Toolbox to display the toolbox. Click the Control Wizards tool (see Figure 10.4) so that it is pressed in. (With the Control Wizards tool engaged, the Wizard helps us build a command button complete with VBA code behind the button.)
2. Click the Command Button tool in the toolbox, and click the *frmCustomer1* form just to the right of the existing First command button. Access places the command button on the form, and the Control Wizard starts by asking what actions you want the new button to perform.
3. Ensure that Record Navigation is selected in the Categories panel.
4. In the Actions panel, click GoTo Previous Record, and then click the Next button.
5. Select the Text option button so that a label appears on the button instead of a graphic. Type **&Previous** in the text box to the right of the Text option button, replacing the existing text. Click the Next button.
6. Type **cmdPrevious** in the text box to rename the button.
7. Click the Finish button to complete the button-building process. The Wizard finishes creating the command button. Simultaneously and invisibly, the Wizard also writes several lines of VBA code and automatically attaches them to the On Click event property for you.
8. Close the property sheet, if necessary, and close the Toolbox by clicking its close button. Press Ctrl+S to save the altered form, *frmCustomer1*. Leave the form open in Design view.

Let's look at the code that the Control Wizard created and attached to the Previous button's On Click event. The next exercise shows you how to view the code attached to an object's event property.

EXERCISE 10.5: VIEWING THE VBA CODE ATTACHED TO A BUTTON'S EVENT PROPERTY

1. Right-click the Previous button you just created, and click Build Event from the pop-up list. The Build Event command tells Access to open the Visual Basic window and to display the default event procedure for the selected object. In this case, the command button is the object, and its default event procedure is the On Click event. Thus, Visual Basic displays the code window showing VBA code behind the On Click procedure (see Figure 10.6).

2. Look around the Visual Basic window, and notice the menus it contains. Hover the mouse over the toolbar buttons, and observe the ToolTips. Don't worry right now about what the code means. We'll examine code in more detail later in this chapter.

3. After you have spent a few minutes observing the Visual Basic window, press Alt+Q to return to Microsoft Access. The Visual Basic window closes, and the familiar Access Database window reappears, along with the form *frmCustomer1* in Design view.

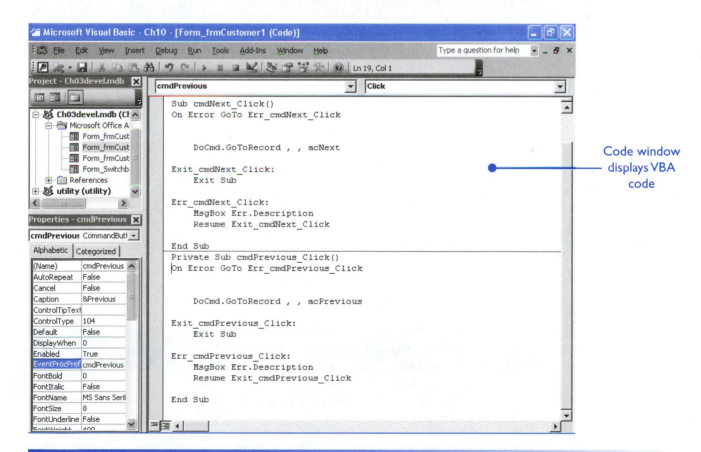

Figure 10.6 Examining a command button's code in the Visual Basic window.

Creating the missing two navigation buttons, Next and Last, is straightforward. To create the Next navigation button that goes to the next record in the customer table, repeat Exercise 10.4 but make these changes to the exercise's steps:

- Step 4: Select GoTo Next Record.
- Step 5: Type **Ne&xt** in the text box to the right of the Text option button. (The ampersand precedes the letter you want to serve as the command's access key.)
- Step 6: Type **cmdNext** to rename the button.

To create the Last navigation button that goes to the last record in the customer table, repeat Exercise 10.4 once again, but make these changes to the exercise's steps:

- Step 4: Select GoTo Last Record.
- Step 5: Type **&Last** in the text box to the right of the Text option button.
- Step 6: Type **cmdLast** to rename the button.

If you want to size the navigation buttons so that they more closely match those shown in Figure 10.2, then take a moment to complete the next exercise.

EXERCISE 10.6: OPTIMIZING BUTTON SIZES

1. In Design view, press and hold the Shift key, click each navigation button, and release the Shift key.
2. Click Format in the menu bar, point to Size, and click To Fit. This optimizes the button lengths to be just long enough to display the buttons' names.
3. Click Format, point to Size, and click To Widest. This step sizes the buttons to a uniform width—the length of the longest button.
4. With all buttons still selected, click any one of the handles in the middle, top edge of a button, and drag it toward the bottom edge to reduce the height of all the buttons slightly. Ensure that you can still see the buttons' labels, however.
5. Rearrange the buttons so that they appear side by side, as shown in Figure 10.2.
6. To make the buttons line up perfectly and have equal space between them, select all four buttons again, click Format on the menu bar, point to Align, click Bottom; and then click Format, point to Horizontal Spacing, and click Make Equal.
7. Press Ctrl+S to save the form.

Now that you have created four navigation buttons of your own, you can eliminate Access's built-in navigation buttons. There's no need for two sets of navigation buttons. Remove Access' navigation buttons by executing the steps that follow.

EXERCISE 10.7: ELIMINATE THE DEFAULT NAVIGATION BUTTONS AND RECORD SELECTORS

1. With *frmCustomer1* still in Design view, press Ctrl+R to select the form.
2. Press Alt+Enter to open the property sheet, click the Format tab, and set the Navigation Buttons property to No.
3. Set the Record Selectors property to No. (Remember: You can double-click any Yes/No property to toggle its value.) When the Record Selectors property is set to No, the record selector arrow disappears from the left edge of a form.

4. Close the property sheet and toolbox, if open.
5. Press Ctrl+S to save the form, click File on the menu bar, and click Close to close the form.

TRY IT

Try out the new form navigation buttons. Open the form in Form view, click the Last button, click the Previous button, and then click the First button. What happens if you click the First navigation button and then click the Previous navigation button? When you are done experimenting, close the form.

Printing a Macro, Macro Group, or VBA Code

You should always save your code prior to testing it. When you close the Macro window after making changes, Access prompts you about saving the macro. By clicking the Yes button, you save the *cmdFirst* macro that you created in Exercise 10.2. Similarly, if you were to make changes to the Wizard-generated VBA code like the code in Figure 10.6, then Access would prompt you to save your changes when you attempted to close the Visual Basic window. If you do not save your code prior to testing it, an errant bit of VBA code can execute incorrectly and may make it impossible to save the changes. For instance, suppose you alter the code in the Last navigation button, return to Form view, and click the Last button to test the changes. If an error in execution of the VBA code occurs, then you can be left staring at an error message in the Visual Basic window and have no easy way to save your latest version of your code.

Part of the process of developing a database system is documenting your work. One part of documenting your developing or completed system is maintaining a printout of all the code that you have written—both macros and VBA. You may want to keep these documents in a notebook along with printouts of forms, reports, queries, and tables. To print a macro, click Macros in the Objects bar of the Database window to display the list of macro names. Then, click the macro name you want to print, and select Print from the File menu. Select the items you want to include in the printout from the list in the Print Macro Definition dialog box. Then, click OK. That's all there is to it. You must repeat this process for every macro you want to print because, unfortunately, there is no way to print more than one macro at a time.

To print VBA code for all the procedures attached to any objects on a particular form, click Forms on the Objects bar of the Database window. Then, click the form name containing the VBA code that you want to print. Click View on the menu bar, click Code, click File on the menu bar, click Print, click the Current Module option (or Current Project to print the code for the entire database), and click the OK button on the Print dialog box. Finally, press Alt+Q to return to the Access database. Figure 10.7 shows an example of the code you created for three of the navigation buttons.

```
Form_frmCustomer1 - 1

Option Compare Database
Option Explicit

Private Sub cmdPrevious_Click()
On Error GoTo Err_cmdPrevious_Click


    DoCmd.GoToRecord , , acPrevious

Exit_cmdPrevious_Click:
    Exit Sub

Err_cmdPrevious_Click:
    MsgBox Err.Description
    Resume Exit_cmdPrevious_Click

End Sub
Private Sub cmdNext_Click()
On Error GoTo Err_cmdNext_Click


    DoCmd.GoToRecord , , acNext

Exit_cmdNext_Click:
    Exit Sub

Err_cmdNext_Click:
    MsgBox Err.Description
    Resume Exit_cmdNext_Click

End Sub
Private Sub cmdLast_Click()
On Error GoTo Err_cmdLast_Click


    DoCmd.GoToRecord , , acLast

Exit_cmdLast_Click:
    Exit Sub

Err_cmdLast_Click:
    MsgBox Err.Description
    Resume Exit_cmdLast_Click

End Sub
```

Figure 10.7   Example code printout.

Access Events

So far, we have looked at one event property, called *On Click*, which occurs whenever a user clicks the object having that property. Other objects besides command buttons have On Click event properties. For example, you can click a form, a text box, or a label. Though clicking such objects is uncommon, they respond by launching the macro or VBA code that is attached to their respective On Click event properties, if any. There are many other events to which various Access objects can respond. Figure 10.8 lists several event properties, when they spring into action, and why you might want to know when the event occurs.

There are more event properties than those listed in Figure 10.8, but the figure contains important event properties that you will need for this chapter. On Change is an

Event Property	Occurs When	Use the Event to
On Change	A control's value changes	Update any other related controls
On Click	A user clicks the mouse on an object	Anything. It is the most used of all events
On Current	A form is opened or requeried	Create more intelligent form navigation buttons
On Delete	A record is about to be deleted	Ensure it is okay to delete the selected record
On Exit	A control loses the focus to another control	Validate the data in a control
On Open	A form is displayed but before the first record is displayed	Initialize form messages and default values

Figure 10.8   Selected event properties and examples of their uses.

event property that occurs when the On Change event occurs. Entering a new value, or changing an existing value, in an object such as a text box triggers the On Change event, which launches the code attached to the On Change event property. The On Current event property is particularly handy whenever you use a form to view or change a table's contents. If you move to and display another record in a form, the On Current event occurs. (Developers sometimes say that an event fires or some action triggers an event.)

Improving Navigation Buttons

One way to improve the four navigation buttons is to change their behavior slightly to help the user. For instance, removing choices that are inapplicable helps users understand which actions are available and which are not. Specifically, when a user clicks the Last button, Access moves to the last record in the customer table. In this case, the Next button has no meaning, because there is no "next" record in the table—you are viewing the last record. Thus it would help users to disable the Next button so that they understand when the button becomes inapplicable. On the other hand, when a user then clicks the Previous navigation button, Access moves to the record just before the last one. In this case, the Next button should be available because there is a next record.

Well-designed Windows applications disable and enable commands and command buttons to indicate when they can and cannot be used. For example, if there is nothing on the Clipboard, then the Paste command in the Edit menu of most Microsoft products is dimmed (light gray), which indicates that you cannot paste anything. You will add similar user convenience features to your four-button customer form.

The next exercise takes advantage of a convenient event property for forms called *On Current*. The On Current event occurs whenever you open a form or Access displays a new record in the form. This is handy, because all four of the navigation buttons cause a new record to display in the form and thus trigger the On Current event.

The next exercise shows you how to write a general-purpose VBA procedure and attach it to the On Current event property, which monitors every record change or form-opening event. It is within that event handling code that your event procedure can gain control and determine if any of the navigation buttons should be disabled or enabled. In preparation for this exercise, open the *Ch10.mdb* database, if necessary, and close all windows except the Database window.

EXERCISE 10.8: CREATING BETTER NAVIGATION BUTTONS

1. Open *frmCustomer1* in Design view.
2. Press Ctrl+R to select the form. Then, click the Properties button on the Design view toolbar to display the property sheet. The property sheet title bar displays "Form" if you have selected the form. The property sheet title bar displays "Section: Detail" for example, if you clicked the dotted background of the Detail section instead of selecting the form as a whole.
3. Click the Event tab in the property sheet, click the On Current event property text box, and then click the Build button that appears on the right side of the On Current property.
4. Click Code Builder in the Choose Builder dialog box, and click OK. The Current event procedure opens in a Visual Basic window.
5. Add the following code to the form's Current event procedure. Be careful to type all new code between the statements *Private Sub Form_Current( )* and *End Sub*. Figure 10.9 shows the Visual Basic window with the following code already entered:

```
'If the CustomerID control is empty, then a new record is being displayed.
'In this case, shift the focus to the Previous button
'and disable the Next button.
'If there is a value in CustomerID, then enable the Next button.


If IsNull (Me.CustomerID) Then
    cmdPrevious.SetFocus
    cmdNext.Enabled = False
Else
    cmdNext.Enabled = True
End If
```

6. Click File on the menu bar, click Close, and Return to Microsoft Access to close the Visual Basic code window.
7. Close the form, and save it when Access prompts you.

TRY IT

Open the form in Form view. Try out the new safeguard built into the form. Click the Last button to go to the last record in the customer table. Click the Next button to open the empty record beyond the last actual table record. If you entered the code correctly in the preceding exercise, the Next button is dimmed, and you cannot click it. Finally, click the First navigation button, and observe that the Next button is enabled again. Close the form.

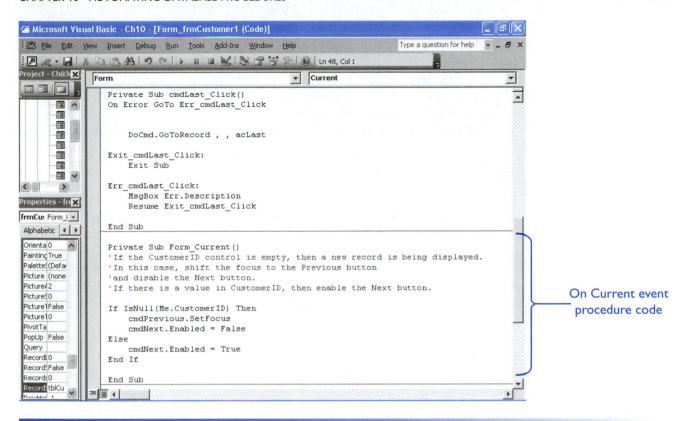

Figure 10.9   Completed On Current event procedure.

What is the code doing? The first four lines of code you typed all begin with apostrophes. This is the way you write Visual Basic comment lines. Everything following an apostrophe on a line is ignored by Visual Basic. The blank line following the comments provides needed visual separation between comments and code.

By using the On Current event property, you gain control of a form whenever the user moves from one record to another—including moving to the last record in the table and the empty record beyond that. You know that the user has pressed the Next button to reach the empty record beyond the last record in the customer table by inspecting the CustomerID control on the form. If the user has moved to a new record, the CustomerID control will be empty. The expression in the first line examines CustomerID to determine if it is empty:

If IsNull (Me.CustomerID)

IsNull is a built-in function available in Access that tests to see if the enclosed object (a control in this case) is empty (Null) or not. We get the value of the CustomerID control of the first record using the reference *Me.CustomerID*. The keyword "Me" indicates to Access that we want to refer to the current object's set of records—in this case, the current object is the form *frmCustomer1*. If the value of CustomerID is empty, or null, then we know that we have reached an empty record.

The expression following the If statement—the statement described previously—is evaluated. It can be either true or false. If it is true, then the statements following "Then" and before the "Else" phrases are executed. If the statement is false, then only the statement(s) between the "Else" and the "End If" are executed. In other words, the If/Then/Else structure provides two mutually exclusive choices, meaning Access will execute one or the other but not both.

What happens if the expression following the If phrase is true? Two statements are executed:

cmdPrevious.SetFocus
cmdNext.Enabled = False

Using the object.method notation, the statement "cmdPrevious.SetFocus" moves the focus to the cmdPrevious button. SetFocus is called a *method*, and cmdPrevious is an object on which the method operates. The result is that the focus first moves off the Next button and to the Previous button. (Recall that an object having the focus is the only object that can accept input—be clicked in this case.) The next statement sets the Enabled property of the cmdNext object to the value of False. Simply stated, the cmdNext button becomes unavailable and appears dimmed on the form.

What happens if the user had pressed the Next button and the second record in the customer display became available in the *frmCustomer1* form? First, the Current event would occur, triggering the code you entered for the On Current event property. The If statement evaluates the expression IsNull (Me.CustomerID) and returns the value False—the CustomerID control is not empty because the second record has a value for CustomerID. Continuing with the code (examine Figure 10.9), only the statement following Else in the If/Then/Else structure is executed: cmdNext.Enabled = True. That statement sets the cmdNext's enabled property to True. This means that the button is available and a user can click it. If you were to omit that statement, then the Next button would remain forever unavailable (dimmed) after the first time a user goes to the new record beyond the last actual record in the customer table.

The statement "End If" marks the end of the If statement. Following the End If statement is the automatically supplied "End Sub" statement, which marks the end of the entire event procedure that responds to the On Current event. One formatting convention is worth noting. Statements on the Then and Else sides of the If statement are indented for readability. It helps you to visually identify which statements belong with which parts of the structure.

IMPLEMENTING DATABASE MANIPULATION BUTTONS

Other useful buttons that can save time for your users and simplify their work include those that update a record, insert a new record in the database, delete an unwanted record, post all changes to a record to the database, and cancel (negate) any changes made to a record. While these tasks can be accomplished by using the Access menus, those menus can be intimidating to anyone not familiar with Microsoft Access. So, we show you how to create the buttons and associated macros to accomplish these important database tasks. We continue to use The Coffee Merchant's Customer form. When you are done with this section, your form (*frmCustomer1*) should resemble Figure 10.2, and all the form's buttons should work correctly.

Creating the Save Record and New Record Buttons

Users want to be able to easily save an edited record and add a new record to a database. You can facilitate these two operations by providing buttons that perform those functions. A very small piece of VBA code implements saving a record. The Save Record command button saves all changes to the current record by executing the Save Record command on the Records menu. It does this with the VBA DoMenuItem command, which invokes existing menu commands to do the work. It is as simple as that.

Let's build the VBA code to be attached to the Save Record button. You can use a Wizard to help you or you can build the button and its associated code yourself. If you choose to build it yourself, then there are two major steps involved. First, place a button on the form; second, create the On Click event property's VBA code to carry out the action. Create the Save Record button by completing the following exercise.

EXERCISE 10.9: CREATING THE SAVEREC BUTTON AND CORRESPONDING VBA CODE

1. Open *frmCustomer1* in Design view, open the toolbox, and click the Control Wizards tool so that it is pressed in—we want the Control Wizard's help.
2. Click the Command Button tool in the toolbox, and click on the *frmCustomer1* form on the right side of the form. Access places the command button on the form, and the Control Wizard displays the first of several dialog boxes.
3. Click Record Operations in the Categories panel.
4. In the Actions list, select Save Record, and then click the Next button.
5. Click the Text option button so that a label appears on the button instead of a graphic.
6. Type **&Save Record** in the text box to the right of the Text option button. (Alternatively, you can simply move to the left side of the text box—so that the insertion point is to the left of Save—and type **&** only.) Click the Next button.
7. Type **cmdSaveRecord** in the text box to give the button a meaningful name.
8. Click Finish to complete the button-building process. The Wizard creates the button and attaches VBA code to the button's On Click event property.
9. Save the altered form, *frmCustomer1*, and leave it open in Design view.

If you want to see the VBA code that Access built for you, then right-click the Save Record button, and click Build Event in the pop-up menu. The Visual Basic window opens. All the VBA code you or the Control Wizard created so far is found in this window. Simply scroll to the top or bottom to view various event procedures. You can display a particular procedure, such as the cmdSaveRecord_Click event procedure you created in the preceding exercise, by clicking inside the procedure you want to view and then clicking the Procedure View button in the lower left corner of the Visual Basic window (see Figure 10.10). Click the Full Module View button to view all the event procedures in the module. When you are done, simply press Alt+Q to return to Access and the customer form.

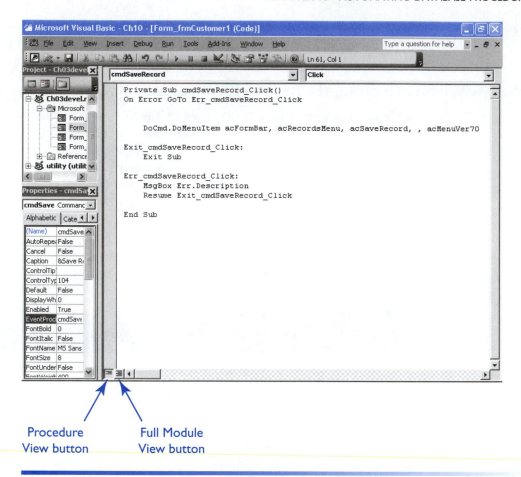

Procedure
View button

Full Module
View button

Figure 10.10 Completed Save Record event procedure.

TRY IT

To test the new Save Record button, let's create a new customer record. First, display *frmCustomer1* in Form view. Click the Records menu, and then click Data Entry to display an empty form. Enter any data you want, but be sure to assign a CustomerID value that is greater than 36000. This way, you will not inadvertently change an existing customer record. Now, click the Save Record button.

Confirm that the record was actually posted to the database. First, click Records on the menu bar, and click Remove Filter/Sort. Next, click the First navigation button, and then click the Last navigation button. After you click the Last button, the new record you just created appears in the form. Figure 10.11 shows an example of a new record. (Soon, we will create and use a Delete Record button to remove the record you entered so that the Customer database remains unchanged.)

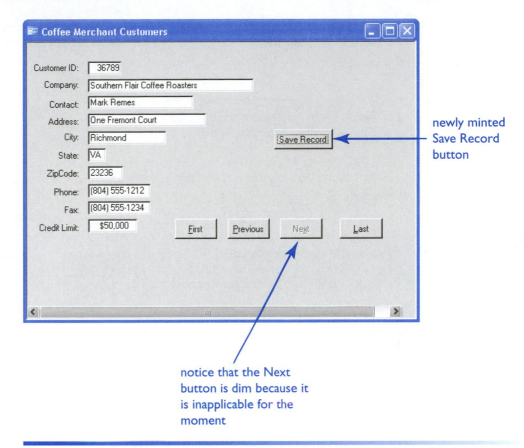

Figure 10.11   Adding a record and saving it with the Save Record button.

The New Record button and associated procedure is equally simple to implement. Repeat Exercise 10.9 but make the following changes in the steps:

- Step 4: Select Add New Record in the Actions list.
- Step 6: Type **&New Record**.
- Step 7: Type **cmdNewRecord** in the text box.

Leave open the Toolbox and the form in Design view, because you will be adding two more buttons in rapid succession. Recall that the ampersand designates the button's access key. Keyboard users can press Alt+N to click the button. Do not be concerned if the Save Record and New Record buttons are not the exact same size or are not aligned correctly. You will take care of all that soon.

Figure 10.12 shows the VBA code that the Control Wizard generated. Here's what it accomplishes. Execution begins with the first line of code following the statement "Private Sub..." The On Error statement simply tells Access that if any type of error occurs, continue execution at the label Err_cmdNewRecord_Click. That label is near the bottom of the sub procedure. The workhorse of the sub procedure is the line

DoCmd.GoToRecord , , acNewRec

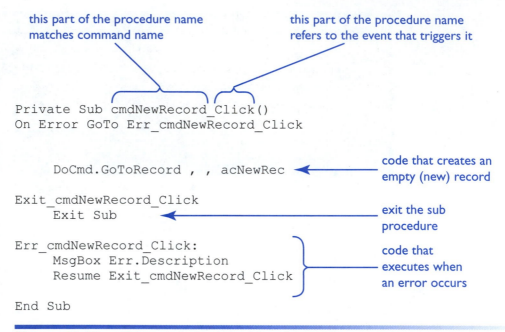

this part of the procedure name matches command name

this part of the procedure name refers to the event that triggers it

```
Private Sub cmdNewRecord_Click()
On Error GoTo Err_cmdNewRecord_Click


    DoCmd.GoToRecord , , acNewRec          ← code that creates an
                                             empty (new) record

Exit_cmdNewRecord_Click
    Exit Sub                               ← exit the sub
                                             procedure

Err_cmdNewRecord_Click:                    ⎫ code that
    MsgBox Err.Description                  ⎬ executes when
    Resume Exit_cmdNewRecord_Click         ⎭ an error occurs

End Sub
```

Figure 10.12   VBA code behind the New Record button.

DoCmd is called an *object*. Following the object is a period and "GoToRecord." GoToRecord is a *method*, which is an action affecting the object to which it is attached. Following the object and its method are one or more arguments. *Arguments* to a method supply additional information about how the method should operate. Commas separate method arguments from one another. You indicate omitted or unneeded arguments by a blank space and a comma. Following the two omitted arguments is the very important intrinsic constant, "acNewRec." An *intrinsic constant* is a character string that has an unchanging value. The intrinsic constant shown in Figure 10.12, acNewRec, indicates that Access should display a new, blank record. The last line that Access executes during normal processing is "Exit Sub." That command terminates the sub procedure and returns control back to Access. Above Exit Sub is a label, "Exit_cmdNewRecord_Click," which is required so that the procedure can pass control to the Exit Sub command if it detects an error and passes control to the error-processing portion of the sub procedure.

Modifying VBA Code

While the Control Wizard does a good job of building VBA code for a variety of predefined tasks, the code can use some refinement. Open *frmCustomer1* in Form view and click the New Record button. Access opens a new record, clearing all the form's controls. Notice that the focus is on the button labeled Previous. We programmed the On Current event to place the focus on the Previous button whenever Access detects that the record displayed has an empty CustomerID. This happens when you click the

New Record button, too. What is the user's next action after clicking the New Record button? He or she will probably click in the Customer ID text box to begin entering information. Simplify things for users by placing the insertion point in the Customer ID field for them. That action is called *setting the focus*. You may remember that we used the SetFocus method in the On Current form property event to move the focus to the Previous button. Let's modify the code behind the New Record button.

EXERCISE 10.10: MODIFYING THE NEW RECORD VBA CODE

1. Display *frmCustomer1* in Design view, right-click the New Record button, and click Build Event in the pop-up list. The Visual Basic window opens and displays the sub procedure attached to the On Click event property.
2. Click the Procedure View button in the corner of the Visual Basic window to zoom in on the cmdNewRecord_Click sub procedure.
3. Click the empty line below the one containing *DoCmd.GoToRecord*, press Tab to indent the line just like the one above it, type **CustomerID.setfocus**, and press Enter.

    As you type, notice that you get help from Access (see Figure 10.13). Note, too, that Access changes the capitalization of "setfocus" to "SetFocus" after you press Enter. That means that you do not need to match the capitalization of objects or methods, because

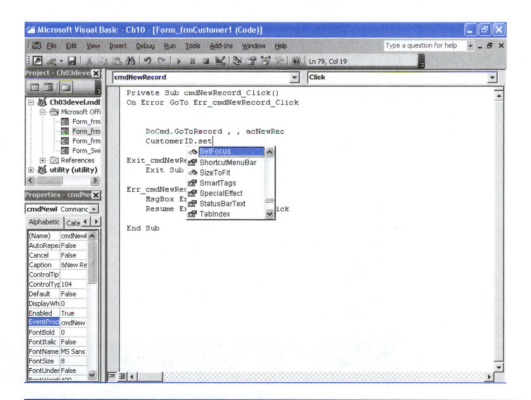

Figure 10.13 Modifying a sub procedure.

Access will do that for you automatically when you move to a new line. This is an excellent way to ensure you have spelled words correctly—type objects' names in lower case. If Access does not capitalize selected letters to match the spelling of an object, then you have misspelled the name.

4. Press Alt+Q to save the VBA code and close the Visual Basic window.
5. Save the altered form.

In step 3 you noticed that as soon as you typed the period (.) following *CustomerID*, Visual Basic displayed a list of an object's methods and properties in a list. As you continue typing, the list automatically scrolls down to the first list member that matches what you have typed so far. If the list highlights the correct item in the list, you do not need to continue typing. Pressing the spacebar when Visual Basic highlights the correct method or property will enter the remainder for you and close the list. You may find this the easiest way to write code. Using this method guarantees that you will not misspell the method.

TRY IT

Observe the changed New Record button. Open *frmCustomer1* in Form view, and click the New Record button. Where is the focus now? If you did Exercise 10.10 correctly, the focus will be in the Customer ID text box.

Creating the Delete Record and Cancel Changes Buttons

The Delete Record button deletes the currently displayed record from the database. In contrast, the Cancel Changes button discards any changes made to the current record, restoring the original record. The difference between the two actions is that the Cancel Changes button restores the original values of a record that has not been posted (saved) in the database. In other words, Cancel Changes allows you to rescind any changes to the current record before the record is saved to the database. On the other hand, the Delete Record button irrevocably removes a record from the database.

Build the two buttons again by using the Control Wizard. First, you will build the Delete Record button by following the steps of an exercise. Following that, you will build the Cancel Changes button by hand without using the Control Wizard (gasp!). Finally, with all four database manipulation buttons in place, you will align them and make them a uniform size.

Follow the steps in the next exercise to create the Delete Record button and associated VBA code.

EXERCISE 10.11: CREATING THE DELETE RECORD BUTTON AND CODE

1. Click Open *frmCustomer1* in Design view, if necessary, and ensure the toolbox is open.
2. Ensure that the Control Wizards button is pressed in (it will be a rust color).

3. Click the Command Button tool in the toolbox and then click on the *frmCustomer1* form on the right side of the form, just below the New Record button. Access places the command button on the form, and the Control Wizard starts displaying dialog boxes.
4. In the Categories list, select Record Operations.
5. In the Actions list, select Delete Record, and then click the Next button.
6. Select the Text option button, click the text box to the right of the option button and to the left of the letter "D", and type **&** just in front of the existing text, *Delete Record*. Click the Next button.
7. Type **cmdDeleteRecord** in the text box to give the button a meaningful name.
8. Click Finish to complete the button-building process. The Wizard creates the button and attaches VBA code to the button's On Click event property.
9. Save the altered form, *frmCustomer1*. Leave the form open in Design view.

The last database manipulation button you will create is called *Cancel Changes*. This button's code is simple enough to not need the help of the Control Wizard. Besides, it's good to practice building VBA code from scratch to get an idea of how it works. You need to complete four steps to accomplish this: Create a button control, place it on the form, create the code that executes when the On Click event occurs, and attach it to the button's On Click event property. Execute the following exercise to build the Cancel Changes button.

EXERCISE 10.12: MANUALLY CREATING THE CANCEL CHANGES BUTTON AND CODE

1. With the toolbox open, click the Control Wizards button so it is not selected. This time we do not want the Wizard's help.
2. Place a command button on the form below the Delete Record button.
3. Right-click the new command button, click Properties in the pop-up list, and click the *All* tab.
4. Double-click the Name property, if necessary, to highlight the entire name, and then type **cmdCancel** to replace the existing name. The Name property is an internal name used by VBA code to refer to the button.
5. Click the Caption property, and then type **&Cancel Changes**. The Caption property contains the text that is on the button's surface—the label that users see on the button.
6. Click the Event tab of the property sheet, right-click the On Click event property, and click Build in the pop-up menu. The Choose Builder dialog box opens.
7. Click Code Builder in the left panel, and click the OK button. The Visual Basic window opens. Access conveniently places the insertion point between the first and last statements of the cmdCancel_Click sub procedure. It is at that position that you will type code that carries out the undo operation.
8. Press Tab to indent the code line, and then type the following line (don't bother to capitalize words):

   DoCmd.DoMenuItem acFormBar, acEditMenu, acUndo

   and press Enter at the end of the code line.
9. Next, type **CustomerID.setfocus** and press Enter. (See Figure 10.14.)
10. Press Alt+Q to close the Visual Basic Editor window and return to the Access database.
11. Click the Save button on the Standard toolbar to save your form and its new command button.

procedure (button) name

event to which the
procedure reacts

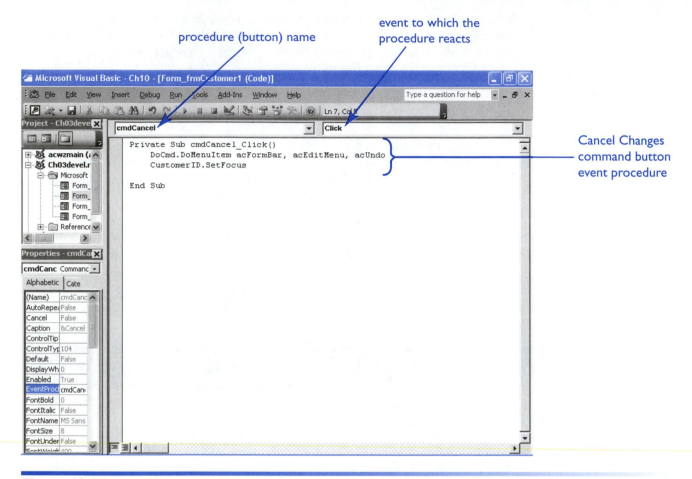

Cancel Changes
command button
event procedure

Figure 10.14   Cancel Changes event procedure.

 TRY IT

Check out the new Cancel Changes button. Switch *frmCustomer1* to Form view, make a few changes to the current record, and click the Cancel Changes button. All the changes you have made will be rescinded, and the record will be restored to its original form.

As you created the four data manipulation buttons, you may not have bothered making them all the same size or even aligning them. We believe that you should defer cosmetic work such as this until after you have done the "heavy lifting" involved with creating buttons and their associated event procedures. Once this is done, you can fix any visual problems. Now is a good time to make the four data manipulation buttons the same size, align them, and make the space between them equal. Simply repeat Exercise 10.6 using the four data manipulations in place of the four navigation buttons.

Change step 6: Align the buttons on their left sides by selecting Format, Align, Left (instead of Format, Align, Bottom); secondly, select Format, Vertical Spacing (rather than Horizontal Spacing), Make Equal. Finally, click Format, point to Size, and click To Widest to size all the buttons to the same width. When you've completed this exercise, your customer form should resemble Figure 10.2. The only features that your form may not have when compared to Figure 10.2 are the rectangles that appear around the two groups of buttons. If you want to add the rectangles, then follow the next Try It. If you choose not to, then close the form design window.

TRY IT

With *frmCustomer1* in Design view, open the toolbox, click the Rectangle tool, and drag the rectangle on the form so that it surrounds the four navigation buttons. Release the mouse. Repeat this for the data manipulation buttons. Save the form design, and close the form design window.

AUTOMATING INTERNAL CONTROL FEATURES

Most database systems provide some built-in validity checking whereby built-in procedures check input values to ensure they are acceptable. Microsoft Access is no exception, providing a Validation Rule for tables, forms, and controls. For example, Access can prevent you from entering a number such as 67.89 in a date field on a form, because Access automatically applies data validation based on a field's data type. If you attempt to enter data that does not match the field data type, Access displays an error message. Other control features built into Access tables include a field's Input Mask, Required, and Validation Rule properties. Although Access' built-in validity checks are powerful in a general way, they simply cannot handle more specific and rigorous data checks. A form's date field is an example. What do you suppose Access would do if you entered an invoice date such as 10/17/2020 and pressed Enter or Tab? Although that date is probably not reasonable for most applications, Access allows you to enter it without issuing an error message.

You can detect and prevent erroneous dates as well as prevent other types of data entry errors that would pass Access' fundamental validity tests. Central to validating data are macros attached to events associated with a field or form to be validated. Access macro statements and VBA code provide powerful features that make elaborate, interfield validity checking easy to implement.

Data validation implemented with VBA code is particularly useful in automating internal controls involving databases that are external to the application. For example, it is not difficult to write a small code block that checks available inventory of an item as the sales order quantity is being entered. When the input quantity exceeds available supplies of an item, a VBA sub procedure can detect the condition and issue a warning message. In other circumstances, VBA code can reduce on-hand quantities to the appropriate value based on the quantity that is entered into an order form. This stock-checking internal control is a business rule you can enforce by writing VBA code and associating it with one of a data field's several event properties.

We show examples of validating a field and enforcing business rules in the two sections that follow. You can use these as models to create your own validity checking and rule enforcement procedures for your accounting applications.

Validating User Input

One example of application-specific data validation is checking data that a user enters on a form *before* you allow the user to post that changed information to the database's tables. For instance, you might want to validate a purchase order date immediately after a user enters it on a form to ensure that the value is reasonable. In the case of any date field, the term "reasonable" is a temporal measure that depends on the application. You might implement this type of date validation at the root—with the built-in Validation Rule property available for each field in the table itself. However, it makes more sense to write code to test values *before* they flow into a table. This is particularly true when you want to *share* the validation procedure across forms and applications within the same database. You can create small VBA sub procedures that can detect certain errors immediately. Frequently, Access does not identify a mistake until you move off the current record. Depending on automatic validity checks provided by Access can delay recognizing mistakes, which can frustrate users who have keyed a lot of data in the meantime.

Chapter 5 introduced you to an Order Entry form, which is pictured in Figure 10.15. Recall that the form fields Customer (customer number) and Salesperson (sales representative) use a combo box to look up and display a list of acceptable values for their respective fields.

Let's create a VBA event procedure that checks the Order Date field on The Coffee Merchant Order form to ensure that the date is acceptable. We will attach the code to the Before Update event property of the Order Date field control. By associating the VBA code with the Before Update event property of the field, Access will automatically execute the code just after the user moves from the Order Date to another control on the form. Triggering the Before Update property means that Access will not move the value that the user typed into the Order Date text box to an internal storage area until the procedure checks the value. When the last value is entered on The Coffee Merchant form, Access then moves all form data from memory where it is temporarily housed into the various tables in the database. The Before Update property is an ideal way to check any field's contents before permitting the change to post to a database.

The *ValidDateCheck* VBA sub procedure checks the Order Date field to ensure it is valid. If it is, then the code permits the focus to move to any form field that the user clicks. On the other hand, the code does not allow the cursor to move from the Order Date control if the date value does not conform to the rules you have established. You will attach the date validation code only to the Order Date control (internally named *txtOrderDate*). If this type of date validation is something you find yourself doing for other controls, then you may want to write a general-purpose date-check code and place

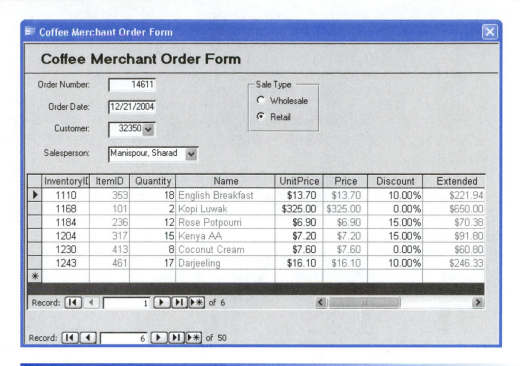

Figure 10.15   The Coffee Merchant order form.

it in the Modules collection. Any code listed in the Modules collection is available for use by any object in the entire database. Code created for any form, like all the code we have created so far in this chapter, is available *only* to the form to which it is attached.

The date validation business rule you will implement is this: Any order date entered into The Coffee Merchant's Order form must be plus or minus 14 days on either side of today's date (inclusive). All other dates (those outside that range) are invalid. This rule, though arbitrary, permits backdating or postdating any order up to 14 days. When an invalid date is recognized, an information message appears and then the user is allowed to correct the date. This may not always be a good policy, but we implement the rule simply to show you how to enforce it. You are free to tweak such rules as you see fit.

Prepare for the next exercise by closing all Access windows except the Database window for *Ch10.mdb*.

EXERCISE 10.13: WRITING VBA CODE FOR THE *BEFORE UPDATE* EVENT PROPERTY

1. Click Forms on the Objects bar, and open *frmOrder* in Design view. Right-click the Order Date text box control (not the Order Date label control), click Properties in the pop-up menu, click the Event tab (if necessary), right-click the Before Update event property, and click Build in the pop-up list. The Choose Builder dialog box opens.

2. Double-click Code Builder from the list of three choices to open the Visual Basic Editor.

3. Press Tab to indent the first line of code, then type **'Validate order date**, and press Enter. That is how you enter a comment line: begin the line with an apostrophe and then type the text. Notice that Access changes the color of comment lines to green. That makes comments easy to distinguish from code.

4. Enter the following code beneath the comment you just typed, pressing Enter at the end of each line. Press Tab as needed to match the indenting shown here. Be aware that the second line in the following code ends with a comma, a space, and an underscore character—in that order.

> **If txtOrderDate < Date - 14 Or txtOrderDate > Date + 14 Then**
> **MsgBox "Date is incorrect. Please reenter.", _**
> **vbOKOnly + vbExclamation, "Error"**
> **Cancel = True**
> **Else**
> **Cancel = False**
> **End If**

5. Press Alt+Q to close the Visual Basic code window, and close the Properties dialog box.

6. Click the Save button on the Standard toolbar to save the altered form. Figure 10.16 shows the Before Update event property VBA code. Your code should match it exactly.

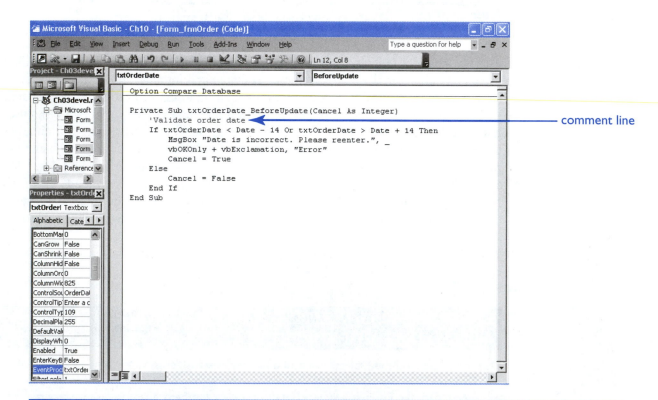

Figure 10.16 VBA code to check user-input order dates.

Before you learn exactly what the code does, let's see if the code works. Always test your work thoroughly before you release it. Follow the next Try It to test the VBA code.

TRY IT

Display *frmOrder* in Form view. Click Records in the menu bar and then click Data Entry to display an empty order form. Type the value **77777** in the Order Number text box. Press Tab to move to the Order Date field. Type the date **10/17/07** in the text box, and press Tab. The error dialog box shown in Figure 10.17 should appear warning you that the date you entered is incorrect. The VBA code you wrote tests the input date to make sure it is within four weeks (two before and two after) of the current date—based on the current date stored on the computer you are using. Click the OK button on the dialog box to remove the dialog box. Next, drag the mouse over the entire Order Date text box, press the Delete key to erase the incorrect date, and type in today's date. Press Tab to move to the Customer list box. Click the list arrow and select any customer's name. Press Tab to move to the Salesperson's text box, click the drop-down arrow, and select any salesperson from the drop-down list. Click the Form View window Close button to close the form.

invalid date
entered to test
date validation
code

error warning
dialog box

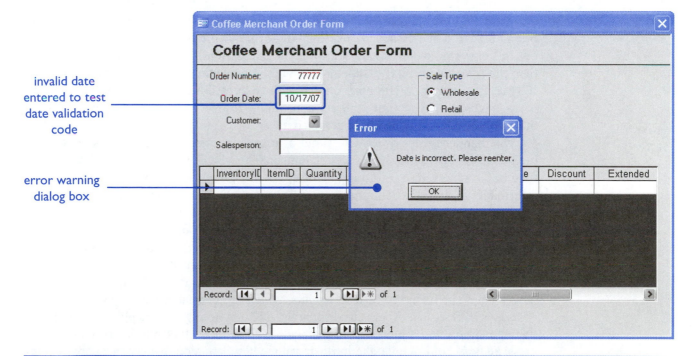

Figure 10.17   Example of an attempt to enter an invalid order date.

What do the lines of the sub procedure shown in Figure 10.16 mean? First, notice that the name of the procedure includes both the form control name (txtOrderDate) and the event procedure (Before Update) to which it is attached. The sub procedure has one argument, on the same line as the Sub statement, enclosed in parentheses. A sub procedure *argument* is a name used to pass information into and out of a sub procedure—a sort of communication pipe linking the inside of the procedure to the code outside the procedure. The sub procedure's argument is called *Cancel* and is an integer. (Arguments are declared in the argument list on the Sub statement.) The second line contains a comment describing what the procedure does. Here, we used a very brief comment. You may want to include multiple line comments to fully explain the purpose of any sub procedures you write. The remainder of the sub procedure is a single statement, believe it or not. The If statement provides three parts as follows:

```
If <conditional expression> Then
    <statements1>
Else
    <statements2>
End If
```

The <conditional expression> is an arbitrarily complex expression that evaluates to either true or false. To validate the date a user enters in the txtOrderDate field, the expression tests whether the value of the date in the control txtOrderDate is prior to today's date (Date) minus 14 days or later than today's date plus 14 days. The word "Date" that appears in the conditional expression is a VBA built-in function that returns the current date, which it gets by interrogating the computer system's clock. Either the expression is true or false. If the expression is true, then that means the date entered is out of range (too old or in the future). If the expression is true—indicating an error—then the first statement(s) (<statements1> in the preceding syntax) are executed in the If/Then/Else statement and none others. If the expression is false, that means the date is reasonable based on your arbitrary constraints. In that case, any statements between the Else and End If phrases are executed.

What happens if the order date is out of range? Access executes the MsgBox statement and then executes the Cancel statement. The MsgBox statement displays a message box on the screen informing the user about an unusual condition or providing an informational message. The message you want to display follows the MsgBox statement in quotation marks. The second argument, separated from the first by a comma, is a bit more complicated. It tells Access which buttons and icons to display on the message box. Because the line is long, we use a *statement continuation* indicator—a blank followed by an underline—to indicate that the statement continues uninterrupted on the next line. (Normally, a statement must be written on a single line, no matter how long it is.) Using *intrinsic constants*, which are constants that appear to be variables, vbOKOnly tells Access to display the OK button only. To display other buttons, you can simply use a plus sign to mathematically "add" other buttons or icons to the message box. For example, the intrinsic value vbExclamation displays a standard Windows exclamation point in the message box. The third argument, "Error", is the text you want to appear in the Title bar of the message box. After displaying a message box using the MsgBox built-in procedure, Access encounters the statement

Cancel = True

That sets the value of the Cancel argument—the variable named in the argument list of the sub procedure—to the value of true. There is a comment in the right part of the line to document the statement. Like the full-line comment, it begins with an apostrophe. The remainder of a line with an apostrophe is commentary. When control returns to the Access form, it causes the cursor to remain in the txtOrderDate control rather than moving to another control on the form. In other words, it cancels the input value and keeps the focus on the control that is in error. Once the code on the "Then" side of the If/Then/Else is executed, control jumps over the rest of the statement and to the End Sub statement. That returns control from the sub procedure back to the Access form.

Suppose the order date value is valid. Then what happens? The conditional expression is false; therefore, Access executes the statement following the Else phrase. The statement

Cancel = False

executes. The If/Else statement code branch accepts the order date and allows Access to move to whatever field the user reaches by clicking the mouse or pressing the Tab key. A comment follows the expression and begins with an apostrophe.

The date range we chose to illustrate validity checking is arbitrary. What we want to illustrate is how to write a simple data validation sub procedure. You can choose to validate dates, numeric values, and even character strings for any number of form fields using the same techniques shown here. Use the date validation method as an example to create similar form field validation tests.

Enforcing Business Rules

Access VBA code is essential for enforcing the many obvious and sometimes subtle business rules. These rules vary from company to company, department to department within a company, and among programs for a single department or division within a company. Business rules might stipulate that a sales order entered by a clerk must be checked against the customer's payment history file before it is approved. Another rule might require that a sales representative's number be included on each sales order form so that the order's origin is easily traced if necessary. Neither of the preceding rules validates data input, because the form fields involved are not subject to range or reasonableness tests. Rather, the tests performed are more subtle and involve information that is not linked to the current form. We show you in this section how to construct these types of business rule tests.

It is important when entering a sales order to check that there is sufficient stock to be able to supply the item being entered. Look at Figure 10.15 for a moment. When you enter "18" in the Quantity column for English Breakfast, an automatic procedure should engage and check the stock on hand to ensure the order can be filled. If less than 18 pounds of the requested item are in stock, then some action should be started to handle the situation. At the very least, a message should appear on the screen warning the order entry person that insufficient stock exists for the particular item. Then, the order entry person can note on the order form that the item is back-ordered. Alternatively, he or she can attempt to locate the requested item in an alternate inventory source. Ideally, the system should also automatically generate a purchase request for additional stock. That purchase request could be an entry in another table that is printed daily to see what stock should be ordered.

We will show you how and where to place a check to ensure stock ordered is available while the order is being processed. For illustration purposes, we will keep the reaction to a stock shortage brief: the process merely warns the data entry person of the shortage. Later, you can embellish the procedure to include a mechanism that creates a purchase order or to simply insert an appropriately identified row in a purchase table.

The exercise that follows shows you how to build a simple VBA procedure that checks each line item quantity value just after it is entered (but before it is placed into the order table). Checking is conceptually simple. VBA code compares the quantity ordered to the item's OnHand value, which is stored in the *tblInventory* table. If the ordered amount just entered exceeds available stock, a warning message displays on the screen. The VBA code that performs the comparison between requested quantity and the actual quantity available is attached to the Quantity column's Before Update event procedure. The Quantity column is part of the *fsubOrder* subform. The subform is embedded in the master form, *frmOrder* (see Figure 10.15). Prepare for Exercise 10.14 by closing all windows in the Ch10 database except the Database window.

We begin by writing the VBA code that performs the stock check. In writing the code, we will use an Access built-in function called DLookup to look up and return the amount of stock on hand for a particular item. The DLookup function interrogates the *tblInventory* table and locates the Quantity value for a user-specified inventory item. The VBA code will display a warning message if the code determines that the amount of the item in stock is less than the quantity requested in the order. Otherwise, the macro returns control to the Order Entry form. (You will also want to decrease the stock on hand quantity in inventory by the amount ordered so that the inventory counts remain accurate. That is left as an exercise for the student.)

EXERCISE 10.14: WRITING VBA CODE TO CHECK AVAILABLE STOCK

1. Click Forms on the *Ch10.mdb* Objects bar, and open *fsubOrder* in Design view.
2. Right-click the Quantity control, click Properties from the pop-up menu to display the control's property sheet, click the Event tab, right-click the Before Update event property text box, and click Build in the pop-up menu. The Choose Builder dialog box opens.
3. Click Code Builder from the list of choices and click the OK button to begin writing code.
4. Press Tab to indent the first line of code; then, type **'Check available stock quantity**, and press Enter.
5. Enter the following code beneath the comment you just typed, pressing Enter at the end of each line and pressing Tab as needed to match the line indent shown below. Remember to

continue the first line by terminating it with a comma, a space, and the underscore character (in that order).

```
If Quantity > DLookup("[OnHand]", "[tblInventory]", _
    "[ItemID]=Forms![frmOrder]![fsubOrder].Form![ItemID]") Then
    MsgBox "Quantity requested greater than available stock", vbOKOnly
    Cancel = True       'quantity requested not available
Else
    Cancel = False      'quantity available to satisfy request
End If
```

6. Press Alt+Q to close the Visual Basic code window, and close the Properties window.
7. Click File, and then click to save the altered form. Figure 10.18 shows the Before Update event property VBA code. Your code should match it.
8. Close the *fsubOrder* subform.

Here's an explanation of the VBA code you just entered. Whenever someone enters into the *frmOrder* subform an item quantity value and then attempts to move to the

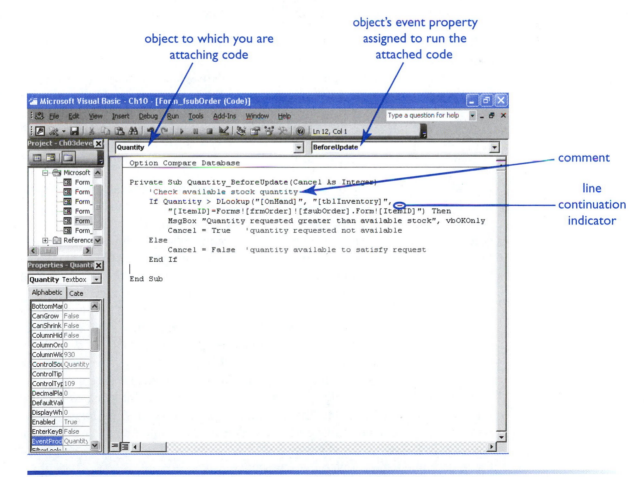

Figure 10.18   VBA code to check order quantity against available quantity.

next field in the order entry detail line, the Before Update event triggers. This causes the Before Update VBA code to take control. Like the previous VBA code you wrote, this sub procedure consists of an If/Then/Else statement that contains two alternative actions. The DLookup built-in function, part of the conditional expression that is tested, has this general form:

DLookup(expression, domain, criteria)

The actual expression used in your code contains "[OnHand]" for the expression argument. This is the column value that is located and returned from the *tblInventory* table. The *tblInventory* table name is the second argument of the DLookup function. It names the table to be searched for the stock quantity. Finally, the third argument indicates which row of the *tblInventory* table to look for. A match between the ItemID of the *fsubOrder* form and the same item in the *tblInventory* table contains the inventory row containing the stock on hand we seek. That criteria argument is the rather lengthy expression:

"[ItemID]=Forms![frmOrder]![fsubOrder].Form![ItemID]"

The notation beginning after the equal sign is the standard way to name a subform field embedded within a form. It requests a match between the order line item identification in the order entry and the inventory item whose primary key is also ItemID.

After DLookup returns a single number—the OnHand value for the chosen inventory item—it is compared to the Quantity value that the user entered. The entire "expression" portion of the DLookup function in a simplified form is this:

[Quantity]>quantity retrieved from the inventory by DLookup

If the preceding condition is true—a larger quantity is requested than is available—then the statements following the word *Then* are executed. In such a case, the MsgBox statement issues a warning message. Notice the lengthy IF statement continues on a second line. Recall that you indicate a line continues by typing a space followed by the underscore character. Continue typing the remainder of the statement on a new line. (It is best to break a statement in a blank space and not in the middle of a character string enclosed in quotation marks.) The second statement, "Cancel = True", passes a true value back to Access when the sub procedure completes. This causes the focus to not move and gives the user a chance to read the warning message and reenter a corrected quantity value. If the quantity requested by the user is *less than* the quantity available in inventory, then the Cancel variable is set to false. Normal processing of the order entry continues when false is returned from the sub procedure.

You could take alternative actions if there was insufficient stock to fulfill the current order. You could update the OnHand column of the *tblInventory* table to reflect how much of the item was taken from stock (negative amounts mean a back-order situation exists). Or you could halt processing. We have shown you one way to deal with the situation—display a warning message.

Now that you have a fundamental understanding of the VBA code attached to the Quantity control's Before Update event property, let's test the code. Experiencing the code in action (triggering a warning message) really drives home how this process enforces a fundamental business rule.

TRY IT

Display the *frmOrder* form in Form view, and click the First Record navigation button for the order form. (Be sure not to click the First Record navigation button for the subform.) The first sales order displays. Execute each of the following steps to see exactly how your newly created business rule catches an attempt to order more of an item than currently exists in stock. Move the mouse pointer to the Quantity column in the last row of the subform corresponding to the *Ethiopia Sidamo* entry. Double-click the current Quantity entry to highlight it. Type the new quantity value, **5000**, and press Tab to enter the value. A warning message appears because there are only 3,440 pounds of Ethiopia Sidamo (item 167) in stock, not the requested 5,000 pounds (see Figure 10.19). Click OK to remove the message box, double-click the quantity value to highlight it, type **4**, and press the Up Arrow key to move off the altered subform record and restore the original value. Close the form.

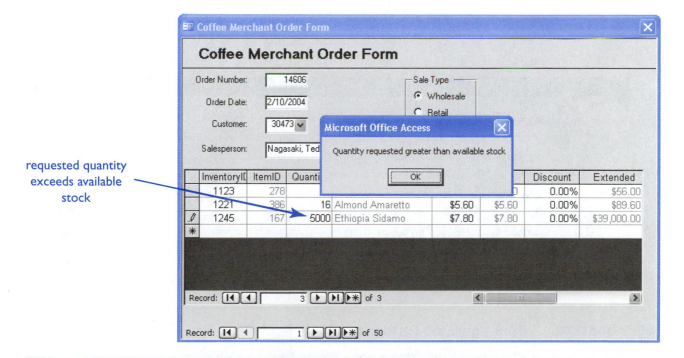

Figure 10.19 The stock-check VBA code in action.

USING A SWITCHBOARD FORM

To add polish to your database application, consider creating a database startup form. A *startup form* opens automatically when a user double-clicks a database application file name to open it. The most common way to provide a simple yet helpful opening screen is to create a form that serves as a main menu. From the opening form, users can click buttons to print reports, open forms, or examine individual tables. We have included a preliminary example of a startup form in your *Ch10.mdb* database. Called *Switchboard*, the form contains three buttons, a graphic, and a bit of text. Figure 10.20 shows the completed Switchboard form. You will begin with a Switchboard form that is almost complete and finish it.

Database designers frequently use the term switchboard for this type of startup form because it contains buttons that allow a user to switch from one part of a database application to just about any other. Like a telephone switchboard, the startup form provides a switching function. Your database contains a preliminary version of the Switchboard form that is stored in the Forms collection of your *Ch10.mdb* database. The only difference between your Switchboard form and the one shown in Figure 10.20 is that the bottom button and accompanying text are omitted on your form. Otherwise, the two forms behave identically. The functional heart of your Switchboard form consists of the three buttons that open selected forms and reports in your database. Clicking the top button opens a customer mailing label report in a Preview window. When you click the button containing an icon of a form—just below the preview customer command button—it displays a Customer form in Form view. With the Customer form, you can review the customers or make changes to them. The third and last button on your preliminary form displays an Employee form. Like the Customer form, the Employee form provides your users a convenient way to either review the employee information or make changes to it.

TRY IT

Before going on, open the Switchboard form to see how it works. Click Forms on the Objects bar, and then open the Switchboard form in Form view. Hover the mouse pointer over the large title "The Coffee Merchant." Within a few seconds, a ScreenTip displays the owner's name and date when the company was established. Hover the mouse pointer over the button next to the label "View or enter customer information." What does the button's ScreenTip display? Finally, try out a switchboard button: Click the middle button to open up a customer form. When you are done examining the customer form, close it by clicking Close button in its title bar. The Switchboard form comes to the foreground. Close the Switchboard form.

Adding an Exit Button to the Switchboard Form

A switchboard-style startup form should also sport a button or menu that allows users to exit the application. Such a button provides a nonexpert a simple way of halting an application and makes the application more polished. You will add another button to the Switchboard form that will exit Access when the user clicks it. To the right of the new command button you will add a label that indicates the purpose of the button. Finally, you will set several form-level properties so that the startup form looks more like a switchboard-style form and less like a record-displaying type of form.

In preparation for the next exercise, open *Ch10.mdb* (if necessary) and close all windows except the Database window.

EXERCISE 10.15: ADDING AN EXIT BUTTON TO THE SWITCHBOARD FORM

1. Click Forms on the Objects bar, and open the Switchboard form in Design view. Open the toolbox, and make sure that the Control Wizards tool is selected.
2. Click the Command Button tool, and then click the form just beneath and aligned with the left edge of the bottom button of the three. The Command Button Wizard begins displaying a series of dialog boxes.
3. Click Application in the Categories list (*Quit Application* is already selected in the Actions list), and then click Next.
4. The Control Wizard asks if you want text or a picture. Unlike other command buttons you created, you want a picture on this command button. The Picture option button and the Stop Sign are already selected. Because those are good choices, simply click Next to go to the next dialog box.
5. Type **cmdExitApplication** in the text box to assign the button a meaningful, internal name.
6. Click Finish. The Control Wizard completes its work and places a new button on your form.

You may wish to align the new button with the existing ones by selecting all the buttons, clicking Format, pointing to Align, and clicking the appropriate alignment command. In addition, you may want to ensure that there is equal spacing between the buttons by clicking Format, pointing to Vertical Spacing, and clicking Make Equal.

Adding a Label to the Switchboard Form

The next step to modify the Switchboard form is to add text to the right of the command button you just added. Users will understand exactly what the button does if there is accompanying text on the form to the right of the button. With the form still in Design view, do the following.

EXERCISE 10.16: ADDING A LABEL TO THE SWITCHBOARD FORM

1. Close the toolbox, and click the label above and to the right of your new button—the label with the text *View or enter employee information*. Selection handles appear around the selected label.
2. Press Ctrl+C to copy the label to the Clipboard. Press Ctrl+V to paste the label onto the form. The pasted label, which is identical to the label you selected in step 1, is enclosed in selection handles.

3. Move the mouse near the edge of the selected label. When the mouse cursor changes to a full hand (thumb and four fingers), click and move the label so that it is to the right of your new button and approximately aligned on its left side with the labels above it.

4. Click inside the label again so that a vertical bar appears. Then, drag across the letters in the label to select all of them.

5. Type **Exit the application** to replace the selected text, and click outside the label to view the results.

6. Click File on the menu bar, click Save As, type **Switchboard2** in the text box, and click OK to save the modified form. Saving the changed form under a new name provides you the opportunity to save the original Switchboard form in case you want to work with it.

7. Open the form in Form view. Your form should match the one shown in Figure 10.20.

8. Click the Design View button on the Design View toolbar to display the form in Design view.

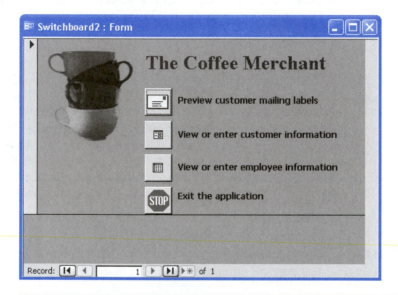

Figure 10.20   Example database application startup (switchboard) form.

The last modification we want to make to the Switchboard form is to tweak a couple of form properties to yield a more user-friendly form. You will set several properties that are assigned to the form as a unit. Changes you will make enhance the form's function and appearance.

Modifying a Form's Properties

Several properties of the Switchboard form are designed to help display database records but are not well suited for a switchboard-style form. The properties are all form-level properties—those attached to the form as a whole. Form properties that you will change on the Switchboard form include these (listed in the order that they occur in the form's property sheet): Caption, ViewsAllowed, ScrollBars, RecordSelectors, NavigationButtons, Dividing Lines, AutoCenter, and BorderStyle.

EXERCISE 10.17: MODIFYING A FORM'S PROPERTIES

1. Ensure that Switchboard2 form is still displayed in Design view, press Alt+Enter (a shortcut) to open the property sheet, click Edit, and click Select Form (or press Ctrl+R, the shortcut to select the entire form). The property sheet Title bar displays "Form," which assures you that you have selected the form rather than a particular object on the form.
2. Click the Format tab on the property sheet.
3. Set the following properties to the values indicated. (They are listed in order, top to bottom, that they occur in the property sheet.) After you set the form properties as shown, your switchboard form will look like a dialog box instead of a database form. Your form's property sheet should match the properties shown in Figure 10.21.

Property	Value
Caption	Switchboard
Allow DataSheet View	No
Allow PivotTable View	No
Allow PivotChart View	No
ScrollBars	Neither
RecordSelectors	No
NavigationButtons	No
Dividing Lines	No
AutoCenter	Yes
BorderStyle	Thin

4. Close the property sheet.
5. Close the Switchboard2 form, and click Yes when asked if you want to save your changes.

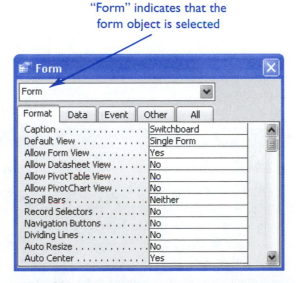

"Form" indicates that the form object is selected

Figure 10.21   Switchboard form property settings.

TRY IT

Test your form by opening Switchboard2 in Form view. Then, click the exit (Stop) button you just created. Access will close both the database and itself, returning control to Windows.

Making a Switchboard Form Open Automatically

A switchboard-style form does not automatically display when a user opens your database. The name "Switchboard" does not impart some special significance to the Access database program. You do not want your database users wondering how to start your elegant database application. Automatically launching a switchboard form—providing an entryway to your application—is a terrific way to help your database users.

The finishing touches needed to complete your database application is to tell Access to launch your Switchboard form automatically whenever Access is opened. The following exercise demonstrates how to do this. If you did the Try It exercise above, then you will have to open your *Ch10.mdb* database.

EXERCISE 10.18: ESTABLISHING A DATABASE APPLICATION STARTUP FORM

1. With the *Ch10.mdb* Database window open, click Tools on the menu bar, and then click Startup.
2. Type **The Coffee Merchant Database** in the Application Title text box. This text appears in the Access application window Title bar in place of "Microsoft Access."
3. Click the Display Form/Page list box arrow, and then select Switchboard2 from the list of forms.
4. Clear the Display Database Window check box. From now on, when users open your database, the Database window will not appear. They do not need it, because your Switchboard form replaces it.
5. Clear the Allow Toolbar/Menu Changes check box (see Figure 10.22). This prevents users from changing any custom toolbars or menus you might create for your application.
6. Click OK to finalize your choices.

TRY IT

Close the *Ch10.mdb* database and Access simultaneously by clicking the Access Title bar's Close button. Now, use Windows Explorer to locate *Ch10.mdb* on your hard disk, and double-click the database file name. Click Open when a Security Warning dialog box appears. What is different about the way Access behaves? If you made all the changes correctly, your *Switchboard2* form opens, but the Database window does not. Notice that the application Title bar contains the text you typed in step 2 of Exercise 18 (see Figure 10.23). Click the Stop button to exit the application and close Access.

database Title bar text   startup form's name

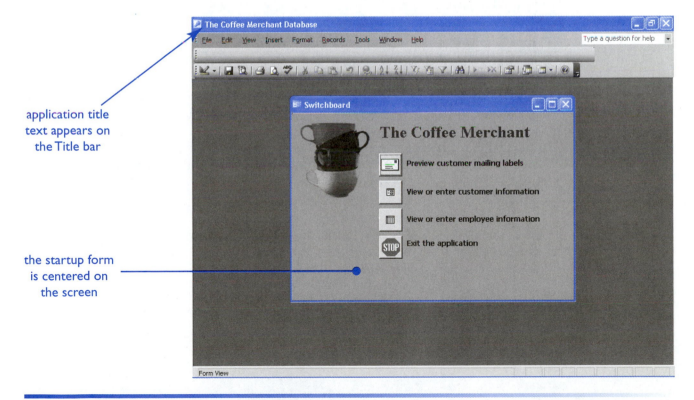

Figure 10.22   Designating a database startup form.

application title
text appears on
the Title bar

the startup form
is centered on
the screen

Figure 10.23   Automatically displaying the startup form.

Now that you have completed your work in this chapter, close all open database windows and close Microsoft Access. Respond Yes if any dialog boxes prompt you to save changes.

 Go to http://perry.swlearning.com for an in-depth tutorial.

SUMMARY

You have learned how to use Access macros and VBA code to automate database procedures to provide form navigation and to perform data tests. You created buttons and linked macros or VBA code to them so that they perform a series of steps. With navigation buttons, you simplified moving around the database rows displayed on a form. You discovered that other database activities can be simplified by making buttons that modify database rows, create new rows, save changes, and cancel changes. Though creating buttons is more work initially, these buttons spare users from learning details about the database system and its interaction language and provide built-in error detection.

Access databases, like other database management systems, support events. Events are recognized when particular conditions exist. A button click is an event, the mouse moving over a form control is an event, and leaving a control by pressing the Tab key is an event. Each of the many events that can occur to an object—a form, a list box, or command button, for example—has an associated event property. You can write VBA code or macros that are assigned to an individual object's event properties that spring into action when appropriate. For example, you can write an arbitrarily complicated bit of VBA code that executes whenever a user clicks a particular command button. The code is attached to the command button's On Click event procedure. Other events such as a form's On Current event provide convenient ways to gain control over a process to validate form fields before Access posts changes to the database.

Data validation and internal controls are important in maintaining a robust database that is free from errors. Creating data validation VBA code is one way to preserve the integrity of your database. You also learned that you could use behind-the-scenes code to automate internal control features. The controls you read about and implemented included validating dates entered in orders and checking stock on hand to ensure that an order can be filled.

QUESTIONS AND PROBLEMS FOR REVIEW

Multiple-Choice Questions

1. When you click a button on an Access toolbar, you change the _____ of that button.
   a. contents
   b. properties
   c. state
   d. location

2. When you click a button, you trigger a(n)
   a. landslide.
   b. event.
   c. happening.
   d. instance.

3. The name for code behind an object that reacts to clicking a button, for example, is called an event
   a. modifier.
   b. handler.
   c. property.
   d. None of the preceding is correct.

4. To attach code to an object such as a button that will trigger whenever anyone clicks the button, you open the object's property sheet and then click which property?
   a. On Click
   b. On Enter
   c. Click
   d. On Mouse Up

5. A collection of macros is called a macro
   a. collection.
   b. procedure.
   c. cluster.
   d. group.

6. An important part of documenting your work is to print your macros. In addition, you should print _____ code.
   a. documentation
   b. VBA
   c. macro group
   d. window

7. You can attach code to what event property to stop the cursor from moving from the current form field if you determine it needs to be corrected?
   a. Lost Focus
   b. Before Update
   c. After Update
   d. canMove

8. You can use what program structure to select from one of two alternative paths in your code?
   a. go to
   b. if then
   c. do while
   d. end sub

9. What special word refers to the current object without using the object's actual name?
   a. This
   b. Mine
   c. Me
   d. Customer.Me

10. An action that affects an object is called a(n)
    a. imperative.
    b. macro.
    c. argument.
    d. method.

Discussion Questions

1. What are the advantages, if any, of using custom-designed buttons to automate a procedure that can be executed by using existing Microsoft Access menus?

2. Describe what advantages, if any, would accrue by attaching field validation code to check whether a field is empty or not. After all, you can check the Required property in the table's Design view to accomplish the same thing. What is the difference in these two approaches?

3. Discuss the meaning and relationship between events and event properties. List at least five form event properties, and briefly describe the event properties. Use Access Help and search for the definition or use of the event properties you choose to describe.

4. Discuss why you might want to disable a command button. For example, under what circumstances would you disable the Next database navigation button? Discuss the exact way you would write a segment of VBA code to disable a button whose name is cmdNext. Also, mention the difference between a button's Caption property and its Name property. Which one displays on the button's surface? Can you refer to a button by its Caption property?

5. Describe in detail the DLookup function (three or four sentences will do). Start by defining its general format: What are its arguments? Then, describe concisely the purpose of the function and where it might prove useful.

Practice Exercises

1. Add another button to the Switchboard2 form to display the order form (*frmOrder* and *fsubOrder*). Add an appropriate label to the right of the new button. Be sure to implement ControlTips both for the new button and the text to the right of the button. The ControlTip for the button can contain a phrase about what the button does. The ControlTip for the label to the right of the new button should display your first and last names.

2. Create a query that joins the tables *tblEmployee*, *tblEmployeeTitle*, and *tblDivisionLocation*. Include the one name field that combines the last name and first name separated by a comma and a space (e.g., Smith, Brian). Include the hire date and birth date from *tblEmployee*. From the *tblEmployee* table, include the Title field. From the *tblDivisionLocation* table, include fields corresponding to city, state, and town hyperlink. Save the query as *qryPracticeExercise2*. Next, create a form from the query and add your own custom First, Previous, Next, and Last navigation buttons (use default pictures, not text, for the buttons). Ensure that all text boxes are sufficiently long enough to display data from the tables. Remove the existing navigation buttons. Remove the Record Selectors and Dividing Lines. Change the form Caption to **Employee Data**, and save the new form as *frmPracticeExercise2*.

3. Create a new form displaying the *tblSalesTaxRate* table in a form. Then, add a field that computes the density of the state (people per square mile) and displays it as a number with one decimal place. Remove Record Selectors and Dividing lines from the form. Change the form's title bar caption to **Tax Rates**. Save the new form as *frmPracticeExercise3*.

4. Create a new form based on the table *tblCustomer*. Include all fields from the table. Add a button to display a blank data entry form. Add another button to save the results once you have entered the data. Change the form title bar text to **Practice Exercise 4**. Save the form as *frmPracticeExercise4*.

5. Open the *Switchboard* form (either the original or the one you modified in this chapter), and add a button to launch Microsoft Word. Modify the form's title bar text to display your first and last names, and save the modified form as *frmPracticeExercise5*. Print the form, and print the code for the button that launches Microsoft Word.

Problems

1. Create a form that allows you to view information in both of the inventory tables *tblInventory* and *tblInventoryDescription* simultaneously. Then, create four navigation buttons labeled First Record, Previous Record, Next Record, and Last Record with associated VBA code that implements the record navigation. Create a group macro that contains all four macros. Print an example of the form (choose any inventory item), and print the VBA code for the four navigation buttons. Be sure to write your name on each page of output.

2. Modify The Coffee Merchant's Order form (*frmOrder*) so that the Order Number and Order Date fields are validated by VBA code. The validation rule for the Order Number field is that the Order Number must be between 15000 and 48000, inclusive. The validation rule for the Order Date field should be changed. Valid dates are between 30 days ago and today's date, inclusive. Both validation routines should display a message box indicating the problem. In no case should the user be permitted to continue filling out the rest of the form until the mistake is corrected. Print the two validation sub procedures and the form.

3. Write an event procedure that validates the ZipCode field in the customer form, *frmCustomer*. The VBA code prevents the cursor from leaving the ZipCode field unless a valid, existing Zipcode is found in the *Zipcodes.mdb database* included in the folder named Supplement on your Companion CD. Ensure that the entered Zipcode corresponds to the correct city and state abbreviation by consulting the *Zipcodes.mdb database*. Include a warning message dialog box that displays if an invalid Zipcode value is entered. The warning dialog box should display the message Incorrect Zipcode entered. Print the VBA sub procedure. Be prepared to demonstrate this code to your instructor.

Index